30° E   **RUSSIA**   140° E
      • Vladivostok

                                                        40° N

      Sea of Japan   38° N

KOREA   J
                                   A
                                   P
                     ○   A
                            Tokyo• N
   n
   • **TSUSHIMA**   Kure•
     ISLAND   •Iwakuni
hima
ait   •Sasebo

       KYUSHU   30° N

   ea   *P   a   c   i   f   i   c*

             O   c   e   a   n

KINAWA

                                              Tropic of Cancer —

   130° E   140° E   20° N

THE BRITISH PART
IN THE KOREAN WAR

VOLUME I

The author of this, as of the official histories of the Second World War, has been given free access to official documents. He alone is responsible for the statements made and the views expressed.

OFFICIAL HISTORY

The British Part in the

KOREAN WAR

Volume I

A DISTANT OBLIGATION

Anthony Farrar-Hockley

LONDON: HMSO

© Crown copyright 1990
First published 1990

ISBN 0 11 630953 9

HMSO publications are available from:

HMSO Publications Centre

(Mail and telephone orders only)
PO Box 276, London, SW8, 5DT
Telephone orders 071-873 9090
General enquiries 071-873 0011
(queuing system in operation for both numbers)

HMSO Bookshops

49 High Holborn, London, WC1 6HB   071-873 0011 (Counter service only)
258 Broad Street, Birmingham, B1 2HE   021-643 3740
Southey House, 33 Wine Street, Bristol, BS1 2BQ   (0272) 264306
9-12 Princess Street, Manchester, M60 8AS   061-834 7201
80 Chichester Street, Belfast, BT1 4JY   (0232) 238451
71 Lothian Road, Edinburgh, EH3 9AZ   031-228 4181

HMSO's Accredited Agents
(see Yellow Pages)

and through good booksellers

British Library Cataloguing in Publication Data
A CIP catalogue record for this book
is available from the British Library

Printed in the United Kingdom for HMSO
Dd290167 5/90 C40 G443 10170

CONTENTS

Page

PREFACE

If a staff officer in the Admiralty or War Office in February 1950, had suggested that a considerable sum must be added to the defence budget in the coming year for operations on the other side of the world, in an area in which the United Kingdom had no interest and to which it was bound by no treaty, he would probably have been borne off for psychiatric treatment. Yet his foresight would have been proven within a few months. The Korean war began on 25th June of that year, and the United Kingdom was drawn almost at once into the conflict. It was a contingency which took the British Government and its military Chiefs of Staff by surprise; the first of many in following years to make unexpected and irresistible claims on money and manpower.

The events of the war seem now remote. At the outset, when forces went into action for the first time under the United Nations flag, when some feared that a third world war was impending, Korea commanded public attention. So it continued during ten months of changing fortunes, until the line stabilised. Two final years of trench warfare attracted few headlines. The rest of the world lost interest in the struggle. Yet it was a full scale conventional war, behind which, to the end, lay the option of the atomic bomb. As to the events of 1939–45, we look back now at those in Korea from 1950–53 with the wisdom of hindsight, sharpened by the scepticism of succeeding generations, yet impaired, perhaps, by the residual prejudices of the swinging sixties and the abiding astigmatism of the 'conspiracy' theorists.

As ever, in the writing of history, it is important to bring into balance what we know now with what was known, believed or felt then. For example, although the state archives of the Soviet Union and the People's Republic of China remain closed, it now appears that Kim Il-sung, the political leader of North Korea, was never the puppet of his great neighbours. On the other hand, the false notion has taken root that the British Government went to war in 1950 because it was politically and financially dependent on the United States, though the evidence of state and other papers, and the word and deed of participants, shows that there were worthier reasons for the decision, not least a determination on the part of Mr Attlee, the Prime Minister, never to use appeasement to buy off aggression. He had learned that from British negotiations with

Hitler. So had the Americans, in their own way. The conclusions drawn from this lesson, intellectual and emotional, encouraged common cause. The United States was reminded that Britain was a valuable but trenchant ally.

These two examples concerning perspective illustrate the fact that the two volumes setting out the British part in the war comprehend the political as well as the military aspects of participation. They include necessarily reference to the inception and development of NATO, which coincided with the outbreak of war in Korea. However, British foreign policy during this period will be manifested across the board and in greater detail in the appropriate volume of 'Documents on British Policy Overseas'. Similarly, while references to economic factors are included among the political, they are more fully covered by Professor L S Pressnell's Official History, 'External Economic Policy Since The War'.

In so far as it has been practicable, I have related political and military events in sequence. Sometimes politics calls the tune, sometimes it is decided by the outcome of battle. Inevitably, the United States features frequently in the account due to the scale of American influence and participation. Even so, because this is not a general history of the war, I have omitted mention of numerous activities including operations of the Americans and other nations where they do not bear upon those of the United Kingdom. I hope none will consider slighted by the omission.

This hope extends importantly to the Republic of Korea. Moreover, I am anxious not to support the curious double standard that has frequently militated in observations and commentary on the affairs of the peninsula. The government of North Korea has from its formation been a communist dictatorship, draconian in character. Recurrent instances of inhuman behaviour by some of its principals, members of the police and armed forces were expected of such a regime by democratic society and, their cause being understood, were in a sense forgiven. The government in the early years of the Republic of Korea was elected by a rough and ready form of secret ballot. Attempts were made to create a democratic state without the least experience. Corruption in the exercise of power was due much to persistent violence and insurgency by the communist front in the south manipulated by the authorities in the north of the country. The problems of the government of the Republic were understood but the concomitant errors were not similarly excused. The Republic was and is criticised without mitigation because it is one of 'us', guilty of not at once striking and maintaining the highest standards of democratic process and institutions. Yet, although the early governments of the Republic were widely judged by many western observers to be unrepresentative and hated, huge numbers in North Korea chose during the war to pass to their administration, walking south as soon as opportunity offered. The armed forces of the Republic, hastily and indifferently trained, given often to breaking in battle during the first year of fighting, rallied to respond with valour against the assumption of power by the government of the North. I regret that the necessary discipline of selection consigns much of the Korean people's struggle to the background.

This first volume is concerned with the decision of Mr Attlee's government to commit land as well as sea and limited air forces to the Korean war, and the British part, in association with members of the Commonwealth, in operations and in political initiatives to bring the war rapidly to an end. It concludes at the point of failure in both endeavours. The second volume will open with an evaluation of that unsuccessful strategy which will serve also as a means of continuity between the two parts. The extent to which the British contribution, within the United Nations extended effort between 1951–53, was successful will thereafter be recounted.

In both parts, I have used the old Wade-Giles system of romanising Chinese words in preference to the modern pinyin. The majority of the translations of documents or works to which I have referred employ this form. The McCune-Reichschauer system of romanisation has been used for Korean names, but without full accentuation. I have also used the Chinese and Korean titles for territorial names: for example, 'North East China', rather than the Japanese 'Manchuria', 'Pusan', rather than 'Fusan'. Unavoidably, some of the documents quoted use Japanese forms, notably in naval usage of names from charts based on the surveys of imperial Japan.

I should perhaps disclose that I was a participant in the war as a captain in the Gloucestershire Regiment. With my comrades in the 29th Brigade, I travelled up and down the peninsula in various seasons, and thus became familiar with the western sector. I have since returned three times to walk the ground of various battles in the Republic, the great majority of which have not been changed by urban or other development. I have not, of course, been back to the north but acquired some familiarity with the north west during a number of unsuccessful escape attempts as a prisoner-of-war of the North Korean and Chinese forces. During recapture and recovery, I had the rare opportunity to live at times among the field forces of both nations and observe something of their conduct and routine behind the line. However, personal impressions tend to bias historical accounts. I have sought to call upon them sparingly.

ANTHONY FARRAR-HOCKLEY

AUTHOR'S ACKNOWLEDGEMENTS

I have had the support and help of many people in the preparation of this book. I thank all those concerned warmly. It is difficult to make a distinction between contributions; all those I have asked for help have readily responded. However, there are some individuals or institutions which have given me a good deal of their time and thought, or have engaged in enterprise on my behalf, and I feel I must mention them by name.

I begin with John Cheatle of the Records Section of the Cabinet Office, whose help was invaluable in discovering what records had been retained and where they might be found. In this connection, I must also thank the Public Record Office at Kew, the Army Records Office at Hayes, and the Common Services (formerly Office Services) Records of the Ministry of Defence for their help. John Andrews, Chief of the Ministry of Defence Library has given me exceptional help over the years in which I have been working on this volume, not only in the provision of books and publications, many of which he has had to obtain specially through distant sites such as Hong Kong, but in arranging translation services in Chinese and Korean. I thank the staff of his library for their help and forbearance. In this association, I must also thank the Historical Sections of the Royal Navy, the Army, and the Royal Air Force, and the Royal Marine Archives. The Libraries of the Foreign and Commonwealth Office, the Staff College, Camberley, and the Royal Military Academy, Sandhurst, have given me much assistance, and, similarly the staffs of the Prince Consort's Library at Aldershot, the Bodleian at Oxford, the British and the London Libraries, and the Soviet Studies Centre at Sandhurst.

I thank all those whose names are mentioned in the source notes for their contribution. Brigadier Boris Eastwood, Colonel Reggie Jeffes, Major R H Cooke, Major G G Norton and Major-General A E Younger scarcely appear among these but they have given frequent advice and material. Alan Moodie, Tony Eagles and Sam Mercer, members of the Executive Council of the British Korean Volunteers Association, have also been most helpful in suggesting or finding me individuals among their number with information about events in which they were participants. I thank them and all those members of the Association for time given up to answering my questions.

The staff of the National Archives and Record Service of the United States in Washington, DC, and at Suitland, Maryland, and in the Library of Congress responded generously to my many calls on their services. The same is true of those who run the Australian National Archives in Canberra, and the Canadian National Archives in Ottawa. In the Republic of Korea, I owe thanks to the Minister of Defence and those who keep the memorial and archives of the Korean War for their help and patience in meeting many requests.

While engaged in writing this volume, I became involved in preparation of the Thames/Channel 4/ABC/WGBH Boston television series on the Korean War. I owe thanks to Phillip Whitehead, the executive producer, for the opportunity to meet many people who took part in the war or scholars who have been engaged in the history of that event. His associates and staff were also very kind to me, passing on many pieces of information about the war or pointing me towards sources.

The Chief of Military History in the United States, and those of his historians concerned with the Korean War have long given me help, Mr William Mossman prominent among them. I have also had the exceptional fortune to enjoy the friendship and continuing assistance of Major-General Jack Huston, formerly Chief of the United States Air Force Historical Department and now a professor at the Naval Academy, Annapolis. I have benefitted much from my discussions with Dr Jeffrey Grey in Canberra and Professor Robert O'Neill in Canberra and Oxford. Kenneth Harris, Lord Attlee's biographer, and Lord Bullock, Mr Bevin's biographer, were kind enough to provide me with data from their research notes relating to the Korean War. I thank the present Lord Attlee for access to his father's papers. Brigadier Anthony Millen took on the task of collecting photographs for this history, a greater problem than he or I expected; the range of official photographs is limited; much has depended on seeking out personal pictures. He has given much leisure time to the work involved. Major S W Cooper spent many hours in checking and substantiating the names of those who were killed in the Korean War or who died as a consequence of service on operations there. I am greatly in their debt.

In the Cabinet Office, Malcolm Mackintosh kindly gave me much help in identifying personalities in the political and military hierarchy of the Soviet Union. The principals and staff of the Cabinet Office Historical Section have provided support over the many years of preparation and been most tolerant of delays in delivery of typescripts. I thank Pat Andrews and Richard Ponman especially in these respects.

My first wife, Pat, died during the main research phase of the history. As on many previous occasions, she took on a host of tasks and filled many gaps in the work in hand. Linda Wood, now my wife, has been involved as researcher and assistant throughout the production. I owe thanks to both which words cannot express.

ACKNOWLEDGEMENTS FOR THE USE OF PHOTOGRAPHS

Thanks are due to those who have kindly permitted their original photographs to be shown in this book at various points in the text. Their titles are shown in each case.

MAPS

xv

PHOTOGRAPHS

1. The Foreign Secretary, Ernest Bevin, addressing the ship's company, HMS *Kenya*, with Captain Brock, and his private secretary (Sir) Roderick Barclay. (Sir Roderick Barclay)

2. Burial at sea from HMS *Jamaica* of the first British servicemen to be killed in the war, July 1950. (Lt Cdr P Sparkes)

3. Firefly flying off from HMS *Triumph* to attack targets in Korea, July 1950. (C D Christmas Esq)

4. Firefly being armed on board HMS *Triumph*. (C D Christmas Esq)

5. HMS *Ladybird*, previously the Yangtse river steamer, *Wusueh*, headquarters ship, in her berth at Sasebo. (Cdr J A de M Leathes)

6. Camouflaged junks on mud flats spotted by aircraft from HMS *Triumph*. (C D Christmas Esq)

7. HMS *Triumph* preparing to enter harbour after operations in Korean waters. (C D Christmas Esq)

8. HMS *Comus* after attack by Stormovik aircraft, 23rd August 1950. (Cdr J A de M Leathes)

9. Close up shows some of the damage. (Cdr J A de M Leathes)

10. 1 Middlesex embark on HMS *Unicorn*, Hong Kong, 25th August 1950. The soldiers were wearing the jungle green tropical uniform which they retained into the winter. (Major B Reed)

11. Farewell address by Rt Hon Malcolm MacDonald, British High Commissioner, South-East Asia, 25th August 1950. (Major B Reed)

12. 1 A&SH arrive in Pusan on the cruiser, HMS *Ceylon*, 29th August 1950. (Hulton-Deutsch Picture Company)

13. 1 Middlesex arrive in Pusan aboard HMS *Unicorn*, 29th August 1950. (Major B Reed)

14. 1 A&SH disembarking from HMS *Ceylon*, 29th August 1950, carrying their bagpipes, 'those contraptions'. (Hulton-Deutsch Picture Company)

15. 1 Middlesex move towards the front line, 3rd September 1950. (Major B Reed)

CALENDAR—1950

JANUARY

Sun	1	8	15	22	29
Mon	2	9	16	23	30
Tue	3	10	17	24	31
Wed	4	11	18	25	
Thu	5	12	19	26	
Fri	6	13	20	27	
Sat	7	14	21	28	

FEBRUARY

Sun		5	12	19	26
Mon		6	13	20	27
Tue		7	14	21	28
Wed	1	8	15	22	
Thu	2	9	16	23	
Fri	3	10	17	24	
Sat	4	11	18	25	

MARCH

Sun		5	12	19	26
Mon		6	13	20	27
Tue		7	14	21	28
Wed	1	8	15	22	29
Thu	2	9	16	23	30
Fri	3	10	17	24	31
Sat	4	11	18	25	

APRIL

Sun		2	9	16	23	30
Mon		3	10	17	24	
Tue		4	11	18	25	
Wed		5	12	19	26	
Thu		6	13	20	27	
Fri		7	14	21	28	
Sat	1	8	15	22	29	

MAY

Sun		7	14	21	28
Mon	1	8	15	22	29
Tue	2	9	16	23	30
Wed	3	10	17	24	31
Thu	4	11	18	25	
Fri	5	12	19	26	
Sat	6	13	20	27	

JUNE

Sun		4	11	18	25
Mon		5	12	19	26
Tue		6	13	20	27
Wed		7	14	21	28
Thu	1	8	15	22	29
Fri	2	9	16	23	30
Sat	3	10	17	24	

JULY

Sun		2	9	16	23	30
Mon		3	10	17	24	31
Tue		4	11	18	25	
Wed		5	12	19	26	
Thu		6	13	20	27	
Fri		7	14	21	28	
Sat	1	8	15	22	29	

AUGUST

Sun		6	13	20	27
Mon		7	14	21	28
Tue	1	8	15	22	29
Wed	2	9	16	23	30
Thu	3	10	17	24	31
Fri	4	11	18	25	
Sat	5	12	19	26	

SEPTEMBER

Sun		3	10	17	24
Mon		4	11	18	25
Tue		5	12	19	26
Wed		6	13	20	27
Thu		7	14	21	28
Fri	1	8	15	22	29
Sat	2	9	16	23	30

OCTOBER

Sun	1	8	15	22	29
Mon	2	9	16	23	30
Tue	3	10	17	24	31
Wed	4	11	18	25	
Thu	5	12	19	26	
Fri	6	13	20	27	
Sat	7	14	21	28	

NOVEMBER

Sun		5	12	19	26
Mon		6	13	20	27
Tue		7	14	21	28
Wed	1	8	15	22	29
Thu	2	9	16	23	30
Fri	3	10	17	24	
Sat	4	11	18	25	

DECEMBER

Sun		3	10	17	24	31
Mon		4	11	18	25	
Tue		5	12	19	26	
Wed		6	13	20	27	
Thu		7	14	21	28	
Fri	1	8	15	22	29	
Sat	2	9	16	23	30	

CALENDAR—1951

	JANUARY	FEBRUARY	MARCH	APRIL
Sun	7 14 21 28	4 11 18 25	4 11 18 25	1 8 15 22 29
Mon	1 8 15 22 29	5 12 19 26	5 12 19 26	2 9 16 23 30
Tue	2 9 16 23 30	6 13 20 27	6 13 20 27	3 10 17 24
Wed	3 10 17 24 31	7 14 21 28	7 14 21 28	4 11 18 25
Thu	4 11 18 25	1 8 15 22	1 8 15 22 29	5 12 19 26
Fri	5 12 19 26	2 9 16 23	2 9 16 23 30	6 13 20 27
Sat	6 13 20 27	3 10 17 24	3 10 17 24 31	7 14 21 28

	MAY	JUNE	JULY	AUGUST
Sun	6 13 20 27	3 10 17 24	1 8 15 22 29	5 12 19 26
Mon	7 14 21 28	4 11 18 25	2 9 16 23 30	6 13 20 27
Tue	1 8 15 22 29	5 12 19 26	3 10 17 24 31	7 14 21 28
Wed	2 9 16 23 30	6 13 20 27	4 11 18 25	1 8 15 22 29
Thu	3 10 17 24 31	7 14 21 28	5 12 19 26	2 9 16 23 30
Fri	4 11 18 25	1 8 15 22 29	6 13 20 27	3 10 17 24 31
Sat	5 12 19 26	2 9 16 23 30	7 14 21 28	4 11 18 25

	SEPTEMBER	OCTOBER	NOVEMBER	DECEMBER
Sun	2 9 16 23 30	7 14 21 28	4 11 18 25	2 9 16 23 30
Mon	3 10 17 24	1 8 15 22 29	5 10 17 24	3 10 17 24 31
Tue	4 11 18 25	2 9 16 23 30	6 13 20 27	4 11 18 25
Wed	5 12 19 26	3 10 17 24 31	7 14 21 28	5 12 19 26
Thu	6 13 20 27	4 11 18 25	1 8 15 22 29	6 13 20 27
Fri	7 14 21 28	5 12 19 26	2 9 16 23 30	7 14 21 28
Sat	1 8 15 22 29	6 13 20 27	3 10 17 24	1 8 15 22 29

CHAPTER 1

A Cabinet Decision

On the morning of Tuesday, 27th June, 1950, the British government held a periodic Cabinet meeting at 11 o'clock. The Prime
Minister, Mr Clement Attlee* was in the chair. The first three
items on the agenda were part of the everyday business of an
administration seeking to recover national prosperity after an
exhausting world war. The fourth was of quite a different kind. It
was marked on the agenda simply as 'Korea'.

Not all Ministers discussing this item in the Cabinet Room of
10 Downing Street that morning were exactly sure where Korea
lay in the Far East. Some of the senior officials present were no
better informed, but one at least had helped a colleague with the
explanation that it lay 'between China and Japan'.[1] Hostilities had
begun there on 25th June between the two states of the peninsula:
the 'People's Democratic Republic' in the north had attacked 'The
Republic' in the south, as a result of which the United Nations
Security Council had called for a 'cease fire'.† Fighting continued,
and a second meeting of the Security Council was shortly to be
held to consider further action. Instructions as to government
policy were needed by the British representatives on the Council
as a matter of urgency.

The Labour government had been returned to power in the
February general election but its majority had sunk to five seats
in the Commons. Struggling to pay off enormous debts incurred
in the second world war, encumbered still with major imperial
commitments, including a counter-insurgency campaign in Malaya,
and occupied with many political, economic and defence problems
in Europe, it is not surprising that an early reaction in many
departments of state in Whitehall was that the struggle in Korea
was a problem which Britain should let others solve. However, the
United Kingdom had been involved during and after the war in
Korean affairs and was in any case now, as a permanent member
of the Security Council, obliged to take an interest in and a share
of responsibility for any attempt at a settlement.

---

*Attlee, Rt Hon Clement Richard, later 1st Earl (1883–1967).
†For the resolutions adopted on 25th and 27th June, 1950, see Appendix A.

First discussion of allied policy for Korea appears to have been in 1943 when Mr Eden* as Foreign Secretary raised the matter with President Roosevelt† and his Secretary of State in Washington in March of that year. Preparing briefs for Mr Eden as to the future of the overseas elements of the Japanese empire, his staff had been reminded that Korea was an early prey in the development of the Greater East Asia Co-Prosperity Sphere; Japan had progressively colonised its weak neighbour since 1897 and annexed it outright in August 1910.

Reporting on 29th March in a telegram to the Cabinet on the substance of his discussion with the President, Mr Eden referred to the topic 'of international trusteeship for certain areas of [the] world'. The subject included '4. . . . (3) intermediate cases like Korea and Pacific Islands . . . Korea and French Indo-China would pass under international trusteeships; for the former the trustees might be the United States, the Soviet Union and China . . .'[2] The reaction of the Foreign Office staff was mixed as to some of the main ideas put forward by the President but 'I hardly think we need quarrel with the suggested solution for Korea, although the trio will hardly be a very happy one and Russia may tend to "jump her claim" before anyone else can arrive on the spot.'[3]

Partly as a result of the discussions in Washington, the national leaders involved in the Cairo Conference in November, 1943— President Roosevelt, Mr Churchill‡ and Generalissimo Chiang Kai-shek,§ included the following promise in their communique:

> The aforesaid three great powers, mindful of the enslavement of the people of Korea, are determined that in due course, Korea shall become free and independent.

The Soviet Union was not a party to this public statement because it was not at war with Japan; but it already had a secret understanding with the other three powers that it would turn upon Japan when Germany had been defeated. Russia was therefore developing ideas as to its claims and interests in the homeland and conquered territories of Japan. Fifteen months later at Yalta, President Roosevelt was floating some of his own thoughts for a Pacific settlement during a bilateral discussion with Marshal Stalin.¶ He remarked that:

---

*Eden, Rt Hon (Robert) Anthony, later 1st Earl of Avon (1897–1977).
†Roosevelt, Franklin Delano (1882–1945).
‡Churchill, Rt Hon Sir Winston Leonard Spencer (1874–1965).
§Chiang Kai-shek, Generalissimo (1887–1975), President of the Executive Yuan of China, 1935–45 and of Nationalist China, 1948–49, 1950–75.
¶Stalin, Joseph Vissarionovich Djugashvili, (1879–1953).

he had in mind for Korea a trusteeship composed of a Soviet, an American and a Chinese representative. He said the only experience we [the US] had had in this matter was in the Philippines where it had taken about 50 years for the people to be prepared for self-government. He felt that in the case of Korea the period might be from 20–30 years. Marshal Stalin said the shorter the period the better, and he inquired whether any foreign troops would be stationed in Korea.

The President then said there was a question in regard to Korea which was delicate. He personally did not feel it was necessary to invite the British to participate in the trusteeship of Korea, but he felt that they might resent this.

Marshal Stalin replied that they would most certainly be offended. In fact he said the Prime Minister might "kill us". In his opinion he felt that the British should be invited.[4]

So it was agreed orally that there should be a trusteeship and that the United Kingdom should be a co-trustee. Nothing was entered in the record because Russia was formally at peace with Japan. For one reason or another, neither leader mentioned the arrangements to the British Prime Minister, his colleagues or their staffs. The Foreign Office did not query future arrangements for this territory because it had been accepted that trusteeship would fall to others.

At the Potsdam conference in July 1945, the subject of Korea surfaced again briefly, albeit a matter overshadowed by the massive problems arising in Europe from the defeat of Germany and, in the Far East, the need finally to overthrow Japanese power. Korea could not be ignored. Its land mass, lying commonly between China, Japan and Russia, was of strategic importance. The United States had huge forces concentrating for the final assault on Japan in which there was a general expectation of bloody and protracted battles. Russian forces would shortly be opening operations in the area. It was clearly necessary to agree boundaries within which the allies would control sea and air space. There was less certainty as to whether it would prove necessary to commit an American land force against the Japanese in Korea; in that July, all efforts were being concentrated on the landing of American forces on Kyushu on the other side of the Korean strait. Even so, it was gradually becoming apparent that at some stage the United States would have to conquer or receive the submission of Japanese forces in the southern area of Korea, now falling within its close operational focus. Thus, while sea and air operational boundaries were being agreed mutually between the United States and Soviet Union military delegations, the United States Army Chief of Staff gave instructions to his chief of operations to look out a suitable boundary to separate the land forces of the two powers as and when they entered Korea.[5]

The British position in these proceedings was one of an associate; a full member, to make a commercial analogy, of the corporation board but a director principally interested in other undertakings of the group. The Foreign Office had prepared several papers on Korea, as for other territories occupied by the Japanese, but the substance of these was historical and the aim simply to maintain a working stock of information. Britain had no direct intelligence sources in the territory. The government declined to have any dealings with *emigré* Korean political groups. When the Russian delegation proposed discussion of Korea by the Council of Foreign Ministers at San Francisco on 22nd July,* the Foreign Office maintained its views that 'our own direct interest is small and if it proves necessary to oppose the Russian proposals we should leave it to the Americans to play the hand'.[6]

The Potsdam meeting ended on 2nd August 1945. The war with Japan continued and so the three allies engaged—China, the United States and United Kingdom—reiterated their policy for the Far East following the anticipated victory. ' . . . the terms of the Cairo declaration shall be carried out . . . '.[7]

Russia still knew nothing officially of the atomic bomb development. The Anglo-American partnership could not be sure what the result would be when the first of these weapons was dropped on 6th August at Hiroshima. When the news of the devastation there reached Stalin he guessed that the Japanese could not long resist such attacks and hastened to establish his claims as a partner in the Far East victory. On 8th August, a communiqué issued from Moscow stated that, 'true to its duty to allies, the Soviet government has accepted the [Potsdam] proposals and has associated itself with the [three power] Allied Declaration of 26th July'.[8] The Red Army began operations against Japan at 0100 hours on 9th August.† Following the dropping of the second bomb on Nagasaki, Japan surrendered on 14th August. It became apparent in Washington that Russian troops would enter Korea ahead of any from the United States. As a hasty, temporary expedient, it was agreed that the 38th parallel of latitude—which roughly divides the peninsula in two—should separate the zones of occupation.[9] The division also placed the capital, Seoul, in the American sector. Elements of the Russian 25th Army‡ entered north east Korea on

*The Ministers were in the United States for the foundation of the United Nations Organisation.
†Local time.
‡Commanded by Colonel-General Ivan Mihailovich Chistyakov (1900–79).

10th August and within a fortnight had completed occupation down to the major northern city of P'yongyang. Apart from a brief initial orgy of looting and rape by the Russian soldiers, control was established peacefully. The Japanese were everywhere at once disarmed and made prisoners, a process completed with occupation down to the 38th parallel on 1st September. A Russian detachment had been in Seoul since 19th August.

The United States occupation force, the XXIV Corps,* did not begin arriving in the south until 8th September and, shortly, military government headquarters were established in Seoul. Late on the ground due to the war burden America carried in the Pacific theatre, the force lacked proper political direction and organisation. Its task was to disarm, assemble and evacuate the Japanese authorities and forces and to maintain military government until the Allied Powers decided on the precise arrangements for the trusteeship on which Roosevelt and Stalin had agreed. The lack of a policy for Korea was due in part to President Roosevelt's habit of developing elements of foreign policy within his private office, He had not shared his thoughts about Korea with the State Department, still less with his successor. They had died with him.

The contrast between the political acumen and objectives of the two occupation forces is manifested by their methods of government.

With the collapse of Japanese power, a national political coalition had surfaced throughout Korea. Its membership was not elected but represented a broad spectrum of the many parties which had been maintained or developed in exile or underground during the forty odd years of Japanese rule. A 'Korean People's Republic' had been proclaimed, and a government formed, though it had little control at national level due to the fact that all the principal departments were still run by the Japanese. At provincial and yet more at county and district level, the coalition's representatives had great influence. It is a matter of interest that the majority of those assuming authority in the northern provinces were members of centre parties or independents, in the southern, predominantly communist or markedly to the left. The focus of the communist party, as with all substantial parties, was Seoul because this was the national capital and all expected it to remain the centre of national power.

The Russian 25th Army had its own organic political staff, concerned primarily with the internal political activities of its units. However, accompanying it was a special political detachment from the headquarters of the 1st Far Eastern Front to organise political

---

*Sent from Okinawa under command of Lieutenant-General John R Hodge, US Army.

5

development within the occupation zone. This was under the direction of a front senior political officer, Major-General A A Romanenko. The official policy of the Soviet occupation authorities was declared in September to be the facilitation of a 'capitalist democratic revolution', a 'bourgeois democratic revolution'. In October, a published statement entitled *'For what purpose did the Red Army come to Korea?'* stressed that the Russian forces were liberators and were not to be the instrument whereby the political system of the USSR would be imposed upon the Korean people as it was not suited to them. The only persons to be excluded from political life were those who had actively collaborated with the Japanese. Everywhere, the all-party councils which had begun to form independently for government at local level were encouraged. Ominously, however, the army commander, General Chistyakov, announced in a proclamation of 12th October that ' . . . Only those who contribute to the progress of the Korean economy and culture through honest enterprise can become patriots and true Koreans'.[10] A narrow definition of 'honest enterprise' was shortly to be developed by the Russian authorities but for the time being their words were taken at face value. Anxieties following the first, limited, Red Army brutalities receded and popular confidence grew in the emergence of an independent democratic nation-state.

In the south, the Americans declined to use or recognise any Korean parties or politicans. All authority was vested in the United States military government and, to make matters worse from the local point of view, those Koreans appointed expediently as police and provincial officials were in many cases individuals who had served the Japanese.

So matters continued until December, the only notable trend being that, in the north, the Russian command progressively increased its political power through the provincial police, which it developed and controlled through Korean placemen, and by forcing out piecemeal political representatives at all levels of government who were not communists or potentially sympathetic to the regime.*

In the south the American methodology provided a common reference point of opposition for all parties and shades of political opinion. In October, the American military government formally declared the Korean People's Republic to be illegal.[11] The zone was administered at all levels by uniformed American officers.

---

*With the Korean Communist Party preponderantly in the south, and notorious for internal squabbling, numbers of Koreans were brought in with the 25th Army to fill key political posts. These were principally from two backgrounds: the 'Russian faction' , Koreans who were Soviet citizens, and the 'Kapsan faction' , former guerrillas based in north east China while operating from the Kapsan mountains, who had spent much of the war in Russia.

Almost from the outset of the occupation, General Hodge and those of his force concerned with civil affairs were confronted by the strength and intransigence of communist political power internally and externally. Internally, factional quarrels notwithstanding, the communists were the most formidable opponents of military government authority, particularly at provincial and lower levels.[12] Externally, the politico-military command in the north progressively diminished co-operation and the use of common services and commerce between the two zones. The only means of direct contact between the commanders, their military liaison detachments respectively in Seoul and P'yongyang, were severed when the Russian detachment was withdrawn abruptly to the north on 11th October 1945.[13] Shortly thereafter the Americans in P'yongyang were obliged by the Russian command to return to the south. Frustrated, Hodge sought governmental action from Washington and on 8th November the American ambassador in Moscow represented formally the need to reopen and develop the Korean economy on a national basis. The situation also caused the State Department to reflect that it would be useful to secure British support in its negotiations.

During the late summer and early autumn, it had become apparent to the British authorities that some kind of agreement concerning trusteeship for Korea had been agreed secretly between President Roosevelt and Marshal Stalin at Yalta. On 17th August, President Truman* was reported by 'The Washington Post' as remarking that the future of Korea had been discussed with the United Kingdom and Soviet Union at Potsdam and that the policy agreed would be carried forward.† On the same day, the American Joint Chiefs of Staff had asked their British colleagues for their ideas concerning forces for Korea in line with the understanding reached at Yalta concerning the quadripartite trusteeship for that area'. The British ideas were negative:

There are no British military interests in Korea and the provision of [British] occupational forces for this area would, therefore, serve no military purpose. While we have no knowledge of any existing undertaking on our part to enter into a quadripartite trusteeship for Korea, we must recognise that we may come under heavy pressure from the Americans to this end; it may thus become politically necessary for us to provide a token force, though on military grounds such provision would be a most undesirable commitment.[14]

---

*Truman, Harry S. (1884–1972). As Vice-President, he had succeeded to the presidency on the death of Franklin Roosevelt in 1945.
†This was an error; the future government of Korea was not discussed at Potsdam.

By 12th September, the United States government had realised that their British colleagues needed elucidation on trusteeship. Lord Halifax,* United Kingdom Ambassador in Washington, reported on that day,

> Member of my staff was asked to visit the State Department to receive an oral communication on the future of Korea . . . there was a proposal to institute a four power trusteeship for Korea until such time as the Koreans become self-governing . . . it was discussed at Yalta but no decision was taken. Mr Hopkins† obtained Soviet agreement to the proposal when he visited Moscow in May 1945 and T V Soong‡ gave China's consent on one of his visits to Washington. Vincent§ apologised for not having consulted us earlier. He also explained that communication was being made orally because all previous consultations had taken place in the same way . . . it would be advantageous if the body appointed to exercise trusteeship functions should take over as soon as possible, thus terminating the present division of Korea on the 38th parallel and replacing the military Government by a civilian one more likely to foster the growing democratic institution . . . .[15]

On 9th October, Mr Bevin,¶ British Foreign Secretary, circulated the proposal for four power trusteeship to those of his ministerial colleagues directly interested. He concluded,

> It is probable that, if the idea of a Four Power Trusteeship is adopted, Australia will wish to take part as a fifth Power. It may be difficult to secure acceptance of this by the United States Government and I have been wondering if, in fact, Australia might not be the fourth member as representative of the whole Commonwealth, instead of ourselves.[16]

No further suggestions were made by the United States for a British or imperial contribution to the occupation force in Korea, either in addition to or coming from the substantial British, Indian, New Zealand and Australian joint force being established in Japan under an Australian commander-in-chief. Korea dropped out of view in Whitehall for some weeks until Mr Byrnes,‖ the American

---

*Wood, Edward Frederic Lindley, 1st Earl of Halifax (1881–1959).
†Hopkins, Harry Lloyd (1890–1946), Franklin Roosevelt's special assistant and old friend.
‡Soong, T V, the western name style of Sung Tzu-wen (1894–1971), Chinese financier and Nationalist Foreign Minister.
§John Carter Vincent was then Head of the Far East Affairs Office, US State Department.
¶Bevin, Rt Hon Ernest (1881–1951).
‖Byrnes, James Francis (1879–1972).

Secretary of State, sent a proposal on 26th November, 1945, for a meeting with Mr Molotov,* Soviet Commissar for Foreign Affairs, and Mr Bevin in December. Three days later, a proposed agenda arrived which included:

4. The establishment of an independent government for Korea.†[17]

Even though there was to be widespread support for such a meeting in and outside Parliament, Mr Bevin did not welcome it. He was closer to the negotiating circumstances. The Council of Foreign Ministers‡ had broken up early in October because of inability to reach any agreement with the Soviet Union. Knowing that the latter wished to make progress, he wanted the initiative for a resumption of negotiations to come from Moscow. Another circumstance which disturbed him was that China and France were to be excluded from the Moscow meeting. Mr Byrnes was insistent, however, to the extent of being prepared to go without his United Kingdom partner if necessary.

In baseball terms, this was a 'squeeze play' : the British government risked being pushed out of the game. By way of maintaining team membership and simultaneously international influence, it was agreed with his Cabinet colleagues that Bevin would go on the understanding that he, Byrnes and Molotov would be meeting to clarify their views as a preliminary to the General Assembly session of the United Nations in January, 1946.[19]

The premise being more or less accepted in Washington and not unwelcome in Moscow, the three ministers met in the Spiridonevka Palace on Sunday, 16th December, 1945. 'Molotov, conducting the meeting, sat leaning forward over the table, a Russian cigarette dangling from his mouth, his eyes flashing with satisfaction and confidence as he glanced from one to the other of the Foreign Ministers, obviously aware of their mutual differences and their common uncertainty in the face of the keen, ruthless and incisive Russian diplomacy. He had the look of a passionate poker player who knows that he has a royal flush and is about to call the last of his opponents.'

---

*Molotov, Vyacheslav Mikhailovich (1890–1986)

†Subsequently item 3 on the agenda and revised by the US delegation's proposals to read: The establishment of a unified administration for Korea, looking towards the eventual establishment of an independent government there.[18]

‡It had been agreed at Potsdam in 1945 that there should be frequent meetings, usually in London for geographical convenience, of the Foreign Ministers of the UK, USA and USSR. As a consequence of American and British representation, the Foreign Ministers of China and France joined the original three at their first meeting.

9

This was the view of George Kennan,*[20] Minister at the United States Embassy. He noted also that Mr Byrnes 'plays his negotiations by ear, going into them with no clear or fixed plan, with no definite set objectives or limitations . . . In the present conference, his weakness in dealing with the Russians is that his main purpose is to achieve some sort of agreement, he doesn't much care what. The realities behind his agreement, since they concern only such people as Koreans, Rumanians and Iranians, about whom he knows nothing, do not concern him. He wants an agreement for its political effect at home. The Russians know this'.

When the Korean item was considered, Mr Byrnes gave notice that he wished to discuss it on the basis of his Ambassador's letter of 8th November; the letter which had represented General Hodge's view. This may have surprised Mr Molotov. He protested that he had had no warning that the questions of Korean government and trusteeship would be approached from this angle—by proposals for local and limited matters such as trade and railways. Where was this to lead them?

As a result of Mr Byrnes making the approach in this way, there is no means of discovering what angle of approach the Soviet Union would have used if it had itself opened. Trusteeship was evidently to be an interim objective but as the national position papers for the conference in the Russian archives are not open to public view it is not clear as to how it was proposed to bring about the formation of a provisional government. However, a candidate for the leadership of the north had already been brought in to Korea by the Red Army: Kim Sung-ju, who had adopted the name Kim Il-sung† Just as the three Foreign Ministers were meeting, this man was succeeding, by a combination of intrigue and strong arm tactics supported by the Russian occupation authorities, to become head of the communist party's 'northern bureau'.[21] From this base, he was to progress to become leader of the North Korean Workers' party, dominated by the communists, and Head of State.

In their sector, the United States had no candidate for zonal or national office and no plan other than the expectation of holding

---

*Kennan, George Frost (1904–), American diplomat, he was Minister Counsellor in Moscow in 1945 and Ambassador to the USSR 1952–3.
†Kim Il-sung born Kim Sung-ju (1912–). For an explanation of the reputation associated with this choice of alias, see 'A Fifteen Year History of North Korea' op cit in source notes, p 34. He was the leader of the Kapsan element entering Korea with the 25th Army.

at some stage democratic elections as an essential step directly or by trusteeship to an independent government of a unified nation*

In this first session in the Spiridonevka Palace, Mr Byrnes said, after some discussion, that 'he was willing to discuss the general subject [of a Korean settlement] and not confine discussion to the text of the [Ambassador's] letter . . . He would tomorrow [17th December] submit a paper enabling the meeting to discuss the actual form of Trusteeship . . .'

> Mr Bevin expressed qualified agreement with the principles in the letter of the 8th November since it was clearly economically advisable to have transport and other services in Korea. But so as not to confuse the issue it was better to discuss the general aspects of the question also. Mr Molotov said that they would await the document to be circulated by Mr Byrnes.[22]

Having examined the United States draft, the Soviet Union now circulated one of its own, placing responsibility on the two military commanders to develop a provisional central government by means of a Joint Commission. To this, with minor amendments, the American delegation agreed.

From the British standpoint, Mr Bevin saw no reason to disagree. Though nobody's poodle, he accepted the Foreign Office advice— 'our own direct interest is small . . .'—and that of the Chiefs of Staff that Korea held no military interest whatsoever for the United Kingdom. Still, Mr Attlee's Administration was committed to maintaining the international responsibilities it had inherited; Korea was to be one of these. As a means of lightening the burden, Mr Bevin gave notice that his government might wish to substitute Australia for the United Kingdom in the trusteeship.

China's agreement having been secured to its provisions, the report of the conference signed on 27th December was published immediately thereafter. It included this section:

III. KOREA.

1. With a view to the re-establishment of Korea as an independent state, the creation of conditions for developing the country on democratic principles and the earliest possible liquidation of the disastrous results of the protracted Japanese domination in

---

*The United States' State Department was not dedicated to trusteeship judging by remarks in a letter from Mr Winant to Mr Bevin on 29th November 1945 (see source note 16). It included this paragraph: 'As to the fourth item, we are prepared to press for the establishment of an independent Korean Government. If that is not acceptable, we would favour a trusteeship under the United Nations for a limited period of time similar to that which we suggested for the Italian colonies'.

Korea, there shall be set up a provisional Korean democratic government, which shall take all the necessary steps for developing the industry, transport, and agriculture of Korea and the national culture of the Korean people.

2. In order to assist the formation of a provisional Korean government and with a view to the preliminary elaboration of the appropriate measures, there shall be established a Joint Commission consisting of representatives of the United States command in Southern Korea and the Soviet command in Northern Korea. In preparing their proposals the Commission shall consult with the Korean democratic parties and social organizations. The recommendations worked out by the Commission shall be presented for the consideration of the Governments of the Union of Soviet Socialist Republics, China, the United Kingdom, and the United States prior to final decision by the two Governments represented on the Joint Commission.

3. It shall be the task of the Joint Commission, with the participation of the provisional Korean democratic government and of the Korean democratic organizations to work out measures also for helping and assisting (trusteeship) the political, economic, and social progress of the Korean people, the development of democratic self-government, and the establishment of the national independence of Korea.

The proposals of the Joint Commission shall be submitted, following consultation with the provisional Korean Government, for the joint consideration of the Governments of the United States, Union of Soviet Socialist Republics, United Kingdom and China for the working out of an agreement concerning a four-power trusteeship of Korea for a period of up to five years.

4. For the consideration of urgent problems affecting both Southern and Northern Korea and for the elaboration of measures establishing permanent coordination of administrative-economic matters between the United States command in Southern Korea and the Soviet command in Northern Korea, a conference of the representatives of the United States and Soviet command in Korea shall be convened within a period of two weeks.[23]

When the idea of a trusteeship reached Korea it was universally rejected by all parties, left, centre and right. If agreed in nothing else, all were certain that full national independence was expected—demanded—immediately, and that suggestion of 'political tutelage' was an insult.

Yet suddenly, in a matter of days, the opinion of the communists and certain of their associates turned completely about. As late as

1st January, 1946, one of their leaders was informing General Hodge of his opposition. By the 3rd, however, he and his comrades were supporting the decision of the Moscow conference. It was widely rumoured in Seoul that the Russian vice-consul there* had relayed instructions from the military government in the north to make the change.† Whatever the truth of the matter and, incidentally, however many of its peripheral supporters the Communist Party in South Korea lost by this *volte face*, the advantage of the change was soon apparent. For when the Joint Commission met in accordance with the Moscow agreement, the Russian chief delegate, General Shtykov,‡ maintained that those political parties—and only those political parties—who accepted that agreement had a claim to legality. All others, by their act of rejection, had disqualified themselves and hence could not as parties take part in elections. If this had been agreed by General Hodge, the only major party left in the electoral field would have been the Communist Party.

He did not agree to the principle but insisted at the first meeting and thereafter that dissent from the Moscow agreement should not disqualify political parties. During the several Joint Commission sessions other impediments to progress arose but this first fundamental disagreement predominated. The Commission was deadlocked. Attempts to disencumber it had now to be taken at a higher level. None were essayed by Mr Molotov. Mr Marshall,§ who had replaced Mr Byrnes as Secretary of State, initiated an exchange of letters with Mr Molotov on 8th April 1947. If this failed, it seemed that the only option was a meeting of the original trustee powers,¶ but the response from Moscow to Mr Marshall gave hope of a readiness to concede acceptance of established political parties in South Korea who were now ready—as most were—to sign a declaration drawn up by the Commission agreeing *inter alia* to uphold the requirements of the original first paragraph of the Moscow decision. The Commission met again. The chief

---

*A I Shabshin.

†A document was subsequently acquired by XXIV Corps intelligence section which was said to have emanated from the north and was addressed to all Korean Communist Party organisations. Its title was '*Instructions to all levels and branches concerning the decisions on Korean problems made by the three Power Conference at Moscow.*' For connected details, see the corps intelligence summary, No, 41, of 23rd June, 1946.

‡Shtykov, Terenty Fomich (1907–64) Colonel-General. Member of the Military Council (ie chief political officer) of the 1st Russian Far Eastern Front.

§Marshall, George Catlett, General of the Army (1880–1959), Chief of Staff of the United States Army throughout the second world war. He insisted, while Secretary of State, on omitting his military rank. He was later (1950–51) Secretary of Defense.

¶The Chinese government made this suggestion in a note to Mr Marshall on 14th April, copied to the United Kingdom. The latter consulted Australia who intimated that they would expect to take the UK's place in the event of a four power trusteeship.

Soviet delegate appeared, however, to have no new instructions when it came precisely to which parties were acceptable for election. In the absence of progress, the United States once again wrote to the Soviet Union, * suggesting now that the Commission should formally report jointly 'the status of its deliberations so that each government may immediately consider what further steps may usefully be taken to achieve the aims of the Moscow agreement.'

In his reply of 24th August, Mr Molotov insisted, on a new tack, that there should be no consultation with those parties and organisations which remained connected with the committee for struggle against the Moscow decision, that there should be no consultation with parties of less than a membership of 10,000, and that persecution of those parties adhering to the original Moscow decision—that is, the parties of the far left—must cease. He did 'not object to your proposal that the Joint Commission should report on the state of its work . . .'.

The United States judged that more issues were being adduced for stalling; wider consultation and support seemed called for. In a note to Mr Bevin on 27th August, the Ambassador in London wrote enclosing a copy of the State Department's response to Mr Molotov, remarking also that 'it is the hope of my government that the government of the United Kingdom may agree to designate' a delegate to four power conversations on Korea. For this was now the option chosen in Washington. All the parties in question, Mr Molotov was reminded on 27th August, had signed the declaration required by the Joint Commission; there was no fundamental disagreement about membership numbers in parties, yet the 'Soviet delegation submitted a list which omitted 24 such parties which claimed total membership of 15,200,000 and refused to consider any other list or alternative proposal . . . ' After two years of stalemate, the United States government felt that a formal report of differences from the Joint Commission would not suffice. The four powers adhering to the Moscow Agreement of 1945 should meet in Washington on 8th September 1947 'to consider how that agreement should speedily be carried out.'. For the first time, it was suggested that 'the United Nations shall be invited to have observers present so that the world and the Korean people may be assured of the wholly representative and completely independent character of the actions taken.'†

While Mr Molotov and Marshal Stalin considered these ideas, Mr Bevin informed his American colleague that the United Kingdom would take part in the four power discussions, and

---

*Correspondence begun on 12th August 1947.
†This letter was signed by Robert Lovett, acting as Secretary of State in the absence of Mr Marshall.

suggested that an Australian representative should also participate. A letter was already en route from Moscow to Washington, however, to say that 'The Soviet government does not regard as expedient your proposal to submit the question of setting up a provisional Korean Democratic Republic Government for discussion by the Governments of the four countries since the Joint Commission is still far from exhausting all its possibilities for working out agreed recommendations'. It alleged also that the United States proposal would perpetuate the division of the country. '. . . the Soviet Government sees no possibility of accepting the proposals advanced . . . '[24]

To the State Department and no less to General Hodge, a return to the unproductive arguments of the Joint Commission seemed pointless. The United States, having informed its co-trustees, the British and Chinese, of the intention, decided to submit the matter to the United Nations. On 17th September the Secretary of State gave notice that '. . . it appears evident that further attempts to solve the Korean problem by means of bilateral negotiations will only serve to delay the establishment of an independent, united Korea. It is therefore the intention of the United States Government to present the problem, of Korean independence to this session of the General Assembly'.[25]

A legal argument followed.[26] The Soviet Union contended that Korea, as a former 'enemy' territory, was outside the aegis of the UN, but the argument could not be sustained due to this simple fact: by its adoption of the Cairo and Potsdam declarations of 8th August 1945, the Soviet Union had accepted that Korea was not an ally but a victim of the former Japanese empire. It was therefore deemed by the Assembly to be a suitable subject for discussion at its second regular session: 'Item 2. The problem of the independence of Korea'.

Much further debate, through the First Committee* and then back once more in the General Assembly, was to follow, in all of which the United Kingdom was the principal or one of several nations in support of the United States' initiative. By 28th October, it was apparent that there was a majority in the Assembly for the holding of elections in each zone under the scrutiny of a Temporary Commission. To this the Soviet Union continued to be opposed. By way of counter proposal, one or another of the communist membership† submitted a significantly different solution based on two contentions. First, representatives of the Korean people should take part in the debate. Second, the election of these representatives

---

*Seven committees had been formed to prepare resolutions for the General Assembly's plenary sessions. The First Committee dealt with political and security matters.
†Byelorussian SSR, Czechoslavakia, Poland, Ukraine SSR, USSR, Yugoslavia.

should be accomplished by 'simultaneous withdrawal of all Russian and American forces respectively at the beginning of 1948, thereby leaving to the Korean people itself the establishment of a National Government of Korea.'

What this would have accomplished is a matter for speculation. Who, for example, was to organise an interim government was left unspecified. If to the two parties alone and they could not agree it seemed likely that the decision would be decided by force of arms. Though the population in the south was twice that of the north, the military forces of North Korea were considerably stronger and more developed.* At the very least, the outcome would be decided by a civil war in which superiority in arms rather than democracy would be the deciding factor, and this was precisely why a majority in the General Assembly, including member nations who could in no circumstances be described as allies or clients of the United States, voted on 14th November 1947 for an electoral commission.†

Nine nations were asked to provide the members of what was to be entitled the United Nations Temporary Commission on Korea (UNTCOK), Australia, Canada, China, El Salvador, France, India, the Philippines, Syria, and the Ukrainian Soviet Socialist Republic. They were to 'travel, observe and consult throughout Korea', in the words of the resolution,‡ to see that those chosen for the National Assembly 'are in fact duly elected by the Korean people and not mere appointees by military authorities . . . ' It was recommended that the elections should be held by 31st March 1948, 'on the basis of the adult suffrage and by secret ballot . . . ' From the National Assembly, a National Government would be formed.

Thus, after more than two years of waiting, it seemed to many Koreans that there was a prospect of national elections leading to the early formation of a national government for the first time since the Japanese formal assumption of power in 1910. In the view of the United States government at least, expectations were lower. Writing to Mackenzie King,§ on 5th January 1948, President Truman remarked,

---

*A defence department, the Provisional People's Committee Security Bureau, had been set up in North Korea on 8th February 1946. Prior to this, however, Korean youths were being sent to the USSR for military training, while others were receiving training by Russian and former guerrilla military instructors inside North Korea.

†By 43 votes to 0. A number of the Scandinavian and Arab countries abstained. The communist membership declined to participate.

‡For the full resolution, see Appendix B.

§(Mackenzie) King, William Lyon Mackenzie (1874–1950), Prime Minister of Canada 1921–25, 1926–30,1935–48. He was deeply opposed to Canada providing a representative on the Commission in Korea, or on any similar international body.

It seems likely that the Commission will be denied entry to Northern Korea and that its work will be confined to Southern Korea where 20,000,000 of the 29,000,000 Koreans live.[27]

So it was to prove. Tens of thousands of Koreans thronged the roads from the airport at Seoul to welcome the Temporary Commission delegates as they arrived successively between 8th and 12th January 1948. A mass meeting was held to welcome them at the city stadium on the 14th under the arrangements of a self-styled 'National Reception Committee' attended by a crowd in excess of 100,000. Great numbers, unable to find a place in the stadium, waited outside. Many of those inside and out had come long distances from towns and villages to join in this expression of satisfaction that Korea was at last to come to nationhood and independence. But the Commission, which had had its first meeting on the previous day,* was already apprehensive of continuing obstacles to both. They were resolved to approach the United States and Russian military commanders in precisely the same manner on the same date. Yet while General Hodge was clearly available to them at any time there were doubts as to whether General Korotkov† in the north would be accessible at all.

On Saturday 17th January 1948, one letter was sent personally to General Hodge; another to General Korotkov was passed to Colonel S V Kornyshev, Russian liaison officer in Seoul,‡ proposing a call by the chairman and a member of the Commission and, in so far as the visit to P'yongyang was concerned, requesting travel facilities. At the same time, United Nations' headquarters transmitted the message for P'yongyang through the foreign affairs office in Moscow. On 23rd January, the following telegram reached the Commission in Seoul transmitting this reply from Mr Gromyko:§

In connection with your letter of 18th January, 1948, transmitting the text of a letter from the acting Chairman of the Commission on Korea, in which he expresses desire to visit the Commander of the Soviet troops in Northern Korea, we find it necessary to remind you of the negative attitude taken by the Soviet Government towards the establishment of the UN Commission in Korea as already stated by Soviet delegation during the second session of the General Assembly of the United Nations.[28]

---

*No representative had been sent from the Ukraine SSR.

†Lieutenant-General G P Korotkov had succeeded General Chistyakov as Russian military commander in North Korea.

‡The liaison missions had been necessarily re-established when the Joint Commission had been instituted.

§Gromyko, Andrei Andreevich (1908–89), Vice-Commissar for External Affairs of the USSR.

No reply was ever received to the letter sent up on the train from Seoul to General Korotkov in P'yongyang.

In the House of Commons in London on 28th January, Professor Savory* put this question to the Secretary of State for Foreign Affairs:

> Will he now state the grounds for refusal by the Soviet Union to allow the Commission established by the General Assembly of the United Nations to enter the zone occupied by the Russians; and whether he proposes to take any action to support the efforts of the Commission to enter the zone in order to assist in the setting up of Korea as an independent state?

This was the point: what did the United Nations now do when a major member declined to accept its decision? There were diverse opinions among the individual member governments. Some believed that UN attempts to unify Korea having failed, the United States and Soviet Union should resume direct negotiations. Others held that the United Nations should not give up but persevere in carrying forward the proposals of the General Assembly; at least to supervise elections in the southern zone.

Argument and counter-argument, political and legal, took time. Considering the extent of consultation that was necessary, it is remarkable that the Interim Committee of the General Assembly† was able by majority vote on 26th February 1948, to direct the Commission to carry out their instructions 'in such parts of Korea as are accessible'. An election was ordered to be held on 10th May and, notwithstanding a number of complaints from the officers of the many local parties, whether participating or not, and many private organisations and individuals among the electorate of ballot rigging, disruption and intimidation,‡ the Commission reported on 25th June:

> . . . its opinion that the results of the ballot of May 10, 1948, are a valid expression of the free will of the electorate in those

*Savory, Professor Sir Douglas Lloyd (1878–1969) was then Unionist MP for Queen's University, Belfast.

†Interim Committee, the body representing the General Assembly when the latter was not in session. Its members then were: Argentina, the Byelorussian SSR, China, Czechoslovakia, Egypt, Yugoslavia, New Zealand, Poland, the United Kingdom, Ukrainian SSR, United States, and USSR.

‡During the run up to the elections, 29th March to 19th May, 589 people were killed in South Korea: 37 government officials and candidates, 150 civilians, 63 policemen, 9 members of police families, 330 'rioters'. On election day, 44 were killed, 62 wounded. These casualties arose principally due to the action of left terrorists and right wing bands including rightist youth terrorist organisations. Subsequent experience shows that political violence, particularly at election times, is common in Korea.

parts of Korea which were accessible to the Commission and in which the inhabitants constituted approximately two-thirds of the people of all Korea.[29]

The Commission had visited about 2% of polling stations, at random and without prior warning. Of 7,837,504 who had registered as voters, 7,036,750 had voted. The electorate of South Korea, representing approximately half the populace, were estimated by the Temporary Commission as being 9,894,000. About three quarters of those eligible to vote had done so; 95.2% of those who had registered had cast a vote. The outcome was a national assembly principally conservative in character, ultra-nationalist and largely right wing. Some members of the international press judged that the electoral process fell far short of the models in western Europe or North America, and it would indeed have been remarkable if a people who had never experienced such a system had immediately been able to practice it. Whatever the allegations about the event, a very large number of voters had expressed their opinion by secret ballot and the consequent accession to power of Syngman Rhee* as Chairman of the Assembly and, shortly, President of the new Republic, was almost certainly as nearly an expression of the wishes of the majority of those who had voted as local circumstances permitted.†

A part of the genuinely democratic political spectrum‡ had boycotted the elections on the basis that they would perpetuate the division of the nation; and whilst this was also the reason given by the left socialists for their own boycott this element, much under the domination of the Communist Party, was aware that it lacked the power to attract the votes of the masses. A number of those in sympathy with the aims of the communists continued to be affronted by its *volte face* on the trusteeship in January, 1946.

A proportion of the seats in the 'National Assembly'—one hundred, calculated on the distribution of population—had been left for representatives from North Korea. Syngman Rhee, not without tongue in cheek, perhaps, pressed those in authority in

---

*Syngman Rhee (1875–1965). This is a western form of the Korean name Yi Sung-man. A veteran politician, imprisoned early as a foe of the Japanese, he had led the Korean government in exile periodically, spending the majority of his exile in the United States. He was then 75 years of age.

†In the Assembly, Rhee's party (the Association for the Rapid Realisation of Independence) had the largest number of seats (fifty-five of one hundred and ninety-eight). He was elected almost unanimously to be Chairman of the Assembly because many of the minor parties and independents believed that there would be an executive Prime Minister who would choose his own ministers. This was not the model adopted.

‡Principally the right wing Korean Independence Party of Kim Ku and the entire centre National Independence Federation Party of Kim Kyu-sik (see also fn (*) on p 20).

the north on 17th July to 'hold free elections' to fill the vacant places. Kim Il-sung and his colleagues responded by ordering a national—as distinct from a regional—general election on 25th August. It was subsequently announced in P'yongyang that 99.97% of the electorate had voted to elect 212 members to a supreme people's assembly; figures which lack independent verification, though elections of some sort had manifestly been held. The parties in the south who had boycotted the elections there were invited to field candidates in the north but, the communist front apart, all declined to do so.* The legitimacy of the assembly in the north in its claim to represent the whole Korean people was questionable also on a broader basis. The majority of the populace lived in the south, roughly 21 million as compared to 9 million in the north. Moreover, refugee movement, despite political and physical diffi- culties, continued to be preponderantly from north to south.† A statement from P'yongyang in late August made the claim that a delegation of 1,080 from South Korea had met in Haeju to elect 360 members to the supreme people's assembly and that this delegation had represented 77.80% of the electorate south of the 38th parallel.‡ These delegates were all from the South Korean Workers' Party, the front organisation of the Communist Party. There had been no public sign of any selection of these representa- tives by ballot, secret or otherwise, in the south and, again, no independent verification of the event.§ Nevertheless, the Soviet Union and its satellites recognised the P'yongyang government as sovereign in the whole peninsula on 12th October 1948. The United States sought to convince its allies that they should do the same for the Seoul government.

In a minor key, the British government had begun to consider this problem as early as 20th July, on the prompting of the Consul- General in Seoul, Captain Holt.¶ Suggesting that recognition would be under examination in London:

---

*Kim Il-sung issued an invitation to Kim Ku and Kim Kyu-sik on 17th June 1948 to attend a conference at Haeju on the 25th. They declined having already protested that 'the northern authorities' had broken promises not to set up a separate government in P'yongyang, and to cut off electricity and water. They had also failed to honour their promise to release from prison Cho Man-sik, leader of the Korean Democratic Party in the north.

†At least 700,000 individuals had come south between August 1945 and September 1948. Not more than 30,000 had moved from south to north. See also Scalapino and Lee, *op cit*, p 380.

‡An account of the election was published in the Russian press of 12th September with a special editorial comment in *Pravda* on 13th September 1948.

§George M McCune and Arthur L Grey cast doubt on the figures claimed for southern voters in *Korea Today*, (Harvard University Press), 1950, pp 246–247.

¶Holt, Captain Vyvyan (later, KBE) CMG, MVO (1896–1960). He had taken up his post on 19th May, 1948. The United Kingdom had maintained a diplomatic representative in Korea since 1884.

. . . during the course of the next three or four months . . . Whatever the Americans may arrange, it is clearly desirable that HM Government should in some way make sure of 'most favoured nation treatment' for British subjects, British trade, British missionary enterprises and British property as a condition of recognising any Government that is set up in Seoul.

In discussion of these *desiderata*, he touched on the first problem to be resolved in the recognition process:

. . . I suppose that one of the complications will be that the government here will claim to be the *de jure* government of the whole of Korea (see for example Article I of the Constitution). This indeed is I gather one of the points that is perplexing the UNTCOK who are sensible of the difficulty of blessing as the government of Korea a body which manifestly has neither title to represent the people North of the 38th parallel, nor any authority over them. I have not been able to find out how the Americans propose to deal with this problem (though it has been announced that the State Department has nominated a diplomatic representative to take up his post in Seoul in the near future) but more information may be obtainable in Washington or London . . .[30]

This despatch discloses that the United States authorities in Korea—General Hodge or his political staff—had neither instructions nor inclination to work closely with their British colleague. However, the State Department had already approached its partners in the trusteeship. The first idea advanced was that, whatever the UN Temporary Commission in Korea might propose, the Seoul government, when formed, should indeed be looked upon as representative of all Korea. The view in the British Foreign Office to this was qualified. 'We shall not, of course, need much convincing that early recognition of the Seoul government "in some form or other" would be correct and expedient . . . But we think that an act of recognition that takes no cognizance of the obvious fact of the division of Korea would be both foolish and improper, and we are anxious that the next step in Korea should be legally unassailable and should carry the widest possible measure of international support'.[31]

From Seoul, Captain Holt reported on 26th July, 'I gather that Australian, Canadian and Indian delegates with United Nations Temporary Commission on Korea are taking the line similar to paragraph 2 of your telegram No 89 but that some others, including the French and Chinese, favour an attitude more in accordance with the views of the United States Government. All wish, however, to avoid a split and a compromise is likely to be worked out. . . General Hodge speaks openly and with some bitterness of pettifogging obstruction where it was least expected, the British Empire'.[32]

Differences of view between the United States and British Commonwealth members were certainly becoming apparent due to the fact that the latter, having no direct administrative or defence responsibility in Korea, did not feel the same compulsion for relief as the Americans, whose Defense and State Departments wished to be shot of a territory governed by a contentious and demanding old man, of a people riven by political factions, possessed of a dynamic seemingly incapable of being harnessed. The only merit of the South Korean state was that its government and evidently the majority of its people abhorred communism, but its ability to resist the north was in doubt.

During discussions throughout the summer and autumn State Department officials in Washington and London spoke and wrote of the need to disengage from Korea, to pass to the United Nations the tedious problem, a residue of the war, which seemed irrelevant to the great political problems developing in Europe.

The United Kingdom was ready to support American disengagement; the problems of managing its own post war economy, imperial responsibilities, and European commitments in an era of Stalinist menace, made it easy to see the American point of view. The Foreign Office had, however, distinct objections to the method of disengaging from Korea. Principally, it was the matter of timing: to recognise Syngman Rhee's government before the General Assembly had pronounced on the validity of the elections would be precipitate. Why not wait for a United Nations' endorsement and recognition of the new government? Presentation to the Assembly would moreover manifest that, while the elections in the south had been a rough and ready expression of democracy, their imperfections had at least been open to observation as distinct from those in the north.

The extent of authority to be accorded to the new government also remained in contention. Syngman Rhee claimed government of all Korea. The United States continued to favour this; assembly and government had, after all, been elected on the terms prescribed by the General Assembly. The USSR had defied the resolutions of the latter in the matter of open elections. The Foreign Office took the view that the South Korean government was neither the *de facto* nor *de jure* authority of Korea as a whole; it governed only the territory and people involved in its election.

A complementary objection was that, by openly considering Syngman Rhee's claim to govern all Korea, Kim Il-sung would be encouraged to make a similar counter claim.

Australia, Canada, New Zealand, South Africa and, to an extent, India, took much the same view as that of the United Kingdom. Sovereign nations all, they were nonetheless ready to let the Foreign Office in London lead in the negotiations subject to consultation,* stage by stage, on matters of principle.

Shortly, the Foreign Office was to discover that its views on the complementary aspect were misconceived. As observed, Kim Il-sung needed no stimulus to claim legitimate authority over the whole Korean nation. Then, to the surprise of departmental officials in the Foreign Office, their legal adviser to an extent substantiated the contrary claim of Syngman Rhee, as interpreted by the United States. Meantime, the United States had, principally as a result of British and Commonwealth objections, reworded its proposal to read as follows:

> . . . the Government of the Republic of Korea which has come into existence at Seoul is entitled to be regarded as the Government of Korea envisaged in the [General Assembly] Resolution of November 14, 1947; and that it functions as such with respect to those parts of Korea where the Commission was in a position to observe elections.[33]

Writing on 28th September to the British Embassy in Washington, the responsible department head† remarked,

> . . . You will no doubt notice with some surprise that we now feel able to support the resolution originally proposed by the Americans; though we still intend to press them to drop it. The reason for this change of attitude lies in the altered interpretation which the Legal Adviser now considers permissible thanks to the weight added to the scales by the second clause 'and that it functions . . .' The pressure on the Americans, exerted both by yourself and by us here, has in fact produced a formula acceptable

*This is remarkable because all these states had broken with the practice of 'imperial defence'—that is, acceptance of the British initiation and coordination of strategic policy through the empire—at the Commonwealth Conference of 1946. Australia, as a Pacific power, had strong views concerning Korea which were not always consonant with those of the United Kingdom. Mackenzie King had sought to keep Canada from any involvement in Korea (or any other distant territory), and his successor's government continued to express doubts about the propriety and value of United Nations involvement in Korea. However, by this stage, there was a consensus among the Commonwealth nations, though India, an Asian power, was inclined to hedge its views.
†Of the Japan Department, which comprehended Korea.

to both parties as far as General Assembly voting is concerned, even if we still differ (as I fear we do) in our attitude towards the South Korean Government's claim to sovereignty in the North.

We doubt whether other interested Governments—particularly India and France—will be able to accept the American resolution, and it is for this reason that we intend to urge the Americans, in Paris lobbies, to refrain from putting forward this controversial resolution. At the same time we shall hope to persuade the Commonwealth Governments to accept our interpretation in case the Americans prove adamant.[34]

Having been forced off its legal and assumptive bases, therefore, the Foreign Office was holding to its position of principle: the United Nations' General Assembly should be asked to validate the 1948 elections which its Commission had observed and judge the extent of authority of the government to which these had given rise.

This course did not involve a great risk of failure. The fifty six member nations whose representatives gathered for the third session of the Assembly at the Palais de Chaillot in Paris in November, 1948, were known broadly to support the event and outcome of the elections in South Korea with the exception of the six comprising the Russian *bloc*. There were, however, pitfalls evident *en route* to the Assembly's vote. The greatest of those was the right of representation of Korean views.

There was a case for hearing a representative from South Korea: the UN Commission provided a point of political contact there. The Russian *bloc* would insist, it was known, on a spokesman for the North expressing views, not simply in sequence with but to the exclusion of the South, whose right to speak was to be denied. A motion to this effect had already been defeated during the second session of the Assembly,[35] but an ambiguity in the report of proceedings gave an excuse to the Russian *bloc* to raise it again.

British Commonwealth Ministers arranged to meet in Paris on 29th September to discuss their ideas concerning the agenda for the Assembly, and Korea was an item in which all had an interest of one sort or another. From this occasion and subsequent consultations between Ministers and officials of the Commonwealth delegations through October into November, 1948, a consensus emerged. They would support the wording of the United States concerning the standing and authority of Syngman Rhee's government, but if this did not carry they would consult to draft another resolution recognising the South Korean administration on a narrower basis. They would, if necessary, agree to admit a representative from North Korea as well as from the South provided that it was clear that in so doing they gave no formal recognition to the government in the North.[36]

The United Kingdom delegation was less enthusiastic concerning the latter idea than others of the Commonwealth. The New Zealanders expressed a view, shared by Australia, that the British were inclined to be overborne by United States views. The Australian, Canadian and Indian governments were not happy about the way in which the Temporary Commission had been drafted to observe the elections. Yet all agreed that the Commission should be continued if that was the wish of the majority of the Assembly; for all were motivated by the wish to do everything possible to bring about the union of the Korean nation and believed that the United Nations were the authority best able to accomplish it.

Although the third session of the United Nations General Assembly began in Paris in September 1948, the Korean question was not debated until the first half of December. As an item for resolution, it was all of a piece with the preoccupations of the North American and European members and, to an extent those of the Orient, including Australia and New Zealand: the settlement of the post-war world. The impasse over Berlin—American and British aircraft were still supplying the city following Stalin's decision to block land access to the city—Russian intransigence over Austria, intervention in Czechoslovakia, interference in the internal affairs of France and Greece, all were creating anxieties to militate in one degree or another for the development of the North Atlantic Treaty. The settlement of the Jewish and Arab struggle for Palestine was being negotiated. The disposal of the former Italian colonies remained to be agreed. India and Pakistan were at enmities over Kashmir. United States attempts at mediation in the Chinese civil war had failed. Disputes between Indonesia and the Netherlands were being referred to the Security Council by Australia and India. Korea seemed to be among the least of international problems.

Yet events in Korea had not stood still following the formation of the governments in the south and north in August and September respectively. The United States Defense Department had continued to press for the withdrawal of its forces from the south. With some reservations the State Department agreed with this policy. A plan was settled to begin the evacuation of troops in August 1948.* On

---

*Movement did not, in the event, begin until 15th September. One infantry regiment remained until 29th June 1949. The cadres of the United States Military Advisory Group (KMAG) remained to help form and to train the South Korean armed constabulary.

18th September, the Soviet Union informed the United States that it was withdrawing all its own troops from the north, the removal to be completed by the end of December 1948, '. . . the Praesidium of the Supreme Soviet expressed the hope that the government of the United States of America will also agree to evacuate American troops from southern Korea within this period.'[37]

Opinions among politicians and officials in Washington were mixed as to what the response should be. It was decided to wait at least until the General Assembly had considered the report of its Temporary Commission in Korea, and the status of the Assembly and national administration in Seoul.

A month later, the 14th Regiment of constabulary in South Korea mutinied at Yosu, in which it was quickly joined by the greater number of the 15th. Several hundred police made captives in the area were murdered together with local civilians labelled as 'reactionaries'. The mutineers were at large for two weeks before forces loyal to the Seoul government succeeded in overcoming them. Late in November, a similar though more localised event occurred elsewhere. In each case, the organisers were communist junior officers and non-commissioned officers, who declared their aim to be the overthrow of the southern authorities, claiming the legitimacy of the government in the north.

Captain Holt reported on 27th November, 'It was, I think, the grim events of the Yosu revolt which frightened the Assembly [in Seoul] into passing the resolution aiming at the retention of American forces . . . '[38] The wish to do so was by no means unanimous. Only 103 (of 198) members were present in the Assembly. Of these, 16 abstained on grounds of principle.

A pervasive wish among many Koreans in the south, politicians and members of the public alike, to be rid of all foreigners did not extend to the government who were in no doubt as to the superiority in numbers, training and weapons of the North Korean forces. The UN Temporary Commission was equally apprehensive of invasion by the north, once the United States field forces had departed. Movement was therefore suspended. Future policy was all to depend on the outcome of the General Assembly's discussion.

The Members of the First Committee, began that discussion on Monday, 6th December 1948, at 10.30 a.m. and completed it a little before 11 p.m. on the evening of Wednesday, 8th December. The debate occupied almost twenty hours, principally on the report of the Temporary Commission, that of the Interim Committee,[39] and the resolution to be put before the General Assembly. The case of the Soviet *bloc** was encapsulated by the Ukrainian delegation's conclusion:

> . . . Firstly, the Temporary Commission had not really been an organ of the United Nations but only a tool of the United States policy for the transformation of Korea into a colony of monopolistic capitalistic interests. Secondly, there had been no free elections held in Southern Korea. Thirdly, the so-called Government of Southern Korea comprised only puppets and their voices should not be heeded by the Assembly. Fourthly, the aim of the Commission which was now being proposed would be to maintain the existing division in Korea, to prevent the unification of the country, and preclude the implementation of the principle of self-determination . . .[40]

The opposing case had been expressed thus by the Australian delegation:

> . . . The United Nations Temporary Commission appointed by the General Assembly in 1947 had been able to observe the situation in South Korea and to co-operate with the United States which exercised authority there. But it had not been able to verify what was happening in North Korea; it had no information, although certain delegations were now alleging, without, however, offering any proof, that the government of that part of Korea represented the entire Korean people. The same delegation had used the Temporary Commission's report to claim that the regime in South Korea was not democratic. That proved only that the Commission had been objective and gave so much more weight to its conclusions, which had been adopted unanimously . . . the statement of the USSR representative to the effect that the South Korean elections had not been free was based on remarks made by certain members of the Temporary Commission during the first few weeks of its existence. That fact alone showed that the members of the Temporary Commission had not been the instrument of any Power, that they had no preconceived ideas and that they had begun their work with an open mind. Furthermore, the Committee should bear in mind that the Commission had decided unanimously that the elections had been free, that there had been no interference on the part of the military authorities of the occupying Power and that the elected government represented the freely-expressed will

---

*This included the Yugoslav delegation. Although Marshal Tito had effectively distanced himself from Russian influence, Yugoslavia continued to vote predominantly with the USSR, the Byelorussian SSR, the Ukrainian SSR, Czechoslovakia and Poland.

of the Korean people. In addition, the Temporary Commission had made every effort to see that a greater degree of liberty prevailed before the elections and to quicken the democratization process in South Korea. The second part of the report of the Commission showed that the measures taken in South Korea had improved the situation and had removed the causes of criticism.

It was true the General Assembly resolution 112(II) of 14 November had not resulted in the unification of Korea. But information had been collected and a democratic government had been formed in South Korea The Australian delegation wished to pay tribute to the officials of the Korean Government who, in spite of 40 years of Japanese dictatorship, had been able to bring about the independence of their country in a remarkable manner.

According to the Australian, Chinese and United States joint draft resolution (A/C.1/426) the Government of South Korea should be considered as the only free government and the Government of North Korea could in no way be considered to have jurisdiction over South Korea. Furthermore, a United Nations Commission should continue the work begun by the Temporary Commission in South Korea. The draft resolution of the three Powers left the way open for the unification of Korea by providing for a withdrawal of the armies of occupation. In short, that resolution would promote the establishment of the independence of a democratic and unified Korea.[41]

At the end, by 48 votes to 6 (the Soviet *bloc*) with 1 abstention, the General Assembly resolved on the 12th December to recognise the government of South Korea—hereafter, officially, the Republic of Korea—as 'having effective control and jurisdiction over that part of Korea where the Temporary Commission was able to observe and consult . . . and that this is the only such Government in Korea;

> *Recommends* that the occupying Powers withdraw their occupation forces as early as possible;
> *Resolves* that . . . a Commission on Korea . . . be established to continue the work of the Temporary Commission . . . in particular to:
> (a) Lend its good offices to bring about the unification of Korea . . .
> (b) Seek to facilitate the removal of barriers . . .
> (c) Be available for observation and consultation . . .

(d) Observe the actual withdrawal of the occupying forces and verify the fact of withdrawal . . .*

After some backing and filling, the new Commission was to be comprised much as before: Australia, China, El Salvador, France, the Philippines and Syria.† Canada had withdrawn; its Prime Minister's wishes had prevailed. The Ukrainian SSR continued to decline to send a representative.

The government in Seoul had now, in the opinion of a majority of the United Nations members, been validated. The United States, which had already appointed a *Chargé d'Affaires* in Seoul, opened an Embassy there. The British raised the status of Captain Holt from Consul-General to Minister. Over half the members of the General Assembly accorded formal recognition during the following months. United States aid was secured by a formal agreement. Some of the politicians and officials in North America and western Europe who had struggled to establish the new Korean state felt that democracy would now flower, and the economy recover within it. Some, including the majority of Australasians concerned, were not so sanguine. The Australian Minister for External Affairs, H V Evatt,‡ had already expressed a wish that the residue of American troops should remain in South Korea,[42] a wish that persisted until the completion of their withdrawal on 30th June 1949. Mr Bevin also had apprehensions of dangers to come. A few months later, while addressing the ship's company of HMS *Kenya*§ on the problems of resisting aggression, he surprised them by remarking that he was 'very worried about the precarious situation in Korea . . . If you ask me where I think we might all be in for further trouble, I believe Korea is the place.'[43]

There were many causes for concern: unabated political factionalism; Syngman Rhee's predilection for autocratic rule; discord and corruption among his ministers; a broken economy; land tenure unreformed; arbitrary policing and justice; persistent violence, of which the most dangerous and widespread stemmed from the north. In the second half of 1949, there were thirty-one incidents of insurrection by communist guerrillas ranging from attacks on police

*For the full text of the resolution see Appendix C.

†Turkey replaced Syria in October 1949, when the Commission's mandate was renewed by UN Resolution.

‡Evatt, Rt Hon Herbert Vere (1894–1965). *Inter alia*, he was President of the UN General Assembly, 1948–49.

§Due to his poor health, Mr Bevin was persuaded to travel to the Colombo Conference by sea from Suez. Although the outlines of a talk about world affairs had been prepared for him by his private secretary, he raised the matter of Korea on his own initiative. His expectation of a crisis in Korea surprised the accompanying members of his staff, who would have judged other areas to be at greater risk.

stations to the attempted capture of towns; and twelve clashes of note along the border between uniformed forces of north and south. The latter were deemed by the United Nations' observers to be responsible for two of the twelve.[44]

By the spring of 1950, the numbers and efficiency of civil police and the armed constabulary, the official title of the army, had grown sufficiently to overcome much of the insurrection and terrorism. The economy, at least in the production of food, was slightly stronger. There was no improvement politically, however; if anything, matters were made worse by Syngman Rhee's attempts to avoid the general election demanded by the constitution.* Pressure from the United States helped him to change his mind.

This was not an easy period for the Korean President. Notwithstanding its advocacy to the Congress of financial aid for his country, the American State Department was ambivalent in its commitment to keep it afloat;[45] Mr Acheson,† who had succeeded General Marshall as Secretary of State, had conveyed as much in a speech to the National Press Club in Washington on 12th January 1950; Mr Lattimore,‡ an adviser on Far East affairs, had recommended that the United States 'should disembarrass itself as quickly as possible of its entanglements in South Korea'.[46] The Defense Department was similarly lukewarm in its support.

Threatened with severance of economic aid, President Rhee abandoned his idea of ruling by decree but sought to persuade the American administration of his need for more money and arms by disclosing that 'North Korean troops were moving in force towards the 38th parallel and that there is imminent danger from the north'.§ There was a grain of intelligence to support the view. Externally and internally, however, the President's public statements were now widely regarded with suspicion. Another high poll at the general election on 30th May brought about the defeat of almost all Syngman Rhee's dedicated supporters. Among the new members were moderate politicians who had previously declined

---

*The National Assembly expired on 31st May, 1950.

†Acheson, Dean Gooderham (1893–1971), distinguished lawyer who held the posts of Assistant Secretary of State, 1941–45, Under Secretary of State, 1945–47, and Secretary of State, 1949–53.

‡Lattimore, Owen (1900–83), Director of the Walter Hines School of International Relations at Johns Hopkins University.

§From the statement of Shin Sung-mo, Defence Minister (and acting Prime Minister) in Syngman Rhee's government to the press in Seoul on 10th May, 1950. See also a statement to the press by Syngman Rhee on 12th May. Although the secretary of the UN Commission in Korea told Captain Holt on 23rd May that this was '. . . "Rubbish", the whole thing is just a stunt to squeeze more military equipment out of the Americans', there had been a well authenticated report of a general clearance of civilians from the northern side of the 38th parallel by the North Korean People's Army during March.

to participate in the hope of reaching an accord with the north but who were now ready to compromise. If on nothing else, there was general agreement with the government in rejecting a proposal for unification by Kim Il-sung on 7th June as a ruse. When the new Assembly met in Seoul on 19th June, a struggle for internal power began and the southern body politic was preoccupied with this when the North Korean People's Army invaded their territory six days later.

.   .   .   .   .

As he sat in deliberation on the consequences of this event in the cabinet room in 10 Downing Street on 27th June, on the other side of the world, Mr Attlee had the disadvantage that the Foreign Secretary was not among his colleagues—Mr Bevin was in a hospital bed—but the Korean problem was not new to him and he had approved British support for condemnation of the North Korean attack expressed by the Security Council on 25th June.* So much he had told the House of Commons on the 26th. The Prime Minister was not now about to ask his colleagues to support formally this line of policy; he was much more the man of independent action than his critics allowed, but events were beginning to run fast and range widely. The North Koreans showed not the least sign of heeding the Security Council's injunction to draw back and the expressed view of the United Nations Commission in Korea was that they would not do so. The United States had that morning advised the British government—and other governments it felt to be concerned†—that 'centrally directed Communist Imperialism has passed beyond subversion in seeking to conquer independent nations and is now resorting to armed aggression and war . . .'[47] On this account, the President was instructing the Seventh Fleet to prevent any attack by Communist China on the Nationalist stronghold of Taiwan—while simultaneously calling upon the Nationalists to desist from armed operations against the mainland; and had directed that military assistance should be expedited to the Philippines and the French forces in Indo-China. A second message had also been delivered to say that the United States would be introducing that afternoon in the Security Council a resolution recommending 'that the members of the United Nations furnish such assistance to the

---

*At the 473rd meeting. The vote was 9:0 in favour with 1 abstention (Yugoslavia). See Appendix A.
†All members of the Atlantic Alliance, Australia, New Zealand, the Philippines and Indo-China.

Republic of Korea as may be necessary to repel the armed attack.' The United Kingdom [together with France and Norway] were asked to support it.

The Cabinet found little difficulty in agreeing to this request. They had reservations as to the encouragement or support they could offer the United States on the first matter. 'Centrally-directed Communist Imperialism' suggested coordination of the threat throughout Asia, for which there was no evidence; indeed, some suggested evidence to the contrary. Linking Moscow or Peking with the North Koreans' attack would in any case be premature and inhibiting to political negotiation. Moreover, if Britain appeared to be engaging in the United States support for Chiang Kai-shek in Taiwan, there might be counter-operations against Hong Kong.

The Foreign Secretary had sent them a message from his bed. He 'doubted whether it would be wise [for the United Kingdom] to try, in any public statement, to isolate the Korean incident from the other matters mentioned in the announcement which the United States proposed to make; for we would not wish to discourage that government from helping us and the French in resisting Communist encroachment in Malaya and Indo-China. In the Security Council, however, it was important that the resolution which the United States was to move should be confined strictly to events in Korea: and we should certainly advise the United States government that, whatever form their own public announcement might take, they should not include in the preamble to their resolution any reference to Communist threats in other parts of Asia which had not yet been brought before the Security Council'. Mr Shinwell,* Minister of Defence, was later to recall that the Prime Minister added a conviction of his own at that point. The United States might be risking a confrontation with the Soviet Union but they were right to be doing it to stop armed aggression. The memory of irresolution in stopping Hitler's aggression was fresh in their minds. The lesson there was to be firm at the outset.

There was also the possibility that, with attention focussed on Korea, the newly established communist government in Peking might be encouraged to invade Taiwan. In any case, they could not conceal the intervention of the Seventh Fleet. Accepting all this, the Cabinet agreed that they would urge the United States in their Security Council resolution to avoid reference to other Communist Asian 'encroachments' which had not been previously

*Shinwell, Rt Hon Emmanuel, later Baron Easington (1884–1986). After an unhappy time as Minister of Fuel and Power, 1945–7, he was moved to the War Office and then promoted following the February 1950 general election, to the Ministry of Defence. He was remarkably popular in both the latter departments and in the armed forces.

identified, and to refrain from suggesting that the North Korean invasion was due to 'centrally-directed Communist Imperialism'.*

From this meeting onwards, the United Kingdom was committed to the armed support of the Republic of Korea in its struggle to remain independent. As the meeting dispersed, the Cabinet Secretary remarked,

'Korea is rather a distant obligation, Prime Minister.'

'Distant—yes,' Mr Attlee replied, 'but nonetheless an obligation.'

---

*The United States agreed to modify the text accordingly.

SOURCE NOTES: CHAPTER 1

1. Johnston, Sir Alexander, GCB, KBE, (Deputy Secretary to the Cabinet 1948–51), conversation with author.

2. FO 371/35366 (U1430/G) Washington 1470 to FO of 28th March 1943.

3. Ibid. Minute on above by Sir M Petersen, 31st March 1943.

4. *Foreign Relations of the United States (FRUS) the conferences at Malta and Yalta 1945*, US Department of State publication, (Washington, 1950) p 770.

5. MacGrath, Paul C, 1st Lieutenant, *United States Army in the Korean Conflict*, (Office of the Chief of Military History (OCMH) Washington, 1948), pp 40–53.

6. FO371/46468 TERMINAL Conference: papers and minutes of San Francisco, July 1945. Minute on F4702/1394/23 of L H Foulds to Sterndale Bennett of 24th July 1945. See also CAB 83/74 UK Joint Chiefs of Staff Committee (COS), Joint Planning Staff (JPS) paper JP(45)217 (Final) of 28th August 1945, giving the same advice.

7. United Nations Documents, 1941–45, p 206.

8. United Nations document A/AC19/W6 of 16th December 1945.

9. See McGrath, op cit, pp 24–25, also Truman, Harry S. *Years of Trial and Hope, 1946–50,* (London, 1956), p 334.

10. Scallapino, Robert A and Lee, Chong-sik, *Communism in Korea*, (London, 1972) p 331.

11. See *History of the Occupation of Korea,* prepared in 1948 by the US XXIV Corps, vol II (of three), Chapter 2. A copy is held by the Chief of Military History, Washington, DC.

12. See, for example, Mead G Grant, *American Military Government in Korea*, Chapters 5 and 9 (London, 1951).

13. *Foreign Relations: The British Commonwealth and the Far East, 1945,* Vol VI, p 1071, US State Department publication (Washington 1969).

14. CAB 79/38, COS(45)210 of 30th August 1945.

15. FO 371/46459 (F6911/2426/23G) Washington 6193 to FO of 14th September 1945.

16. Ibid. Foreign Office memorandum FE(M)(45)10 of 9th October 1945, (intialled 6th October).

17. CAB 120/201 John G Winant, US Ambassador in London to Mr Bevin of 29 November 1945. For the background to the Byrnes initiative, see also the file of private papers of E Bevin as Foreign Secretary, 1945–6 (FO 800/501).

18. CAB 133/82 Moscow Conference proceedings, 1945, p 82.

19. CAB 128/2 Cabinet meeting, CM(45)60 of 6th December 1945.

20. Kennan, George F, *Memoirs (1925–50)* (Boston, 1967), p 287.

21. Suh Dae-sook *The Korean communist movement, 1918–48*, (Princeton, 1967), pp 318–329, also Kim Ch'ang-sun *Puk Han siponyon-sa (A Fifteen Year History of North Korea)*, (Seoul, 1961) pp 55–6, and O Yong-jin, *Hana ni-chung-on (An eyewitness account)* (Pusan, 1952), pp 141–143.

22. CAB 133/82 Moscow Conference proceedings, p 39.

23. Ibid, final agreement.

24. *Summary of events relating to Korea,* Annexes D and E contain useful extracts of these letters, HMSO Cmd 8078 (London, 1950).

25. FO 371/63838 (F12771/54/81) New York 2562 to FO of 17th September 1947. Connect also with Washington 5078 to FO, 17th September 1947.

26. For a commentary, see *International law and Korea*, Keeston, Manchester Guardian, 29 and 31 July, 1950.

27. Pickersgill J W and D F Foster, editors *The Mackenzie King Record, IV: 1947–1948*, (Toronto, 1970).

28. *Summary of events relating to Korea*, op cit, Annex G.

29. United Nations A/AC/19/66, Addendum 3, (Vol II, Annex VII)

30. FO 371/69943 (F10751/511/81), Letter from HM Consul-General, Seoul to FO, 20th July 1948.

31. FO 371/69942 (F8868/511/81), FO minute of Japan and Pacific Department circulated to United Nations, Political etc and Legal Adviser, 28th June 1948.

32. FO 371/69943 (F10339/511/81) Seoul No 58 to FO of 26th July 1948.

33. FO 371/69945 (F12637/511/81) Paper attached to letter from Washington 476/48 to FO of 6th September 1948.

34. Ibid, Minute FO to Washington 28th September 1948.

35. See verbatim United Nations record of 200th Meeting of the First Committee of the General Assembly, p 20.

36. FO 371/69945 (F13357/511/81), Final day of 200th Meeting of the First Committee of the United Nations General Assembly.

37. *Korea, 1945–8* (A Report on Political Developments and Economic Resources with Selected Documents), p 22, (US Department of State publication 3305); also *Background of Information on Korea*, (Report of the Committee on Foreign Affairs Pursuant to House Resolution 206), p 17, US Congress, 1950.

38. FO 371/69949 (F17776/511/81), Seoul 117 to FO of 27th November 1948.

39. Numbered in United Nations documentation respectively as A/575, A575/Add.1, Add.2, A/583.

40. 236th meeting of the United Nations General Assembly Interim Committee dated 8th December 1948.

41. 231st meeting of the United Nations General Assembly Interim Committee dated 7th December 1948.

42. For the background, see *Australia in the Korean War 1950–53, vol I: Strategy and Diplomacy*, Robert O'Neill, (Canberra, 1981), p 9.

43. Barclay, Roderick, *Ernest Bevin and the Foreign Office, 1932–69*, (London, 1975), p 68.

44. See Foreign Office file FK 1015/81 (FO 371/76258).

45. For the basis of this commitment, see Truman, op cit, p 347.

46. However, see *FRUS* Volume VII (Washington 1976) p 67 fn 1. For the text of Mr Acheson's remarks to the Press Club, see *Documents on International Affairs, 1949–50*, (RIIA, London), pp.96–108.

47. *FRUS* op cit, p 186, United States Department of State (USSD) 3124 to London of 27th June 1950.

CHAPTER 2

A Surprise Offensive

From the afternoon of 27th June 1950, the Korean war began to engage a small but important part of the machinery of government in Whitehall: in the Cabinet Office, the Foreign Office, the Defence Departments, in Commonwealth Relations, the Home Office, the Ministry of Labour, Departments of the Law Officers, and of course the Treasury. An immediate problem for the first four of these was the lack of information as to what was actually happening in the war zone. Captain Holt signalled the first bare facts from Seoul, but within forty eight hours was apprehensive of North Koreans entering the capital and so destroyed his cyphers. It had been in any case difficult for him to obtain facts in a city wild with rumours. At short notice, the government left for Taegu, 200 road miles to the south. The United States Embassy was at full stretch maintaining links with ministries in transit and the United States Military Advisory Group (KMAG), and the evacuation of its own and other nations' dependants, while simultaneously seeking news from various sites to keep Washington informed of events. Washington was also receiving news from the KMAG directly and via the headquarters of General MacArthur* in Tokyo. Not surprisingly, there were intermittent contradictions between what the Defense and State Departments received. On one point there was no disagreement, however: they had all been taken by surprise.

That surprise was the product of remarkable secrecy. Post-war evidence, by no means comprehensive or wholly trustworthy, suggests that Kim Il-sung proposed military invasion to Stalin early in 1949, and discussed the matter with Mao Tse-tung† in the October of that year; that Stalin consulted Mao Tse-tung, who began his first and only visit to Moscow on 16th December, and approved the operation in February 1950.[1] The communist guerrilla war in the southern half of Korea was losing momentum; by early 1950 it was being defeated by the local security forces. Despite

---

*MacArthur, Douglas (1880–1964), United States General of the Army, Allied Commander-in-Chief of the South West Pacific, 1942–45. In 1950, he was the Supreme Commander, Allied Powers in Japan, as chief of the occupation forces, and the United States Commander-in-Chief of its armed forces in the Far East (but not of the Seventh Fleet).
†Mao Tse-tung (1893–1976), Chairman of the Chinese Communist Party.

political hiccoughs, the United States government was evidently determined to provide financial aid to the Republic of Korea on a long term basis. There was no prospect of the communists and their associates coming to power by *coup de main* let alone popular vote. Kim's earlier expectations, therefore, of winning the south by subversion and intimidation showed no sign of realisation. On the other hand, by the end of 1949 the United States seemed increasingly unlikely to engage its armed forces in such distant sites as Korea; indeed, in January 1950 the Secretary of State appeared to confirm this explicitly*. The North Korean People's Army (NKPA) had a clear superiority in numbers and experience over its counterpart in the south. Its field army was then in excess of 100,000, of whom about a quarter had fought with the Chinese communist forces. Several thousand others had received extensive technical training in the Russian Army. A number of its senior officers had fought with that Army in the second world war, albeit in junior posts.[2] Staff colleges and other training establishments in North Korea had educated a comprehensive structure of officers from 1946 onwards.

None of this was matched in the armed forces of the south. Some of their leadership had served in the imperial Japanese Army but the majority were novices. Multiple political influences, language difficulties between American instructors and Koreans, and frequent deployment against guerrillas were among the many causes of delay in bringing into being a matured body with accomplished and disciplined leaders and staffs.[3]

The North Koreans had fighter-ground attack aircraft and light bombers; the south had none. The north had tanks; the south had none. The artillery of the North Korean People's Army outranged that of the Republic of Korea[4], was greater in strength and, in many cases, weight of shell†. President Syngman Rhee did not help this situation. Occasional emotional threats to invade the north if a political solution was not found chilled those in Washington responsible for providing him with arms, equipment and other war

---

*Addressing the National Press Club in Washington on 12th January 1950, Dean Acheson remarked, 'The [United States'] defensive perimeter runs along the Aleutians to Japan and then goes to the Ryukyus. We hold important defensive positions in the Ryukyu Islands, and these we will continue to hold . . . The defence perimeter runs from the Ryukyus to the Philippine Islands'. Korea was thus excluded. This speech complemented another by President Truman on 5th January relating to the decision of the United States not to interfere in the expected struggle for Taiwan between Nationalist and Communist Chinese forces.

†The NKPA had by June 1950 more than 100 120-mm howitzers with a range of 12,500 yards; over 200 76-mm guns with a range of 14,000 yards and a further 240 76-mm self-propelled guns and howitzers. The ROK Army had 90 105-mm guns with a range of just over 8,000 yards, and 115 57-mm guns with a range of 5,500 yards.

supplies for defence. The fact that he did not have the means was small comfort.

Notwithstanding their superiority in arms at the end of 1949, the North Korean People's Army lacked a sufficiency of the items needed to sustain an offensive campaign, particularly as there were plans also to expand by a further four divisions and two tank units. From February 1950 Stalin began to provide the increments for these objectives*. Much of the reinforcing war material was necessarily moved from Russia into North Korea across the railway system of North-East China; the Japanese had deliberately neglected communications between Korea and Russia during their long occupation of the former. Some items were also shipped by sea through the north east ports such as Hungnam and Wonsan but, because it was believed that this route was watched, shipping was restricted.

For their part, the Chinese resumed the return of Korean veterans, begun on a large scale in July 1949. In February and March 1950, about 12,000 crossed the Yalu river into their homeland. The majority of these formed what was to become the North Korean 12th Division. A few weeks later the activation of the 10th Mechanised Division began, while certain newly trained regiments were detailed to be ready to join selected border constabulary brigades to form the 13th and 15th Divisions. All these were to be ready for operations in June†.

The end of June was chosen for the opening of the invasion so as to permit the transplantation of rice shoots in the summer rains. It was expected that operations would be completed by the first rice harvest in August. Early in June, Kim Il-sung took a personal hand in the preliminary campaign of political deception. He proposed publicly on the 3rd that, as 5,300,000 Koreans had signed a petition for immediate peaceful unification, the national assemblies south and north should be merged on an equal basis and that preliminary consultations should be held during the 15th–17th with national elections in August. He stipulated that President Syngman Rhee, his ministers and principal officials were to be excluded from any part in this process and, equally, the United Nations Commission. As was to be expected, the President declined to abdicate. Resettling after this excitement, the newly elected Assembly in Seoul returned to negotiating for internal power. The North Korean People's Army began its deployment for war.

---

*Numerous items of North Korean equipment including armoured vehicles, captured later, bore Russian manufacturing dates 1949/50.

†For respective orders of battle in June 1950, see Appendix D.

Secrecy had been preserved in the north by close restriction of numbers privy to war planning in P'yongyang, which was supervised by Russian officers.[5] Principal orders were drafted initially in the Russian language. When the time came for these to be disseminated among the tactical formation commanders, they were carried 'by hand of officer'; nothing relating to them was permitted to be referred to by radio or telephone.

As deployment began, it was put about among the junior ranks that a large scale exercise would shortly be taking place, but this did not entirely deceive them. For one thing, the Russian military advisers were withdrawing from regiments when, normally, during exercises, their number multiplied in the field army. For another, there was not only a great deal of dumping forward of ammunition and fuel stocks but these began to be broken out on a grand scale. Fusing of shells was set in hand. No nation, however well supplied, can afford such preparations unless it expects shortly to be at war.

There was no such activity in the south. By chance, two Australian observers from the United Nations Commission toured the Republic of Korea's positions on the 38th parallel from 9th to 23rd June*. The report of their observations included the following:

1. The South Korean Army in all sectors is disposed in depth. The parallel is guarded on the southern side only by small bodies of troops located in scattered outposts together with roving patrols. There is no concentration of troops, and no massing for attack at any visible point . . .

5. The South Korean Army does not appear to be in possession of military or other supplies that would indicate preparations for a large scale attack. In particular, there is no sign of any dumping of supplies of ammunition or petrol, oil, lubricants in forward areas. Roads generally are little used and apart from a convoy of trucks taking a company from Kangnung westwards . . . no concentration of transport was anywhere encountered . . .

7. There is no indication of any extensive reconnaissance being carried out· northwards by the South Korean Army, nor is any undue excitement or activity observed at the Divisional Headquarters or at regimental levels to suggest preparation for offensive activity. The observers were freely admitted to all sections of the various Headquarters and Operations rooms . . .

---

*Major F S B Peach and Squadron-Leader R J Rankin were indeed the only two military observers with the Commission. Other nations had not responded to its request on 2nd March to contribute to a team to 'observe and report any development which might lead to or otherwise involve military conflict in Korea'.

8. The observers made a special point of enquiring what information was coming in regarding the situation north of the parallel. In some sectors it had been reported that civilians had recently been removed from areas adjoining the parallel to the north to depths varying from 4 to 8 kilometres. Another report received during the night of Thursday 22 June at the regimental headquarters in Ongjin was to the effect that there was increased military activity in the vicinity of Chwiyari, about 4 kilometres north of the parallel. No reports, however, had been received of any unusual activity on the part of the North Korean forces that would indicate any imminent change in the general situation on the parallel.[6]

This report was written in Seoul on Saturday, 24th June. It is a testimony not only to the light manning of the parallel by the Republic of Korea but equally to the excellence of North Korean political and military security. All the extensive military and civilian movement that had taken place had been largely undetected: the emplacement of weapons, the breaking out of ammunition to tank, gun and mortar sites, the distribution of fuel and rations, the setting up of main and reserve communications necessary to the opening of a coordinated offensive had been successfully concealed. The assault echelons of two corps were hiding on that Saturday in towns or villages, factories, railway tunnels, woods or scrub. They would emerge from these after darkness late on the Saturday evening to march to their respective start lines, gun or mortar areas. Several groups of guerrilla and raiding forces were already embarked in fishing boats ready to put to sea at dusk *en route* to landings on the east coast at dawn.

From 0400, then, on the overcast, showery morning of Sunday, 25th June, artillery and mortar fire opened progressively from west to east along the parallel lasting, in some areas, for an hour, in others about 20 minutes. As soon as each local bombardment ended, the infantry assaulted the foremost South Korean localities along the border as others, from behind, passed through to begin engagement of the deeper defences. Wherever the ground suited their use, tanks advanced with the infantry. The task of the invading force was made easier in the western sector because a substantial number among the defence garrisons was away on weekend leave.

The attack in the west was mounted by the North Korean I Corps. Its principal task immediately was to capture Seoul and, with the prospect of operating in more open country, it had been allotted the greater number of the 150 Russian T-34 tanks committed to the battle. The II Corps attacked in the eastern sector, advancing simultaneously on the Ch'unch'on-Hongch'on central road junctions. Somewhat to the surprise of senior commanders in both corps, the resistance of their southern compatriots grew steadily during the 25th to the point that the advance was several times brought to a prolonged halt. The Republic of Korea's infantry fought doggedly. Lacking effective anti-tank weapons, they sought heroically at a number of points to destroy the T-34s by placing explosive charges under or on to the tanks engaging them. Engineers joined these actions. The American 105-mm field guns were well served by the Republic of Korea's gunners who inflicted many casualties among the NKPA's infantry during the latter part of the 25th and throughout Monday, 26th June, as across the front line the remnant of the foremost defenders fell back upon their divisional main positions, and the latter swelled out to full strength with men hurrying back from leave. Within the next twenty four hours, however, three circumstances were to bring about an early and disastrous defeat.

The first was that there were only four field divisions forward* in defence, the remaining three being well to the south, engaged in counter-guerrilla operations or the completion of training. Those forward had to cover the whole front while their enemy, superior in numbers and quality of arms, possessing the initiative, was able to attack, concentrated, at selected points. The second was the lack of a tactical air force, indeed of any air defences. Third, the high command of the Republic of Korea's Army (ROK Army) was incapable of conducting operations.

Sound arrangements had been made in Seoul to resist a variety of North Korean attack options, and with the four forward divisions maintaining their integrity in withdrawal a sustained defence would have been possible and perhaps even a counter-attack developed from within Seoul. The plan made, however, was implemented precipitately and failed. By the evening of 27th June, the two divisions in the eastern sector were withdrawing independently, lacking any coherent instructions from the ROK Army Headquarters. Those in the west, though reinforced by elements arriving from the south, were in a retreat rapidly becoming a rout. North Korean mechanised forces were moving through Uijongbu towards Seoul—had, indeed, reconnaissance forces in the northern outskirts of the capital. Within, the city roads were choked by military traffic and refugees pressing towards the huge bridge spanning the river Han on the southern edge. Rumours, doubts, anxieties, lack of

---

*The almost indefensible enclave on the Ongjin peninsula in the extreme west was held by an independent force which, by pre-arrangement, was withdrawn by sea on attack. In Seoul, there was also the Capitol Division, but this was principally a ceremonial and guard formation.

decision and organisational arrangements then brought about one of those events common in the opening days of a surprise offensive. The crowded Han bridge was blown precipitately by engineers of the defending army.* Not only were hundreds killed upon the demolished spans; almost half of the ROK Army, and more than half of their transport, heavy weapons and equipment, were lost on the northern bank.

This disaster took place between 2 and 3 a.m. on 28th June, Korean time—between 5 and 6 p.m. in London, 12 noon and 1 p.m. in Washington and New York on 27th June. By that time, several decisions were in train to relieve the Republic of Korea's difficulties, though the magnitude of these was then unperceived.

President Truman had authorised the use of United States naval and air forces against North Koreans operating below the 38th parallel, and the release of such arms, ammunition and equipment from American stocks in Japan as General MacArthur judged could be spared and usefully used by the ROK forces. Of his own initiative, Admiral Brind†, Royal Navy, Commander-in-Chief of the Far East Station, had sent the following signal to Vice Admiral Joy‡, United States Naval commander, Far East, (COMNAVFE):

Should like my ships to take part in any humanitarian mission you may desire and I hope you will tell [my] Flag Officer Second-in-Command, Far East Station if there is anything else they can do to help you.[7]

To his second-in-command, Rear Admiral Andrewes§, he sent instructions which indicated that he was putting the greater part of his fleet into position in case they should be needed for more active operations:

Korea. Fleet may be called upon for action under United Nations Charter. All available ships at your disposal for this purpose if so ordered operating under Comnav F.E. [sic] Malayan and Hong Kong Forces are to be kept at present strength.

---

*The chief of the Army engineers was later executed for this action but was widely—and still is—believed to have been a scapegoat.

†Brind, Admiral Sir (Eric James) Patrick, KCB CBE RN (1892–1963). He was at this time at sea, en route to Hong Kong from Japan, where he had been visiting his ships. He had sent the major part of the Far East Fleet there to give the officers and men relief from the summer heat of Hong Kong and Singapore. By arrangement with General MacArthur, they were to be attached to his naval forces of occupation under Admiral Joy.

‡Joy, Vice-Admiral C Turner USN, (1895–1956). He was later to be the first chief UN delegate to the armistice talks in Korea.

§Andrewes, Rear-Admiral W G (later Vice-Admiral Sir William KBE) CB DSO RN (1899–1974). It was his function, as second-in-command, to command the fleet at sea.

2. Recall *Triumph* [light fleet carrier] to Japanese waters. Inform me when you need *Unicorn* [support carrier] with Reserve Aircraft.

3. Operations under para 1 above are to have a precedence over Yangtse and Amoy patrols which should remain in force for as long as practicable.[8]

Admiral Andrewes noted later '9. . . . I drove to Tokyo to see Commander Naval Forces, Far East. He informed me that he took a serious view of the situation on land in Korea, and that he did not at the moment require British ships to help with the evacuation or any other humanitarian duty, as all British and United States nationals who wished to leave Korea had already been evacuated. He was anxious not to have too many ships in Japanese ports as he did not know what the immediate Russian reaction might be to any direct intervention by United Nations Forces.'[9] The lesson of Pearl Harbour was not lost upon the American admiral.

He was not alone in his apprehension of general war; ministers, officials, defence staffs in Washington, London, Paris, Canberra and many other capitals were debating whether Russia would intervene by direct military action in support of the North Koreans. On balance, the early conclusion was that it was less, rather than more, likely that they would do so; and a few, like President Truman and Mr Attlee took quickly and independently the view that whatever the risk of confrontation in Korea, it must be faced. The idea that Russia was creating a diversion in Korea was also widely considered: Lord Tedder* reported from Washington that the Chairman of the American Chiefs of Staff, General Bradley†, 'suspected that the next move [by the Soviet Union] might well be in Iran and that the sooner our Governments decided what action they would take in such circumstances the better'[10], a view coincidentally held in the State Department and the Foreign Office. Such ideas were encouraged by reflection on the earlier withdrawal of Russian international delegations from two important points of contact. In January, 1950, Mr Malik‡ had removed himself and his staff from the Security Council when the latter declined by majority vote to displace the representative of Nationalist China

---

*Tedder, Marshal of the Royal Air Force Arthur William, GCB, 1st Baron Glenguin (1890–1967). After holding a series of high commands in the second world war, Chief of the Air Staff in 1946–49, he was appointed head of the British Joint Services Mission in Washington in 1950.

†Bradley, Omar Nelson, General of the Army (1893–1981), an army group commander in the second world war he became Chief of the United States Army Staff in 1948, and Chairman of the Joint Chiefs of Staff in 1949.

‡Malik, Yakov Alexandrovich (1906–80) head of the Russian delegation to the United Nations. He was later Ambassador to the United Kingdom

and open the seat to the newly established People's Republic. The Russians were still absent from the Council in June. In May, Lieutenant-General K N Derevyanko and Ambassador Panyushkin had withdrawn from the Allied Council in Tokyo in order to have consultations and leave in the Soviet homeland. They were still consulting and holidaying in June. When, on 27th June, the United States Ambassador in Moscow sought an interview with the Soviet Foreign Minister or his deputy to make representations about the war in Korea, he was informed that neither was available.

Without Russian participation, then, the Security Council met on the afternoon of the 27th. The galleries of the council chamber were packed with delegation supporters, officials and members of the public as the President, Sir Benegal Rau*, opened the meeting by reading the latest news of the war sent by the Commission in Korea†.[11] He could not then deny himself a brief expression of an idea he had earlier aired to some of his colleagues informally, that a meeting between heads of state—he had in mind President Truman and Marshal Stalin no doubt—would be advantageous. For many, he suggested, saw in the events of the last two days an introductory phase to 'a third world war, with all its horrors. A terrible burden therefore rests upon us as the body charged with the primary responsibility for the maintenance of international peace . . .'. A meeting between the respective Prime Ministers of India and Pakistan had recently eased the tension between the two countries, he reminded them, but then forbore to press this example upon his fellow members; he knew that the majority were persuaded that they were past the point of conciliation.

The United States representative now put this latter point in the plainest terms to the Council. '. . . the North Korean authorities have completely disregarded and flouted the Council's cease fire and withdrawal order of 25th June . . . The most important provisions of the Charter are those outlawing aggressive war. It is precisely these provisions which the North Korean authorities have violated. . . The Republic of Korea has appealed to the United Nations for protection. I am happy and proud to report that the United States is prepared as a loyal member of the United Nations to furnish assistance to the Republic of Korea.' He proposed formally that '. . . the members of the United Nations furnish such assistance to the Republic of Korea as may be necessary to repel the armed attack and to restore international peace and security

---

*Rau, Sir Benegal Rama (1889–1969), Indian Civil Service. While acting as his country's representative at the UN, he was also Governor of the Reserve Bank of India.
†This had been sent late on 26th June. Next day, after a vain attempt to establish contact with the Korean government in Suwon, the Commission was evacuated by United States aircraft to Japan.

in the area. It was, he said, the logical consequence of the resolution adopted by the Council two days before and the subsequent events. President Truman's statement, amended to meet the suggestions of the British Cabinet, was then read to the Council.

The Yugoslav representative made a counter proposal: the two Korean elements should again be called upon to cease hostilities. There was still time for mediation and to that end a North Korean representative should be invited to join them*. 'Much agitated', in the view of a member of the British delegation, the South Korean spokesman appealed to all members for immediate assistance; the resolution adopted on 25th June had made the moral stance of the United Nations clear. 'That moral judgement must be backed by the power of enforcement.' The remaining speakers, Nationalist China, Cuba, Ecuador, Norway and the United Kingdom among them, gave full agreement to this. It was time to vote.

The Egyptian and Indian representatives, however, regretted that they lacked instructions and so the Council adjourned at 5.10 p.m. to give them an opportunity to obtain them. Yet, when they resumed at 10.25 p.m. that evening, neither Mohammed Fawzi Bey for Egypt nor Sir Benegal Rau for India had, as they said, been able to make contact with their respective governments, statements widely believed by their international colleagues to mean that their governments had not made up their minds what to do†. After a brief consultation with the remaining members and the Secretary-General, Trygve Lie‡, the President called for voting. The United States resolution was carried 7:1, the Yugoslav resolution was lost 7:1, Yugoslavia being in the minority in each case§. As this business was concluded, it was rising 1 p.m. in the afternoon of 28th June in Korea, 4 a.m. in London on that same day.

When the news of the Security Council's resolution reached the British Chiefs of Staff—the First Sea Lord and the Chief of the Air Staff in London, the Chief of the Imperial General Staff in Australia on tour—their reaction was common: it was right in principle to support the Republic of Korea by armed intervention but difficult for the United Kingdom to do so. Notwithstanding withdrawal from substantial garrison commitments in the Indian sub-continent, Greece and Palestine, the greater part of the armed

---

*Next day, the Yugoslav government in an unattributable press briefing explained its apparently 'indefinite attitude' in the Council by expressing the view that 'otherwise the Cominform would seize the opportunity of proving that Yugoslavia had gone over to the West and the USSR would exploit this to increase its pressure on Yugoslavia.'[12]

†For confirmation of this, see page 50.

‡Lie, Trygve, (1896–1968), Norwegian statesman, first Secretary-General of the United Nations, 1946–52

§See Appendix A.

forces were still engaged world wide. Counter-guerrilla operations were continuing on an increasing scale in Malaya. Hong Kong was believed to be threatened by the People's Republic of China; a brigade had recently been sent there as a reinforcement from the United Kingdom by way of deterrence. A British army and a tactical air force were in the British zone in Germany, with associated line of communication and base elements in France, Belgium and Holland; a commitment which was expected to expand as a consequence of British accession to the Atlantic Alliance*. Then, the British Chiefs, like their colleagues in the Foreign and Commonwealth Relations Offices, were apprehensive of other Russian adventures: into Iran, for example, Yugoslavia or Scandinavia. In London and Washington there was a notion that Stalin was seeking to draw out the Atlantic powers to a Far Eastern sideshow. Here was the rub: the blaze might be in Korea just now but if he started fires elsewhere over the range of oceans and continents they would run out of fire brigades†.

Asked by the Cabinet on 27th June, 'what practical steps the United Kingdom could take to assist the Republic of Korea', the Chiefs' short answer might have been 'not much'—the jocular suggestion of the First Sea Lord when they met to consider their response. Next afternoon he spoke more formally and fully to the Defence Committee of the Cabinet, meeting in the Prime Minister's room in the House of Commons.

The Chiefs welcomed the United States' intervention in Korea and in the Taiwan strait. Though they doubted that action by sea and air forces alone would restore the situation in Korea, the only British forces available speedily and without endangering commitments elsewhere were the warships currently in Japanese waters under Admiral Andrewes. Ministers accepted their recommendations, though there was dissent on some peripheral proposals and a clear warning that the Royal Navy was not to join American operations in the Taiwan strait. The Foreign Office was to report the British government's decision to the Security Council, the United States and the Republic of Korea. The Commonwealth governments should be asked 'to take any action to the same end which they might think appropriate.' The Defence departments should implement the decisions made in their sphere. The Prime Minister said he would inform the House of Commons at once

---

*With the United States and France, the United Kingdom was a founder member of the Atlantic Treaty, compacted on 4th April 1949, which led to the North Atlantic Treaty Organisation. Among other commitments, the UK was expected to commit seven divisions to Germany. It then had two in position.

†For a view of the Russian threat in the Far East see the appreciation of the Commissioner-General and Commanders-in-Chief of 27th June 1950.[13]

about the naval deployment; he had made arrangements to make a statement almost as soon as their business was completed. 'It was a customarily brisk meeting; Mr Attlee expected Ministers to have read and digested the memoranda beforehand.[14] Forty minutes after assembling, politicians, officers and officials were going their separate ways.

The Defence Committee was functioning on lines developed in the first and second world wars. The Prime Minister had taken the chair. The members were those concerned with matters of inter-related defence and oversea policy: the Foreign Office; the Treasury; Labour; the Ministry of Defence, the three single Service departments and the Ministry of Supply (defence procurement). In view of other implications—Hong Kong and Malaya, for example—the Secretary of State for the Colonies was in attendance and, similarly, the Secretary of State for Commonwealth Relations. The officials and advisers invariably present were the Secretary of the Cabinet and the Chiefs of Staff. The secretariat was comprised of the Chief Staff Officer to the Minister of Defence, his deputy, and a representative of the Foreign Office.

As Minister of Defence, Mr Shinwell was the Cabinet member responsible for the coordination of defence matters, though he was not at all concerned with the day to day running of the Admiralty, the War Office or the Air Ministry, whose Secretaries of State, whilst not Cabinet members, answered on most purely single service matters directly to the Prime Minister. His Chief Staff Officer, Air Marshal Sir William Elliot*, was the principal link between the Cabinet and the Chiefs of Staff. He attended the meetings of the latter as an associate member—as did his Foreign Office colleague on the Committee—incumbent of a post requiring him to be the point of common contact, the prime agent for the transaction of politico-military policy by government. He had few exclusive subordinates but a number who acknowledged his part in the direction of their affairs. The Joint Planning Staff—the JPS—was such a body. So too, to the extent that they served the defence establishment, were the directors of single service intelligence, with the Joint Intelligence Staff, the JIS. The Joint Administrative Planning Staff, the JAPS, was a complementary element in this field of joint staff work.

As a consequence of the Defence Committee meeting in the House of Commons the Joint Planning Staff was instructed to prepare, in conjunction with the Joint Intelligence Staff, two reports:

---

*Elliot, Air Marshal (later, Air Chief Marshal) Sir William, GCVO KCB KBE DFC RAF (1896–1971).

(i) on the implications of the situation in Korea on Formosa [Taiwan], Hong Kong and British interests in south-east Asia generally.

(ii) examining the likelihood of further Russian attacks elsewhere and the measures which should be taken to meet such attacks.[15]

This was not going to be an easy task in as much as the intelligence available was deficient; the Directors of Intelligence reported to the Chiefs of Staff on the afternoon of the 28th that almost all information about Russian movements was at least three weeks old. They had no adequate intelligence about events inside the Soviet Union.[16] Direct information about what was happening in Korea continued to be fragmentary.

Air Marshal Elliot had remarked in a signal to Lord Tedder in Washington on 26th June, 'We are, as you can imagine, very lacking in information about Korea . . . and again on the 27th,

> Most of our information on the situation in Korea comes from the UK [Diplomatic] Liaison Mission in Tokyo as the result of an unofficial arrangement with G2 [General MacArthur's intelligence staff]. Without this we should virtually know little more than appears in the Press. We are under orders to produce a daily report of the situation for the Prime Minister. This being so it would be most helpful if you could urgently obtain Bradley's agreement to General MacArthur being told to authorise this channel officially and tell us all he can.[17]

The Director of Military Intelligence was similarly signalling direct to the Army attaché with the diplomatic mission in Tokyo.

The flow of political information was better. Ambassadors and High Commissioners round the world were reporting frequently their activities and impressions concerning the Korean hostilities; and while these were inevitably productive of indirect material their contributions were valuable to the policy and intelligence staffs.

Sir Alvary Gascoigne*, head of the UK mission in Tokyo, had sent the following on 26th June, a telegram which reflected the limits of his own relationship with General MacArthur:

> Allison, State Department official accompanying Mr Dulles†, gave [my] Counsellor in strictest confidence the following at 1315

---

*Gascoigne, Sir Alvary Douglas Frederick, GCB, KCMG (1893-1970) was the British Government's representative among the Occupying Powers in Japan. As no peace treaty had been concluded with Japan it was not a sovereign state, and had no diplomatic missions accredited to it.

†Dulles, John Foster (1888-1959) lawyer, diplomat and statesman, American Secretary of State (1953-59).

hours today regarding the Supreme Commander's reactions to events in Korea.

2. A conference took place last night between the Supreme Commander and Mr Dulles at which General MacArthur expressed his surprise that the North Korean attack should have taken place at this particular juncture and in such blatant fashion. The general was confident that provided he was given a moderately free hand he was in a position to cope with the situation . . .

3. Meanwhile some measures have already been taken. Supplies . . . are now being loaded for arrival at Korean ports in two or three days. Aircraft are also being despatched for use of South Korean Air Force. They will be manned by Koreans unless Koreans show themselves incapable of making good use of them, in which case the provision of American crews will be considered . . .[18]

From the British Consul in Shanghai came the information that,

On June 26th the North China Daily News published Reuter's report from Tokyo of June 25th under the headline "North Korea declares war on South Korea". For this the editor was verbally spanked by the Foreign Affairs Bureau [of the government in Peking] and ordered to suspend publication for three days . . .[19]

The High Commissioner in Delhi was discovering the reason for the Indian avoidance of voting at the Security Council meeting on 27th June:

I asked Bajpai* today what was the attitude of his Government about the Korea situation.

2. He said he had only had a hurried talk with the Prime Minister [Pandit Nehru †] last night and again this morning and no clear policy had so far emerged. The Prime Minister seemed to be inclined to take no action because he stood a good chance to lay himself open to criticism that if he supported one particular side he would be guilty of aligning himself with one particular bloc . . .

3. I naturally pointed out that failure to condemn aggression would strike at the whole basis of Membership of the United

*Bajpai, Sir Girja Shankar KCSI KBE CIE (1891–1967) Secretary-General (Permanent Secretary) in the Ministry of External (Foreign) Affairs, 1947–52.
†Nehru, Pandit Jawaharlal (1889–1964). First Prime Minister and Minister of External Affairs when India became independent in 1947.

Nations Organisation and could not conceive how India could possibly attempt adoption of a neutral policy in such a matter. Bajpai did not argue this rather obvious truism but said that the Prime Minister was in such a hurry that he had not had time to put to him what he called 'the other side of the medal'.[20]

Sir David Kelly, British Ambassador in Moscow, reported on 28th June,

Today's press again publishes selection of agency reports from all sources, and Truman's statement is adequately summarised. First comment has appeared in form of Pravda leader . . .
2. Main points made are (a) United States action constitutes ''direct acts of aggression'' against Chinese and Korean republics and (b) absence of any United Nations authority for steps announced by Truman.
3. No hint is given of Soviet intentions and article seems clearly intended to hold position while policy is decided. Reference to aggression against China is however somewhat ominous in view of terms of new Sino-Soviet Treaty [of February 1950].

Mr Hutchison, *Chargé d'Affaires* in Peking*, signalled on 29th June

. . .My first tentative and personal views of the situation as seen from here are (a) the attack by the North Korean forces upon South Korea was arranged through Russian influence to prevent possible American implication in and an imminent invasion by 'People's Liberation Army' of Formosa (b) the strength and extent of American reaction has been a shocking surprise and will prove a grave embarrassment to the People's Government (c) these developments may have consequences very seriously affecting our position in this country now and in the future.
2. As regards (a) I had indeed considered reporting my view that the press campaign here which preceded the attack on South Korea was probably indicative of immediate imminence of invasion of Formosa . . . absence during the past few weeks of General Chu Teh† from meetings . . . also seemed to indicate that the invasion of Formosa would soon be attempted.

---

*Hutchison, (later Sir) John Colville (1890–1965) was head of the United Kingdom Mission in Peking negotiating the establishment of full, formal inter-governmental relations with the new People's Republic of China. The talks were protracted and the mission was drawn into the conduct of everyday business, an arrangement which for the time being suited both governments.
†Chu Teh, Marshal of the People's Republic of China (1886–1976), professional soldier who was an early collaborator with Mao Tse-tung. He commanded the People's Liberation Army during the civil war, was a Vice-Chairman of the Party Central Committee, the Military Affairs Committee and the Politburo.

3. As regards (b) it seems incredible that the authorities would have permitted the publication on 25th June of the letter from four Kuomintang Generals* calling upon the people and troops in Formosa to rise because "the eleventh hour is approaching" had they had any reason to suppose that America would actually intervene to prevent invasion. . . . More generally, I still feel that the Chinese Government have had every intention of keeping clear of international hostilities (or even serious entanglements) at least until they firmly establish internal political, social and economic conditions on a sound basis . . .[21]

From Australia and New Zealand there had been welcome news as Mr Attlee announced in the House of Commons on the 29th:

Honourable Members will probably have learned by now with gratification that the Australian government has decided to place Australian naval vessels at present in Far Eastern waters at the disposal of the United States authorities on behalf of the Security Council . . . [and the] statement of the Australian Prime Minister† in support of President Truman's declaration.

I have seen press reports that the Australian government is not proceeding with the withdrawal of its occupation forces from Japan until the present emergency is past. ‡

The New Zealand government have stated their firm support for the action which has been taken by the United States and have offered to make certain New Zealand naval forces available. . .

MPs were already aware that Canada was in similar accord.
A British Commonwealth naval force, considerably more than a 'token' , was thus in process of forming up. Immediately, at the end of June and in early July, it comprised:

HMS *Triumph* —light fleet carrier
HMS *Belfast* ⎱
HMS *Jamaica* ⎰ cruisers
HMS *Consort* ⎱
HMS *Cossack* ⎰ destroyers
HMS *Alacrity* ⎱
HMS *Black Swan* ⎰ frigates
HMS *Hart* ⎰

---

*Who had come over to the People's Republic.
†Menzies, the Rt Hon (later Sir) Robert Gordon (1894–1978).
‡Following the defeat of Japan, a British Commonwealth Occupation Force was established there. By 1950, however, Australia was the only member still disposing forces which included a warship, an infantry battalion and an air squadron. The Australian government had earlier decided to withdraw this by the end of 1950.

Fort Charlotte ⎫
Green Ranger ⎭ Royal Fleet Auxiliaries

HM Hospital Ship *Maine*

HMAS *Bataan* —Australian destroyer, arriving

HMAS *Shoalhaven* —Australian frigate*

Committed to join:

HMNZS *Pukaki* ⎫
HMNZS *Tutira* ⎭ New Zealand frigates

The British element of this force had been formally committed by a signal from the Admiralty instructing Admiral Brind to 'place the Royal Navy at present in Japanese waters at the disposal of the United States naval commander for Korean operations [Vice-Admiral C. Turner Joy] in support of the Security Council resolutions.'[22] When Admiral Brind responded that this instruction might prove restrictive, excluding him from operating with the United States Seventh Fleet in the Formosa strait, he was told by the First Sea Lord that operations in this area were in no circumstances to be permitted because they might stimulate a reaction by the Peking government against Hong Kong. The need for a clear definition of commitment had arisen in part because, on the 29th June, it had become apparent that General MacArthur, as United Nations Commander-in-Chief, was extending air operations north of the 38th parallel without the authority of the United States government.[23]† On learning of this at an evening briefing by Air Marshal Elliot, Mr Attlee had become concerned that commitments might become extended casually. He was unhappy at the information they had of events and intentions and sent for Lord Fraser‡, First Sea Lord and the senior member of the Chiefs of Staff Committee, to ask him to obtain on a personal basis, through Lord Tedder in Washington, American ideas for future operations.[24]

On the 30th, the Chiefs signalled the head of the British Joint Services Mission (BJSM):

> Prime Minister is anxious to obtain some idea of the American plan of Campaign in Korea as indeed we are, since British and Commonwealth forces are now taking part.
>
> 2. We assume that the American intention is to clear the territory up to the 38th parallel. The following questions are therefore relevant:

---

*Shoalhaven had been on duty in Japanese waters as part of the Commonwealth Occupation Force committment for five months and was in process of being relieved by *Bataan*.

†For an illuminating account of General MacArthur's musing on this matter, see 'With the Australians in Korea' , ed. Norman Bartlett (Canberra, 1954) pp. 170–174.

‡Fraser, Admiral of the Fleet Bruce Austin (1888–1981), 1st Baron Moseley, Fraser of North Cape, GCB KBE.

(a) What American forces are immediately available and what reinforcements are envisaged.

(b) Is it the intention to use land forces if this become necessary.

3. As the Americans have committed themselves to restore the *status quo* the US Chiefs of Staff are doubtless making some appreciation of what this is likely to entail including the timing. We would be very grateful for their views on this in due course.

4. We realise that the US Government cannot commit themselves at the present time but we are most anxious to know unofficially the way the Chiefs of Staff are thinking. A preliminary indication of their views early next week would be of the greatest value.'[25].

A reply came within hours from Lord Tedder:

Following points arose in personal talk with Bradley on his return from the White House.

2. Immediate action in Korea is to put combat group by air and sea to secure port on SE coast. Bradley's view is that of the four [occupation] divisions in Japan MacArthur could with safety employ two in Korea if necessary. If more were to be needed in Korea their places in Japan would have to be filled from US. President has authorised employment of US naval and air forces North of the 38th parallel against the Northern Korean forces.

3. At this morning's meeting at the White House which was a non-party one representing all parties and both Houses [of Congress] hope was expressed that all nations would make some definite contribution to the UN forces in Korea even though the main burden inevitably American and such contributions in most cases merely token ones. Bradley said that UK and Commonwealth contributions widely and genuinely appreciated, both as regards their promptitude and scale. He realised our already heavy commitments in Far East but said that if repeat if a land force contribution however small could be added it would have excellent political effect in sealing even more firmly our complete unity on this issue.

4. Bradley said his view, and I understand the US Chiefs of Staff view, is that the Soviet has no desire for a war at this stage. On the other hand this affair is a warning to us to overhaul our plans and preparations against the major threat and we touched on problems of higher direction, command, state of present planning purely in exploratory fashion.

5. Am sure I need not emphasise that above was all given in confidence on purely personal basis . . .[26]

With this the Prime Minister, his colleagues, foreign and defence staffs were, for the time being at least, content; the more so as Lord Tedder also indicated agreement in Washington to the immediate passage of all information on Korean events to the British Joint Services Mission, and approving similar arrangements for the British mission in Tokyo with General MacArthur's headquarters.

Mr Attlee and Mr Bevin were content, too, that a proper military command arrangement was developing because, in parallel with the communications between the chiefs on either side of the Atlantic, other ideas had been suggested. Sir Gladwyn Jebb*, who had now assumed his post as United Kingdom delegate to the United Nations, reported on 29th June:

> . . . The Secretary-General was this afternoon [the 28th] on the point of circularising all members of the United Nations requesting them advise him of assistance which they intended to offer to the Security Council . . .
>
> 2. On receipt of this intelligence Mr Gross [US delegation] called on M. Cordier [UN international staff] and induced him to hold up all action temporarily. . .
>
> 3. . . . the reasons which had induced the United States Delegation to intervene were as follows:
>
> (a) They wanted to avoid creating embarrassment for Government such as the French who would in practice be able to contribute little or nothing.
>
> (b) More importantly, they did not wish any offers of assistance to be transmitted *to the Security Council itself.*
>
> (c) . . . if Mr Lie insisted on sending out his circular telegram it should in the United States view be made clear that the offer of assistance was to the Government of the Republic of Korea in the latter's capacity as "victim of aggression". The United States Government believe in fact that the Security Council could not be so to speak "operational" for the simple reason that the necessary agreements had not yet been concluded under Article 43 of the Charter.
>
> 4. In telling me this Mr Gross hastened to add that his Government were of course deeply grateful for the offer of assistance contained in the Prime Minister's statement . . . it was essential for His Majesty's Government to act quickly . . . It remained a fact, however, that as they saw it the arguments against using the Security Council for any organisational or operational purposes were very cogent.

---

*Jebb, Sir (Herbert Miles) Gladwyn (later, 1st Baron Gladwyn of Bramfield), GCVO GCMG CB (1900–).

5. . . . he had just told Mr Chauvel* [French Delegate] as well as the [Council] secretariat that the United States Government were strongly opposed to any effort to make use of the [United Nations] Military Staff Committee in connexion with the present crisis. Quite apart from the fact that the Military Staff Committee was not capable of doing any practical work an impossible situation would arise if the Russians suddenly turned up and demanded to see any plans which the Military Staff Committee had been preparing.

6. Finally Mr Gross said that the State Department felt strongly that there should be no formal or informal designation of General MacArthur as Supreme Commander or indeed of the United States as so to speak the executive power of the Security Council. It was quite true that in practice things might work out in this last direction but the United States Government did not want to be involved in any legal tangle as a result of such designation being formally made . . .[27]

'Legal tangles' were just what the British government and all those with whom they were associated in the decision to aid the Republic of Korea did not want. Among a range of incipient counter-moves, the Russians were developing an argument that the Security Council's resolution was invalid in the absence of the Soviet Union's delegate. The Foreign Office replied, *inter alia*, to Sir Gladwyn Jebb on 29th June, '. . . We are urgently considering the implications of the Secretary-General's proposal which clearly might give rise to difficulties. A further telegram on this point and an exposition of the legal position will follow as soon as possible . . .[28]

Ideas on the legal position were soon being aired more widely. The Commonwealth Relations Office (CRO) informed Australia, Canada, Ceylon, India, New Zealand, Pakistan and South Africa later on the 29th June,

In absence of Soviet Union from Security Council, we have been considering whether to make some direct approach to Soviet Government. Anglo-Soviet Treaty of 1942 might have provided grounds for such an approach, but in view of passages on the treaty in ''Statment on the North Atlantic Pact'' issued by Soviet Ministry of Foreign Affairs on January 29th 1949, we have concluded that it would be wiser to avoid reference to it. On the other hand we are reluctant to expose ourselves to accusation that at time like this we have made no attempt to

*Chauvel M. Jean, Hon. GCMG GCVO DCL(Oxon) (1897–1979), distinguished French diplomat and author.

establish direct contact with Soviet Government. We have therefore instructed United Kingdom Ambassador in Moscow to seek
urgent interview today with highest available Soviet official and
urge Soviet Government in general terms to cooperate in effecting
a peaceful settlement of Korean conflict.

2. If Russians should question competence of Security Council
to take decisions in their absence, United Kingdom Ambassador
has been instructed to point out that Article 28 provides that
Security Council should function continuously. Absence of one
member cannot of course be allowed to frustrate object of this
Article and cannot therefore be regarded as any more than an
abstention on any vote which might be taken. It is now accepted
practice of Security Council that an abstention by a permanent
member even on a question of substance does not (repeat not)
count as a veto. Russians have themselves on occasion subscribed
to this practice.[29]

Next day, Sir Gladwyn Jebb advanced another thought on this
matter:

. . . Abstention is essentially a discretionary act of the permanent
member concerned and it would be difficult for the Council to
assume that it has taken place particularly when the permanent
member has declared in advance that it will consider all such
decisions invalid. A stronger legal basis for argument might
therefore be that the Soviet Union cannot claim the rights of a
permanent member under Article 27 (III) of the Charter so long
as it fails to perform its duties under Article 28. I do not suggest
that we should necessarily adopt this alternative line . . . but
you may wish to consider it.[30]

The challenge by the Soviet Union to the legality of Security
Council proceedings in its absence was to continue, intermittently,
for many months. An early jibe from Moscow that, in any case,
the vote for the United States resolution to aid the Republic of
Korea was passed by only six clear votes was muted when India
declared its support on 29th June 1950*.

Far removed from these high considerations, the fighting in
Korea continued. Briefly checked by the obstacle of the Han river,
the North Korean People's Army was well on its way to the ancient
city of Suwon by the end of the first week of the war. Behind, in
Seoul, terror was mounting. A sizeable minority of communist
front agents and supporters had surfaced. Under the direction of

---

*This contention was based on the vote of seven being opposed by one (Yugoslavia) with
two abstentions (Egypt and India).

political officers from the north, aided by newly established 'peoples' committees' at all levels, ROK government officials, police and private citizens were being arrested summarily, mostly to be shot as political enemies, some to be kept alive for a time under torture to confess to crimes against the state. Many, including humble folk, were shot as they sought to prevent their property being looted.

Captain Holt had remained in the Legation compound after sending out all but two members of his staff on the morning of 27th June. He believed that he should stay at his post to represent British interests when the Kim Il-sung regime was established. With George Blake, Vice-Consul*, and Norman Owen, Pro-Consul, he was joined there by Commissioner Herbert Lord of the Salvation Army and Father Charles Hunt. Apart from occasional visits by looters and communist officials they were left in peace until the evening of 2nd July. As they were about to sit down to dinner then in the dining room of the residency, the two legation cars which had been stolen earlier drove in with a mixed bag of North Korean police, political officers and soldiers. The five men were arrested. As they were driven into captivity, the sack of the Legation began.

---

*George Blake returned to the United Kingdom after the war and was later found to be a Soviet agent. Sentenced to 42 years imprisonment in 1961, he escaped with external assistance. He now lives in the Soviet Union.

SOURCE NOTES: CHAPTER 2

1. For the background and sources, see author's article in *China Quarterly*, June 1984. Also Robert O'Neill, op cit, pp 12–20.

2. See for example *The Russian faction in North Korea*, Asian Survey, April 1988, Lee Chong-sik, pp 270–288.

3. Sawyer, Robert K, *Military Advisers in Korea: KMAG in peace and war*, (Washington, 1962), Chapter IV gives details.

4. For details of the NKPA armament, see Appleman, Roy E, *South to the Naktong, North to the Yalu*, (Washington, 1961), pp 11–18.

5. For details of the extent of the Russian presence in the North Korean Government and Armed Forces, see *North Korea: case study of a takeover*, (United States Department of State, 1951).

6. Contained in Annex B to UNCOK Report, 1950 to the Fifth Session of the United Nations General Assembly. See also the Review Article by Colonel F S B Peach in the Australian Defence Force Journal No 56, January/February 1986.

7. Case 11554 Vol 19, Flag Officer Second-in-Command (FO2i/c) summarised Reports of Proceedings (RoPs) No 1, 25th June–9th July 1950, Signal CINC FE Station to COMNAVFE of 260431Z June 1950.

8. DEFE 11/193, Signal CINC Far East Station to FO2i/c of 261350Z June 1950.

9. Case 11554, vol 19, FO2i/c cit, RoPs No 1 25th June–9th July 1950, paragraph 9.

10. DEFE 11/193, BJMS, Washington to MOD London AWT19 of 262254Z June 1950.

11. Ibid, for details, see CRO 88 to Governments of Canada, Australia, New Zealand, South Africa, India, Pakistan, Ceylon of 27th June 1950.

12. Ibid., Belgrade 525 to FO of 28th June 1950.

13. Ibid, GHQ Far East Land Forces (for British Defence Co-ordinating Committee (Far East) (BDCC(FE)) to MOD (for Chiefs of Staff) SEACOS 70 of 272030GH June 1950.

14. The Hon K G Younger, MP (Minister of State, Foreign Office, 1950), conversation with author.

15. DEFE 6/13 see paper JP(50)85F of 11th July 1950.

16. DEFE 4/32 Annex to COS(50)98th meeting on 28th June 1950.

17. DEFE 11/193, MOD DEF 455 to BJSM, Washington of 261235A June 1950 and MOD DEF 463 to BJSM Washington of 271815A June 1950.

18. Ibid, Tokyo 468 to BJSM, Washington 26th June 1950.

19. Ibid, Shanghai 652 to FO of 28th June 1950.

20. Ibid, UK High Commission New Delhi 1762 to CRO of 28th June 1950.

21. Ibid, Peking 940 to FO of 29th June 1950.

22. Ibid, Admiralty signal to CINC FE Station of 281720A June 1950.

23. Ibid, See also the memo of Air Marshal Elliot COS 817/29/6/50 to First Sea Lord (1stSL/CNS), Chief of the Air Staff (CAS) and Vice-Chief of the Imperial General Staff (VCIGS) of 29th June 1950.

24. Ibid, Air Chief Marshal Elliot's memo to PM 826/30/6/50 30th June 1950.

25. Ibid, MOD(for Chiefs of Staff) COS(W)816 to BJSM, Washington (for Lord Tedder) of 301705A June 1950.

26. Ibid, BJSM, Washington AWT12 to MOD of 301912Z June 1950.
27. Ibid, New York 629 to FO of 29th June 1950.
28. Ibid, FO 727 to New York of 29th June 1950.
29. Ibid, CRO A.97 to High Commissioners of 29th June 1950.
30. Ibid, New York 640 to FO of 29th June 1950.

CHAPTER 3

The Sea Flanks

In those days, visitors to the cinema expected to see a newsreel before the main programme. British companies already had pictures of ships of the Far East fleet at sea and thus, soon after the announcement that the Royal Navy was engaged in Korean operations, these were shown, a voice commentary over one remarking:

'The navy's there! Within a few days of the opening of the Korean war, our men and ships, acknowledged to be among the finest in the world, were representing Britain . . .' Grey hulls were seen steaming through oriental waters, a cruiser's guns swinging on to an unseen target; a carrier appeared with its aircraft, wings folded, lined up on deck neatly for some peace time display.

This piece of minor opportunism no doubt inspired confidence among the watching cinema audiences in Britain but in some degree it was misleading. Admiral Sir Patrick Brind's fleet was undermanned, and some of the warships were ill-equipped or supplied for the many and wide ranging tasks to which they were to be committed. For example, the aircraft in the carrier, *Triumph*—Fireflies and Seafires*—were obsolete. Catapulting arrangements for the former required so much preparation as to make its launching by this means scarcely worth while.† Their armament was limited. A wind speed of 34 knots over the deck was needed to launch Fireflies with 500 lb bombs, but if they were in light airs, *Triumph's* engines could not bring her up to that speed. 'In spite of application as long ago as December 1949,' the captain reminded the Commander-in-Chief, 'we still have no bomb racks for the Seafire 47. Now, when it is too late, the Admiralty announce that some are being provided.'[2] Aside from air defence cannon, therefore, the only weapons available for fitment were rockets. Among aircraft and warships alike there were communications problems due to obsolescent equipment, requiring high maintenance or, where new radios had arrived, a want of maintenance manuals.

---

*The Firefly I and the Seafire 47

†'. . . very little Firefly I catapulting has been done because the catapult is always required for launching the Seafire 47. It takes about 2 hours to fit the legs to the trolley for launching the Firefly I, their catapulting rate is slow and the catapult is then useless to the Seafire until converted back again,' the captain later reported.[1]

There were numerous ammunition difficulties and, in *Triumph*, a serious defect in the starboard propellor shaft. This last item excepted, most of the problems arose from the deployment of a fleet underfunded and over committed. In any case, *Triumph* was only a light aircraft carrier. The Royal Navy component of the United Nations force was thus inclined to look admiringly at the advanced systems of their United States counterparts, notably in the fleet carrier, *Valley Forge*.*

Even so, Admiral Andrewes, his small staff, captains and ships' companies were not daunted by the constraints arising from these weaknesses; indeed, they had lived with them for so long that they were accepted as a part of life. Their ships were basically sound and they sought readily to maintain the high standards expected of them. Commitment to active operations was widely welcomed. Even those men due for release from their term of service—almost all members of the fleet were regulars—were not discontented when, shortly, they heard they were to be retained compulsorily for a time; the common reaction to their captains was to ask that a term should be set to this retention.†

Neither captains nor admiral knew what that might be just then. There were many questions at the outset of the emergency to which only the enemy or their sponsors could provide an answer: how long, for example, would operations continue; to what extent would an air offensive develop and, similarly, a submarine offensive?

As earlier remarked, the apprehension of being caught concentrated in harbour by a surprise air attack influenced Admiral Joy to disperse his forces while he discovered how best they could contribute to the struggle for South Korea. Admiral Andrewes therefore instructed his squadron‡ to refuel and to join him at sea to the south of Japan as quickly as possible. On 29th June, the first United Nations naval plan[3] was issued and ships were disposed as follows:

---

*The USS *Valley Forge* carried 100 aircraft, a mixed complement of 86 propellor (Corsairs and Skyraiders) and jet (Panther) types, with a high variety of armament options, plus 14 helicopters and specialist models.

†Later fixed as one year.

‡Although Admiral Andrewes' function as Flag Officer, Second in Command, was to command the Far East Fleet at sea, he was also designated as commander, 5th Carrier Squadron. From 27th July he became effectively a squadron commander, in as much as he was preoccupied with that part of the fleet detached for Korean operations.

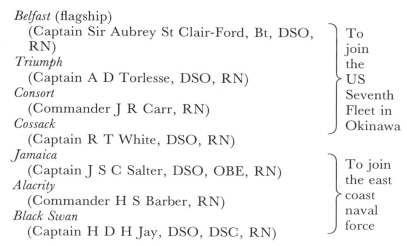

The frigate *Hart* (Commander H H Mulleneux, DSC, RN) was to move to Tokyo to provide communications between Admiral Joy, commander, naval forces, Far East, and his British component; and the hospital ship, *Maine*, (Master: Captain S G Kent, OBE) was to take up station at Kure, a port on the Inland Sea in southern Japan.

The northern element of the Seventh Fleet was then concentrated at Buckner Bay in Okinawa. The Fleet Commander, Vice-Admiral Struble,* welcomed Rear-Admiral Andrewes aboard his flagship, the cruiser *Rochester*, on 1st July. The information they had about the land battle was poor; negligible in so far as the activities of North Korean forces in the zone behind the fighting line were concerned. They knew nothing about the enemy's army bases north of the 38th parallel. Although all ships had adequate charts for navigation purposes, including those of the coastal areas, the maps of Korean territory for aircrew were not much superior to those of a schoolroom atlas. But such intelligence as was available suggested that there would be a good deal of North Korean traffic southward along the few main roads, and that there was a likelihood of coastal craft, armed and otherwise, supporting the advance south, perhaps involving strategic landings. They had the means to find and strike these. No less importantly, they had the means of striking from the sea airfields deep in North Korea. Aside from helping the overall effort, success in these areas would reduce the danger of air attack upon themselves. Admiral Struble therefore proposed to move the American and British carriers and their

---

*Struble, Vice-Admiral Arthur Dewey, USN (1894–1960) had returned hurriedly on 29th June from his daughter's wedding in Washington to confer in Tokyo with General MacArthur and Admiral Joy.

escorts north into the Yellow Sea at once with the object of attacking North Korean shipping, troops, supplies and communications, and airfields known to them. If nothing else, their operations against this range of targets would inhibit enemy progress, and they would gain information for General MacArthur's intelligence picture, itself far from complete.

Between 1630 and 1700 hours that afternoon, the British carrier group sailed northwards from Buckner Bay, the American an hour and a half later. Next morning, the two squadrons made a rendezvous between 1030 and 1100. 'It all seemed familiar joining up in formation as it was just what we had done so often during the [joint] exercises in March with very similar forces. We didn't feel out of things and we were already getting back into the easy use of American signal books.

'Once joined up,' Admiral Andrewes remarked later, 'all the normal routines of flying off anti-submarine patrol aircraft, the transfer of Staff Officers and orders by helicopter and so on went on continuously. The force moved northward at about 22 knots . . .'[4] The *Valley Forge* was able to sustain 33 knots but *Triumph* could not do more than 23 at maximum and had to restrict her steaming at full speed because of her defective starboard propellor shaft. 'It had originally been intended to divide the force during the night of 2nd/3rd July, allowing the United States part with the greater speed of the *Valley Forge* to reach a point some 40 miles to the northward of the British group. I did not care much for this plan,' Admiral Andrewes reported, 'as it would have complicated many things particularly communications and so I was glad that we made such good northing during the day and night of 2nd July that it became clear that the whole Task Group could continue to work together' . . .[5]

In operational terms, Admiral Struble's command was Carrier Task Force 77.* His subordinate elements were the United States 3rd Carrier Division under Rear-Admiral Hoskins,† designated Carrier Task Group 77.2, Captain C W Parker's eight American destroyers, Carrier Task Group 77.4, and the British squadron, Carrier Task Group 77.5.‡ Tactical command of naval air operations fell to Admiral Hoskins. Between 0545 and 0615 on 3rd July, he launched eight Corsairs, twelve Panthers and sixteen Skyraiders

---

*For details of UN Naval Forces see Appendix E.

†Hoskins, Rear-Admiral J M , USN. He was given tactical command of air operations not so much due to seniority as the fact that he was a pilot. Admiral Andrewes was not. It was a canon of the United States navy that carrier-borne aircraft should be commanded by an aviator.

‡Cagle and Manson (The Sea War in Korea, USNI, 1957, p 37) show the British squadron split, an initial concept which was changed at Admiral Andrewes' request.

from *Valley Forge* to attack airfields in and around the North Korean capital, P'yongyang, nine Seafires and twelve Fireflies from *Triumph* to strike Haeju airfield close to the coast along the 38th parallel. The American aircraft had the more distant target because they had better endurance or speed—the propellor driven Skyraiders and Corsairs could remain aloft for four hours on a sortie, the jet Panthers for two but their speed enabled them to go much further in this time. The Americans were thus able to operate over radii up to 200 miles, the British about 120—somewhat less if they were required to reconnoitre the target area extensively beforehand.

The *Valley Forge* aircraft destroyed fuel, ammunition and other facilities with a variety of aircraft on the ground and two Yak-9s in the air. The Seafires and Fireflies found no aircraft at Haeju but fired their rockets into hangars and other buildings. That enemy were about was manifest from slight damage to two of the aircraft by small arms fire. That afternoon, as *Valley Forge* aircraft made sorties against railways and bridges in the area of P'yongyang, the British carrier provided the combat air patrols (CAP) and anti-submarine patrols (ASP) over the force, maintaining station just below the 37th parallel, about 80 miles from the Korean coast.

On leaving Okinawa, the original plan had been to withdraw the carrier force after a single day of air strikes; the United States authorities were anxious to have their one carrier in the western Pacific ready to intervene in the Taiwan Strait at short notice. But the news from the land battlefront caused COMNAVFE to signal even as they steamed northward,

> . . . continue strikes past the first day in view of the rapidly deteriorating Korean situation. Highest priority to be given to rail facilities in vicinity of Kumch'on, Sariwon, and Sinanju . . .

Accordingly, both *Valley Forge* and *Triumph* launched strikes again on the 4th, the Americans continuing to attack targets in the P'yongyang area, the British rail targets and a motor column of troops round Haeju and Yonan—the admirals do not appear to have liked the sites chosen in Tokyo for their operations.* On this occasion, Task Force 77 turned south after recovering the aircraft. Admiral Andrewes, however, was not to return to Okinawa. COMNAVFE had signalled him on 3rd July that a blockade was to be established by the Royal Navy on the west coast, by the

---

*Consideration was given to attacking the railway between Sinmak and P'yongsan but it was beyond the Fireflies' range. On this second occasion, anti-aircraft fire was more intense. Although all aircraft returned safely, four Skyraiders were hit, one of which crashed on landing into waiting aircraft, while a damaged Seafire limped in on one wheel.

United States Navy on the east. He therefore decided to return to Sasebo to establish a headquarters there and make arrangements for this task. A regrouping of his ships would evidently be necessary and, as a first step, he took *Consort* and *Cossack* with him, leaving *Triumph* and a newly joined destroyer, *Comus* (Lieutenant-Commander R A M Hennessy, RN) with Admiral Struble. In Japan he expected to be able to find out the extent of commitment of his ships working with the Americans off south east Korea.

The cruiser *Jamaica*, with *Alacrity* and *Black Swan* following, had moved east to join the flag of Rear-Admiral Higgins* on 30th June. The flagship, *Juneau*, was not easy to find. Radio messages had multiplied progressively as the crisis deepened; the numbers of radio operators and radios in the main headquarters were insufficient to transmit them hour by hour. The Services' system of giving a precedence to each 'signal'—a text to be despatched— was designed to cope with peaks of traffic by relegating items at the lower end, marked 'Deferred' or 'Routine', in favour of those in the ascending scale 'Important' 'Immediate', 'Emergency', and 'Flash'. Even though only a limited number of officers were permitted to use the last two, the operators' desks were soon laden with 'Flash' signals. As a consequence, much necessary working information remained unsent, and amongst these was the instructions to *Jamaica* as to where she would find Admiral Hoskins on *Juneau*.

Captain Salter was not of a mind to steam in a circle while awaiting information, however. He had acquired the general whereabouts of *Juneau* and set off to find her in an area roughly 80 miles square, confident in his radar. Clearing the Shimonoseki Strait at 0830 on 1st July, he discovered the *USS Collett*, which directed him to meeting the flagship just south of the 38th parallel at dusk. *Alacrity* and *Black Swan* joined them at midnight.

Formal arrangements for blockade were not then in force but there was little expectation of ocean going merchant ships—as distinct from coastal craft—running supplies to North Korea through their immediate operational waters. Admiral Higgins' force was to deny landings to the North Korean People's Army, and to give gunfire support to the Republic of Korea's army to the limit of range ashore.

'I was afraid we were in for a very tame cruise when we were detached,' a young officer wrote home to his parents later that month, 'but as it happened our ships with the Americans have had plenty of excitement. Early on [2nd July] the weather cleared and four North Korean motor torpedo boats suddenly came at us very

*Higgins, Rear-Admiral J M, USN, was then commander of Task Group 96.5.

bravely. They had absolutely no chance against our guns, though one managed to escape so fast that *Black Swan* could not catch it. In the next few days we were shelling enemy coastal craft and other targets, sometimes coming under shellfire from their guns on shore . . . I feel my education as a naval officer is progressing fast!. . .'[6]

The task group operated for eight days between Yangyang, just north of the 38th parallel, and Cape Imwon-jin close to the 37th. *Black Swan* was raked by the fire of two Ilyushin-10 aircraft of the NKPA and all ships came under shellfire from the shore at one time or another, mostly ineffective, except for one engagement against *Jamaica* in the area of Cape Imwon-jin on 8th July. A salvo caught her while she was firing at military vehicles 3,000 yards distant along the coast road. Shell splinters killed or mortally wounded an able seaman and five soldiers among other casualties, the first British servicemen to fall in the war.*

These operations were inhibiting the movement south of the North Korean 5th Division which, due to the lie of the high and jagged Taebaek mountain range, was almost wholly confined to the east coast road as it moved to capture the important road junction at Ulchin. They also diminished the continuing landings from the sea of a North Korean raiding unit, the 766th Independent Regiment, though the harbour walls at Chumunchin protected those enemy trawlers and sampans which managed to scurry into its safety.† Although the British ships had no fleet support at sea to refuel or otherwise resupply them, a presence was maintained by bringing *Hart*‡ into their company so that when one ship was replenishing at Sasebo, two others were on station. *Alacrity* had been detached from 3rd July to begin the blockade of the west coast.

Meantime, Admirals Joy, Andrewes and Higgins had been meeting in Tokyo to settle longer term arrangements for maritime operations. It was agreed that the Canadian and New Zealand warships approaching the maritime operations zone would join

---

*The soldiers, from the Royal Artillery and 1 Middlesex, had been embarked among others in Hong Kong for the summer cruise, an annual arrangement of inter-service goodwill. When *Jamaica* was ordered into operations, all volunteered to help with ammunition supply and were engaged in this duty when they were hit. Charts show Imwon-jin as Rimuon-ma.

†A team of political officers, destined to disembark at Ulchin to establish the political authority of the North Korean government in that area, were among those sheltering in Chumunchin. As part of the planning for the war, groups had been prepared to take over local government of every district, county and province of South Korea.

‡The demand for ships necessitated the cancellation of *Hart's* instructions to undertake the communications role in Tokyo (p 63).

those of Britain and Australia in a Commonwealth squadron,* and that, in principle, ships from nations other than the United States would also be allocated to this force as they arrived. By this means, the respective sea flanks, west and east,†would be covered by balanced forces, though units from either would be exchanged temporarily as contingencies demanded. The exception to the division by nation of origin would be the frigates escorting transports into Korean ports. These would be pooled.

Just twelve days after the North Korean attack, then, Admiral Andrewes began to establish the British and Commonwealth naval headquarters and base at Sasebo on the west coast of Kyushu, the most southerly of the major Japanese islands. It had an excellent harbour but the port was only of medium size and the slender US naval facilities, due to the emergency, were overloaded. In everything, the Americans were ready to share what they had, but from these beginnings to the end of their participation in the Korean war the British were constrained by the need to spend as few United States dollars as possible. The constraint applied equally to the Australian and New Zealand servicemen whose national treasuries were tied to sterling, a 'soft' currency. Thus, even in the sailor's clubs in Sasebo—and equally for those with the Seventh Fleet in Okinawa—nothing could be bought because payment could only be made in dollar scrip. Fortunately, the Sasebo Shipbuilding Company, the third largest in Japan, was eager to find work and could be paid from occupation funds in which the United Kingdom had a share; and the British Commonwealth Occupation Force offered administrative support, chiefly with transport. Immediately also the fleet support ships were well stocked and able to meet most needs, though ammunition expenditure from ships' guns soon brought extraordinary demands.

In Singapore, the Commander-in-Chief and his staff sought to foresee the squadron's needs. Communications between the two commanders and the staffs were happily without the vexing assumption that the senior necessarily knows better than the man on the spot, sometimes a feature of distant operations. Equally, those in Korean waters did not abuse the sympathy of their base by making extravagant demands. For example, Sir Patrick Brind favoured the idea of sending the maintenance carrier, *Unicorn*, (Captain H S Hopkins, OBE RN), to a permanent station in Japan for aircraft repair and replenishment, a course favoured also by his

---

*Although common operating procedures, training and to a considerable extent equipment, made this arrangement desirable, the Commonwealth governments had left grouping to General MacArthur, effectively to COMNAVFE.
†The west coast was allotted to Admiral Andrewes because of his greater dependence on distant bases, Hong Kong at 1,079, Singapore at 3,000 sea miles.

staff, but he insisted on consulting Admiral Andrewes. The latter, having discussed the idea with Captain Torlesse, commanding *Triumph*, took the view that it would be better to disembark the aircraft repair element of *Unicorn* to work at HMS *Simbang*, the naval air station ashore at Singapore, then to use *Unicorn* to carry aircraft stores and replacements forward and to bring back those for repair at the base. There was no fully suitable site in Japan for *Unicorn* and in any case Admiral Joy persisted in his wish to keep the carriers out of Japanese ports. They had long planned to make *Simbang* the Far East air base and work there would be uninterrupted by the local operational situation. Not unimportantly, the Japanese bases were already over full; *Unicorn* would add to the burden of domestic maintenance. The Commander-in-Chief at once agreed with these representations and thereafter the supply and servicing of naval aircraft continued on this basis through the war.

There was similar cooperation on an inter-service basis. As operations opened, Admiral Andrewes realised that he needed an air transport link of his own with Hong Kong. A Royal Air Force Sunderland was detached for this purpose. A little later, following a request to London, a larger detachment was sent for maritime patrolling.[7]

One requirement could not be met so urgently: a headquarters ship for Admiral Andrewes. His flagship at sea continued to be the carrier or one of the cruisers because of their greater communications and accommodation facilities, but these were too important to keep tied up alongside a jetty in Sasebo. No doubt he might have found buildings ashore for a headquarters but they would have required a complete fit of radios, auxiliary power, security and other facilities. A depot ship would have been ideal but none was available. As a first solution, the Commander-in-Chief sent his dispatch vessel, HMS *Alert* (Commander R de L Brooke, DSO DSC RN) a converted Loch Bay class frigate, which reached Sasebo on 3rd August. For the longer term it was decided to hire or buy a ship. A Yangtse river steamer, the SS *Wusueh*, was taken up from trade, refitted and commissioned as HMS *Ladybird*, relieving the *Alert* about six weeks later.

The operational area defined for Admiral Andrewes' Commonwealth squadron, now Task Group 96.8, was bounded by latitude 39°30'N, longitude 128°E:* effectively, from the mouth of the Ch'ongch'on river on the north west coast of Korea southward along the main shore and coastal islands turning eventually east

---

*Due to the delay in all signal traffic, Admiral Andrewes did not receive his full orders, sent by COMNAVFE on the morning of 3rd July at 0745 hours until he returned to Sasebo on 14th July. He then discovered that the southern patrol limit was to be latitude 37°N and that *Triumph* and *Comus* were to return to his command.

until reaching a line 55 miles west of Pusan. Leaving aside *Triumph* and its escort *Comus* which were to remain with Admiral Struble's carrier group, and a contribution to the group escorting ships from Japanese to Korean ports, he had eight ships with which to carry out his orders. He defined these to his captains as follows on 8th July:

1. To enforce the blockade of the coast occupied by the North Koreans.
2. To prevent infiltration by sea on coasts held by South Koreans.
3. To provide naval support as required against North Korean maritime forces or land targets.

To effect these operations, at least three ships were required to be on station twenty four hours a day, every day, in all weather. He needed some sort of reserve. The group was therefore divided into three task units (TU), to rotate on patrol.

TU 96.8.1 *Belfast, Cossack, Consort,* commanded directly by Admiral Andrewes.

TU 96.8.2 *Jamaica, Black Swan, Alacrity,* commanded by Captain Salter of *Jamaica.*

TU 96.8.3 *Kenya,* (Captain P W Brock, RN) and *Cockade,* (Lieutenant-Commander H J Lee, DSC RN), both recently arrived, commanded by the captain of the cruiser, *Kenya.*

The absence of a third ship in the last task unit would be made good from further reinforcements.

In the morning twilight of 9th July, Admiral Andrewes took his force of three ships to establish the blockade, hitherto maintained on an opportunity basis. *Cossack* was detached temporarily to Pusan to pick up a Korean liaison team for each ship—'the value of having a Korean aboard who spoke reasonable English enhanced the value of our intelligence gathering fivefold,' was remarked by one of *Cossack's* officers. 'You slip alongside a junk in the darkness and unless it actually has people on board wearing uniforms there is no way of knowing who they are. All right, you send a party over to make a search. Set aside the need for a gas mask when you go below decks because the smell of fish, garlic and pickled turnip is enough to take the colour out of your shirt, two or three people with powerful lights can be reasonably sure that there are no weapons on board or mines, say. We later found that North Korean junks spying would dump their weapons on a buoy until they were needed. But fortunately they were mostly poor people trying to make a living fishing. The problem was, you couldn't tell whether they had anything of value to tell you—Korea wasn't a country where many people spoke English' . . . [8]

A Korean naval liaison team would not necessarily include anyone who spoke adequate English, however; there were a number of officers who could read and write English well but who found it very difficult to understand the spoken language. It was often necessary to employ a civilian as an interpreter, frequently a university teacher from among the refugees. These men had to be taken on trust as there was no means of screening them. The captain of *Cossack* did not like the look of those offered to him on 9th July. 'I embarked only the naval members and warned everyone to speak English slowly and clearly to them.'

Just before first light next day, having passed through a rainstorm, TU 96.8.1 was off Inch'on. Admiral Andrewes reported that, 'It was hoped to pick up any shipping that might have been trying to make the entrance to Inch'on at first light, and the sweep was made sufficiently close inshore to sight both the main channel and the Flying Fish Channel, and explore the islands. Apart from a few junks which were engaged in fishing, nothing was seen. The Unit was therefore turned to seawards again to intercept any shipping on passage As we went north, HMS *Cossack* was detached to pass inside the islands of the Techong group. It was as empty inside as out'. . .[9]

During the night they swept the sea route between the Chinese port of Luda (Dairen) and the entrance to Chinnamp'o, port of the North Korean capital, P'yongyang. In the previous week, *Cossack* had contacted a British merchantman, the SS *Houston City*, in these waters but, as the blockade rules were not then clear, had let her proceed.* Now the sea was empty. They steamed south again, through the Techongs, surveying again the channels winding between mud banks up to Inch'on, 20 miles distant. This was important work; the extraordinary tidal range on these shores, interacting with the rivers, caused frequent changes of the sea bed.

Several junks were closed and inspected: there was only fishing gear aboard. One crew, however, reported that 'armed Communists had seized PENG YONG TO [Paengyong-do],' the most northerly of the Techong Group, 'armed with light weapons only.'[10] As planned, they beat back to the north, *Consort* taking a turn to inspect the eastern side of the islands. The lookouts saw nothing but some of those on watch wished that they had a helicopter aboard.

The Task Unit continued to steer an irregular course in these waters which might conceal submarines or be attacked from the air. They rounded Changsan Got† and passed the island of Ch'o-do beyond which, inshore, channels and mud banks led up to Chinnamp'o. It was then necessary to turn away; the sea was full

---

*The SS *Houston City*, a British merchant ship belonging to the Reardon Smith line, was en route from Yokohama to Luda.
†Referred to by the UN Navies as Choppeki Point.

of islands and shoals. As before, they patrolled to the northern limit in darkness to minimise risk of air attack in an area so close to the enemy airfields.

When they returned towards Inch'on on 12th July, TU 96.8.1 paid a small price for a pattern of activity repeated. *Cossack* began the inspection of the coastal side of the Techongs. 'The ship had barely been lost to sight behind the islands when I received a report that she was being engaged by shore batteries . . . a short but evidently hot engagement ensued in which HMS *Cossack* silenced two guns.'[11] The North Koreans fired ten rounds, *Cossack* 140 from her 4.5-inch guns. The destroyer suffered no damage.

They were approaching the end of the patrol. Delayed by an unsuccessful search for the crew of an American B 29 which had parachuted into the sea,* they set course for Sasebo on 13th July as TU 96.8.2 took their place.

It was now mid-July. Though checked briefly from time to time in encounter battles, the North Korean People's Army continued inexorably down the peninsula despite the supremacy of the United States forces in the air and the engagement of its 24th Infantry Division. As Admiral Andrewes arrived back from patrol in Sasebo on 14th July, the Kum river defences were being enveloped and Taejon was imminently threatened. A second American division, the 25th, was arriving from Japan to reinforce the centre and plans were advanced to land another, the 1st Cavalry.

The naval reinforcements Admiral Andrewes had expected were in or about to join operations: the cruiser *Kenya*, the destroyer *Charity* (Lieutenant-Commander P R G Worth, DSC RN), the Australian destroyer *Bataan* (Commander W B M Marks, DSC RAN), and the Dutch destroyer *Evertsen* (Lieutenant-Commander D J van Doorninck) But within a matter of days he knew that he would lose *Belfast, Comus, Alacrity* and *Black Swan,* and shortly thereafter *Cossack* and *Shoalhaven* (Lieutenant-Commander I H MacDonald, RAN). He was thus eager to have news of the three Canadian destroyers and two New Zealand frigates en route. For commitments were growing; among them, the requirement for escorts with the swelling volume of troops and stores crossing from Japan to Korea. HMAS *Shoalhaven*, engaged in this work from the outset, had been joined by *Hart; Alacrity* and *Black Swan* were being sent as reinforcements. There were reports that numerous North Korean forces were apparently attempting an outflanking movement via the south western road and rail routes. Admiral Andrewes was directed to patrol the Kunsan approaches. He shared also the concern of his American colleagues concerning the more direct

*The survivors were picked up by Captain Salter's task unit as it came on to the patrol.

threats to the principal port of Pusan through Taegu, and down the east coast to P'ohang.

It is an indication of the uncertainties and misperceptions of those difficult days for the generals and admirals in Tokyo that plans had been developing early in July to outflank the advancing North Koreans by putting part of the United States 1st Cavalry Division—a light mechanised formation—ashore at Kunsan or even Inch'on. 'A few short days,' the American naval historian remarks, 'demonstrated the visionary aspects of the idea . . . the problem came to be not one of throwing the 1st Cavalry Division against the enemy's flank, but of getting this force into Korea while there remained some Korean territory to get into.'[12] The remaining major port of Pusan was grossly overloaded with traffic. P'ohang was chosen as the landing site, though there began to be expectations that the North Koreans might be there first. An assault across beaches was prepared.

Ever ready to contribute to the action, Admiral Andrewes had meantime volunteered the services of *Belfast* and, briefly, *Cossack* to join the shore bombardment of the North Korean 5th Division, largely confined by the mountains on the east coast route. This force was continuing to press the inferior numbers of Colonel Kim Chong-won's 23rd ROK Infantry Regiment. The British ships joined Admiral Higgins' action against the enemy line of communication—principally vehicles moving southward, store and supply dumps—using direct observation from ships or observers in aircraft. When no targets could be seen, they shelled sections of the cliff face, bringing rocks down on to the winding shore road. But when they sought to aid the local defence clinging to the road junction at Yongdok, it was soon apparent that the warships' fire relied more on luck than skill. They could not discriminate between friend and foe and there was no communication with the defence ashore. A gunnery officer from *Juneau*, Admiral Andrewes' fleet gunnery officer, Commander H R Law, RN, and army artillery liaison officer, Captain Keith McQueen, RA,* solved this problem.

They landed in a whaler at Kokodo and made their way to the American KMAG fire control centre supporting Colonel Kim Chong-won. They gave the American artillery officers a naval radio and took one of the army sets back with them. This provided a double direct link, so that targets could be identified and adjustments of fire requested. From 18th July, accuracy improved markedly as the struggle continued for Yongdok. On the evening of the 20th, the two British officers with American colleagues were once again landed and made a simple fire plan with the 23rd Regiment

*As one of the Army passengers, Captain McQueen had volunteered for this duty.

and its KMAG. Next morning, for an hour from 0530, *Belfast, Juneau,* and three United States destroyers pounded the disputed ground. The hills surrounding the town were stripped of trees, Yongdok and close villages were reduced to rubble. They had, however, helped to deny the advance to P'ohang, where the 1st Cavalry Division landed without opposition on 18th July.

Valley Forge and *Triumph,* which had been brought to the south east coast to support the landing were released as soon as it was clear that there was no opposition to the division. The carriers separated. Admiral Andrewes returned to Japan. Admiral Struble sailed north to strike the major oil refinery at Wonsan.

As July came to an end, the three Canadian Tribal Class destroyers arrived under Captain J V Brock, DSO DSC CD RCN,* in HMCS *Cayuga,* with HMCS *Athabaskan,* (Commander R P Welland, DSC CD RCN), and *Sioux,* (Commander P D Taylor, DSC CD RCN). The two New Zealand frigates were also entering operations, HMNZS *Pukaki* (Lieutenant-Commander L E Herrick DSC RN) and *Tutira* (Lieutenant-Commander P J H Hoare, RN).† Admiral Andrewes was delighted to be allocated at the same time the French frigate *La Grandière* (Commander Urban E Cabanie). This made good the losses to his force due to the imminent return of *Shoalhaven* to Australia and five of the British ships to the bases of the Far East Fleet. With the arrival of Rear-Admiral Hartman from the United States‡ it was also possible to establish a central headquarters at Sasebo for command and control of the blockade on the two coasts and the escorts between Japan and Korea, an arrangement long asked for by Admirals Andrewes and Higgins. Each was anxious to direct more closely the operations on his particular coast. They were sensitive to the implied criticism of General MacArthur's staff that the North Koreans were using coastal waters as the principal routes for battle supplies.

The basis for this notion was twofold. The Far East Air Force claimed to have destroyed many of the roads and railways entering the battle area from the north, yet supplies were still manifestly being delivered. It was reasoned that they must therefore be carried in coastal shipping. The air force reported many sightings of enemy coastal steamers, trawlers, and sampans. 'If this is true,' Admiral Andrewes remarked to a conference of his officers in the fourth

---

*Not to be confused with Captain P W Brock, captain of the cruiser *Kenya.*
†Officers on exchange with the Royal New Zealand Navy.
‡Rear-Admiral Charles C Hartman, USN.
The new arrangement was upset for the American element when he was required to command a division of the Seventh Fleet in the Taiwan strait. Returning later, he alternated as east coast commander.

week of July, 'we must quickly put a stop to it.' He had maintained three ships on the blockade patrol for many days of the month but expected that with *Triumph* shortly returning to his flag, her aircraft would complement his surface forces. Royal Air Force Sunderlands, a detachment of three flying boats from 88 Squadron at Hong Kong, were shortly to begin operations from the American base at Iwakuni and although they were able to operate only at night,* their presence would also enhance surveillance of the operational area. Admiral Andrewes' patrol force, redesignated Task Element (TE) 96.53 within Admiral Hartman's Task Group 96.5, intensified its search for blockade runners.

Meantime, as the line ashore was driven yet further back towards Pusan, and with the news that a fresh North Korean division was advancing down the west coast, General MacArthur directed that naval air should add its weight to that of the 5th Air Force in an effort to stabilise the battle. The carrier force put to sea at midnight on 24th July, *Triumph* abandoning further repairs to her defective stern gland. It was a worthy but largely pointless response. The North Korean 6th Division had indeed travelled on the south western roads to Sunchon but by the time the carriers were within range they were at their destination. The American naval aviators searched a bare countryside while their British comrades maintained the combat air and anti-submarine patrols. Turning to support the troops in immediate contact with the enemy, they were almost wholly frustrated. There were no communications with those on the battlefield at first, and even when these were established the maps held by naval pilots were so different to those of the air force that target references given by the light spotter planes took too long to pick up.† There was an urgent need for trained liaison teams with the army units on the ground, using naval radios for direct contact with the naval aircraft. None existed.‡ After striking out behind the contact zone from a stormy sea, the Seventh Fleet withdrew to Japan, *Triumph* and *Comus* still among them. An unsatisfactory period was not improved when an American B-29

---

*There were no air gunners available to the Royal Air Force and it was feared that the Sunderlands would be vulnerable to air ambush by day fighters from North Korean airfields. To have kept these wide ranging flying boats within the radii of the carrier aircraft would have made them almost valueless.

†Admiral Struble had several times warned GHQ that the carrier aircraft could not intervene effectively in close support of the Army until communications had been established with the troops on the ground and the Fifth Air Force tactical operations centre in Korea.

‡At an allied conference to resolve this problem, Lieutenant-Commander P B Jackson, RN, commander of the air group on *Triumph*, suggested that his army ground liaison section (65 CBGLS) could operate as an air contact team, a suggestion adopted by the Seventh Fleet but not taken up due to the return of *Triumph* to Admiral Andrewes. (See also Cagle and Manson, op cit, p 54).

shot down a Seafire flown by Commissioned Pilot D R White, RN, 'for no very apparent reason', in the opinion of Captain Torlesse.*[13]

Determined to see for himself what was happening on the west coast, Admiral Andrewes set out in *Belfast* with *Bataan* and *Charity* as Task Unit 96.53.1 on 28th July. There had certainly been recent attempts by the North Koreans to move supplies through coastal waters but none of these had succeeded. The western half of the ROK Navy, operating under Commander Lee Hae-yong from its base in a tank landing ship in the remote south west islands of Taehuksan, had sunk three North Korean motor craft south west of Kunsan on 22nd July. The interceptor, a small minesweeper, had been attacked next day by an armed North Korean launch in the same area. On the 27th, Commander Lee in a former submarine chaser, PC 702, in company with PC 703, had ventured almost 200 miles north from his base, extending his patrol through the mud banks to Inch'on, which they had bombarded. *En route* home, they had overtaken some miles out to sea a convoy of twelve sampans filled with ammunition, which they sank while driving off several armed launches.[14] It was clear, however, that they were taking excessive risks. It was the typhoon season. North Koreans were now occupying the entire south west so that there were no close friendly ports in which to find shelter. The Admiral arranged that the ROK Navy should operate at shorter ranges and that his patrols would help with supplies and technical support as often as possible.

On 1st August, *Bataan* observed a group of junks at about 6 p.m. closing the coast in the Haeju gulf just south of the 38th parallel. It was half tide and ebbing. The channels to the shore lay between mudbanks. Commander Marks decided to put *Bataan* in stern first so that he could get out more readily in emergency and shortly one arose. Still 4 miles out, the flash of artillery ashore was spotted. Seconds later, there were shell splashes nearby. Full ahead was ordered by the captain, but in the change from slow astern steam pressure was momentarily lost. After a long pause painful to the ship's company, the engines turned and they drew away, returning fire. A duel followed for about a quarter of an hour, the shells on ship and shore straddling their targets.[15] *Belfast* closed from seaward on hearing the firing and fired 56 rounds from her 4- and 6-inch guns before the light faded.

---

*To facilitate recognition, all naval aircraft had broad bands painted on their wings and rear fuselage, as used in Europe for Operation 'Overlord,' 1944–45. Despite this, Mr White was fired on when he closed on the beam of the FEAF B-29. Neither navy nor air force knew of the other's operations in the area.

More deliberately, Mokp'o and Inch'on were bombarded on 2nd and 5th August. The first of these, in the extreme south west of Korea was a possible port for seaborne supplies; the second was known to contain North Korean forces. Flying in two United States naval P-2V Neptunes, Lieutenant-Commander T D Handley, RN, and Captain J M Thompson, RA, spotted for the 4.5-inch guns of *Cossack* and *Cockade*. Almost 1,000 rounds were fired at the oil refinery and its tanks, railway sidings and rolling stock, warehouses and wharfs. The town appeared to be deserted. On the 5th, with the same air spotting arrangements and under cover of a pair of American naval fighters, *Belfast* and *Kenya*, supported by *Cossack* and *Charity*, bore in via the Flying Fish channel to Inch'on on a flood tide. The rocks and shoals on the approaches to it are numerous, the mud banks shifting. The range of the tide is between 25 and 32 feet. The tidal currents are strong. The charts they were using were out of date.* Taking up position at a range of about 20,000 yards from the town and port, *Kenya* anchored, *Belfast* under way in the tide but keeping station with a danbuoy, the two cruisers opened fire with their 6-inch guns just before 0930. In the next hour and three quarters, they fired 415 rounds on barracks, the power station, railway sidings and oil stores, the latter catching fire. There was no reaction, no sight of an enemy.[16]

It may be that the quick and relatively heavy response of warships to fire from shore, such as that following the attack on *Bataan*, had persuaded the North Koreans to lie low when these appeared. For there clearly were enemy shore batteries in place,† and port operations attempting to run supplies south but these were defeated by the close cooperation between Admiral Andrewes' ships and Commander Lee's inshore patrols. From 5th August, three barrier stations were established off the headlands between 38°08' and 36° 45'N. On the 9th, Commander Lee's base was advanced to Ochong island, 40 miles west north west of Kunsan. The successes in intercepting single and small groups of boats did not, however, satisfy GHQ that this route was being denied. Admiral Joy's headquarters continued to receive air force reports of '300 supply junks moving south', 'large freighter unloading in Mokp'o harbour', of freighters or coastal vessels at Inch'on. Consequent searches found 'supply junks' were South Korean fishermen. The ships reported unloading in harbours were checked, reported as sunk or stranded by the navy but were soon featuring again in air force 'sightings.' 'This forenoon,' Captain Brock reported from

---

*Many were based on Japanese surveys dated 1934 with marginal post-war corrections.
†Firings of star shells were observed frequently at night round the port area.

Kenya, 'Wednesday, 9th August, two Operational Immediate signals originated yesterday from COMNAVFE were received, reporting sightings by B-29 aircraft on the previous day, Monday 7th August. Despite certain discrepancies, three of the four sightings reported could hardly have been anything but HMS *Kenya* and *Cockade*, and one of the two . . . was either HNMS *Evertsen* or wildly improbable.'[17]

The irrepressibility of the idea that the North Koreans were pouring supplies through the south west ports was due in part to faulty passing of information by some of the headquarters. For example, the Far East Air Force had not passed on information to its B-29s operating up the west coast that friendly carriers were in that area. Ships' companies felt cut off from land operations because no one realised that they were both professionally and personally interested in what was happening ashore. Indeed, GHQ in Tokyo frequently complained to the Army headquarters there that it also was kept short of information. It is a common experience in war that current, accurate information is all too rare: all concerned contribute to the omission. Korean operations were no exception.

At the end of July and in the first week of August, there were reports of submarine contacts. The echoes reached the State Department and Foreign Office.

A telegram passed on 4th August from the latter to Sir Oliver Franks,* British Ambassador in Washington,

> We have been informed by the Admiralty that the United States Naval Commander in the Far East has ordered the ships under his command, including His Majesty's ships, to attack and drive off unidentified (that is, submerged) submarines in the Korean area. The British Naval Commander-in-Chief, Far East Station, has represented to him that this might involve the risk of sinking a Russian submarine allegedly on a peaceful mission, and that it would be desirable to issue a general warning to warships of powers not engaged in the conflict to avoid the area. The United States Commander put this suggestion to [his] navy department, who turned it down on the grounds that such a general warning could be construed as an unjustifiable restriction on the use of the high seas by neutral warships.
>
> 2. To sink a Russian submarine without having given such warning, however, would not only be unlawful but might also be considered an aggressive act by some of the other United Nations. Although it is not normal to sink neutral warships in a belligerent area, even after such a warning, no submerged

---

*Franks, Sir Oliver Shewell (later, Lord), OM GCMG KCB CBE PC (1905-)

submarine could have a reputable reason for entering the battle area, and the Admiralty consider that the United Nations Commander has every right to warn submarines off for this reason . . .

3. You should, therefore, unless you see any objection, ask the State Department if they could arrange with the Navy Department for a warning to be issued in order to legalise any sinkings which may result . . .

4. His Majesty's ships will, of course, obey the United States' Commander's orders in any case but it seems desirable that there should be legal cover for the action contemplated.[18]

It was now discovered that Admiral Joy's instructions had originated from the Chief of Naval Operations* in Washington:

In the view of the United States government, these instructions are entirely justified by the inherent right of self defense and sufficiently explicit to minimise the risk of sinking a Russian submarine on a peaceful mission. It is also the opinion of the United States Government that the issuance of a general warning to all warships of powers not engaged in the conflict to avoid the necessarily broad area related to the operations in Korea would be an undesirable restriction on the use of the high seas by warships of those powers, and would not have any legal effect in addition to that given by the inherent right of self defense.

2. . . . State Department official observed that as submarines always have the first knowledge of presence of surface forces, any submarine on a peaceful mission has adequate time to take evasive action, or indicate its pacific intentions.[19]

The policy was therefore that any submarine submerged and in the location of any of the United Nations' warships in Korean operations would be attacked. As it happened, false alarms apart, submarine contacts diminished. Admiral Andrewes was immediately thankful as *Triumph*, after 10 days in dock, was ready to join the west coast blockade.

The Fireflies and Sea Furies were now able to undertake operations of enterprise. They reconnoitred extensively, confirming what the destroyer captains had suspected: small North Korean vessels were lying up among islands by day under camouflage. The disguise took the form of tree branches covering decks and rigging, stuck into the funnels of those which had them. They were attacked with rockets. Attacks were also made on North Korean

---

*Admiral Forrest P. Sherman, USN (1896–1951).
Chief of Naval Operations is chief of the naval staff.

patrol craft and minesweepers at Chinnamp'o. A secondary but nonetheless substantial benefit of *Triumph's* presence was that other ships on station were able to range more widely—investigating merchant ships on ocean transit, picking up the crew of a Neptune shot down over Chinnamp'o, and boosting operations with Commander Lee—without abandoning areas of sea to North Korean blockade runners. The night patrolling of the Sunderlands extended the cover.

Triumph could not remain on station indefinitely, however. Her absence was noted by the North Koreans ashore, and at 0712 hours on 23rd August, Lieutenant J A Palmer, RN, officer of the watch on *Comus*, spotted two aircraft on the port beam about 2 miles distant. The destroyer was patrolling the Inch'on approaches, heading north east. Cries of warning came also from the port look out and the depth charge sentry; they recognised the pair as Ilyushin *Stormovik 2* fighter bombers which, turning in, showed red stars in white roundels on their wings.* They were clearly North Korean aircraft. As the captain, Lieutenant-Commander Hennessy, came running out of his sea cabin in boots and pyjamas in response to the order for action stations, the *Stormoviks* had turned in behind *Comus,* dropping to 100 feet above her wake. The leader began to rake her with cannon fire before dropping four bombs, hitting 'down the port side abreast the whaler. The ship was lifted considerably by the explosion and a heavy amount of black water landed on the bridge . . . I ordered full speed ahead,' the captain reported, 'and commenced to alter course violently to starboard by which time the second aircraft was attacking in a similar manner to the first and was being engaged by all Bofors guns and the starboard Oerlikon.† The bombs from the second aircraft dropped one cable ahead of the ship and did no damage.

'The forward boiler room had been holed on the port side and the compartment flooded rapidly.'[20] The first aircraft returned to attack with machine guns before following the second into the clouds, under fire from *Comus's* air defence weapons. Remarkably, there was only one casualty: Leading Stoker Mechanic James Addison, killed instantly at his station in the boiler room.[21] Such an incident reminded all ships' companies that in the absence of air cover they were vulnerable to hit and run raiders.

Escorted by *Consort* and covered by an air patrol, *Comus* made her way back slowly to Kure for repairs to the huge hole on her waterline, from which the sea tore every temporary patch rigged

---

*The ship's Type 291 Air Warning Radar did not pick up the approaching aircraft, partly because of positioning, partly because it was a short range equipment best used in cooperation with those of longer range in larger ships.
†Oerlikon, a heavy machine-gun of Swiss design.

by her damage control parties. Her absence constrained west coast operations, particularly as *Evertsen* had been holed on a submerged rock on 9th August, necessitating withdrawal. For there were many additional calls for ships beyond the varied demands of the blockade. Two nights before the air attack on *Comus,* she and *Consort* had been covering clandestine landings from the USS *Horace A Bass,** north and south of Kunsan.

A young rating on *Consort,* reflecting the general wish to have more information, remarked to a chief petty officer as they peered into the darkness of the night watch that he would 'like to be in on what the Americans are up to.'

'That's nothing to do with you', the chief reproved him. 'Nor ever likely to be.'[22] In this, unwittingly, he was in error.

---

*A destroyer escort converted to be a fast transport.

SOURCE NOTES: CHAPTER 3

1. Case 11554, Vol 15, *Triumph*, RoPs 2nd–5th July 1950, para 14.
2. Ibid, para 15.
3. COMNAVFE United Nations Operations Order 5–50.
4. Case 11554, Vol 19 FO2i/c, FE RoPs (summarised), No 1, 25th June–9 July 1950, para 20.
5. Ibid, para 21.
6. AJC, personal letter of 10th July 1950, shown to author.
7. CAB 21/1988, Minute from Elliot to Minister of Defence on 'Flying Boat Reinforcements for Korea' of 10th July 1950.
8. BNB, interview with author in March, 1979.
9. Case 11554, Vol 19, FO2i/c, RoPs cit, para 4.
10. Ibid, para 5.
11. Ibid, para 8.
12. Field, James A jr, *History of United States Naval Operations: Korea*, (Washington, 1962), p 102.
13. *Triumph*, RoPs cit, 22nd July–1st August 1950, para 6.
14. Field, op cit, p 127. (See also ROK Navy Records, Western Operations July/August 1950, in ROK Historical Institute.)
15. *Bataan's* report of engagement, Australian Naval Office 585/202/622. See also British Naval Staff History op cit p 34.
16. Fo2i/c cit, RoPs No 3, 29th July–10th August 1950, para 33–44 and Case 11554, Vol 9, *Kenya* Patrol Report dated 19th August 1950.
17. *Kenya*, cit, Patrol Report 19th August 1950.
18. DEFE 11/198, FO 3529 to Washington of 4th August 1950.
19. Ibid, Washington 2186 to FO 10th August 1950.
20. Case 11554, Vol 6 *Comus* and FO2i/c, cit RoPs No 4 8th August–2nd September 1950, para 86–89.
21. Anderson, F R (formerly EME, RN), conversation with author, April 1986.
22. TAC, conversation with author, September 1985.

CHAPTER 4

Searching for Peace: Squaring for War

As the shock occasioned by the North Korean invasion receded and the immediate political and military responses were effected in London, the Foreign Office had to cope with a number of consequences arising from the government's decision to join a unique alliance in war while simultaneously pursuing the possibilities of an early, honourable peace.

As noted, the precise basis of collective right under the Charter to rally the United Nations to the defence of the Republic of Korea, and in the absence of a permanent member of the Security Council, had to be agreed with allies.[1] Similarly, there had to be agreement on the article under which there was a commitment to hostilities. The United Kingdom was engaging in war even though military operations would be of a limited nature. But in terms of international law, it was not as simple a matter as going to war with like-minded allies as in 1914 or 1939, or even in standing against a potential aggressor with allies as in the Shanghai International Settlement in 1932.

On this occasion, the members of the Security Council had to agree from the outset which, of several articles, should be applied to the particular circumstances in Korea. Sir Gladwyn Jebb reported from New York that views differed. The United States suggested that they were engaged in an enforcement action under Article 42.* The British apprehended that this assumption would remit operational control of the gathering UN forces to an enforcement committee with Trygve Lie, the Secretary-General, acting as chief of staff. Sir Gladwyn, joined by his French colleague, M. Chauvel, suggested that this was militarily impracticable and politically inexpedient. The Security Council members in session as the enforcement committee would include Yugoslavia, and Nationalist China whose involvement in Korea would exacerbate problems with Mao Tse-tung's *de facto* government of the People's Republic of China. Britain and France proposed that they should proceed under Article 39 because the Security Council had

---

*For the text of connected Articles of the UN Charter (28, 39, 42, 43, 46, 47 and 106) see Appendix F.

recommended active support to the United Nations' membership, as distinct from *deciding* on it. Foreseeing itself as the major contributor of military forces and resources, and concomitantly wishing these to operate under an American Commander-in-Chief responsible to the Joint Chiefs of Staff in Washington, the United States came to accept this reasoning.

There were besides a number of minor aspects for negotiation. The most contentious involved the use of United Nations' insignia: statesmen earnestly weighed whether sailors, soldiers and airmen should wear United Nations' armbands; they became concerned with the rules for flying the United Nations' flag among participating contingents. None was more touchy in this debate than the British. When, finally, the comprehensive resolution concerning command and control was ready to be put to the Security Council there was some backing and filling as to who would sponsor it. The United States was reluctant to do so because it arrogated much responsibility to its government. The Norwegians, who held the presidency currently, felt it wrong to be so closely involved when it had no forces to offer. The British and French obliged, putting the following to the Council on 7th July:

The Security Council . . .
1. Welcomes the prompt and vigorous support which governments and peoples have given . . .
3. Recommends that all Members . . . make such forces and other assistance available to a unified command under the United States.
4. Requests the United States to designate the commander of such forces.
5. Authorises the unified command at its discretion to use the United Nations' flag in the course of operations . . .
6. Requests the United States to provide the Security Council with reports as appropriate on the course of action taken under the unified command.[2]

Yugoslavia, Egypt and India abstained when this resolution was adopted by an otherwise affirmative vote of the Council. Next day, as expected, President Truman 'designated General Douglas MacArthur as the Commanding General of the military forces which the members of the United Nations place under the command of the United States pursuant to the United Nations' assistance to the Republic of Korea . . .'

One of the first requests to be made by the newly appointed Commander-in-Chief was a blockade of supplies to the North Koreans, a measure which required somewhat more than an adaptation of the well tried wartime rules. There was always the possibility that Russian warships might attempt to escort merchantmen into North Korean ports. It is a measure of the failure of both sides involved in the war to understand the other's cast of mind that while the United States and its principal allies decided that they would not in any circumstances be the first to open fire on a Soviet escort, Stalin had already decided that he would not hazard either warships or merchantmen to supply the North Koreans as he expected that they would be fired on.*

More widely, the United States sought to complete denial of strategic supplies to North Korea and to its other neighbour and supporter, the People's Republic of China. Russia, with its European satellites, was already the subject of an embargo in these particulars by North America and western Europe, one of several counter-measures to contain Stalin's cold war. To ensure that strategic goods did not pass into Russia via the Far East, the United States and Britain approached France, Belgium and Holland during the summer of 1949 to prohibit items commonly agreed† also to China and North Korea. At the same time, the United Kingdom was making similar proposals to the sovereign Commonwealth states. Negotiations were still in hand when the Korean war opened. It seemed to the United States that the time had come to abandon leisurely diplomacy: action was needed. Moreover, having ordered their own oil companies to cease supplying their products to China and North Korea, they expected Britain and other allies to do the same.

To the British government, the snag in all this was China. The policy of His Majesty's Government in the Far East throughout this period was inhibited by anxiety about the aggressive potential of the Communist authority established in Peking: in general terms, that Mao's regime would, from the ousting of Chiang Kai-shek's Nationalist forces from the mainland in October 1949, begin to destabilise the hemisphere; in particular, that the People's Liberation Army would occupy Hong Kong. Amongst senior officials in the Foreign Office including the Permanent Secretary, Sir William Strang, there was a view that this might be avoided if the western powers with Australia and New Zealand would recognise and work with the People's Republic which, however unwelcome, was manifestly in control of the mainland of China. To do otherwise, they concluded, would in any case leave Mao no option but closer

---

*For reasons of security, Stalin had previously reduced sea movements to North Korea in the early part of 1950. See Ch 2, p 39.
†There were two lists of strategic materials:
   ia. which comprised items to be denied absolutely;
   ib. which indicated items whose movements should be noted.

cooperation with the Soviet Union.*[3] Hence, a United Kingdom diplomatic mission had been established in Peking to negotiate a full, formal relationship between Britain and China. Political and emotional influences in the United States combined in another direction; the accession of communism had ended an honourable, longstanding love affair between China and America. Republicans and Democrats were implacably opposed to recognising the Peking regime.

When the British Cabinet met on 4th July it considered how it should respond to the United States' urgent proposals to embargo all exports to North Korea and strategic items to China, to which was now added oil. There was no difficulty concerning North Korea: the President of the Board of Trade would make the necessary order prohibiting cargoes from the United Kingdom, the Secretary of State for the Colonies for shipments from Singapore and Hong Kong. But action of this sort against China made many of those at the Cabinet table uneasy. They were comforted to learn that the Foreign Office had informed Washington that oil exports to China were for local consumption and negligible. The only company concerned, Shell, had been asked not to increase its sales. As to strategic exports, they agreed to defer a decision.

Mr Bevin, still in hospital, did not see the minutes of this meeting until 6th July. He was vexed by the item concerning China. Writing to the Prime Minister, he reminded him of Britain's continuing joint action with the United States in urging others to extend the embargo to China. To stand aloof from control of strategic exports in the Far East in current circumstances would open His Majesty's Government to an accusation of bad faith by its allies.

3. The possibilities of adverse repercussions in China appear to be negligible. The imposition of the controls would involve no overt discrimination against China. The United Kingdom licences are already required for the export of all items in question to all destinations (including China) other than the Commonwealth, USA and most OEEC† countries.

4. The flow of strategic items through Hong Kong and Singapore to China is believed to be of negligible proportions at present. It is, however, certain that the psychological effect of our refusing

*This mirrored the opinion of Pandit Nehru. Recognition of China—and incidentally of Bao Dai's regime in Viet Nam—by the Pacific and south-east Asian states was one of Mr Bevin's objectives at the Colombo conference in January 1950.

†The Organisation for European Economic Cooperation, established in April 1948, as the counterpart to the United States' Economic Cooperation Administration (ECA) for the Marshall Plan.

to impose the controls proposed by the United States [will] create resentment out of all proportion to their practical effect, and would seem to have no advantage in the context of our policy towards China.[4]

The Prime Minister was already of the same mind. In matters of overseas policy the combination of Mr Attlee and Mr Bevin was irresistible. The Cabinet agreed to prohibit strategic exports to China; but that did not provide for oil, a fact of which Mr Bevin was, immediately, unaware.* The United States government was very much aware of it, however, and had not in the least been satisfied with the soft answer of the Foreign Office concerning 'negligible' amounts for Chinese domestic use. North Korea's only supply lines were now through Russia and China.

Lord Tedder signalled from Washington on 10th July that he had been approached on the denial of oil by the American Air Force Under-Secretary.

> . . . I suggest that the validity of the 'domestic use' argument is very doubtful in case of Communist Government. It would be unfortunate to say the least if in the event of a serious debacle in South Korea there could be even a vestige of an excuse for the import of British oil being quoted as one of the causes . . .[5]

The Chiefs of Staff took this warning seriously. In Mr Bevin's absence, the Foreign Office quibbled: there was no statutory power to deny oil to China; in any case, China might take reprisals if Britain acted in an apparently discriminatory way, and this might include action against employees of Shell inside Chinese territory. On 13th July, Sir Oliver Franks advised that,

> When I saw Acheson today he raised the issue of British oil exports to China. He expressed the strong hope that we should see our way quickly to stop these exports. He felt no one could be sure that they would be used for civilian purposes only and that they might well free other oil entering from Russia for Korea. I think he also feels that this is one of the issues where the American people will not be able to understand our present attitude. In this I am bound to agree with him.[6]

The figures for oil supplied through Hong Kong for the first six months of the year had by now become available: 26,000 tons of petrol, diesel, kerosese and lubricants, a modest total but enough

---

*The only oil products on List 1 were aviation spirit and certain high grade lubricants.

to suggest to a number of American newspapers* that American boys in Korea were in danger of being killed due to the supply of British oil to the enemy there. More immediately worrying was the discovery that a British tanker, the MV *Fusus*, was en route from Hong Kong to Tientsin with motor spirit. At this point, an official in the Ministry of Fuel and Power conceived a solution which satisfied all parties.

On the grounds of special needs for Korean operations, the Admiralty should requisition all fuel stocks in Hong Kong and, as necessary, any stocks arriving there should be subsequently appropriated. As a part of this requirement, the *Fusus* should be intercepted and her cargo impounded. There would thus be no fuel available for export to China.

The idea was at once adopted. The Americans found it useful as a means of protecting the employees of their own companies in China;† the press were either satisfied with the news of requisitioning or lost interest in the story. To ensure that there were no further problems, all oil products were at Britain's urging added to list 1a of strategic exports.

During the course of these events, other activity in Washington and London was directed towards bringing the hostilities in Korea quickly to an end. Both governments believed that this could only be achieved by persuading Stalin to recall Kim Il-sung's forces to the 38th parallel. Pursuing this aim in association, and commonly confused by a concurrent Indian peace initiative, their endeavours were dogged by differing perceptions as to issues, and as to status.

The United Kingdom and United States had ended the world war five years previously as victorious and nominally equal partners. Although President Roosevelt had sought intermittently during the war to treat alone with Marshal Stalin in the settlement of international political problems, there was recognition in the State Department that this had had certain adverse consequences. Even so, in the years following the dissolution of close partnership, the United States had completed its emergence as a super power. It had assumed responsibilities, as in Greece, which Britain could no longer underwrite; and had responded to the British proposal that America should take the lead in an Atlantic alliance which included a major military commitment to the defence of Europe. The United States had been the benefactor of western Europe with the Marshall Plan, of which the United Kingdom was a beneficiary. In the nature of such relationships, donors, however generous, are apt to assume the attitude of the patron. It was therefore vexing to the

---

*Chiefly the Hearst chain.
†Caltex and Standard-Vacuum.

governmental apparatus in Washington that ministers and officials in London continued to behave as if they were partners still of the first rank. It was not that they wished the British to withdraw from the role of a world power; quite the contrary, their policy making assumed its continuance. Equally, they looked upon Britain as their prime partner in Europe. On major issues, however, the United States expected that the lesser partner would leave initiatives to the greater. Dean Acheson, Secretary of State, later wrote,

> The British Foreign Office had long believed, more than evidence seemed to warrant, that it understood the Russians and could negotiate with them compromise solutions of difficult situations.[7]

Whilst Mr Attlee and Mr Bevin were determined to maintain the close partnership with the United States, of which they were assured from 1947 onwards, and recognised the limitations of British power, they saw themselves nonetheless very much as independent partners still. As earlier remarked, they had not hesitated to take a contrary or otherwise differing view on security issues, to which they had sometimes won United States agreement. It had seemed perfectly natural that they should seek in succession to the United States an indication of the Russian attitude to and intentions in the North Korean invasion, and were encouraged to persevere when the American Ambassador in Moscow, Admiral Kirk*, received on 27th June from the Russian Vice-Minister of External Affairs no more than the expression of the view that, 'the Soviet Government adheres to the principle of impermissibility of inter-ference by foreign powers in the internal affairs of Korea'.[8] As mentioned, Sir David Kelly had to wait until 6th July before he, too, saw Mr Gromyko. After preliminaries, the latter remarked that the United Kingdom 'knew the position of the Soviet Govern-ment from the documents which have been published but Soviet Government wished for a peaceful settlement and therefore asked me if I had any proposals. I said that all I asked for was the use of their influence with the North Korean Government, that I would report at once what he said and that I would ask to see him again if I received any further communication from him . . . .'.[9]

At this stage the Russian response, limited as it was, excited some hope in London and Washington—with whom full details were at once shared—that Stalin might be considering the option at least of halting the North Korean People's Army where it stood. Mr Acheson sent the following for Mr Bevin on 7th July:

> (1) Although it is impossible to be certain that this is not an attempt to confuse issue and weaken our common resolve, we

---

*Kirk, Vice-Admiral Alan G, USN (1888–1963).

89

are inclined to regard this as a serious approach designed to find way to end Korean affair without undue prestige loss to USSR but presumably for price as yet undisclosed.

(2) We agree that any move which might lead to peace should have the most serious consideration. However, we believe it important not to appear over anxious and we are not willing to bargain away positions in exchange for termination of aggression against South Korea . . .

So far, then, the United States was ready to see the British carry negotiations forward, though,

(8) If British Ambassador is asked whether he is representing views of United States, it is suggested he make it clear that he is speaking for his own government but if Gromyko has any comments or views which he wishes to have transmitted to other members of the Security Council, his government would be glad to assist.[10]

But from the outset, Mr Acheson insisted that two principles should be maintained. First, the price—'the price as yet undisclosed'—might well be the admission of the People's Republic of China to the United Nations or recognition of its sovereignty over Taiwan. The United States would not make any concessions in this matter. Second, any arangements for peace must carry forward the United Nations' policy for reunion of Korea under supervision of its commission.

Before Mr Acheson's message had reached Mr Bevin in his hospital room, from which he was conducting the businesss of the Foreign Office from 6th July, the following was reported by the news agency *Tass* in Moscow on the morning of the 7th,

A representative of the British Foreign Office stated at a press conference in London on 5th July that England [sic] had addressed, through the Ambassador in Moscow, a proposal for the peaceful settlement of the Korean question, and that England was awaiting a reply from the Soviet Government*. *Tass* is authorised to state that, in the course of his talk with a representative of the Ministry of Foreign Affairs of the USSR, the British Ambassador delivered to the Soviet Government no proposal for the peaceful settlement of the Korean question and confined himself to expressing the hope that the conflict would be settled

*What actually passed at this briefing was as follows. The official conducting it was asked by a correspondent whether any reply had been received from the Russian government as a result of Sir David Kelly's approach. He answered, 'There has been no reply'.

in due course. It is clear that the statement of the British Ambassador in Moscow does not require any reply from the Soviet Government.

Though some members of the Foreign Office believed that this manifested a Russian disinclination to discuss peace in Korea, others argued the contrary: the Soviet government was signalling that negotiations would continue if there were specific proposals including, by implication, a *quid pro quo*. Within the Office, however, the import of the publication was subsumed in broader considerations as Mr Bevin sent Mr Acheson his own thoughts on Sir David Kelly's meeting with Gromyko, which crossed those of Mr Acheson in transit to him.

'If the Soviet government genuinely desire a peaceful settlement,'

he instructed Sir Oliver Franks by telegram on the 7th,

. . . it is possible that they in fact would agree to use their influence in the manner suggested. I cannot foresee precisely how they would extricate themselves from the difficult position in which they have placed themselves, but Soviet ingenuity could no doubt find some face-saving device.

We must expect however that if the Soviet Government do show a readiness to cooperate in re-establishing the *status quo* in Korea, they will almost certainly raise the question of Formosa [Taiwan] having regard to the situation which the President's declaration of 27th June creates. It also seems to us, that the question of Chinese representation in the United Nations would be raised and become acute, the Russians arguing that they could not play their part in the Security Council with [the People's Republic of] China not represented.

I think that Mr Acheson and the United States' Government should appreciate, and I put it to them very frankly, the way I see the situation which is as follows.

The United States have the whole-hearted backing of world opinion for the courageous initiative they took to deal with the aggression in Korea. I do not believe they could rely on the same support for their declared policy in connexion with Formosa. Not only would many powers, particularly Asian powers, dislike the prospect of an extension of the dispute which might follow if [the People's Republic of] China were to attempt an attack on Formosa, but some undoubtedly feel that, now that the Central People's Government are in control of all Chinese territory, it would not be justifiable, in view of the pledge under the Cairo declaration, to take steps which might prejudice the ultimate handing over of the territory to China. India especially, as Mr Acheson will have heard from the United States Ambassador at Delhi, is very sensitive on this aspect of United States policy. In general I think the United States Government would be wise in their public statements to concentrate on the Korean issue and play down the other parts of the President's statement of 27th June, otherwise there may be a risk of a breach in the international solidarity happily achieved over Korea.

Thus the latest Soviet move has forced us to ask ourselves the question what the attitude of the United States would be if the Russians agreed to help in restoring the *status quo* in Korea in return for United States readiness to reconsider their present declared attitude in regard to Formosa.

Finally I want Mr Acheson to know that I am keenly alive to the possibility, and even likelihood, that the Soviet move has a sinister significance. For example, the Russians, knowing there is a divergence of policy between Great Britain and the United States in regards to China, may well calculate that their move may increase the divergence. We must both be on our guard against this. Moreover, the move may be no more than a manoeuvre in the Soviet peace campaign, launched with the object of courting a refusal, though personally I am inclined to doubt this. Finally we must bear in mind that a restoration of the *status quo* in Korea may merely result, in the long run, in a development similar to that in Czechoslovakia. Clearly there can meanwhile be no relaxation in the military effort.

Mr Acheson will understand my feeling that this is a time for us to be frank with each other. I know that he will answer me with equal frankness.[11]

This message, handed to the Secretary of State by Sir Oliver Franks during the afternoon of 8th July, exacerbated Mr Acheson's resentment and, to an extent, his apprehensions, stimulated by British reluctance at that juncture to prohibit oil exports to China. In seeking to run its own course, the British Foreign Office was willing, it seemed, to sacrifice allied solidarity. From his own staff he knew that the senior officials concerned in London disagreed with United States' policy towards China but he was surprised that Mr Bevin seemed now to have been won over largely to their view. In personal discussions earlier in the year, Mr Bevin had indicated that he was far from committed to it.

Next day, the news from London was more encouraging. 'I called at the Foreign Office this morning,' the American Ambassador reported by telegram on the 8th, 'and had a preliminary conversation with Younger* and later with Prime Minister who called at the Foreign Office.' They discussed Acheson's telegram:

> Prime Minister stated that British thinking was consistent with ours: that they would despatch a holding telegram to Kelly. . .
> 3. Speaking entirely off the record and personally I suggested to Prime Minister that very probably one of the prices which Soviets would demand for using their influence . . . would be agreement that Communist China be seated in Security Council . . . Communist representative in Security Council might result in a real estate swap of South Korea for Formosa. Prime Minister replied that British had been thinking along this same line and that the position of HMG would be that the question of Korea and admittance of Communist China to Security Council were wholly separate.[12]

While this telegram relieved Mr Acheson's anxiety, it seemed to indicate that the British Prime Minister and Foreign Secretary were out of step. It was not so. Mr Bevin had given, as was his method, oral instructions on the 6th as to what he wished to say to Mr Acheson. This was the day when, contrary to the advice of his officials, he expressed the view that List 1 exports should be prohibited to China. Possibly, being unwell still, he did not perceive the implications of his wording on the 7th; certainly he protested later that he had not intended to propose appeasement of the Russians. Mr Attlee's visit to the Foreign Office was made after consultation with Mr Bevin, probably because he was specially sensitive just then to the need for Anglo-American accord—he had sent a personal message to President Truman on the 6th on the need to define together strategic objectives and policies in the Far East relative to Korea. The Foreign Office, rather than No 10, Downing Street, was chosen as the meeting site to avoid creating, in Mr Bevin's words, an impression 'in the public mind that high level Anglo-American conversations of a dramatic kind were being held.' The Prime Minister, *en route* to the Farnborough air show, thus slipped into the Foreign Office by a side door.

The British record of the meeting is not of the same character as that described by Mr Douglas to Mr Acheson. Whilst agreeing that there must be no appeasement of the Russians, the Prime Minister urged 'that the United States should not get into a position where whites could be represented as contending against coloured

---

*Younger, Hon (later Sir) Kenneth (Gilmour), (1908–76), Minister of State at the Foreign Office. He was not on close terms with Mr Bevin and often held different views on matters of policy. However, in Mr Bevin's absence, the Prime Minister maintained control of major policy.

races.'[13] The essential difference between Mr Bevin's written and Mr Attlee's spoken remarks was that the latter was able to make clear in a dialogue that the British government were not going to offer concessions to Stalin to end the Korean war.

By 8th July onwards, then, British and American policy for the negotiations in Moscow were generally in tune. In due course, Mr Acheson replied strongly* to Mr Bevin's message, received and accepted Mr Bevin's assurance that he was opposed to bargaining with Stalin, and himself hastened to explain a misleading phrase of his own.[14] By 14th July both men were clear that while they did not agree on the American stance over Taiwan and China's seat in the United Nations, these matters were discrete from settlement of the Korean problem. Friendship between them was restored. Both had been under strain, Mr Bevin physically, Mr Acheson overburdened by work—Sir Oliver Franks noted on 8th July that he was 'well, but taut'.

In this same period, India was involved in a peace initiative of her own. Although several leading members of the Congress party have been credited with this enterprise, there is little doubt that the originator was the Prime Minister, Pandit Nehru. In High Commission and Embassy, Britain and America were aware of stirrings in this direction but appear to have believed that these were simply part of India's persistent unease about the Far East situation. A hint that anxiety was heightening came to London from Mr Hutchison, the British *chargé d'affaires* in Peking, who reported that 'Indian Ambassador told member of my staff on 6th July that he had received a telegram from his Government . . . that they thought it inevitable that a major war would develop out of the Korean situation. HM Consul-General in Shanghai reports that the same day the Indian Ambassador instructed the Indian Consul-General [there] to destroy his cyphers . . .'.[15] What the Indians had not revealed was the delivery of an enquiry by Pandit Nehru as to whether the People's Republic of China would use its influence for peace in Korea if it was admitted to the UN. In Moscow, the Indian Ambassador was asking the government whether, given China's admission, Marshal Stalin would support a Security Council resolution for peace in Korea.

Admiral Kirk was then told of this latter approach and pressed the Indian Ambassador to inform Sir David Kelly also to avoid unnecessary complexity in the British explorations. Shortly, Mr Nehru appealed officially to Washington and London to support

---

*In terms described by E M Nicholson to the Lord President (Herbert Morrison) as 'this powerful and well-merited rebuke', an illustration of the fact that not all senior officials disagreed with United States' policy in the Far East.

his idea of Communist China's admission to the UN as the key to a Korean peace settlement.

China's reply was generally affirmative, though it made the point that the issue of its place in the United Nations and its Security Council had nothing to do with the Korean war. Stalin returned this message:

> I welcome your peace initiative. I fully share your point of view as to the expediency of a peaceful settlement of the Korean question through the Security Council, the participation of the representatives of the five great powers including the People's Government of China being indispensable I believe that to reach an early settlement of the Korean question it would be expedient in the Security Council to hear representatives of the Korean people.[16]

In a message to Mr Attlee immediately thereafter, Mr Nehru suggested that the reply was 'most encouraging . . . My honest belief is that Moscow is seeking a way out of present tangle without loss of prestige . . . there is a real chance of solving Korean problem by enabling Peking government to enter and Soviet government to resume its place in Security Council without insistence on conditions. This may be an act of faith but the gravity of the alternative seems to justify it. In view of urgency of matter I shall be grateful for earliest possible answer.'[17]

Although he had disclaimed to this point any wish to become a principal in peace negotiations,[18] Pandit Nehru had now assumed such a role. The British Prime Minister, who had set out his objections only four days previously to the course proposed, now reiterated with the agreement of his Cabinet these views with specific reference to Marshal Stalin's note:

> I think this is an appropriate moment, [he wrote to Mr Nehru on the 18th], for us all to consider the position in which we shall find ourselves if we accept the procedure outlined by Stalin in his communication to you. There are variations of attitude and outlook amongst us which must, I think, be taken into account if any agreed solution is to be reached.
>
> The first point which strikes us about Stalin's message is that it totally ignores the fact, which you yourself accept, that the present conflict in Korea is the result of aggression by North Korea . . . You have said in your message of 14th July that you find it difficult to believe that the North Korean invasion was staged in order to compel the United States and United Kingdom to admit the New China into the Security Council . . . I think

that assessment is correct, but now Stalin is making precisely that a condition for the settlement of the Korean affair. But he does not indicate any real intention to settle the Korean question in any way which would satisfy the rest of the world. He merely makes the suggestion that the ''representatives of the Korean people'' (presumably North Korea) should be heard in order to reach an early settlement. This suggestion does not really deal with the main question of the North Korean aggression . . .

The question of Chinese representation in the United Nations seems to us a separate issue. . . Whether you and we agree with [the United States] point of view or not, the fact remains that for them now to recede from their position as a concession to bring about the termination of aggression by North Korea would be something United States public opinion could hardly be expected to swallow. I think we shall put ourselves in a very difficult position if we make such a proposal. As is usual in the case of aggression, the aggressors are having the best of it for the time being. Americans are being defeated and American blood is being shed . . .

You say that if after the Soviet Union returns the Security Council and the New China is admitted, they abuse the veto, the world will hold them guilty of imperilling world peace. I would agree that the world would see then clearly where China and Russia stood, and that there would be some advantage in clarifying the issue. But let us see what would happen in practice if Russia and the New China took their place in the Security Council. Were they to veto future Security Council resolutions relating to the aggression of North Korea, United Nations action to stop aggression would be frustrated. This is the price we might have to pay for demonstrating the non-cooperation of Russia and China.

. . . I should feel very considerable difficulty if I were asked to try to influence [the United States] in that direction. If the issue is raised in the Security Council I still think that China would not get the requisite number of votes. There is no indication that Egypt, Cuba or Ecuador would change their minds. The result would then be that the Soviet Union would seize upon this as an excuse for not using their influence with North Korea to stop the fighting. We would then find ourselves exactly where we were before . . . [19]

Mr Nehru was affronted privately by this rebuff and another from the United States. He was not altogether pleased with the Russian government when it published, without warning during these exchanges, his correspondence with Marshal Stalin. A view among the diplomatic community, widely held, that Stalin had decided to take such modest profits as were offered by the negotiations was reported to him and may have caused him to suspect that he had been misused. Any immediate prospect of bringing the Korean war to an end by Russian intervention seemed unlikely when the details of the Anglo-Soviet negotiations were also published in Moscow on 20th July. These included a note handed to Sir David Kelly on the 17th with much the same message as that given to India.[20]

In later years, the question has sometimes been asked: was there a chance of peace at this time; was Stalin, surprised perhaps by the speed and range of the United Nations' response to the North Korean invasion, looking for an acceptable way to return to the *status quo ante;* and did he then overplay his hand in seeking concessions? The Russian government has not yet opened its archives to provide answers to these questions. Any judgement must meantime take account of a factor relative to this and all other traffic passing to or from the British Foreign Office and Washington Embassy. Three officials were working in or in close association with both: Guy Burgess, Kim Philby and Donald Maclean. They were subsequently discovered to be traitors*. Details of all policy discussions and decisions concerning the negotiations may well have passed to the Russian government. Is it too fanciful that this was the reason why, when Sir David Kelly was in discussion with Mr Gromyko, he noticed a slight smile on the latter's face?

.   .   .   .   .

Within a few days of the attack upon South Korea, Mr Attlee apprehended that America and Britain, united in the essential aim of resisting aggression there, were less than coordinated elsewhere. It was true that the American and British Foreign and Defence Departments perceived at once the possibility that Stalin was deliberately staging a diversion in Korea and were mutually apprehensive of Russian ventures in other parts of the world, but it was evident that, singly and collectively, their intelligence was at best patchy and often late, their policies for common action, agreed in some theatres such as Germany, were at variance in others.

---

*Burgess was in the Foreign Office Far Eastern Department and Philby in the British Embassy in Washington at this time. Maclean was in the British Embassy in Cairo, until May 1950, from which he was posted in November 1950, to head the North American Department of the Foreign Office. Burgess and Maclean were suspended from duty on 1st June 1951, after their flight to Moscow. Philby was 'retired' under suspicion of complicity with them. He was finally unmasked—and fled to the Soviet Union—in 1963.

Difficulties in obtaining a clear statement from Washington about its strategy in Korea and the differences of view concerning recognition of the People's Republic of China and Taiwan were the weighting factors which persuaded the Prime Minister to write to President Truman on 6th July, though he tactfully omitted to mention these too precisely:

I have been giving much thought to the problems which are likely to face us as the situation in Korea develops. These problems are of course primarily military but they are likely to have increasingly wide political implications . . .

3. A particular aspect of the situation in Korea which is causing us concern is that the Russians have involved the Western Powers in a heavy commitment without themselves playing an overt part, and there are other areas in the Far East where the same tactics are open to them. You have already made known your concern with Indo-China and Formosa [Taiwan]. There is some reason to think that Communist-inspired activities in Malaya have already been stepped up in tune with the Korean affair. And we cannot ignore the possibility of a Chinese attack on Hongkong.

4. . . . . I understand your military advisers have already expressed the view that Persia may again become a danger spot. We should consider whether the opportunity may not be taken of relighting the fire in Greece. And there may be other areas of potential trouble.

5. . . . No-one can attempt to provide precisely in advance for every eventuality. But I hope you will agree with me that we should look ahead as far as we can and reach some agreement as to our common policy in these areas in the event of further outbreaks.

6. . . . Other Governments, in particular the French, may be concerned, but it will suffice if they are informed as and when the situation demands.

7. . . . I would therefore like to suggest to you that you should authorise the appropriate United States authorities to discuss these problems with Lord Tedder in Washington.

8. It seems to me that such talks cannot ignore the political implications. I should therefore be glad to hear whether you would propose that the Department of State should be associated with these talks. . . .[21]

On 8th July, President Truman replied,

I, too, have been giving a great deal of thought to the problems which may arise as the situation in Korea develops, and agree with your suggestion that these problems be explored between us.

I note that you intend to send a representative of the UK Chiefs of Staff to advise Lord Tedder. I agree entirely that the political implications . . . are of the greatest importance, in fact in some respects they are preeminent. For this reason I have asked Ambassador Jessup* to be associated with General Bradley in conducting the talks on our side . . .

I am in entire agreement with your thought that these talks should be conducted in the greatest secrecy and note your observation that it will suffice if the French and other interested Governments are informed as and when the situation demands . . .[22]

Mr Acheson did not altogether welcome this development—his anxieties about the British attitude to the negotiations in Moscow were rising just then—and, later, he was to dismiss the talks as adding nothing of value to their labours. That judgement, made with much hindsight, is partial. The talks at least clarified the strategic planning assumptions of both sides and probably softened United States views on the rearmament of west Germany. They also focussed British attention on the fact that America was growing anxious about the provision of troops for Korea. By the time the British supporting members† arrived on 18th July, the principal interest of the Americans in meeting them was to secure a British land force for General MacArthur's command.

In a full, wide-ranging brief for their negotiators, the Foreign Office and Chiefs of Staff had continued to argue against this though, led by the Chief of the Air Staff, they were coming to recognise that the British response overall might have to be widened. Writing to Air Marshal Elliot on 14th July, Sir John Slessor noted that, 'A matter which is not covered in the Foreign Office paper (for the Washington talks)[23] is what happens if the Americans have a disaster in Korea and have to stage a Dunkirk, leaving (inevitably) a lot of American prisoners and equipment in enemy hands.'

2. In view of their pronounced intention of clearing Korea to the 38th Parallel it seems inevitable that they will have to stage

---

*Jessup. Dr Philip C (1897–1978), then an Ambassador at large for the United States Government.

†Major-General (later, Lieutenant-General Sir) Harold Redman (1899–1986), Director of Military Operations in the War Office, and Mr M E, (later, Sir Esler) Dening (1897–1977), Assistant Under-Secretary at the Foreign Office. Just prior to the opening, it was decided that Sir Oliver Franks should lead the talks in Washington, rather than Lord Tedder, due to the primacy of the political content. Representatives of the Joint Intelligence Staff followed later for consultations with their United States counterparts.

a full scale invasion to get back to Korea. This will absorb enormous resources and take a long time. Meanwhile other danger spots in the Far East—such as Indo-China—to which those resources *should* be directed, will presumably have to go short, while the possibility of obtaining any American support for danger spots elsewhere, such as Persia, will be correspondingly reduced.

3. In one way, therefore, nothing would suit the Soviet book better than to see the US committed to a minor *Overlord** in Korea. Meanwhile, within the country the Communist regime would be consolidating, and when the American invasion came it would be represented as aggression . . . Indeed, it is somewhat bizarre that, to liberate a country about which no-one cares very much (except on a point of principle) and restore a regime which was a pretty rotten one, the United Nations should have to undertake a major effort to weaken their ability to meet other "Koreas" elsewhere—to say nothing of a major Soviet attack.

4. Nevertheless, the effect on American—and indeed on United Nations prestige in Asia in particular and throughout the world in general of an unredeemed failure of the first collective move to resist armed aggression would surely be such that any acceptance of defeat seems impossible. . .

6. . . . if this United Nations action to stop aggression in its infancy and prevent a really major aggression in at most a few years time is to succeed, the United Nations must place themselves virtually on a war footing now. The United States are already mobilising some of their National Guard (TA)† Divisions and are returning some of their civil industry to a war production basis. I do not suggest in any detail what corresponding action we should take, but the purpose of this note is to suggest that we have got to face more drastic measures and something much nearer a return to a war economy than anything we have even yet considered . . .[24]

At the following meeting of the Chiefs of Staff on 17th July, Sir John suggested that air power might save the South Korean people much of the suffering that would follow a long clawing back of their territory by a conventional land campaign and, by implication, reduce the bill for soldiers:

For example, the Allies might announce their intention in advance of bombing certain selected towns in North Korea. The

*Overlord: title of the allied invasion of Normandy, 1944.
†TA—the British Territorial Army comprising part time volunteers roughly equivalent to the National Guard.

inhabitants would be given adequate warning to evacuate and the Allies would then destroy by precision bombing with High Explosive, one or two of the towns that had been warned—and so on until North Korea agreed to withdraw behind her own frontier. It would appear that there were a considerable number of good industrial targets in North Korea . . .[25]

This concept, essentially the same as a strategy used between the wars by the Royal Air Force to maintain internal security in certain imperial territories, was warmly supported in the committee . . . It seemed to offer an option within the existing United States resources,* which might obviate the need for any further British military contribution to Korea; the more welcome as the Secretary-General of the United Nations had just pressed, on behalf of the United States, the need for reinforcements, particularly land forces.[26]

At the Foreign Office, Sir Pierson Dixon was not quite so enthusiastic:

> . . . I do not presume to discuss the merits of strategic bombing, [he wrote to the Chiefs on 21st July], 'but I am inclined to think that at this moment it might have a bad effect on our relations with the Americans if we broached with them a plan based on the assumption that they would be driven out of Korea. We do not want to seem defeatist, nor to interfere with MacArthur; nor of course would we like it if the Americans thought we were seeking an excuse not to make a contribution on the ground.[27]

Lord Tedder, to whom General Redman had mentioned the idea, had already asked General Bradley 'if they had considered the possibility of using air power on lines suggested by the Chief of Air Staff,' though without the context of ejection from the Korean peninsula. 'Bradley took the point and agreed that it deserved careful consideration once the position was stabilised'. But from the American point of view such suggestions were incidental. They had put three divisions into Korea and had in train arrangements to insert another three. With these, naval and air supremacy, General Bradley believed that they would be able to hold a 'reasonable bridgehead even though it would involve a perimeter covering Pusan of some 150 miles. As regards further action', Tedder reported, 'there would inevitably be delay of some months since they are anxious not to launch advance until the

---

*It was known that the United States Far East Air Force had a group of strategic bombers, one of medium bombers, and three of fighter-bombers available for operations at that time. Naval carrier aircraft would add weight to these.

force available is strong enough to ensure rapid and decisive defeat of the North Korean forces. They wished to insure against any possibility of the North Korean forces being merely driven back to the 38th parallel with a stalemate resulting . . .'[28] Bradley stressed the need for considerable forces,

> not only to secure rapid and decisive result when advance became possible, but also to keep secure very lengthy Lines of Communication which would be subject to guerrilla attacks.
> 2. With regard to scale of such assistance from other UN countries he said that units of battalion strength upwards would be of genuine assistance. In view of present estimate, that a period of some months would necessarily elapse before advance could be launched, reinforcements would be valuable even though they might not be able to arrive in Korea for some time. But an early public announcement of the intention to send such reinforcements would be of immense political value . . .[29]

Sir Oliver Franks' report of the meeting to the Foreign Office remarked,

> . . . It was quite clear that the question of United Nations forces for Korea was foremost in the American mind and I would judge that as a result of the representations made to us we shall now be expected to respond with at any rate a token force. There was no doubt in our minds that what was said to us had been carefully thought out before-hand and had the highest authority . . .[30]

Indeed it had. The United States government were undertaking notable appropriations of money and manpower to deal with the Korean operations, now clearly perceived as a nut requiring reinforced crackers*. They expected their allies to go some way down the same road. Sir Oliver Franks, closely in touch with opinion in the American government and society, was so convinced of the need to send British soldiers to join those of the United

---

*The President sent a special message to the Congress on 19th July recommending an increase in the statutory size of the armed forces, mobilising elements of the National Guard and reservists, and authorising an additional US$10 billion for defence together with certain special measures related to war manufactures.[31] The speed with which the costings were produced was due to work following a National Security Council report, NSC-68, recommending re-armament following the development of the Russian atom bomb in 1949.

States in Korea that he took the exceptional step of writing direct to the Prime Minister on the subject on 15th July:*

> . . . for some ten days now there has been a steady increase in interest, questioning and criticism in Washington on this subject. It spreads through all branches of the government and press. In the last two days it has spread outside Washington and has reached editorial columns in out of town newspapers. On this I wish to make one comment. Too often in the past we have taken our time to make a decision with the result that often, when we have done what was in line with American ideas, we have got no credit or approval for it; the decision has followed upon and seemed to be extracted from us by the massive discussion, criticism and pressure that has been built up in the US . . .[32]

Mr Attlee passed this without comment to the Foreign Office, in which there was already general agreement that the political considerations for sending British troops to Korea were becoming irresistible However, miffed that their man in Washington was approaching the Prime Minister direct, the Permanent Secretary asked Sir Oliver for a formal expression of his views. He was also aware by this time that the United States did not want to make a formal request, government to government, preferring that the United Kingdom should make an apparently spontaneous offer of troops.

Sir Oliver sent a long and unequivocal response, stressing American reliance on its partnership with Britain.[33] The Prime Minister now put it informally to the Foreign Office and Defence Departments that they could not expect special collaboration with their American partners, manifest in such events as the consultations just completed in Washington and an impending meeting of the combined Chiefs of Staff, if the British role was to be restricted principally to advice. On 24th July, he chaired a meeting of the Cabinet Defence Committee at which, by pre-arrangement, the Chief of the Imperial General Staff, Sir William Slim, spoke for his colleagues. They had reconsidered the question, he said,

> Although in their view it was still militarily unsound, they recognised the strong political arguments . . . it would be wrong to send less than a Brigade Group. Nothing less would achieve the political objective . . . It should be a mixed force—perhaps

---

*He excused the approach on the grounds of Mr Bevin's absence from London on convalescence.

an Armoured Regiment* equipped with Centurion tanks, an Anti-Tank Regiment . . . a Field [artillery] Regiment and three Infantry Battalions. To this could perhaps be added the contribution which New Zealand was thinking of furnishing, e.g., a medium artillery regiment. There would be at least some military advantages in sending this force: it would be an exercise in finding the strategic reserve which the War Office were always trying to constitute, and it would provide a practical test for certain weapons, especially the Centurion tanks. The force could not be constituted in a day and it might be necessary to call up perhaps some 2,000 reservists, especially signallers, of which the Army was very short. The American Command . . . would probably not want reinforcements until the battle was stabilised and they were in a position to counter-attack. The despatch of our Brigade Group was not therefore urgent which would allow us at least two months in which to make the necessary preparations . . .

The minutes of the meeting noted that the Committee:
(2) Agreed that this Brigade Group should not be formed at the expense of the Hong Kong Garrison.
(3) Invited the Secretary of State for War to examine and report any measures required for the calling-up of reservists.
(4) Agreed that the decision of the Committee should be made known to Parliament in the course of the defence debate [on 26th July].
(5) Invited the Minister of State [representing Mr Bevin] to inform the United States Ambassador, in confidence, in the meantime and to notify the Secretary-General of the United Nations at the time of the debate in Parliament.
(6) Invited the Prime Minister to notify the Commonwealth Prime Ministers.
(7) Instructed the Chiefs of Staff to notify Lord Tedder.[34]

Next day the whole Cabinet endorsed its Defence Committee's decisions. A British land force would take part in the Korean war.

---

*The British military term *regiment* had already occasioned misunderstanding. The United States, like many Armies employing the continental system of organisation, uses it to describe a formation of troops approximating to a brigade. Knowing that there was an 'armoured' or 'tank regiment' in Hong Kong, General Bradley's staff had expressed a wish to have such a potentially powerful force in Korea. But the British usage implies a battalion when used for the cavalry and armoured forces, the artillery (and now also the engineers and signals). For the infantry, a *regiment* connotes a group with a territorial or other special connexion, often long standing, which fields battalions. This custom not only confused allies but some officials in Whitehall and, later, the enemy in Korea.

SOURCE NOTES: CHAPTER 4

1. DEFE 11/193,FO 502 to Moscow of 28th June 1950.
2. UN S/1588 of 7th July 1950.
3. See FO 371/76386, (W 5572/3/500G) PUSC (32), 'The United Kingdom in SE Asia and the FE', and Sir Pierson Dixon's internal minute (in relation to note 14) of 12th July 1950.
4. CAB 21/1949, Foreign Secretary to PM 50/33 of 7th July 1950.
5. Ibid, BJSM Washington AWT 15 to MOD of 102210Z July 1950.
6. Ibid, Washington 1948 to FO of 13th July 1950.
7. Acheson, Dean, *The Korean War*, (New York, 1971) p 35.
8. FRUS, op cit, United States State Department (USSD) Moscow 1767 to USSD of 29th June 1950.
9. DEFE 11/95, Moscow 567 to FO of 6th July 1950.
10. FRUS, op cit, USSD 83 to London Embassy of 7th July 1950.
11. Ibid, FO 3092 to Washington of 7th July 1950.
12. Ibid, London Embassy 156 to USSD of 8th July 1950.
13. DEFE 11/195, For an account, see FO 3105 to Washington of 8th July 1950.
14. For details, see *FRUS*, op cit, USSD 132 and 133 to London Embassy of 10th July 1950; and DEFE 11/96 Washington 1946 to FO of 13th July 1950.
15. DEFE 11/195, Peking 1008 to FO of 7th July 1950.
16. See FO 371/84089 (FK1022/142), FO 3244 to Washington of 18th July 1950.
17. For details, see Ibid (FK1022/142), FO 3245 to Washington of 18th July 1950.
18. See, for example, DEFE 11/195, Delhi 1836 to CRO of 8th July 1950 and 1842 of 9th July 1950.
19. For details, see FO 371/84089 (FK1022/142), FO 3246 to Washington of 18th July 1950.
20. DEFE 11/196, Moscow 620 to FO of 17th July 1950.
21. DEFE 11/193, FO 3070 to Washington of 6th July 1950.
22. *FRUS*, op cit, USSD 121—London Embassy of 8th July 1950.
23. CAB 131/9, DO(50)55 of 10th July 1950.
24. CAB 21/2102, letter from Sir John Slessor to Air Marshal Sir William Elliot of 14th July 1950.
25. DEFE 4/33, COS(50) 112th Meeting of 17th July 1950.
26. See DEFE 11/193, New York 704 to FO of 14th July 1950.
27. DEFE 11/196, letter from FO (Sir Pierson Dixon) to Secretary of Chiefs of Staff Committee dated 21st July 1950.
28. Ibid, BJSM AWT23 to London of 202359 July 1950.
29. Ibid, BJSM AWT22 to London of 202023 July 1950.
30. FO 371/84089 (FK1022/198), Washington 2022 to FO of 21st July 1950.
31. United States Public Papers of the Presidents of the United States: Harry S Truman, 1950, p 527.
32. FO 371/84089; (FK1022/165), letter from Sir Oliver Franks to PM dated 15th July 1950.
33. Ibid, (FK1022/22), Washington 2036 to FO of 23rd July 1950.
34. CAB 131/8, DO(50) 15th meeting of 24th July 1950.

CHAPTER 5

Money, Men, and Materials

In taking the decision to send troops to Korea, the Prime Minister was well aware that there would be elements within the Labour Party who would be uncomfortable as a consequence, some dismayed by it. The reactions among several Ministers, he knew, lay within this range. It was not that the Party was pacifist in character—though there were staunch pacifists among its membership—or inhibited by vestigial loyalties to the international communist camp; quite to the contrary. Rather, that the Party was dedicated to the extension of equal opportunities and benefits among all sections of the community. The problem was that the policy needed additional funds. In broad terms, the government had been devoting the limited sums it could muster from an economy debilitated by the recent world war to its capital reconstruction and social programmes. When the Defence Committee met in the Prime Minister's room in the House of Commons on 24th July, and when the Cabinet discussed their conclusions on the 25th and 1st August, it became clear that the needs of defence would be met at the expense of these programmes.

The defence budget for 1950–51 was £780 million and forecast to remain at that for the following two years. Mr Shinwell advised that this was in any case too low a figure: production costs of weapons and associated items were rising; in order at least to retain the regular content of the armed forces it would be necessary to raise service pay.* To the requirements of funding exemplary defence commitments to the Western European Union and the newly-fledged North Atlantic Treaty Organisation, they had now to consider the extraordinary expenditure which would arise in the Korean war. Sir Stafford Cripps, Chancellor of the Exchequer, made the following proposals to his colleagues as a result of the representations made to him by the Minister of Defence. An additional £100 million would be made available for contingencies— about £30 million of which would be spent in the remaining nine

---

*Both the Labour and Conservative Parties intended to return progressively to voluntary manning of the services after the second world war. In the interim, conscripts would serve in home stations, regulars overseas. However, there were insufficient numbers to implement this policy. In 1950 the regular content of the forces was diminishing.

months of the financial year, the balance in 1951-2. A further £100 million should be available for improvements in service pay: £10 million in the current year, £30 million in each of the following three years. Adding the new sums which the supply departments* expected to spend, the bill was as follows:

£million	1950-51	1951-52	1952-53	1953-54
Budget adjusted	£780	£800	£780	£790
Contingencies	30	70	30	30
Pay/manning increases	10	30	30	30
Armament increases	4	175	293	342
Totals:†	£824	£1,075	£1,133	£1,192

The Chancellor said that:
the United States Government had asked the Governments of all the other North Atlantic Powers to provide them, before 5th August, with particulars of the nature and extent of the increased effort they were willing and able to undertake in increasing their armed forces and their military production, and of the further military production programmes which they could initiate with American financial assistance . . . in answering the second part of the enquiry by the United States Government, we should take the following line. We should state that by decisions already taken or likely to be taken in the near future we were committed to defence expenditure of about £820 million in 1950-51 and £900 million in 1951-52. We considered that on general economic grounds an annual expenditure of £950 million on defence was the most we could afford in 1951-52 and in the following two years. If, therefore, we were to undertake the additional programme indicated above, we must ask for United States assistance to cover the difference between an expenditure of £2,850 million over the three years [3 x £950 million, 1951-54] and total programme of £3,400 [£1,075 + £1,133 + £1,192 million], ie, we should ask for United States aid to the extent of £550 million . . . in the form of free dollars which we could either hold or use to make purchases in any part of the world. . . .

Ministers should recognise that the resources required . . . could not be provided without some reduction in Government expenditure, some additional taxation or some reduction in capital investment, or a combination of all three.

---

*Defence procurement was the responsibility of the Ministry of Supply, but the three service departments operated within it through the Controller of the Navy, the Master-General of the Ordnance, and the Controller of Aircraft.

†There was an additional commitment of £137 million to civil defence over the four year period. Overall, the increases involved a rise to 10% of the national revenue.

Mr Bevan,* Minister of Health, objected:

Our foreign policy had hitherto been based on the view that the best method of defence against Russian imperialism was to improve the social and economic conditions of the countries threatened by Communist encroachment. The United States Government now seemed to be abandoning this . . . in favour of a military defence. He believed that this change of policy was misjudged, and that we should be ill-advised to follow it. The United Kingdom could perhaps support the burden . . . without fatal damage to its economic and social structure. He doubted, however, whether the same was true of France and some of the other countries of Western Europe. If, as a result of this further military effort, their economic and social standards were still further reduced, their ability to resist the domestic threat of communism would be seriously prejudiced.

If the Cabinet now endorsed the proposal . . . defence expenditure at an annual rate of £950 million over the next three years, he foresaw very great difficulties for the Ministers responsible for social services. They would be forced to accept reductions in the Government's civil programmes; their only freedom would be to decide which of those programmes would suffer first or most. If some increase in defence expenditure was inevitable, would it not be better to take the line that there could be no reduction in our existing level of expenditure on social services and capital investment and to allocate to defence the increase in the national income which was expected to accrue from increased productivity?

In reply, it was pointed out that, if the whole of the increment from increased productivity were allocated to defence, this would involve a much larger defence expenditure than that proposed. . . . In fact, however, the product of future increases in industrial productivity had already been taken into account in the social and economic programmes to which the Government were committed. . . .

. . . some Ministers felt that the greater danger was that the proposals might appear, to the United States Government and to public opinion on both sides of the Atlantic, to take insufficient account of the dangers of the present international situation. Since the end of the war much had been done, by way of disposals of ammunition and surplus stores, which Ministers would never have countenanced if they had known that we should be faced so soon with a prospect of becoming involved in war. . .[1]

---

*Bevan, The Rt Hon Aneurin (1897-1960).

In later years, it became a verisimilitude in Whitehall that rearmament for the Korean war crippled the post war recovery of the British economy. This notion is false in as much as it ignores the fact that the decision to rearm was principally to meet obligations to the Atlantic Alliance. Though not insignificant, the cost of sending forces to Korea was fractional and brief; an unexpected but essential expense in resisting expansion by the communist powers. It ignores also the advantage to the British Treasury of acquiring additional 'free' dollars—United States dollars it could spend at its own discretion—at a time when it was critically short of this 'hard' currency.* For the United States quickly agreed to meet the additional sums requested by the British government. The efforts of the supply departments were not distorted by the deployment of a naval force or the fielding of a British brigade group, though Korean operations made irresistible and often inconvenient demands upon them as they sought to expand and modernise the Royal Navy, the Army and Royal Air Force to perform both their longstanding imperial and new NATO roles. Even if the needs of Korea had been predominant, they would have been unable to provide quickly, in a matter of a few months, any quantity of new weapons or equipment: the defence manufacturing base had shrunk and enlargement, however modest, required time. Yet more time would be involved in the design, development, trial and modification, acceptance and manufacture of new items. Purchase overseas was not an option, beyond existing contracts; there was no supplier of consequence in the sterling area, and in the United States new supply was dedicated to national rearmament. Almost all of the ammunition used was of war manufacture and some, at least, over a period, would have have exceeded its shelf life.

For the Service Ministers and Chiefs of Staff, the immediate difficulty in the Korean commitment was not war supplies but manpower. At the meeting of the Defence Committee on 24th July, the First Lord of the Admiralty, Lord Hall,† had indicated that to maintain the Far East Fleet in operations would require another 1,300 ratings. There was also a shortage of aircrew in the carriers:

Later there would be requirements for manning minesweepers and for bringing some further ships into commission. These requirements might amount to 3,000 men. It would be necessary to delay all releases and call up pilots and observers, and also

---

*Impoverished by the war and lagging in exports, the United Kingdom had been short of dollars since 1945. Despite an attempt to make it so in 1949, sterling was not freely convertible as an international currency.

†Hall, Rt Hon George Henry, 1st Viscount Hall of Cynon Valley (1881–1965)

ratings from the Royal Fleet Reserve. This could be done by proclamations and a declaration to the House of Commons. . . .[2]

'Delaying releases' in the Royal Navy meant delaying the departure from the service of regulars whose contractual term of active duty had expired. It did not apply to national service men.* In any case, the political difficulties of extending the eighteen months period of national service were such as to deny its application to a single service.

Whilst there was no opposition to delaying regular release or recalling regular reservists, in all the discussions concerning services manpower during July, Mr Shinwell was adamant that an extension of the term of national service was neither right nor politically acceptable. The programme of national recovery required more men; conscription disposed a huge pool of commercially unproductive labour and any extension of it increased the pool at the expense of national output. Politically—indeed as a matter of ideology— the party wanted to be rid of conscription.† He was not alone in maintaining this view but by the 31st the contrary opinion of the Chiefs of Staff was hard to resist. 'You asked me to let you have for the Minister's information a short note on personnel requirements,' Sir John Slessor wrote on 21st July:

2. The first point to realise is that the RAF today is some 20,000 men short of establishments. These establishments are *not* lavish for our present commitments. We quite definitely have not got any 'fat' on the Air Force—we had two years ago but it has all been sweated off.

Within that problem is the more important one of the unbalance of trades and the very serious shortage in some of the really key trades without which the others cannot keep aircraft in the air . . . for instance, in January this year Wireless Fitters were only 50% of establishment, as were Radar Fitters (air);

---

*The Royal Navy was not short of recruits but had deliberately, as a means of economy, accepted a reduced peacetime establishment. Its seagoing complement was by design almost wholly regular but re-engagement had fallen from the pre-war figure of 60% to 25%. The Army requirement in 1950–51 for NS men was 117,000, that of the Royal Air Force, 49,000. The numbers enlisting or extending on regular engagements were falling—the regular Army was only 107,000 at the outbreak of the Korean war. In March 1950, the Minister of Defence arranged an inter-service working party to enquire into why conditions of service were not attracting volunteers. It was due to report in October.

†When it became necessary to introduce a Bill for national service in peacetime, the Labour Party was split. Although the vote in favour on 1st April 1947 was 386 to 85 against, the majority was owed to the Conservatives voting with the government. There were many abstentions by Labour members, and numbers of those in the Party who voted for the Bill said they did so under protest.

Electricians about 60% of establishment and Ground Wireless Mechanics 65% . . .
4. To match the very costly orders to make up deficiencies of material included in our 'shopping list'—for instance about £34 million in the next two years for reserve fighters complete with their radar spares, long range tanks, ammunition, fuel etc,—we must make up the corresponding deficiencies in our personnel. . . .[3]

The Chief of the Air Staff remained convinced that:

12.(a) We must retain a far higher proportion of regulars now due for discharge . . . and (b) the RAF can only meet its minimum foreseeable commitments if the term of National Service is increased to 2 years.[4]

When the Committee of Service Ministers met on 31st July, Mr Strachey,* Secretary of State for War,

doubted whether the international situation was as yet sufficiently serious to offset the great political difficulties involved in extending the period of National Service as suggested. In his view, the effect of pay increases for the regular Forces should be tried first and quickly; the extension of National Service could be considered later if this failed or if the international situation deteriorated.[5]

But the Chief of the Imperial General Staff had to disagree with his Minister. He had already advised him privately that changes in recruiting trends were rarely quick. Now he reminded the meeting that,

The Army had had to provide a number of Forces for special operations, for example Hong Kong. There had been a severe strain on their limited manpower resources. The result was that, to provide troops for Korea would mean, in addition to stopping the discharge of time expired regulars, calling up no less than one fifth of the Regular Army Reserve and thus greatly jeopardising the Army's mobilisation plans.† He did not think this was a proper risk to be taken . . .[5].

Slightly to their surprise, the Service Chiefs discovered two supporters in the Prime Minister and the Minister of Labour,

*Strachey, Rt Hon John (1902-63)
†This proportion involved recalling half the Army's reserve of infantry.

George Isaacs.* The latter agreed with his officials that, if they had to find manpower for military service, it would be better to hold on to young men, largely untrained for civil industry, than to call up large numbers of reservists, many of whom were skilled artisans. The Prime Minister let it be known that he did not believe there would be acute political difficulties in extending national service. It was not a matter of feeling safe from immediate dissent in Parliament—the Commons had recessed for the summer after a prolonged session. He believed that there was a general apprehension in the country of a threat to peace and stability and one of his aims, when he made a ministerial broadcast on 31st July, was to focus the international picture:

> . . . The attack by the armed forces of North Korea on South Korea has been denounced as an act of aggression by the United Nations. No excuses, no propaganda by communists, no introduction of other questions can get over this fact. Here is a case of aggression. If the aggressor gets away with it, aggressors all over the world will be encouraged. The same results which led to the second world war will follow; and another world war may result. That is why what is happening in Korea is of such importance to you.
>
> The fire that has been started in distant Korea may burn down your house.

By this time, most Ministers had followed their parliamentary colleagues on holiday, many believing that the increased defence budget they had agreed on 1st August would await the return of Parliament in the autumn. But manpower had to be found for Korea at once: the Army staff in particular needed to know which of several options to adopt for the brigade group to be despatched. The manpower question was linked to services pay policy; whatever classes of men were to be involved—regulars, recalled regular reservists or national servicemen—it was in every way desirable that all should know what improvements were to be made in their pay and allowances if their service was to be extended. Mr Gaitskell, Minister for Economic Affairs,† noted in his diary, on Friday, 11th August 1950,

> In the last few days my biggest headache has been increased pay for the forces. This has been round the corner for some time and we set aside 30 million a year for it in the calculations

---

*Isaacs, Rt Hon George Alfred (1883–1979)

†Gaitskell, Rt Hon Hugh Todd Naylor (1906–63). He was not a member of the Cabinet but was often in attendance as the second senior Treasury Minister.

of the three-year programme. Increases were foreshadowed in the Defence Debate by Shinwell and the P[rime] M[inister] and the last thing the Chancellor did (before leaving) [going on holiday] was to write Shinwell an angry letter about the failure of the Ministry of Defence to consult the Treasury on proposals which they had just announced were nearly ready. This was just before the Bank Holiday weekend. During that weekend, on the Sunday [6th August], the PM's Private Secretary rang me up and said he had been instructed to tell me of a letter which the PM had sent me, saying we must get on with the question at once and get it settled before the end of the next week.

When I came back to London after the holiday I found that our boys in the Treasury had only just received the details of these proposals and that they amounted to far more than the £30 million contemplated. I then went into work with the Service Ministers and Minister of Defence. After a lot of talk I finally got them to agree to figures which involved £40 million as against £55 million which their own proposals would have cost.

Meanwhile, however, they had circulated—contrary to an understanding with us—their original proposals to the Cabinet. When I went into the meeting which was called to discuss this I noticed the Chiefs of Staff were present, and I had a strong suspicion that they had been round to the PM . . . It was a bad Cabinet, many of the more responsibly minded Ministers being away, such as the Lord President* and Dalton,† Harold Wilson‡ and Patrick Gordon Walker.§ And, of course, it was flooded out with Service Ministers and Chiefs of Staff, so perhaps it was not surprising that I was routed . . . .

. . . The PM smoothed me down: said he agreed with my fears, and it was more or less arrived at that in future in any such situation I would go and see the PM beforehand. He said, 'I would like to have backed you up on this first occasion.' Nevertheless, I feel it was his influence more than anything which made the decision go the other way.[6]

Although the Cabinet began with the discussion about forces' pay, it became evident that they must decide first whether national service was to be increased: an extension of 6 months would add

---

*Rt Hon Herbert Morrison (later, Lord Morrison of Lambeth) (1888–1965).

†Dalton, Rt Hon Hugh (later, Baron Dalton) (1887–1962), Minister of Town and Country Planning.

‡Wilson, Rt Hon Harold (later, Lord Wilson of Rievaulx) (1916–), President of the Board of Trade.

§Gordon-Walker, Rt Hon Patrick (later Lord), (1907–80), then Secretary of State for Commonwealth Relations.

80,000 men to the strength of the Army and Royal Air Force which, without a penny increase in pay rates, would add £16 million to the pay vote. Mr Shinwell remarked that 'he was now fully convinced that this increase was urgently needed', and with the Chiefs of Staff gave the Cabinet two prime reasons why they should put the proposal to Parliament for legislation:

1. The danger of a general war had increased and the difficulties they had had to put together a brigade group for Korea illustrated 'the parlous plight in which the Army found itself.' The additional 50,000 men which would accrue to the Army would permit the disposal of three divisions in Germany, filling of vacancies in other overseas garrisons and a small strategic reserve at home.
2. The increase of 28,000 men in the Royal Air Force would largely fill ground crew vacancies and permit flying training for national service men.

Mr Gaitskell lost the argument that the cost of pay increases should be limited to £40 million as against £56 million because the need to recruit regulars persisted. The Cabinet Minutes noted that '. . . it would be lamentable if the current large expenditure of defence was rendered in part nugatory to effect a saving of the order of £15 million a year.'[7]

The Prime Minister had hitherto resisted suggestions from the Conservatives that Parliament should be recalled because, as he remarked to the Chief Whip, until the conclusion of Cabinet discussions, there was no fresh defence policy to debate. But now they had decided on these important issues he was not going to be caught by a public demand from the Opposition. The Cabinet agreed that an emergency meeting of both Houses would be arranged for 12th September. The Prime Minister would broadcast to the forces on 23rd August, announcing then what they proposed for national service and what they had decided about pay.

None would be more eager to hear what he had to say than the men of the 29th Independent Infantry Brigade Group, preparing to enter the Korean war.

·   ·   ·   ·   ·

The headquarters of the 29th Brigade was at Colchester. Its commander was Brigadier Thomas Brodie, aged 46 in the summer of 1950, who had seen a good deal of active service, including command of a Chindit formation in Burma during the second world war. With the departure of the 27th Brigade to Hong Kong in 1949, the 29th had assumed the role of 'imperial strategic reserve,' the one balanced force at the disposal of government for contingency operations outside the United Kingdom or Germany. It was 'balanced' in as much as it comprehended elements of all arms—infantry, armour, artillery, field engineers, signals and the administrative services—supply and transport, ordnance, a medical and dental element for the recovery and treatment of casualties, and electrical and mechanical engineers for the recovery and repair of the brigade's hardware. However, it was weak in two respects: all units were manned to 'lower establishment'—between a half and two thirds of 'higher establishment', the strength required for war; and some units were partly or wholly committed to other duties under distant commanders. When the brigade was warned on 28th July that it was being committed to Korea, it was not clear where the extra men were to come from and whether all the units on which they had a claim were to accompany them.

The meetings of the Defence Committee and Cabinet in late July and early August clarified the ground rules as regards manning. The Army staffs* were thereafter able to develop them, though some weeks were to pass before arrangements were complete. In sum, these provided that the regular content of each unit would go to Korea with the exception of officers committed to essential courses such as the staff college, and soldiers under 19 years of age. Regular officers and men about to leave the service into the reserve would be retained compulsorily.

As many officers as were needed would be recalled from the regular reserve of officers; other ranks from Class A and as many as were needed from Class B of the reserve.† National service officers and men over 19 would be permitted to volunteer if they would agree to extend their service by 6 months (a Type 'C' engagement).‡ Alternatively, they would be able across the Army to volunteer for a further 18 months service, a special short term regular engagement, Type K (for Korea). Recruiting offices were authorised to enlist others for Type K who had left the service but had completed at least eighteen months active duty.

On 8th August, a conference was held in the War Office to coordinate the *Acanthus* project—the codename for the assembly

---

*The General Staff was concerned with the policy relating to units by type and identity to be sent to Korea and the numbers by ranks and duties involved. The Adjutant-General's Staff was responsible for terms of service including new engagements, posting of individuals and the recall and interests of reservists.

†Class A contained men who had been most recently at active duty, Class B those who had been away longer.

‡The extension of national service to 2 years could not be effected compulsorily until Parliament gave authority on or after its recall on 12th September.

and despatch of a British land force to Korea. It was comprehensive and successful to the extent that it was never again necessary to call such a wide number of representatives together before the brigade departed.*

The projected date of departure, however, seemed too distant to the Minister of Defence. It was to be 1st November. '. . .a great deal of the value of the action we are taking will be lost if we must wait a further 2½ months before the force begins to move,' Mr Shinwell wrote to the Secretary of State for War on 10th August. 'Every effort must be made to speed up the programme and I should like you to consider whether the embarkation date could not be advanced to 1st October.'[8] The General Staff then prepared one of those papers which offer several options, all but one of which are so unattractive as to make the exception irresistible.[9] It proposed a departure date on 1st October and this was accepted.

In Colchester, to the south on Salisbury Plain and in the north west, the activity of 29 Brigade was intense. Its 'order of battle'— complement—comprehended fifty one units great and small, beginning with brigade headquarters and ending with a NAAFI detachment; in all, 416 officers, 8,564 other ranks and 102 civilians.† Units were involved in drawing up the volume of additional weapons, equipment, stores and clothing consequent upon expansion to 'higher establishment'.

A more persistent task was receiving the reservists arriving in small groups by every train. At Colchester, many of these were carried from railway station to barracks by a taxi driver who chaffed his passengers on their recall to soldiering until, in the middle of the second week, he received his own recall papers and was driven by a colleague into barracks. There, like those who had preceded him, he was issued with a complete scale of 'home service' clothing, and donned for duty hours the familiar battledress blouse, trousers, anklets and studded boots, A denim suit was issued for work in barracks. With his recalled comrades he resumed the evening activity of applying blanco to webbing, polish to brass and leather.

The reservists were men who had completed at least seven years service and were thus experienced in a range of weapons and duties. There was an excess of military tradesmen, recalled essentially to make up numbers—for example, vehicle mechanics found themselves employed as drivers; but on the whole unit arrangements were such as to relate skills and proclivities to existing vacancies.

---

*See Appendix G.[10]
†These figures included first reinforcements for casualties. For the full order of battle, see Appendix H.

The process of absorbing individuals who had settled over some years into civil life and, in many cases, married and begun to raise families since leaving the Army, was less of a problem than had been expected. An early meal of bad meat prompted a brief general protest in the cookhouse of one unit. In a few cases, recalled officers were understandably irritated by pointed reference to their lack of peacetime uniforms or ignorance of ceremonial, but most of this stemmed from a handful of very junior regular officers, exceptionally from the odd myopic among the more senior regimental officers. It was largely overcome by common sense and the occasional sharp word from commanding officers. Otherwise, within a matter of days, the reservists were indistinguishable at their work from regulars. No doubt, behind these outward appearances, there were anxieties and cares, but these were mitigated by three factors. Where there were extraordinary circumstances in favour of releasing an individual—what the Army termed a 'compassionate case'— they were investigated rapidly and decisions made quickly. About two in every hundred were sent home permanently. Cases of physical disability were also settled without delay: three per cent were discharged as unfit for active service. Secondly, everyone was engaged in hard work preparing for operations. These experienced men knew that survival on the battlefield is enhanced by skill and fitness. Finally, a great many of those brought back were buoyed up, as they were later to own, by the environment of comradeship, an aspect of life they had missed in civil life.

The infantry, the largest element of the Army and in the brigade, were the most difficult to reinforce. A battalion of the Bedfordshire Regiment originally disposed was so low in numbers of regular soldiers that it had to be replaced by the 1st Battalion, Royal Northumberland Fusiliers, which was the demonstration unit at the school of infantry. Reinforcement of all battalions—the other two being, respectively, the 1st Battalions of The Gloucestershire Regiment and the Royal Ulster Rifles, should have been effected from the reservist pools of their recruiting regions but, due to poor regular recruiting throughout the Army noted earlier, these were insufficient. The balance of numbers were made up by arbitrary postings.

The armoured units, the 8th Hussars and C Squadron of 7th Royal Tanks, had proportionately fewer numbers from other sources. The artillery—a field regiment, a heavy mortar battery, a light anti-aircraft battery, and a specialist radar unit—had a broader base of reservists but, since all recalled reservists retained their former highest substantive rank, found themselves with a surplus of non-commissioned officers. In such case, as also in the squadron of field engineers, regular NCOs with acting rank were obliged to revert to a lower one.

The whole force began intensive training: refresher training on an individual basis progressing through minor collective activities to each unit training as a whole. Finally, under Brigadier Brodie's arrangements, all arms exercised together as a formation.

Yet even before this training programme began, the government and Chiefs of Staff received from General MacArthur an appeal for more immediate help. Between 13th July and 4th August, ten divisions of the North Korean People's Army had succeeded, despite the air superiority of the United States, in smashing through the defences of three American divisions and seven of the South Koreans, overrunning the south west of the Korean peninsula, closing to within 10 miles of Taegu, where the government of the Republic of Korea and the United States army headquarters was located, and bringing their forces within striking distance of the United Nations's base and port at Pusan. There were many reasons for this situation, not least the difficulties of the raw South Korean Divisions and the unavoidable piecemeal committal of their American allies. The fact was that the United Nations' bridgehead in Korea was threatened. Air Vice-Marshal Bouchier,* who had just arrived in Tokyo as British liaison officer to General MacArthur, reported on 10th August,

> As expected MacArthur's first question was how soon will British brigade go into Korea. I said my personal impression was that the earliest it could arrive was in four months time. He said the urgent requirement for now and the immediate future was to get more men into Korea with rifles. At present they are flying in from America five hundred troops a day by chartered four-engined civil aircraft. . . Gist of his off the record remarks was that a little got in fast was better than a lot later on. . .[11]

This signal did not entirely surprise the Chiefs of Staff or Ministers; they received briefings several days a week based on the reports sent from the outset of hostilities by the Army and Air Attaches with Sir Alvary Gascoigne's diplomatic mission in Tokyo.† The grave news arriving early in August almost certainly prompted Mr Shinwell to urge the War Office to hasten the departure of 29

---

*Bouchier, Air Vice-Marshal (later, Sir) Cecil Arthur KBE CB DFC Royal Air Force, (1895–79), who had served with the British Commonwealth Occupation Force, Japan, 1945–48 was recalled from retirement because of this previous experience and acknowledged *rapport* with General MacArthur. For his directive, see Appendix J.
†There were also intermittent reports from the British diplomatic representative in Korea, (Captain Holt's successor) Mr H R Sawbridge.

Brigade. But in deciding to despatch the latter, government had been motivated primarily by political considerations. Now they were being asked to send a contingent rapidly on military grounds. Political or military, the CIGS maintained, and his colleagues agreed, that to send forces simply 'with rifles' was pointless; they would be dependent on United States support in every detail, and even if the Americans gave them unlimited support weapons and heavy equipment for use on arrival they would have to be trained in their use. Discussions about accelerating the departure of 29 Brigade had shown that, with the airlift available, it would take a month to fly out one battalion with personal weapons only from England to Singapore. '7(a) . . . . To achieve this all present operations will have to cease and there will be no reserve of transport aircraft for any other emergencies. It is unlikely that the British Overseas Airways Corporation* will be able to assist without major interference to their routine schedules.'[12]

Early in their discussions, the Chiefs of Staff felt that the gravity of the news from Korea notwithstanding, they had to ask their American colleagues whether they agreed with General MacArthur's request: the latter was renowned for hyperbole; it was only a matter of days since General Bradley had reassured Sir Oliver Franks and Lord Tedder that the British contingent would be needed for a break out battle from the Pusan bridgehead. The reply came on the evening of 16th August,

> Joint Chiefs of Staff have just discussed. As I rather expected they stress extreme urgency of reinforcement from point of view of stemming present attack. They are concerned primarily regarding present situation where they are still dangerously thin on the ground but also as regards danger of stalemate in the tip of South Korea when winter conditions prevent large scale movement.
> 2. For your private information they have denuded Okinawa, Hawaii, Puerto Rico and Panama of their garrisons. As Bradley metaphorically expressed it, "a platoon now would be worth more than a company tomorrow.". . .[14]

Next day, the Chiefs signalled the British Defence Co-ordinating Committee in the Far East:

> . . .we have decided to recommend to Ministers today that two infantry battalions and the necessary command element should

---

*BOAC, the British national airline flying trunk routes. Although it had no reserve of aircraft beyond that needed to sustain scheduled services, it had apparently a surplus of aircrew which the Ministry of Civil Aviation proposed offer to the Royal Air Force or the United States civil airlines engaged in troop movements.[13]

be despatched from Hong Kong to Korea as soon as possible. We have further recommended that 29 Brigade should still be despatched from UK to operations in Korea. When 29 Brigade is committed it is our intention to withdraw the two battalions and the command element which we are now proposing should be sent . . . .[15]

This signal suggests that the Chiefs were united in their ideas about the deployment of troops to tasks but, throughout the second half of August, they were not. The First Sea Lord wished to send a brigade from Malaya to Korea, preferably the Royal Marine Commando brigade, a force which lay within his particular responsibility, he reminded his colleagues.[16] He was already arranging to meet a request from the American naval Commander-in-Chief for contributions to an amphibious raiding force by forming a new commando from within his own resources,[17] and was influenced by the fact that a United States marine division was forming up in General MacArthur's command.* The Chief of the Imperial General Staff—the CIGS—and the Chief of the Air Staff—CAS—opposed this: Britain was engaged in active operations in Malaya as important, in their view, in countering communist expansion as in Korea. The disagreement persisted through ministerial agreement to the despatch of 27 Brigade from Hong Kong. Lord Fraser then withdrew.[18]

One reflection they shared commonly at the end of this period. The 'rapid' response to General MacArthur's appeal propelled 27 Brigade into the Korean battle within a fortnight.† Within this period, reports from the Tokyo headquarters ranged intermittently between deep anxiety and supreme confidence. A suspicion grew in the Defence Ministries and the Foreign Office that they were dealing with a volatile high command.

Yet the home team were not guiltless in impulsive reactions. On 17th August, the British diplomatic Mission in Tokyo reported that,

United States Far East Air Force intend in the immediate future to 'take out' the five major cities of North Korea including P'yongyang. Leaflets warning civil populations will be dropped prior to mass bombing . . . .[19]

At once the overseas and defence policy makers in London took alarm: the British Missions in Washington and Tokyo were

*As the result of the United States' extensive disarmament programme post 1945, its two marine corps divisions were too weak to engage in operations. From their total numbers, a composite brigade was formed and, later, swelled by recalled reservists, a division.
†See Chapter 6.

instructed to make urgent representations that operations of this sort would be counter productive, particularly as the Russian representative had just resumed his seat in the Security Council. Lord Tedder cooled this fever somewhat in his own first reaction:

> . . . Fully appreciate vital political considerations which must govern air operations of the nature apparently proposed which in fact amount to one of air action as a directly political weapon. I do not question the validity of the view that in present circumstances the political arguments against such action are overriding. I must however remind you that . . . we were briefed to outline to the Americans air action on these lines and though that proposal envisaged such action under somewhat different conditions, there is little or no difference in principle between that proposed and the operations the Americans now plan. . .*[20] Enquiry disclosed that there were no plans for 'area bombing'— the original report from Tokyo was based on the proposal of a planning officer who believed wrongly that his superiors would accept it. There had, however, been some discussion as to whether civilians should be warned when strategic targets in or near towns were to be attacked.†[21]

Due to the excellent relationships developed by Sir Oliver Franks and Lord Tedder with their American colleagues, there was no resentment of this ill-founded intervention. In any case, there was much goodwill for the British ally in Washington as the news was received that the militarily small but politically important 27 Brigade was preparing to leave Hong Kong for Pusan.

---

*See pp 100–101, particularly Sir J Slessor's statement on 17th July.
†The idea was abandoned later because it would have made it possible for the enemy to lay air ambushes for the attacking aircraft.

SOURCE NOTES: CHAPTER 5

1. CAB 131/8, DO (50) 15th Meeting, and CAB 128/18, Cabinet 50 and 52 (50). See also Williams, Philip M, ed, *Diary of Hugh Gaitskell* (London, 1983) pp 194-5.

2. CAB 131/8, DO (50)15th meeting, and CAB 131/9, DO (50) 59: 'Royal Navy— Manpower requirements in the Far East.'

3. DEFE 7/1927 (f 4), Minute from the Chief of the Air Staff (CAS) to Sir Harold Parker of 21st July 1950.

4. Ibid.

5. Ibid (f 11), Meeting of Standing Committee of Service Ministers, 31st July 1950. (See also WO216/344).

6. Williams, op cit pp 196-7.

7. CAB 128/18, Cabinet 53 (50). See also CAB 129/41, CP (50) 188.

8. CAB 21/1988, f 40A, Minute from Minister of Defence to Secretary of State for War of 10th August 1950.

9. WO 216/344, Brief for Vice-Chief of the Imperial General Staff (VCIGS) on 'The Implications of accelerating the date of departure of 29 Independent Infantry Brigade Group to Korea'.

10. DEFE series, MOı Collection, see Acanthus Meeting No 1 on 8th August 1950 reference 79/Mob/9527(SD2)

11. DEFE 11/198, Tokyo (Bouchier) CAB 1 to MOD (Chiefs of Staff) 100629 August 1950.

12. WO 216/344, Brief for VCIGS (as 9 above).

13. CAB 21/1988, Minister of Civil Aviation to Minister of Defence of 4th August 1950 and see also reply from Air Ministry to Minister of Defence (for Minister of Civil Aviation) of 24th August 1950.

14. DEFE 11/199, BJSM, Washington AWT37 to MOD (Chiefs of Staff) of 161711Z August 1950.

15. CAB 21/1988, MOD COSSEA 760 to GHQ FARELF of 171791oA August 1950 and DEFE 11/199, WO (MO2) 42340 to GHQ FARELF of 151800A August 1950.

16. DEFE 11/199, Minute 1895 of 16th August 1950 from First Sea Lord to Chief Staff Officer, MOD.

17. CAB 21/1988, Minute 1888 of 15th August 1950 from First Sea Lord to Minister of Defence.

18. Ibid, Minute on 'Possibility of certain reinforcements to Korea from Malaya' of 12th September 1950 from Secretary to COS to Minister of Defence and MSS annotation thereto.

19. DEFE 11/199, Tokyo 967 to FO of 17th August 1950.

20. Ibid, BJSM, Washington AWT 39 to MOD of 172314Z August 1950.

21. Ibid, BJSM, Washington AWT 41 to MOD of 181530Z August 1950 and Washington 2256 to FO of 18th August 1950.

CHAPTER 6

27th Infantry Brigade to the Naktong

The 27th Infantry Brigade had arrived in Hong Kong in July 1949, aware that it might soon be on active service defending the frontier of the colony with China. For in the summer of that year the People's Liberation Army, sweeping south against the crumbling forces of Chiang Kai-shek, was occupying the province of Kwangtung. Mao Tse-tung had made it clear that he did not respect the agreement with previous governments of China, one of the several 'Unequal Treaties' contracted with western powers in the previous century, whereby the United Kingdom leased the mainland New Territories until 1997 and held the remaining areas in perpetuity. There was a possibility, therefore, that an attempt might be made to take the colony by force of arms. The number of troops available to the local communist field army for this purpose was so great, however—and the memory of the Japanese invasion of 1941 so painfully abiding—that neither the British Governor nor the military commander were hopeful of conducting a successful defence, even with the addition of 27 Brigade.

Though the government in London was no more optimistic about the outcome of an attack on the colony, it was convinced that the territory must be actively defended, and be seen to have the means to fight. This policy sought to dissuade the Chinese communist authorities from engaging in an international adventure at a time when they had immense problems in establishing political authority internally, and in reconstruction. It was hoped that the economic advantages to the new regime of maintaining the *status quo* would weigh against the inclinations of their political ideology and national pride.

As the summer passed, this aspiration seemed to be realised. The Chinese provincial administration and military were vigilant but not aggressive. In the following months, there were no signs of civil disturbances being fomented within Hong Kong. Still, in midsummer, 1950, all was quiet on the frontier; the city and environs 'at peace . . . busy crowded streets, pretty girls, rickshaws, T bone steaks, wonderful beaches, sampans'.[1]

The 27th Brigade had earlier been formed and was still commanded by Brigadier Basil Aubrey Coad, an officer of the Wiltshire

Regiment who had seen a good deal of campaigning before and during the second world war, in which he commanded an infantry battalion and brigade in action. The CIGS described him in 1950 as 'a good plain cook', and meant it as a compliment.[2] His principal units were the 1st Battalions of the Royal Leicestershire Regiment, the Middlesex Regiment and the Argyll and Sutherland Highlanders, all, due to the shortage of manpower, on the lower establishment. They formed part of the 40th Division, the Hong Kong field force. Almost three quarters of the brigade were national service officers and soldiers, many of whom had been posted from basic training just prior to embarkation. It was thus a relatively raw force. Hong Kong provided opportunities to develop military skills, particularly those of the infantry rifle companies.* The training of the 3-inch medium mortar and Vickers medium machine-gun crews, and of the pioneers, signals, transport, medical and quartermaster's elements, which each battalion had to support it, was largely confined to the basic level.† From time to time, the 40th Division exercised its role across the bare south China hills overlooking the colony.

When the Korean war broke out a year after the arrival of the brigade, there had been a considerable turnover of national servicemen in their ranks; new drafts had arrived to replace those due for release at the end of the eighteen months term of compulsory service. The regular officers and non-comissioned officers were once more extending the skills of youths barely nineteen. Rumours that they would shortly be sent to Korea were soon plentiful, but these stopped as soon as the announcement was made that 29 Brigade was being committed to the task.

The Governor and military commander were thus surprised when, late on Friday, 18th August, instructions arrived in Hong Kong from Singapore to mount Operation GRADUATE: the greater part of 27 Brigade was to be sent to Korea as the British Army contribution until 29 Brigade arrived. On the basis of strengths and numbers of national servicemen, the Royal Leicesters and Argylls only would be despatched with the expectation that the 3rd Battalion, Royal Australian Regiment, would join them in Korea from Japan to make up the balance of infantry. Advanced

*A 'rifle' company is the main fighting sub-unit of an infantry battalion: it closes with the enemy in attack; it holds ground in defence. The personal weapons of its complement—130 at war strength—were then rifles, machine carbines or pistols. It also had nine light machine-guns, and three light mortars among its three rifle platoons; and three PIATs—projectors, infantry, anti-tank. For the battalion organisation see Appendix K.

†The continual turnover of national servicemen among these support and administrative elements, as in the rifle platoons, the strict rationing of training ammunition for the support weapons, and the demands for manpower to meet guard and domestic duties within their own camps and in the garrison, denied opportunities for advanced training.

parties would travel to Korea by air via Japan, the main bodies by sea. Further details would follow.

Although, in the Foreign Office view, 'The risk of an attack on Hong Kong was remote',[3] it was decided to restrict news of the move to a very small number until a public statement was made in London.* Brigadier Coad was inevitably one of those informed but he was warned that the information was to be restricted for the time being to himself and his brigade major.† As he represented,[4] however, the weekend was beginning and many individuals were out of barracks; there would be arrangements to make. It was agreed that the commanding officers must be told.‡

This was wise but insufficient. Security seals inevitably began to leak—for example, the brigadier had to cancel golf with a member of his staff, who then came in to the office to find the brigadier at work on a holiday; a clerk had to be housed in a specially secure room to account for incoming correspondence. Brigade headquarters notified a conference next morning 'to discuss a matter which cannot be divulged on the telephone'. As curiosity was prompted, the erosion of security began. All the Korean rumours were revived.

By the evening of Sunday, the 20th, the brigadier had had almost more information than he wanted: the Middlesex had been substituted for the Leicesters—though the commanding officer of the former had yet to be told; several different organisations for active operations had been notified and more were to come. There were numerous contradictory instructions about the means and routing of transportation and other administrative arrangements. A personal appeal by Brigadier Coad on the 19th to reduce secrecy, strongly supported by his local military superiors, had been relayed to General Harding in Singapore, who at once persuaded his colleagues of the need for wider disclosure. Company commanders and others were informed on the 20th. On Monday, 21st August, the two commanding officers, Lieutenant-Colonel Andrew Man of the Middlesex and Lieutenant-Colonel G L Neilson of the Argylls, were permitted to brief everyone in their battalions of the general intention. Some of those who heard them had only just returned to camp from the fleshpots of Hong Kong, a weekend to be

---

*This was to be issued at 2330 GMT, 20th August (0730 Hong Kong time on the 21st) and include the reassurance that replacements would shortly arrive in the colony—actually, one battalion diverted at sea from Singapore, an armoured car squadron and a field engineer squadron from Malaya.[5]

†The title then of the principal staff officer of a British (or Commonwealth) brigade.

‡Having just completed a periodic divisional exercise, many non-operational items were crated for storage—a standing procedure for frontier deployment. The commanding officers were able to stop the process of unpacking.

remembered. For they were to embark for Korea on 23rd August, brigade headquarters and the Middlesex in the maintenance carrier *Unicorn*, the Argylls in the cruiser *Ceylon*. Advanced parties would be carried in United States transport aircraft.

There was a flurry of list making and packing and conveying. Field units are accustomed to moving with everything they possess: personal belongings, weapons, equipment, tools, transport, office machinery, records, technical stores, reserves and spares of almost every item needed to meet a range of foreseeable contingencies. They required a shipment of ammunition because the calibres of their weapons did not match those of the Americans. Rations would be provided from the United States Army supply organisation but a special issue of tea was made to provide for British tastes. Because they were going into operations, the colours of the battalions, the silver and certain other purely regimental property were to be left behind. Most of the heavier vehicles were also to remain in Hong Kong to reduce the burden of transportation; wheeled load carriers above 1-ton were to be provided by the United States Army on their arrival.

It was also necessary to reorganise. All those under nineteen years of age were to be left in Hong Kong, but fighting strength needed to be raised. Moreover, if there were heavy casualties early in action, they could not rely on the arrival of replacements quickly. The infantry at least must be reinforced. Volunteers were readily found from other units in the garrison.* The four rifle companies in each battalion were reduced to three, but each company was thereby raised to about two thirds war strength.† The number of support weapons and crews, and regimental signallers, were similarly strengthened. But there were still serious deficiencies; there was no artillery, no engineer element; the Royal Signals serving brigade head-quarters had no additional manpower to cope with the increase in stations to be manned. The brigade lacked its own second line transport, medical unit, ordnance field park.‡ A visitor remarked to a member of the brigade staff that their organisation was 'pretty light'.

---

*For example, the Argylls received 17 from the Royal Leicesters, 25 from the King's Own Scottish Borderers, 38 from the South Staffordshire, 53 from the King's Own Shropshire Light Infantry.

†Higher (war) establishment of an infantry battalion was 38 officers and 945 other ranks with 9 officers and 176 first reinforcements in the theatre. The commander-in-chief, General Sir John Harding, insisted that the minimum strength of each battalion within 27 Brigade must be 27 officers and 618 other ranks, including an attached medical officer and 22 other ranks of the Royal Army Medical Corps (RAMC), tradesmen and specialists from the Royal Army Ordnance Corps (RAOC), Royal Electrical & Mechanical Engineers (REME), Army Catering Corps (ACC), and Army Physical Training Corps (APTC)

‡For the brigade order of battle, see Appendix K.

'Too light,' was the answer. We're in danger of floating to Korea like a bunch of balloons.'

At length, after a late change of the date of departure, and a final decision that the light vehicles including tracks would follow separately in a special transport, together with the drivers, the main body of the force embarked at Holt's Wharf, Kowloon, on 25th August. The Middlesex were aboard the fleet support carrier, *Unicorn*, (Captain H S Hopkins, OBE RN), the Argylls on the cruiser, *Ceylon*, (Captain C F J Lloyd-Davies, DSC RN). They were to be escorted by the Australian destroyer, *Warramunga*, (Commander O H Becher, DSO DSC RAN).

'Are you ready for action?' a friendly voice called from the crowd which had come to see their departure that evening.

'I'm ready for a rest,' a joker of the Middlesex called back. It was true. The soldiers had been engaged in reorganising and sorting and packing and loading for many hours a day. They had been addressed by the Commander-in-Chief and were shortly to be wished God speed by the British Commissioner-General for South-East Asia, Malcolm MacDonald.* In one group or another, all had been given farewell parties from the Governor to the girls in the down town bars.

At about 6.30 p.m., all secured below, the two warships began to move away from the wharf, played out by the pipe band of the King's Own Scottish Borderers. The pipes of the Argylls and the band of the Royal Marines on *Ceylon's* quarterdeck responded. If there were sentiments common among the soldiers aboard, they were of excitement and apprehension.

The two battalions were commanded by the respective seconds-in-command, Major R A Gwyn of the Middlesex, Major K Muir of the Argylls. The commanding officers emplaned next morning with the brigadier and thirty others, selected as advanced parties, in a United States transport aircraft for Japan. Passing the warships, the aircraft circled and dropped a flare.

·   ·   ·   ·   ·

The American proposition in July that 'a platoon now will be worth a company tomorrow' was based on the distinct possibility that the United Nations' front in Korea would crumble unless it was rapidly reinforced. The Republic of Korea (ROK) forces had not recovered from their extraordinary losses on the Han river in late June. For the next two to three weeks, they were little more than an armed rabble, scarcely under control except where, locally,

---

*MacDonald, Rt Hon Malcolm John (1901–1981)

leaders of outstanding quality were able to maintain it. Of the original seven field divisions and the Capital Division, none had more than one third of their original complement. Among three divisions, there were only 11 artillery pieces and ten 81-mm mortars, the latter entirely without sights.

It was fortunate that General MacArthur had appointed from 12th July a brave and tenacious officer to command the troops in Korea, Lieutenant-General Walton H Walker.* Short and thickset, he resembled slightly in features and much in character a bulldog. His Eighth Army headquarters in Japan was moved across to serve him on the battlefield. Much due to his arrangements and drive, and the response of the Korean Military Advisory Group, the ROK forces were reorganised and re-equipped. The Koreans themselves, despite their lack of experienced officers, carried forward dynamically the resuscitation of a moribund military body. By the end of July, the ROK Army had been formed into two corps, each of two divisions in the line, with a fifth division on the east coast. None were able immediately to withstand a determined thrust by the North Korean People's Army (NKPA). Most of the newcomers were men taken off the streets and given a few hours training, but they were capable of manning areas of the defensive perimeter and resisting patrol actions or probing attacks.

This function was essential because the United States divisions which had been arriving over several weeks were not, by their own admission, widely successful. The more they were obliged to spread themselves to underpin the ROK section of the front, the greater the danger of their own collapse. By the third week in July, General Walker had accumulated the 24th Infantry Division, the 1st Cavalry Division† and, most recently, the 25th Infantry Division, about 33,000 fighting troops in all. Yet the term 'fighting troops' describes their designated function rather than their capability. The great majority were young men engaged in their compulsory military service. They were well-equipped but poorly trained; occupation forces who had been drawn more into garrison administration and security in Japan than the extension of their basic skills, and softened by the perquisites of their environment. At a few days notice, they had been sent to Korea and were almost immediately engaged on wide frontages against a spirited, accomplished foe. It is not surprising that they were often ineffective, occasionally given

---

*Walker, Lieutenant-General Walton Harris (1889–1950), a regular infantry officer of the United States Army. He commanded the IV Armoured and XX Corps in the second world war.

†Expecting that the 1st Cavalry Division would essentially remain in Japan for occupation duties, Eighth Army headquarters had posted 750 senior non-commissioned officers from it in June to the 24th and 25th Divisions.

to panic.[6] Throughout July, the United Nations' line was pushed back 10–15 miles a day, no mean pace of advance for an enemy moving for the most part on the marching boot.

General Walker was not a man to despair but confessed one evening to his chief of staff that he had to 'find some fresh ideas'. He had been constantly moving about the forward area of the battlefield to coordinate his divisions, plugging holes with regiments or even battalions from his slender reserve. In his Dakota aircraft, he had flown 'low and slow' over areas being abandoned unnecessarily, encouraging or exhorting from the door those in the line.[7] The withdrawals continued. Towards the end of the month, he was obliged to consider the necessity of moving his headquarters from Taegu back to Pusan, a notion that brought General MacArthur to Korea on 27th July.

The two high commanders met privately. There is no record of their conversation, but in the headquarters mess at lunch afterwards, the Supreme Commander remarked that there would be no evacuation from Korea, no Korean Dunkirk.[8] General Walker carried this theme to his divisional commanders and the KMAG. On 29th July, he told the commander of the 25th Division and his staff that,

. . . We are fighting a battle against time. There will be no more retreating, withdrawal, or readjustment of the lines or any other term you choose. There is no line behind us to which we can retreat. Every unit must counterattack to keep the enemy in a state of confusion and off balance. There will be no Dunkirk, . . . no Bataan, a retreat to Pusan would be one of the greatest butcheries in history. We must fight until the end. Capture by these people is worse than death itself. We will fight as a team. If some of us must die we will die fighting together. Any man who gives ground may be personally responsible for the death of thousands of his comrades.

'I want you to put this out to all the men in the Division. I want everybody to understand that we are going to hold this line. We are going to win.[9]

A similar exhortation was given to the other divisions and passed down to everyone in the fighting units. Some took it as an order that they would fight in their positions to the 'last man and last round of ammunition', and were not much comforted as a consequence. But the majority and, most importantly, the seasoned leaders remaining,* read more carefully and accepted the spirit of

---

*A high proportion of those killed or wounded in these early battles were battalion and company commanders, regimental and battalion staff officers and senior non-commissioned officers.

the army commander's message.[10] Withdrawal did not come suddenly to an end, but the pace and extent of it slowed. By 4th August, it came to a halt on the northern and western extremities of what was to be called the Pusan Perimeter.

Further United States forces were arriving. The 5th Marines reached Pusan on 30th July, the leading regiment of the 2nd Infantry Division next day. Just in time. Two divisions of the NKPA had carried out a series of marches round the western flank of the Eighth Army, moving by night, resting in hiding from the dominant United Nations air power by day. Following its share in the capture of Taejon, the North Korean 4th Division under Major-General Lee* had been directed southwards on a 100 miles march to turn eastwards through Kochang. Major-General Pang's† 6th Division, mounted in trucks, had undertaken a bold sweep to capture the whole of south-western Korea between 5th and 28th July. Gathering together on this date and reinforced by the 83rd Motorised Regiment, it then began to drive eastwards in daylight, taking advantage of two days of rain clouds which restricted aerial observation and attack. Its first objective was Chinju, a meeting point of roads and the railway. The second was Masan, a small port on the Korea Strait. Most important was the target of Pusan, the United Nations only major entry port, 65 road miles to the east.

It is probable that if Kim Il-sung had been less concerned with gathering in the short term the huge territorial prize in the south-west, defended only by scattered detachments of police and home guards, and had driven in upon Pusan through Chinju and Masan during the third week of July, he might have won the war in a mighty manoeuvre of encirclement. But he did not.

When the 4th and 6th Divisions attacked at the end of July into the first week of August, the defences were no longer manned solely by a depleted, under equipped and demoralised American 24th Division, dispersed in packets over main approach routes to the south of the 1st Cavalry Division. There were still huge gaps in what was represented to be the main line of defence, but the 25th Division had entered the critical area immediately west of

---

*Lee Kwon-mu, Major-General, born in Yenchi, North-East China in 1910, he attended a Russian military school in 1934 and thereafter served with the Chinese Communist Forces, rising to various senior military posts in the Korean element of the Chinese People's Liberation Army up to May 1947, when he returned to North Korea.

†Pang Ho-son, Major-General, born in Korea in 1910, he joined the Chinese Communist Forces and became, during the second world war, the political officer of the Korean 166th Division in the Chinese Fifty Sixth Army. When this division returned to North Korea in July 1949, he became its commander.

Masan with the Marine Brigade* behind it. The 2nd Division from Hawaii were arriving progressively at Pusan.

An American counter-attack on 7th August from Masan coincided with the renewed offensive of the NKPA 6th Division. The North Koreans had the advantage because they had closed up to the American positions secretly during the two preceding nights and, in places, infiltrated them. The upshot was a bloody struggle throughout the next seven days. The high temperatures of August— there was, unseasonably, little rain or cloud cover during the month—led to many cases of heat exhaustion among the Americans, but they also lost high numbers of killed and wounded† and much equipment. Clear skies, however, enabled the ground attack aircraft of the United States Fifth Air Force, the Navy and Marine Corps to add their weight of fire to the battle by day. At the end of it, the Americans were everywhere driven back to their start lines but the North Korean 6th Division with its motorised reinforcement had failed to break in.

This news was a consolation to General Walker, for his line was already under heavy attack in three other areas: across the lower Naktong river; on the main route from Waegwan to Taegu; and down the east coast.

The western side of the Pusan perimeter defences lay principally on the winding Naktong river. It was a convenient obstacle, 800 yards wide—sometimes more—and mostly too deep to be waded by men or vehicles. The 24th Division engineers had destroyed all but one selected bridge and similarly all ferries and other boats along its banks. About 30 miles north of Masan, as the crow flies, the river swings westward for five miles before resuming its south easterly course, creating a huge bow. Into this area on the night of 5th/6th August, the NKPA 4th Division attacked, thrusting its whole fighting force across over the next four days. Rafts were brought forward for vehicles. Several 'underwater bridges'‡ were made to provide for a continuous flow of traffic. The companies of the 24th Division on the hills overlooking the river line were separated by as much as three miles, such was the frontage. They were thus unable to see one another, let alone offer mutual covering fire. A second flow of replacements was just being drawn in by them when the fighting began, and some of these newcomers, arriving in darkness, became casualties before they could see their

---

*The 5th Marines were the infantry element of this brigade.
†HM Hospital Ship *Maine*, the only hospital ship then in the theatre, treated and evacuated to Japan 1,845 American casualties between 16th July and 16th August 1950.
‡Underwater bridges, much in use by Soviet military engineers in the second world war, were built of rocks and logs creating, in effect, a ford. They were not easily distinguished from natural shallows from the air and very difficult to destroy once in place.[11]

comrades' faces in daylight. An intense struggle began to hold the enemy and to maintain open the supply routes to the rear through Yongsan, on which North Korean road blocks began to appear. Operations were not helped by attempts at counter-attack, ordered by divisional and army headquarters, which were impracticable in terms of time and scale. Yet General Walker's persistent demands for offensive action had this merit: they made clear beyond doubt that the policy was to fight where they stood.

North and south of Waegwan, in order, the NKPA 8th, 1st, 13th, 15th, 3rd and 10th Divisions, with the 105th Armoured Brigade in the centre, broke in across the Naktong and the north western area of the perimeter to envelop Taegu. Their blows fell principally upon the 8th, 6th and 1st ROK Divisions, and the American 1st Cavalry Division. The river was shallower in this area; lacking the August rains, the level was falling. Wading became possible at certain sites. Two underwater bridges for vehicles were constructed prior to the North Korean operation. Widely separated feint attacks drew the defenders out during the first week of August before the main offensive opened. The struggle for possession of the dominant heights among the huge, rolling scrub covered hills developed from the 9th August. Small but important armoured battles began along the continuous valleys between them.

Almost simultaneously, two North Korean Divisions, the 5th and the 12th, with the 766th Independent Infantry Regiment, had been attempting to force a way down the east coast corridor. With one or all of these separated offensives, Kim Il-sung hoped to bring the campaign to a victorious close. The following exhortation from the political office at army headquarters was found on the body of a North Korean colonel on the Taegu front,

> Kim Il-sung has directed that the war be carried out so that its final victory can be realized by 15th August, fifth anniversary of the liberation of Korea . . .
>
> Our victory lies before our eyes. Young soldiers! You are . . . able to participate in the battle for our final victory . . . the capture of Taegu lies in the crossing of the Naktong River . . .[12]

Similar messages had been given to the NKPA forces in the east. Descending from the mountains there, the 5th Division isolated the ROK 3rd Division on the coast. The latter held on for a time, supported by naval gunfire, but had to be evacuated by sea. Further south, the 12th Division and the 766th surprised the defences north of the An'gang-ni—P'ohang-dong road and infiltrated to the edge of Yonil fighter airfield. General Walker, assisted by the ROK Army headquarters, formed various task forces from regular and *ad hoc* units to recover the area. It was not easy to do with so many demands at Masan, on the Naktong and west of Taegu.

The battle to recover the Naktong crossings ended successfully on 19th August. Fighting for Taegu and Masan continued until the end of August. But General Walker did not underestimate the determination and calibre of his enemy. His two armies* were still insufficient to create a continuous line of defences. He was again taking replacements directly from basic training establishments in the United States.

It was in these circumstances and against this background, that Brigadier Coad's 27th Brigade arrived at Pusan on 29th August.

Air Vice-Marshal Bouchier was following the advance of Operation GRADUATE with keen interest. When he had carried the news of the commital and imminent entry of 27 Brigade to General MacArthur, the latter was moved to make a brief speech referring to the 'historic unity of the Anglo-Saxon peoples'.[13] Hyperbole apart, he was relieved to know that other national army contingents were arriving at last to reinforce the American and ROK troops. The British were, he told Bouchier, 'to be sped like an arrow' to Korea.

On the 27th, accompanied by the air marshal, Brigadier Coad reached Taegu. 'General Walker and Partridge of the 5th Air Force had flown to Pohang . . . We therefore had initial conference with Chief of Staff . . . After lunch, Walker returned. Apologised for circumstances which had prevented meeting us at air base which had been his intention. Walker gave us the warmest possible welcome . . .'.[14]

'I've been greatly looking forward to this moment,' he remarked. 'We are all delighted to have the British here, and I want you [Coad] to know that if you have any difficulties you can get to see me at any time.'[15] The brigade was to be looked after by the 24th Division, the army commander told his visitors, but would not be put into battle until its members had completed instruction on the United States anti-tank rocket launcher†, had a chance to visit units in the line to observe operating conditions, artillery and air

---

*The ROK Army, though not part of Eighth Army, was under General Walker's operational command.

†To replace the PIAT with its limited range. The first United States troops into Korea had been equipped with the second world war 2.36-inch rocket launcher—the original Bazooka—which had not proved effective against the Russian T34 tank. It was replaced by the 3.5-inch model for use in rifle and support platoons. Several had been flown to Hong Kong with 20 rounds of live ammunition to enable the Middlesex and Argylls to familiarise themselves with the weapon during the sea voyage. It had been agreed that instructors, a general issue of launchers, and live ammunition would be made available in Korea to carry training to completion.

support procedures, and had received its essential light transport, expected in six or seven days. With these assurances, the advanced party were moved to establish a concentration area between Kyongsan and Chain, ten miles south east of Taegu, 'a delightful area of tree covered hillocks and a wide, stony stream bed with clear flowing water in which we bathed thankfully after the heat and dust of travelling.'[16]

The warships carrying the main body were now approaching. Just after noon on the 29th, watched by Brigadier Coad and the two commanding officers on the quay, *Unicorn* and *Ceylon* came alongside. As they made fast, a United States Army band played briskly a song then popular, 'Silver Dollar', before changing tempo to 'God Save the King', in which they were joined by a ROK Army band and a choir of Korean school children, the result of much practice during the earlier part of the morning. Despite the youth of so many of the British soldiers, the force impressed the various onlookers, including a large element of the press corps, and an official delegation from the National Assembly of the Republic, the only admiral in the ROK forces among them. 'They marched ashore as if they were still on parade,' Ralph Izzard of the London *Daily Mail* noted. 'And they all looked fighting fit.'

The Argyll pipers, notable in their white tunics and regimental kilts among the various uniforms on the quay, began to play, and quickly became the focus of interest. Asked to comment by an American journalist why there was no band from his own regiment, Lieutenant-Colonel Man of the Middlesex replied, perhaps defensively,

'Well, the Scots need those contraptions to fight with.'

A member of his battalion soon cut a dash, however, by disembarking with a tennis racquet and golf clubs on his shoulder.

A few of 27 Brigade's jeeps and light trucks had been carried in *Unicorn* and these were unloaded on to the quay with kitbags, first line ammunition* support weapons, and other field equipment— what was known to the British units as their 'G10'†. In the dock sidings, two railway trains were waiting to carry the force to Kyongsan station.

The welcoming ceremonies over, there was considerable work to be done. Personal baggage and 'G10' had to be manhandled for loading into the trains, and the trains had to be cleaned. Passenger and freight wagons had recently been packed with refugees. Assisted

---

*First line ammunition (supplies or equipment) is that element required for immediate use in operations; that is, the ammunition with the fighting weapons plus a small unit reserve. It is continually topped up from the second line held under brigade or divisional control.
†The schedule of weapons and equipment authorised for a field unit is listed on Army Form G1098, appropriate to arm of service.

in comradely fashion by the Royal Navy, who were the sole source of cleaning materials, this work was undertaken over some hours. Working, or resting in the adjacent godowns, all the newcomers were beset by a noisome smell from the numerous open sewers of the refugee areas nearby combined with the wood smoke of thousands of humble cooking fires. All were glad to escape at last, the Middlesex at 1830, the Argylls at 2330. The brigade headquarters elements, military police and other small detachments were divided among them.

During the next two days, living in the open or under makeshift shelters was no hardship. Unit cooks provided a hot breakfast and evening meal, bread and cheese or 'some form of exotic American tinned meat' or cold sausage at midday. The soldiers maintained their fitness by running along the local tracks or climbing the hills. They extended their knowledge of the Bazooka. Personal clothing was divided between what was required immediately for battle in the remains of summer, and what would be needed for the formidable winter ahead. Plans were made to begin liaison visits to the American units in the line. Thus passed two days.

Suddenly, the agreeable tempo of preparation was transformed. The failure of the NKPA to break open decisively the United Nations line had brought urgent instructions from Kim Il-sung to his formation commanders in the field. The extent to which time was running against them was inescapable. The United Nations forces were building up their numbers and their base. The North Koreans had lost far more killed and wounded than the United States or ROK defenders realised just then, both in combat and, to a lesser but still significant extent, from attacks in rear by the Fifth Air Force. By the end of the first week of August, this loss approached 60,000.[17] Having impressed some 20,000 recruits from the south Korean countryside they occupied, the NKPA had about 68,000 in fighting formations, the local recruits being capable of elementary duties only.* By that time the United States, notwithstanding 10,000 casualties, had 35,000 officers and men in combat.†
The ROK Army, having lost 70,000 battle casualties, had about

---

*This figure excludes the numbers in the North Korean base, north of the 38th parallel, the Front and two corps headquarters, and the lines of communication. Recruits impressed in South Korea represented about one third of the total. These men were given elementary training in the use of a rifle and grenades. Some received further instruction during 'quiet' hours' in the line in the working of the light machine-gun.
About a third of the NKPA casualties were inflicted by the ROK divisions.
†The United States figures exclude the Pusan base, line of communication and army headquarters, and Far East Air Force units in Korea. Casualties relate to killed, wounded and prisoners. The many heat stroke casualties quickly rejoined their units from medical aid stations.

73,000 in its divisions. But though more numerous, General Walker had still to spread his soldiers along the entire perimeter, the inevitable consequence of being on the defensive. The NKPA could mass superior numbers at selected points, the moral and physical advantage it enjoyed from persistence in offensive action. It was on this basis that the western press and radio continued to report 'wave upon wave' of enemy,[18] and the common opinion remained that the United Nations were heavily outnumbered.

This situation obtained still at the end of August. American air supremacy had slowed and to an extent diminished the flow forward of men and materials by rail and road but not sufficiently to deny offensive action by the North Koreans. Infantry reinforcements marched the last hundred miles into the battle line. Twenty one new T34s and 200 members of an independent tank battalion arrived by railway from the tank training centre in P'yongyang in mid-August.[19] Once in the forward area, many portable items were cross loaded on to ox carts taken from the local community, and troops obliged to move in the open by day dressed often in the white jackets and trousers of peasants. By 31st August, thirteen infantry divisions and elements of four brigades, including armour, had been brought to readiness. They totalled 98,000.

There were still sufficient experienced leaders among this total at all levels, predominantly the ardent veterans from the Chinese Communist Forces. At 2330 on 31st August, they struck again in the Masan area and across the bulge of the lower Naktong; at 1800 on 2nd September across the upper Naktong, in the mountains north of Taegu, and in the north east of the perimeter.

No doubt General Walker would have preferred to have kept his promise to give 27 Brigade a week to settle in to the environment and methodology of the American battlefield, but in the crisis of a renewed North Korean offensive this had to be abandoned. Brigadier Coad regretted the change but understood the reason for it. What vexed him were the frequent changes of orders that followed, often due to impulsive judgements and careless staff work in some of his superior headquarters. He noted that 'With very few exceptions the American staff officers never leave their HQs, even to visit lower formation HQs, and never in our experience did any staff officer come to look at any ground'.[20] Placed under command of Major-General Gay and the 1st Cavalry Division, on 2nd September, he was surprised to find numerous press correspondents at regimental and divisional headquarters, 'who, in spite of the urgency of the situation, stopped us to take photographs and then crowded into the Command Post to hear the General's orders'.[21]

---

*The ROK figures include specialist troops such as the ROK marines but exclude the (then) small training and administrative base and ROKA headquarters.

After three changes of plan, and contradictory orders from army and divisional headquarters, 27 Brigade was committed to the Naktong line on 4th September. It was to relieve the 3rd Battalion of the American 23rd Infantry, holding the left flank of the 1st Cavalry Division sector.* Taegu lay barely ten miles to the north east.

The division had a huge frontage, 35 miles in length. 27 Brigade now took responsibility for about 10 miles of it. The Argylls were to hold the southern area, the Middlesex the northern. Brigadier Coad was given a battery of 105-mm and another of 155-mm guns, and a platoon of Sherman tanks, a generous share of the divisional support resources. No less important was the attachment of a Tactical Air Control Party (TACP) from the 5th Air Force.

Taking over a sector of a defensive line is never an easy matter, often conducted, as on this occasion, in darkness to avoid alerting enemy observation posts. Reconnaissance parties spent the day looking at as much of the ground as could be reached without exposure. In the evening the main bodies came forward in American trucks. With the dusk, companies set off in single file along rough tracks until these petered out. Thereafter they marched by compass across the hill slopes, seeking to make as little noise as possible as they passed through scrub and dwarf oaks. The 3–inch mortars and the Vickers medium machine-guns were sited to cover both the company perimeters and the wide gaps between them but, with such frontages, there were considerable tracts of ground through which the enemy could pass unseen, unheard and unthreatened in the darkness.

At sunrise, everyone was standing to arms. The Argylls' take over had not been trouble free. The American guides to their distant, left flank company, had lost their way. Elsewhere, a subaltern coming into his platoon position from a brief walk round the approaches, surprised and was shot by one of his own sentries. For the Middlesex, with the greater frontage, the morale and effectiveness of the company of ROK civil police holding two miles of the river bank on their right was a problem.

The arrival, late on 8th September, of the the greater part of the brigade's jeeps and other light transport, together with the tracked carriers of the two battalions, eased the internal transport problem. Brought up on railway flat cars from Pusan, to which they had been carried in a merchant ship, the vehicle group at one point had been shunted into a siding to give way to a train with a higher priority. Lieutenant Geoffrey Norton of the Middlesex went

---

*This battalion belonged to the United States 2nd Division, but had been placed temporarily under command of the 1st Cavalry due to the length of its line.

to see the local American movements officer. He discovered that the load comprised eight large ice cream machines, and was able to persuade him that 27 Brigade's vehicles were more urgently needed.

If all these were minor events compared to the huge struggle to the north and south, where American and ROK forces were locked in battles to maintain the perimeter's integrity, the British front was not inactive. A watchful and aggressive defence was at once established. Observation posts by day, listening posts and reconnaissance patrols by night on both sides of the river established that there was considerable movement across their front. The American guns and British mortars in support were frequently engaged against these targets. The air force confirmed local Korean reports that an extremely large force of the NKPA was forming up in the hills to the south of the Argylls. An early fighting patrol clashed with one of its outposts.

In the run of these events, working options were developed. The Argylls' left flank company was difficult to supply; air drops were insufficiently accurate. Korean porters were brought into service across the front, the first of many to provide a dependable line of supply. American helicopters were used when available to evacuate wounded. And the 230 Korean police, poorly armed, indifferently led, were successfully controlled in the northern sector by Corporal Field of the Middlesex, chosen because, as a former prisoner-of-war, he spoke a little Japanese, a *lingua franca*. His command of two groups was dubbed 'Army Groups A and B'.

A police battalion under Major Gwyn, aided by a subaltern, several warrant and non-commissioned officers of the Middlesex, was organised to counter the NKPA elements seeking to infiltrate eastward through the gap between the British brigade and the United States 2nd Division to the south. '. . . one column [under CSM Seabrook] included 100 men armed only with two grenades each. Arms were diverse and varied from Yank rifles to Russian and Japanese ones. One mortar was found and used with deadly effect despite the fact that it had no sights and the wrong calibre bombs were used. Major Gwyn issued all his orders through a most inefficient interpreter and held frequent order groups in which the recipients of the orders closely resembled Balkan bandits'.[22]

There were losses due to shell and mortar fire, in vehicle accidents on the narrow tracks, in patrol clashes on either side of the Naktong. The veterans rehoned their martial skills; the novices began to acquire them.

SOURCE NOTES: CHAPTER 6

1. Shipster, J N Colonel, *The Diehards in Korea*, memoir, The Middlesex Regiment, p 2.

2. Field-Marshal Sir William Slim, conversation with author.

3. DEFE 4/35, COS(50)131st meeting on 17th August 1950.

4. Major-General Coad, A B, (using his personal notes), conversation with author.

5. DEFE 11/199, COS to GHQ FARELF (for BDCC(FE)) COSSEA 761 of 18th August 1950 and MOD (Chiefs of Staff) TOK4 for Tokyo (Bouchier) 191500A August 1950.

6. Appleman, op cit, Ch XII

7. See Thames Television series, The Korean War, 1988, Programme 2 of six (hereafter, Thames TV).

8. Appleman, op cit p 207.

9. Ibid p 207–8.

10. Mayo, Walter L, jr, Colonel, conversation with author.

11. DEFE 11/199, Tokyo 1032 to FO 23rd August 1950.

12. 1st Cav Div G-2 WDS Report August 1950 (USNA Suitland).

13. Bouchier reminiscence to Field-Marshal Lord Harding (passed to author by the latter). See also DEFE 11/199.

14. DEFE 11/200, Tokyo (Bouchier) CAB 17 to MOD (Chiefs of Staff) 280515A August 1950.

15. Coad, conversation with author.

16. 1 Middlesex war diary, annex.

17. Appleman, op cit, p 263.

18. Appleman, op cit, p 264.

19. *History of the North Korean Army*, Headquarters Far East Command, Military Intelligence Section, General Staff publication, 1952, p 80.

20. Coad, conversation with author, and Coad's report on 'The Operations of 27 British Infantry Brigade', (hereafter, Coad Report), annex to 27 Bde war diary, 1950.

21. Ibid.

22. Shipster, op cit, pp 10–11.

1. The Foreign Secretary, Ernest Bevin, addressing the ship's company, HMS
   Kenya, with Captain Brock, and his private secretary (Sir) Roderick Barclay.
   (Sir Roderick Barclay)

2. Burial at sea from HMS *Jamaica* of the first British servicemen to be killed
   in the war, July 1950.
   (Lt Cdr P Sparkes)

3. Firefly flying off from HMS *Triumph* to attack targets in Korea, July 1950.
(C D Christmas Esq)

4. Firefly being armed on board HMS *Triumph*.
(C D Christmas Esq)

5. HMS *Ladybird*, previously the Yangtse river steamer, *Wusueh*, headquarters ship, in her berth at Sasebo. (Cdr J A de M Leathes)

6. Camouflaged junks on mud flats spotted by aircraft from HMS *Triumph*. (C D Christmas Esq)

7.   HMS *Triumph* preparing to enter harbour after operations in Korean waters.   (C D Christmas Esq)

8. HMS *Comus* after attack by Stormovik aircraft, 23rd August 1950.
    (Cdr J A de M Leathes)

9. Close up shows some of the damage. (Cdr J A de M Leathes)

10.　1 Middlesex embark on HMS *Unicorn*, Hong Kong, 25th August 1950. The soldiers were wearing the jungle green tropical uniform which they retained into the winter. (Major B Reed)

11.　Farewell address by Rt Hon Malcolm MacDonald, British High Commissioner, South-East Asia, 25th August 1950. (Major B Reed)

12. 1 A&SH arrive in Pusan on the cruiser, HMS *Ceylon*, 29th August 1950. (Hulton-Deutsch Picture Company)

13. 1 Middlesex arrive in Pusan aboard HMS *Unicorn*, 29th August 1950. (Major B Reed)

14. 1 A&SH disembarking from HMS *Ceylon*, 29th August 1950, carrying their bagpipes, 'those contraptions'. (Hulton-Deutsch Picture Company)

15. 1 Middlesex move towards the front line, 3rd September 1950. (Major B Reed)

CHAPTER 7

A Stroke of Genius

Unique among his peers in service and seniority, General MacArthur had for long been an object of suspicion to governments of the United States and anxiety to her Joint Chiefs of Staff. These apprehensions, surfacing intermittently during the second world war, receded somewhat in the years 1945–50, in which he had been occupied with the affairs of Japan. They were recurrent following the outbreak of the Korean war. The problem was that great accomplishments underpinned the status he assumed. Vain and devious, he was besides a man possessing the experience, breadth of vision, and readiness to take risks necessary to turn defeat into victory.

During the first week in July, when it became evident that the Republic of Korea must rely upon the United States to defend its territory, General MacArthur drew upon his experience as a strategist. He possessed superiority in the air and supremacy at sea. Assuming that the first contingents he despatched would halt and draw upon themselves the NKPA round Taejon, he decided to land a force behind the enemy at Inch'on. This was Operation 'Bluehearts', a plan stillborn as the North Koreans successively forced back the American intervention and threatened to overwhelm it.

Even so, he declined to contemplate the loss of the Pusan bridgehead or to abandon plans and preparations for striking behind the enemy. His demands on Washington for the stripping out of their resources were not conceived with the aim of simply pushing the North Korean divisions back across the 38th parallel but of pulverising them where they lay. On 23rd July, just after the fall of Taejon, he signalled Washington that he now intended to use the 5th Marines and 2nd Division in 'major amphibious operations', which would be exploited by an airborne assault.* Once established ashore, the Eighth Army would break out from the bridgehead. As MacArthur informed Washington,

---

*The 187th Airborne Regimental Combat Team was mobilising in the United States for Korea.

Although the exact date of D-day is partially dependent upon enemy reaction during the month of August, I am firmly convinced that an early and strong effort behind his front will sever his main line of communication and enable us to deliver a decisive and crushing blow . . . . The alternative is a frontal attack which can only result in a protracted and expensive campaign to slowly drive the enemy north of the 38th Parallel . . .[1]

Next day, 24th July, at a teleprinter conference, he assured the Chiefs that 'barring unforeseen circumstances, and with complete provision of requested replacements, if the full Marine Division is provided, the chances to launch the movement in September would be excellent.[2] They did not ask for—and MacArthur did not offer—details of the site he had in mind for the landing. Their attention was rivetted by the simpler and more immediate issue of whether or not the line in Korea, retiring still despite the arrival of the 25th and 1st Cavalry Divisions behind the 24th, would hold, and how much more would be needed to make it secure.

Stabilisation of the defence line was also the preoccupation of MacArthur's staff through the remainder of July and August. As earlier recounted, the 2nd Division and 5th Marines were drawn essentially into the Naktong line. Only the 7th Division and the residue of the marine division remained uncommitted. The 7th had posted almost 10,000 of its officers and men to the divisions in Korea. It would not receive replacements until 1st October and must then train as an entity. The second and third regiments of the marines and their supporting air squadrons would not be available until November or December. Indeed, the decision to send a marine division at full war strength, including supporting air squadrons, was not taken until early August.

General MacArthur was scarcely a commander to wait upon difficulties, however. He had already directed General Walker to draw Koreans* in to reinforce the Eighth Army divisions. Over eight thousand were sent to the 7th Division in Japan in August. All American infantry and artillery reinforcements from the United States were allotted to the 7th during the last week in August and the first in September. The divisional strength rose to 24,845, though less than half of these were effectively trained for battle. The United States Marine Corps needed no urging to hasten the Washington timetable. The United States Navy had sufficient amphibious craft to lift the force. Assuming that General Walker's

---

*Most of these were civilians, young men gathered off the streets by the police. One, returning home from fetching medicine for his wife, arrived in Japan with the medicine in his pocket.

144

army in Korea could hold the North Koreans, the operation could be mounted. But was it feasible?

Feasibility depended upon satisfaction of three conditions: the holding power of the Eighth Army; numbers sufficient to command the zone chosen; and the ability to land these numbers effectively.

General MacArthur was determined that the Eighth Army would hold; hence his declaration to General Walker at their meeting in late August that there would be no 'Dunkirk' in South Korea. He seems to have been confident that they would continue to hold even when he removed the marine brigade from the bridgehead early in September during the resurgent North Korean offensive.

Of course, he had a wider view than the army commander who was occupied with the detailed control of the tactical battle at that time,* and a better appreciation of the effect of the Far East Air Force's attacks in rear of the NKPA. His judgement was validated by events. The bridgehead forces were not only able to hold and weaken the greater part of the NKPA without the marines and, for a fortnight, without casualty replacements, but to develop also a capability to break out when the Supreme Commander's amphibious operation—'Chromite'—was launched. There were, therefore, two complete divisions, the 1st Marine and the 7th, together with other force troops—additional artillery, engineers, signals and administrative elements—grouped as a new formation, X Corps, for Chromite.†

These were matters entirely within General MacArthur's prerogative. So was his choice of a landing site; but in this he needed to carry others with him, including the United States Navy. His staff had produced two other site options for consideration but neither offered the strategic dividends of Inch'on, close to the enemy line of communication and the national capital. As a location at which to put 70,000 men ashore with their fighting equipment and supplies, however, it had numerous disadvantages. At Inch'on, the tide falls more than 30 feet twice a day. The port lies on a narrow channel between great banks of mud which become exposed as the tide falls. Spring tides would be necessary to provide sufficient water for the landing ships to reach their beaches; the dates and times of these narrowed severely the range of options for the operation. Sea walls hazarded an initial assault and the disembarkation of vehicles and stores.

At a conference in his headquarters on the evening of 23rd August, General MacArthur's staff laid out the landing options

---

*Lacking any corps headquarters at that time, General Walker was obliged to act as both corps and army commander of the United Nations forces, while simultaneously directing the ROK Army.
†187 Airborne RCT was not a part of these but was kept as General MacArthur's reserve.

and his plan to capture Inch'on with the 1st Marine Division, through whom the 7th Division would pass, both formations going on subsequently to retake Seoul and Kimpo airfield. The Eighth Army would break out from the Naktong line and the NKPA would be crushed between the two forces. Among the senior officers listening to this exposition were two of the national Chiefs of Staff, Admiral Sherman and General Collins.* Both were uneasy due to the physical difficulties of the Inch'on site. But when MacArthur had himself spoken for some thirty minutes at the end of the briefing, with his habitual eloquence, yet in a quiet and conversational way, they were won over by his arguments that it offered the best options in place and in effecting surprise.

Next day, removed from the immediate force of MacArthur's personality, when there had been time for informal discussions, there were second thoughts. A naval and marine proposal to land at a fourth site near Inch'on was put to the supreme commander but he rejected it

'For a five dollar ante', he concluded, 'I have an opportunity to win $50,000, and I have decided that is what I am going to do.'[3]

'I wish I had that man's confidence,' Admiral Sherman remarked before he returned to Washington.[4]

On the 28th August, the Joint Chiefs signalled,

> We concur after reviewing the information brought back by General Collins and Admiral Sherman in making preparations and executing a turning movement by amphibious forces on the west coast of Korea, either at Inch'on in the event the enemy defences prove ineffective, or at a favourable beach south of Inch'on if one can be located . . .[5]

This left MacArthur and the Chiefs of Staff separate loopholes for escape if such should arise.

Among several extraordinary features of Operation Chromite, two are particularly remarkable. The first is the speed with which it was mounted. Tide and autumn weather conditions dictated a narrow range of dates in mid-September for D-day, the 15th being finally selected. This gave less than three weeks to convert a planning study, albeit advanced, to the detail of operation orders, to assemble the ships, and to prepare the 7th Division and force troops who had no experience of such an operation—indeed, had no experience of operating together at all. Commanders and staffs were to draw heavily upon the preliminary work done by the

---

*General J Lawton Collins, US Army (1896–1963)

United States, such as the secret reconnaissance from the USS *Horace A Bass* on 21st August,* and the continuous chart correction work of Admiral Andrewes' squadron. Fortunately, the burden of the assault on the North Korean positions would fall upon the experienced shoulders of the United States Marines.

Second, it is extraordinary that the plan did not become known to the enemy. The security arrangements became increasingly ineffective within the theatre. The list of those admitted to knowledge of the operation was too restrictive; speed of mounting required a considerable number to undertake detailed planning. As a consequence, the list was of necessity enlarged daily. Soon, no one was quite sure who was and who was not on it. False assumptions were made which led to unwitting revelations. Some on the outside became so suspicious and hence inquisitive about what was going on that associates brought them in to avoid piecemeal leakage of information. Air Vice-Marshal Bouchier, for example, became aware that Admiral Andrewes had been brought to Tokyo on 31st August for a 'special' briefing. When he asked the subject, the admiral said, 'Are you on the list?' He was not but managed to persuade a colleague that he should be. Next day he sent the Chiefs of Staff a top secret, high precedence signal marked 'EYES ALONE'.† It contained the general plan of Chromite, and continued:

> 8. Above is the quickest appreciation of this major offensive which if successful may well be the beginning of the end of this war. I have got it from the American Planners here but have not yet been told by MacArthur or Chief of Staff who considers it of the greatest secrecy. I have read Navy plans for this operation and unless something of the greatest importance happens to make [a] postponement essential it will take place as planned. Request you do not compromise my source of information . . . .[6]

The Chiefs of Staff respected the request, though they were soon also to be informed about Chromite by Admiral Andrewes through Admiral Brind; Admiral Andrewes had been appointed a task force commander in the naval force. After private discussion among themselves, they informed the Minister of Defence and Prime Minister.[7] The latter said that he would find the right moment to inform his other colleagues.[8]

---

*See p 81.
†'Eyes Alone'—to be seen only by the addressee(s) named or one holding a specific appointment(s).

The Foreign Office learned of Chromite on the 14th September because the naval *attaché* in the Embassy had attended Admiral Joy's final briefing on the 12th and had passed the details on to Sir Alvary Gascoigne next day.[9] Similarly, Sir Oliver Franks in Washington was told about Chromite on the eve of its launch. Still, it would seem that Philby and Burgess in their offices were unaware of the event until a late hour, perhaps too late to inform their Russian controllers.[10] In Japan, however, the information may have become known to North Korean agents; the Japanese leader of a group was captured with details a week before D-day.[11] By then, however, the headquarters, base units and ports were awash with rumours; Chromite had been dubbed 'Operation Common Knowledge'. What was clear was that a large scale amphibious operation was being prepared. Exactly where it would take place was not so widely known.

It has been suggested since that the North Koreans were expecting an attack because mine laying was just beginning in the Inch'on area. This was in hand on another basis. A large consignment of Russian sea mines had been received during July by the NKPA and during August they were being distributed for laying at Chinnamp'o, Haeju, Inch'on, Kunsan and Mokp'o. Inch'on was garrisoned by two battalions of North Korean marines and two batteries of 76-mm guns. Many of the men in these units had recently been conscripted locally. Behind them, the 87th Regiment covered Kimpo airfield and the approaches to Seoul. This was not a recent deployment. An engineer team, using local civil labour, was just beginning work on seaward defences, but similar activities were taking place at the same pace at ports north and south. Though it is probable that the high command in P'yongyang had some information that a landing was being prepared, there is nothing to indicate that they knew when and where it would take place.

While men, materials and ships were made ready, a typhoon passed across Kobe, damaging cranes and cargo on the docksides, tearing ships from their moorings. Soon, another was seen to be approaching. In haste, the fleet put to sea. Many ships, especially the older landing ships, had an extremely uncomfortable twenty four hours on passage through mountainous seas.

As the screening forces began to take up their station for the protection of the main body, HM frigate, *Whitesand Bay*, (Lieutenant-Commander J V Brothers, RN), was engaged in a deception operation at Kusan. On board were 120 officers and men of the United States Army, 2 officers and 14 men from the Royal Navy and Royal Marines. At nightfall on the calm and cloudless night of 12th September, *Whitesand Bay* began to run in for the coast at 16 knots. At 2228, she stopped about 2 miles from the shore. The captain later reported,

> . . . the troops disembarked and paddled ashore in their rubber dinghies.
>
> 12.   At 0023, 13th September, machine gun and Browning Automatic Rifle fire was observed . . . . It was known that no tracer ammunition was carried by our own troops. At about 0040 the Seaguard detected the rubber dinghies returning.[12]

By half past one that morning, all were back aboard except for the colonel commanding the force and eight other Americans. After a quick pooling of information, the consensus was that the missing party had bumped into an enemy detachment on high ground at the northern end of the beach, for this was the area from which two machine-guns had suddenly fired, the source of tracer rounds. But those returning believed that some at least of the others might have successfully withdrawn in the darkness to an emergency collection point on Sokutei-to. *Whitesand Bay's* motor cutter and a dinghy were sent to this island, which was searched without success.

Lieutenant-Commander Brothers now felt the burden of his command. Dawn was approaching and he was within range of enemy guns ashore. Running in the night before, his ship had hit an underwater obstruction which had damaged his hull, putting his anti-submarine gear out of action. These factors weighed heavily for a withdrawal. But he could not bring himself to abandon the missing nine until the last possible moment. As a precaution, he signalled to ask for support from *Triumph* at dawn but the range was too great for her aircraft.[13] If he waited until daylight, therefore, he would have to cope with enemy action on his own. Then, at 0445, a light flashed the emergency signal from Sokutei-to, and at almost the same moment the seaguard reported a dinghy approaching from the south. The cutter, still in the water, went off to tow this alongside. It contained five of the missing number, one mortally wounded. A further two were picked up from the island. One man was known to be dead, another seriously wounded ashore. But they could wait no longer. Lieutenant-Commander Brothers 'retired to seaward at 17½ knots.'

American, Australian, British, Canadian, Dutch and French ships, combined in Joint Task Force 7,* had been moving towards the Inch'on area since 10th September. Admiral Struble was in overall command. Wide ranging air reconnaissance and surveillance was being conducted by Task Force 99, which included the Royal

---

*For details of the force, see Appendix L

Air Force Sunderlands of 88 and 209 Squadrons. Three United States fast carriers with escorts comprised Task Force 77 which was to maintain air supremacy across the whole objective area, and to complement close interdiction and ground attack from the air during the lodgement. Admiral Andrewes commanded the ships blockading the east coast and covering the approaches from seaward, Task Force 91. Close inshore were the light craft of the ROK Navy. At the heart of the command was the main attack force, TF 90: the flagship USS *Mount McKinley,* two escort carriers with US Marine Corps aircraft embarked, the bombardment force, screening and protective ships, minesweepers, specialist ships, supply and hospital ships, and the transports and freight vessels carrying the X Corps led by the 1st Marine Division. In all, eighty five warships, more than one hundred others, were steaming into position. The British hospital ship, *Maine,* was kept initially at Sasebo, ready to come forward to collect casualties at sea, and to provide an emergency centre for casualties among the landing force until shore facilities were established.

Arriving in the objective area, Admiral Andrewes' Task Force divided into two groups. The northern (Task Group 91.1) was required to maintain the blockade and coastal watch, and to provide air cover during the middle phase of the passage. During the landing, it was to operate to the west and north of the Inch'on area, providing protection against submarine attack, offering air defence, air observers—'spotters'—for naval bombardment, and interdiction as required. The southern (Task Group 91.2) was to provide escorts on passage, and then to maintain the southern element of the blockade. ROK patrol craft and minesweepers were to operate in coastal waters under command of *Charity* (north) and *Sioux* (south).

To the west and south, the frigates, *Mounts Bay, Whitesand Bay, Tutira,* and *Pukaki* formed part of the outer screen under United States command.

Air attacks began on 10th September, dropping napalm—fire bombs of jellied petrol—on to the outlying defences on the island of Wolmi-do. On the morning of 13th September, D-day minus 2, a day of sparkling sunshine, *Jamaica* and *Kenya* joined with USS *Rochester* and *Toledo* for shore bombardment. By 0900, they were moving up the Flying Fish channel towards Inch'on. Anxiety during planning that a succession of air raids and ship bombardments, two full days before the landing, might alert the North Koreans to the precise site had been set aside by Admiral Struble: the risks to the marines were great enough; he was not going to put them ashore without crushing anything that looked like an enemy position. It was also fairly remarked that aircraft and warships had, at random intervals, raided and shelled Inch'on on several previous occasions.

> The wind was easterly, quite fresh, and the visibility excellent, [an officer aboard *Kenya* wrote in his diary next day]. The approach was unfriendly . . . all the mudbanks were exposed, however, as we were due to reach our bombardment positions at low water. The idea was that if the North Koreans had brought up any number of guns we—and even more so the American destroyers preceding us—would be withdrawing on a rising tide. It is not a very attractive area, mud and low rocks wherever one looked, very flat for Korea, though one could see mountains in the distance . . . *Jamaica* remained under way during the bombardment but we were at anchor throughout the afternoon.[14]

The six United States destroyers had been designated 'sitting ducks'. Approaching to within 800 yards of Wolmi-do, they expected to draw fire, and indeed were soon targets for the North Korean batteries, most of whose guns had survived the earlier air attacks. One destroyer, the *Henderson*, also discovered a line of floating mines which appeared to be moored. Alerted to this danger, destroyers and cruisers shot at these targets, some true, some false, through the day, with light calibre weapons. A number exploded obligingly.

Captain Salter reported,

> 5. It had been intended that aircraft should spot for the four cruisers, who had an elaborate and detailed schedule of targets for bombardment; but in the event two aircraft only were available, communications were bad and sharing proved to be impracticable: *Jamaica* carried out an area bombardment of such targets as could most readily be observed from the ship. The lack of an aircraft to spot was most disappointing and made one feel that the bombardment was really rather a waste of ammunition . . .[15]

On *Kenya*, Captain Brock had much the same opinion and after half an hour decided to weigh anchor 'to get the guns on to a suitable bearing.' But it was not rewarding; they were firing at low lying targets at ranges in excess of 7 miles.

> 10. The other cruisers also appeared to be having their own difficulties with the result that the destroyers, who were engaging with great gallantry at close range abreast of, and above,

Inch'on, had a thin time of it. Three were hit or sustained casualties and had to retire. The remainder were then recalled and withdrew at high speed.[16]

After a night at sea, the force returned on the morning of the 14th. As a result of discussions aboard the bombardment flagship the previous evening, each cruiser had an aerial spotter. *Jamaica* fired 283 rounds from her 6-inch guns, *Kenya* 320. The force retired in mid-afternoon, confident that they had destroyed the artillery on Wolmi-do, and pleased to be able to stand down part of each ship's company; for they had an early start next day.

At 0100 on D-day, 15th September, the ships carrying the first assault group of marines began the journey up the Flying Fish channel. Soon, the cruisers were following.

10. . . . Passage through the narrows, [Captain Salter remarked] this time with the full flood under us and in the middle of the night—promised to be interesting but in the event was no more than that: the night was not dark, there being few clouds only, and visibility was good. By 0525, just as the Eastern horizon was beginning to show signs of the coming dawn, all four cruisers were [back] in their bombardment anchorages, . . . and at 0545 all four opened fire on previously allotted targets. From this time on and for the rest of the day there was incessant bombardment from the sea and from the air: before long there was a pall of smoke over the whole area and it was quite impossible to tell what was going on. *Jamaica* was supplied by *Triumph* with a succession of spotting aircraft who ranged the countryside and reported targets: the most notable result was a hit on an ammunition dump which produced by far the most spectacular explosion of the day . . .[17]

As the numbers of transports entering the anchorage grew, *Kenya*, by prearrangement, moved out, but not before firing 385 6-inch and 205 4-inch shells. Disappointed at leaving, Captain Brock was able to tell the ship's company that the marines had captured Wolmi-do. A second wave came up on the next high tide to break into the town defences an hour before sunset. The sea walls were not easily breached but the majority of North Korean troops in the area were either overcome or had withdrawn by midnight. Unloading continued under lights from the landing craft lying on the mudbanks as the tide ebbed. Much equipment had to be cleared before the succeeding flood brought in the next instalment of the force.

Occasional bursts from light calibre weapons, though falling short of the ships anchored inside the channel, indicated that North

Korean troops were still active on the mainland and a few of the islands nearby.

14. *Jamaica's* berth was no more than 1,500 yards from the nearest land—an island.' Captain Salter 'had intended to land a small party on the bluff . . . whose sole purpose would have been to deter any would-be snipers who tried to get near enough to be a nuisance—but I changed my mind when I saw that the weather was deteriorating . . .' *Jamaica* found 'an excellent berth 15 cables further north . . .

15. The night was wet and unpleasant. Armed sentries were posted around the ship as a precaution against boarders, small charges were fired in the water at irregular intervals of about half an hour to deter under water saboteurs, the hands were kept at the second degree of readiness (having been at first degree since 0400) . . . A sudden deterioration in the weather and a signalled threat of gusts of wind of 45 knots caused me to veer more cable during the middle watch—this of course had the effect of inducing a calm which lasted throughout the rest of the night: ten rounds of 6–inch were fired five times during the night at irregular intervals, directed at targets prescribed in the operation orders . . . Apart from this, the night (afloat) was uneventful.[18]

That same wet evening, Admiral Andrewes was 60 miles distant from the cruisers, in the Yellow Sea. From a station west of Inch'on, he had moved to the south for the night to avoid the many ships converging on the port area.

Reviewing *Triumph's* activities, he was satisfied that her limited ability for air operations had been exploited to the full. The number of Seafires and Fireflies serviceable rarely exceeded twelve. To avoid continual changes of role, six Fireflies had been committed to air spotting and fitted with two 45–gallon overload tanks, providing each aircraft with two hours over the target area. The aircrew had performed well, the more creditably as less than half of them had previously put their classroom knowledge of this work to a practical test. Reserving two aircraft for combat air patrol—defence of the carrier itself—left four for other operations. When Admiral Struble had asked that *Triumph* should undertake spotting for the British cruisers, Admiral Andrewes had been obliged to withdraw from air reconnaisance to the northwest. But with four aircraft, it was possible to continue with blockade patrols. Four Seafires had been ranging up to Chinnamp'o, attacking small craft including a 500–ton freighter.

'Operations have been satisfactory so far,' he noted in speaking to some of his officers that evening. It would be several days before they could be confident that the landing had been completed and perhaps several weeks before the manoeuvre could be judged a success. Opinions on *Triumph* were divided about the North Korean capability and will to intervene in the air. Those who asserted that it would be suicide to challenge the aerial might of the augmented American Seventh Fleet were reminded of *kamikaze* attacks in the second world war.

Next day, Saturday, 16th September, events seemed to confirm those who believed that Seoul would be recaptured within a week. There were no calls for fire from *Jamaica*, though the spotters flew long and low over the target area, bringing back to Admiral Andrewes first hand reports of the progress of the advance, and incidentally collecting bullet holes. The clearance of Inch'on was completed. Those suspected of being North Korean soldiers or sympathisers were rooted out ruthlessly by ROK marines. The distracted inhabitants, some of whom had lost all their possessions in the bombardment* or in one or another of the fires which had broken out, began the process of resettlement. But, on the Sunday, there was an unpleasant, if minor, surprise.

20. First degree of AA [anti-aircraft] readiness was assumed at daylight, as usual, [Captain Salter reported]. At about 0555 . . . a single aircraft—taken to be friendly—flew normally and slowly from north to south down the line of ships anchored in the approach channel to Inch'on, at a height of about a thousand feet. Shortly afterwards it dived gently, passing over the US Hospital Ship *Consolation*, towards USS *Rochester*: it dropped two bombs close astern of *Rochester* and was followed by a second aircraft, which also attacked the *Rochester* with bombs. The first aircraft then wheeled around and gave the impression that she might have designs on HMS *Jamaica*: she was taken under fire with 4-inch and close range weapons, apparently thought better of her intentions and made off over the islands to the south. The second aircraft came at *Jamaica* from a relative bearing about red 20 and was taken under fire with close range weapons: the enemy returned the fire, raking *Jamaica's* port side with tracer and machine-gun fire, did a vertical bank, turned sharply to port, passed over the forecastle and crashed in the water about thirty yards from the ship. There were three casualties in

*Admiral Struble had reminded the Joint Task Force in his orders that 'The Seoul-Inch'on area is inhabited by our South Korean Allies, and our forces plan to utilise facilities in this area. Unnecessary destruction will impede our progress'. Bombardment and air attack was to be confined to specific areas in which enemy positions were identified. Bombardment records show that these instructions were heeded. Even so, as a number of North Korean positions were in inhabited areas, civilian lives were lost and much property was damaged.

Jamaica [one mortally wounded] . . . and there were a number of lucky escapes; one disturbing feature was the fact that the 1-inch armour plating which forms the back of Y [gun] turret was penetrated by a 15-mm solid armour piercing bullet: there was one man only inside the turret and he suffered no more damage than a grazed leg but he was considerably surprised . . . No markings were seen: one was a Yak 3 and the other a Stormovik Il-10 . . .[19]

The bombardment work of the cruisers in support of the landings was by this time almost at an end; the troops ashore were expanding the bridgehead to the limit of the warships' range. In case of attacks from the flanks—particularly from the north—Captain Thompson, RA, had been sent ashore with a small detachment to act as British naval gunfire support officer (NGFSO) with the 1st Marine Division. The last calls were met by *Jamaica* to support attacks by the leading marines, 12 miles to the east.

By 19th September, Admiral Andrewes was making preparations to redeploy his forces. They had been distributed to cover the landing and capture of the beach head for X Corps, and this had been accomplished, though much of this formation was still afloat. Warships on station, troop carriers, vehicle, store and supply ships, and specialist clearance vessels approaching or returning from Inch'on, were in such numbers that, 'Between 0100 and 0300 on 18th September the sea in our vicinity bore a striking resemblance to Hampstead Heath on August Bank Holiday,' Admiral Andrewes observed.[20] 'What is remarkable is that the whole of the movement in and out of the port was conducted without further orders.' All the ships concerned were following their particular instructions from the operation order—well, not quite all. On the night 16th/17th, *Triumph* had come across 'an LST bound for the battle but far off her course, and were able to direct her towards Inch'on, Had she gone on she might well have started a private invasion of her own in the Gulf of [the] Yalu.'[21]

As *Triumph* departed for Japan, her aircraft flew blockade missions and spotted for *Ceylon*, which was remaining as the command ship. Having had no immediate part in the landings like her sister cruisers, *Ceylon*'s company was happy to be sent to engage a target on the 20th: gun positions on Fankochi Point,* the southern extremity of the Ongjin peninsula, seventy miles north west of Inch'on. Her captain assumed command of the blockade force, the destroyers *Concord* and *Charity* in the north, the three Canadian destroyers in the southern sector.

---

*This is the Japanese name for the Korean coastal feature Tungsan-got.

The ROK vessels were under Canadian orders, a patrol craft and two inshore minesweepers. With much enterprise, Captain Brock had used these with his own ships to discover what was happening among the many islands, large and small, between Inch'on and Kunsan. In places, small numbers of North Koreans—or their South Korean sympathisers—were rooted out on the evidence of local inhabitants. But what became increasingly apparent was the destitution of some of these fishing communities kept from catching fish, their prime source of livelihood, either by communist authorities ashore, who believed that fishermen would pass information about them to the United Nations naval forces, or those same naval forces who feared that they might be laying mines or other obstacles as the time for Chromite approached.

Captain Brock set in hand the first of several measures to relieve the islanders, establishing fishing zones, arranging for the delivery by Commonwealth warships of rice and other essentials, tasks which were assumed by the ROK Navy during October.

The frigates, with two ROK inshore minesweepers, under Captain Unwin of *Mounts Bay*, continued their work in an arc round the south west approaches to Inch'on, challenging and identifying every ship, day and night, that entered their patrol zone. They were required to provide cover against aircraft attack, surface attack by warship or civilian craft on suicide missions, submarine attack, and mine hazards. None of these transpired but the hit and run air attack at Inch'on on *Jamaica* reminded ship's companies that every approaching aircraft had to be identified at an early point in its approach. It was arduous work which continued until 14th October. By that date, *Mounts Bay*, *Whitesand Bay*, HMNZ Ships *Pukaki* and *Tutira* and the French Ship *La Grandiere* had been at sea for 32 days and under way for all but two or three of these.

Many congratulatory signals, a feature of naval life at the end of operations, were received by Admiral Andrewes for the forces under his standing command. General MacArthur's was characteristic,

My heartiest felicitations on the splendid conduct of the Fleet units under your command. They have added another glamorous page to the long and brilliant histories of the Navies of the British Commonwealth.[22]

More revealing, perhaps, was the report signalled by Admiral Brind to the First Sea Lord after visiting the base in Japan as the first of the Commonwealth ships came in immediately after the Inch'on operation:

I have seen General MacArthur, Admirals Joy and Struble, and spent four days at Sasebo. From what I have seen myself and heard on all sides, the Commonwealth ships under Andrewes have met all calls made upon them exceedingly well and have made a great reputation for themselves. They have reached a high standard of efficiency, the bearing of the ships' companies is most creditable and health is good. Andrewes himself plays a much larger part than commanding the Commonwealth forces, for his experience and counsel are used to the full and are greatly appreciated . . .[23]

SOURCE NOTES: CHAPTER 7

1. MacArthur as US/UN CINCFE to Department of the Army (DA) for Joint Chiefs of Staff (JCS), C-58473 23rd July 1950, (US National Archives and Record Services (USNARS) CM IN 14839).
2. Teleprinter conference JCS-CINCFE, TT 3573 of 24th July 1950, (USNARS).
3. Schnabel, James F, *Policy & Direction: The First Year*, (OCMH Washington, 1972) p 150, and Heinl, Robert Debs, *Victory at High Tide*, (London 1972), pp 42 and 43.
4. Cagle, Malcolm W and Manson, Frank A, *The Sea War in Korea*, (US Naval Institute, 1957) p 76.
5. JCS-US/UN CINCFE 89960 of 28th August 1950,. (USNARS CCS 382-21 Korea (3-19-45) sec 49).
6. DEFE 11/200, Bouchier to Chiefs of Staff UK, TRAIN 1 of 011909 September 1950.
7. Field-Marshal Lord Slim, conversation with author.
8. Shinwell, conversation with author.
9. Admiralty Case 11554, Vol 18, Third RoPs from Naval Adviser of September 1950 (NA 41/912/50 of 28th September 1950, pp 3 and 4)
10. Manchester, William, *American Caesar*, (London 1979) pp 597-8, fn. See also Costello, John, *Mask of Treachery*, (London, 1988), p 534.
11. United Press report in *Washington Post*, 15th May 1951.
12. Admiralty Case 11554, Vol 16, *Whitesand Bay* RoPs, 8th-15th September 1950.
13. Ibid, Vol 19, FO 2i/c FE Summarised RoPs No 6, 12th-21st September 1950, reports erroneously on this matter.
14. Private diary extract made available to author.
15. Admiralty Case 11554, Vol 9, *Jamaica* RoPs for 12th-19th September 1950.
16. Ibid, *Kenya* RoPs for 12th-26th September 1950.
17. Ibid, *Jamaica* RoPs for 12th-19th September 1950.
18. Ibid, para 14.
19. Ibid, para 20.
20. Ibid, Vol 19, FO 2i/c FE Summarised RoPs No 6 12th-21st September 1950, paragraph 47.
21. Ibid, para 42.
22. British Naval Staff History—British Commonwealth Naval Operations Korea 1950-53 (BR1736(54) 1967) p 64.
23. Ibid, CINCFE Station (Brind), personal signal to First Sea Lord of 081025 October 1950 p 86

CHAPTER 8

Break Out

The struggle for possession of the Pusan perimeter continued into the third week of September. The United States' front was broken on a number of occasions, necessitating the use of engineers as infantry. In the south, the 25th Division was forced out of almost all its defences and the road to Masan, twice open to the enemy, was recovered with difficulty. Along the Naktong, North Korean divisions forced further crossings and enlarged their bridgeheads. Errors and omissions, sometimes a want of spirit, among the Americans were outweighed by extraordinary courage and fortitude. Losses here, as elsewhere on the perimeter, were the highest for any similar period in the war. With these the total had risen to almost 20,000 American officers and men.

The 27th Brigade, in the centre of the Naktong line, was in danger of being drawn into an intense struggle, in which it would be heavily outnumbered. The 'large number of enemy' in the bulge on the Naktong below the Argylls was the 10th Mechanised Division, a formation which had seen no action prior to 12th August, but had lost heavily during its attempts to cross the Naktong on a broad front.[1] By the 9th September it had settled into the southern half of its original objective, a hill mass above the east bank of the river. Though two of its regiments were weak, the third was largely intact; and it still had the majority of its supporting artillery. Despite serious losses, therefore, it had the means to break out during these days but continued to spar in local, small scale actions.* Major Gwyn's ROK police—'Roly's Force'—having contained the numerous small enemy detachments from this source attempting to infiltrate towards the road and railway running south from Taegu, progressively drew in to observation posts overlooking the north eastern face of the 10th Division's concentration area. The chain provided Brigadier Coad with a reliable source of early warning of enemy movement.[4]

---

*It had been ordered to 'destroy the enemy in Taegu city in coordination with the 3rd Infantry Division'.[2] Some evidence suggests that the division held back because it was awaiting instructions to exploit a complete breach of the American line by the other divisions. The Far East Command intelligence staff later assessed its failure to move 'as a result of poor intelligence'.[3]

The enemy was not quiet to the north. A few miles upstream from the Middlesex, the 1st Cavalry Division was driven back towards Taegu. The threat of a break in their line was sufficient to persuade General Walker to withdraw the main body of Eighth Army headquarters to the south, leaving a tactical command post in the threatened city for himself and the 5th Air Force commander. North east, several of the ROK divisions seemed ready on occasions to break completely, and the reason is quite clear: so many of their officers and men were still no more than raw levies. Capable of watch and ward while others manoeuvred round them, they lacked the expertise and thus the confidence to stand against deliberate attacks. General Walker continued to underpin them with American detachments. Part of the burden was taken up by those ROK formations, such as the 1st Division, which were held together by vigorous leadership.

The strain on General Walker was immense. As the enemy offensive was rekindled, his casualty replacements were withheld for the 7th Division for Chromite. The 5th Marines were withdrawn for the same operation. But he had one huge advantage over his foe. He commanded great resources in fire power. Although there were occasions when artillery ammunition had to be rationed until the next supply ship arrived in Pusan, his field (105-mm) and medium (155-mm) batteries were more numerous and able to deliver fire more effectively than those of the North Koreans. There were times when one or more of these batteries were embattled: NKPA infantry which had infiltrated or broken the defensive line brought the guns under small arms fire. In some places, gun and command post crews fought them off hand to hand. But the effects of these incursions were not as great or as lasting as the frequent air attacks upon the North Korean batteries. Now and again the air failed due to weather—recurrent rain clouds—pilot errors, or more calls than the squadrons could respond to, but mostly the American aircraft, augmented by an Australian squadron, intervened decisively in the close combat on the ground and struck at the North Korean gun lines, headquarters, supply and communication areas behind. They struck with cannon fire, with high explosive rockets and bombs, and with napalm tanks each containing 110 gallons of petrol. As the naval and marine air support moved to support Chromite,* General Stratemeyer† secured two additional fighter/ ground attack squadrons to strengthen the 5th Air Force.

---

*The Pusan perimeter became so close to collapse while the Joint Task Force was *en route* to Inch'on that two carriers were recalled part way to augment the close air support of and interdiction for the Eighth Army.
†Stratemeyer, General George E, (1890–1970), Commander, Far East Air Force 1949–51.

Despite the use of his fire power to the limit of capability, and the continual drawing in and expenditure of reserves, General Walker's army was not in a position of superiority on 16th September, the day that he was to begin to break out towards the Inch'on bridgehead. The selected junction point was 180 miles distant as the crow flies, a good deal more by road over mountainous country. It was fortunate that, just at this time, he had some relief in his personal direction of the battle. Two corps headquarters had arrived to form the I and IX Corps. The former, under Major-General Frank W Milburn, was ordered to assume responsibility for the main thrust northwest.

Two routes were available to I Corps. The first lay along the main road—single track but metalled—Taegu–Waegwan–Kumch'on–Taejon–Suwon and onwards to Seoul. It ran for 160 road miles across the grain of the high Sobaek mountain range but descended towards more open country, parallel with the west coast, for the remaining 120 miles to the edge of Seoul. An advance by this means would also cut the immediate escape route of the NKPA in the south west region.

The other route followed a secondary road, part stone metalled, aligned initially north, then north west. From Taegu it passed through Tabu-dong–Naktong-ni–Sangju–Ch'ongju to Seoul. For the greater part, this road rises and falls through a series of steep mountain passes and valleys until it strikes the main western road on the coastal plain ten miles south of P'yongt'aek. It offers excellent opportunities for defence by small numbers, and was initially rejected on this account.

General Coulter with IX Corps consisting of the 2nd and 25th Divisions was to break out through the south west, sweeping the region, destroying the enemy which stood against him, forcing back those who withdrew on to I Corps. General Milburn, with the 1st Cavalry, 24th Division, 5th Regimental Combat Team, 27 Brigade and the 1st ROK Division, was to strike through Taejon to join X Corps.

The mountainous road up the centre of Korea, and the east coast road to the north east were allocated to the ROK Army as lines of advance. I ROK Corps followed the central, II ROK Corps the coastal route.

After ten days in their defensive locations, the British brigade was ready for more active operations. They had brushed successfully with the enemy. They had become accustomed to the ways of their allies. In relative terms, the brigade was also approaching a better organic balance; for in addition to the vehicles for the battalions and brigade headquarters, 'A' Troop of 27 Light Battery, Royal Artillery, equipped with four 17-pounder anti-tank guns, and 11

Field Workshops, REME, had joined from Hong Kong. An ordnance field park, carrying a reserve of equipment and spare parts, clothing and tools, would be with them by the end of the month. The Australian maintenance base, setting up in Pusan, was obligingly sending ammunition in short supply, principally for the 3-inch mortars. From this source first came the very welcome news that the 3rd Battalion, The Royal Australian Regiment—3 RAR—would be with them in about two weeks.

Brigadier Coad received his first instructions about the break out operation on the afternoon of 13th September from the 1st Cavalry Division. The I Corps chief of staff came to see him on the 14th.[5] The overall plan was to attack towards Waegwan on two routes: 5th Regimental Combat Team up the river bank from a position about six miles south of the town; 5th Cavalry Regiment up the Taegu-Waegwan road. A river crossing would then be made by 27 Brigade behind 5 RCT, through which 24th Division would pass towards Kumch'on. Seizing a bridgehead of sufficient size might be 'a problem with only two battalions,' Coad noted, 'but cheerfully accepted by all, and planning commenced'.[6] For his own security, and to test the Eighth Army view that there were very large forces immediately across the river from him, he ordered the Middlesex and Argylls to reconnoitre the opposite bank and to raid selected enemy locations.

Next day, the crossing plan was changed. They were to cross at the ferry site immediately downstream from Waegwan. New plans were made. In any case, they had to withdraw from an area which was under enemy surveillance and, in the case of the Argyll's left flank, close to the NKPA 10th Mechanised Division. Arrangements for their relief were tentative An assurance that the ROK police would remain in their positions was not comforting; without Major Gwyn and his Middlesex henchmen, it was unlikely that any would stay in the line. Mindful of the strength of their North Korean neighbour relative to their own, the brigadier and commanding officers apprehended the possibility of a running battle commencing on the present ground as they moved to their new location.

Plans and provisions for the river crossing remained sketchy. There would be very little time to reconnoitre the crossing site to the north, still to be cleared of the enemy, before the leading elements of 24th Division appeared. The assault force would be crossing in boats provided by the American engineers, but the British soldiers would be paddling and steering them. They had never seen the American type. Promises that several would be sent for practice were unfulfilled. Brigadier Coad was not optimistic when he returned to his headquarters on the evening of the 15th. He had been to visit 5th Cavalry, and found that they had been forced back 1,000 yards from their start line. They reported an enemy battalion with two tanks behind them.

D day was Saturday, 16th September; H hour was at 0900. It was a miserable morning, overcast with intermittent heavy rain. An American bombing raid on the enemy positions was cancelled accordingly. There was no rumble of distant gunfire from the north. All seemed strangely quiet. At about 4 p.m., Major Alan Hunter, DAA&QMG,* who had been sent to find an assembly area for the brigade close behind 5 RCT, returned to say that the RCT had advanced 3,000 yards up the east bank of the river, driving in outposts, but was now held up by enemy on a main feature. From them he had learned that the 5th Cavalry had regained and crossed their start line but had been forced back to it. Half an hour later, the Cavalry Division ordered 27 Brigade to withdraw from the line.

Brigadier Coad was mystified by this instruction. 'The advance was plainly blocked. There was no mention of anybody coming to relieve us. Why open up a large tract of ground to the enemy while we sat somewhere else doing nothing?'.[7] He asked for confirmation that they were to abandon the position and received it. Units were immediately told. Brigade headquarters had itself completed packing when a further message came from divisional headquarters at 2030 hours cancelling the previous order. The brigade was to remain in position.

Withdrawing safely without relief from a defensive line, even one at a distance from the enemy, is never a carefree matter. In addition to the hazard of random shelling or mortaring during darkness, there is the possibility that, as companies come out of their trenches, an enemy patrol or raiding party may coincidentally launch an attack. On the night of 16th September, each company thinned out progressively, but the moment had to come when the last element abandoned the position to join the remainder waiting at an assembly point in rear. There, a final check was made to ensure that every member of the company, including attached members of support company, such as Vickers machine-gunners, was present. If there were wounded, these would have to be carried on stretchers until a point was reached both accessible to transport and sufficiently distant to risk the sound of a vehicle engine.

On being told to reoccupy their positions, the two battalion commanders at once instructed by radio their companies moving across the dark hills and tracks to return as quickly as possible. Few had far to go. None encountered the enemy. But the radio of

---

*Deputy Assistant Adjutant- and Quartermaster-General, the appointment of the principal administrative staff officer of a British or Commonwealth brigade at that time.

the Argylls' left flank company was screened by intermediate ridges as it descended. Colonel Neilson had replaced C Company in this position by A several days previously because the remoteness imposed additional burdens on the occupants. All ammunition, tools and equipment not essential to the final hours had been removed by Korean porters in preparation for abandonment. Even so, the company was obliged to carry considerable weights of reserve ammunition in addition to each personal fighting load.

The orders to cancel the move were sent out on the Argylls' radio command net at 2100. As A Company made no acknowledgement, an officer from battalion headquarters was sent to intercept it but failed, not surprisingly, on what was a very dark night. At 0330 on the morning of the 17th, in heavy rain, the company column reached the head of the jeep track, and at 0400, Major Wilson, the company commander, drove in to report at battalion headquarters. Noting his sodden state, Colonel Neilson told him to rest and dry out in a nearby village until the afternoon. A platoon from C Company was sent to reoccupy temporarily the A Company battle location.

As expected, the ROK police units disintegrated with the withdrawal of the Middlesex leadership; the commander and some of the officers made at once for Taegu. Major Gwyn spent the 17th rounding them up, restoring them in darkness that evening to their former posts. It had been a trying Sunday.

On the 18th and 19th, sensing some change in the British sector, the NKPA increased their shell and mortar fire upon it. Several small enemy patrols felt their way each night along the forward defended localities. In A Company of the Argylls, a larger force attempted to break in, finally concentrating on 1 Platoon, holding a hill peak, one hundred yards by one hundred and fifty, overlooking the river. Its commander, Sergeant J Robertson, very coolly told his little force, alert in their two man slit trenches, to remain completely quiet in the darkness as attempts were made about 0445 to cut a way through his perimeter wire. During this process, considerable small arms fire and grenades came into his position. The North Koreans grew bolder, some standing up to shoot. At the same time, the sky was lightening. At about 5 a.m., on Sgt Robertson's orders, quietly passed, his platoon suddenly responded with an outburst of fire, killing ten of their attackers, driving off the remainder.[8]

During the night of the 19th, Major John Willoughby's D Company of the Middlesex raided the far bank, capturing two prisoners, members of the NKPA 3rd Division. Yet, although North Koreans were evidently on either side of the water in their sector, apart from the 10th Division, their numbers were considerably less than army intelligence had assessed. General Milburn had reached a similar conclusion.

It was clear at I Corps headquarters on the evening of 16th September that neither 5 RCT nor 1st Cavalry Division were going to reach Waegwan for at least 36 hours. General Milburn decided that he would cross the Naktong while these two formations were pushing forward, probably attracting the greater number of NKPA in the vicinity. On the Sunday, 17th September, therefore, he ordered the 24th Division to make a crossing in the area of Hasan-dong, a ferry site seven miles south of Waegwan. It had just been cleared by 5 RCT. By the time General Church, the divisional commander, reconnoitred the river bank, a further suitable site, to the north, was also being cleared. He decided to put two regiments over simultaneously during the night of the 18th. His 21st Infantry Regiment would cross at Kumnan-dong, upstream; the 19th Infantry below at Hasan-dong. But movement problems delayed the plan. The assault boats of the 21st pushed off into the river at 0530 on the 19th September, those of the 19th Infantry at 1600 that afternoon. NKPA shell, mortar and machine-gun fire killed and wounded about one hundred and seventy at the two sites. After an anxious day, particularly at Kumnan-dong, lodgements were made and reinforced during the night. Wheels and tracks began to cross by engineer ferries.

On the 20th, General Milburn placed 27 Brigade under the 24th Division to assist in the exploitation of its crossings.[9] A battalion of 7th Cavalry was to take over the British sector that night.

Unaware of the various changes of plan, Brigadier Coad expected still to be making a river crossing. With very little information, he instructed his units to make ready for a night withdrawal on relief and decided to see the commander of the 19th Infantry Regiment whose headquarters he had discovered. He was looking for up to date information and received an item he had not expected. Briefed on the two river crossings in progress, mention was made of a British move west of the river to capture Songju. These orders were confirmed during the early afternoon at a meeting with General Church. The aim was to open an alternative road to Kumch'on in case of a delay at Waegwan. In any case, he was to protect the left flank of the 24th Division's advance on the main axis. As soon as it arrived on the west bank, the brigade was to be supported by five Sherman tanks, four 105-mm self-propelled guns, and three batteries of 155-mm guns. Coad reckoned that he could begin crossing during the afternoon of the 21st.

Having had, as it were, a rehearsal, the two battalions left their positions quickly and quietly as their reliefs were guided into place. It was a clear, cold night. The Middlesex were the first out. Their only complication had been the withdrawal of a platoon of D Company, left as a foothold on the west bank of the Naktong after their raid. There was also the grave matter of a missing member, Second-Lieutenant Jeffrey Bucknell, the intelligence officer, who had not returned from a reconnaissance.* Several unsuccessful searches had been made for him. The Argylls were inevitably held back by the wait for their left flank company. Each in its own harbour area at last, the battalions were delighted to find a hot breakfast waiting for them.

The forward concentration area of the brigade was close to the river. Vehicles and men were shielded from enemy observation by a long high embankment as they drew into it between 1 and 3 p.m., the Middlesex being the first to arrive. The soldiers sat in groups, smoking and talking while reconnaissances and orders proceeded. In the distance there was the continuous noise of traffic, occasional shouting, and, far off, the rumbling of artillery. Now and again came the distinctive noises of enemy shells or mortar bombs bursting somewhere nearby.

The Middlesex had been in the area for about three quarters of an hour when orders came down to move: they were to cross the river to capture two hill features on the road to Songju. Enemy was holding up an American reconnaissance company there. The Argylls would follow. On such basic information, the private soldiers fastened their webbing belts and braces, slung on their small packs, picked up personal arms and whatever other share they had of the platoon's loads—Bren light machine-gun, light mortar, anti-tank rocket launcher, or the ammunition for these, light radio or telephone and cable—and set off in a long single file, marching towards the ferry.

It was now 4 o'clock in the afternoon. It had been the expectation of General Church and his staff that the lower crossing area would by this time be completely clear of enemy fire, and that the British brigade would pass over the river quickly and easily, the men by footbridge, vehicles on a ferry rigged by the divisional engineers. Certainly, the semicircle of low hills overlooking the crossing site had been cleared of enemy and the pass, 2,000 yards to the west of the bridge, was held by a company of the 19th Infantry Regiment The divisional reconnaissance company had pushed on 2,000 yards beyond the pass towards Songju but had been brought to a halt by shell and anti-tank fire. From a re-entrant in the hills about a mile south of Songju, several guns—two of which were later discovered to be Russian self-propelled 76-mm SU76—fired at

---

*He had gone out alone to reconnoitre a patrol task. His body was later discovered on the river bank.

intervals on the crossing and the area immediately behind. Several pairs of aircraft had attempted to find then during the morning and early afternoon without success. These were the fortunes of war.

Captain John Shipster of the Middlesex noted that:

> At 4 o'clock in the afternoon, the commanding officer, company commanders and platoon commanders, covered by a platoon of A Company, crossed the Naktong by way of a very rickety footbridge. This [original] bridge had been demolished by the Americans earlier in the campaign Since then it had been patched up and its 300 yard length consisted of cement slabs from the old bridge, sections of assault boats and rubber floats, bits of wood and metal and sandbags. On arrival at the far side of the river, this party was carried forward on tanks and armoured personnel carriers to where the US unit was held up. A, B and D Companies followed on foot, carrying what they could.[10]

Shelling killed one and wounded four of those on the footbridge. Otherwise, the marching column of the Middlesex moved unscathed over the pass towards Songju. Lieutenant-Colonel Man aimed to capture the first of the two hill features he had been given as objectives before nightfall but, even though he had taken his officers forward for the necessary reconnaissance, time was against him.

The Argylls, following an hour later, lost two to shellfire on the crossing. Their B Company took over from the Americans holding the pass while the remainder moved to the north side of the road to harbour for the night. What both battalions lacked was their vehicles, support weapons, reserve ammunition and food. Almost all of these items were still on the far bank.

Shelling had slowed the loading and movement of the ferry. It received a direct hit. Repaired, its engine broke down. During darkness, only three jeeps and two tracked carriers were transported over. The B Echelons* and Korean porters of the two battalions, aided by parties sent back from the rifle companies, 3-inch mortar, Vickers machine-gun, signal platoons, drums and pipers, manhandled essential items across the footbridge throughout the night, creating a dump on the west bank.

The battalions' support weapons were vital for operations next day, the 22nd September. The divisional reconnaissance company

---

*Each battalion's transport was divided into three echelons: 'F' Echelon with the fighting element, mostly jeeps and carriers; 'A' immediately behind, including company light trucks; 'B' principally the heavier vehicles including the greater part of the reserve ammunition, rations, petrol, oil and lubricants, spares and stores.

agreed to provide fire support from some of its light Chaffee tanks, but the forward observation officers for the American artillery had not arrived when the Middlesex attack began.

The battalion was roused by its sentries while it was still dark on the 23rd. All had slept fully clothed and with their boots on, glad to be wrapped in a lightweight blanket and groundsheet during the cool night. These latter items were rapidly rolled and strapped on to packs. Darkness and the ferry problems having baulked the capture of their objectives the night before, Colonel Man wished to attack as soon as it was light, daylight being necessary for the direct fire support of the tanks.

Immediately beyond and above the battalion, north of the road to Songju, lay a large feature rising to 1,000 feet. Its crest was about two and a half miles from the southern foot, on to which the Middlesex had encroached the previous night. Half a mile along their route to the top, a round hill at the centre of three spurs offered an outpost to the enemy; and the British sentries below had heard sounds of digging on it through much of the night. The hill feature was called Middlesex Hill, the outpost, Plum Pudding.

Now, with first light, a platoon of B Company, led by the tall figure of 2nd Lieutenant Christopher Lawrence, moved uphill through dwarf fir trees at a smart pace, gratified to hear their 3-inch mortars bombs exploding on Plum Pudding and the steady tack-tack-tack sound of a pair of Vickers machine-guns firing along their right flank. As they drew closer, two tanks began firing for them from the valley floor. This weight of fire, in conjunction with the speed of the platoon's approach, carried them to the edge of the enemy position which they captured by close fighting with small arms and grenades. At once, the remainder of B Company advanced to join them, securing a start line for D, which had been ordered to capture the top of Middlesex hill.

The advance to this objective went at a steadier pace; the distance was greater, the approach steep. Moreover, all prospect of surprise had gone; the enemy in the main hill defences knew well that an attack against them had begun.

Major Willoughby's D Company passed Plum Pudding about 0800. By 0930, the leading platoons were obliged to cross a piece of flat, open ground just below the final steep ascent, part of which came close to the vertical. Reckoning that they would find it difficult to make ready for the assault on this slope, Major Willoughby decided that they should fix bayonets before the climb. This accomplished they entered the open area. Midway, they heard the sound of shells passing close overhead which were soon bursting on their objective, Immediately, this seemed a godsend. But then some of the guns in rear advanced the range so their shells began to fall on the reverse side of the hill. Major Willoughby still could not move forward as a proportion of shellbursts continued immediately above, but he became anxious that some of the North Korean positions below ground might be able to engage them in the open, and he asked Colonel Man on the radio to stop or adjust the fire.

Colonel Man could not control it. The fire was coming from a 155-mm battery behind the Naktong and was being directed by the pilot of a Mosquito light aircraft overhead. He had no means of speaking to the pilot. But after some time a nearby officer of the 24th Division reconnaissance company learned of the problem and said that the tank radios could speak to the Mosquito. Firing was stopped by this means. Supported by the 3-inch mortars, D Company hastened across the remaining open ground to climb the face of the summit.

Breathless, first one, then a second platoon reached the edge of the topmost ring contour, Major Willoughby among them. A number of the enemy slit trenches and their occupants had been hit but about twenty survivors of some forty defenders of the hilltop were still active. Two platoons closed with them, Brens firing to support the riflemen searching out each enemy post. This took them about an hour, Between 11 and half past the report came to battalion headquarters that they were in possession of the top.

Yet Major Willoughby was too experienced a soldier to claim the battle was won. Occasional bursts of machine-gun fire were passing over their heads from the north and north west. Then, the Mosquito pilot had evidently seen targets immediately beyond him. He had an unpleasant feeling that the main NKPA strength lay on the reverse slope of the hill. While he was arranging a reconnaissance, the young platoon commander nearest that slope stood up unwarily on the crest and was immediately shot dead at comparatively close range. Subsequent observation from several points confirmed that there were numerous enemy positions running back from about 150 yards distance to two subordinate crests on spurs 1,000 yards away, north and north west. Although all these were on lower ground, the enemy there were dug in; those attacking them would have to come over the northern crest and out into the open. Moving up as close as he could and occupying a former enemy trench, Major Willoughby discovered that he had lost radio contact with battalion headquarters and the mortars. To gain any covering fire he had to communicate with his only clear link, the foremost two light tanks, who could speak by radio to B

Company of the Middlesex who could speak to battalion head-quarters. Arrangements had to be kept very simple as they inched their way downhill to clear the reverse slopes.

Not for the first time, Major Willoughby reflected thankfully on the spirit of his young conscript soldiers, and their responsiveness. 'They had the amazing idea that I knew how to get them out of every situation!' By 1430 he had made very limited progress and recognised the danger of being counter-attacked at short notice by an enemy almost twice his size. As he was wondering how he could hasten matters, two or three Americans came wriggling over the hillside to join him. They were an artillery observation post.

Within a few minutes, the situation was transformed. Possession of the higher ground was once more an advantage to the Middlesex: Major Willoughby could select and strike at targets without moving his small force into the open. The first round the American lieutenant put down was into the centre of the enemy positions. The whole medium battery under his instructions then fired three rounds from each of its guns on this range and bearing, doing considerable damage Next, the entrenched machine-guns on the distant spurs were silenced. One by one, the remaining strong points were picked off, D Company closing up to clear those nearest to them. Fifty minutes after the arrival of the first shell, the North Koreans streamed off the hill. Sixty dead were counted in their positions. D Company had lost five killed, seven wounded, one mortally. Even though the enemy seemed to have disappeared, Major Willoughby asked for reinforcements for the night. Colonel Man sent him A Company. It was just as well. Next day the North Koreans tried to retake the feature, somewhat indecisively, and were quickly thrown back. This was a happier outcome to their operation than that of the Argylls across the other side of the valley.[11]

The advance to Songju was held up by enemy positions both left and right of the road. Middlesex Hill was on the right. On the left, across a narrow section of the valley, was Song-san, rising to almost 1,300 feet—marked as 390 metres on the map—with a subsidiary, Point 282, about one mile north east, a height overlooking the road. Reviewing the ground on 22nd September and better informed as to the enemy strength in the area, Brigadier Coad decided against his first, more ambitious plan for breaking the opposition and reaching Songju that day. Meeting Lieutenant-Colonel Neilson about midday, they considered outflanking Song-san by a western loop, but the route of such a march would extend them into equally broken country under enemy observation. The idea was therefore abandoned. With limited means, Brigadier Coad decided to capture Point 282, for this was in range of the weapons they had to hand. It was agreed that Point 390* would have to be cleared thereafter provided that they had American artillery support. The fire control teams for the guns had not then arrived. Waiting on the conclusion of the Middlesex attack, Colonel Neilson decided that he would facilitate his own by capturing a low intermediate feature, rising to Point 148.[12]

Feeling somewhat naked in front of the enemy observation posts on Song-san, A Company set off at 1430 to this end, surviving inaccurate though occasionally close shelling. Major Wilson, the company commander, had all the battalion's support weapons covering him and was further comforted, as they ascended the eastern end of the ridge, by an arrangement he had made with the commander of a troop of tanks, an American master-sergeant. The five Shermans,[†] dispersed among nearby hillocks, would give him covering fire on to the objective. He had loaned this friendly non-commissioned officer one of his radios so that they might speak directly as circumstances demanded. By 4 p.m., supported generously by the tanks' guns, Major Wilson and his three platoons were in occupation of Point 148 and its outcrops without losing a man, a small party of North Koreans having withdrawn ahead of them.[13]

This event ran concurrently with the final stages of the battle for Middlesex Hill. The American artillery observer teams had joined the Argylls—as also the Middlesex—and had completed arrangements to support the attack on Point 282. But in view of the strength encountered by Major Willoughby, Brigadier Coad did not want the Argylls struggling for the high ground as darkness fell. He postponed the attack until the morning of the 23rd.[14]

The Argylls used the following hours of darkness for their preparations. The 3-inch mortars were brought forward into pits newly dug behind A Company. Advanced positions were made by the Vickers machine-guns on the flanks. A few more vehicles had trickled across the Naktong—the ferry site was still under random fire—and together with two tracked vehicles loaned by the American reconnaissance company, the quartermaster and regimental sergeant-major completed the delivery of the battalion's ammunition reserve. B and C Companies settled themselves by midnight in the area immediately behind A. Covering and carrying, digging and deploying, occupied much of the night; but most of the battalion managed several hours sleep. At 0400 those resting were wakened.

---

*Shown on some maps as Point 388 or 389.
†It is probable that these were the five Shermans allocated to 27 Brigade by 24th Division for the advance to Songju, but the master-sergeant had received no orders to this effect.

Colonel Neilson established his headquarters on the eastern end of A Company's ridge. B and C Companies shook out and drew towards their start line, a track in the valley overlooked by A Company, facing north west the spurs leading up to Point 282. All was quiet on this still morning. Delayed for a few minutes in gathering a platoon which strayed in the darkness, they crossed the track at 0520, C Company on the left of B, passed over dry rice paddy, and began the ascent to their objective, roughly a mile distant.

When they were about halfway up, there were several bursts of fire from above—probably a response to noises in the dark. However, they caused the advancing columns to stop briefly, and when the advance resumed a platoon from each company inadvertently crossed the other in the gloom.

In twilight, at about 0550, the leading platoons of B Company reached an open stretch just below the final ridge. Turning right, they surprised an enemy position. A number of North Korean soldiers were eating their breakfast in the open. Surprised themselves, the Argylls had the advantage of being ready for action, opening fire quickly, killing those who stood to fight. They guessed that they had wounded some of those who ran off because they were seen to fall and be dragged away by others. Perhaps warned by this commotion, a second enemy position, passed unwittingly in the shadows, fired on two of the B Company platoons, obliging them to work back to clear it. At 0618, Major A I Gordon-Ingram, the company commander, reported that they had captured Point 282. They had killed fifteen North Koreans and cleared them from their route and objective. He had lost one killed and five wounded, amongst them two of his platoon commanders.

C Company under Major J M Gillies arrived at 0630, short of a platoon which was found to have joined B Company. The two majors agreed that 'Baker' Ridge, which included Point 282, would be held by four platoons; C Company would hold on 'Charlie' Ridge, behind and to the left, with two. Some men were instructed to dig slit trenches, others concentrated the casualties in a sheltered site. Evacuation was going to be a problem because the hillsides were too steep for the use of stretchers. The only effective method of carrying down the deadweight of a man was in a groundsheet, and this required four soldiers. A request was sent to battalion headquarters for bearers and a resupply of first aid equipment, particularly morphine syrettes. While this was in hand, Colonel Neilson ordered Major Gillies to advance to capture Point 390 and the ridge on which it stood, 2,000 yards distant across an intermediate saddle, as soon as basic defence work was completed against counter-attack, and the artillery plan was finalised. It was 0815.

Battalion headquarters had moved to Point 148. A Company had stood down for a wash and breakfast. A few minutes later, what appeared to be a desultory mortar fire fell upon the hilltop Argylls. It was almost certainly ranging fire. At 0830, there were mortar bursts in concentrations. Thanks to their trenches, casualties were limited.

Meantime, Major Kenneth Muir had found himself something to do. His role as the battalion second-in-command in operations was—as it is now—an unrewarding one: to be ready to replace the commanding officer if he should fall sick, be wounded or killed; otherwise he must stand to one side until and unless some temporary, extraordinary task should arise for him, a rare occurrence. Many a red blooded second-in-command has secretly wished that his colonel would be removed by a painless, briefly incapacitating wound so that he might have his hands on the wheel for a few glorious days.

At battalion headquarters, Major Muir saw an option for employment, albeit humble. The carrier party sent forward to bring back the B and C Company wounded had lost its way and been told to return. He suggested to Colonel Neilson that he should take charge of a second group forming up to replace them. They reached Point 282 at 0900.

By this time, enemy guns as well as mortars were firing on the positions. The American artillery observation parties were trying to get a Mosquito up to find the guns but, in the hope of destroying their observation posts, were shelling Point 390. The total of Argyll wounded had grown to almost thirty, too many for the bearers under Major Muir. Some of C Company were detached to assist them. Recovering the casualties to the collection point took some time because of the intermittent fire, but this was completed by 1000. However, in the hour since Major Muir had arrived, the whole battalion had become threatened.

Just after half past nine, brigade headquarters was informed by 24th Division headquarters that its artillery support was being withdrawn. Only one of the batteries originally offered had been made available and this was now required elsewhere. When Major Douglas Reith, the brigade major, protested, he was reassured by a divisional staff officer that the guns would remain until reliefs could be found. In fact, the battery was already moving and at 0945 the observation parties were returning to the Naktong crossing. Thereafter, there were no weapons in support which had the range to reach Point 390 or the routes from it towards 282.

At 1000, the foremost platoon of C Company—part of the Baker Ridge defences—reported that a small party was approaching through the scrub. The platoon commander said that he was waiting until they were closer so that he could see the enemy clearly before opening fire. North Korean mortar and shellfire began to increase once more after a lull. Below the hill, A Company observed enemy parties coming from the west and south west. Soon they were involved in a struggle to hold on to Point 148. Colonel Neilson's third rifle company was no longer a reserve in his hand.

At 1045, a much larger force than expected drew upon the C Company outpost, 'the scrub is full of them' came over the radio. The battalion 3-inch mortars fired into this location while two sections from B Company reinforced the platoon. The two Brens they carried helped to rebuff the attack, but other North Korean groups were working their way round the left flank. When the platoon officer and sergeant were wounded Major Muir had the platoon withdrawn into the Baker Ridge perimeter. Using B Company radio, he spoke to Colonel Neilson, proposing that he should take command of the hilltop defences in which the two companies were becoming increasingly intermixed. He was confident that they could hold Point 282, given ammunition resupply, but they were sitting targets for the enemy artillery and mortars. Without fire support beyond their immediate defences, they had no potential for offensive action.

The colonel at once agreed that Major Muir should take command on the hill, and informed him that he had asked for an air strike on and immediately around Point 390. Ammunition would be brought up by the C Company men who had helped to carry down the wounded. Shortly after this, the news came that three Mustangs would make air strikes about noon.

Still subject to shell and mortar fire at intervals, the hilltop force waited. Major Gordon-Ingram with B Company and the much reduced forward platoon of C continued to hold the Point 282 area, Baker Ridge. Major Gillies was commanding the remaining twenty five of his company, covering the rear. They had placed out the white panels used to indicate the presence of friendly troops to aircraft.

A Mosquito came overhead about noon. The Argyll battalion headquarters had no means of talking to the pilot but were reassured by its arrival: full map references had been sent with the request for air support and it was evidently observing Song-san. Unknown to them, an air contact team had arrived to control the strike, though the officer with it had selected an observation site some distance in rear. The three Mustangs came overhead at 1215 and began to circle Song-san, apparently looking over the ground. Then, in single file, the aircraft ran in towards the hilltop, releasing napalm tanks and firing their guns. But these weapons did not hit the area of 390. They fell upon 282. Baker Ridge was suddenly covered in flames and black smoke. The Mustangs returned. Major Muir stood up, waving a panel at the leading pilot but they fired rockets into Baker Ridge, pulled away and, in a final pass, attacked A Company below.

All this happened very quickly. The Mustangs probably left the area by 1220, certainly by 1225. On the hill, some of the wounded had been killed. There were many newly wounded. Some managed to walk back to the collecting point. Those gravely burned were the most difficult to lift down the hillside to the regimental aid post. A small party took up positions on the foremost part of Charlie Ridge: Major Muir, Major Gordon-Ingram, Captain Penman, Company Sergeant-Major Collett and about six soldiers.

Looking forward to Baker Ridge, they saw the petroleum flames subsiding, and saw also one small outcrop which was being approached by a party of enemy. They were being fired on by a lone rifleman, Private Watts, who had somehow survived. As long as he was active, the ridge was in Argyll hands.

Calling to Major Gillies for covering fire, Major Muir drew in a scattered number behind to join his group and led them all forward, cheering, to join Watts. The North Korean sortie was driven back, but small arms fire from three widely separated points in the scrub to the west and south west indicated the presence of others.

Major Muir reported the recovery of the hilltop. Colonel Neilson gave him authority to stand or withdraw at his discretion in the event of another enemy attack. But his second-in-command was in no mind to give up the ground. C Company had been strengthened by returning bearers. They went scavenging for weapons and ammunition with the dead or in abandoned positions.

Suddenly, as North Korean soldiers were glimpsed moving towards them through several patches of scrub, there was a storm of small arms fire. Every defender found a weapon to use. Major Muir and Major Gordon-Ingram manned a light mortar. A burst of automatic fire hit Major Muir, knocking him to one side, mortally wounded.

The accuracy of the Argyll's fire and the support of the 3–inch mortars below again drove the enemy back. Major Gordon-Ingram found that he had ten comrades fit to fight, though some were wounded, three Bren light machine-guns and ammunition for a magazine apiece. Covered by two of these, he drew the remainder back to Charlie Ridge. They dragged with them those who could not walk. He found Major Gillies with about the same strength. On the radio, he asked Colonel Neilson's permission to withdraw and for as many carrying parties as could be mustered to bring down the remaining casualties. The answer was that forty or fifty were on their way. Battalion headquarters had been stripped out, drivers, clerks and pipers, the adjutant and intelligence officer, and eager helpers from the Middlesex were just then approaching the hilltop. The Middlesex regimental aid post was treating casualties in parallel with that of the Argylls.

It was a deliberate withdrawal, not a rout. The area was searched for anyone left alive. There were none. Major Gordon-Ingram's party then withdrew covered by those with Major Gillies. During the late afternoon, when company rolls had been checked, it seemed that their losses had been about ninety.* Reorganised on the basis of two rifle companies, 1st Battalion, The Argyll and Sutherland Highlanders settled for the night round Point 148, ready for whatever was required next day.[15]

.   .   .   .   .

That evening, 23rd September, Brigadier Coad drove to divisional headquarters to see General Church. Expecting to continue operations on the 24th, he asked for artillery support, but the general said he had none to spare: every gun was needed to maintain the advance towards Kumch'on on the main axis. A platoon of heavy mortars might be available.

General Walker was present during this meeting. He and Coad had met on the road and a full account of 27 Brigade's experiences had been told. 'When I left the headquarters, I felt more confident, in spite of General Church's unhelpful attitude, because General Walker intervened several times to say, "Well, we must look at that," when we were talking about fire support. Anyway, next day, we were sent a battery of anti-aircraft guns [for use in the ground role], better than nothing. I am sure we owed that to General Walker.'[16]

What the brigadier did not know was that General Walker had signalled details of the disastrous air strike on the Argylls to General MacArthur, and had asked the 5th Air Force for an explanation. The result was a visit on the 25th by Air Vice-Marshal Bouchier and the chief of staff of the 5th Air Force, the first of many senior officers and officials who came to hear a first hand report of the accident.

Air Marshal Bouchier's account, hastily scribbled as he journeyed, signalled to the Chiefs on 26th September, concluded,

---

*Actual losses were: 13 killed/died of wounds, including Major Muir; 73 wounded (with an additional soldier wounded on the Naktong crossing). The battalion was unable immediately to certify the casualty list because several men were 'missing', and the practice was to wait 72 hours before officially declaring an individual to be in this category. For example, two men, believed missing, made their way back off the hill on the 24th. Major Muir was later awarded the Victoria Cross.

13. Spoke to General Partridge in Taegu yesterday about accident. He is conducting investigations. From his remarks it appears to me, firstly, that American Fighter Calculation Control Team were not close enough up to battalion on the hill crest because they could not get across a small river . . . secondly, some confusion, possibly caused by the fact that spotter aircraft had different scale of map to that used by Ground Control Team; thirdly, accident appears to have been caused mainly by officer of Ground Control Team making a mistake in hill crest which was required to be attacked in spite of the fact that spotter pilot in the air reported back that the hill crest ordered by ground Control to be attacked was clearly showing the right ground recognition signals and that friendly troops appeared to be in occupation of it. After the aircraft in the air had been told by Ground Control that enemy often copied our ground signals and hill crest in question was the one to be attacked, it appeared that the aircraft finally attacked our positions. American officer-in-charge of Ground Control was immediately replaced and I assume appropriate action will be taken after completion of American investigation.

14. General Partridge and Walker have expressed personally their . . . condolences to Brigadier Coad also the American Minister* to the British Ambassador here. I tried to suppress original press release knowing it would probably be exaggerated and sensational in the home press, but it had been released before I even heard of the accident. Everyone in high places here deeply sorry and concerned about it and greatly appreciative of attitude I thought you would wish me to adopt in the circumstances.[17]

Next day, in his situation report, he added,

13. British Brigade continues to secure the Songju area south west of Waegwan where there are numerous pockets of enemy by-passed and dug in on high hills that area. Brigade are in great heart and have taken accidental bombing of their positions without turning a hair.

14. I am repeatedly pressed by FARELF [Far East Land Forces] to send back direct to Adjutant General at War Office names of Highlanders killed or wounded by American accidental bombing of them because British Press is stated to be likely to publish radio photographs of the men of the Highlanders who were casualties in this incident. If possible, suggest War Office veto

---

*Ambassador William J Sebald, the United States diplomatic representative at General MacArthur's headquarters.

publication of all photographs and names until War Office is officially notified of names and release is made to the Press by the War Office.

15. I am replying to FARELF'S most urgent signals to me for release of this information that it is impossible for casualties of "missing" to be forwarded to them or anyone else until . . . missing for 72 hours. Moreover, the Brigade find it extremely difficult to separate casualties to Highlanders on 23rd September as between those resulting from 2 assaults on hill crest and Highlanders subsequent withdrawal from it and the casualties which resulted from actual accidental bombing.

16. In any case I strongly suggest that casualties resulting from the bombing should be classified as having been caused in action with the enemy, some as result of accidental bombing. It is invidious and unnecessary and unkind I suggest to publish, in any form, the names of those who died and went missing and were wounded solely as a result of accidental bombing . . .[18]

The Chiefs replied on the 27th September,

We are very concerned at delay between occurrence of casualties of 27 Inf Bde and receipt of names by War Office. For example, by evening 26th September War Office had not received names of casualties sustained by the Argyll and Sutherland Highlanders as result of bombing attack on 23rd September. As incident was given great publicity and, indeed, a radio photograph of wounded appeared in Press on 26th September, inability of War Office to inform next of kin has given rise to considerable criticism and naturally caused distress to relatives.

2. Understand from C-in-C FARELF that American military authorities have refused to allow opening of special wireless link between 27 Inf Bde and Hong Kong, which was sent for the particular purpose of reporting casualties.

3. You should represent to General MacArthur importance of our point of view of getting quick notification of casualties, particularly as there is no censorship in Korea which can hold up Press reports, and press for authority to be given to 27 Bde to open immediately direct wireless link to Hong Kong.*

4. We entirely endorse attitude you have adopted over this incident and agree proposal . . . to report casualties as "killed in action".[19]

---

*As a line of argument to secure agreement to the opening of the direct radio link to Hong Kong, the C-in-C FARELF advised Air Vice-Marshal Bouchier of the arrangements during the Italian campaign in 1944–45, when a large number of such links had been operated without serious complications.[20]

By the end of the month, the radio truck to provide direct communication to Hong Kong was in Korea and operating. The Chiefs of Staff were not wholly correct in saying that it had been provided 'for the particular purpose of reporting casualties'; General Harding had sent it because he was acutely aware of 27 Brigade's isolation. The first foreign force to arrive in Korea, other than the Americans with their immense administrative and communications presence in the theatre, they were waifs in a far country. No doubt their families and the authorities needed to know details urgently of casualties, but the brigade needed immediate access to their home base for other important reasons, spare parts or supplies urgently required, for example, without having to send for these through one or more signal relays.

The attack on the Argylls brought the matter of a direct signal link to a head, the one fortunate outcome of this unhappy incident. But whilst the grievous mistake of their ally continued to occupy high military and political circles for some days thereafter, Air Vice-Marshal Bouchier was not far wrong in saying that the British force had accepted it 'without turning a hair'. During the following day it was a recurrent topic of heated conversation among all ranks; yet the feeling passed quickly. Though they would not forget it, they could forgive it. What angered the more senior officers, principally the commanding officers and the brigade commander, was the abrupt and thoughtless withdrawal of artillery support while they were engaged closely with a strong North Korean force known to include guns of its own. Clearly, the opening and exploitation of the main axis was a first priority for the 24th Division, but this was not threatened when the guns were ordered away. From this time onward, Brigadier Coad never trusted General Church again, and dreaded the prospect of being placed under command of the 24th Division.

He was gratified, therefore, on the day following the Argylls' action, to revert to direct command of I Corps, and this arrangement continued when 27 Brigade began to move forward warily on 25th September towards Songju. It was understood that they would link up with the 19th Infantry Regiment in or around the town, on which the latter were advancing from the north west. Mines were encountered—several brigade headquarters vehicles were destroyed—but the majority were either spotted and lifted or destroyed by fire from the Shermans of the friendly master-sergeant.

The British task during these last days of September was to protect the left flank of I Corps as its divisions pushed ahead with increasing speed. The North Korean line had been broken open. Evidence came to hand that they had been fighting the 10th Mechanised Division with elements of the 3rd and 7th Divisions.

Stragglers were rounded up by the Middlesex and Argylls, deserters came in of their own accord. Many of the survivors of these last battles, however, put on civilian clothes to escape, either to their homes in South Korea from which they had volunteered or been levied, or to pass through the hills to the north. Combing out an extensive area of territory, the British companies also discovered considerable stocks of serviceable small arms, artillery, ammunition and equipment, some dug into caches which were disclosed by local villagers. The enemy defeat in this area at least was not due to a lack of the means to resist.

Reinforcements began to arrive: on the 28th a draft from all the Highland regiments joined the Argylls; on 1st October, a company from The Queen's Regiment in Germany became part of 1 Middlesex. These additions were very welcome but could not compare in weight with the appearance of the 3rd Battalion, The Royal Australian Regiment. A force of volunteers, it was eager for action. Its officers and men had a professional look about them. Most importantly, they provided that third fighting element without which a brigade's potential is continually constrained. On his own initiative, Brigadier Coad informed I Corps headquarters that the title of his formation was, with immediate effect, to be 27th British Commonwealth Infantry Brigade.

SOURCE NOTES: CHAPTER 8

1. US Army Allied Translator and Interpreter Section (ATIS) Research Supplement Interrogation Reports, Issue 104 (North Korean 10th Division), pp 44–45, (US National Archives, Suitland)

2. Ibid, Issue 96 (North Korean 3rd Division), and 104, p 46.

3. *History of the North Korean Army*, cit, p 69.

4. Coad, personal notes and conversation with author.

5. Ibid, Coad Report, cit, p 4., and war diary, 27th Infantry Brigade, 13 September 1950.

6. Coad Report.

7. Coad, personal notes and conversation with author.

8. Conversation with Major (now Brigadier) A R D G Wilson, and war diary, 1 A&SH.

9. Coad's report and war diaries 1 MX and 1 A&SH. These conflict with Appleman, op cit, p 556. The former are correct as to the date.

10. Shipster, op cit, p 11.

11. Major (now Major-General Sir John) Willoughby, Lieutenant-Colonel (now Colonel) A M Man, Coad, conversations with author.

12. Coad, and Wilson, conversations with author, and war diary 1 A&SH. There is a conflict over timings.

13. Wilson, conversation with author, and war diary, 1 A&SH.

14. Coad, conversation with author, and war diary, 1 A&SH.

15. Conversation with Coad, Captain John (now Colonel, the Viscount) Slim, 2Lt (now Lieutenant-General Sir Alexander) Boswell, Wilson, and war diaries, 1 A&SH, 27 Brigade, and US I Corps, including report of Lt Col Thomas C Gillies, and FEAF Operational History, Vol I, US Air Force Historical Archives, Washington DC.

16. Coad, personal notes and conversation with author.

17. DEFE 11/201 Tokyo (Bouchier) CAB 59 to MOD (Chiefs of Staff) of 261043 September 1950.

18. Ibid, Tokyo (Bouchier) CAB 61 to MOD (Chiefs of Staff) of 271442 September 1950.

19. Ibid, MOD (Chiefs of Staff) TOK 22 to Tokyo (Bouchier) of 271132A September 1950.

20. Ibid, Note by VCIGS reporting on British Army Casualties in Korea, Annex to COS(50)157 of 27th September 1950.

16. 1 Middlesex moving into Naktong river positions, 3rd September 1950.
(Major B Reed)

17. View of Naktong river from 27 Brigade positions, September 1950.
(Major B Reed)

18. Naktong river positions of A Company, 1 Middlesex, September 1950.
(Major B Reed)

19. HMAS *Bataan* and HMS *Kenya* oiling from RFA *Wave Prince* before the
Inch'on landing. (C D Christmas Esq)

20. The support line at Inch'on. (C D Christmas Esq)

21. Approaching Inch'on. (Ken Cox Esq)

22. Inch'on as seen by an aircraft of HMS *Triumph* on the date of landing.
(C D Christmas Esq)

23. Royal Air Force Sunderlands at their Iwakuni base. (Royal Air Force
Official Photograph)

24. Major Kenneth Muir, VC, The Argyll and Sutherland Highlanders.
(Argyll and Sutherland Highlanders Museum)

25. A Korean peasant coming into Waegwan after the battle.
(Lt Col H R Jeffes)

26a–b. Bringing wounded Argylls down from Point 282. (Associated Press)

26c.   An Argyll & Sutherland piper brightens the march south from Kunu-ri,
        November 1950. (Argyll and Sutherland Highlanders Museum)

26d.   A Company, 1 A&SH, attack south of Sariwon, 17th October 1950.
        (Associated Press)

27.   At Kimpo airfield—'The officers' mess'. (Major B Reed)

28.   At Kimpo airfield—'The other ranks dining hall'. (Major B Reed)

CHAPTER 9

War of Words

In the high summer and early autumn of 1950, General Walker and his soldiers might have been forgiven for thinking that the world outside Korea was in suspense, awaiting the outcome of their struggle. Of course, it was not so. The Korean war was merely another ball in the air with which the jugglers in government had to cope. For Britain, productivity, the strength of the pound, its involvement in an incipient European Economic Community, the development of NATO as a defence against the Russian threat, were among the policy pieces requiring continuous attention. At home, despite popular support for the Prime Minister personally, there were continuing signs that the 'floating voter' was coming to associate the Labour administration with restraint and restriction as a matter of philosophy rather than expediency.*

The Korean war was not an item which could be dealt with at discretion, however. The Soviet Union retained a number of political as well as military options in its conduct. On 28th July, Tass reported,

> Members of the Security Council again assembling July 28 . . . Speakers limited themselves to short remarks in which they obligingly approved Austin's† report. After statements [by] representatives of France, England [sic], Cuba, India and Ecuador, President Sunde‡ closed meeting and set new meeting for July 31. This decision of Sunde provided delegates of Anglo-American *bloc* with opportunity to continue hurried behind-scenes negotiations and hold new meeting before representative of USSR Malik occupies post of Presidency on August 1 when turn of representative of Soviet Union to preside in Security Council begins§.

---

*The Party, divided broadly between those who wished to consolidate on achievements and those who wished to advance from them, collectively recognised the need for a new manifesto. The National Executive Committee met in July to discuss ideas.

†Austin, Warren Robinson (1877–1962) (Senator), US Representative to UN 1947–1953.

‡Sunde, Arne (1883–1972) Norwegian Representative to the UN.

§UN Security Council rules of procedure provide that the Presidency 'shall be held in turn by members in the English alphabetical order of their names for one calendar month'. (Chapter IV, Rule 18).

By this oblique means, the United Nations membership was acquainted with the news that Russia intended to resume its seat among them.

On 31st July, the Council voted on a joint French-Norwegian-United Kingdom resolution to provide aid to Korean refugees,[1] and then considered a draft put before it by Senator Austin, the United States delegate:

> The Security Council:
> Condemns the North Korean authorities for their continued defiance of the United Nations;
> Calls upon all States to use their influence to prevail upon the authorities of North Korea to cease this defiance;
> Calls upon all States to refrain from assisting or encouraging the North Korean authorities and to refrain from action which might lead to the spread of the Korean conflict to other areas and thereby further endanger international peace and security.

No call was made to vote on this proposal at once. The United States asked simply that it should be placed on the agenda for the next meeting.[2] Out of session, as *Tass* had predicted, the 'Anglo-American *bloc*' came together. Sir Gladwyn Jebb sent this telegram to London:

> After Security Council meeting today it was announced that Malik's agenda for meeting tomorrow would contain two items:
> (1) Recognition of the representative of the Central People's Government of China as the representative of China.
> (2) Peaceful settlement of the Korean question.
> 2. We had a long meeting with French, Norwegian and United States delegations to discuss tactics at tomorrow's meeting. We all agreed that Malik's proposed agenda was not acceptable since it was clearly designed to link the question of Chinese representation with that of Korea. It appeared that his object was to make a proposal on the lines of that made by Stalin to Nehru and Gromyko to Kelly. The main discussion was on whether we should attempt to get an early vote to amend agenda or to alter the order of the items or whether we should (group undeciphered) a debate on the adoption of the agenda itself. I suggested that from publicity point of view it would be best for Senator Austin to make a strong statement on the adoption of the agenda in which he would insist on the separation of Chinese representation from Korea and on necessity for the Council to deal with Korea first and consequently with United States motion tabled at this afternoon's meeting. Malik would presumably

reply and in doing so reveal his hand. Debate might well last until 6 p.m. when the meeting could be adjourned without any decision being reached or the agenda being adopted. We should then be in a position to consult our governments in the light of Malik's statement.

3. After consultation with State Department, Gross agreed in general with this procedure. He said that from their own point of view United States Government would not be sorry to see a vote taken on the question of Chinese representation at tomorrow's meeting since the vote would presumably confirm the decision reached last January. . . . State Department were however concerned lest postponement of Chinese representation question for a definite period of say three days might lead to undesirable press speculation. They hoped therefore that if there were postponement the reason for it should be clearly stated namely that the question of aggression in Korea must be dealt with first.

4. Only point on which there is still some lack of agreement is on the manner in which tomorrow's meeting should terminate. State Department at present feel that there should be a vote to reverse order of Malik's two items and to place the item on peaceful settlement of the Korean question under the existing Korean Item, which is now before the Security Council. I think this would be a mistake because it might give Malik the opportunity of walking out of the Council before we have had time to consider his statement and after all we cannot say in advance whether it will be wholly unacceptable or not.[3]

A telegram from the Foreign Office crossed with this.[4] Mr Bevin, back in office from his convalescence at Eastbourne, apprehended that the American proposal was weaker than that passed in late June and the first part of July and that, seeking now to condemn North Korea again and isolate it, was not only unnecessary but also offered the Soviet Union a chance to exercise its veto. A second aspect was that calls to 'refrain from action which might lead to the spread of the Korean conflict to other areas and thereby further endanger international peace and security' might provide a basis for accusations of American interference in Taiwan. Still, Mr Bevin accepted that this was not an issue on which to divide with the Americans. He was more concerned that they should be ready to counter any propaganda line which might be followed. Late on the 31st, the following had also been sent to Sir Gladwyn Jebb:

Judging from trend of Soviet propaganda (and excluding the obvious) Malik is quite likely to take the line:

(A) that the Council's decisions on Korea were taken on the United Nations Commission on Korea's reports which were themselves based only on information provided by government of Korean Republic*.

(B) that American action in Korea is part of general American aggression against Asia which must be expected to spread to China, Persia etc., (and has already done so as far as Formosa is concerned). He may also refer to Stalin's reply to Nehru (and imply that freedom-loving peoples of the world support the line taken by Russia, China, India).

2. With regard to (A), preparations for aggression by North Korea against the Republic [of Korea] can effectively be traced back to formation of National Front in June, 1949, from which point the agitation and propaganda for 'unification' was built up to a high pitch, including the provocation of UNCOK just before the outbreak of hostilities. It was during this period that sabotage squads and partisans began to be organised and were referred to in North Korean propaganda as 'springing up' spontaneously. My immediately following telegram [No 901, not shown here] contains extracts from North Korean broadcasts illustrating the aggressive intentions of North Korean Government and on inadequacy of South Korean forces even for the maintenance of public order (which gives lie to Communist allegations of Korean Republic's intentions). Note also that Communist propaganda concentrates mainly on UNCOK's first report: you may therefore like to refer to the others.

3. In connexion with (B), it is important to bring out Asian and particularly Indian Government's support for the Security Council's verdict and action. We must not let the Russians manoeuvre us into a position of opposition to Asia generally. You may find an opportunity to remind the Council that the Asian delegates on UNCOK, including the Indian, helped to draw up that Commission's report.

4. Malik may or may not refer explicitly to the Partisans of Peace†. You can doubtless develop a general case. It seems to

---

*This was an erroneous belief. Actually, the United States Embassy in Seoul was informed of the invasion by KMAG officers with the forward ROK divisions. This information was passed *inter alia* to UNCOK.

†Partisans of Peace were an agency of the immense propaganda operation organised by the Soviet Union and supported by national communist parties throughout the world to prevent the formation of the Atlantic Alliance and NATO. A number of eminent people from Europe and North America who were neither Marxists nor members of the communist party led others unwittingly into a 'front' as the Partisans, from which sprang a 'world congress' in Paris, in April 1949, on a spurious basis of national delegacy. Similar to the Popular Front of the 1930s, the World Peace Movement was later used to promote the Stockholm Peace Appeal of 1950.

us important *not* to contrast peace propaganda with aggression in Korea, but to treat them as two sides to the same medal, the Peace Offensive being exploited to prevent others from coming to the aid of North Korea's victim.

5. Specifically you may find the following two points useful:

(1) the Partisans of Peace Propaganda organisation is being used now not in support of the action taken by the whole machinery for the maintenance of peace represented by the United Nations, but to frustrate it; and

(2) it is being used actually to incite dock workers not to transport arms in implementation of that peace making organisation's decisions.

6. My second immediately following telegram [No. 902, not shown here] contains extract from Soviet History of Diplomacy published in 1945, in which the Soviet authorities described in penetrating terms the purpose of a Peace Offensive such as they are running.[5]

The 1st of August 1950 was a Tuesday. When the Security Council met at 3 p.m. on that day it at once became evident that the Russian President intended to be combative. 'Before adoption of agenda,' Sir Gladwyn Jebb reported that evening, Mr Malik 'ruled that the representative of Kuomintang group was not representative of China and could not therefore participate in meetings of Council . . .'[6] India and Yugoslavia assented. The United States, United Kingdom, France and Norway argued that the ruling was invalid. They were supported by Egypt, Cuba and Ecuador. The vote against the chair was therefore 7 to 3.

Mr Malik then, in Sir Gladwyn's words, 'attempted to declare agenda adopted', namely:

(1) Discussion of the representative of the Central People's Government of China as the representative of China.

(2) Peaceful settlement of the Korean question.

The advantage of the United States' reserved resolution was now employed:

15. . . . Austin at once intervened. He said that he noticed agenda did not contain item which the Council had been discussing at its last meeting. Rules required that unfinished business should be placed on agenda. There was a United States resolution pending and council's understanding had been that it would be discussed at today's meeting. He also objected to inclusion in today's agenda of Chinese representation issue.

United Nations had devoted great attention to Korea and had sent army into field there. All other issues were secondary and no delay or diversion should be allowed. It was highly inappropriate for the Council to concern itself with this other question which was not linked in any way with the Korean problem. Agenda as at present drafted might create impression that the two issues were linked together. That impression must be removed . . . .[7]

These two matters, the Chinese seat in the Security Council and the securing of a cease fire in Korea, were to occupy the Council throughout August without being resolved.

As regards China, the British government maintained its view that Generalissimo Chiang Kai-shek's authority was valid only in Taiwan and certain off-shore islands, and that Mao Tse-tung's government effectively ruled the mainland of China. On what Sir Oliver Franks was to describe as 'a difficult day in Anglo-American friendship', the British vote was cast on 3rd August with Russia, India, Norway and Yugoslavia in favour of including discussion of Peking's claim on the agenda. It was largely a gesture. The Foreign Office was aware that five votes would be against the motion, those of the United States, [Kuomintang] China, Cuba, Ecuador, and France. As expected, Egypt abstained. But it was made clear that the United Kingdom had not shifted from the view that the issue was wholly unconnected with Korea and should be discussed after the Korean item. Attempts by Mr. Malik to invite China to join the Council for discussion of the war issue were vigorously opposed by Britain.[8]

When the Council considered Korea, the Russian proposal was to summon delegations from both North and South Korea. The objection to this was that the Council had already declined to accept representations from the former until the NKPA had been withdrawn behind the 38th Parallel. Any change from this position might be construed as weakening the Security Council's resolution of 25th June; and certainly would not speed a cease fire, so much desired by the ROK and United States forces through the difficult days of August when the defensive perimeter seemed close to collapse. The Republic of Korea had a constitutional right under Article 32 of the Charter to a place at the table when aggression against it was being discussed.

Throughout the month, Mr Malik sought by aggression, sophistry and abuse of the Council's rules of procedure to invalidate or override the Council's resolution of 25th June. Whether by chance or purpose, these methods, which prevented any progress in the negotiations, enraged the United States delegation and some of its associates in the State Department in Washington. There was talk among them of the need for exceptional measures, formally naming Russia as the aggressors in Korea, or the 'impeachment' of Malik for the misuse of the presidency. Sir Oliver Franks discussed their frustration during informal meetings with Mr Acheson; and both men agreed that they had to avoid impulsive reactions. Britain and America, France and Norway, were anxious to avoid giving the Russians the opportunity to use their veto on a substantive motion which would negate or reduce the scope of the United Nations intervention in Korea. They were anxious to deny Russia the opportunity to withdraw once more, a tactic which, hindsight suggests, the Russians were unlikely to adopt. Occasional private discussion out of committee brought no progress. An Indian initiative to form a sub-committee of the Council's non-permanent members to seek solutions came to nothing—the Foreign Office and state department kept closely in touch on this matter, as did their representatives in New Delhi.

By the middle of August, Malik had achieved this if nothing else: his opponents had negated every proposal he had made without putting forward any new ideas of their own. Russian propaganda made much of this but its effect was less than the United States and United Kingdom feared; to an extent because the rationale was flawed but principally because the general public in western Europe and North America was simply not interested in fine debating points at Lake Success. It was scarcely more acceptable in India and hence to much of Asia. The Indian external affairs ministry suggested that the best course would be to talk out the period of Russia's presidency. Britain and, as time passed, the United States, came to the same conclusion. Lengthy speeches were therefore made by Sir Gladwyn Jebb and Senator Austin reiterating the facts and the constitutionality of the United Nations enterprise in Korea. Mr Malik countered extensively. He did not hesitate to further occupy their time with a complaint that American aircraft had bombed Communist China, or to seek the presence of representatives from Peking on a complaint concerning Taiwan. Throughout the remaining sessions of August, the Council chamber in session was occupied with rhetoric.

This outcome may have been an objective of Russian policy. As early as 4th August, Sir Gladwyn Jebb had advised the Foreign Office that, 'In any case, it seems increasingly obvious that . . . Malik is waiting on military events.'[9]

When the Russian seat was resumed in the Security Council on 1st August, General Walker was struggling to throw back the North Koreans from the approaches to Masan, to regain the territory lost east of the Naktong and to hang on by any means to Pohang and its adjacent airfield. It was during the previous weekend that he had advised his divisional commanders that there would be no more withdrawals, that they must all stand and fight. When the month ended, the situation seemed little better—and, indeed, with Taegu closely threatened, General Walker was no less anxious about the integrity of the Pusan perimeter. But the hierarchy of the State and Defense Departments in Washington knew that Chromite was proceeding. The first of the British land contingents was about to arrive in Korea. Troops were following from other countries. And this was all of a piece with their confidence in General MacArthur's unwavering assurance that he would defeat the North Korean People's Army in the field.* As early as July, the State Department had prudently begun to look towards better military times: what should be done politically if there was a cease fire and the North Koreans withdrew behind the 38th parallel; what could be done if the North Korean forces should be destroyed? The British Foreign Office was asked for their views, and this prompted Mr Bevin to order a full appreciation of prospects and options, gathering together incidentally several drafts of papers on such matters as policy options in the event of Russian air intervention in North Korea. Shortly, both governments agreed that this work should be tabled for the meeting of the British, French and United States Foreign Ministers due to take place in New York on 14th September. After earlier soundings, preliminary discussions between senior officials of the three countries began on 1st September.

Mr Bevin put his appreciation to the Cabinet as a memorandum on 31st August:

> . . . The subject of Korea is on the agenda for the forthcoming Tripartite Ministerial Talks in New York,† and the memorandum was drafted primarily with a view to its use in that connection. I have already sent a copy to Washington for use by Sir Oliver Franks in the preliminary official discussions.

---

*When a politically contentious message sent by General MacArthur to the Veterans of Foreign Wars became known to the President, Mr Truman discarded the idea of dismissing him, partly on political grounds but also because he was essential to the successful conduct of the Korean war. Ordered to withdraw the message, MacArthur believed that this was due to British influence. Mr Bevin certainly instructed Sir Oliver Franks to ask for withdrawal, but Mr Acheson had already decided for himself that this was essential.[10]

†Though important, the Korean war was not the principal subject of the meeting. The three states were primarily concerned to organise NATO as an allied military command. A difficult matter was the extent to which West Germany (the Federal German Republic) should be rearmed to take a part in this. Though France was opposed to German rearmament, the Korean war had shown that commitments of the powers outside Europe made it unlikely that they could collectively field forces strong enough for a credible defence against those of the Russian *bloc*.

2. Subject to the agreement of my colleagues, I would propose to pursue discussions of the political settlement in Korea on the lines discussed in the attached memorandum not only with the United States and France but also with the Commonwealth and other friendly countries.[11]

The paper began, 'On any realistic view, it is difficult to be optimistic about the future of Korea' but this was the remnant of an original which Mr Bevin had thought altogether too gloomy.[12] He had redrafted numerous sections himself. Even so, the long term problems were seen to be formidable.

. . . It can be assumed that the Soviet Union will only co-operate in any United Nations proposals for Korea in so far as she believes that she will be able to further her own designs by doing so. Indeed, the Soviet Union will be implacably opposed to the establishment of a genuinely democratic and independent government of a unified Korea. Any new democratic State established at the end of the present hostilities in a part or the whole of Korea will, therefore, need a protracted period of tutelage and protection and will be a constant prey to attempts at internal subversion.

2. It is of the first importance that the impressive degree of unanimity over Korea in the United Nations should be maintained and that, at every phase, action should command the widest possible support from the Governments and peoples of all non-Communist states, especially those in Asia. It follows, therefore:

(a) That the United Nations should endeavour to make arrangements for Korea which are palpably just and reasonable even though they may prove in practice difficult of attainment.

(b) That if these arrangements are in fact frustrated, it should be clear to the world who is responsible.

3. . . . It will of course be difficult to make detailed plans for the political future of Korea until a later stage in the fighting. Much might, for example, depend on whether the North Korean armies suffer almost total destruction in the South, or whether substantial forces succeed in retiring in reasonably good order beyond the 38th parallel. In the former case, it is conceivable that in the absence of more direct Soviet intervention, the administration in North Korea might disintegrate of itself.

4. A statement of objectives would be unlikely to achieve its purpose unless it envisaged something more than the mere restoration of the authority of the present government (even though this was set up under United Nations auspices) and a

return to the previous precarious *status quo*. A limited objective of this kind would satisfy neither world opinion nor the Korean people. In any case, the United Nations can hardly abandon their declared objective of working for the establishment of a unified and democratic government. The statement might perhaps, therefore, take the form of a resolution in the General Assembly recommending that as soon as the military situation permits all possible steps should be taken to implement previous Assembly resolutions on the subject and to secure the holding under United Nations auspices of elections in Korea on a national basis with a view to the establishment of a unified, independent and democratic Korean Government. It would be more appropriate for such a resolution to be passed in the General Assembly than in the Security Council, since the Assembly has hitherto been responsible for political arrangements in Korea. Moreover, a resolution in the Assembly . . . could not be vetoed by the Soviet Union. . . .

5. A resolution on the above lines would not necessarily commit the United Nations to the view that United Nations forces should eventually pass beyond the 38th parallel and occupy the whole of North Korea, which is a question which will have to be left for later decision in the light of the developing military and political situation. But it would emphasise the continuing desire of the United Nations to bring about the unification of Korea on a democratic basis, and if, in the event, this proves impossible of attainment, the responsibility will be made clear.

6. Whatever decision may eventually be reached on the question whether the United Nations forces should proceed beyond the 38th parallel, there may be doubt whether such action (apart of course from such minor incursions as may be necessary in the course of military operations conducted from the south) could be justified on the basis of the Security Council's Resolution of 27th June. Action under the Resolution is for the purpose of repelling the armed attack on the Republic of Korea, and consequently action beyond the 38th parallel would be legitimate for this purpose. But permanent occupation would be another matter. In the view of many members of the United Nations, the Republic of Korea derives its legality from the elections held in 1948 under the supervision of a United Nations Commission, and has no title to sovereignty in those parts of Korea where it proved impossible to hold elections, and where, therefore, it has no claim to be representative. It is known that President Syngman Rhee considers that his Government is the Government of all Korea and is fully entitled to exercise jurisdiction throughout the peninsula. If these pretensions were to be accepted, there

would be no necessity for new elections; but they are, in fact, unlikely to find favour with many members of the United Nations, and any proposal based on them would be calculated to cause a split in the ranks of the democratic Powers. Indeed, if there is to be any question of United Nations forces operating on any extensive or semi-permanent basis beyond the 38th parallel, it is considered essential that such action should be taken only after some statement of general objectives has been made on the lines discussed in paragraph 4 above. It might also be desirable for the General Assembly resolution contemplated in paragraph 4 above to recall the recommendation contained in the Security Council Resolution of 27th June and to carry it a stage further by recommending that the necessary steps should be taken, under the aegis of the United Nations forces, to promote conditions of stability and security in which the required rehabilitation of the whole area can be begun.

7. The Soviet Union would view United Nations military operations in North Korea as an attempt to extinguish by force the satellite 'People's Republic' she has established there. Soviet reactions to such operations cannot be foreseen, but the risks of Soviet (or possibly Chinese) intervention would be increased, since Soviet prestige would suffer if she were to stand by and let her satellite be destroyed. It is believed that the Soviet Union wishes to avoid provoking a major war, but she might none the less pour in an increased supply of arms and equipment and arrange for the despatch of increased numbers of 'advisers'. She might even arrange for the despatch of a 'volunteer' force, perhaps composed of Russians or Chinese or both, to aid the North Koreans. The resulting situation, which would be much like that which developed during the Spanish Civil War, would be full of explosive possibilities.

8. It is conceivable that irrespective of any intention on the part of the United Nations forces to penetrate North Korea, the Soviet Union may decide, once it has become clear that the North Korean offensive has failed either:

(a) to reoccupy Korea without warning down to the 38th parallel (a move which could not fail to intensify the dangers of the situation, and might even lead to war); or

(b) to propose in the United Nations that since United States forces are now back in South Korea Soviet forces should reoccupy the North to assist in restoring peace. . . .

9. . . . Soviet occupation authorities would, in so far as this might be practical in the light of the outcome of the present hostilities, endeavour to utilise this period to rearm and re-equip the North Koreans. Once they had done this they might be able

to withdraw and a situation would result in which the unification of Korea would only be possible if the United Nations were themselves prepared to take the initiative in resuming hostilities. Such a step would, of course, be unthinkable and the situation would be very much what it was before the North Korean attack. . . . the Soviet Union might well decide to forego any further overt assault on South Korea. But South Korea would, as before, be subject to continuous attempts at internal subversion.

10. Another possibility is that the Russians may resuscitate the proposal originally adopted at the Moscow Conference in December, 1945, for a Four-Power Trusteeship for Korea. . . . the grounds for rejection would be clear, viz.: that the problem of Korea had become a matter for discussion by the United Nations. If the Soviet Union were to introduce a proposal into the United Nations seeking United Nations endorsement for the revival of the Four-Power Trusteeship proposal, the best grounds for rejection might be that this was an inappropriate and retrograde step, since the Koreans had already had an opportunity to demonstrate their capacity for self-government. It would be easy, at the same time, to expose Soviet motives for introducing such a proposal.

11. On the assumption that new national elections throughout Korea eventually prove possible, it would be necessary for the United Nations forces to remain in Korea at any rate until the elections had been held. Once the North Koreans have been defeated (and they appear in fact to be so deeply committed in the South that their forces may be largely destroyed far to the south of the 38th parallel), and on the assumption that neither the Russians nor the Chinese enter North Korea, the next step would be to endeavour to establish contact with the North Korean authorities. It is considered that the present United Nations Commission in Korea would not be a suitable body for this purpose, and that it would be preferable for the United Nations to set up in the first place an *ad hoc* group, preferably composed predominantly of representatives of Asian states, to function as a Truce Commission and to be charged with the task of conducting preliminary discussions with representatives of the Korean people regarding the political future of Korea. They might appropriately be attached to the United Nations military command for this purpose, and associated with any discussions that may be held with a view to the termination of hostilities and the restoration of order. . . . It would also be desirable for the North Koreans to be told that the United Nations forces would prevent violent retaliation against innocent citizens of the North, and that people should return to their jobs

and the administrative machine continue to function as before for the time being. It is to be hoped that it would thus be possible to arrange for the United Nations forces to enter North Korea unopposed.[13]

In two concluding paragraphs, the memorandum proposed that the new United Nations Commission should be 'composed of members of real weight . . . predominantly of Asian members, perhaps with a first-class British Secretary-General', though all members should be drawn from states which had contributed to the United Nations forces. To settle the new unified Korea on course, the Commission and military forces should be expected to remain for at least twelve months. Even so, 'conditions in Korea will remain unsettled and the possibility of serious civil disturbances from time to time cannot be excluded. An armed attack on the new government from within would, of course, be a civil war, and it would therefore be extremely difficult for the United Nations to intervene.[14]

With hindsight, some of the political policies suggested in this paper smack of naivety, not least in their underestimate of Kim Il-sung. The idea that, with or without an army in being, he would have treated with a United Nations Commission as the head of the 'North Korean authorities', encouraging the people he controlled to continue quietly with their daily affairs while an international electoral commission made arrangements for a fully democratic election is scarcely credible.

It is scarcely credible now because Kim's character and capacity for survival has been manifested. Then, he had been in power for less than five years. In the circumstances of the time, the paper had the merit of looking at the range of options. However, when they came to consider it on 4th September, Mr Attlee's Cabinet had to defer formal approval because there were believed to be 'legal difficulties of transferring consideration of this question from the Security Council to the General Assembly . . .'[15]

The United States were also anxious to avoid a precipitate referral to the assembly which might undo the Security Council's resolutions of the 25th and 27th of June. This aside, their position, eventually consolidated as a National Security Council policy paper, tended to view the problem more subjectively;[16] any solution would, inevitably, be paid for largely by the American taxpayer and, contrary to the repeated accusations of the communist camp, they were anxious to minimise their presence in Korea if they could not altogether abandon it. They wanted to be sure that no opportunity should be lost to reduce their commitment as soon as possible. On the question of crossing the 38th parallel, the Defense and State

Departments contained more hawks than doves, amongst the former, John Foster Dulles. There was dogged support for Syngman Rhee's government and the republic's National Assembly. But as contacts with the British and French proceeded, at first informally, often at middle-ranking level, ideas were modified. The British continued to press for predominantly Asian membership of the supervisory commission but wisely forebore to mention the thought that its chief should be British; India was sensibly substituted. The French were anxious to move deliberately 'a step at a time', when the North Koreans were overcome militarily.

On 6th September, the three allies came to an agreement on the procedure for dealing with the Korean settlement between the Security Council and the General Assembly. Article 12 provided that while the Security Council was exercising its functions during a dispute, the General Assembly should make no recommendation on the matter unless the Council requested it to do so. However, while the Security Council should continue to reserve to itself the consideration of 'a complaint of aggression against South Korea', the Assembly could legitimately discuss another item, 'the independence of Korea'.[17]

The briefing memorandum prepared for Mr Acheson on 14th September relative to his meeting with Mr Bevin and M. Schuman indicates the extent to which State Department ideas had moved towards those of their British and French colleagues.

During the preliminary tripartite discussions general agreement was reached on the following points:

1. Every effort should be made to maintain the present impressive degree of unanimity in the UN on the Korean question.
2. UN forces should not be committed to proceed north of the 38th parallel without prior UN direction. This would not preclude tactical operations incident to actions south of the 38th parallel.
3. UN forces should not proceed north of the 38th parallel if Soviet or Chinese Communist forces have occupied North Korea to the 38th parallel or if major Soviet or Chinese Communist combat units have engaged or clearly intend to engage in hostilities against UN forces.
4. The General Assembly should formulate its broad objectives and intentions with respect to Korea at an early date, emphasizing the necessity of implementing previous UN resolutions directed to the achievement of the independence and unity of Korea.

5. A commission of representatives of senior rank with a high percentage of Asian members should be formed to make recommendations to the UN on problems relating to the establishment of an independent and unified Korea, including the holding of elections.

6. UN forces with strong Asian participation should be retained in Korea during the period of readjustment following the cessation of hostilities.

7. Continued UN political and economic assistance to the Korean Government will be necessary.

Agreement with the British and French should be sought as to the future competence of the present Government of the Republic of Korea in the following sense:

(a) the continuity and sovereignty of the ROK should continue to be recognised over Korea south of the 38th parallel.

(b) the validity of the elections previously held by the ROK under UN supervision should not be challenged.

(c) elections under UN supervision should be held, when opportunity offers, in Korea north of the 38th parallel for the ultimate extension of the ROK in that area.

With reference to paragraph 2, above, the US position as established in NSC 81/1* may be summarised as follows:

Operations north of the 38th parallel for the purpose of the occupation of North Korea would be undertaken only after consultation with and approval of United Nations members. The UN forces now have a legal basis for conducting operations north of the 38th parallel to compel the withdrawal of the North Korean forces behind this line or to defeat these forces. However, the UN Commander, before undertaking such operations, including amphibious and airborne landings or ground operations in pursuance of a rollback, would, in view of the risks involved, obtain further authorisation from Washington.[18]

The level of agreement was such that, when the three Secretaries of State met on 14th September in the Waldorf-Astoria in New York, discussion of a Korean settlement occupied no more than a few minutes of their time. Mr Acheson, Mr Bevin and M. Schuman

---

*NSC81/1 was the National Security Council paper relating to 'United States courses of action with respect to Korea' (19). Dated 9th September, its conclusions were approved by the President on the 11th. It took account of war measures to be adopted if the Soviet or Chinese Communist forces directly entered the fighting. It anticipated that the UN Commander would receive authority to continue operations into North Korea provided that there had been no entry by Soviet or Chinese Communist forces and no announcement or expressed threat of it. The UN Commander was to be given authority to plan the occupation of North Korea but would do so only with the explicit approval of the President, who would consult and obtain the approval of members of the UN.

'approved the understanding reached by their Delegations in this matter'.[20]

In Moscow, the progress of the Korean war had also been under review. North Korean losses in men and materials were well known to the Soviet General Staff. Despite the efforts of the NKPA, the United Nations line had not effectively been broken. Reinforcements were continuing to arrive at Pusan, including those of other nations. The United States had air superiority throughout Korea, enjoyed indeed air supremacy for the most part. United States defence stocks were apparently sufficient to replace all losses and the nation's expanding defence industries would assure all conceivable demands for replenishment. If the NKPA should be defeated, would the United Nations forces—in particular, the United States forces—advance to the borders of China and Russia?

In August, a conference took place in Peking between senior officers of the People's Republic of China and the Soviet Union. Principals among the latter were Marshal Shtemenko, Chief of Staff of the Army, and from the Far East Command, Marshal Malinovsky, Commander-in-Chief, Lieutenant-General Glazovsky, air commander, and Major-General Bilizov, air defence commander. One result of this meeting was the establishment of a joint planning staff in Shenyang in the middle of September. The Russian Lieutenant-General Derevyanko was appointed chief of staff, Lieutenant-General Han Hsien-chu deputy chief.[21]

These arrangements were almost certainly of a defensive nature, though the landings at Inch'on doubtless added to their importance. There is no evidence that additional Soviet troops were deployed to the border area other than the three additional divisions which had reinforced it just prior to the opening of the Korean war. The Chinese were still intent on the recovery of Taiwan, the principal subject of their propaganda campaigns; all forces which could be spared from 'bandit suppression', that is, counter-revolutionary operations on the mainland, and from economic recovery projects, were concentrated for amphibious operations against the island. The only formations in North East China which had no territorial connection were the 50th Army and the 66th. The first was a former Kuomintang body which had surrendered *en masse* during the civil war, had had its officers changed and then been employed with Lin Piao's Fourth Field Army. In June, after the capture of Hainan island in the south, it had moved back with the Fourth to the north east, the latter's parent region. More difficult to explain was the movement into the Fourth Field Army area of the 66th Army. It had been sent into concentration areas round Shenyang in early July, when it began intensive training.[22]

Like the British, French and United States governments, Stalin and Mao appear to have decided to wait upon events before making any further political decisions on Korea.

SOURCE NOTES: CHAPTER 9

1. DEFE 11/197, New York 765 to FO of 29th July 1950.
   767 of 29th July 1950.
   773 of 31st July 1950.
2. Ibid, New York 773 to FO of 31st July 1950.
   769 of 31st July 1950.
   776 of 31st July 1950.
3. Ibid, New York 775 to FO of 31st July 1950.
4. Ibid., FO 903 to New York of 31st July 1950.
5. Ibid., FO 900 to New York of 31st July 1950.
6. Ibid., New York 778 to FO of 1st August 1950.
7. Ibid.
8. United Nations document S/PV/.482 and 483.
9. DEFE 11/198, New York 794 to FO of 4th August 1950. This view was already held by Sir Esler (formerly Mr M E) Dening, the Assistant Under-Secretary (AUS) responsible in London.
10. Sir Oliver Franks, conversation with author.
11. CAB 129/41, CP(50)193 of 31st August 1950.
12. Shinwell, conversation with author, included this comment: 'Ernie thought some of the Foreign Office seemed to enjoy all the worst news they could find . . .'.
13. CAB 129/41, CP(50)193 of 31st August 1950, Annex.
14. Ibid.
15. CAB 128/17, Cabinet 55(50), p 6. FO 1401 and 1402 to New York of 23rd September 1950.
16. See, for example, in the United States National Archives series 795.00:

Defense memo of 31 Jul 50	/7–3150
State (Butler) memo of 1 Aug 50	/8–150
State (Dulles) memo of 1 Aug 50	/8–150
Defense memo for NSC of 7 Aug 50	/8–750
State (Allison) memo of 12 Aug 50	/8–1250
State (Butler) memo of 15 Aug 50	/8–1550
State (Jessup) memo of 17 Aug 50	/8–1750
CIA memo of 18 Aug 50	/8–1850
State (Kennan) memo of 21 Aug 50, and (Allison and Emmerson)	/8–2150
State memo for NSC of 23 Aug 50 and internal (Sandifer)	/8–2350
State (Barco) memo of 25 Aug 50 and McConaughy	/8–2550
State draft of 31 Aug 50	/8–3150
State draft of 30 Aug 50	/8–3050
Position paper on Korea for tripartite meeting of Foreign Ministers in September (SFM D-7/3a)	/8–2850
Preliminary tripartite conversations	/8–3050
of 30 Aug 50 and 1 Sep 50	/9–150

17. Tripartite memo of 6 Sep 50   /9–650
18. SFM D-7/3a Revised, 14 Sep 50   /9–1450
19. United States Executive Secretariat Files, NSC/81/1   /9–1450
20. Tripartite conference minute 4

21. Huang Chen-hsia, *Chung-kung chun-jen chi (Mao's Generals)*, (Hong Kong, 1968), pp 441 and 687.
22. China Quarterly No 98, June, 1984, pp. 289–90.

CHAPTER 10

To Cross or Not to Cross

Operation Chromite occasioned the admiration of the British Cabinet's Defence Committee, but its outcome revived differences between its political and military constituents. These were not at all what popular imagination might have expected.

The Prime Minister and Foreign Secretary favoured enterprise in the continuation of operations, the Chiefs of Staff restraint. The reason was simple. The Chiefs were burdened with commitments for which they lacked the resources. They were expected to muster a substantial contribution to the NATO land and air forces in Europe and maritime forces in the Atlantic; and to have in hand reserves for contingencies in the Middle and Far East, and in Africa. They were not the makers of overseas and defence policy but its agents. This role obliged them to be realists; it tended equally to inhibit their judgements.

Mr Attlee and Mr Bevin were the policy makers The two men were commonly influenced by historical factors in their responses to events in Korea during that summer and autumn of 1950. They believed that Stalin had been frustrated in his attempts to extend Russian power into northern, western and southern Europe by the alliance of the European democracies and the United States. It seemed in every way probable to them that Stalin had decided to try his hand at an extension of power on the other side of the world, in Korea. Abandonment of South Korea to military conquest by the North, as earlier observed, would have encouraged Soviet political adventurism and discouraged small nations on whom his shadow might fall. The arguments against intervention seemed very similar to those which had proved so disastrously wrong in countering Hitler's adventurism in the nineteen thirties. There were the associated factors of keeping the United States as an international partner, of avoiding the rebuffs to the American government which had helped to prolong isolationism in that same decade; and of adherence to the charter of the United Nations to prevent its decline into the impotence of the League of Nations.

Mr Bevin's policy paper of 31st August* manifests the risks involved in the occupation of North Korea by the United Nations

*See pp. 190–195.

forces but, somewhat diffidently, recognises the need to do so in order to unify and democratise the Korean nation. But having gone so far, he and the Prime Minister came to accept that, if they were constrained altogether or too long by their fears, they and their allies risked losing not only their objective but even the long term independence of South Korea.

While the Chiefs of Staff saw the desirability of a political settlement in Korea, they believed the cost of assuring it would be too high.

A letter from Air Marshal Bouchier concerning General MacArthur's future plans made Sir John Slessor, Chief of the Air Staff, apprehensive that they might be drawn into 'an unlimited engagement' in Korea. He became more anxious when he received a copy of the Foreign Secretary's paper. In discussions with his Minister and colleagues, he warned that they were in danger of dissipating the United States dollars provided to recover their economic health and to help build their defences against Russia. On 14th September, just prior to the Chromite landings, he wrote to the members of the Chiefs' committee,

2. What is the object of the exercise? I think the Americans would agree with us that we have really no strategic interest in Korea whatever. Politically I know our object is to see an independent, unified and democratic Korea as a result of free elections under UNO auspices—we can keep our tongues in our cheeks as to the extent to which any Korean regime would in fact ever be democratic or, for that matter, independent with Communist China and Russia just across the Yalu.
3 But we certainly do not want to be let in for a very big and prolonged commitment to maintain forces throughout Korea maintaining law and order.
3. . . . On the broad strategic view the more and the sooner we can reduce our forces in Korea and have them available either to deal with further Russian 'proxy' wars on the Korean model elsewhere, or to strengthen the European front, the happier we shall be. We shall no doubt have to maintain some forces in South Korea for a long time to come, to ensure that Russia or China does not immediately nullify all we have fought for there. That doesn't mean maintaining forces there strong enough to withstand a Russian or Chinese attack . . .[1]

These remarks occasioned a discussion of policy in Korea at the Chiefs' meeting on 20th September, attended by Lord Tedder, on leave from Washington. He said that,

. . . the result of the present conflict would be to leave Korea in a state of chaos and that practically all the industrial resources of North Korea would have been destroyed. If the United Nations were to take the line with the Koreans that they did not wish to leave the country in the state of waste . . . they might be able to revive the whole of Korea as a single entity.[2]

They were all agreed that, while 'the problem was mainly a political one'—Field-Marshal Slim's words—the military factors should be taken note of:

. . . Unless instructions were issued to General MacArthur there was a grave danger of forces being moved forward into North Korea without the implications of such actions having been fully studied. One result of such action might be to provoke the Russians or Chinese Communists to invade North Korea.[3]

Reflecting on this advice, passed to him in New York on 24th September by Air Marshal Elliot, Mr Bevin observed later to Sir Esler Dening[4] that it took no account of his and the Prime Minister's apprehension that if they did not go into North Korea the Russians or Chinese would be likely to come in anyway to resuscitate the North Korean government and armed forces.

By the end of September, the landing at Inch'on and the break out from the Pusan bridgehead had broken the North Korean People's Army. Prisoner tallies for the Eighth Army moving north soon exceeded one thousand a day and by the end of the month were approaching two thousand. The ROK forces were capturing as many. As the North Koreans crossed the 38th parallel, the strongest battalion numbered 97 officers and men, many had less than 50.[5] Divisional strengths were reduced to two to three thousand. Behind them they lost in action or abandoned almost all their tanks and other vehicles, artillery and mortars.[6] Stocks of ammunition, rice, and medical equipment were discovered in their wake. Several thousand North Koreans, including civil administrators and police security forces, withdrew into the Ciri mountains in south west Korea. The greater number exfiltrated east of Seoul, up the central mountain chain.

The United Nations forces had indeed broken the NKPA, but they had not altogether destroyed it. Those that evaded capture were its most zealous members. Wherever they could, they attempted to hold blocking positions to delay the pursuit. Some of these were briefly effective; but although all were either overcome or forced to move on again such small actions were enough to make it clear to Eighth Army and X Corps, and hence at General

MacArthur's headquarters, that the final destruction of the NKPA had not yet been accomplished.

A troop of tanks from 1st Cavalry Division reached the X Corps bridgehead on the morning of 27th September. From that moment, the army and corps were linked. But they did not become one. General Walker and his staff very much wished that this should be the outcome of their contiguity. So did General MacArthur's staff. The Commander-in-Chief had other ideas.

Looking at his map as the break out progressed, General MacArthur was struck by the spine of formidable mountains continuing north across the 38th parallel which separated the eastern section of the country from the western. He was anxious that his field forces should not be confined in a western corridor and obliged to engage in a series of frontal attacks, or to leave the mountainous eastern sector as an open corridor for guerrillas. He was later to say that he doubted the ability of his supply and transport services to provide for an army of three corps through Pusan and Inch'on. Roads and railways in the south required much work for the carriage of heavy traffic, principally due to air attacks on them over three months.* The operational and logistic dangers would be avoided if he should put X Corps ashore on the north east coast in the area of Wonsan and Hamhung. From that area, they could strike west towards P'yongyang, the North Korean capital, a force to cut behind any attempt by the NKPA to hold on or below the River Taedong.

There may be some suspicion that this reasoning was influenced by a wish on General MacArthur's part to display again his brilliance as a strategist. It is also unfortunate that none of his senior staff officers, his naval and army commanders, felt able to approach him with a contrary opinion. But with his judgement triumphantly vindicated at Inch'on, it is doubtful whether he would have accepted either an argument of principle or of circumstance to change his decision. In principle, and particularly where there is only one tactical air force, field operations in a theatre are better controlled by one land commander and staff working in exclusive partnership with their air associates. As a matter of circumstance, while the port at Wonsan would be useful, there were already indications that the area would be heavily mined. No doubt these could be overcome but, ship losses apart, there would be a time penalty for clearance. MacArthur's aim in putting X Corps ashore there was to reduce time in his advance against a broken foe.

---

*As the break out operation progressed, General MacArthur ordered a reduction—shortly, the cessation—of air strikes on roads, bridges, railways and tunnels in the battlefield interdiction zone to avoid further damage to facilities that would be needed for the advance.

The idea of a landing on the north east coast was certainly in the Commander-in-Chief's mind by 26th September; he instructed his staff to produce an outline plan for it on that day. He did not doubt that the Joint Chiefs of Staff would agree to the necessity of crossing the 38th Parallel and, as he expected, he received confirmation in a provisional directive on the 27th:

. . . you will continue to make special efforts to determine whether there is a Chinese Communist or Soviet threat to the attainment of your objective, which will be reported to the Joint Chiefs of Staff as a matter of urgency.

2. Your military objective is the destruction of the North Korean Armed Forces. In attaining this objective you are authorized to conduct military operations, including amphibious and airborne landings or ground operations north of the 38th Parallel . . . provided that at the time of such operation there has been no entry into North Korea by major Soviet or Chinese Communist Forces, no announcement of intended entry, nor a threat to counter our operations militarily in North Korea. Under no circumstances, however, will your forces cross the Manchurian [North East China] or USSR borders of Korea and, as a matter of policy, no non-Korean ground forces will be used in the north east provinces bordering the Soviet Union or in the area along the Manchurian border. Furthermore, support of your operations north or south of the 38th Parallel will not include Air or Naval action against Manchuria or against USSR territory.

3. In the event of the open or covert employment of major Soviet units south of the 38th Parallel, you will assume the defense, make no move to aggravate the situation and report to Washington. You should take the same action in the event your forces are operating north of the 38th Parallel and major Soviet units are openly employed. You will not discontinue Air and Naval operations north of the 38th Parallel merely because the presence of Soviet or Chinese Communist troops is detected in a target area but if the Soviet Union or the Chinese Communists should announce in advance their intention to reoccupy North Korea and give warning, either explicitly or implicitly, that their forces should not be attacked, you should refer the matter immediately to Washington.

4. In the event of the open or covert employment of major Chinese Communist units south of the 38th Parallel, you should continue the action as long as action by your forces offers a reasonable chance of successful resistance.

5. In the event of an attempt to employ small Soviet or Chinese Communist units covertly south of the 38th Parallel, you should continue the action.

6. You should immediately make an intensive effort, using all information media available to you, to turn the inevitable bitterness and resentment of the war-victimized Korean people away from the United Nations and to direct it towards the Korean Communists, the Soviet Union, and depending on the role they play, the Chinese Communists.

7. On the principle that the treatment of POW's shall be directed towards their exploitation, training and use for psychological warfare purposes, you should set up on a pilot plant scale interrogation, indoctrination and training centres for those POW's now in your hands in Korea.

8. When organized armed resistance by the North Korean forces has been brought substantially to an end, you should direct the Republic of Korea forces to take the lead in disarming remaining North Korean units and enforcing the terms of surrender. Guerrilla activities should be dealt with primarily by the forces of the Republic of Korea, with minimum participation [sic] by UN contingents.

9. Circumstances obtaining at the time will determine the character of and the necessity for occupation of North Korea. Your plans for such occupation will be forwarded for approval by the Joint Chiefs of Staff.

10. You will also submit your plans for future operations north of the 38th Parallel to the Joint Chiefs of Staff for approval.

11. The Joint Chiefs of Staff understand that instructions are now being formulated on the Governmental level regarding:

   a. Armistice terms to be offered by you to the North Koreans in the event of a sudden collapse of North Korean forces; and
   b. Course of action to be followed and activities to be undertaken during the post-hostilities period.[7]

An additional paragraph had been inserted at the suggestion of Mr Acheson:

As soon as the military situation permits, you should facilitate the restoration of the government of the Republic of Korea, with its capital in Seoul. Although the government of the Republic of Korea has been generally recognized (except by the Soviet *bloc*) as the only legal government in Korea, its sovereignty north of the 38th degree parallel has not been generally recognized. The Republic of Korea and its armed forces should be expected to cooperate in such military operations and military occupation as are conducted by United Nations forces north of the 38th degree parallel, but political questions such as the formal extension of sovereignty over North Korea should await action by the United Nations to complete the unification of the country.[8]

Next day, 28th September, a press report reached Washington that the Eighth Army planned to halt ROK divisions on the parallel for 'regrouping'. General Marshall, who had been appointed Defense Secretary in President Truman's Cabinet,* signalled the following to General MacArthur on the 29th:

For his eyes only. Reference present report of supposed announcement by Eighth Army that ROK Divisions would halt on 38th parallel for regrouping: We want you to feel unhampered tactically and strategically to proceed north of 38th parallel. Announcement above referred to may precipitate embarrassment in UN where evident desire is not to be confronted with necessity of a vote on passage of 38th parallel, rather to find you have found it militarily necessary to do so.[9]

This message was sent before General Marshall became aware of developments on the diplomatic network between China and India, and India and the United Kingdom.

Following the tripartite meetings, Mr Bevin and his staff had been occupied with the General Assembly meeting at Lake Success. His—and the Prime Minister's—aim was to get a resolution through the Assembly as soon as possible to state clearly what the United Nations intended to do in North Korea. Mr Acheson was of the same mind. The British Cabinet approved a draft on 26th September[10] which was agreed on the 28th by the United States.[11] The Australians, consulted belatedly and surprised by its 'wider terms', made useful proposals which included the need to specify details of the states which would form the United Nations Commission for the Unification and Rehabilitation of Korea (UNCURK).[12] Both America and Britain were anxious that Australia should be one of these, India another.

A copy of the draft was sent to India through the British High Commission on 26th September[13] with the following message from Mr Bevin to Pandit Nehru:

. . . We have now reached the stage where military operations may come to a successful conclusion at a very early date. The question of Korea is likely to come up in the First Committee

---

*He replaced Louis Johnson on 20th September 1950.

of the United Nations General Assembly during this week and it is therefore urgently necessary to consider what is to be done there. After very careful thought we have drafted a resolution which we believe to be constructive and which is designed not only to cover the immediate future but also the long term settlement of the Korean problem. This I believe to be in accordance with your own desires. We should like to sponsor this resolution and we very much hope that India together with other Powers will join with us in doing so. We have good reason to suppose that the United States would support the resolution though for obvious reasons they would not wish to take the initiative.

2. You will see that the resolution contemplates the contingency that United Nations forces may enter North Korea but that it very carefully defines their functions there. I feel strongly that if the authority of the United Nations is to be established we cannot be content with restoring the *status quo*. The 38th Parallel is an imaginary line on a map which has neither political nor military significance on the ground. The General Assembly of the United Nations has already declared as its object the unification of Korea and it is highly improbable that this object can be achieved if North Korea is permitted to remain as a separate entity. When the United Nations Commission envisaged in the draft resolution is established I hope it will be able to ensure that free elections are held throughout Korea and I think that we must then accept the government established by those elections.

3. Certain member states of the United Nations may fear that the movement of United Nations forces into North Korea will precipitate war with Russia. Our own view is that if Russia wants war she does not need Korea as an excuse but we have so worded our draft resolution that the non-provocative nature of the entry . . . is clearly demonstrated . . . .[14]

Meantime, another signal on this subject was being considered in New Delhi. Mr Panikkar,* Indian Ambassador in Peking, reported:

Last night [26th September] General Nieh Jung-chen, Chief of Staff in overall charge of military planning under Chu Teh dined with me. He was emphatic that Chinese Government will not take lying down continuous provocation of Americans meaning violations of Manchurian territory by aeroplanes, They consider

*Panikkar, Kavalam Madhava (1895–1963).

they have no option but to resist if America does not stop this. When I pointed out dangers to China through overwhelming air action from all sides his reply was 'We could not help it'. His point of view which probably reflects military opinion here is that China can no longer remain patient. I told him that whatever the outcome of such conflict, experience of Korea showed that not a single industrial establishment will be spared and that Chinese economy will suffer for many years to come. He seemed certain that America and Western Nations will not be able to spare troops for a major land campaign and that wars cannot be won by aerial bombardment.

2. Polish Ambassador who had been urgently recalled for consultation and returned only four days ago elaborated the point later that Korean fighting will soon develop into a major conflict as China will consider American Army on her Manchurian flank as a grave menace to her and will give indirect help on a large scale to North Koreans. This view finds some support in Chou En-lai's* protest to Security Council which emphasises that China does not propose to sit with folded hands in face of aggression against her territory . . . .[15]

On reflection, Mr Panikkar added,

There was one sentence on Chou En-lai's talk with me on 21st to which I did not then attach much importance. He said 'since United Nations claim to have no obligations to us we also have none to them'.[16]

These details, *verbatim*, accompanied Pandit Nehru's response to Mr Bevin during the evening of 27th September.

. . . You will appreciate for yourself the gravity of the news that he [Panikkar] has given us. I am sending a personal appeal to Chou En-lai urging moderation and restraint. If that appeal is to have any chance of success then we must avoid all action that might precipitate the entry of New China into the armed conflict in Korea. That any decision or even suggestion that United Nations forces will move beyond 38th Parallel is likely to precipitate what might be world catastrophe is, I fear, more than probable. . . . The limitation of the military operations by United Nations forces north of the 38th Parallel as you suggest— your High Commissioner mentioned that it was not intended to go beyond 40th Parallel north—will, in my judgement, not prove . . . satisfactory to Peking in present circumstances . . . .

---

*Chou En-lai (1892–1976), principal political associate of Mao Tse-tung, Prime Minister of the People's Republic of China.

I recognise that military developments in South Korea lend urgency to a decision as to how the future of Korea should be settled. I would suggest that at this stage such action should be limited to announcement of objectives namely creation of a united free Korea on the basis of free elections under the auspices of the United Nations and an offer to the North Koreans to discuss with them ways and means to this end provided that they cease hostilities immediately. . . .[17]

Mr Nehru does not seem to have been aware that the United States Government had drafted a statement to the North Koreans to end hostilities, a text discussed with Britain and other allies. It was to be used by General MacArthur on 1st October. Whether Mr Nehru knew or not, he made no suggestions as to how the United Nations should proceed if the North Koreans ignored it. But the Indian viewpoint shifted during the passage of telegrams during the next few days as Mr Loy W Henderson, the United States Ambassador in New Delhi, made evident:

29th September. Nye, UK HICOM [Lieutenant General Sir Archibald Nye, High Commissioner] informed me noon today of latest developments in correspondence between UK and India re Korea.
2. . . . I understand British are keeping [State] Department fully informed. Nye gave Bajpai last evening [second] message from Bevin in reply to Nehru's message to Bevin of preceding day. In this note Bevin expressed doubt Peking would be so foolish as to intervene in Korea at this stage and pointed out unless UN forces entered North Korea there seemed to be no way to effect unification of Korea. . . . Nehru took position that it would be dangerous to assume Peking leaders were bluffing when they intimated Communist China might intervene in Korean situation. He agreed to support resolution similar to that proposed by British [in the General Assembly] provided it did not sanction entrance UN forces into North Korea. Note indicated that appeal to North Korea to cooperate with UN in carrying our purposes of resolution would not be appeasement and pointed out that if North Korea refused decision could then be made as to future course of action.
3. I called on Bajpai shortly after Nye's visit. . . . I understood that British were taking lead in formulating resolution on Korea for General Assembly and that it was my impression Department preferred that discussion with India re this resolution be conducted through British channels. Bajpai said he had similar impression and then outlined conversations which had taken place

between UK and . . . Delhi during last two days. He showed me Nehru's latest reply to Bevin, asked if I had any comments. I replied in negative. . .[18]

30th September. Bajpai read to me this evening text of GOI [Government of India] telegram to Panikkar, Indian ambassador in Peiping [Peking], in which GOI outlined US suggestions received through Bevin* for settlement any legitimate claims arising from US bombing. . . . GOI expressed willingness to appoint representative if Peiping was agreeable to act with Swedish representative in investigation and assessing damages.

2. Bajpai said GOI considered US generous and could not see how in face of it Peiping could continue to maintain US was not doing all it could reasonably be expected to do to compensate China for any damage which US planes might have inflicted on Chinese territory. . . .[19]

30th September. Bajpai sent for me late this afternoon to discuss further problems re Korea. He read to me latest communication received this morning from Bevin and Nehru's reply thereto.

2. Bevin referred to recent changes which had been made in text of proposed UK resolution and expressed hope GOI could *now* co-sponsor it.† Bevin stated UK had not meant to convey in previous message belief that Peking was bluffing in making threats, but rather opinion that Communist Chinese leaders were too statesmanlike to push China into war with UN forces.

3. Nehru's reply indicated that although GOI might not *oppose* resolution, it would make clear in GA [General Assembly] that it would be preferable for UN before sending armed forces into North Korea to give North Koreans opportunity to lay down arms and to undertake to cooperate loyally with committee proposed in resolution in carrying out aims of UN.

4. Bajpai undertook explain what present position GOI is along following lines:

(a) GOI agrees that under SC [Security Council] resolutions of June, UN forces have right to enter North Korea for military purposes. It believes, however, that in interests of peace, UN forces before entering North Korea should give North Koreans chance to lay down arms and to undertake to permit UN to take jurisdiction over area for purpose of carrying out program set forth in draft resolution.‡

---

*Accepting that the United States had accidentally bombed targets in North East China, Mr Acheson proposed that the United Kingdom might convey to China, perhaps through India, that it was willing to pay compensation, subject to investigation and assessment by representatives from India and Sweden. Mr Bevin put this to Mr Nehru on 28th September.[20]
†For the final form of the resolution, see Appendix M.
‡See General MacArthur's proposal on pages 215 and 230.

(b) Period during which this chance should be given could be so short that North Koreans would not be able to gain material advantage militarily for respite.

(c) It is not intent of GOI to *oppose* resolution. It may abstain or it may even vote for it. Its final decision depends upon facts brought out during discussions in GA and on international developments.[21]

On 30th September, Chou En-lai made a speech in Peking to the Council of the Central People's Government which included these words,

. . . On the pretext of the situation in Korea, it [the United States] despatched its naval and air forces to invade the Taiwan Province of China . . . Time after time, it sent its air force . . . to intrude into the air over the Liaotung Province of China, strafing and bombing, and sent its naval forces . . . to bombard Chinese merchant shipping on the high seas.

By these frenzied and violent acts of imperialist aggression, the US Government has displayed itself as the most dangerous foe to the People's Republic of China. The US aggressive forces have invaded China's borders and may at any time expand their aggression. MacArthur, Commander-in-Chief of American aggression against Taiwan and Korea, has long disclosed the aggressive designs of the US Government and is continuing to invent new excuses for extending its aggression . . .

. . . The Chinese people enthusiastically love peace, but in order to defend peace they never have been and never will be afraid to oppose aggressive war. The Chinese people absolutely will not tolerate aggression, nor will they supinely tolerate seeing their neighbours savagely invaded by the imperialists. . . . Whoever attempts to exclude the nearly 500 million Chinese people from the UN, and whoever ignores and violates the interests of this one fourth of mankind and fancies to solve generally and arbitrarily any Far Eastern problems directly concerned with China, will certainly break their heads.

Arrangements were made to publish these remarks nationally and internationally on 1st October.* On that day also, General MacArthur, as arranged, made his injunction to the North Koreans:

---

*The speech was published in *Jen Min Pao [People's Daily]* on 1st October and *World Culture*, though the section concerning Korea was omitted in the first edition; and by the London *Times* and New York *Herald Tribune* on 1st October, and the New York *Times* on 2nd October 1950. Liaotung Province adjoins north west Korea.

To the Commander-in-Chief, North Korean Forces:
The early and total defeat and complete destruction of your armed forces and war making potential is now inevitable. In order that the decisions of the United Nations may be carried out with a minimum of further loss of life and destruction of property, I, as the United Nations Commander-in-Chief, call upon you and the forces under your command, in whatever part of Korea situated, forthwith to lay down your arms and cease hostilities under such military supervision as I may direct—and I call upon you at once to liberate all United Nations prisoners of war and civilian internees under your control and to make adequate provision for their protection, care, maintenance and immediate transportation to such places as I indicate. North Korean Forces, including prisoners of war in the hands of the United Nations Command, will continue to be given the care dictated by civilized custom and practice and permitted to return to their homes as soon as practicable. I shall anticipate your early decision upon this opportunity to avoid the further useless shedding of blood and destruction of property. (Signed) Douglas MacArthur.[22]

At this juncture, there was general agreement among the participants in and supporters of United Nations military operations that the Commander-in-Chief had the right to undertake these north as well as south of the 38th Parallel as a matter of overspill. Some, notably India, but intermittently the British, seem to have apprehended that there would be a general onrush northwards at any moment. Few, including the United States Government, seem to have realised that North Korea's stubborn defence of Seoul, resistance at other points, anxieties concerning guerrilla action and, not least, logistics, made any precipitate movement almost impossible. Certainly, neither General MacArthur nor his immediate subordinates in the field were thinking of unimpeded pursuit. Fighting in the northern outskirts of Seoul did not end until 28th September. The I Corps then had to complete the relief of X Corps and wait for relief by IX. Stocks of ammunition, petrol, oil lubricants, engineer stores including bridging, food and medical supplies had to be transported forward while the Inch'on port and associated administrative base, 'ASCOM City',* was established. Moreover, the area between Seoul and the parallel had to be cleared and prepared for advance, a task which included the crossing of the River Imjin.

However, there were other forces ready to cross into North Korea at the end of September, and not simply in overspill

---

*ASCOM—nickname for the Army Supply Command base.

operations. These were the divisions of the ROK I Corps. On 21st September, as the North Korean forces in the north eastern sector of the Pusan bridgehead were showing signs of exhaustion, ROK Army headquarters was instructed plainly by President Syngman Rhee that its divisions under direct command were to fight their way to the 38th Parallel and to keep advancing until they reached the Yalu river.[23]

The 3rd Division of the ROK I Corps was foremost on 30th September. It patrolled across the Parallel that afternoon and, next day, the leading battalions followed. They were not moving on President Rhee's instructions, however, but those of Eighth Army Headquarters. Far from wishing to conceal this development, the staff flew a group of newspaper correspondents to Kangnung to follow the ROK troops movement. The news of the crossing was published in New York on 2nd October, ahead of an official statement from General MacArthur's headquarters that ROK troops were in North Korea from the 3rd. The ROK divisions— the 3rd was joined by the Capital Division—were in occasional contact with North Korean forces; and, as has been noted, the passage of South Korean troops into the North was not classified by either side as 'provocative'.

This view was underlined that evening during an interview in Peking between Mr Panikkar and the Chinese Prime Minister. The former had been summoned just after midnight to a meeting at the latter's residence. In an urgent signal, the Indian Ambassador reported early on 3rd October,

. . . as the question of Korea has become suddenly important he [Chou], desired that you should know his views fully. He said he was in full agreement with statement you [Nehru] had made to the press* and that he was equally anxious that Korean issue should be settled peacefully. But he added if the American army crosses 38th parallel China will be forced to take immediate steps. He said that obviously America no longer attaches value to three power decision not to cross 38th parallel and United Nations may find itself faced with a *fait accompli* dictated by MacArthur. That he said will mean definitely enlargement of the war. Chou En-lai said that he considered it to be of supreme importance that the Korean war should be localised and a peaceful solution found. China will put forward her own sugges- tion for peaceful solution and will be glad to discuss with us.

*This referred to a statement by Mr Nehru at a news conference on 30th September which proposed a peaceful settlement of the Korean problem and his views that there should be no crossing of the 38th Parallel 'till all other means of settlement have been explored'.

I asked him whether the issue could not be localised and an attempt made to find a solution acceptable to all parties, even if military action is extended to North Korea. He replied that if American authorities decided to cross the boundary then it will be clear that they have elected for war and not for peace and China will be forced to act accordingly. . . .[24]

Mr Panikkar was later to record,

I returned home at 1.30 where my first secretary and cypher assistant were waiting. . . . I was fully satisfied that as Chou En-lai had claimed that the Americans had crossed the parallel, the Chinese troops which had been concentrated in Manchuria had also moved across the Yalu into North Korean territory. In the morning I contacted Hutchison, the British Minister, and told him briefly how matters stood . . .[25]

This information reached London on 3rd October, initially from Peking,[26] later from the High Commission in New Delhi.[27] The news was at once passed to the State Department. Focus sharpened on China. By this time, a series of intelligence assessments had been made in Britain and the Commonwealth powers involved, in the United States and France.[28] These were generally in agreement that, if the United Nations stayed out of North Korea, Russia would intervene to resuscitate Kim Il-sung by one means or another; if they went in, there would be no danger of Russian physical intervention. China was another matter. The violent language used by Chou on 30th September was no more extreme than that in much Communist Chinese—or Russian—propaganda. High colour was used for dramatic effect. Disregarding the theatricals, views were evenly divided among officials and military advisers as to whether the Chinese were bluffing.

Marshal of the Royal Air Force Sir John Slessor had already reiterated his ideas on 2nd October that 'the risks involved and the inevitable military commitment . . . more than outweigh the political advantages to be obtained.' He continued in a note to his colleagues:

2. I find it hard to understand Mr Bevin's view (telegram 1188 of 25 Sep [not shown]) that if we stop at the 38th parallel and leave N. Korea as an entity Russia will virtually have triumphed and the whole UN effort will have been in vain.

I should have thought that the complete defeat of this obviously Soviet-inspired Communist aggression, the destruction of the whole North Korean industry and the elimination of the north [Korean] Communist Army represents a triumph for the UN on any count.

3. I think that any boost to UN prestige in Asia resulting from successful UN operations in North Korea would be more than offset by the strong nationalist feeling throughout Asia against Western intervention north of the parallel. The Asiatic Powers backed us in resisting the aggression against S. Korea; it is already clear that we should not have their backing for an occupation of North Korea.

4. I still think that, while unification of all Korea under UN is no doubt desirable, the one *essential* is that the UN position in Korea must be no worse than if the invasion had never happened. As long as Communism makes no gains to offset the calamitous losses it has now suffered, we should only seek to extend those losses if we are sure that the cost of doing so is commensurate with the advantages to be gained. . . .

5. The Americans say they propose to remain approximately South of the 40th parallel (telegram 1200 of 25 Sep [not shown]). This takes them to the Chinese border on the West, and involves the occupation of territory not much smaller than South Korea.

But (though it includes Pyonghyang [sic], the NK Capital) it still excludes another area of NK not so much smaller than SK. It avoids contact with the Russian border, but apart from that why does it make sense to have to cross one arbitrary line on the map and stop short of another? If the NK 'People's Republic' does not collapse as a result of the operations South of the 38th parallel, I see no reason to imagine it will be allowed by the Russians to do so as a result of operations south of the 40th. There will still be a NK 'People's Republic' North of the 40th parallel which will be a harbour and base for Russian and Chinese backed NK guerrillas, who will be just as much a curse to the UN occupying forces South of 40° as those in the present NK will be to UN occupying forces South of 38° North. The UN forces necessary to protect the imaginary line of the 40th parallel will have to be stronger (it is longer and, if anything, less naturally defensible than the 38th). And the forces required to maintain law and order, suppress guerrillas etc, will be much larger.

We are probably in for something like another Malaya even in South Korea. By going North, we merely increase that commitment by about 100%.

6. Finally it is clear that by operating North of the 38th parallel we run really serious risks of extending the war by the intervention of Communist China—and possibly also Russia. Even if China does not overtly intervene, it seems clear from Chou En-lai's speech on Oct. 1st [30th September] that they will give

every sort of covert support to the North Koreans, and thus enormously increase our military commitment there.

7. It may be argued that this is too narrow a military view, and that failure to 'make the Russians realize they are up against it' will only, in the long run, lead to increased military commitments elsewhere. I do not believe this is true; and against it must be set the *certainty* that to occupy North Korea will greatly increase our military comitments in an area in which we have no strategic interest whatever.[29]

The Joint Intelligence Staff were told to produce a geographic brief for the Chiefs before their next meeting. They summarised their views that,

(a) the greater part of North Korean heavy industry, in so far as it had survived, lay below the 40th Parallel, but the main electricity generators were to the north.
(b) the principal lateral road and all linked rail communications lay south of the 40th Parallel The north eastern mountains would in any case be difficult to control.
(c) P'yongyang and the food growing areas of the country lay below the 40th Parallel.[30]

They might have added that an advance to the 40th Parallel would also permit the construction of a defensive line on the narrowest part of the peninsula, one of its attractions to the United States military planners. This was also in the mind of Field-Marshal Sir William Slim[31] who remarked at the next Chiefs' meeting on 3rd October, after the news of Chou's midnight meeting with Panikkar had arrived, that the

. . . eventual military commitment would be greater if the United Nations remained South of the 38th Parallel than if they were to go forward. If it was decided to occupy the whole of Korea then we should only need to maintain sufficient forces to control guerrilla operations in the whole area. On the other hand, if the United Nations forces were confined to the area South of the 38th Parallel, not only should we have to maintain forces to deal with the guerrillas in South Korea but we should have to maintain sufficient forces to stop large scale incursion from the North.
Lord Fraser said that in his view the United Nations forces should go as far North as was necessary in order to prevent the North Koreans from building up for a major attack. . . .[32]

The Chiefs were no longer quite of the same mind on this matter. At the end, they agreed that the requirement to localise the conflict persisted, as did the need to bring matters to an end as quickly as possible in order to be able to deal with greater disturbances elsewhere. Recognising, perhaps, that in finding this common ground they were close to banalities, they accepted that what was needed immediately was information from Washington. What was going on in Korea along the parallel? The Foreign Office pursued the question that afternoon:

> . . . If the Chinese should in the event intervene, it would seem very difficult to localise the conflict.
>
> 2. Obtain urgent clarification from the United States Government on the following points:
>
> (a) whether (i) South Korean forces have actually crossed the 38th parallel as reported in the Press and if so whether on their own initiative or on instructions from the United Nations Command;
>
> whether (ii) United Nations forces other than South Korean have in fact already crossed the Parallel.
>
> (b) have any instructions been issued to General MacArthur regarding this [authority for crossing] or are any contemplated? We have noted from Tokyo telegram No. 1341 (of September 27th)[not shown] that General MacArthur told Sir A. Gascoigne that he had received the most definite instructions from the President himself that he was not to send United Nations forces across the Parallel without explicit instructions to do so.
>
> 3. It is difficult for us to formulate views until we have the answers to the questions listed above. In general, however, our objectives are still
>
> (a) to localise the conflict and
>
> (b) to bring the Korean affair to an end as soon as possible, including the withdrawal of United Nations Forces, so that they may be ready to deal with the possibility of more serious trouble elsewhere.
>
> 4. At the same time we cannot risk a repetition of aggression from North Korea. If North Korean military machine has already been so damaged as no longer to constitute a serious threat then, as we see it, (and pending clarification of points enumerated above) there is everything to be said for settling the Korean question by political rather than military means. There seems to be force in Pandit Nehru's statement of September 30th [to the press] . . . provided that delay does not jeopardise the military situation and give time to the North Koreans again to become a military menace. . . .[33]

This telegram owed little to ministerial direction; Mr Attlee and Mr Shinwell were at the Labour Party conference at Margate, Mr

Bevin returning by sea from the United States. It reflects the anxieties of the senior officials and military officers. It was a part of the long running international minuet being danced round the parallel crossing question. In Washington, as in London, meetings were being held, internal and external memoranda were being exchanged by departments The factors were reviewed repeatedly. Sir John Slessor was not the only participant with apprehensions of Asian dissent, though Pakistan, Burma, Thailand, and the Philippines were showing no signs of it. If Indian opinion was worried by the prospect of entry to North Korea it was equally worried by the prospect of China invading Tibet. Mr Acheson and Mr Bevin, with much else to occupy them, were content to let the minuet continue until it was brought to an end in the General Assembly.* For Britain, the Minister of State, Mr Kenneth Younger, had been left in New York by Mr Bevin to see matters to a conclusion.

Discussion of the Korean question in the General Assembly was in the First Committee forum on 2nd October. On that day, Mr Vyshinsky, the Russian Foreign Minister, supported by the delegations from the Ukraine, Byelorussia, Poland, and Czechoslovakia, proposed this resolution:

The General Assembly recommends:

1. To the belligerents in Korea that they immediately cease hostilities.

2. To the government of the United States and the governments of other states that they immediately withdraw their troops from Korea and thereby establish conditions which would secure for the Korean people the possibility of enjoying the inalienable sovereign right to settle freely the internal affairs of their state.

3. That after the withdrawal of foreign troops and for the purpose of establishing a government of a unified and independent Korean state, all-Korean elections to a national assembly be held as soon as possible on the basis of an expression of the free will of the population of all Korea.

4. A parity commission composed of North and South Korea shall be elected at a joint assembly of the deputies of the Supreme People's Assembly of the People's Democratic Republic of Korea

*Learning on 4th October of Chou's warning to the Indian Ambassador, Mr Bevin sent instructions to New York (Younger) and Washington (Franks) to seek the agreement of the United States to inviting a representative of the People's Republic of China to attend the General Assembly discussion of the Korean settlement. Mr Younger and Mr Acheson believed that the debate was too far advanced to introduce such a radical change, and the former represented this to Mr Bevin. The United States memorandum of their conversation also manifests his view that if the Chinese 'wanted to take part in the ''poker game'', they would have to put more on the table than that' [the warning].[34]

and of the National Assembly of South Korea to organise and conduct free all-Korean elections to the national assembly of all Korea. . . .

5. That a UN Committee, with the indispensable participation in it of the representatives of states bordering on Korea, be established to observe the holding of free all-Korean elections to the national assembly.

6. That for the purpose of rehabilitating the Korean national economy which has suffered from the war, the Economic and Social Committee urgently draw up, with the participation of the representatives of Korea, plans for providing the necessary economic and technical aid to the Korean people through the United Nations Organisation.

7. That after the establishment of the all-Korean government the Security Council consider the question of admitting Korea to membership of the United Nations Organisation.[35]

These were similar to the proposals put by Mr Malik in August to the Security Council. As Professor Whiting has remarked, 'Considering the military situation, the Soviet demands were high: cessation of hostilities presumably at the parallel, removal of American troops before the establishment of a unified government, parity for P'yongyang and Seoul despite Seoul's larger constituency, and the admission of Peking to UN supervision of elections'.[36] To which might be added the inclusion of the USSR as a supervisor. In an attempt to reconcile this resolution with that sponsored by the United Kingdom and others—the eight-nation proposal'*—Sir Benegal Rau proposed that a special committee should be formed to draft a compromise. This failed to attract the necessary majority.† On 4th October, the First Committee rejected the Russian resolution 46:5, and approved that of the 'eight-nations' 47:5.‡

Meantime, a signal from Air Vice-Marshal Bouchier of 4th October had reached the Chiefs of Staff. The following made them anxious,

3. An amphibious assault will be launched against objectives on the east coast probably at or near Wonsan . . .

7. Concurrently with the establishment of a firm bridgehead at Wonsan it is probable that the 8th Army of General Walker will advance to capture P'yongyang and that we should hold firmly

---

*The eight nations were Australia, Brazil, Cuba, the Netherlands, Norway, Pakistan, the Philippines, and the United Kingdom.

†32 against, 24 in favour, 3 abstaining.

‡Negative votes were Russia, Byelorussia, Ukraine, Czechoslovakia and Poland. There were seven abstentions, Egypt, India, Lebanon, Saudi Arabia, Syria, Yemen, Yugoslavia.

a line running across the peninsula north of P'yongyang to the north of Wonsan. . . .[37]

This had been preceded by information from the military *attaché* in Tokyo of military columns moving south from the border of North East China. That evening Air Marshal Elliot travelled to Margate to see the Prime Minister and Minister of Defence to tell them of the Chiefs' reactions. He left this minute with Mr Shinwell for the record:

After my conversation with you over the telephone this afternoon, I spoke to the First Sea Lord, who agreed that the Chiefs of Staff should hold a short meeting this afternoon to consider the situation arising out of the information sent to us by our Ambassador in Tokyo, and by Air Vice-Marshal Bouchier, that General MacArthur proposed to carry out an amphibious operation for the invasion of North Korea on the 10th October.

2. This meeting was held at 5 p.m. this afternoon with the First Sea Lord in the Chair, CIGS, DCAS (CAS being absent) and Mr Scott (Foreign Office) present. The views of the Chiefs of Staff can be summarised as follows:

. . . (ii) Any crossing of the 38th Parallel by United Nations troops will clearly risk an extension and aggravation of the war.

(iii) The military situation may, however, be such as to necessitate a crossing of the 38th Parallel in due course, but the Chiefs of Staff are of the opinion that there is no *immediate* military need for such a crossing.

(iv) They therefore advocate that General MacArthur should be instructed to pause on the 38th Parallel for a limited time—say 7 to 14 days—and that this pause should coincide with an immediate announcement to the North Koreans to surrender within that period.

(v) The announcement will continue to say that if the North Koreans fail to surrender within the stipulated period, the United Nations forces will then cross the 38th Parallel in order to effect their surrender by force.

(vi) The announcement will make it clear that in crossing the 38th Parallel the United Nations will have no intention of carrying out a permanent occupation of Korea.

(vii) Whilst the United Nations forces under General MacArthur pause on the 38th Parallel, South Korean forces should be allowed to continue their advance and tactical air action against military targets should also be permitted.[38]

The Chiefs met again on the 5th October, when they were joined by Sir Roger Makins* from the Foreign Office. The latter said:

that he had had a short talk with the Foreign Secretary before the latter had left for Margate. Mr Bevin felt that we were faced with a very difficult and delicate situation.

General MacArthur, using mainly American Forces, had just succeeded in restoring the situation in South Korea and was about to launch an operation for the capture of the enemy capital.

If we were to intervene, and such intervention would have to be on the highest level and in very strong terms, there was always a danger that this military opportunity might be lost and that we should be blamed by the Americans for any military difficulties that ensued: for example, the North Korean forces might use any respite which they were given to re organise their resistance. On legal grounds the view was held that General MacArthur would be justified in crossing the 38th Parallel and it would appear, although the situation was somewhat confused, that the Americans had given General MacArthur authority to advance. The latter had already made one call on the North Koreans to surrender and it would be, perhaps, inadvisable for him to make a second appeal so soon after the first.[39]

The Chiefs, notably the Chief of the Air Staff and First Sea Lord, felt that they must continue to warn the Government of the dangers of carrying operations northward, though they recognised the delicacy of interfering. They would continue to ask that a final call for surrender should be made, preferably by the United Nations itself, and that everything should be done to localise any intervention by the Chinese, for example, by continuing to confine air operations to Korea. Sir Roger promised to pass these views to Mr Bevin on his return from Margate that evening.[40]

Sir Oliver Franks had now received the series of queries and proposals relating to the development of military operations in Korea, including those prompted by the British Chiefs. He was anxious to discuss these with the State Department and, Mr Acheson being away in New Haven, he met with Ambassador Jessup and Mr Dean Rusk,† Assistant Secretary of State on Friday, 6th October. The United States record shows that they began by discussing the localisation of fighting:

1. . . . We replied that it continues to be US policy to localize the Korean fighting and mentioned to the Ambassador [Franks]

---

*Makins, Sir Roger Mellor, KCMG, then Deputy Under-Secretary at the Foreign Office.
†Rusk, Dean (1909–), later, Secretary of State, 1961–69.

our efforts to settle the Yalu bombing incidents, the public statements we have been making to reassure Communist China and the Soviet Union as to our intentions in Korea, and indirect messages we have attempted to get to Peiping [Peking] privately along the same lines.

2. The second question was whether General MacArthur had clear instructions not to attack targets in Manchuria [North East China] and Siberia and that such attacks should not be delivered without full consultation. We told the Ambassador that such was the case.

3. The third question related to the gap between General Assembly action and any major move on the part of non-Korean UN forces beyond the 38th parallel. Mr Bevin attached considerable importance to there being a gap in order not to bring into question the good faith of many delegations voting in favour of the resolution in the Assembly. We replied that we did not have precise information but that we understood that there would be some gap if the Assembly moved promptly to pass the resolution. The Ambassador said that General Bradley had confirmed to Lord Tedder that there would be such a gap, but 'not a large one'. It was agreed that the US and UK Delegations at Flushing [Lake Success] should use every effort to insure prompt passage of the Resolution on Saturday [next day].[41]

The discussion then turned to two telegrams which Mr Bevin proposed to send to Mr Nehru, the first directly for his information and encouragement towards the terms of the 'eight-power' resolution, the second with a message which Mr Nehru might send on to Peking. Mr Bevin, tired and ill after his visit to New York followed immediately by a speech at the Labour Party conference, was anxious to make a last effort to persuade China to hold back, and India to join wholly in the unification of North Korea under the United Nations command. It was clear to him that the United Kingdom and United States must be in step on their tactics: 'I am anxious to know whether [Mr Acheson] concurs in their terms or whether he has any suggestions or amendments,' he had instructed Sir Oliver. Mr Rusk noted that,

Ambassador Jessup and I confirmed that the line of this telegram accurately reflected our own attitude . . . We stated that we were confident that we reflected Mr Acheson's views and that we saw no reason to attempt to get in touch with the Secretary in New Haven.[42]

As soon as this information was passed back to London, three telegrams were sent to Sir Archibald Nye, British High Commissioner in New Delhi:

As we see it the two main objectives in Korea are:
(a) to localise the fighting
(b) to restrain Peking.
2. As regards (a) we are disturbed at the implications of further fighting in Korea and of possible extensions beyond Korea. We have put to the Americans the vital need to confine operations to Korea itself and we have stressed the importance of timing any possible future operations (should they be militarily necessary) so as to to enable the Resolution to make its maximum impact.
3. As a result of our approach to the Americans we have been informed that they entirely agree on the need to confine the conflict to Korea. As regards timing the Americans took our point but pointed out that logistics and other military considerations must be borne in mind. As we understand it the American intention is that, as soon as the Resolution is passed, General MacArthur will again address the North Koreans by leaflet and other means calling upon them to lay down their arms, inviting them to co-operate with the United Nations to build a united, independent and democratic Korea, assuring them of just treatment and promising them United Nations relief and rehabilitation for the whole of Korea.
4. These two preceding paragraphs are for your personal information only and should not be communicated to the Government of India.
5. As regards (b) of paragraph 1 above—restraining Peking— we consider that the best method of approach would be to ask Pandit Nehru to bring to the notice of the Chinese through the Indian Ambassador in Peking a statement of our intentions which may also probably be said to represent those of many member states of the United Nations. My two immediately following telegrams therefore contain:
(a) a message from the Foreign Secretary to Pandit Nehru and
(b) a second message from the Foreign Secretary to Pandit Nehru in a form suitable for transmission at Pandit Nehru's discretion to the Central People's Government [of China].
6. Please take the earliest opportunity of passing these two messages to Pandit Nehru. It is possible that in the course of today's proceedings in the General Assembly on the 8–Power Resolution a statement will be made by one of the sponsors (or even perhaps an amendment adopted to the Resolution itself)

providing for the United Nations Commission set up under the Resolution to associate itself with other Governments closely interested in the solution of the Korean problem (ie, the Chinese) If this occurs you will receive from the United Kingdom Delegation New York by emergency telegram further information based on the above which you should bring immediately to Pandit Nehru's attention with reference to the third paragraph of the second message. . .[43]

Foreign Secretary to Pandit Nehru. *Begins*. I have been giving much thought to the recent reports which you have been good enough to send me from your Ambassador in Peking about China's misgivings about developments in Korea and the movement of United Nations forces northwards. I know that both you and we are in complete agreement regarding ultimate objectives, and I particularly regret that you have not felt it possible to associate India with the Resolution sponsored by the United Kingdom and other powers now before the General Assembly. I fully share the concern you have shown regarding any extension of the conflict. Armed intervention by China would indeed be a great catastrophe, more particularly if this were to come about as a result of her misapprehension of United Nations intentions.

2. In view of the disastrous consequences which would follow from any precipitate action by China I feel that every endeavour must be made to remove any misunderstanding. I wonder therefore whether you would consent to instruct your Ambassador in Peking to tell the Central People's Government what our intentions really are. These are set out in my immediately following telegram. I have no objection, if you so desire, to the text of that telegram being shown to the Chinese but naturally I leave this entirely to you.

3. I sincerely hope that you will be able to agree to your Ambassador in Peking being the bearer of some such message and thus using your great influence with China once again towards reaching a settlement which is of such vital importance to Asia.[44]

Second message [for Peking].

We have been considering most carefully the statements of the Central People's Government regarding recent developments in the Korean situation. These show their concern about the future movements of United Nations forces in Korea and their fear that these forces may become a potential threat to China's security. We have also noted their wish to be a party to the final settlement of the Korean problem. In the light of this I feel it would be useful for me to take this opportunity to tell you how

I—and I venture to believe many member states of the United Nations—view the present situation.

2. Our primary objective, with which I know you are in agreement, is to achieve as soon as possible a unified, independent and democratic Government for the whole of Korea. We can make no real progress towards this until the fighting comes to an end. This could be brought about at once if the North Koreans laid down their arms. If they will not do so, then the United Nations Command has no alternative but to prosecute the campaign in order to prevent any recurrence of the threat to the peace of Korea. You will recall that under the Security Council Resolution of June 27th, the Commander of the United Nations Forces has the task of re-establishing international peace and security in the area. While there can be no doubt that these necessary military objectives must be achieved, there is no intention on the part of the Unified Command to take any action which could be construed as a threat to China's security. In fact it is the intention to withdraw all operational forces as soon as possible, to retain no military bases or installations, and to keep United Nations Forces in Korea no longer than is necessary for the purposes of holding elections and setting up a new democratic government for the whole of Korea as stated in the 8 Power Resolution. I also believe it to be the intention of the Unified Command that no troops other than Korean will be disposed near the China frontier.

3. I fully appreciate China's desire to be associated with all steps that are taken to secure a peaceful and final settlement of this problem. Her close historical association with Korea and her common frontier make this to my mind essential. I am sure that the United Nations Commission which is to be constituted under the 8 Power Resolution will accord the most careful consideration to the views of the Central People's Government.[45]

While these signals were being put into final order, Mr Bevin sent this final thought and instruction to Sir Archibald Nye in New Delhi:

2. At your discretion I would like you to impress on Nehru that I have taken all the measures open to me to localise the conflict in Korea to bring about a peaceful solution. I have endeavoured to take into account and to meet the apprehensions of the Peking Government. I have also done my best to keep in step with Nehru throughout this affair.

3. I cannot do more than I have done to avert Chinese involvement in Korea.[46]

These remarks might equally have been addressed to Mr Acheson. The General Assembly passed that day, 7th October, the resolution which Mr Bevin had conceived as a way forward. It recommended that:

I.

(a) All appropriate steps be taken to ensure conditions of stability throughout Korea,

(b) All constituent acts be taken, including the holding of elections, under the auspices of the United Nations for the establishment of a unified, independent and democratic Government in the sovereign State of Korea,

(c) All sections and representative bodies of the population of Korea, South and North, be invited to co-operate with the organs of the United Nations in the restoration of peace, in the holding of elections and in the establishment of a unified Government,

(d) United Nations forces should not remain in any part of Korea otherwise than so far as necessary for achieving the objectives specified at (a) and (b) above,

(e) All necessary measures be taken to accomplish the economic rehabilitation of Korea . . .*[47]

But Mr Bevin felt no great sense of triumph.[48] At a late hour he had come to believe that they should make one more attempt to draw in the Communist Chinese Government. On reflection, he realised that such a change was not only unacceptable to the United States but was unlikely to result in anything but interminable and probably fatal delay. He was more firmly persuaded by the Chiefs of Staff that a pause of a week or two on the 38th Parallel following the passing of the resolution might have been sufficient to hold the Chinese back from intervention. At heart, however, neither he nor Mr Attlee believed that there was any alternative to occupation of North Korea by the United Nations Military Command in order to carry through the programme of elections and economic assistance under the United Nations Unification and Rehabilitation Commission.

An occupation solely by the Republic of Korea's divisions was not a feasible option. As is now known, Kim Il-sung had no intention of becoming a caretaker during a United Nations occupation. President Rhee's mandate did not extend across the parallel, despite his assertions; and there was a manifest danger that ROK forces would take revenge on all identified with Kim Il-sung's

*For full text, see Appendix M.

229

regime for the atrocities his forces had committed in the south. Then, there was no guarantee that, having reached the Chinese and Russian borders, the ROK forces would have been free from engagement by the People's Liberation Army on the one side or the Red Army on the other. Even under some measure of American control by their KMAG advisers, the ROK Army would have been unable to create the conditions of political stability for free elections.

Two days later, on 9th October, General MacArthur made a second radio broadcast to Kim Il-sung and his forces:

> In order that the decisions of the United Nations may be carried out with a minimum of further loss of life and destruction of property, I, as the United Nations Commander-in-Chief, for the last time call upon you and the forces under your command in whatever part of Korea situated, to lay down your arms and cease hostilities. And I call upon all north Koreans to cooperate fully with the United Nations in establishing a unified, indepen-dent and democratic government of Korea, assured that they will be treated justly and that the United Nations will act to relieve and rehabilitate all parts of a unified Korea. Unless immediate response is made by you in the name of the North Korean Government, I shall at once proceed to take such military actions as may be necessary to enforce the decrees of the United Nations.[49]

United States forces were already in North Korea by this date, having crossed on the 7th. The advance was negligible but the event of crossing was made much of by the international press corps who watched or were briefed on the event under the arrange-ments of Eighth Army headquarters. The world was therefore left in no doubt that Americans were over, fighting as they advanced.

Even so, Pandit Nehru's wish, and that of the British Chiefs of Staff, for a final cease fire call was to an extent satisfied. There was time for Kim Il-sung to agree to end hostilities and accept the United Nations offer of elections. But he had no intention of doing so. Still at P'yongyang, he had already made arrangements to withdraw to Sinuiju, at the mouth of the Yalu, immediately across the river from North East China. He sent no official response to General MacArthur's message but made plain in a broadcast of his own on 10th October that he rejected it. It is interesting that, in all the thought devoted to this option, none had been given to the effect of an immediate refusal.

The Foreign Ministry in Peking also issued a statement on the 10th which repeated that, 'the Chinese people cannot stand idly by when such a serious situation has been created by the invasion of Korea by the United States and its accomplices. . .'.[50] The international press corps was not granted facilities in North East China to discover exactly what this warning portended.

SOURCE NOTES: CHAPTER 10

1. DEFE 5/21, COS(50) 152nd Meeting of 20th September 1950, Appendix.
2. Ibid, minutes.
3. Ibid
4. Dening, conversation with author.
5. Eighth Army of the United States in Korea (EUSAK) War Diary, Provost Marshal's section, 16 Sep-1 Oct 50. GHQ, Far East Command Allied Translator and Interpreter Section Research Supplements, and Interrogation Reports of individual formations, NKPA, September, 1950. See also the Republic of Korea Military Archive, Seoul, Capture and Interrogation of Prisoners-of-War, September, 1950. (Korean language only).
6. Ibid
7. United States Joint Chiefs of Staff (JCS) signal 92801 of 27th September 1950, personal to CINCFE, (USNARS Suitland).
8. State Department telegram 615 of 26th September 1950, Secretary of State to Acting Secretary of State, FRUS, cit, p 785.
9. JCS signal 92985 of 29th September 1950, The Secretary of Defense to the CINCFE, (USNARS)
10. CAB 129/42, Cabinet CP(50)216 of 26th September 1950.
11. Minutes of Ninth Meeting of the US delegation to the UN General Assembly, 28th September 1950, (FRUS Vol VII, pp 799-802).
12. Australian Department of External Affairs New York delegation to High Commission, London, telegrams 40 and 41 of 25th September 1950. Canberra to High Commission, London 4690 of 26th September 1950, (Department of Foreign Affairs (DFA), Canberra, File 3125/5/5.
13. DO 35/2838, Commonwealth Relations Office (CRO) to UK High Commission, India, (India) 2113 of 26th September 1950.
14. Ibid, CRO to India 2114 of 26th September 1950.
15. Ibid, UKHC India to CRO 2749 of 27th September 1950.
16. Ibid
17. Ibid, UKHC India to CRO 2754 of 27th September 1950.
18. FRUS Vol VII, US Embassy New Delhi to State Department 803 of 29th September 1950.
See also, DEFE 11/201, CRO to UK HC India 2114 of 26th September 1950 UK HC India to CRO 2748 and 2749 of 27th September 1950 New York to UK HC India 168 27th September 1950.
FO 371/84098 (FK1023/362), UK HC India to New York 2765 of 28th September 1950.
19. FRUS Vol VII, US New Delhi to State Department 812 of 30th September 1950.
20. See letter from Mr Acheson to Mr Bevin of 28th September 1950, (USNARS 795.00/9-2850).
21. FRUS Vol VII, US New Delhi to State Department 813 of 30th September 1950.
22. FO 371/84101 (FK1022/432), UN 126/639/50 to Sir G. Jebb of 30th September 1950.
23. Associated Press report from Pusan, 19th September 1950.
24. DEFE 11/201, UKHC India to CRO 2804 and 2805 of 3rd October 1950.

25. Panikkar, K.M., *In Two Chinas*, (London, 1955), pp 110-1.
26. DEFE 11/201, Peking to FO 1529 of 3rd October 1950.
27. See 24.
28. DEFE 11/201, See, for example, JIC appreciation in FO to Washington 4313 of 29th September 1950.
29. DEFE 11/201, Note to First Sea Lord and CIGS from CAS of 2nd October 1950, as follow up to Appendix to COS(50)152nd Meeting of 20th September 1950, for consideration at 160th Meeting on 3rd October 1950, DEFE 5/21.
30. DEFE 11/201, See also loose minute 'Advantages of holding a line on the 40th Parallel', JIB2 of 3rd October 1950.
31. Slim, conversation with author.
32. DEFE 5/21, COS(50)160th Meeting of 3rd October 1950.
33. DEFE 11/201, FO to Washington 4396 of 3rd October 1950.
34. Memo of the meeting of the US delegation to the UN General Assembly on 4th October 1950, USNARS 795.00/10-450.
35. UN document UNA/C. 1/SR.348.
36. Whiting, Allen S., *China Crosses the Yalu*, (New York, 1960), pp 112-113.
37. DEFE 11/201, Tokyo (Bouchier) TRAIN 4A to MOD (COS) of 4th October 1950.
38. DEFE 11/201 and 202, Copy sent to COS under MOD 1298/5/10/50 of 5th October 1950.
39. DEFE 5/21, Mins, COS(50)162nd Meeting of 5th October 1950.
40. Ibid.
41. Memo of conversation between Mr Dean Rusk and Sir Oliver Franks on 6th October 1950, USNARS 795.00/10-650.
42. Ibid.
43. DO 35/2838, CRO to UKHC India 2236 of 7th October 1950.
44. Ibid, CRO to UKHC India 2237 of 7th October 1950.
45. Ibid, CRO to UKHC India 2238 of 7th October 1950.
46. Ibid, CRO to UKHC India 2242 of 7th October 1950.
47. UN document A/PV.249
48. Dening, conversation with author.
49. *Bulletin*, US Department of State, 13th November 1950.
50. Radio Peking broadcast (English language), 11th October 1950. See also Peking to London 1568 of 12th October 1950, DEFE 11/202.

CHAPTER 11

Pursuit to the Yalu

Nine days passed between the end of the fighting for Seoul and the crossing of the 38th Parallel by the American 1st Cavalry Division. By this latter date, 7th October, IX Corps had stretched its boundaries north to include the capital, and the bulk of X Corps had been withdrawn to embark at Inch'on, or was in process of being withdrawn by air, road and rail. Helped by Korean military engineers and civil labour, the Army engineers had managed to repair enough bridges, restore enough track, to reopen surface lines of communication. But the road surfaces were riddled with potholes. There were scarcely enough resources to reinforce crumbling shoulders, none for resurfacing.

The 27th British Commonwealth Brigade was warned on the 4th that it was to move north of Seoul. Advanced parties, heavy weapons, ammunition and equipment were to travel by road. The remainder of the brigade—the 'marching' element—was to be lifted by air from Taegu to Kimpo, a simple enough plan. There were, however, immediate practical problems. I Corps headquarters could only provide transport to lift one battalion. The aircraft were due to take off at 0800 from Taegu, 25 miles distant over a circuitous one way route. Two round trips by the American trucks would just be feasible in the time available; three would not. Not for the first or last time in the campaign, the stores and supply trucks—B echelon—were emptied to carry the third battalion. Departure of the first flight was delayed until 1200—just as well, the sandbag bridge over the Naktong south of Waegwan had been partially swept away by floods after a night of heavy rain. One column of trucks was delayed while it was repaired. The officer commanding the leading element of the brigade, arriving just after noon, expected to be met by an angry air commander at the head of a line of waiting aircraft. A rifle company clerk recalled,

Actually, when we got there, they were quite surprised to see us. Many of the planes had arrived earlier in the day but the tail of one of the C119s had collapsed on landing and they were inspecting all the others as they came in. That took time. Besides that, they all had to unload their cargoes. Then we heard that

235

one of the aircraft had been given the wrong fuel. So no one was really ready for us much before 2 p.m. Our company commander stopped sweating.[1]

3 RAR departed first in a mixture of C54s and C119s. Last to arrive were the Middlesex. The brigade war diary recorded that they 'were flown off throughout the night, the last plane taking off at 0400 hrs. To the delighted astonishment of Major Alan Hunter, the DAA&QMG,* who was in charge of the British arrangements, the entire event was accomplished without a single written order or authority from any source:

> The whole of the airlift was organised by one captain of the US Air Force and was very well organised as far as the men were concerned. Meals were available and even a stage show was in progress during the early part of the evening.[2]

As the loading approached its end, it was discovered that there were 15 men in excess of seats. Major Hunter, due to board the last aircraft wondered how he was going to leave Taegu. To his further surprise, the Air Force Combat Cargo Command sent a C47 immediately to pick up the residue.

At Kimpo, facilities were scant. As each battalion arrived, it settled on open ground on the airfield perimeter. Tents were improvised with groundsheets. A distant water point, owned by the United States Marines air wing, was found and, an unexpected luxury, a row of hot showers, which they were invited to use next day. Each man had his rations and a small stove fuelled by blocks of solid methylated spirits, 'Tommy cookers'. Latrines were dug, security picquets posted. The three battalions with a fragment of brigade headquarters settled to a delightful rest.

They fared better than the road parties, jolting over 260 miles of potholes to Kimpo. Brigadier Coad and his commanding officers continued into Seoul to find the headquarters of I Corps. There they received a personal briefing.

General Milburn's corps had been ordered to assemble north of the Imjin river preparatory to conducting operations northwards.[3] The 1st Cavalry Division, with 27 Brigade under command, was to advance up the main Seoul-P'yongyang highway—a single track road—and railway line. The 24th Division was to cover the left or western flank, 1 ROK Division the eastern. The much vaunted crossing of the parallel by American forces on 7th October was made by reconnaissance patrols. General Gay did not give his

---

*See fn to p 163.

orders for the advance until 0900 on the 9th,[4] at which time some of his units were still skirmishing below 38°. The movement of the division's fighting and administrative transport was delayed due to the scarcity of roads and tracks, all of which had been mined; the North Koreans had made good use of the nine day pause in the pursuit.

Brigadier Coad came to divisional headquarters on the 10th to resolve a number of queries about his role. By that date, his brigade was concentrated in and around Kaesong, ready for action. Whatever numbers of North Koreans remained to deny an advance in the western sector, Brigadier Coad felt 'pretty confident—we were at our strongest, and the main body had had a short rest'.[5] The Middlesex now had four rifle companies, the Argylls three as a result of being reinforced.* 3 RAR numbered more than 1,000. The latter had lost several of these in mine accidents just after their arrival. They had also had a small number of reverse 'desertions'—men who, believing that the war was coming to an end, had set off singly or in pairs to join the foremost American forces for a taste of battle. These zealots were recovered, suffering no more than a sharp rebuke.

General Gay, who had been chief of staff to General Patton during the second world war, was determined to emulate his old commander by driving forward to the limit of his resources. But he had been warned by General Milburn that the hills were full of NKPA detachments, fighting as guerrillas,† so that he must flush out the ground on either side of the highway as he advanced or risk having his line of communication cut. There were besides formed bodies of the enemy ahead, thought to be in the old North Korean frontier defences. To achieve the double aim of rapid progress with a general clearance of the frontage, the divisional plan placed 8th Cavalry Regiment in the centre to clear the highway, sent the 7th in a loop westward across the River Yesong, and the 5th looping east to brush shoulders with 1 ROK Div before it returned to meet the 7th above Kumch'on. 27 Brigade was to clear a minor road spotted from the air by a Mosquito light aircraft, advancing within 5th Cavalry's arc.

---

*The Middlesex were 640 all ranks on that day, the Argylls, 587.

†Advancing in the central and east coast sectors, the lines of communication of I and II ROK Corps had been cut frequently by small enemy parties. During the rail and road journey south to Pusan, parties of X Corps were attacked by forces several hundred strong. The Argylls were mortared as they drove north to Kaesong. Guerrilla attacks by uniformed soldiers of the NKPA, isolated by the break out, in company with former local guerrillas, continued to disrupt the resettlement of the countryside for many months, involving savage treatment of civilians believed to be supporting the Government, and equally savage reprisals by Government—principally police—forces against those thought to be assisting guerrillas.

The Middlesex set off at 1315 on the 11th October from a harbour area 2 miles north east of Kaesong. They were in trucks, following 5th Cavalry's column. Ideas of a grand sweep of their own declined. They crawled along in fits and starts as the leading elements of the 5th halted to deal with small enemy parties or suspicious sightings. By dusk they had moved five miles, when it was discovered that the track which was to carry them away from 5th Cavalry was not fit for vehicles; even as a footpath it came to a dead end in a nearby village. Frustrated, Colonel Man turned his battalion back to its starting point.[6]

During the next few days, all three battalions swept areas of the countryside in the area of the 38th Parallel, sometimes below, sometimes above it.* There were many reports of enemy from the villagers, and patrols were led to where caches of arms and ammunition had been hidden by the NKPA. In some areas, villagers had been killed by the withdrawing soldiers for actual or fancied acts of hostility. The Middlesex found several groups of two or three bodies whose hands had been tied behind their back before being shot in the head. 3 RAR were shown eight in one group. Prisoners were taken, mostly stragglers. Among three surrendering to the Australians was a soldier who threw a grenade from his raised hands. Lieutenant Philip Bennett kicked it away— he and another soldier were slightly wounded by fragments as it exploded at a distance—and the thrower was shot dead.[7]

All evidence showed that numbers of enemy were being flushed from the brigade area and some were crossing by night to the west of the highway between Kaesong and Kumch'on. The Argylls established several posts on the highway, but those manning them saw only streams of American trucks running north and south.

1st Cavalry Division's initial plan had been brought to a successful conclusion by intermittent hard fighting and some remarkable leadership. Kumch'on had been captured, the Yesong crossed to the west. Namch'onjom, thirty miles north, had been stormed. At this point, the road turns westwards towards the large town of Sariwon, an important North Korean military training, supply and communications centre. 7th Cavalry had reached an intermediate point, the small town of Sohung, on 16th October. Even so, this pace was not up to General Milburn's—or General Walker's— expectations. Prisoners of war identified themselves as being members of the 19th and 27th NKPA Divisions opposing 1st Cavalry, with others from the 43rd Division west of the Yesong.[8] But the intelligence staff knew that the first two had until very recently

---

*Lieutenant-General Sir John Harding, Army commander-in-chief in the Far East, and Air Vice-Marshal Bouchier, visited the Brigade during these operations.

been brigades and, despite reinforcement by half trained recruits, were unlikely to have a divisional potential in numbers or weapons. The 43rd Division was a coastal defence formation; its men were in process of elementary training. 1 ROK Division, overtaking 1st Cavalry on the right, appeared to have a tougher foe in the residue of 17th Armoured Division. On 15th October, a very wet day, General Milburn ordered General Church to come up on the left of the Cavalry, with the aim of reaching Sariwon through the Ongjin Peninsula. The two divisions were to race for the town. Whichever got there first would be given the right to capture the enemy's capital, P'yongyang.

No doubt this encouragement of rivalry was meant well. As ever on the battlefield, however, the fostering of competition between friends tends to distract those concerned from the aim of defeating the enemy. What might have been a spectacular corps encirclement became instead a *meleé*.

Before this character was imposed on operations, General Gay had warned 27 Brigade to take the lead as the first phase ended. On the 15th, divisional orders were issued. Brigadier Coad gave his own to commanding officers at 1130 on the 16th. He was relieved to have what he termed his 'own axis', at last, 'a proper job to do; we had been been at the edge of things too long'.[9] Under command was 90th Field Artillery Battalion of 155-mm howitzers— three batteries—89 Tank Battalion, and a company of 72 Combat Engineers. Expecting to be advancing for three or four days, and bearing in mind his instructions for speed, he arranged to split these American units between his battalions, making each a 'battalion group', a mixed force of infantry, armour and engineers. The second group in each column would be prepared to pass through the first at short notice; the third would lie back in reserve, ready to take the lead. Two of the howitzer batteries would always be in firing positions, the third either firing or moving forward. Within battalions, commanding officers similarly allotted resources to rifle companies: each had a tank platoon, a 3-inch mortar and a medium machine-gun section. The leading company had the engineer platoon, augmented by the battalion assault pioneers, ready to clear mines or other obstacles. An important element lacking was troop carrying transport. Without it, the column would be confined to the marching pace of the rifle companies. I Corps had only sufficient to lift two battalions. Once again, stores, equipment, reserve ammunition and rations had to be unloaded from the B echelons to provide passenger carriers, an arduous task which left these items stranded by the side of the road with a few storemen until they could be collected during the night.

The Argylls, who had fortunately been in a comfortable base in the largely undamaged town of Kaesong, were warned to take the lead on 17th October. However, they had first to get on to the highway, packed with traffic. It took seven hours to force a way in. The Argylls arrived in their concentration area, a river bed about a mile to the east of Sohung, at 7.30 p.m. on the 16th October. Lieutenant-Colonel Neilson, the commanding officer, at once went forward to liaise with the battalion commander of 7th Cavalry holding the village.

Next morning, the Argylls group started off at 0647, led by A Company under Major David Wilson. The countryside was empty after they passed through Sohung: no one was working in the fields; there were no carts on the roads. A self-propelled gun to a flank, shot at by the tanks, turned out to be a burned out hulk. In the next eight miles, they passed a number of North Korean trucks, abandoned with empty petrol tanks, before coming to twin villages, Hungsu-ri and Sinwon-ni. From the former, snipers opened fire prematurely at long range. The tanks tried to blow or burn them out by high explosive but this did not work. The leading platoon dismounted, shooting into the housetops as they passed down the streets or forcing out snipers with smoke grenades. The tanks were among them, firing the .50 calibre machine-guns on their turrets. One Highland soldier was killed at almost point blank range. Some of the snipers escaped to the west; those who stayed were killed in their positions. This incident took an hour of the morning. There were more snipers at Masan-ni, the next village, but this time infantry and tanks closed at once, clearing the much smaller collection of buildings in about twenty minutes. All four snipers were killed.[10]

By 2 p.m. they were ten miles on. The Argylls' commanding officer was not pleased to be joined by three American generals and a jeep load of newspaper reporters. General Gay had sent forward the visiting I Corps chief and assistant chief of staff with Brigadier-General Frank A Allen jr, his own deputy. They had invited a press party to join them. Colonel Neilson did not respond with enthusiasm to the suggestion that he was leading a race with the 24th Division for Sariwon.

That objective was now less than five miles distant from A Company, but at half past two they heard firing immediately ahead. Major Wilson recorded the sequence of events shortly afterwards:

> . . . the leading tank was fired on by an anti-tank gun and small arms. At that point the road ran round a bend and from the company headquarters jeep I could see at least 40–50 enemy

running away [to the left of the road] out of an orchard. I directed the fire of the [platoon] commander's tank on to these and he engaged with machine-gun and high explosive.

At this moment the liaison aircraft which had been flying ahead of the column chose to land in front of the [platoon] commander's tank impeding further progress down the road and there then developed a gap of 800 yards between myself and my leading platoon into which the press and visiting generals rapidly infiltrated. This did not aid the general conduct of the battle.

Brigadier-General Allen came running forward, waving his map, shouting, 'They're in that orchard, rake 'em, blast them out of there!' His ADC climbed on a tank to give fire directions to which, fortunately, no one paid much attention.[11] Major Wilson remarked that,

> 13. Very shortly after the opening burst of fire the commander of the second tank in the column was seriously hit, and the wireless of the leading tank went out. I was still, however, in touch with the forward platoon commander and ordered him to engage the enemy.[12]

It took some thirty five minutes from the opening North Korean round until the remainder of A Company was in position to deliver the *coup de grâce* to the road block, a position manned by about seventy NKPA soldiers with an SU-76 anti-tank gun. In this time, orders had been issued to the tanks, the mortar and machine-gun sections, the second and third rifle platoons in A Company, all of whose commanders had joined Major Wilson and the artillery forward observer for hasty orders in the roadside ditch. The artillery had ranged and begun to fire for effect, the mortars had bedded in their base plates behind another orchard, the machine-gunners had doubled to the site chosen for their tripods, and the infantry platoons were in their respective positions.

The actual assault took about eight minutes. A combination of fire and close quarter battle killed forty two of the NKPA on the site without loss to the Argylls. Seven haggard prisoners were taken. The remainder had escaped, perhaps into Sariwon.

As this little battle was ending, Colonel Neilson took the remainder of the battalion group into the town. He was anxious to secure it before dark. So was Brigadier Coad. His plan was to block the road with 3 RAR five miles beyond Sariwon to catch any enemy attempting to slip through during the night. The Mosquito light aircraft had spotted enemy in position in a small pass just north of this location and Lieutenant-Colonel Green was instructed to attack it with his Australians next morning.[13]

Sariwon lies on the main railway to P'yongyang. At that time, an outlying section of the township had developed round the station, junction and marshalling yard a mile to the south of the original site. Scattered small dwellings, shops, and several concrete military warehouses filled the gap between. The whole had been repeatedly attacked from the air. Although some buildings were still undamaged, including those on one side of the barracks, the remainder were ruined.[14]

The Argylls dismounted short of the railway suburb, which B Company began to clear. C Company and the tanks led the remainder into the town centre. They were surprised to see men in civilian dress and a number of women and children moving about or looking out from buildings, despite rifle shots nearby. Tanks and jeeps parked in the streets. The Australians had some difficulty in finding a passage as they followed C Company, advancing through the central section to the northern end.

Brigadier Coad found Colonel Neilson by some ruined buildings in the gap between the town and the railway suburb. The light was beginning to fail. Much of the town had not been cleared. Confirming his plans for 3 RAR, the brigadier ordered the Argylls to secure the south and south western town exits for the night, anticipating the arrival of North Koreans withdrawing in front of the 24th Division. The colonel gave instructions for B Company, clearing snipers from the one point of high ground west of the railway suburb, to secure the highway into the town. He intended to bring back C Company to block the southern road. A Company, just arriving after clearance of its battle site, would fill the ground between them. As C Company would take some time to return from the northern edge of Sariwon, Colonel Neilson called up the company second-in-command, Captain Colin Mitchell, to show him the exact site he wished C Company to occupy. Unwisely, as it transpired, he decided to take Major J B M Sloane, the battalion second-in-command* with him on this short reconnaissance

At about ten minutes to six that evening, then, these various activities were proceeding. Suddenly a vehicle appeared from the south east. This was the opener of a night of surprise encounters. It was a Russian truck packed with North Korean soldiers. Both sides were surprised but began to exchange shots as the North Koreans drove north through Sariwon.

Colonel Neilson and his party were driving off after this excitement when they met a second enemy truck approaching from the eastern side of the railway. To Colonel Neilson's vexation, his Sten

---

*Major Sloane had brought out the reinforcements from Scotland, and became second-in-command in place of Major Muir.

machine carbine jammed, but others in his party with B Company opened fire and a grenade was thrown into the back of the vehicle. It crashed to a halt, all twenty occupants dead.

Off again went Colonel Neilson with his reconnaissance party in three jeeps. Coming up the highway, on either side, was a long column of soldiers—more North Koreans! Those at the head of the column opened fire at them briefly but on the colonel's orders they accelerated down the road towards Chaeryong at high speed. The split column of about two thousand enemy soldiers extended for several miles. A few souls among them turned to stare after the speeding vehicles but most trudged on, incurious. Some minutes thus passed before the three jeeps cleared the tail end. Driving on until they were quite alone, the group found shelter down a side road.

The North Korean column continued into Sariwon, apparently unaware that it had fallen. A and B Companies were deploying into their night positions, C Company were returning through the town. Word passed that marching troops were approaching. Some expected the Middlesex. The North Koreans, seeing Europeans in cap comforters, thought they had fallen in with Russians. 'Russki, Russki!' they cried. 'Russki!' called back the Jocks nearest, puzzled, now thinking that the newcomers were members of 1 ROK Division. But each became suddenly aware that the other was the foe: shots broke out, the North Koreans scattered through the streets, and then 'the whole town seemed to explode with firing. The wonder is that none of us were hit—as much by our own rounds as those of the Gooks.'[*][15]

At some stage, this column found an empty road on the north side of the town and resumed their march along the highway. A light flashed briefly at the roadside:

I was in an apple orchard with WOII[†] W A M Ryan and six guides awaiting the arrival of the ration vehicles, [said Major Ferguson, second-in-command, 3 RAR] when coming up the road from the rear we heard the tramp of marching feet.

. . . When the column was abreast of me I flashed on the jeep lights to see who it was. The officer at the head of the column called out 'Russki!' just as one of my guides fired off his Owen gun.[‡] The column dispersed, taking up fire positions. I asked Lieutenant-Colonel Green for the loan of some troops and,

---

[*]'Gook' is the Korean word for people. The British used this term for Koreans as 'Yanks' were used for Americans.
[†]Warrant Officer Class II.
[‡]The Owen gun was a 9-mm calibre machine carbine, designed and manufactured in Australia.

although he doubted my statement, he did in fact give me Major G M Thirlwell, MC, and his [B] company to clear them out.

Major Thirlwell, an interpreter and I mounted a tank and drove down the road. Through an interpreter we told the North Koreans they were surrounded and gave them two minutes to give themselves up. They were the longest two minutes of my life. A deathly hush fell over the area and you could hear your own heartbeats. Finally, the North Koreans surrendered and the bag for the night was 1,982 prisoners plus some anti-tank guns and a host of LMGs, MMGs and mortars.[16]

B Company's night operation had not ended. When the ration vehicles arrived, they included a Russian truck among them. Lieutenant E O Larsen found an officer inside with two female and twenty three male soldiers. He made them get out and march. More marching North Koreans had by this time appeared:

. . . Ahead of us we saw a Russian truck bogged down. An officer loaded with red tabs called to us 'Russki!' and indicated that he wanted his truck pulled out. As I tried to take his pistols he started yelling and within a minute gooks were running in all directions. Our fellows opened up and killed a few but the chap in red tabs got away.[17]

The two girls were probably the same pair encountered by Captain Robin Fairrie, mortar officer of the Argylls. A Russian truck had come up alongside his own earlier and a girl in the back had asked for his Balmoral. Some of his soldiers close by were equally asked for keepsakes and, aware that they were heavily outnumbered, passed these over. This North Korean party apparently believed that they were Russians and passed on without hostility.[18]

Back in Sariwon, the adjutant, Captain Slim, and the intelligence officer, Lieutenant Boswell, disturbed at the absence of Colonel Neilson and Major Sloane, called in Major Gordon-Ingram, the senior company commander, to take command. He drew the three companies in close together, enclosing as many of the vehicles as possible among the ruins. This was a sensible arrangement. Parties of North Koreans, looking for food and transport on the line of march, came into the town throughout the night and brushed periodically with the Argyll's outposts.[19]

Further north, 3 RAR were contacted by 1st Battalion, 7th Cavalry Regiment. The regiment having worked its way along a minor road to the east during 17th October, had reached the highway at Hwangju. General Gay ordered it to send a unit south to make contact with 27th Brigade and trap with them the hundreds of North Koreans spotted by aircraft as they made their way through the hills. During the afternoon, the 1st Battalion captured a detachment of horsed cavalry moving towards 3 RAR. Then it came upon the ambush position which Colonel Green was preparing to destroy next day. Persuaded by a ROK interpreter that the Americans were Russian troops, this enemy body came out to greet them and were taken prisoner. Seeing their apparent surrender, hundreds of North Korean soldiers came in from the hills immediately to the east to do likewise. Others, whose movement could be clearly seen to the west, continued to fire small arms at long range until dusk when, suddenly, they too surrendered *en masse*. They totalled seventeen hundred, with thirteen women nurses.[20]

Lieutenant-Colonel Peter D Clainos, commanding 7th Cavalry, made radio contact with 3 RAR at 1945[21]. Moving south slowly with his horde of prisoners in darkness, his 1st Battalion moved through the pass, switching on their leading vehicle lights for identification as they neared Colonel Green's positions. He was later to say that he heard a disgruntled Australian remark, 'Now what do you make of this? Here we are all set for a coordinated attack in the morning, and the bloody Yanks come in at midnight from the north, with their lights burning, and bringing the whole damned North Korean Army as prisoners.'[22]

Next morning, 18th October, 3 RAR were ready to move at 0630. They had risen at 5 o'clock, washed, shaved, packed their kit and made some sort of breakfast. There was much to be done before getting on to the transport. Disposal of their own mass of prisoners had to be effected—many were sent back in empty supply trucks and this required the despatch with them of guards. Fortunately, the 7th Cavalry formed a temporary concentration area for those awaiting removal and the Australians' residue of prisoners were added to them.

The capture of Sariwon by 27 Brigade had effectively won General Milburn's P'yongyang Stakes for 1st Cavalry Division. It was given pride of place on the highway; 24th Division was ordered to stand fast a few miles below Sariwon. General Gay sent a letter of warm congratulations to Brigadier Coad for the advance of forty miles in the day. His gratitude was not boundless, however; the British Commonwealth force was not going to be first into the North Korean capital. The brigade was to switch to the left flank on reaching Hwangju, and just to make sure that there was no doubt about it, General Gay was waiting for 3 RAR when they reached the town to tell Lieutenant-Colonel Green to turn left off the highway.[23] The remainder of 27 Brigade was taken off the road for the time being, immediately south of Hwangju. Traffic jams were frequent as 7th Cavalry moved north and the 5th attempted to enter from the east. The Australians, deliberately limited in range by Brigadier Coad to prevent their isolation, made contact with an enemy company in Samgap'o. A Company under Major Gordon, supported by the American tank squadron, briskly cleared the village and hill spur behind it. Five North Korean soldiers were killed, three captured, with no loss to the Australians or American armour.

During the 18th, 7th Cavalry were held up on the P'yongyang highway, ten miles to the north. General Gay decided to hedge his bets: 27 Brigade should be prepared either to continue as flank guard or, if necessary, to close up to assist in overcoming those blocking a shallow pass at Hukkyo-ri The brigade was therefore given road priority across the improvised river bridge at Hwangju from 0600 to 0900 on the 19th. Brigade headquarters and the Middlesex set off along the highway. For lack of transport, the Argylls marched, following 3 RAR. But Hukkyo-ri and its exits to the north had already fallen.[*] Brigadier Coad was instructed at 1130 to move altogether on the flank. They were free of traffic blocks as a consequence but the route was often 'little more than a muddy path. Many of these could not take the loads; we spent hours hauling trucks out of ditches.'[24] There was heavy rain intermittently throughout the day. 3 RAR warned that the route was getting worse not better: the rest of the brigade was obliged to return to the highway, fit into the rare gaps in the traffic stream, and pick up the western road north of the Hukkyo pass. It was one of those tedious days when there is no action but no rest. The Argylls, for whom transport had been produced during the day, were the last to come in to harbour in heavy rain at 0330 on the 20th.

That afternoon, 3 RAR had been opposed briefly by fire from a group of armoured vehicles. Their accompanying tanks returned the fire and subsequent clearance by the infantry found one Russian T-34 destroyed, another with an SU-76 abandoned. Both had dry petrol tanks.

P'yongyang had now fallen. A company of 5th Cavalry entered the outskirts of the city shortly after 11 a.m., following a brief final encounter with an NKPA detachment. 1 ROK Division were pacing them after a series of forced marches, and actually crossed the River Taedong into the heart of the capital ahead of 1st Cavalry Division. The Americans had been held up because all the bridges were blown. Major-General Paik Sun-yup, approaching from the south-east, knew where he would find a crossing place.

---

[*] The NKPA opposing the Australians at Samgap'o were part of the same force opposing 7th Cavalry at Hukkyo-ri

'I am a native of P'yongyang, he told the commander of the 5th Cavalry when they met. 'I know the fords.'[25]

Led by the Middlesex, 27 Brigade arrived in the south western outskirts of P'yongyang at noon on 20th October. They had entered that morning the lower valley of the River Taedong, passing into flat, open country. As elsewhere, the rice paddy contained only stubble. Rice straw was stacked along the dividing walls. Maize fields were thick with dead stalks.

> . . . many barracks and police stations were passed along the route which suggested, together with the type of country travelled over, that this was a military training area. The civilians, who came out to cheer and applaud the advance of UN Forces in our area, appeared genuinely enthusiastic by their welcome. This was perhaps good training on their part and merely due to a deeply engrained respect brought about through the years of dealing with the military![26]

Brigadier Coad did not know that P'yongyang had fallen and half thought that his brigade might have bypassed the enemy on the highway. His radio 'rear link'* to 1st Cavalry Division was not working. Though the Middlesex reported the presence of American soldiers as they reached the suburbs, none of those encountered knew the location of 1st Cavalry Division headquarters. He ordered his units to concentrate until fresh orders arrived. There was a general hope that they might have a few days to service their weapons, vehicles and equipment, for everyone to take off their boots while resting, and to find a bath or shower unit. Major Willoughby of the Middlesex later recalled, 'A few of the young soldiers newly arrived as reinforcements had the extraordinary idea, because it was a Friday, that we might have the week end free!'.[27]

Next morning, 21st October, brigade headquarters discovered that its radio link to 1st Cavalry Division had disappeared. The 24th Division had been ordered to lead the advance but, as it was still well to the south of P'yongyang on indifferent roads, 27 Brigade was to carry forward the pursuit until General Church's division caught up.

At levels of command below the division, the American practice was to issue orders in the form of a map 'picture'. Objectives, routes, boundaries, enemy and friendly forces would be sketched

---

*Each unit or formation in the field is sent a radio by its next higher authority which is an 'outstation' on that authority's 'command' net. The subordinate terms it its 'rear link' to the superior. The 'rear link' from 27 Brigade to 1st Cavalry Division operated inadequately throughout its advance to P'yongyang.

out on the respective map sheets and marked, as appropriate, with dates and times or other necessary details. A master trace or 'overlay' would then be made for reproduction on a duplicator. Each subordinate element would receive a copy, and trace the details on to its own maps. Despite some shortcomings, it was a satisfactory method of issuing orders quickly; but like the more conventional form of written orders, its success depended upon a sufficiency of information and accuracy in what it depicted. Brigadier Coad was accustomed to the British system of verbal orders, supported if advisable by brief written instructions, or full written orders supported by maps or traces. He disliked the United States single trace method because, it seemed to him, those sent to his brigade invariably lacked details he needed to know.

Thus, on 21st October, a staff officer from I Corps arrived at his headquarters early in the morning with an 'overlay' which instructed him to advance with his brigade as rapidly as possible to the Chongch'on river, to cross it and to seize the town of Chongju. The latter was seventy five miles distant up the main highway. There were no details as to the whereabouts or plans of 24th Division, under whose command he now came. 'Also on the trace a circle was drawn about Sukch'on marked "187 Airborne Combat Team". I had no information of any airborne landing'.[28]

He should have been told that General MacArthur had launched a parachute operation by 187 Airborne Regimental Combat Team, aiming to cut off the withdrawal of North Korean officials—optimists in Tokyo thought these might even include Kim Il-sung—and the remnant of the North Korean People's Army in the western sector. He hoped, too, to recover American prisoners-of-war in their hands. It was a promising idea, one that would have had a better chance of succeeding if he had had a complete airborne division. As it was, anxious not to project the lightly armed parachute force too far from his leading ground forces, the Commander-in-Chief held them back too long. They were not dropped until the 20th. By that time, 1st Cavalry Division had been committed to the security of P'yongyang and Chinnamp'o so that relief depended upon the rapid advance by 6 ROK Division and, as noted, 27 Brigade.

The airborne plan comprehended a simultaneous drop in two zones. The first, DZ (drop zone) William was on the main road to the Chinese border close to Sukch'on, about thirty miles north of P'yongyang. This was the most distant from UN forces. The second, DZ Easy, was twenty miles to the east of William and close to the town of Sunch'on. A railway ran through both sites. The majority of the RCT dropped on William at 1400 on the 20th

October; the 2nd Battalion Group on Easy at 1420. The 6 ROK Division was then within sight of DZ Easy.

Brigadier Coad later reported,

> There was only a one way sand-bag bridge over the river at P'yongyang and after a request we received priority from 1200 to 1400 hours.
>
> We started about 1100 hours with the Argylls in the lead and the first difficulty was the large number of sand-bag road barriers on our road to the bridge. They were formidable obstacles about 10 feet high* and required vehicles to do a double turn to get through them. This proved too much for some of our [tracked] carriers and several delays occurred.
>
> The scene at the bridge was chaotic, traffic was trying to cross in both directions. The Chief of Staff, 1st US Corps, was standing near the bridge doing nothing about it. After a few chosen words he and my Brigade Major and some American police sorted the muddle and my Brigade eventually got over.
>
> I also enquired about 187 ACT [Airborne RCT] and was told by the Chief of Staff that our first task was to link up with them. This information was passed to the Argylls.[29]

At Kambuk, a few miles to the north of P'yongyang, the 27 Brigade military police had established a lonely traffic post; they were briefly the point of the United Nations force. The road divides here, forking right to Sunch'on, left to Sukch'on, the lower Ch'ongch'on crossings and Chongju. Lieutenant-Colonel Neilson stopped his leading company at this site, pausing to collect his column together after the impediments of the city.

From Kambuk, they did not have to fight for a place on the road as they forked left. The land was empty again except for occasional burned out vehicles and, in one or two villages, parties of old men, women and children cheering and waving. Brigadier Coad, who had also paused at Kambuk to see the Australians arrive, then followed the Argylls. For almost two and a half hours the advanced and main guards pushed on at about eight miles an hour. At 4 p.m., the column turned north west out of a long river valley. Crossing the flood bank, the tanks led through low hills which closed as they progressed. The road looped. Vehicles came briefly under sniper fire from the hillsides. Tank fire scattered those engaging them.

Brigadier Coad drove up to find Colonel Neilson:

---

*These barriers were part of the North Korean defence works. Kim Il-sung's orders had envisaged a street by street defence of the city.

We were coming into hilly country and I didn't want to try driving through in the dark. For one thing, I still had no idea of precisely where the airborne troops were, though [I] Corps had sent a message to say that they thought there was a company in Yongyu. I told the Argylls to stop just short of the town.[30]

The brigade plan for the 22nd required the Argylls to clear Yongyu, through which 3 RAR would pass to advance to Sukch'on. Colonel Neilson put his companies out on the hilltops surrounding the loop in the road and sent a patrol to Yongyu to contact whomsoever they might find there from 187 Airborne. An officer and two soldiers departed on this latter task, a matter of some delicacy not simply in avoiding enemy ambush but in avoiding a firefight with American outposts. They successfully contacted K Company of 187, commanded by Captain Claude K Josey, established in some scattered houses on the northern edge of Yongyu and Hill 163 immediately above. This small force had moved south during the day, capturing Hill 163 after a sharp fight with North Koreans who were seen to withdraw east and south. Their main battalion position was about two miles to the north. They believed that there were several large enemy detachments nearby as another airborne company of the battalion had been driven into the hills from Op'a-ri during the afternoon.[31]

This was a useful warning. Actually, they had all entered an area occupied by 239 Regiment, the last NKPA element to leave P'yongyang. Its task was to delay the UN advance up the main highway but by the evening of the 21st October it was aware that there were UN forces to the north and south. About a thousand strong, three hundred of the regiment were hiding in Yongyu.

Returning to his headquarters, Brigadier Coad met an American colonel from I Corps Headquarters, who said he must

. . . attack Yongyu. As it was now dark, I refused and asked what he was doing. He said he had been sent up to liaise between myself and the airborne and had been with the leading company of the Argylls. He was highly excited and disappeared, but I was to see more of him.[32]

At midnight the NKPA in Yongu attacked K Company, breaking into its headquarters. Captain Josey and several others were wounded in hand to hand fighting but managed to eject them. The battle sounds were heard clearly by the Argylls. Half an hour after this ended, a small number of enemy attacked A Company, killing two and wounding two of their number by grenades. The Argylls quickly drove them off, killing one, wounding another. Soon a second outbreak of firing was heard from Yongyu followed by what sounded like cheering. Major Wilson and his company feared that K Company had been overwhelmed. In fact, the parachutists had lost their roadblock position below Hill 163 but had managed to draw into a tight perimeter on the northern edge of Yongyu.[33]

As soon as it was light, A and C Companies of the Argyll and Sutherland Highlanders began clearing the town. Using high explosive and white phosphorous grenades to run down snipers, many buildings soon caught fire. None of the battalion was hit and a considerable number of prisoners were taken. Captain Josey's embattled parachute company was relieved at the far end of the town. The colonel from corps HQs then caused some confusion by ordering the leading Argyll platoon to advance with tanks to relieve 187 RCT but fortunately this scheme was quickly counter-manded by Colonel Neilson.[34]

As planned, C Company of 3 RAR under Captain A Denness emerged from the smoking streets with D Company of the American 89th Medium Tank Battalion at 7 o'clock to continue the advance.

The main body of 187 Airborne was thought to be on the highway between the 55 and 56 northing grid lines. Because this was so imprecise, artillery fire could not be used to support Captain Denness in any immediate action in case of shelling friendly troops. For reasons not apparent, 3 RAR's mortars had not been brought forward in support. Still, C Company had eighteen Shermans; they were scarcely lacking in firepower.

A mile from the town, light mortar and small arms fire was opened on them from an apple orchard five hundred yards to the east. Leaving one platoon on the road, Captain Denness hastened to the hillside with the other two while the tanks fired their guns and machine-guns by direct observation. The speed and dash of the Australians was remarkable. Many of the North Koreans made the error of leaving their trenches as the assault force covering fire was at a height. They suffered accordingly. Four of C Company were wounded.

Lieutenant-Colonel Green had been close behind C Company as the attack took place and decided to clear the entire ridge of high ground overlooking the highway. While C Company flushed out the survivors of its attack from straw in the paddy fields, A and B Companies climbed the ridge. D Company, rearmost in the column, was ordered to advance on foot along the road. The forward element of battalion headquarters concentrated in the apple orchard.

Prisoner-of-war reports indicate that a substantial number of 239 Regiment were, as earlier assessed, recently trained conscripts, a qualification which accounts for their errors in abandoning trenches at the wrong moment. But they had among them experienced leaders. On this account alone, the NKPA remained a dangerous foe. Suddenly, a counter-attack was mounted on the apple orchard from the east. Three of Colonel Green's rifle companies were moving away from him to the west and north; none were immediately to hand. Instructing D Company to come to his relief, the colonel gathered his headquarters back to back to hold their ground. Three were wounded before the enemy were driven off.

In this action as a whole about one hundred and fifty of the NKPA were killed, two hundred and thirty made prisoner, some wounded. With those engaged by the Argylls, the total of killed exceeded two hundred. Prisoners captured, and those surrendering exhausted through the day, totalled five hundred.

C Company moved on with the tanks and contacted 503rd Parachute Battalion. They were warmly welcomed by the Americans who were very short of ammunition after a morning battle. Then the Middlesex arrived. They had been ordered to push on to Sukch'on to complete relief of the 187 Airborne. By nightfall, the battalion was in a defensive position a mile to the north of the town. At Yongyu, brigade headquarters attempted to ease the circumstances of a crowd of refugees, some of whom were wounded. Rice straw was brought in to provide warmth and a hot meal was provided from a share of the military rations.[35]

Next day, 23rd October, the whole brigade came up to the Ch'ongch'on river at Sinanju, which the Argylls found to be clear of enemy. Chongju, their objective, lay thirty miles along the highway, across the Ch'ongch'on and the lesser stream of the Taeryong. The road and rail bridges across the Ch'ongch'on, eight hundred yards wide at this point, had been destroyed. The I Corps chief engineer had insufficient bridging to hand but could provide assault boats. The Middlesex, warned for the crossing, were told that they must establish a bridgehead next morning.

The river was tidal, falling twelve feet on the ebb. There were, however, no tide tables. 'A frightened local was found who gave us the [tidal] information after a good deal of difficulty, by using sign language and drawing diagrams in the dust with a stick.'[36] Opinions varied as to what these foretold. Some thought he indicated high tide on 24th October at 0700, others thought 0900. Colonel Man decided to cross at 0830, his best option for slack water. The United States engineers carried the assault boats to the bank on the evening of the 23rd but omitted to bring paddles for half the number. The crossing did not begin until 9 o'clock, by which time it had become evident that,

. . . the only opposition from the North Koreans was the great press of villagers and local dignitaries who streamed down the far bank to welcome the regatta . . .

. . . The first flight . . . were immediately swept upstream and ultimately reached the far bank simultaneously with the local mayor and great hosts of little men in white carrying enormous flags who, too, had experienced some difficulty in forecasting the exact point of disembarkation.

The second company was more fortunate, and a slackening tide gave them a pretty fair run with a very fine and less breathless concentration of local dignitaries to help them ashore.

The third company started off well with slack water, but in a few minutes the necklace of boats began to show ominous signs of sagging downstream, and once more the reception committee was on the move . . . on to what turned out to be an island close to the far bank with a sort of Noah's ark ferry waiting for them. By this time the tide was streaming out and the ferry grounded in mid-channel with the rear half of the Company. One by one they had to be dragged ashore through fathomless black mud.

The last company went one better . . . its headquarters in the mud on the far bank, half the Company aground in mid-stream and the other half disappearing in the direction of the Yellow Sea.[36]

Local fisherman helped to gather in the stragglers.

. . . by nightfall defensive positions had been occupied covering the main bridge from Sinanju. There were many signs of recent enemy occupation and the bridge had been covered by well dug-in positions and field pieces sighted for direct fire. Many of these had been abandoned and most of the houses contained weapons and ammunition.

Although the battalion had safely gained its objectives it was without its supporting arms, its transport, its rations and its blankets.[37]

The temperature dropped well below freezing point that night, adding to the discomfort of the Middlesex. But their occupation of the middle ground between the Ch'ongch'on and the Taeryong rivers was an essential step in the advance which Brigadier Coad meant to continue on the 25th. The 24th Division was closing up behind his column. General Church planned to split his axis at Pakch'on, sending 5 RCT north to Taech'on, 21 RCT west behind 27 Brigade to Chongju. In a telephone conversation with Brigadier

Coad, the divisional chief of staff stressed that operations were approaching a successful conclusion; 'one final stroke will do it'. The news the Middlesex passed back of abandoned positions, and the gathering of sixty-six prisoners-of-war—mostly deserters and stragglers—in the Sinanju area contributed to the impression of an enemy in the final stages of disintegration.

1 ROK Division had arrived in Anju on 23rd October to find the road bridge damaged. The engineers expected to have it repaired for light wheeled traffic by the 25th. A ford was found for armour three miles upstream. Learning that 27 Brigade's American engineer company were unable to raft even light vehicles, General Paik agreed on the 24th that 27 Brigade could use the road bridge for a period next day and its armour the ford.[38]

By 4 p.m. on the 25th, 3 RAR with their comrades, D Company of the 89th Tanks, had passed through the Middlesex to reach the village of Kujin, in which the road turns west across the Taeryong to continue through Chongju to the Chinese border. But the centre span of the Taeryong bridge had been demolished. The column halted and the battalion's 3-inch mortars came into a firing position. Lieutenant A Morrison with two sections of his 4 Platoon crawled across the wreckage to the far bank, covered by the remainder of B Company and the tanks. The Mosquito light aircraft of the tank battalion scouted beyond.

On the other side of the river, the road runs through a ridge rising steeply from the river bank. As Lieutenant Morrison's party advanced to the foot of the ridge, fifty NKPA soldiers were seen coming down from the right with their arms up. They were closing on the Australians when rifle and light machine-gun fire came from the high ground, directed apparently on those surrendering. Lieutenant Morrison's party returned fire while taking in the ten North Koreans nearest to them—the remainder had scattered.

During the unfolding of this little event, Colonel Green had sent D Company from the rear of his column to clear Pakch'on, a mile and a half to the north* and to look for a bridge or ford in that locality. At 1700, they reported that they were entering the town.

About this time, the Mosquito returned with the news that there were two companies of enemy on the ridge across the river. Colonel Green at once recalled Lieutenant Morrison and instructed A and B Companies to prepare to assault these positions. A fire plan was arranged by the American artillery and his own mortars. Immediately, he asked for an air strike on the target.

---

*Two of the brigade's Royal Military Police section, engaged in route signing, inadvertently preceded 3 RAR into Pakch'on. They were fired on and wisely withdrew just before D Company arrived.

The ACT—the United States Air Force air contact team— produced a quick response. A pair of F-8os appeared at 1715, quickly identified and attacked the targets. The light was now fading, however; the guns and mortars took up the bombardment.

Major Brown reported that he had cleared Pakch'on, taking two hundred and twenty five prisoners without opposition. The American engineer platoon with him had found a damaged under- water bridge which they believed they could repair. An Australian platoon was left to protect them at this work. At 1900, A and B Companies crossed the Taeryong by the wrecked bridge, climbed the ridge in moonlight and began to dig in. The enemy appeared to have withdrawn.

This idea was dispelled within half an hour. From 1930 and intermittently throughout the night North Koreans in various strengths counter-attacked. Colonel Green sent a platoon of C Company across the river to reinforce the ridge positions. Although casualties were relatively light, there were difficulties in evacuating them across the river. The wounded were hand carried on stretchers to the broken span of the bridge, where, under the arrangements of the drum-major,* Sergeant T M Murray, each stretcher had to be lowered twenty feet into a boat, which was then hauled by ropes to the opposite bank. From time to time, the bridge was fired on. The first boat sank. The last was swept against the concrete piling and also sank. Sergeant Murray dived into the icy water to rescue the wounded occupant.

Occasional shelling of Kujin by armour piercing rounds indicated an SU-76 in the enemy force, but there had been no report of tanks until, at 0400, two T-34s approached A and B Companies with several wheeled vehicles and about sixty infantry. One of these moved round to fire on A Company, the other closed on B Company headquarters. This was the first close encounter of the Australians with armour and, in their excitement, those armed with rocket launchers forgot to move the safety catches to the firing position. But a combination of shells and mortar bombs, intensified by the small arms and grenades of those on the ridge, threw back the enemy. After dawn, two Russian jeeps were found with a motorcycle, all undamaged.[39]

Among the dead was a lieutenant-colonel, Kim In-sik, who had commanded the reconnaissance battalion of the 17th Tank Brigade since 23rd October, probably because of exigencies; he was primar- ily a culture—that is, a political—officer. His diary showed that on the previous day,

---

*The operational task of the drummers and buglers was stretcher-bearing. They were attached to the regimental aid post.

. . . it seems that our infantry and tanks preparations were late before the enemy. The demands of the front line were for ammunition. To supply ammunition efficiently, it is necessary to perfect the rear supply lines. Since morning, members of the Culture Section were sent out to recruit local farmers and retreating soldiers for transportation purposes. The problem of clothing for the soldiers has not been solved, however. I promised to take action for the night of 25 October 1950. From yesterday the enemy's air attacks have increased. It seems they are supporting the ground troops who will probably cross the river and advance. We are in a bad position. The time for the overall counter plan is here before us now. A new culture propaganda plan was established to change the tide of battle from defence to attack. General plans and instructions were made and three important staff members were present. Former staff members were replaced. Plans for assignment and reassignment of culture staff members were completed. Yesterday I met the Corps Chief of Staff and Brigade Commander and conferred about the education of the men . . .[40]

Lieutenant-Colonel Kim's diary showed that the 17th Tank Brigade, with twenty tanks, had been ordered not to withdraw from the Chongju defences, the line of which was indicated in a map found on his body. They had also been enjoined to look out for 'local rebellions'.

In spite of enemy interruptions at Pakch'on during the night, the American engineers continued their work on the underwater bridge. Tanks were able to wade there at 1100 on the 26th, though the water was still too deep for wheeled vehicles. Brigadier Coad put two companies of the Argylls across against minor resistance and passed the Middlesex through them to connect with 3 RAR. Wheeled vehicles followed that night. Although North Korean patrols attempted to harrass the brigade's outposts and a few shells fell into the perimeter, it was a quiet night.

The experiences of the 25th and 26th, taken with air reports on the morning of the 27th, persuaded Brigadier Coad that, despite their losses, the forces ahead still included tanks. He decided to advance in shorter bounds, clearing high points *en route*.[41] The Middlesex, temporarily under command of Major Gwyn, moved west at 0900 on the 27th October. Three miles beyond the Australians, they were fired on from the village of Yongsong-ni, which was promptly struck from the air. C Company advanced to clear it. The houses began to blaze as they entered and were soon exploding; the village was filled with enemy ammunition. C Company reeled back temporarily. In the smoke, the company commander's carrier was hit by a tank which crushed one of Major Favelle's legs. They were now entering a circular valley, principally dry rice paddy. On the far side, where the highway entered a small pass, North Korean tanks and infantry held a crossroads. Major Gwyn moved his companies forward in succession steadily under air strikes, artillery and mortar fire. D Company, moving through C, which had captured the cross roads, found that the enemy had withdrawn. By the early afternoon, the whole area was taken without further loss—three members of the battalion had been killed in the initial clash and three were later wounded. Thirty five enemy soldiers had been killed, a further eighty prisoners were captured. Ten enemy tanks and two SU-76s had been knocked out in the Middlesex engagement.[42]

While this battle was developing, brigade headquarters received air reports of an enemy force three or four hundred strong approaching Pakch'on from the north. Brigadier Coad left the Middlesex area to confer with Colonel Neilson. The Argylls, now concentrated on the west bank, were warned to cover the town. But as a reconnaisance was being made for new positions, 5th Regimental Combat Team appeared, ready to advance north to Taech'on. It was a timely relief.[43]

27 Brigade was now able to bring its headquarters, howitzers, and baggage across the Taeryong* and concentrate on capturing Chongju. The Argylls took the lead on 28th October. Between 0800 and the last hour of daylight, the battalion advanced fourteen and a half miles, occasionally skirmishing with enemy infantry and knocking out an SU-76. Tanks spotted in ambush ahead by the Mosquito were knocked out by air attack called in and directed by the ACT. They were halted four miles from Chongju. The following entry appears in the 27 Brigade war diary for the 28th:

> During the evening, an officer PW was brought in and interrogated . . . He gave information that he was of the 2nd Battalion, 17th NK [Tank] Brigade. He had 50 men with him at Napch'ongjong [cleared by the Argylls about noon] where he received orders on night 27/28 October to withdraw to Sonchon [30 miles beyond Chongju] . . . and that his Brigade was to withdraw to that area. On withdrawing his men to the Chongju area, he met three tanks and was given a message from his commanding officer that he was to return with the tanks to Napch'ongjong and engage the advancing UN forces. When the leading elements of 1 A&SH approached his force, they scattered

---

*During this move, a road shoulder collapsed, toppling the operations staff truck into a deep watercourse. Inside the vehicle, Major Reith, the brigade major, and a signals NCO, Corporal Rudge, were killed.

and fled. He gave details of the composition of 17 NK Brigade and stated that the 1st Battalion had been engaged in bitter fighting on the bank of the Taeryong river 48 hours previously, and had suffered severe casualties . . .

Chongju seemed now almost within 27 Brigade's grasp. It was an important railway and road junction, but more important to the brigade it had been their long range target for some days. Brigadier Coad proposed to 24th Division that, once it had been taken, 21 RCT might, as had been mooted, pass through and give the brigade an opportunity to rest and maintain its equipment. Although they had not all been engaged every day in battle, they had been living in clothing and equipment continuously since taking over positions on the Naktong, apart from the brief stand easy at Kimpo. Many still lacked winter clothing. Shirts, under-clothing and socks were in tatters, boots wearing out.

Still, Chongju had yet to be taken. Having limited resources, the enemy had apparently two options in its defence: to hold forward on the hills to the east of the River Talch'on, or to defend the west bank, the town and hills on either side. On the morning of 29th October, 3 RAR advanced to discover which of these sites the local NKPA commander had selected.

D Company under Major Brown led the column with two platoons of tanks. Their axis lay along the highway. One thousand yards beyond the Argylls forward posts the hills ended on a north-south valley containing rice paddy. As the the leading tanks prepared to cross this towards the main feature on the far side, the brigade's familiar friend, the Mosquito light aircraft, reported that there were at least four tanks on that feature both left and right of the highway. Lieutenant-Colonel Green stopped D Company and ordered air strikes.

Eight pairs of F80s and F51s* attacked targets on the high ground during the next three hours, using napalm, rockets and .50 calibre machine-guns. Nine tanks and two self-propelled guns were claimed as destroyed.† During this time, Colonel Green gave orders for a full attack on the hills and his force deployed to carry it through. The 155-mm howitzers of 90th Field Artillery Battalion and 3 RAR's 3-inch mortars began to fire concentrations.

---

*The propellor driven F-51 Mustang was better suited to ground attack, having a greater range and load potential than the faster, jet driven F-80 Shooting Star. The former could carry two 110 gallon napalm tanks and six 5-inch rockets. The latter normally carried the same napalm but only had rockets if the range was short. Both had six .5-inch machine-guns and could carry bombs at a sacrifice in radius of action. The Army believed that the slower F-51 was more accurate in attack.

†Actually, as discovered on the ground later, four T-34s and one SU-76.

D Company advanced with its tanks to capture the feature south of the road. Once this was gained, A Company under Captain W J Chitts was to capture its extension to the north. D Company closed at 1430. For two hours infantry and tanks clawed their way on to the high ground through scrub and occasional clumps of stumpy pine trees. Half the tanks, lying to the right on a hillock captured with 10 Platoon, shot to cover the infantry entering the enemy positions. The infantry sought the enemy armour and self-propelled anti-tank guns dug deep into hides to warn the tanks of their location. Inevitably, they were not always successful; for one thing the American tanks were within range of T-34s and SU-76s to the north of the highway. A Sherman was hit by an armour-piercing round. But the tanks followed the infantry closely. However, one bold Australian, Private J H Stafford stalked a T-34 and opened fire on it with his Bren light machine-gun, luckily setting fire to petrol cans on the hull. The two rifle platoons, attacking a superior number of enemy, searched out the entrenched enemy through the afternoon under the responsive fire of the howitzers and mortars. At 1630, Major Brown reported on his radio that D Company group was in possession of the the hill.

Almost immediately, A Company with two tank platoons began to attack the enemy to the north of the road. It had been a general hope in 3 RAR that, with D Company to the south, the adjoining feature would be abandoned. But although fire now fell upon the second objective from two sides, it took A Company an hour of hard fighting to secure it. Colonel Green had said some sharp words to his battalion about rocket launcher handling two days before. Now the two Bazooka men with 3 Platoon responded, knocking out three T-34s.[44]

Brigadier Coad had spent the afternoon watching the progress of 3 RAR's battle. Early on, he called forward Colonel Man to give preliminary orders for an advance by 1 Middlesex into Chongju next day.[46] But after his departure, he became apprehensive. The 3 RAR success in capturing the western valley exits by 1730 was an important step in the advance to Chongju, though quite a costly one; they had lost nine killed and thirty wounded in the process. The accomplishments of the day had not, however, carried them on to the hill features overlooking Chongju. When he was called back to 24th Division headquarters at 1730, a drive of 35 miles, he was not altogether in a happy frame of mind. 'I suppose I half expected a massive battle to get into Chongju, and I was by no means certain that we would be relieved at the end of it.'[46]

On arrival at Divisional HQ, I was asked by the Divisional Commander whether I would like to be relieved. A difficult question I thought, as the relieving Regimental Commander was also present. I pointed out that we were all right to go up to the Yalu, but we were slowing [up] and as speed was essential, fresh troops would obviously go faster.

It was then decided that 21 RCT should pass through us, once we had secured Chongju, which I undertook to do by 1500 hours the following day.

On my return to my HQ at about midnight [actually, 2330], I found the situation was not as good as I had hoped. 3 RAR were still on their first objective where I had left them and they had been counter attacked again at 2100 hours, but were firm.

I therefore ordered 1 Middlesex to attack to the north of 3 RAR as soon as possible in the morning, 3 RAR to conform their forward movements with them. 1 A&SH to be ready to pass through and clear Chongju.[47]

3 RAR were counter-attacked twice during the night. The first onslaught succeeded in getting right through a platoon position in A Company but was ejected. The second, against D Company, described by Major Brown as a 'banzai' charge, was defeated about 2200 by artillery and mortar fire brought down in prearranged defensive fire zones.* Thereafter, the night was uneventful for 27 Brigade.[48]

Next day was sunny, both in the weather and the course of operations. The Australian attack and its defeat of the counter-attacks of the night had broken the enemy locally. One hundred and fifty North Koreans were found to be dead in their area. By 11 a.m., the battalion had advanced, skirmishing but without loss, to overlook the valley of the Talch'on, killing a further twelve and capturing ten soldiers, some of whom were evidently stragglers. The Middlesex, meantime, had pushed forward on the extension of 3 RAR's high ground to the north, a move which carried them to the river bank without contest. The Argylls forded the river in the afternoon with two platoons of Shermans to find Chongju empty.

Warned by the Mosquito that there were enemy tanks to the west of the town, the Sherman platoons became cautious. It was 1700 before Chongju was finally reported clear, when, welcome sight to 27 Brigade, the tanks and infantry of 21 RCT began to move past and beyond them on the road to the Yalu river.[49]

---

*As a matter of routine, a unit taking up a defensive position selects the approaches which menace it most. The map coordinates of these are notified to the artillery and/or mortars as specific targets—then known as 'DF' (defensive fire) 'zones'—so that they can respond quickly when fire is called into one or another. One or two were classed as 'DF(SOS) tasks'. Artillery or mortars laid their sights on these whenever they ceased firing on other targets so as to be able to respond immediately on demand.

Close security was observed by the brigade as it settled for the night; for though they were now in divisional reserve, their experience since arriving in Sariwon suggested that groups of the NKPA might yet appear on their doorstep out of the night by design or accident. Still, apart from the Middlesex, who were detailed to move to Taech'on next day, it was 'a relief to know that we would not be moving again immediately, and that someone else was ahead of us'.[50] Lieutenant-Colonel Green was one of a number to the east of the river who decided to turn in early for sleep. He had retired to his tent when,

> At 6.10 p.m., just on dusk, six high velocity shells, presumably fired by a marauding self-propelled gun or tank west of Chongju, hit the battalion headquarters area. The headquarters was protected by being sited on the reverse slope of a hill overlooking the Talch'on river and five of the shells exploded harmlessly on the forward slope. However, the sixth cleared the crest and hit a tree, exploding very close to Lieutenant-Colonel Green's tent. The Commanding Officer was asleep on a stretcher and was badly wounded in the stomach by a shell fragment . . .

He was taken by road to a MASH—mobile army surgical hospital—at Anju, but the wound was mortal. He died there on 1st November.[51]

The Middlesex had moved on 31st October, as instructed, to Taech'on, to provide a reserve force on 24th Division's northern axis. After being held up by a bulldozer broken down on the road above Pakch'on, the battalion arrived in the town at 1500. As they arrived, the advanced party were bringing in two prisoners who had been driven from a hiding place by local citizens. One of them was a North Korean lieutenant. The other was a Chinese soldier.[52]

SOURCE NOTES: CHAPTER 11

1. RMP, conversation with author.
2. 27 Bde War Diary (WD), 5th October 1950.
3. Eighth United States Army in Korea (EUSAK) Operation Order (OO) 103. of 3rd October 1950 (USNARS, Suitland).
4. Appleman, op cit, p 623.
5. Coad, conversation with author.
6. Man and Major (now Brigadier) D B Rendell, conversation with author, and letter from Man.
7. 3rd Battalion, The Royal Australian Regiment (3 RAR) War Diary (WD), 13th October 1950.
8. Appleman, op cit, p 623.
9. Coad, Coad Report, Pt III, p 1, and conversation with author.
10. Wilson, conversation with author.
11. Appleman, op cit, p 644.
12. 1 A&SH WD, 17th October 1950, Appendix J.
13. Coad, Coad Report, Pt III, p 1, and conversation with author. 3 RAR WD, 17th October 1950.
14. Major (now Major-General J B M Sloane), conversation with author. The author was in Sariwon shortly after these events.
15. Boswell, and R Stone, conversations with author. 1 A&SH WD, 17th October 1950.
16. Bartlett, Norman, *With the Australians in Korea*, (Canberra, 1954), p 29.
17. Ibid, pp 29-30.
18. Stone, conversation with author, Bartlett, op cit, p 29.
19. Boswell, conversation with author. 1 A&SH WD of 17th October 1950.
20. US 1st Cavalry Divison (Cav Div) WD, 17th October 1950 (USNARS, Suitland).
21. 3 RAR WD, 17th October 1950.
22. Appleman, op cit, p 646.
23. 3 RAR WD, 18th October 1950.
24. Major (now Lieutenant-Colonel) H R Jeffes, conversation with author.
25. General Paik Sun-yup, conversation with author. Quoted also in Appleman, op cit, p 651.
26. 27 Bde WD, 20th October 1950.
27. Rendell, conversation with author.
28. Coad Report, Pt III, The Advance from P'yongyang, p 1.
29. Ibid.
30. Coad, conversation with author.
31. Wilson, conversation with author. 1 A&SH WD 21st October 1950. Appleman, op cit, pp 658-60.
32. Coad Report, Pt III, The Advance from P'yongyang, p 1.
33. Wilson, conversation with author. Appleman, op cit, pp 658-60.
34. Wilson, conversation with author. Coad Report, Pt III, The Advance from P'yongyang, p 2.

35. 3 RAR WD and 27 Bde WD, 22nd October 1950. O'Neill, op cit Vol II, PP 35-37

36. Coad Report, Pt III, The Advance from P'yongyang, p 3.

37. Shipster, op cit, pp 20-23.

38. Paik Sun-yup, conversation with author and 1 ROK Div WD. Coad Report, Pt III, The Advance from P'yongyang, p 4 does not tell the whole story of this arrangement.

39. 3 RAR WD, 26th October 1950. O'Neill, op cit, pp 41-44.

40. 3 RAR WD, October 1950, Appendix 3.

41. Coad, conversation with author. 27 Bde WD, 28th October 1950.

42. 1 MX WD 27th October 1950.

43. Coad, conversation. 1 A&SH WD, 27th October 1950.

44. 3 RAR, 29th October 1950. O'Neill, op cit, pp 47-49.

45. 1 MX WD, 29th October 1950.

46. Coad, conversation with author.

47. Coad Report, Pt III, The Advance from Pakch'on, pp 1-2.

48. 3 RAR and 27 Bde WD, 29th October 1950

49. 3 RAR and 1 A&SH WD, 30th October 1950. Appleman, op cit, p 682.

50. Jeffes, conversation with author.

51. 3 RAR WD, 30th October 1950. O'Neill, op cit, pp 50-51.

52. 1 MX WD, 31st October 1950.

29. Lt-Gen Sir John Harding with Lt-Col Man, CO, 1 Middlesex, Brigadier Coad, Comd 27 Brigade, and AVM Bouchier, Chiefs of Staff's representative with General MacArthur, 15th October 1950. (Major B Reed)

30. B Company, 1 Middlesex, aground in Ch'ongch'on river, 24th October 1950. (Major B Reed)

31. 1 Middlesex crossing the Taeryong river, 26th October 1950. (Major B Reed)

32. C Company, 1 Middlesex, 27th October 1950, advancing towards Chongju. (Major B Reed)

33. Lt-Col Neilson, CO, 1 A&SH, with Brigadier Coad and Lt-Col Man after
the award of the DSO to the latter, November 1950. (Major B Reed)

34. 1 RUR disembarked from *Empire Pride* on the quay at Pusan, 5th November
1950. (Brigadier M N S McCord)

35. 1 RUR move by train from Pusan to Suwon, November 1950. (Brigadier M N S McCord)

36. Pte Clarke of 1 Middlesex brings in a Chinese deserter with a safe conduct pass, November 1950. (Major B Reed)

37.   D Company, 1 Middlesex, ride up to Kunu-ri pass, November 1950. (Major
      B Reed)

38.   D Company, 1 Middlesex, moving to positions at Kunu-ri supported by
      five US tanks, November 1950. (Major B Reed)

39. D Company 'O' Group, 1 Middlesex, below Kunu-ri pass, November 1950. (Major B Reed)

40. D Company, 1 Middlesex, advance uphill to final positions at Kunu-ri, November 1950. (Major B Reed)

41. Members of Drysdale Force (41 Independent Commando, RM) returning to Koto-ri after the convoy battle en route to Hagaru, 30th November 1950. (Royal Marines Museum)

42. Supply drop at Koto-ri, 4th December 1950. (Royal Marines Museum)

43. 41 Independent Commando, RM, hampered by refugees as they withdraw from Koto-ri, 10th December 1950. (Royal Marines Museum)

44. Members of the Commando moving to embark on the USS *General Randall*, during the evacuation from Hungnam, 12th December 1950. (Royal Marines Museum)

CHAPTER 12

Home by Christmas

While the Eighth Army was pushing into North Korea, and X Corps was progressing towards landing at Wonsan, President Truman made arrangements to meet General MacArthur. Periodic congressional elections were due in November 1950. In keeping with a reputation for contumacy, General MacArthur had made a series of statements since June which were at odds with government policies, the most recent being his letter to the Veterans of Foreign Wars in August*. It would clearly be politically advantageous if, in a personal encounter, the Democrat President could effect a *rapprochement* with the Republican general.

Mr Truman was a shrewd politician. However, other factors prompted him. He had a clear idea as to the loyalty owed to the presidency by an officer of the armed forces, indeed by any subordinate to a superior in the service of the state. He wanted to assert this. Then, contrary to the opinion of Mr Acheson, who believed that General MacArthur was irredeemably corrupted by power, the President expected to improve the general's judgement by widening his perspective of domestic and Atlantic developments. In a personal account of his eight years in office, he remarks that until October 1950 he and General MacArthur:

> . . . had never had any personal contacts at all, and I thought he ought to know his Commander-in-Chief† and that I ought to know the senior field commander in the Far East. I have always regretted that General MacArthur declined the invitations that were extended to him to return to the United States, even if only for a short visit, during his years in Japan. He should have come back to familiarize himself with the situation at home. This is something I have always advocated for our foreign service personnel—that they should spend one year in every four in their own country. Then they would understand what the home-folks were thinking.

---

*See p 190.

†The President of the United States of America is *ex officio* Commander-in-Chief of the armed forces.

. . . The Peiping [Peking] reports of threatened intervention in Korea by the Chinese Communists were another reason for my desire to confer with General MacArthur. I wanted to get the benefit of his first-hand information and judgement.

For a short time, I thought of flying to Korea to pay our troops there a brief visit*. I realized that MacArthur would feel his place in those perilous days was near his forces and that he would hesitate to make the long trip across the ocean for what might be only a few hours' talk. I suggested therefore that we meet somewhere in the Pacific and Wake Island was agreed on as a good location.[1]

Crossing the international date line, The President's party reached Wake Island at 6.30 on the morning of Sunday, 15th October. It was a lonely outpost, principally a refuelling stop for Pan-American Airlines. President and General travelled in 'an old two door sedan' to a private meeting in the office of the airport manager.

The General assured me that the victory was won in Korea. He also informed me that the Chinese Communists would not attack and that Japan was ready for a peace treaty

Then he brought up the subject of his statement about Formosa to the Veterans of Foreign Wars. He said that he was sorry if he had caused any embarrassment. I told him that I considered the incident closed. . . .

The two men continued to talk alone for about an hour on the Far East and Europe:

The general seemed genuinely pleased at this opportunity to talk with me, and I found him a most stimulating and interesting person. Our conversation was very friendly—I might say much more so than I had expected.

A little after seven-thirty, we went to another small building where other members of our parties had gathered. . . . Admiral Radford, Ambassador Muccio, Secretary of the Army Pace, General Bradley, [Ambassador at large] Philip Jessup and Dean

---

*He was dissuaded from doing this because it might have required him to venture north of the 38th Parallel, and would certainly have obliged him to meet and enter discussions with President Rhee, who was insisting on his right to visit the north.

Rusk from the State Department, Averell Harriman, and Colonel A L Hamblen from General Bradley's staff.*[2]

The larger meeting lasted for about an hour and a half. Much of the conversation, running freely without an agenda, concerned the rehabilitation of Korea and continued support for President Rhee and the National Assembly on the basis of the elections supervised by the UN Commission, but with a recognition that the United Nations insistence on new elections in the north must be honoured. The following points concerning Korean operations emerge from the record:†

General MacArthur: . . . I believe that formal resistance will end throughout North and South Korea by Thanksgiving [23rd November]. . . . It is my hope to be able to withdraw the Eighth Army to Japan by Christmas. That will leave the X Corps, which will be reconstituted, composed of the Second and Third Divisions and UN detachments. I hope the United Nations will hold elections by the first of the year. Nothing is gained by military occupation. All occupations are failures. (The President nodded agreement.) . . .

The President: What are the chances for Chinese or Soviet interference?

General MacArthur: Very little. Had they interfered in the first or second months it would have been decisive. We are no longer fearful of their intervention. We no longer stand hat in hand. The Chinese have 300,000 men in Manchuria. Of these, probably not more than 100/125,000 are distributed along the Yalu River. Only 50/60,000 could be gotten across the Yalu River. They have no Air Force. Now that we have bases for our Air Force in Korea, if the Chinese tried to get down to P'yongyang there would be the greatest slaughter.

---

*Mr Acheson did not approve of the meeting and asked to be excused. As Secretary of State, he suggested that Jessup, Rusk and Harriman, together with Muccio, would provide all necessary departmental advice. The Foreign Office view of General MacArthur was influenced by Mr Acheson's strong mistrust of him.

Also present were Charles G Ross, the President's press secretary, Colonel Matthews of the Army staff, Major-General Courtney Whitney and Colonel Laurence E Bunker of General MacArthur's staff.

†Ambassador Jessup had brought his secretary, Miss Vernice Anderson, to type the anticipated communique. Sitting in the next room, of which the door was later alleged by General MacArthur's staff to have been ajar, she took full notes of the meeting in shorthand, reportedly on her own initiative. General MacArthur's military assistant had been stopped from making notes by Mr Ross, and there was no other manifestation of minute taking, though a number of those at the table made personal notes. General Bradley later asserted that a record of the 'substance of statement' was compiled by the presidential party on the journey home, and that he sent five copies of it to General MacArthur on 19th October.[3]

With the Russians it is a little different. They have an Air Force in Siberia and a fairly good one. . . . They are probably no match for our Air Force. The Russians have no ground troops available for North Korea. They would have difficulty putting troops into the field. It would take six weeks to get a division across and six weeks brings the winter. . . .

Mr Rusk: Not long ago, Bajpai spoke to Henderson about a suggestion Nehru was turning over in his mind. This would be placing Indian and Pakistani troops along the Korean-Manchurian and Korean-Soviet frontier to act as a buffer between these countries and the US forces in Korea. While they were talking, Nehru sent for Bajpai who returned shortly thereafter saying that Nehru had dropped the whole idea. We might think this over in case Nehru comes up with it or something similar in the future. I wonder if General MacArthur thinks such a plan would be dangerous?

General MacArthur: It would be indefensible from a military point of view. I am going to put South Korean troops up there. They will be the buffer. The other troops will be pulled back south of a line from 20 miles to the north of P'yongyang to Hamhung. . . .[4]

The two groups parted, the presidential aircraft *en route* for Hawaii and then San Francisco, where Mr Truman was to make a speech about Korea referring, incidentally, to 'a man who is a very great soldier—General Douglas MacArthur'. The general returned to Tokyo and the conduct of the war.

Immediately, both the President and General MacArthur appear to have been pleased with the outcome of their meeting. The President believed that he had developed a mutual understanding with the general, politically and personally. He was satisfied that the war would soon be over and the objectives for which the United States and its allies among the United Nations had been struggling would be realised. General MacArthur believed that he had won the President's confidence. It encouraged his notion that events were following the pattern of his struggles in the Pacific during the second world war: early crises; final victory. The reports awaiting him from the battle front did not upset his expectations.[5]

Two days after his return to Tokyo from Wake Island, he abandoned constraints on UN forces approaching the Chinese and Russian borders. As a part of the orders to cross the 38th Parallel, a 'MacArthur Line' had been established on 27th September, beyond which only ROK forces would be permitted to operate. It ran from Chongju through Kunu-ri and Yongwon to Hamhung. But with X Corps still at sea, there were signs that the ROK forces available might be insufficient to take control of the extensive frontier provinces. On 17th October, the line was shifted to within thirty to forty miles of the borders.[6] On the 24th he cancelled all restrictions on the movement northward of non-Korean forces.

When the Joint Chiefs of Staff pointed out that this was not in accord with their directive of 27th September, General MacArthur replied that General Marshall's supplementary message of the 29th had advised him to 'feel unhampered tactically and strategically' in operations north of the 38th Parallel* 'I am fully cognizant of the basic purpose and intent of your directive, and every possible precaution is being taken in the premises. The very reverse, however, would be fostered and tactical hazards might even result from other action than that which I have directed. This entire subject was covered in my [sic] conference at Wake Island.'[7]

Those attending the conference from the Defense and State Departments could not agree with this last point, though some conceded that a re-reading of the C-in-C's remarks might indicate his intention. The Joint Chiefs decided not to press the point. The war was apparently almost over. Instructions had just been issued to halt the flow of reinforcements, including those of other nations, to the Far East.[8] General Walker had asked for the supply of bulk ammunition to Korea to be terminated.[9] The President began by telling the press that he did not recall this specific agreement at the Wake Island conference but almost immediately reversed his position by remarking that he would not allow any part of North Korea to become a 'privileged sanctuary'.[10]

Yet, as these exchanges were taking place, there was news from the front that a sanctuary might yet be preserved. Two of the ROK divisions, the 6th whose leading elements were almost on the southern bank of the Yalu, and the 1st, at Unsan, had killed and captured on 25th October small numbers of soldiers clearly identified as Chinese.

For reasons unknown, Air Vice-Marshal Bouchier omitted to mention the modifications and final abolition of the MacArthur Line to the Chiefs of Staff in London, but he signalled the following on the appearance of Chinese on 27th October.

1. There is no evidence whatever that any Chinese Communist troops have crossed over South of Yalu River and are in conflict with our force advancing Northwards to Manchurian border. I make this positive and authoritative statement to negative any exaggeration and alarmist reports . . . made here by some newspaper men. Such reports are generally based upon a single

*See p 209.

unconfirmed statement made by a single enemy prisoner of war who does not know what he is talking about. Moreover because intervention now by the Chinese would be a sensational world news item the more irresponsible newspaper men here tend to magnify 10 times such totally unconfirmed reports.

2. The fact is that a day or two ago a solitary prisoner captured at Unsan which is about 20 miles North-East of Sinanju claimed that his unit, the 60th Regiment of Third Chinese Division consisting of 2,000 Chinese and 150 Koreans, crossed Yalu River at Sinanju [presumably, Sinuiju] on 19th October. . . .

3. For the last 18 months the Chinese have been combing out Koreans who have fought in their armies in China to build up North Korean Army (group undeciphered since the) commencement of this war. Since the start of the Korean war however no more than a steady trickle over the border has been going on.
. . .

9. American 1st Marine Division of 10th Corps landed yesterday at Wonsan. American 7th Division are afloat and may land at Wonsan or Hungnam or possibly small port of Iwon still further north. Latter completely free of mines whilst Hungnam in process of being swept. It is however not improbable that this Division may be ordered to land as far North up the East coast as Ch'ongjin sometimes called Seiwin if this port found to be free of mines. 10th Corps have ordered South Korean 1st Corps to organize at once a flying column of not less than one regimental combat team and to move very fast along East coast to North Korean border [with Russia]. Similar orders given to 1st Marine Division to go rapidly to the border to the North-East. 10th Corps are smarting under the delay of their landing at Wonsan and trying to make up time and distance lost. . . .[11]

This message reached London just ahead of a Reuter's report from Tokyo of 'unconfirmed reports that 40,000 Chinese have been thrown into North Korea to prevent United Nations getting control of Yalu [electric] power plants feeding Manchuria's war industries.' For a little while, the I Corps intelligence staff could scoff with their colleagues at Eighth Army and General Headquarters in Tokyo that this was the wildest of rumours. On the 26th, the manifestation of Chinese soldiers at Unsan and Kojang was still explained as,

further reinforcement of North Korean units with personnel taken from the Chinese Communist Forces [CCF], in order to assist in the defense of the border approaches.[12]

Over the next week, these 'reinforcements' were sufficient to rout the 6 ROK Division in the far north and oblige General Milburn to commit 1st Cavalry Division to bolster 1 ROK Division at Unsan. They obliged him to extend a protective flank as the ROK II Corps collapsed on his right. To the east, General Almond's X Corps was similarly engaged with forces initially assumed to be Koreans who had served with the Chinese. As on the I Corps front, however, the problem with that assumption was that captives taken from them spoke no Korean, only Chinese. They owned to being members of Chinese formations. As the fighting extended—became, indeed, for a time critical—the question of nationality was, immediately, overtaken at corps level by anxiety concerning numbers. How many of these 'reinforcements' had entered North Korea?

The answer was known by General P'eng Te-huai*. He had been called to Peking in August to discuss with Russian representatives the establishment of a joint staff in Shenyang†. In his autobiography‡, he states that,

At noon on 4th October, Peking suddenly sent an aircraft with orders for me to board it and go immediately to Peking to attend a conference—I was not to delay even for a minute. I arrived at the Chungnanhai at about 4 o'clock on the afternoon of that day and found the Central Committee was already in session discussing the question of sending troops to aid Korea. Other comrades told me that, after Chairman Mao [Tse-tung] had allowed everyone to emphasise clearly the circumstances which did not favour the sending of troops, he said something to this effect: 'There is reason in everything you say, but when others find themselves at a moment of national crisis, for us to stand watching on the sidelines, it is still difficult to bear in one's heart.' I had only just arrrived and did not have an opportunity to speak, but in my heart I felt that we ought to send troops to Korea. . . .

On the following day, in the afternoon, the Central Committee reconvened in the Yinien T'ang and, after the other comrades had spoken, I said a few words: 'Sending troops to aid Korea

---

*P'eng Te-huai (1898–1974), Marshal of the People's Liberation Army. A soldier of fortune who joined the Communist camp in 1928, he rose to command the North-West, later, First, Field Army in 1946. Dismissed in 1959 for opposing Mao's policies, he was imprisoned in 1966 during the Cultural Revolution until his death. In 1978, as a result of the reforms after Mao's death, his reputation was restored.

†See Chap 9, last two pp.

‡*P'eng Te-huai tzu-shu* was published after his rehabilitation and is compiled from various writings concerning his life and including some material from the many 'confessions' he was called upon to make in prison. Chapter 14 is particularly concerned with Korea.

is vital; defeat for Korea will amount to a postponement of victory in the War of Liberation by several years. If the Americans are positioned on the bank of the Yalu River and in Taiwan, then, if they want to start a war of invasion, they can always find a pretext whenever they like'. The Chairman decided that I should go to Korea, and I made no attempt to evade the responsibility. After the meeting, someone remarked to me: 'It seems that you still refuse to give up in old age!'[13]

Since the meeting in August, a number of arrangements had been completed. The joint Sino-Russian headquarters had been established at Shenyang. The 13th Army Group, a body which formed part of Fourth Field Army in North East China, had been engaged in intensive training. Its distribution of weapons and equipment, a jumble principally of Japanese and United States origin but with elements of Russian, Czech, British and Danish, had been rationalised. Under the command of Li T'ien-yu*, it comprised four armies†,the Thirty Eighth, Thirty Ninth, Fortieth, and Forty Second, to which had been added the Fiftieth and Sixty Sixth. The whole had been overposted to a strength of 200,000 men in eighteen divisions and a regiment of cavalry, part on horses. Another army group, the 9th, had been brought up from the adjacent area of the Third Field Army. Its commander. Sung Shih-lun‡, had only three armies in his force, the Twentieth, Twenty Sixth, and Twenty Seventh, but each of these contained four divisions numbering 130,000 in all. In course of forming was a 'Special Army', an artillery formation of four divisions equipped with United States and Japanese 155-mm howitzers. Four air divisions were to provide tactical support.[14]

These were the forces available to P'eng in the first week of October for deployment into north Korea. At some stage, it had been necessary to decide in Peking upon the status of those members of the PLA—the People's Liberation Army—joining the fighting across the Yalu. A clash with United States forces was inevitable. If the soldiers were avowedly a part of the forces of the People's Republic of China, a state of war with America might be

---

*Li T'ien-yu, (1910–), a veteran of the Long March, renowned on the battlefields against Japan and the Kuomintang, he was appointed to command the 13th Army Group in 1950.

†An 'army', translated from the Chinese word *jun*, corresponded to the corps in the United Nations Eighth Army

‡Sung Shih-lun, (1909–), trained as a professional officer under the Kuomintang, he was chief of staff to P'eng Te-huai in 1930, was expelled from the Communist Party for failure to suppress a mutiny but subsequently reinstated. However, he was mistrusted, suspected of favouring a united front with the KMT. His zeal and success in the civil war of 'liberation', and the support of P'eng, earned him promotion to the command of the 9th Army Group in 1949.

the consequence, an outcome to be avoided. Moreover, fighting by China's armed forces against those of the United Nations might be taken by some of the contributing states as confirmation that the People's Republic was unfit to replace the Kuomintang in the UN at the very time when Peking was advancing, albeit slowly, towards that goal. It was therefore decided that a simple fiction should be employed: the Chinese military entering Korea would do so as volunteers; men so apparently incensed by the wrong being done to their Korean neighbours that they came of their own volition to aid them. No matter that these 'volunteers' were manifestly in formed bodies, conforming to PLA orders and discipline, supplied from PLA depots, many scarcely aware that their unit had 'volunteered' collectively. Just prior to leaving China, each soldier, irrespective of rank, removed the red star from his cap and assumed his new status. Thus the Chinese People's Volunteers (CPV) came into being.[15]

This was the simplest of the military problems to be overcome in the matter of intervention. More difficult was the discovery from the remnants of the North Korean high command of the enemy's locations and strengths, where surviving units of the NKPA were operating, and to what extent they could be relied upon to fit into an encounter battle plan. A comprehensive concept of operations, the 'first phase' of intervention, was needed. There was the problem of how overall command was to be exercised. There was a requirement to find sufficient crossing places on the Yalu for the considerable intervention force, and to conceal this and all movement from American air reconnaissance.

Some work had been undertaken since mid-September on the logistic arrangements. By 12th October, at the latest, executive orders were received at Shenyang to launch the first echelon of the CPV.

The marching columns crossed the wide stream of the Yalu by night over the principal bridges: from Antung to Sinuiju, close to the river mouth, from Chi-an into Manp'ojin almost 200 miles east north east upstream. Between these areas, use was made of river barges to ferry men and supplies across to Pyoktong; but the light ferries at other points were allocated for the most part to Koreans, military traffic, government officials and private citizens seeking refuge in China. Control of the considerable number of Chinese soldiers was evidently well organised. Routes were signed, report centres were distributed along the line of march together with temporary field kitchens and supply points. Each division had sent over advanced parties. Liaison groups had been established with the North Korean headquarters at Kangyye, with garrison and tactical field headquarters. All communications were effected by telephone. The radio listening posts of the United Kingdom and United States thus received no intimation, coded or open, of the huge numbers travelling south in the darkness.[16]

The prime requirement of the first echelon was to stop the United Nations Command from driving out the remnants of the North Korean People's Army and closing up to the Sino-Korean border. A counter-offensive by China in such circumstances, necessitating an assault across the Yalu waters, would have been formidable. This military consideration aside, it would have been politically much more difficult for China to justify the launching of military forces from her territory, manifestly under national arrangements. It was plain to Peking that there was not much time to establish blocking positions in depth; the United Nations' divisions were approaching from the 38th Parallel at a fast pace. Advanced parties crossed on the night of 12th October* and the movement organisation deployed at the same time. Main bodies began to cross between the 17th and 25th.

The overall plan was to put two armies over as quickly as possible at Manp'ojin and the remainder at Sinuiju. The Forty Second Army came over first at the former as it had the furthest to march: it was to block the roads leading north west from the Changjin Reservoir†, one hundred marching miles from the river crossing site. Behind it came the Thirty Eighth to block movement north of Huich'on. From Sinuiju, the Fortieth Army marched towards Pukchin to block the road from that junction to Pyoktong. The Thirty Ninth followed it to deploy astride the roads running north from Unsan and Taech'on. As soon as the exits were clear, the Sixty Sixth and Fiftieth crossed in succession to cover the rear of the Thirty Ninth and Fortieth and to support the North Korean armoured elements on the west coast highway at Pakch'on and Chongju. The last to cross were the completed formations of the Special Army, the 1st Motorised Artillery Division and two of the three regiments of the 2nd.

In the short autumn the nights were lengthening, air temperatures were dropping rapidly after dusk each day. Dressed in khaki cotton uniforms padded with cotton wool, shod in what may best be described as padded basketball boots, their feet enclosed by footrags, the Chinese soldiers marched quietly and patiently through the nights, up and down mountains, on main roads, on side roads and tracks. Like the Roman legions, they sought to march the shortest distance between two points irrespective of

---

*Major-General William F Dean, captured at Taejon in July, under guard 20 miles north of Huich'on on 13th October, saw a group of Chinese soldiers. These were probably advanced parties.[17]

†This is more familiarly known by the Japanese title, Chosin.

contours. Rest halts were few; not for them the western practice of ten minutes halt in the hour.

The foot had been the primary means of transport for most of them throughout their lives, the back and shoulders for load carrying. Machine-guns and mortars, light or medium, were carried by their crews, broken down into parts where practicable. The divisional howitzers* were carried on pack horses, and in many regiments the heavy mortars also. But where there were insufficient animals, the mortar-men had to carry their weapons and ammunition, aided by porters whose loads were borne on either end of a pole. Each soldier had a personal weapon, grenade, personal ammunition—normally eighty rounds—a haversack with washing kit, spare foot rags, sewing kit and other minor personal possessions together with a small enamelled eating bowl, metal spoon and chopsticks. Each had a waterbottle and rations for five to seven days, tea, ground soya bean flour—'the simple food'—a little sugar, and perhaps a small tin of fish or meat paste. But these rations were to be husbanded; field kitchens were to feed men at least as far as Korean soil. The first supply detachments had been put out to provide a second-line source. As often with soldiers, however, according to prisoners-of-war, some men ate their reserve rations on the march and ran out before the next supply was due.

The Forty Second Army left a division to cover Manp'ojin. A small force, possibly part of the cavalry, covered Sinuiju. Each division provided air sentries during its night movement. The moment an aircraft was heard a sentry fired his rifle and shouted 'Fijilella!' Every man, horse and vehicle was at once halted, remaining still until the engine noises faded. Once in Korea, movement of any sort in daylight was forbidden. Any shelter that could hide men from aerial observation was used, and since the columns tended to avoid the towns, Korean villages were packed with soldiers before dawn. The success of this simple discipline was absolute. The seven armies entered Korea without disclosing their presence to United Nations aerial observation.[18]

Thus early contacts on the ground occasioned considerable surprise. The single Chinese soldier captured by 3 ROK Division on the Changjin Reservoir on 25th October made no attempt to deny his nationality but gave misleading information. Sixteen prisoners taken on the 28th reported correctly that they were from 124th Division, Forty Second Army, 13 Army Group. Over these same three days, the prisoners taken by 6 and 1 ROK Divisions were unmistakably Chinese to their captors.

---

*Divisional pack howitzers were of three types: the Japanese 70-mm, American 75-mm, or Russian 76.2-mm.

A flutter of unease was felt among the South Korean soldiers at the outset of these encounters. In the preceding weeks of break out and pursuit they had been developing a confident stride as success followed success in pushing back the North Koreans. Some of those in the ROK service were men originally from the north. They knew well that the Russian and Chinese borders were not far from the reservoirs. All had been told that, once the border was reached, Korea would be unified and the war over. Now they had Chinese in action against them. Each was aware of the size and power of China. The manifestation of this power was as daunting to the ROK soldiers as to their officers.

From that first day of contact, 25th October, apprehensions grew. The ROK 6, 8 and 7 Divisions crumbled as their scattered regiments were caught in ambushes and then out manoeuvred by elements—often as small as a battalion—of the Fortieth and Thirty Eighth Armies. Triumphant, these two began to march south through the broken line of the ROK II Corps, turning south west when they reached the Ch'ongch'on river. The ROK collapse uncovered the right flank of the United States I Corps, the more dangerous for General Milburn as his right hand divisions, 1 ROK and two thirds of 1 Cavalry, were fighting to retain Unsan.

The Thirty Ninth Army had turned from successful ambush of 1 ROK Division to the offensive. On 1st November, it advanced in daylight, hoping to obscure its movement from the air by fires ignited in the pinewoods to the north and north east of Unsan. Huge clouds of smoke, carried by the light north wind, spread above them.

They were too eager, however; the columns outstripped the smoke clouds. Yet others, to the east of Unsan, had no cover at all. Now they were exposed to the weight of the tactical air force and the ground forces' artillery. Some pilots of the United States Fifth Air Force found dense columns of men and pack animals, occasionally even groups of vehicles, and fell upon them with bombs, cannon, and napalm. The forward artillery observers of the United States 1st Cavalry and 24th Divisions, now on either side of the Ch'ongch'on, were able to fire not only their own guns but those of the corps and army artillery coming into action. On the evening of 1st November there was general confidence in Eighth Army headquarters that the advancing enemy—whether Chinese or not—would be destroyed on the front of I Corps. The urgent task now seemed to be the stabilisation of the ROK II Corps before it lost any more ground on I Corps' flank.

An equally urgent requirement, had they but known it, was the containment of the Thirty Ninth Army's 115th and 116th Divisions attacking and enveloping Unsan. Driven to ground by air and artillery in the afternoon, they were ready despite considerable losses to resume the attack soon after dark. Heavy mortars and multi-barrel rockets—the Russian BM21 'Katyusha'*—were brought into previously reconnoitred positions at nightfall. Regimental columns set off shortly afterwards for target areas. This was a tactical operation at which the Chinese excelled, the silent approach followed by the 'three fierce actions'—fierce fire, fierce assault, fierce pursuit. The mortars opened on prearranged targets once small arms fire was exchanged at points of contact. Attacks were resumed north and west of the town.

Daylight observation had suggested that there were gaps in both the American and ROK regiments defences round Unsan. These were exploited by Chinese battalions moving alone to attack the defences from the rear. Elsewhere battalions or companies blocked roads to the south.

The foremost regiment of 1 ROK Division, upon whom rockets and mortars were heavily concentrated, was broken up by assaults before midnight. The 8th Cavalry remained in its positions, subject to attacks from west, north and east. Before midnight, the approach of 'thousands of troops'—the report of refugees adding weight to late afternoon air observations—on his right, decided General Milburn to withdraw from Unsan. But despite best endeavours, the fighting elements of the 8th were caught in the road blocks as they attempted to retire. Successively, the 5th and part of the 7th Cavalry Regiments were drawn in to restore control but were unable to do so. By 3rd November, 1st Cavalry Division was withdrawing behind the Ch'ongch'on. One doughty battalion of the 8th held out in position until the 6th November, after which a number of survivors scattered to make their way back south through the mountains. The Regiment had lost nineteen officers and almost six hundred soldiers.[19]

While the 115th and 116th Divisions of the Thirty Ninth Army had been assailing the defenders of Unsan, the 117th was marching south east by way of Yongsan-dong. On its right, lying back to the north west, was the leading division of the Fiftieth Army. Moving towards Kusong and Taech'on by night, it was preceded by an advanced party to liaise with local NKPA groups. On 31st October, aided much by air strikes, the United States 5 RCT captured Kusong from a mixed force of North Koreans and Chinese, predominantly the former. Because of continuing success, the regimental commander was not much concerned by the nature of his foe. He had the Yalu river in his sights. Similarly, on the western highway to Sinuiju, 21 RCT had reached Chongo-dong on

---

*The batteries formed part of the motorised artillery of the Special Field Army.

1st November, confident that it would soon cover the remaining eighteen miles to the great river. To their consternation, the commanders of both 5 and 21 received orders from their parent, 24th Division, at midnight on 1st November to withdraw to the Ch'ongch'on.

Orders for Brigadier Coad arrived at Chongju at 1115 on 1st November. 27 Brigade was to remain in divisional reserve but to withdraw immediately to Pakch'on, with the exception of the Middlesex. That battalion was to remain at Taech'on, covering the road junction for 5 RCT as it withdrew behind the Ch'ongch'on. Harbour parties set off before 1300. The remainder gathered to wait for transport, which lost its way and did not arrive until mid-afternoon. Half of the trucks were still missing. The Argylls, at the head of the column, departed with brigade headquarters and the Royal Artillery anti-tank troop, leaving 3 RAR to follow.

Settled in Pakch'on, Brigadier Coad was summoned at 2130 to 24th Division headquarters, on the edge of the town. He entered the operations staff tent, crowded with excited officers:

[I] eventually found the Divisional Commander by the map. His words to me were, 'Coad, the Chinese are in. World War Three has started'. I was told to join the Middlesex in Taech'on with the rest of my Brigade the next day. . . . I pointed out to the Divisional Commander how isolated Taech'on was, in fact my Brigade was to be 25 miles out in the blue. He said he would put in an RCT in behind me, which in fact he did, but within an hour or so, they were withdrawn for another job.

By 1415 hours on 2nd November, Brigade Headquarters and 1 A&SH had joined up with 1 Middlesex and the transport had been sent back for 3 RAR, who were still at Chongju. A certain number of dead Chinese were lying in and about the positions occupied by 1 Middlesex, the first we had seen.

B Echelon had been ordered up, to be near us when we were in divisional reserve, this was ordered back over the Ch'ongch'on river again to Anju.

By about 1800 hours, after various orders and counter orders, it appeared that the Corps had decided to withdraw south east of the Ch'ongch'on river, that 27 Brigade would withdraw through a bridgehead formed by 24th Division . . .

No news or contact had been made with 3 RAR and Division said they would hold them at Pakch'on. 40 vehicles were to be sent to us, to arrive between 1200 and 1400 hours the following day [3rd November], and a Reconnaissance Squadron was to be sent to cover our withdrawal. . . .

At 2215 hours a message was received by devious means that by 2030 hours no transport had arrived for 3 RAR who were still at Chongju. By then we had no contact with Division, a highly unsatisfactory state of affairs. A little earlier, three Chinese came and surrendered to the 1 Middlesex, and said that there were 1,000 further up the road.[20]

They were evidently a good deal further up the road than these words suggested; for that night the Argylls' ration truck passed through Taech'on unwittingly, missing its waiting comrades, motored on north through Kusong where, doubts arising in the mind of the ration corporal, it turned south for Chongju. Chongju was empty of troops. 21 RCT had passed through, leaving 3 RAR holding the line and beginning to feel rather lonely. Fortunately, their trucks had at last arrived and they had driven to Pakch'on, where they were joined by the Argyll ration truck just after dawn.

On that morning, 3rd November, there were fresh orders for the brigade. It was not to withdraw into divisional reserve south of the Ch'ongch'on but to hold the left forward section of a bridgehead. The overlay which set out these instructions was so scanty that Brigadier Coad departed at once to see General Church or his chief of staff. A minor but vexing consequence of the change was that unit harbour parties were now twenty miles south of the river in the area of Suk'chon. The brigadier took battalion intelligence officers with him to prepare for the arrival of their units.

While Colonel Neilson was giving out the revised plan at 1030, sustained machine-gun fire was heard to the south east. Observation in that direction showed that it was directed upward at friendly aircraft. The minds of the officers in conference became troubled. If there was an enemy force as near as that, might not the road south be closing to them? The troop carrying trucks were due to arrive at 1200, but experience suggested that they might not be punctual. Brigadier Coad had given instructions that units should not wait indefinitely but march out in company with their fighting vehicles at 1400. Colonel Neilson consulted with Colonel Man. They decided to ask permission to commence withdrawing immediately.

The brigade commander was still on the road and out of radio contact, but soon an American liaison officer arrived. He had news that aircraft had observed considerable numbers of troops moving on Taech'on from the north and north west. Brigadier Coad had told him to pass orders to begin withdrawing immediately. A further message informed the brigade major that 3 RAR had been instructed to secure the cross roads at Kasan with a company, and confirmed that transport was *en route* to the southern side of a pass five miles south of Taech'on. On this basis, without any enemy interruption, the brigade withdrew into its new area round Pakch'on. The only impediment was 21 RCT. It had harboured immediately west of Kasan for the night and began moving into the 27 Brigade column as it reached the crossroads in the late afternoon.[21]

By 3rd November, General Walker was successfully reinforcing his eastern flank. The ROK 7th and 8th Divisions of the ROK II Corps had been reorganised and returned to the line, facing east. Behind them, General Milburn had placed his 2nd Division and a regiment from 24th Division in depth. 1 ROK Division extended the line to the west.

General Walker had at first agreed to the complete withdrawal of 24th Division behind the river lines but, on reflection, decided to hold a bridgehead beyond both the Ch'ongch'on and the Taeryong. Accepting that a number of Chinese had come into Korea, the idea was growing—on the scantiest evidence—that they numbered only six divisions. These would be defeated where they stood. He expected to bring IX Corps into the line later in the month to resume the advance. Thus 27 Brigade and 19 RCT found themselves in parallel, the first round Pakch'on, the second to the east.

In parallel but not side by side. The weakness of the position was that there was a gap of six miles between 27 Brigade's right and the 2nd Battalion of 19 RCT, its nearest neighbour. General Church was aware of the situation but had only one other formation, 21 RCT, in hand and believed, no doubt correctly, that he must retain it as a reserve. I Corps promised him all or part of 6 ROK Division for the bridgehead when it had been resuscitated after its losses close to the Yalu. He placed his deputy, Brigadier-General Garrison H Davidson, in command of the bridgehead forces, grouped as Task Force Davidson.

What none of these commanders then knew was the extraordinary movements of their Chinese foe at that time. The third division of Thirty Ninth Army, 117, was marching south to attack the eastern end of I Corps line, unaware that Fortieth and Thirty Eighth Armies were approaching along the Ch'ongch'on from the east. Fighting resumed from the 4th November against the combined ROK and United States forces from Won-ni, through Kunu-ri, to the junctions of the routes south to Sunch'on. It spread to 1 ROK Division, then to the 1st and 2nd Battalions of 19 RCT on the night of the 4th/5th. General Church had to launch 21 RCT to recover their ground.

On 4th November, all had been quiet in 27 Brigade's positions. The Middlesex were holding Pakch'on and the high ground immediately north and east. 3 RAR and the Argylls were holding positions covering the approaches west of the river. A battalion of American field artillery, the 61st with 105-mm howitzers, moved into support, dispersing its batteries in the the broad strip of rice paddy south of Pakch'on. Concerned that the enemy might infiltrate between his forward defences to seize the northern end of the Ch'ongch'on crossings, Brigadier Coad had ordered the Argylls to place one company with mortars, anti-tank and machine-guns eight miles to the rear. It was to hold open the low pass at Maenju-dong, and to provide a fire base.

A Company had this role. From Maenju-dong the road to Pakch'on runs north into the broad rice paddy and was cut by several streams spanned by concrete bridges, small but essential to the passage of wheeled traffic. Down this road, throughout the 4th, huge numbers of refugees were moving, a pitiable stream of families laden with such of their food and household goods as they could carry. Even though, with rare exceptions, they had received nothing but help from the local people, including those who had formed themselves into anti-Communist 'home guards', the British Commonwealth soldiers were uneasy that among their numbers might be North Korean troops in civilian clothing.

Before dawn on the 5th, all units in the brigade heard sounds of battle to the east—this was the attack upon 19 RCT. At about 8 o'clock, Major Wilson heard firing to the north and saw at a distance, from one of his hill posts, white smoke bombs bursting to the right of the road. He had, however, been told clearly by the brigade commander that his task was to hold Maenjung-dong. Accordingly, he was

. . . wandering slowly back to my own area determined not to meddle in anyone else's battle when a Tank Company Jeep drove up at speed and an officer leaned out and said, 'Are you Major Wilson, A Company Commander? Your Colonel wants you to attack the road block at once.'[22]

A difficulty was that Major Wilson did not know where the road block was and discovered that he had no communications working: his direct telephone line to brigade headquarters had been cut and his radio to his battalion was not communicating. While he was gathering the greater part of his small force—some had to be left behind to hold the position—four tanks appeared. On the radio of one of these he was able to talk to Colonel Neilson.

The Chinese had established a considerable number of men on the road in the general area of 61st Field Artillery Battalion. One objective appeared to be a concrete bridge two thousand yards south of the Argylls' battalion headquarters in Kujin, another, C

Battery of the 61st. Brigadier Coad had ordered the Argylls to clear the road as quickly as possible.

B and C Companies, Colonel Neilson told Major Wilson, were being drawn back from the west bank of the Taeryong. They would attack south in succession with tanks. A Company was to attack north at once. Rudimentary arrangements—all that was possible in the circumstances—were made to minimise the danger of shooting at one another as the two forces closed. Air support had been called for and was on its way.

It was now about 0840. Two American trucks coming up the road were commandeered and, using these and two of the tanks, A Company set off at 9 led by the other two tanks. A mile and a half to the north they came upon 'an inspiring sight'. C Battery had formed a perimeter round its guns and was resisting hotly attacks being pressed by Chinese who had crept up stream beds and behind the paddy bunds. Its commander, Captain Howard M Moore, had brought one howitzer, then a second, into action over open sights. Their fire was daunting but inadequate, however, to knock out more than a fraction of the many small groups of assaulting infantry closing upon them. Shellfire from another battery, directed by a Mosquito, helped to stem the onslaught. Yet the position was still critically threatened. The battery had lost two killed and seventeen wounded, and was becoming worried about its stock of small arms ammunition when, at 9 o'clock, the leading tanks with A Company arrived, followed shortly by the remainder of Major Wilson's force.

The battery area was soon cleared. Chinese withdrawing north along the railway were shot at by the tanks. To the east, a hill dominated by the flat paddy was captured by the Argylls shortly after 1000. Leaving a reinforced platoon on its summit, Major Wilson withdrew the remainder of his group, twenty in all, to the road, where the 3-inch mortar and machine-gun sections were established. On the tank radio, he heard that the attack by B Company and its tanks had started on the other road block.[23]

The 61st Field Artillery were now firing for this battle. After a hot encounter, in which Major Gordon-Ingram the company commander was wounded, the Chinese were forced back, leaving a number of dead close to the road. Some of these had demolition charges which had clearly been intended for the concrete bridges. Survivors were seen running into the hills to the east and Colonel Neilson ordered B and C Companies to take up positions on that flank to protect the road. The area fell quiet.

The battle was far from over, however. At 11 o'clock, A Company's hill was heavily attacked and half a dozen killed and wounded. Withdrawal was made possible by the sustained fire of the two Vickers medium machine-guns close to the road.

Through the morning, the Mosquitoes reported that a large number of enemy were in the hills in rear of 27 Brigade. Brigadier Coad felt that it would be foolhardy to remain so far forward; the Chinese would surely cut the road again during the night and their strength seemed to be growing.

I didn't fancy the idea of fighting our way out against a force my own size on the 6th when I could probably get out without too much of a struggle on the 5th. However, I had to speak to Davidson, of course. We couldn't simply fall back without consultation. Actually, he had no idea and said I should do whatever I thought best. I pointed out that we were not giving up the bridgehead altogether, but coming into a tight defensive perimeter on the hills overlooking the north bank of the river [Ch'ongch'on].[24]

The brigade plan was threefold. While the Argylls held the road open, 3 RAR would recapture the hill taken and lost by Major Wilson's company; the Middlesex would pass through to sweep and occupy the hills east of Maengjung-dong; and the Argylls, rearguard to the brigade, would follow to occupy the right of the defensive position.

3 RAR withdraw across the Taeryong at 1130. As it marched down the road, air strikes occupied the enemy's attention*. At 1400, after a few rounds of mortar fire had fallen in their forming up place, the leading two companies, A under Captain Chitts, B under Captain Laughlin, began their advance across the rice paddy from the road.

Initially there was nothing to be seen; but as soon as the infantry began the ascent fire was opened from the higher ground and the hills to the south and east. Supported by their mortars and machine-guns, and four tanks standing off near the road, it took an hour to capture the feature. Lieutenant Larsen, who had led the crossing at the Taeryong bridge in the previous week, was among those killed. Colonel Walsh put D Company through on to the hill to the south. By 1600, the whole of the battalion was on its final objective.

Right behind them, the Middlesex came through to find that their ground was unoccupied apart from one small feature. In failing light and a bitter wind, the greater part of the brigade's transport and the 61st Field Artillery then withdrew across the

*By chance, the aircraft involved in the later stages were Mustangs from 77 Squadron of the Royal Australian Air Force.

Ch'ongch'on. The Argylls drove south with a platoon of tanks to find their advanced parties waiting to lead them out on to their new plot of North Korea, and were unimpressed when these guides told them that they had been mortared and shot at occasionally. Still, few doubted that they would hear more from the Chinese during the night.

As was customary, every member of the brigade stood to arms from dusk until full nightfall. Night double sentries were then posted while the remainder sought rest. About an hour later, C Company of 3 RAR, astride the road to Pakch'on, dug into rice paddy bunds, came under sustained mortar and machine-gun fire, which increased to embrace battalion headquarters a few hundred yards to the rear. Then trumpets began to sound* and whistles. Out of the darkness across the paddy came a strong attack on C Company and, almost simultaneously, against A and C Companies holding the hills they had captured that afternoon. All three reported hot fighting and limited penetration of their positions.

Lieutenant-Colonel Walsh rapidly became anxious that he might lose his whole force. He ordered a general withdrawal to the road and railway crossing about a mile to the south.

This change of position, relayed to brigade headquarters, was unacceptable to Brigadier Coad. It opened the left flank of his defences. He told Colonel Walsh to return his companies to their original locations.

This was not practicable. A Company under Lieutenant L G Clark—Captain Chitts had been wounded in the afternoon attack—had just fought its way clear of the enemy, likewise B. Their positions, and those of C, were now occupied by superior enemy numbers. They concentrated at the railway crossing. However, D Company had not been attacked at all and was able to climb back to the top of Hill 63.

At 2200, Brigadier Coad arranged for the former RAR positions to be shelled and mortared. The Middlesex were instructed to put a standing patrol on the southwestern side of the Maenju-dong pass until the RAR had sorted themselves out and were in a position to take on the task themselves. This small operation, involving the commitment of ten men into a black night thirty minutes after they had been wakened, was done extraordinarily well.

The radio conversation between brigade headquarters had been heard by the other two battalions. All were apprehensive of a second attack but none came. In the morning, Brigadier Coad

---

*Though often referred to as a 'bugle', the Chinese instrument was actually a trumpet, similar to those in use by European cavalry.

relieved Colonel Walsh of his command and appointed Major Ferguson in his place.[25]*

In the morning, too, it became apparent from the dead left on the battlefield that they had been assailed by a mixed force of Chinese and North Koreans. As the day of 6th November lengthened, a more notable circumstance became apparent: the enemy had departed. By the afternoon, ground and air news from elsewhere confirmed that this was a general disengagement.

---

*This decision was confirmed by the (Australian) C-in-C British Commonwealth Occupation Force, Lieutenant-General Sir Horace (Clement Hugh) Robertson, KBE DSO (1894–1960).

SOURCE NOTES: CHAPTER 12

1. Truman, op cit, Vol II, pp 384-88.
2. Ibid, pp 386-87.
3. Ibid, pp 386-7. FRUS, Vol VII, Korea, p 948, fn. Whitney, Courteney, *MacArthur: His rendezvous with history*, (New York), 1955. Acheson, op cit, pp 61-62.
4. FRUS, Vol VII, pp 949-59.
5. Manchester, op cit, pp 598-599.
6. United Nations Command Operation Order No 4, 17th October 1950, (USNARS, Suitland).
7. Appleman, op cit, p 670-671. FRUS, Vol VII, p 995-996, CINCFE C67397 to Department of the Army (DA) for JCS of 25th October 1950 (USNARS, Suitland).
8. FRUS, Vol VII, pp 997-1000, Memo by the Deputy Assistant Secretary of State for Far Eastern Affairs to the Deputy Secretary of State of 26th October 1950.
9. Appleman, op cit, p 669.
10. Manchester, op cit, pp 599-600.
11. DEFE 11/202, Tokyo (Bouchier) CAB 90 to MOD (Chiefs of Staff) of 270827 October 1950.
12. Appleman, op cit, p 677.
13. *P'eng Te-huai tzu-shu*, (Peking People's Publishing House), 1981, p 257.
14. Ibid, p 259. US Far East Command (FEC) ATIS. Interrogation Reports (Enemy Forces), issue 17, p 186, and Enemy Documents, Issue 29, p 84, FEC Intelligence Digest No 6 16th-31st August 1951, and No 8, 16th-30th September 1951, and vol 1, Issue No 4, 1st-15th February 1953, pp 26-38 (USNARS, Suitland). George, Alexander L, *The Chinese Communist Army in Action*, (Columbia University Press), 1967, chap 1. Griffith, Samuel B, *The Chinese People's Liberation Army*, (London), 1968, chap 7. Whitson, William W with Huang, Chen-hsia, *The Chinese High Command*, (London), 1973, pp 248, 324, 355-356, Charts E and G.
15. Joshua Chance, conversation with author, and author's conversations with members of the Chinese People's Volunteers (CPV), notably Nieh Jung-chen.
16. Ibid
17. Dean, William F, *General Dean's Story*, (London), 1954, p 138.
18. Author's conversations with and observation of members of the CPV.
19. Appleman, op cit, pp 707-708. Author's conversation with Colonel Walter L Mayo jr, and Captain Clarence L Anderson.
20. Coad Report Part IV.
21. 27 Bde unit war diaries, November, 1950. Coad, conversation with author and Report, Part IV.
22. 1 A&SH war diary, November, 1950, and Appendix thereto.
23. Ibid
24. Coad, conversation with author, and Coad Report, Part IV.
25. 27 Brigade unit war diaries, November, 1950. Coad, conversation with author. O'Neill, op cit, Vol II, pp 63-64.

CHAPTER 13

The Dual Enigma

As Air Marshal Bouchier's signal of 27th October to the Chiefs of Staff indicated, General MacArthur and his staff did not accept initally the reports that Chinese soldiers were engaged in the fighting. General MacArthur had convinced himself that there would be no intervention; his staff were not of a mind to hold another opinion. By 1st November, however, the manifestation could no longer be ignored. The United Nations Commander-in-Chief then began to come to terms with their presence, easing open the curtain of his disbelief to admit selected images. On 2nd November, he thought that the Chinese Government probably 'had only limited objectives in mind'. A flood of new and accumulated evidence persuaded him to signal the Joint Chiefs of Staff on the 4th that various objectives could be foreseen:

> First, that the Chinese Communist Government proposes to intervene with its full potential military forces, openly proclaiming such course at what it might determine as an appropriate time; second, that it will covertly render military assistance, but will, so far as possible, conceal the fact for diplomatic reasons; third, that it is permitting and abetting a flow of more or less voluntary personnel across the border to strengthen and assist the North Korean remnants in their struggle to retain a nominal foothold in Korea; fourth, that such intervention, as exists, has been in the belief that no UN forces would be committed in the extreme northern reaches of Korea except those of South Korea. A realization that such forces were insufficient for the purpose may well have furnished the concept of salvaging something from the wreckage.
>
> The first contingency would represent a momentous decision of the greatest international importance. While it is a distinct possibility, and many foreign experts predict such action, there are many fundamental logical reasons against it and sufficient evidence has not yet come to hand to warrant its immediate acceptance.
>
> The last three contingencies or a combination thereof, seem to be the most likely condition at the present moment. . . .[1]

On the 5th, the day on which 27 Brigade fought its way south from Pakch'on, he decided to make Chinese operations his own cause by issuing a communique that was as much political as military: '. . . the Communists committed one of the most offensive acts of international lawlessness of recorded history by moving without any notice of belligerency, elements of alien Communist forces across the Yalu river into North Korea . . .'[2]

Mr Acheson was irritated by this publication, of which he had no prior knowledge. He did not welcome General MacArthur's political judgements at any time, least of all when he was developing a political counter strategy. An initial step in this process was to lay before the Security Council the catalogue of Chinese military operations against the UN forces on land and in the air, including anti-aircraft fire from the Chinese side of the Yalu.[3] On the 6th, news from Tokyo further disturbed him:

Shortly after ten o'clock this morning Mr Robert Lovett [Under-Secretary of Defense] came over from the Pentagon with an urgent message from General Stratemeyer [Commander of the Far East Air Force]. This message reported that the Air Forces had been ordered to take off at one o'clock p.m. Eastern Standard Time today on a bombing mission to take out the bridge across the Yalu River from Sinuiju (Korea) to Antung (Manchuria). They were to use radio controlled bombs and would attempt to bomb the Korean side of the bridge.

Mr Lovett expressed his view that from an operational standpoint he doubted whether the results to be achieved would importantly interrupt traffic and the danger of bombing the city of Antung and other points on the Manchurian side of the river were very great.

Mr Rusk [Assistant Secretary of State for Far East Affairs] explained that we had a commitment with the British not to take action which might involve attacks on the Manchurian side of the River without consultation with them. He also said that the British Cabinet was meeting this morning to reconsider their whole attitude towards the Chinese Communist Government and that ill-considered action on our part might have grave consequences. He also told Mr Lovett that we had filed General MacArthur's report concerning Chinese intervention with the United Nations Security Council and had asked for an urgent meeting tomorrow or Wednesday at which we were going to present a resolution calling on the Chinese to cease activities in Korea thus attempting to get UN support for any action which might be necessary in the event of their refusal to accept the UN action. He also mentioned the possibility of Russian involvement under the Sino-Russian Treaty.

After some discussion, we [Acheson, Lovett and Rusk] all thoroughly agreed that this [bombing] action should be postponed until the reasons for it were more clearly known. . . .[4]

Mr Acheson decided to inform President Truman, who was in Kansas City that morning. The President recorded that:

. . . the matter before them was of such importance that they felt an immediate decision was necessary. . . .
I told Acheson that I would approve the bombing mission only if there was an immediate and serious threat to the security of our troops. . . .[5]

The upshot was that the Joint Chiefs sent an order to General MacArthur to cancel the bombing and to inform Washington what circumstances made such an operation necessary.[6]

Mr Acheson had asked Mr Bevin on 1st November for his views on putting to the Security Council a resolution framed 'to restrict the area of hostilities.'[7] On the 5th—in a message despatched on the 6th—he carried the matter further:

. . . We have officially ignored Soviet arms and advisers 'volunteers' from Manchuria and other assistance in the past, even though the whole world knew the facts. We did so in order to leave the other side a way out. I doubt that it is possible to treat organised Chinese units on the same basis, even though there has not been an official espousal of these units by the Peiping regime. . . .
It seems to us therefore that we should ask for an early meeting of the Security Council for not later than Wednesday of this week, to discuss the reports from the United Nations Command. At this meeting, our debate should be directed towards localising the conflict and should be geared to a short and simple resolution along the lines of the resolution vetoed by the Soviet Union on the same subject in August* A proposed draft resolution is being forwarded by separate message.
We welcome the information that you are working on a draft resolution and would be glad to give it most sympathetic consideration. I am sure our purposes in the present situation are very close together. You will notice that our draft resolution takes into account a number of the points raised by your message of 3rd November. . . .[8]

*See pp 184–189.

In that message, Mr Bevin had expressed agreement that the involvement in combat of Chinese military units in Korea could not be ignored on the basis that they were 'volunteers'. But, as he explained in the Cabinet discussion of the subject on the 6th, his principal points were that China should not be provoked to the point of widening hostilities throughout Asia by the application of penalties such as sanctions, and that all options should be explored to persuade the government in Peking to draw back.[9] The Chiefs of Staff, notably the Chief of the Air Staff, were less temperate.

Signals from Air Marshal Bouchier from 30th October onwards had increased their apprehensions of a major involvement in Korea. Following his rejection of Chinese intervention on the 27th, the identification of prisoners on the 30th and 31st required a first shift of outlook:

> . . . The foregoing should not be taken as an authoritative statement that the Chinese forces are in any sense now officially engaged in this war. Practical evidence so far to hand combined with official statement made some time back by the Chinese Communists to the effect that they would come in if we crossed the 38th Parallel makes it however reasonable assuming that an appreciable number of Chinese soldiers in an unofficial capacity have crossed south of the border and joined up with the enemy. These additional Chinese troops are probably not sent south openly or in any organised military formation whatever and although their numbers at present are not at all serious neverthe- less there have been sufficient numbers to put new and unexpected life into the pattern of North Korean resistance during the last few days. . . .[10]

On the 2nd and 3rd November, he reported air intervention and yet more evidence of Chinese troops which were bringing the United Nations advance to a halt. At this point, the question of 27 Brigade's future employment arose. The 29th Brigade was arriving and, on the basis of the previous understanding, 27 would return to Hong Kong—indeed, after capturing Chongju, all ranks were told that they would shortly be leaving Korea. Preliminary arrangements for transportation were being made. In a second signal on 3rd November, Air Marshal Bouchier suggested that

> . . . it would be at least a military embarrassment for General MacArthur in order to keep his promise to have to withdraw and to concentrate Brigade in a rear area by 15th November or in sufficient time to ensure that the 27th Brigade are up-lifted at Pusan in the same ship[ping] which brings the British 29th Brigade into Korea.

3. Without any hint whatever from American sources here I feel it is my duty to submit to your judgement that the British Chiefs of Staff may wish me to represent to General MacArthur your particular request, in view of changed military situation in Korea, that General MacArthur may feel quite free to retain the British 27th Brigade until such time as . . . the British 29th Brigade have concentrated and moved up to take over in line. . . .[11]

Against this background, the Chiefs of Staff signalled Lord Tedder on 6th November:

You will understand that we are anxious about the Korean situation and we shall be grateful if you could discover from Bradley what are the US intentions in respect of an advance to the Manchurian and Russian frontiers of Korea when it becomes possible. We should like to know under what directive MacArthur is operating or whether he is deciding his own policy in this respect.

2. We originally understood that it was the intention that only South Korean forces should advance north of a line approximately Chonju [actually Chongju]–Wonsan. We were thus assured only about a fortnight ago by US Chiefs of Staff that MacArthur had orders that anyway US and British troops should not go nearer than 30 miles of Northern Frontier. We are not clear whether in fact they have done so, but Bouchier repeatedly refers to 'our advance to the Manchurian border'. Does this mean US or British troops as well as South Koreans? . . .

3. On Bouchier's representations we have offered, in view of present situation, to leave 27 Brigade in Korea, and our commitments are growing. We feel we are entitled to know under what instructions MacArthur as UN Commander is operating. Present situation looks like letting us in for what we have feared since Inch'on landing, namely at best prolonged containment of large UN forces in Korea at expense of really important commitments elsewhere; and at worst continuation of large scale warfare with Chinese with consequent risk of spreading the conflagration in the Far East. We are becoming anxious about repercussions in Hong Kong and Malaya.[12]

The Foreign Office had advised the Chiefs 'not to take too strong a line' with their American colleagues: 'the situation is delicate while we are negotiating with the State Department'. But the British Chiefs knew that Lord Tedder had a longstanding relationship with

General Bradley* which permitted a more forthright approach than was customary in international diplomacy. 'Discussed Korea with Bradley on his return this afternoon,' Lord Tedder replied on 8th November.

> The intention to avoid direct conflict with China is more firm than ever and that issue is of course now with the United Nations. As Bradley said 'What we want is to be able to get together with these people and talk things over—if it is the power station and dam on the Yalu they are worried about we could come to an arrangement'. Bradley does not speak of Chinese divisions in the way in which General Walker does as quoted in CAB 103† but there is plenty of evidence of continual and very heavy movement down the Yalu eastward. In view of this after consultation with the State Department MacArthur has today been authorised to attack the eastern end of the main bridges across the Yalu with orders to avoid flying over the border. In the course of another three or four weeks the Yalu will probably be frozen over and bridges will no longer be essential. The other danger is the fighter attacks by Yaks and MiGs‡ which are increasing and are undoubtedly coming from across the border and which from a purely military point of view can only be effectively dealt with at their source.
>
> 2. Since the heavy reinforcement of N Korea forces has developed it is clear that the original endeavour to differentiate between the South Korean forces and the UNO forces is no longer possible and the idea of the South Koreans alone dealing with the final stage has become academic.
>
> 3. As Bradley put it, the problem in Korea now is not one of holding this or that terrain, but of destroying the armed forces in North Korea. MacArthur still thinks he can do this.
>
> 4. In conclusion, it is clear that Bradley and the US Chiefs are as concerned about the dangers of the present situation as we are and for much the same reason.[13]

General Bradley spoke from the heart. The American Chiefs, like their associates in the State Department, wanted to be done

---

*As Deputy to General Eisenhower in Europe, 1944-45, Lord Tedder had tended to take the part of General Bradley against his fellow army group commander, Field-Marshal Montgomery.

†In this signal of 7th November, Air Vice-Marshal Bouchier had quoted General Walker's opinion that three of the People's Liberation armies were in the field against him.

‡The piston engined Yak-3s were the same type of Russian fighter/ground attack aircraft which had attacked HMS *Jamaica* at Inch'on. The MiGs were MiG-15s, jet fighters, which had only entered squadron service in the Russian air force in 1949. Their appearance surprised the Fifth Air Force.

with the war as quickly as possible. Where they differed from the British was in their ideas about operational options.

Field-Marshal Slim remarked at the Chiefs of Staff meeting on 7th November that if the Chinese intended to expel the United Nations from Korea, it would be difficult to stop them. The answer to the latest development might be for their land forces to stabilise themselves on a good defensive line and then for the problem to be negotiated by political means.[14] During the National Security Council Meeting on the 9th, General Bradley said that it might not be possible to hold the United Nations positions without attacking the air bases inside north east China, though the Chiefs recognised that such an extension would require United Nations agreement. The further back they held, the easier it would be to maintain their line but withdrawal might affect the South Koreans' will to fight.

By this date, Mr Acheson was aware that the British might propose a buffer zone in North Korea to separate the UN forces from the Chinese frontier. At the NSC meeting, he floated an alternative concept: a demilitarised strip ten miles deep on either side of the Yalu, administered by the United Nations Commission but policed by a constabulary drawn from outside the existing United Nations forces. He gave his support, meantime, for the continuance of military operations up to the border but without aerial sorties into Manchuria.[15]

While this meeting was taking place, Sir Gladwyn Jebb was engaged with the resolution which would call upon the Chinese to withdraw from Korea:

> Americans informed us this morning [9th November] that they intended to add an additional paragraph to their draft resolution which had been authorised by the President as well as by Mr [General]* Marshall and Mr Acheson which would affirm the intentions of the United Nations forces to hold the Chinese frontier in Korea inviolate and to protect legitimate Chinese interests in the frontier if the Chinese withdrew and refrained from intervention.
>
> 2. . . . The French considered however that the proposed United States wording was somewhat too threatening and the following redraft was agreed after a joint Anglo-French-American discussion:
>
> 'Affirms that it is the policy of the United Nations to hold the Chinese frontier with Korea inviolate and fully to protect Chinese legitimate interests in the frontier zone;

---

*During his incumbency as Secretary of State, General Marshall had dropped his military title deliberately. He made no rule about it when he later became Secretary of Defense.

'Calls attention to the grave danger which continued intervention by Chinese forces in Korea would entail for the maintenance
of such a policy.'

3. The idea behind the above addition seems a good one. On
reconsideration it appears to us that it might however be useful
to make it clear that any violation of the frontier would only be
undertaken in so far as it might be necessary for attaining the
specific purposes of the United Nations in Korea. We propose
therefore to suggest to the Americans and the French the
substitution for their second paragraph above of something on
the following lines:

'Recognises that the maintenance of such a policy in the face of
continued Chinese intervention in Korea will seriously hamper
the attainment of the objectives which the United Nations is
determined to accomplish in Korea.'. . .[16]

That evening, Mr Bevin replied.

Though the proposed addition to the draft Resolution is in
accordance with the basic principles of the United Nations policy
in Korea, it seems to me unnecessary and inadvisable at the
present juncture to make an affirmation in such categorical
terms. It might for example entail a specific United Nations
guarantee of the Korean/Chinese frontier with the possibility of
increased military commitment in the future.

2. I have considered this point afresh since receiving the following telephoned text from you of proposed further amendment
replacing that mentioned in paragraph 3 of your telegram . . .:

But recognises that if Chinese intervention in Korea continued
the United Nations may be forced to reconsider this policy in
order to attain the objectives in Korea which it is determined
to accomplish.

3. This latest amendment might well be interpreted as an
ultimatum to China and I cannot accept it.

4. On the evidence at present available to me I do not think
that the time has yet come to authorise General MacArthur even
by implication to take action in Manchuria. Before giving my
approval to any such authorisation it would be necessary to
consider the consequences most carefully.

5. You should therefore explain to the French and Americans
that I still regard it as of great importance to endeavour to
secure the maximum support for the Security Council Resolution
and that I am averse to the inclusion of anything which might
be interpreted by the Chinese or others as an ultimatum.

6. I would prefer the resolution to stand without any addition
(ie as in your telegram . . .) but if Americans and French are
insistent I am willing to accept the redraft agreed upon after

Anglo-American-French discussion, the text of which was given in your paragraph 2. . . .[17]

This telegram indicates Mr Bevin's ideas as to how China should be persuaded to draw back from hostilities in Korea: by negotiations without unilateral concessions but also without threats; and the gathering of wide support for the resolution among the United Nations membership which would formally identify and warn China. He hoped that India, disenchanted by the Chinese invasion of Tibet, might become a sponsor, but Mr Nehru was distracted by developing an initiative of his own. Cuba, Ecuador and Norway joined Britain, France and America, the 'six nation' sponsors.

In the matter of negotiations, Mr Bevin believed that the presence of the Chinese Communist delegation at the Security Council table was essential. In a move which took the Russians by surprise, the British delegation put a compromise proposal* to the Council at its meeting on 8th November:

> The Security Council decides to invite, in accordance with rule 39 of the rules of procedure, a representative of the Central People's Government of the People's Republic of China to be present during discussion by the Council of the special report of the United Nations Command [on Chinese intervention] in Korea.[18]

The proposal was adopted by eight votes to two (China and Cuba) with one abstention (Egypt). Russia voted for the resolution even though Sir Gladwyn Jebb intimated that its adoption would not necessarily mean that they need wait upon the arrival of the Peking delegation before discussing the detail of Chinese military operations.[19] This success was diminished by the refusal of the Peking government on 12th November to take up the invitation, but they were coming to Lake Success anyway to represent their complaint of aggression by the United States in isolating Taiwan. It was felt that this would provide opportunities for private negotiations on Korea.

Officials in London and Washington, and a day or so earlier also in Canberra, began to consider options for the separation of the two sides in North Korea. Almost certainly as a result of an informal exchange between the War Office and Foreign Office, a United Press representative in London reported on 8th November that 'Britain will ask United States to let Chinese Communists

---

*The Russian delegation originally proposed the following, defeated at the 8th November meeting, 'The Security Council decides that during the discussion of the Korean question it shall be necessary to invite the representative of the People's Republic of China'.[20]

occupy a buffer strip of North Korea'. The main thrust of the story was false but not 'without foundation' as the Foreign Office stated when it had unsuccessfully sought for its origin at the request of Sir Oliver Franks. In a telephone call, he was advised that the CIGS had in mind the creation of a demilitarised zone in North Korea. Sir Oliver passed this to Mr Acheson.[21] Lacking this advice, General MacArthur took the UP report at face value. He was not best pleased that the Joint Chiefs had cited the need to consult the British Government when they ordered him to postpone the bombing raid on Sinuiju, and now scorned the British idea of a Chinese occupied zone as appeasement similar to 'the historic precedent in the action taken at Munich on 29 September 1938 . . .'[22]

On 10th November, there was further talk of a demilitarised separation zone from the United States. Sir Oliver Franks reported,

At a very conservative estimate (which has all along been the line taken by State Department) there are now 35,000 Chinese troops in North Korea. Estimates made on basis of commanding General's [MacArthur's] reports could bring figure up to 60,000 or 70,000 but evidence from prisoners (48 have now been captured) is not of sufficient weight to support these higher figures. No reliable assessment of position will be possible until United Nations forces have resumed contact in strength with their opponents. Commanding General's opinion is that Chinese and North Koreans are regrouping for an attack against centre of the line. State Department are surprised that Communists have not reacted strongly to the almost total destruction of Sinuiju.

2. Rusk confirmed that MacArthur is under the strictest instructions not to destroy Suiho dam, despite fact that its concrete highways afford passage across river. A military operation against this utility is only to be taken on specific direction from Washington.*

3. Rusk said that United States Government was most anxious that Chinese authorities should be made aware that what United Nations forces were doing in Korea could not possibly lead to a threat to the sovereignty of China. . . . Repeated assurances by Americans in authority seemed, however, to make no impression on the Chinese Government and Rusk wondered whether His Majesty's Government, through, say, yourself [Mr Bevin],

---

*In authorising the Sinuiju bridge bombing on 6th November, the Joint Chiefs forbade the violation of Chinese air space and any attack upon Yalu dams or power plants. On 9th November, they advised General MacArthur that, as a consequence of Chinese intervention, his directive might be changed. Both these signals produced what Mr Acheson described as a 'manic reaction'.[23]

would be disposed once more to make a statement calculated to assure the Chinese of our good faith in these matters. . . .

4. State Department officials are turning over in their minds a proposal for a nonbelligerent band North and South of Yalu. If this could be arranged they would suggest facilities for United Nations Commission to inspect freely both zones. Special arrangements might perhaps be negotiated for Korean-Siberian frontier, or, more probably, that area would have anyway to be kept out of these calculations. This is only a thought at the moment but if you have views the State Department would be grateful to receive them. . . .[24]

Field-Marshal Slim and his colleagues were fast developing such views, carrying the Foreign Office and Cabinet with them. They were disturbed by the news that General MacArthur was preparing 'a reconnaissance in force'. They took this to mean a resumption of the advance to the Yalu. Essentially, none of them believed that this line could be held against the ground strength the Chinese could muster. At the Cabinet on 13th November, Sir John Slessor reiterated the view that the total occupation of Korea was not worth a major war. Given the United Nations' air superiority, unlikely to be lost to Chinese and North Korean air forces, a shorter line to the south could be held:

. . . With this in view the Chiefs of Staff Committee favoured the withdrawal of United Nations forces to a shorter line across the neck of the country, running from Chongju to Tokch'on, roughly along the 40th Parallel. In addition to being a much shorter line to defend, this would have the great advantage of leaving a buffer area to the north, on the Korean side of the Manchurian frontier, in which military targets could be attacked from the air without the grave international risks involved in making air attacks on targets within Manchuria. It might be possible to declare this buffer area a demilitarised zone, with the reservation that any offensive concentration of Chinese or North Korean troops within that area would be liable to air attack. A cease-fire might be arranged on the basis of that line, pending the result of discussions in the Security Council. Meanwhile, United Nations forces would be free to clear up the guerrilla activities to the south.

The Foreign Secretary said that this proposal . . . was in accordance with his political objectives. He was anxious to prevent the United States Government from being led by their military advisers into policies which would provoke further intervention by China. . . .*

In the following discussion the following specific points were made:

(a) The proposed buffer area should be wholly within North Korea. There were some indications that the political authorities in the United States might be thinking in terms of a buffer area including some part of Manchuria; and the Cabinet were not disposed to support such a proposal.

(b) Who would be responsible for administering this buffer area? Would it be possible to arrange that, at an early stage, the Chinese should be associated with its administration?

The Foreign Secretary said that he would like further time to consider this aspect of the problem.[25]

The Cabinet instructed the Foreign Secretary, Minister of Defence and Commonwealth Secretary to instruct and inform their various overseas representatives and contacts concerning the buffer-zone policy. An essential element of this was that the zone should be backed by a tenable United Nations defensive line. Mr Bevin sent instructions to Sir Gladwyn Jebb, Sir Oliver Franks, and Sir Oliver Harvey in Paris. The Chiefs of Staff instructed Lord Tedder to discuss the idea with General Bradley at the same time as Sir Oliver raised it with Mr Acheson. The Commonwealth Secretary passed details under special disclosure instructions to the Governments of Australia, Canada, India, and New Zealand through the resident British High Commissioners.[26]

Sir Gladwyn Jebb responded on the 14th:

. . . I feel that, broadly speaking, your proposed new line offers much the best chance of some eventual solution. On the other hand, and with great deference, I feel that this solution is unlikely to be achieved by the tabling in the Security Council of some new resolution on the lines now proposed. My reasons are as follows:

(A) The achievement of any demilitarised zone in the north of Korea must, as I see it, be a result of a *negotiation*. It is most unlikely to come about as a result of some unilateral declaration. Since the Peking Government have refused to attend meetings of the Security Council at which this question is discussed, any resolution we put forward will almost certainly be vetoed by the Soviets and rejected by them.

---

*Mr Bevin advised his colleagues that his prospects of persuading the United States to adopt the buffer zone policy would be helped if he could offer a generous subscription to the costs of Korean rehabilitation. The Treasury was thinking in terms of £5 million but agreed 'in the last resort' in negotiations to £12 million.

(B) Withdrawal of draft resolution altogether at this stage and its replacement by one which is clearly much milder from the Chinese point of view, would no doubt have an effect on United States opinion which can only be assessed by the Embassy.

(C) The existing resolution as modified will of course probably be vetoed if it is put to the vote next week, but this really in itself does not matter very much, since the representatives of Peking will not be present . . . In any case a vote on the resolution in the Council will not in our view prejudice subsequent negotiations for the sort of settlement which you contemplate.

(D) . . . This could either be of course with the representatives of Peking or with the Russians or indeed with both, though I imagine that you will not wish any approach to be made to the Russians (whose general objective would seem to be to maintain the tension rather than diminish it) except in some specific point affecting their interests in the frontier zone. If, however, such negotiations are to have any prospect of success, the solution . . . should be allowed to emerge from the negotiations themselves and cannot so to speak be laid down in advance before the negotiations start.[27]

Sir Oliver Franks did not at once pass on the proposal. As he explained to Mr Bevin on 14th November:

As there appear to be still several days before resolution has to be voted on, and in view of Sir Gladwyn Jebb's comments in his telegram . . . to you, I decided to await your further views before speaking to Acheson.

2. At first sight I think there is attraction in Sir Gladwyn Jebb's suggestion that the achievement of a demilitarised zone in North Korea should result from *negotiation* and that it is unlikely to come about as a result of unilateral declaration. If we exclude (as I agree with you that we must) the possibility of getting the Chinese to agree to a demilitarised zone north of the Yalu we are depending on what might appear, especially to the Middle West, to be a unilateral concession. With the results of the recent election in mind it would, I think, be extremely difficult for Acheson, at this stage to accept the proposal . . .*

3. It is relevant to the foregoing that United Nations forces are shortly to resume their offensive which, if successful, should in

---

*The Democrats had had substantial losses in the November elections. During the campaign, the Republicans had strongly criticised the weak attitude of Mr Truman's administration in foreign policy, notably in Asia. The Middle West was then a stronghold of Republicanism.

a short time give them possession of most of the ground south of the Yalu.[28]

Mr Bevin pressed by return for Mr Acheson's views. He had just received advice via the United States Embassy in London that it might be necessary to permit United States aircraft to engage in 'hot pursuit' into north east China—the pilots of the 5th Tactical Air Force were growing impatient as they saw aerial intruders withdrawing on challenge into the sanctuary of Chinese air space. They were also pleading that their safety was imperilled by strict observation of the boundary.*[29]

'I put your ideas . . . to Acheson this afternoon, Dean Rusk and Freeman Matthews [Deputy Under Secretary of State] being present,' Sir Oliver reported to Mr Bevin on the evening of 15th November:

. . . He was in complete agreement with [your] general view of the situation . . . He therefore regarded the proposals with sympathy and active interest.

3. His great difficulty is to find out and assess Chinese intentions. If they intended to hold and dominate part of Northern Korea or even to push back United Nations forces to the south then an approach such as the one you have in mind could effect nothing. If on the other hand Chinese intentions are limited and they are preoccupied with worries about Manchuria and their legitimate interest in the supply of manpower to Manchuria from the power plants on the Korean side of the Yalu River then the kind of approach you have in mind is constructive and helpful.

4. Since at present it was not possible to find out about Chinese intentions by talking to them the only way open to us was military probing. For this and other reasons he did not feel that the course of operations in North Korea could be suspended or interrupted at this stage. Such a course would involve the commanding general of the United Nations forces in grave risks if the Chinese used any time given to them to build up their offensive power.

There had been a general discussion of points of detail in application; certain questions needed to be answered. Overall, Mr Acheson promised to give immediate and detailed consideration to the proposals. Sir Oliver concluded,

---

*This message remarked that 'we are not asking for concurrence of [British] Government because we believe the highly limited application would turn . . . upon military necessity . . .' Even so, Whitehall 'reactions' were requested.

7. It was noteworthy that Acheson and his associates at no point raised the issue of getting the Chinese to agree to a parallel demilitarised zone north of the Yalu as I thought they would do. From this and from the general tenor of the talk it seemed to me that they are very deeply troubled about the present situation and its possibilities.[30]

They were very deeply troubled because Mr Acheson knew that, politically, any move that looked like a unilateral concession would endanger the administration, particularly if it was not supported by the armed forces. It was manifest that any instruction to General MacArthur to draw his forces back, even on a limited basis, to a permanently defensive line would occasion an intense and probably public argument between Tokyo and Washington. The danger to his command would be cited as a strong argument against such a move. The Joint Chiefs of Staff would not wish to impose a policy which endangered their forces. Yet, the Secretary of State had no other ideas to offer. However grudgingly, he was carried forward by the hope that General MacArthur, who had never failed to secure ultimate victory, might do so again.

Quite apart from the political difficulties of the American Government, Mr Bevin accepted that the buffer zone initiative was not suitable as a replacement for the Security Council motion in draft. But it was soon to acquire support from some members of the State Department as the best option for negotiations, led perhaps by the United Kingdom, which it was hoped to have out of session with the Chinese delegation when it arrived for the Taiwan debate.[31]

The immediate disadvantage was that the Chinese seemed in no hurry to appear—24th November was the date rumoured—while General MacArthur was pressing ahead with the opening of his offensive. If he would not heed the proposal of the British Chiefs of Staff to pause until negotiations with the Chinese had been attempted, there could at least be insistence that 'hot pursuit' by American aircraft across the Chinese border was to be forbidden. Australia, Canada, France and New Zealand were among the United Nations membership who came to oppose it with the United Kingdom. The basic objections that aerial intrusion into China would widen the conflict and make negotiation more difficult were persuasive in themselves. Weight was added to them by advice from Mr Hutchison that the Russian Embassy in Peking had given notice that United States 'bombing' in North East China would be resisted by Soviet aircraft.[32]

On 17th November, Mr Bevin advised Sir Oliver Franks and Sir Gladwyn Jebb that he had arranged to make a statement in the House of Commons which would publicise again the determination of the United Nations to maintain the integrity of the Chinese border. 'But the situation is so serious that I think we ought to go further than making governmental declarations.' In addition to preparing direct contacts with the Chinese delegation in New York, he sought immediate action in Peking. 'Though Mr Hutchison has no *right* of access to the Chinese Government of matters of general policy,' he advised Mr Acheson on 17th November,

> 5. . . . I propose to instruct him to try to see Chou En-lai (even at the risk of inviting a snub), or at any rate the highest available responsible official, to convey a statement on the general lines [of the statement to the House of Commons]. . . . I do not propose to convey to the Chinese Government an indication of our proposals and ideas for a demilitarised area. If however the Chinese should give any opening to Mr Hutchison in the course of conversation about future possibilities in the frontier area, I would ask him to enquire from them (as being an enquiry from him personally) whether they have ever given any thought to the idea of a demilitarised area in North Korea and if so, whether they would like him to convey any suggestions regarding this to me.
> 6. I also propose to inform Pandit Nehru of the approach which Mr Hutchison will be making . . . and shall ask him to consider sending instructions to the Indian Ambassador in Peking to make a parallel approach.
> 7. Finally, I propose to instruct His Majesty's Ambassador in Moscow to inform the Soviet Government, in view of their declared interest in the maintenance of peace, of the views of His Majesty's Government on the gravity of the situation in the Far East. Sir D Kelly would *not* raise the question of a demilitarised zone . . .[33]

Unfortunately, the buffer zone plan was already known to both the Soviet Union and China. As Mr Bevin's telegram was *en route*, Sir Gladwyn Jebb telegraphed London and Washington in the late evening of the 17th,

> . . . Katz-Suchy of the Polish Delegation [to the United Nations] today approached Fry of Reuters and informed him that Polish Delegation had received information through certain channels to the effect that the Chinese Government would be prepared to discuss withdrawal of their troops from North Korea on the following terms.
> (a) creation of a 40 mile deep buffer zone south of the border, to be administered by the North Korean authorities;

(b) withdrawal of the United States Seventh Fleet from Formosan waters;

(c) withdrawal of recognition of the Chinese Nationalists by the United States;

(d) cessation of all Military and material assistance to the Chinese Nationalists by the United States.

2. Fry has himself informed United States Delegation of foregoing.[34]

In the welter of Korean and much other business, this news does not appear to have attracted much attention. Both the British and United States foreign departments at New York and in Washington appear to have thought that this might be just a rumour, overlooking the fact that satellite agencies of the Soviet Union were not permitted to while away idle hours by passing random information. They released news in deliberately chosen words at precisely directed times. The opening phrase, 'through certain channels' should have been a reminder of that. The object of the release, whether for example it was to test the market or simply to convey that Russia and China knew what was mooted, was as deliberately obscured.

On the 18th, Sir Oliver Franks sent Mr Acheson's reactions. Although the Secretary of State's mind was moving in very much the same way as yours, he had a reservation.

4. . . . he felt strongly that a short delay before these approaches [to Peking, Moscow, and Pandit Nehru] which you have in mind took place would be advantageous. He felt that in two or three days he would have a much clearer view on these important tactical issues and asked me to beg you most earnestly to consent to a temporary postponement of action under these proposals.[35]

What Mr Acheson did not say was that he had asked the Swedish Government on 13th November to convey through their Ambassador in Peking a message of assurance as to the United States' respect for the territorial integrity of China and the Yalu river facilities.[36] He made no mention of this to Sir Oliver Franks. But on reflection, however, the latter decided that his own report to Mr Bevin did not say enough. He sent this amplification to the Permanent Under-Secretary, Sir William Strang, that same evening:

In the course of our conversation it emerged that Acheson expected the general offensive of United Nations forces in Korea about November 22nd to November 24th. I put it to him that this meant he was asking Mr Bevin to postpone his approaches to the Chinese and Moscow until very near the time of the start of the offensive.

2. Acheson then said he, Lovett, General Bradley and Bedell-Smith [sic]* had gone over the intelligence situation in the last two days. Bedell-Smith had said that a good deal of information had come in which, judged for example by the tests applied by the Japanese to Russian intentions and preparedness in 1944 and 1945, showed that the Russians had considerably raised the level of their preparations in the last fortnight or ten days. Bedell-Smith did not argue from this that the Russians intended war but that their activities reflected the increase of tension in that part of the world.

3. The Chinese according to Bedell-Smith had moved three armies from South China to Manchuria. They had also strongly reinforced the whole length of the Korean border. They had put between 75,000 and 100,000 men across the border into Korea. There was a very considerable concentration of Chinese troops round the central [Yalu] reservoirs big enough to suggest they intended to try to break through the centre of the United Nations line

4. Bedell-Smith could not infer from this whether the Chinese intended only a strong defensive action in Korea or more than that. He thought the only useful question to ask was what the Commanding General of the United Nations forces should do. There were three possibilities: he could stay where he was, go forward or move backwards. American military opinion was that the decision between these possibilities could not be made 7,000 miles away from the scene of operations. The position had to be left to the General Commanding in the light of his general directives.

5. Acheson then went on to say that he was seriously concerned about the situation and that his mind moved along lines parallel to that of Mr Bevin. He did not think the American Chiefs of Staff would take it on themselves to try to tell MacArthur what to do in a military way—they were too far off and too ignorant of the ground and the general possibilities Acheson himself was therefore working at a political directive which he hoped to complete and clear with the Defense Department and the American Chiefs of Staff by Monday November 20th latest which would not make the conquest or occupation of the rest of North Korea a requirement on the Commanding General. He would

---

*Smith, General Walter Bedell (he did not hyphenate his name) (1895–1961), war time Chief of Staff to General Eisenhower. Head of the Central Intelligence Agency 1950–53.

be required as before to unify the large part of Korea which he had occupied and to hold elections and equip a Korean Army of ten or twelve divisions as rapidly as he could. The political directive could not however specify what from a military point of view the Commanding General should or should not do in the unoccupied part of North Korea in order to fulfill his mission.
6. I formed the clear impression that Acheson was very troubled about the timing of the planned offensive. It may coincide almost exactly with the arrival of the Chinese delegation in New York and will thus form an unhappy prologue to whatever talks may develop. I also formed the clear impression that Acheson is not in a position and is not willing to attempt to overcome the strong objections of the American Chiefs of Staff to telling the Commanding General in Korea how to conduct his military operations there. They feel for reasons given above that the decisions must be left to him.[37]

Mr Bevin had no intention of reviving the Korean issue with the Russians before he had a response from Peking, but it was too late to delay his instructions to Mr Hutchison or Sir Archibald Nye. The latter saw Mr Nehru on the 20th, interested him in the idea of a buffer zone and received a promise that 'he would issue the necessary instructions to Panikkar as requested by Foreign Secretary and that he would instruct him not to make any reference to our demilitarisation proposals in discussion with the Chinese Government'.[38] Mr Hutchison was received at the Foreign Affairs ministry in Peking on the afternoon of the 22nd. He was seen by the Vice-Minister, Chang Han-fu, and the head of the West European and African Department, who accepted Mr Bevin's message and listened with 'grave attention' as he propounded the idea of a demilitarised zone:

5. . . . Chang asked whether this was my own suggestion or whether I was putting it forward as a suggestion made by His Majesty's Government. I repeated that I was putting it forward tentatively as my own suggestion. He then asked what I meant by a demilitarised zone. I said I had in mind a sort of cushion on the Korean side of the border in which fighting would cease and from which military units would be withdrawn. Finally he enquired who would keep order in such a demilitarised zone. I replied that I had only so far thought of the possibility of such a zone in a general way and had not considered it in detail, but that I would suppose that the local North Korean authorities would be responsible for keeping law and order in the Zone. (I fancy that he had thought I might suggest that the United Nations authority should administer the demilitarised Zone).

6. The pertinence of his question suggests that the idea was not new to him, and the impression is that the Chinese are already considering some such possibility . . .

9. Chang then said that he would convey to Chou En-lai both your message and also the substance of what I had personally said.

10. I feel sure that he fully appreciated the urgency of the matter . . .[39]

With this offer, political initiatives to separate the forces of China and the United Nations in the northernmost Korean provinces came to an end. Of course, this was not immediately apparent. Much as reviews and discussions had continued in the search to find another solution to crossing the 38th Parallel after the crossing was inevitable, notions persisted in Washington, London, and to a lesser extent in Paris, Canberra, and New Delhi that 'mutual interests' or 'reason' might yet throw up a political option to contain the struggle in terms of territory and time.

In London, the Chiefs of Staff pressed again for a delay in General MacArthur's offensive—a week might suffice. As Field Marshall Slim contended,

It seemed that the war [in Korea] was largely regarded in the United States as a domestic affair, and that decisions . . . were coloured by the internal political situation . . . There was indeed a fallacy in the conception of advancing to a military objective in the form of a line on the map, since in the process the combat zone must inevitably spill over that line. There were various other military arguments . . . which had already been put to the Americans. All these arguments should be presented afresh . . . with the additional point that account must be taken of British public opinion . . .[40]

They resolved to ask the Prime Minister and Defence Minister to send personal messages to President Truman and General Marshall respectively urging this brief restraint.* But the proposal overlooked a factor of which Mr Attlee was aware: there were limits to his influence with the President of the United States. A personal message seeking to change United States policy should be sent by a British Prime Minister only if it conformed to one of two criteria. Either it should have some reasonable chance of success, or it should relate to a matter so crucial to British interests that, regardless of potential influence, a contention had to be expressed.

*This form of action was proposed by Mr Robert Scott, the Foreign Office representative present.

306

Though sympathetic to the Chiefs' apprehensions, he did not believe that they satisfied either of these criteria. Mr Bevin was of the same mind.[41] It may be that he disliked in principle the recurrent intromission of the Defence Ministry. In any case, he had other irons in this particular fire: the issue of 'hot pursuit'; the Security Council resolution on Chinese intervention, to which he was thinking of tying the buffer zone proposal; direct negotiations in Peking as a response to Mr Hutchison's contact—then proceeding—or with the Chinese delegation on its arrival at Lake Success. A military delay was in every way desirable but scarcely to be realised. The Chiefs might send their views to Lord Tedder, who would doubtless convey them to Sir Oliver Franks.[42] At the same time, he would instruct Sir Oliver in his own way. 'There is general anxiety on all sides in the House of Commons,' he telegraphed on the afternoon of 22nd November, 'lest General MacArthur should commit the United Nations forces in Korea to large scale hostilities with the Chinese. The questions put in the House (see Hansard for November 16th) indicate what is in the minds of Members.'

2. I shall have to deal with this, possibly quite soon, and in any case during the debate on foreign affairs due to take place next week.

3. Whilst I have had certain indications of the nature of the instructions issued to General MacArthur, eg, in regard to civil affairs, even these have been communicated to me for my secret information. . . . This places me in a most difficult and embarrassing position. There is a campaign going on in Korea in which British forces are engaged; the command of the forces is ultimately subject to the United Nations through the Agency of the United States Government (Security Council Resolution of 7th July) and the objectives of the Commander must be those set out in United Nations Resolutions. Despite this the United Nations has no real say in the instructions issued to the Commander, and I am not at liberty to disclose such information as I have. Parliament and the British public are entitled to expect that the objectives of the United Nations Commander in the field are no more and no less than the stated objectives of the United Nations as expressed in its Resolutions. They are, moreover, entitled to feel confident that whereas in this case one member government (the United States Government) is acting as agent for the United Nations for the purpose of issuing instructions to the United Nations Commander, such instructions are confined strictly to the attainment of the declared United Nations objectives. I am aware that under the American military

system it is customary to leave more latitude to the Commander in the field than under the British system. But the same principles apply whether the Commander is acting on his own initiative or under instructions. I can reasonably claim that it is not in the public interest to disclose the precise nature of the instructions issued to him. I must, however, be careful not to leave the impression that the reasons why the instructions are not made public is either because these give General MacArthur more latitude than a strict fulfilment of the United Nations Resolutions would justify or that quite simply we have no knowledge of their contents.

4. I recognise that General MacArthur must be given discretion (within the broad limits outlined above) to conduct the campaign on the lines he thinks best. I recognise also that in view of military requirements and with the Russians back in the Security Council there can be no question of the latter issuing detailed military instructions or of his being required to seek such instructions from the Council through the representatives of the United States.

5. All this, however, does not meet my particular difficulties. I should therefore like you to explain these urgently to Mr Acheson and ask him how we can best overcome them. Public opinion here is getting restive and it is of very great importance that I should be able to assure the House *first* that the objectives of General MacArthur are no more and no less than the objectives of the United Nations, *second* that proper consultation is taking place and *third* that General MacArthur through the United States Government is in fact as well as in name the agent of the United Nations.

6. There should not be much difficulty in giving the first and third assurances. The main problem arises over consultation. The Commander's view of military necessity may prompt him to action going beyond his Mandate without the United Nations being given the opportunity to consider its political implications. As regards this, I feel that we should press the United States Government to agree:

(i) to consult confidentially at least those member States of the Security Council who are providing forces in Korea on any contemplated action of this character and

(ii) not to issue instructions to the Commander to proceed unless those States consulted express their agreement to what is proposed.

If we get an assurance on these lines (which I feel is our due) I shall, during the course of the Debate, be able to tell the House that there is a satisfactory arrangement in force regarding consultation, though of course I would not propose to divulge any details. I would consult as to the words to be used.

7. I should be glad if you would speak to Mr Acheson urgently.[43]

Mr Bevin may have had a false impression of Mr Acheson's power at this juncture. Manifestly, he had more power than Mr Bevin to influence United States policy and was dedicated to a political solution to the Korean problem, not least the Chinese intervention. He was far from a devoted admirer of General MacArthur. He and his associates were heedless neither of British ideas nor domestic problems arising from partnership in the war. In responding to the sense of impotence which lay behind Mr Bevin's request for assurances, however, two difficulties, previously noted, constrained Mr Acheson. The first was that he saw no other clear solution to their difficulties than a military victory—the seizure of the northern Korean provinces. Given their possession, the United Nations Commission would be able to put in hand the union of Korea. Second, he was by no means sure that the President and the Defense Department were able wholly to control General MacArthur.

In this latter consideration, both domestic politics and the American tradition to its distant commander-in-chief militated. But beside these was the reluctance of the Joint Chiefs to change or define more precisely their instructions because they were overawed by the seniority, standing, and potential for success of the remarkable veteran in Tokyo. General Marshall was not affected in this way; his standing was no less than that of General MacArthur's. But he was inhibited by feelings of loyalty to the military tradition and recognition of the President's domestic difficulties.

The day before he received Mr Bevin's message on consultation, reluctant acceptance of the military option obliged Mr Acheson, at a meeting with the Defense Department, to concur with a renewed offensive. Even so, he pointed out with Mr Rusk 'the anxiety which other friendly members of the UN felt about [the United States] becoming more deeply involved perhaps finally in war with Communist China'.

General Marshall expressed satisfaction that Mr Acheson had stated his belief that General MacArthur should push forward with the planned offensive. He expressed some doubt about the establishment of the [demilitarized] zone and assumed that if one were established south of the River another would have to be established to the north. If there were a UN Commission, it would have to have military protection. He preferred to consider first the political action based on the premise that General

MacArthur will succeed in his pending military offensive. The time for making political proposals would be after MacArthur had had such a success.

Secretary Acheson pointed to the possibility that there might be partial success without either complete success or failure. He noted that we had discouraged the UK from pressing its proposal for a zone. He noted the difficulty of securing agreement on a demilitarized zone on both sides of the border. The zone on the south side only would be better than continuing the war but we would want to be sure that the zone was not being used for the build up of further Chinese forces.

Mr Lovett raised the question whether instead of negotiating for a zone it would not be better as a matter of fact if General MacArthur withdrew to a defensible line after pressing his offensive forward successfully to the River.

Secretary Acheson stressed the need for finding a way of terminating the Chinese intervention in the war and also stressed the sensitive area of the northeast province from the Soviet point of view. From the point of view of our partners in the UN, it is desirable to find some kind of an agreement and we are searching for something which would be useful instead of harmful to General MacArthur.

General Marshall stressed again the desirability of our making proposals while the UN Forces are advancing instead of waiting until other members of the UN advance proposals which might be unacceptable.

General Vandenberg, at this point and later, emphasized his doubt whether we could find any solution which would satisfy the Chinese Communists . . .

The meeting discussed defensive zones and lines once the Chinese border had been reached. There was general agreement that the river would not be a useful line:

After Secretary Acheson, General Marshall and Mr Harriman withdrew . . . The Chiefs seemed to agree that if it was decided that it would be desirable to concentrate on the line which General Collins had indicated [the high ground overlooking the river from the south] some changes in MacArthur's directive would be desirable. . . .

Mr Lovett raised the question of the possible use of Chinese Nationalists . . .

Mr Rusk pointed out that it was most likely that the British would refuse to have their troops fight along side of Chinese Nationalists against the Chinese Communists and suggested that

10,000 British troops were of more value than 30,000 Chinese in Korea. . . .[44]

Notwithstanding his willingness to represent the British point of view to his colleagues and a measure of sympathy for it, Mr Acheson found the burden of the Anglo-American partnership heavy over the next few days. He was frustrated by the limitations of his own position in respect of Korea. He gave a bland reply to Mr Bevin's request for assurances on consultation, but found it more difficult to look reasonably at his proposals to air the buffer zone idea when the debate on the six-power resolution on China was resumed in the Security Council. After several exchanges of view, Mr Bevin agreed to suspend this idea until the Chinese Communist delegation under General Wu Hsiu-chuan attended the Council. But this was not enough for Mr Acheson. On 24th November, he instructed Mr Julius C Holmes, *Chargé d'Affaires* in London, to pass a further personal request to Mr Bevin:

> . . . Since the [Chinese Communist] delegation arrived today and since there will probably be a meeting of the Security Council early next week, I wish to lay before you in more detail than was possible in the brief message transmitted through Sir Oliver Franks on November 21st why I have the gravest apprehensions regarding the presentation of any such proposal [concerning a buffer zone] pending such clarification and reconsideration of the situation following General MacArthur's offensive.[45]

In six paragraphs, he set out the sum of the arguments against dividing American and British public opinion on the war, and coincidentally of providing the Chinese Communists with 'a starting point for negotiations to obtain something much more favourable to them and as an indication of the greatest weakness on our part. . . .'

He was so 'deeply conscious of the gravity of the ensuing days and of the far-reaching consequences of any misstep' , that he took the extraordinary step of adding a postscript for Holmes. 'Department believes it might be useful for you to discuss the general lines of the above with Salisbury* and Eden'.[46] Fortunately, Mr Holmes was able to report on 25th November that Mr Bevin 'had no desire to upset the applecart. . . . In light of Bevin's helpful attitude, I feel it would serve no useful purpose to talk with

---

*Salisbury, Robert Arthur James Gascoyne-Cecil, 5th Marquess of (1916–82), then leader of the Conservative opposition in the House of Lords, and with Anthony Eden, Conservative foreign affairs spokesman in the Commons, powerful in the opposition hierarchy.

Salisbury and Eden as suggested in last paragraph . . ., and in view Foreign Minister's delicate situation re opposition particularly in connection with Parliamentary Foreign Affairs debate scheduled for coming week, such action might have most unfortunate repercussions. . .'.[47]

On the same day, General J Lawton Collins, Chief of Staff of the United States Army, signalled General MacArthur. As ever in their communications, the phraseology reflects the respect for the appointment and trepidation of the man. Mention of Allied concern about developments, is made in such a way as to suggest its use as a stalking horse.

> Following from JCS. Other members of United Nations indicate growing concern over the possibilities of bringing on a general conflict should a major clash develop with Chinese Communist forces as a result of your forces advancing squarely against the entire boundary between Korea and Manchuria–USSR. This might not only result in loss of support within United Nations and leave US standing alone but would also involve increased risks of a military nature. Proposals in UN suggest unwelcome restrictions on your advance to the north since some sentiment exists in UN for establishing a demilitarised zone between your forces and the frontier in the hope of thereby reducing Chinese Communist fear of UN military action against Manchuria and the corresponding sensitivity on the part of the USSR with respect to Vladivostok. . . .
>
> The consensus of political and military opinion was that there should be no change in your mission, but that immediate action should be taken at top governmental level to formulate a course of action which would permit the establishment of a unified Korea and at the same time reduce risk of more general involvement. On the assumption that your coming attack will be successful, exploratory discussions were had to discover what military measures, which you might in any event wish to take, might lend themselves to political action which would reduce tension with Peiping and the Soviet Union and maintain a solid UN front. The following represent a search for such measures:
>
> 1. After advancing to or near Yalu, you might secure the position which you had just achieved by holding forces on terrain dominating the approaches from the Valley of the Yalu, from its mouth to approximately the position now held by the 17th Infantry. These forces would be principally ROK troops while other UN forces would be grouped in positions of readiness to insure the holding of the established line. This, of course, would be contingent on the cessation of effective enemy resistance.

2. The above position would be extended to the Japan Sea along a general line approximately east from the 17th Infantry's position with an outpost at Chongjin, which would be the limit for the present of your advance to the northeast.

3. It was thought that the above would not seriously affect the accomplishment of your mission.

4. UN forces would continue to make every effort to spare all hydro-electric installations in North Korea; destruction of these facilities could result only as incident to resistance from enemy forces.

5. The United Nations Commission for Unification and Relief in Korea (UNCURK) would, at the appropriate time, enter into negotiations with appropriate representatives to insure an equitable distribution of hydro-electric power.

6. In the event that the Chinese forces did not again attack in force across the Yalu, the conduct of orderly elections in North Korea and the unification of the country could proceed in accordance with UN action.

7. Ultimate handling of the extremely sensitive Northeast Province would await further UN procedures . . .

Since there are many political and military implications involved in these ideas and since other nations would be involved, no action along these lines is contemplated until full opportunity has been given for further consideration of your views, final decision by the President, and possibly discussion with certain other governments.[48]

This advice was not well received by General MacArthur: it bore on his prerogative and vexed his sense of mission. It was also at odds with the character of his Communique No 12, issued as the offensive began on the 24th. *Inter alia* this remarked that

The United Nations massive compression envelopment in North Korea against the new Red Armies operating there is now approaching its decisive effort. The isolating component of the pincer, our Air Forces of all types, have for the past three weeks, in a sustained attack of model coordination and effectiveness, successfully interdicted enemy lines of support from the north so that further reinforcement therefrom has been sharply curtailed and essential supplies markedly limited. . . .
If successful this [operation] should for all practical purposes end the war, restore peace and unity to Korea, enable the prompt withdrawal of United Nations military forces, and permit the complete assumption by the Korean people and nation of full sovereignty and international equality. It is for this we fight.

On the 25th, as all formations reported successful progress, he rejected all the military suggestions made to him by General Collins—'In the first place from a military standpoint my personal reconnaissance of the Yalu River line yesterday* demonstrated conclusively that it would be utterly impossible for us to stop upon commanding terrain south of the river . . .'—and then picked off the political considerations. He concluded with an advisory note of his own:

> . . . By resolutely meeting those commitments and accomplishing our military mission as so often publicly delineated lies best— indeed only—hope that Soviet and Chinese aggressive designs may be checked before these countries are committed to a course from which for political reasons they cannot withdraw.[49]

The game was afoot, therefore, without strategic limitations in Korea. Indeed, the line of the Yalu on the ground and in the air was the only absolute limitation remaining when the offensive began. Now we know that the advancing UN soldiers were about to be drawn into a violent clash of arms in strategically and tactically disastrous circumstances, the wisdom of hindsight prompts the question, as so frequently, why was it allowed to take place?

From a military point of view, General MacArthur was correct in stating to the subsequent Congressional Hearings[50] that he could not stay where he was; with the Eighth Army and X Corps separated in positions of hasty choice, that would have invited destruction. He had either to go on or draw back. Politically, as recounted, there were many reasons against drawing back, though the British Chiefs set out the military and political advantages in so doing. With hindsight, were they right?

From a purely military point of view, there can be little doubt that the ground roughly below the 40th Parallel offers in commanding features, distance, communications and adjacent supply sources perhaps the best purely defensive line in the peninsula. Politically, it also retained a considerable part of North Korea. But any idea that Russia and China, to say nothing of Kim Il-sung, would have permitted the establishment of a demilitarised zone in the remainder of the northern provinces is highly questionable.

Dean Acheson was to reflect upon the dual enigma which faced the United Nations in Korea immediately after the intervention of the Chinese—'What were the facts about Chinese military presence in North Korea and what were Chinese intentions? (The first would throw light on the second)'.[50] Experience of dealing with the Soviet

---

*After visiting Eighth Army on the Ch'ongch'on on 24th November, General MacArthur flew up to the Yalu in his unarmed C-54 transport before returning to Japan.

Union, and recent American experience of dealing with the leaders of the revolution in China, had made it apparent that, as opponents, each would press any advantage to its limits. From the evidence available, Chinese troops had come into Korea to stop the United Nations forces from advancing to the Yalu. Having halted the UN divisions in October, P'eng Te-huai drew his armies back because divisions were becoming dangerously dispersed.[52] He needed also to redeploy, taking account of the second army group crossing into Korea. With these forces to hand, there was no question of pulling back across the river, surrendering the northern provinces, at best, to a United Nations Commission. Drawing back American troops without necessity might have stocked some political furnaces in the Middle West of the United States; it was contrary to every principle of the Russian and Chinese leadership.

A buffer zone was never a practicable idea. Those who conceived or supported it were as remote from realities as those who apprehended that China had the capability to make war throughout Asia when its agriculture was struggling and its manufacturing resources exhausted after many years of war with Japan and between Nationalist and Communist factions. Clearly, the Communist camp was informed that a demilitarised zone might be a United Nations objective—perhaps by the United Press—but whenever it had been revealed, as Mr Acheson remarked to Mr Bevin, '. . . it would be taken by them as a starting point for negotiations to obtain something much more favourable for them . . .'[53]

The concept was wisely abandoned by Mr Acheson for the reasons he set out at the time. It was clung to by Mr Bevin, probably because it was the only initiative in his hand at a time when he felt singularly powerless. It divided the two frustrated Secretaries of State at a time when the stimulation of the one by the other might, as on other occasions, have produced something more fruitful.

Mr Bevin's illness may also have contributed to his inabilities in the partnership. Korea apart, he had an immense range of work, which included the struggle to develop the European element of NATO in the face of a Russian challenge and a divisive French scheme. But this said, what political policy was waiting for Mr Bevin or Mr Acheson to pick up to solve the Korean problem while the United Nations armies prepared to resume their advance?

There being no peaceful political solution, Mr Acheson was obliged to accept that 'war is the continuation of policy by other means'. Probably the best option would have been to encourage General MacArthur to put into practice his first idea after the October check, 'a reconnaissance in force'. Feeling out the Chinese positions while closing up and reserving his main forces would certainly have offered the United Nations forces a better opportunity to defeat the Chinese People's Volunteers than a general advance on to ground chosen by the waiting foe. When this led to a United Nations reversal, the British Chiefs' original idea of a robust defensive line on the 40th Parallel on which Chinese and North Korean waves would dash themselves under skies commanded by the United States Air Forces would have been politically a better refuge than a similar line on the 38th. Preparation of a northern line would have been prudent during the standfast between the end of October and 24th November. But by the 24th, General MacArthur had raised a popular cry, 'Home for Christmas!'

SOURCE NOTES: CHAPTER 13

1. CINCFE 68285 of 4th November 1950 to JCS (through Department of the Army (DA)), (USNARS, Suitland).

2. DEFE 11/202, CINCUNC Communique No 11 of 5th November 1950, Washington to FO 3007 of 5th November 1950.

3. Secretary of State (S of S) 476 of 5th November to the US Mission at UN, USNARS 795. B/11–550.

4. Memo of conversations by S of S, 6th November 1950 USNARS 795. 00/11–650.

5. Truman, op cit, Vol II, p 397.

6. JCS 95878 of to CINCFE 061147 November 1950, (USNARS, Suitland).

7. DEFE 11/202, Washington to FO 2950 of 1st November 1950.

8. Ibid, Washington to FO 3005 of 6th November 1950.

9. CAB 128/18, Cabinet 71 (50) of 6th November 1950 and Sir A Johnston, conversation with author.

10. DEFE 11/202, Tokyo (Bouchier) to MOD (Chiefs of Staff) CAB 94 of 311123 October 1950.

11. Ibid, Tokyo (Bouchier) to MOD (without reference) of 031618 November 1950.

12. DEFE 11/203, MOD (Chiefs of Staff) to BJSM Washington COS(W)894 of 061710 November 1950.

13. Ibid, BJSM Washington to MOD AWT 71 of 082241 November 1950.

14. DEFE 5/21, COS (50) 176th Meeting.

15. Truman, op cit, Vol II, pp 402–3.

16. DEFE 11/203, UK New York to FO 1659 of 9th November 1950.

17. Ibid, FO to UK New York 1944 of 9th November 1950.

18. United Nations document S/184.

19. DEFE 11/203, UK New York to FO 1668 of 8th November 1950. See also FRUS, 1950, Vol VII, Korea p 1096.

20. UN document S/189.

21. O'Neill, op cit, Vol I, pp 136–7. Shinwell, conversation with author.

22. FRUS, p 1108. See also Article by Peter N Farrar, 'A pause for peace negotiations: The British Buffer Zone Plan of November, 1950, p 69, in The Korean War in History, ed. Cotton and Neary (Manchester, 1989).

23. JCS95949 of 6th November 1950 to CINCFE and JCS96060 of 8th November 1950 to CINCFE (USNARS, Suitland). James F Schnabel, Policy and Direction, The First Year, The United States Army in the Korean War, (Washington DC, 1972), pp 250–2.

24. DEFE 11/203, Washington to FO 3048 of 10th November 1950.

25. CAB 128/18, Cabinet 73 (50).

26. DEFE 11/203, FO to Washington 5028 of 14th November 1950. Commonwealth Relations Office (CRO) to UK HC New Delhi 2612 of 14th November 1950, and to all High Commissioners 359 and 360 of 15th November 1950.

27. Ibid, New York to FO 1720 of 14th November 1950.

28. Ibid, Washington to FO 3079 of 14th November 1950.

29. Ibid, FO to Washington 5066 of 15th November 1950. See also FRUS pp 1144, S of S to Embassy in UK 2487 of 13th November 1950 to London.

30. DEFE 11/203, Washington to FO 3089 of 15th November 1950.

31. Ibid, New York to FO 1763 of 16th November 1950.

32. Ibid, Peking to FO 1805 of 12th November 1950.

33. Ibid, FO to Washington 5123 and 5124 of 17th November 1950, and to Peking 1890 and 1891 of 18 November 1950.

34. Ibid, New York to FO 1780 of 17th November 1950.

35. DEFE 11/204, Washington to FO 3133 of 18th November 1950.

36. Memo, Clubb to Rusk, 10 November 1950, USNARS A795. B/11-1050, Memo, Rusk conversation with Swedish Ambassador to US, 13th November 1950, USNARS 693. 95/11-350.

37. DEFE 11/203, Washington to FO 3131 of 18th November 1950.

38. DEFE 11/204, New Delhi to CRO 3524 of 20th November 1950.

39. Ibid, Peking to FO 1882 of 23th November 1950.

40. DEFE 5/21, COS (50) 182nd Meeting.

41. Shinwell, conversation with author.

42. DEFE 11/204, MOD to BJSM Washington WE7 and 8 of 23rd November 1950.

43. Ibid, FO to Washington 5194 of 22nd November 1950.

44. Memo of conversations by US Ambassador at Large Jessup, 21st November 1950, USNARS 795.00/11-2150.

45. S of S 2752 of 24th November 1950 to US London Embassy, USNA795. 00/11-2450.

46. Ibid

47. US London Embassy 3076 of 25th November 1950 to S of S, USNARS 795. 00/11-2550

48. Chief of Staff, United States Army (CSA) WAR 97287 of 24th November 1950 to CINCUNC/CINCFE, (USNARS, Suitland).

49. CINCUNC C-69808 of 25 November 1950 to JCS, (USNARS, Suitland).

50. Military situation in the Far East, Hearings of Armed Services and Foreign Relations Committees of US Senate, 82nd Congress, 1st Session, (Hearings) vols i-v, Washington, 1956.

51. Acheson, op cit, pp 64-72.

52. Author's article cit, China Quarterly.

53. See 45, above.

CHAPTER 14

'. . . the great army sweeps all before it, Who dares gallop ahead, sword in hand? None other than our great General P'eng.'
(Mao Tse-tung)[1]

Throughout October, the 29th Independent Infantry Brigade Group and the British administrative tail—all fifty-five major and minor units—had been approaching Korea by air and sea.* Brigadier Brodie reported to General MacArthur's headquarters on 26th October. Once, the staff there had looked for him urgently; now they were uncertain as to how his large brigade would be employed. 'It is difficult to be sure what we are getting into: some Americans here seem to think the war will be over before we arrive,' the brigadier wrote home to the War Office.[2] Air Vice-Marshal Bouchier, who discussed prospects with him, believed they would be used in the occupation role. Sir Alvary Gascoigne, and Lieutenant-General Sir Horace Robertson, Commander-in-Chief of the British Commonwealth Occupation Force, were unwilling to make a guess. From a temporary base in a Tokyo hotel, Brigadier Brodie visited General Walker in Korea and went forward to see Brigadier Coad in the field. Both these commanders believed that, at the very least, they would be engaged for many weeks in counter-guerrilla operations.

Well ahead of these movements, 'Battle Inoculation Teams' from the brigade began arriving in Japan early in September. They travelled in Hastings aircraft of Royal Air Force Transport Command, night stopping on a journey of five days from southern England. American Dakotas carried them into Korea. Three or four officers and non-commissioned officers had been sent from units of the fighting and supporting Arms—infantry, armour, artillery, engineers and signals—to acquire impressions of the battlefield and the working methods of the United States Army. They were to be attached to American units, principally within

---

*See Appendix N. In the mistaken belief that chartered ships could not be sent into the Korean war zone, it had originally been intended to land the force in Japan for embodiment, prior to transportation in American ships to Korea.

the 25th Division, then involved in the fighting prior to the Inch'on landing. After two weeks, they were to gather at Eighth Army headquarters under Colonel B A Burke, the deputy brigade commander, to pool their experiences. The majority would then fly to Singapore to board the troopship of their respective unit, imparting their knowledge on the final run to Pusan[3].

The plan worked well. The teams were eager to make use of the brief time available and impatient of a delay caused by rainstorms on the night of their arrival. It was still raining on the following morning, by which time some of the 'pup tents' provided as temporary shelter were collapsing. Colonel Burke, who had joined only a fortnight before from the Austrian occupation, had a brief moment of regret among his swamped canvas and sodden possessions.

'To think that a month ago I was living in a royal palace, the uncrowned king of Vienna!'[4]

Soon they dispersed to their host units among the soaring hills, bumping in vehicles over potholes, scrambling occasionally across scrub covered slopes, or wet fields in the intensely cultivated valleys. Almost all came under fire, and none more gladly than Second Lieutenant Henry Cabral of the Glosters, recently commissioned from the Royal Military Academy, Sandhurst. A North Korean bullet grazed his left forearm during an attack one afternoon. 'What luck,' he called to a surprised American comrade, 'I'm battle inoculated!' Captain Desmond Holmes of 55 Squadron, Royal Engineers, earned himself newspaper headlines by taking forward orders to an isolated force whose radio had been destroyed. 'The bravest man I know,' the local commanding officer told reporters that evening.[5] The teams' own reports, to Colonel Burke and to their units as they returned, were of a traditional infantry war.

Next came the advanced parties, coordinated by the brigade DAA&QMG, Major Boris Eastwood. Their task was to find accommodation in the locations selected by Eighth Army, to borrow American transport until the brigade's vehicles arrived, to acquire intelligence information and maps.

Seven troopships and twenty four store and vehicle ships carried the sea parties.* Aboard the former, corporals and below were accommodated on 'flats'—decks below the water line—which contained racks for bedding, and 'sea' kit bags, the only containers available for clothing and personal belongings. Long mess tables and benches were fixed to the decks. Hammocks were slung throughout the space at night for sleeping. There was just sufficient

---

*See Appendix P.

room to permit a man to climb in or out of his hammock without disturbing his neighbour and to offer, along each row, a passage way to the washrooms and latrines—the 'heads' in ship's parlance. Ventilation was provided by dorades and air scoops on deck; stale air was drawn out by motorised fans. The cramped conditions and heat were tolerable in cold weather and moderate seas, but trying in the tropics, and wretched in heavy weather when numbers of men were seasick. Officers, warrant officers and sergeants were packed into cabins, some of the latter also on 'flats', but had the advantage of separate messing and sitting accommodation on the upper decks.

A glimpse of life aboard is caught by brief entries in the war diary of the 1st Battalion, The Royal Ulster Rifles.

1st October. 1945 hours. *Empire Pride* left Liverpool bound for Korea. The battalion was addressed by the Rt Hon John Strachey, Secretary of State for War.

2nd October. A private of 26th Field Ambulance [travelling with the RUR] threw himself overboard. Search abandoned after two hours.

3rd to 7th October. No training commenced owing to heavy seas running.

8th October. Church Services at 1030 hours. Good attendance.

9th October. Training commenced at 1145 hours. PT, training films and firing of small arms at targets from aft of ship.

Training was not delayed because of late rising. Getting up, visiting washrooms and heads, stowing kit, serving and clearing breakfast, cleaning and inspection took a considerable time each morning. There were periodic lifeboat and fire drills. But the voyage was not an endless series of miseries for the junior ranks: there were deck games and tugs-o'-war; and, best of all, long easy hours yarning or card playing in deck spaces as the ship ran through calm waters in warm weather, with the option of sleeping on deck in these conditions. The canteen sold cheap cigarettes and beer. There was mail waiting, and shore leave, at Aden, Colombo and Singapore. Even so, after six weeks on the sea, most looked forward to the end of the voyage. For the Royal Ulster Rifles, 'On the morning of the 5th of November, the mountainous coastline of Korea came into sight, although partly hidden by squalls of rain.'

By midday, the *Empire Pride* was anchored in Pusan harbour and, while she waited her turn to go alongside, the men on board took their first look at the bleak harbour, the squalid township beyond and, in the distance, the dark and rugged mountains stretching away inland to the north. . . . In the late afternoon the Battalion disembarked and marched to the railway station, there to entrain for Suwon, where the Brigade was to form up.

It was dark by now and the chaos and muddle in the pitch blackness of the station were unbelievable. All those stores— petrol for cookers, rations, and water—necessary for the two hundred-mile journey north to Suwon (reputed to take four or five days if all went well) were to have been placed on the train before the battalion's arrival. In fact, of course, they were not there, and it was only after a frantic search round a strange town in the darkness that they were eventually assembled . . . evidently the British supply organisation was not yet functioning.[6]

It was not functioning because the units required to make it do so were, like the RUR, in process of arriving, but in a matter of two weeks the organisation was beginning to operate.

In and around the Brigade Administrative Area at Suwon were the eighty 3-ton trucks of 57 Company, Royal Army Service Corps, augmented by relief drivers, and a platoon for the collection and issue of rations, petrol, oil, lubricants and ammunition. Nearby was the Ordnance Field Park, responsible for obtaining, receiving and issuing weapons, equipment including radios and telephones, vehicle and other spare parts, batteries and clothing. 10 Infantry Workshop complemented these services. 26 Field Ambulance provided an advanced dressing station,* and a medical centre. It had the means to send forward casualty collecting posts close to fighting units. A mobile dental team was attached to the field ambulance. Within the Administrative Area a Royal Engineers Postal Unit was established, and a Field Cash Office. These elements, under their respective commanding officers, were controlled by the DAA&QMG to provide for the needs of the forward elements.

Behind the brigade was the British Korean Base and Forward Maintenance Area under Colonel A M Rowlandson. They had been organised to provide the depth of administrative support for 29 Brigade but would also do so for 27 as long as it remained in the field. For the 8th Hussars, a Forward Delivery Squadron held a reserve of armoured fighting vehicles and crews. 'K' Reinforcement Holding Unit set itself up to provide a buffer of reinforcements for forward units to replace casualties.

The unfolding of this organisation was a great relief to Lieutenant-General Sir Horace Robertson. As recounted, he had

---

*With a field surgical and a transfusion team.

been in command of the residual, and by then wholly Australian, British Commonwealth Occupation Force (BCOF) in Japan when the war began. To reduce defence costs, he was instructed in May 1950 progressively to close his facilities and prepare for withdrawal homeward, but further action was suspended with the outbreak of the war in Korea. By July, his limited resources were being called upon to help Admiral Andrewes' squadron. By early August, it was plain that Australian, British, New Zealand and probably Canadian land forces would be committed to Korean operations; indeed, he was aware that the United States Government advocated a combined British, Australian, and New Zealand force for Korea. But more immediately he foresaw that,

Whatever happens, a base here is necessary and this implies a chain of supply right forward to the front line including some advanced base in Korea. . . . Any suggestion that each portion of the Empire should be separate and distinct must mean a large overhead to each with the establishment of separate bases. The waste of effort . . . appears to me to have nothing to commend it.[7]

This sensible observation should have prompted immediate consultation and an early resolution of the evident base requirement. It did not. The fault lies with the British Government and Chiefs of Staff.

Overall, the error arose from the outlook of the Government. While accepting that Australia and New Zealand were sovereign powers, the authorities in London continued to behave as if the old arrangements for imperial defence obtained.

The first mistake was the manner of appointment of Air Vice-Marshal Bouchier. It was perfectly reasonable for the Chiefs of Staff to appoint their own man to General MacArthur's headquarters; they wanted someone sufficiently senior to obtain information directly from General MacArthur and his Chief of Staff by working within the headquarters, and to whom they could send detailed and, if necessary, blunt instructions. It did not occur to them to ask Mr Menzies to appoint General Robertson to this post because he was, as a commander-in-chief, at once too senior and inevitably in a different relationship.

The Australian Government was not so much offended as surprised by the speed of the appointment and despatch of the air marshal. General Robertson was incensed by it. An experienced and highly competent soldier, he was also self seeking and umbrageous. He had some reason in this matter; Bouchier's relationship with General MacArthur would diminish his own. Moreover, it was not simply a matter of false pride. Under the occupation terms—in force until a Japanese Peace Treaty was concluded—the Commander-in-Chief, BCOF, had responsibility for the enforcement of law and order over all British Commonwealth citizens in Japan.

Second, a curious assumption was initally made in London that the British force in Korea would be supplied and administered from Singapore. When it became evident that the distance was too great, a second and equally faulty idea arose that use would be made of the BCOF facilities as required, and as a matter of course.[8]

The first movement for change came from General Sir John Harding. It was apparent to him as soon as he was ordered to despatch 27 Brigade that it should have a base in Japan.[9] He sent a member of his staff to see General Robertson to see what was available, and agreed when the latter declared that the brigade could not rely totally, as Air Marshal Bouchier suggested, on American support. In making emergency arrangements to supply Brigadier Coad's force, General Harding expected that the British base units sent with 29 Brigade would merge with those of BCOF. The War Office did not take this point.

General Robertson was meantime venting his feelings to Canberra. 'I feel that we are just being made use of on the one hand,' he signalled on 27th August, 'and being insulted and slighted on the other'.[10]

General Rowell,* Chief of the Australian General Staff, was inclined to agree. From the outset of commitment, he had sought to proceed on a basis of cooperation with the British in Korea. In the first half of August, with General Stewart,† his New Zealand colleague, and General Cassells,‡ head of the UK Services Liaison Staff in Australia, he had agreed that 'the existing facilities of the present BCOF base should be utilised. . . .'[11] But he had expected that there would thereafter be some consultation about the way in which the expanded organisation should take place, and the division of costs. The war notwithstanding, he was under continuing pressure from his own ministers and financial officers to cut Australian outgoings in Japan.

On 31st August, he sent a personal signal to Field-Marshal Slim:

We always talk very glibly about the way we cooperate but when it actually comes to the practical test, we have a special facility for doing the opposite. I suggest in the present circumstances

---

*Rowell, Lieutenant-General Sir Sydney Fairbairn KBE CB (1894–1975).
†Stewart, Major-General Sir Keith Lindsay, KBE CB DSO (1896–1972).
‡Cassells, Major-General A J H (later Field-Marshal Sir James) (1907–).

the more or less complete sidetracking of BCOF is a case in point. . . .

As things stand today Commander-in-Chief BCOF is under no obligation whatever to afford British troops any facilities. In actual fact your people are compelled to use our signals and cipher staff and I have no doubt that very soon Bouchier or Coad will be asking for . . . hospital accommodation and the like. Under no circumstances would we refuse these facilities but we would very much prefer to have their use planned for . . . I suggest to you that it is not too late to put this business on the right basis and so prevent what can only become a quote buggers muddle unquote in which the only people to suffer will be the soldiers.[12]

The field-marshal made enquiries and discovered that this contention was wholly justified. He was the more vexed as during his visit to Australia in June and July he had agreed with General Rowell on the advantages of mutual cooperation. Replying that he was 'in complete agreement with everything you say'[13] he informed his colleagues in the Executive Committee of the Army Council* what had happened and they at once agreed that they must all consult fully with the Commonwealth contributors to Korea. The CIGS issued orders through the Vice-Chief to ensure that information on all matters of mutual interest was to be shared with Australia and New Zealand.

The problem, however, was to change attitudes as much as anything. For example, immediately after the CIGS's orders were issued to the War Office staff, the Director of Military Operations (DMO) was still seeking to limit General Robertson's function and to maintain Air Marshal Bouchier as the prime channel of instructions to the formations in Korea.[14] It was not that the DMO was an insubordinate officer; simply that he could not immediately adjust to the idea of Australian direction of British forces' administration in the field.

Clearly, for that and other reasons, it was necessary that the three governments—Australian, British and New Zealand†— should agree a directive to General Robertson which set out clearly his responsibilities The process of doing this continued for well over two months.

---

*The Executive Committee of the Army Council (ECAC) consisted of the CIGS, Adjutant-General (AG), Quartermaster-General (QMG), Master-General of the Ordnance (MGO), and Vice-Chief (VCIGS). They met frequently to run the day to day policy of the Army.
†It was then by no means sure that the Canadians would join a Commonwealth force. General Robertson was therefore at the outset to represent the Chiefs of Staff of these three. For his directive and that of Brigadier T Brodie, see Appendix Q.

It was delayed in part because of the need to produce a comprehensive administrative plan. Tasked to prepare this, the Australian Joint Administrative Planning Committee concluded that the expansion of BCOF was unnecessary except, perhaps, for the General Hospital at Kure. Otherwise, an advanced base in Korea would be able to cope with all foreseeable demands. This was an embarrassment to General Rowell, who was relieved when the War Office in London proposed reversion to Robertson's original concept. Even so, the plan was not tabled until 8th November.[15]*

A more manifest delaying factor was the role of Air Vice-Marshal Bouchier. The British Chiefs insisted that he must stay as their representative with General MacArthur; the Australians believed that this ran counter to the idea of a single senior officer representing them collectively in Japan. Eventually there was agreement that Bouchier should stay solely as a channel of communication and information for the United Kingdom and entirely without responsibility for the troops in the field or base.[16] Even when this impediment was removed, the British asked for a delay in manifesting the plan to the Americans until arrangements to include Canadians in the force were concluded.[17] By that time, the British troopships were disembarking in Pusan. Fortunately, given the necessary declarations of intent, General Robertson had thrown his energy and skill into organisation of the base and forward maintenance.

Almost unnoticed, a small, specialised British unit joined General MacArthur's command shortly after 27 Brigade. It was 41 Independent Commando, Royal Marines.

They had arrived in response to General MacArthur's request in July for a British component in an American raiding organisation† and were thus, in the interests of commonality, to be provided with United States weapons, equipment, and field uniforms, though they retained their green berets. Ten officers and two hundred other ranks gathered from volunteers in Britain and drafts for the Commando Brigade in Malaya[18] now joined a further forty naval and marine volunteers from the Far East Fleet. The commanding officer, Lieutenant-Colonel D B Drysdale, MBE RM, arrived in Tokyo on 5th September with an advanced party.

The base was at Camp MacGill, close to Yokosuka on the south west point of Tokyo Bay. Three hundred and twenty American seamen, marines and soldiers, and three hundred South Koreans, were in training there under the command of Lieutenant-Colonel

---

*The plan is set out at Appendix R.

†A Special Air Service detachment was to contribute to this component but the regiment had been reduced post-war to a single Territorial Army unit, the Artists' Rifles. As volunteers were being mustered, the war seemed to be ending in Korea and the project was abandoned.[19]

Louis B Ely. Designated the 'Special Activities Group', a detachment from this force, including a troop from the Commando, undertook the raiding operation with HMS *Whitesand Bay* on the west coast of Korea just prior to the Inch'on landing. They also attempted to capture Kimpo airfield as the United States Marine Division went ashore, but were defeated by tidal flow and mud flats.

For a brief time in October, there was an inter-Service squabble as to who should own the Special Activities Group. The United States Army claimed them. Admiral Joy succeeded in keeping them within his command. His trump card was that he had the ships from which they would be launched. The USS *Perch*, a submarine transport, had been modified to carry one hundred and sixty raiders, and two fast surface transports, the USS *Horace A Bass* and *Wantuck* adapted for clandestine operations.

On the night 1st/2nd October two troops of 41 Commando* landed from *Perch* on the east coast above Hungnam. They mined two adjoining railway tunnels, becoming involved in a running battle as they withdrew. On the 6th/7th, the other troops under Major D L S Aldridge, second-in-command to Colonel Drysdale, landed from *Bass* and *Wantuck,* demolishing a railway tunnel and large culvert just south of Songjin, and another railway tunnel in Kyongsong Man, twenty miles south of the port of Ch'ongjin. All these involved transporting quantities of limpet mines and explosives ashore in rubber dinghies through surf and currents, then manhandling them to the respective sites.[20]

It was an encouraging development for the Commando but a few days after Colonel Drysdale returned to Camp MacGill on 7th October—he had been with the raiders on *Perch*—it was apparent that the options for distant coastal raiding were fast diminishing. The UN forces were engaged in what everyone believed was a victorious march to the Yalu. Previously, he had resisted a suggestion that his unit should fight with the United States Marine Division. Now he felt that, if it did not, there would be no action at all. But the Marine Division was embarked for the landing at Wonsan. There was neither room for them aboard the transports nor a role in the landing. Besides, they might find themselves relegated to occupation duties within a matter of weeks. He decided that the Commando should revert to training in conventional war skills—as distinct from those for raiding—but wait to see what happened in North Korea.[21]

By the time this training concluded at the end of October, the 1st Marine Division was ashore in north east Korea but still far

---

*The Commando comprised a headquarters, three—later four—rifle troops, a support troop and an assault engineer troop.

from the Yalu. There was even some talk of an encounter between a marine regiment and Chinese troops. At Colonel Drysdale's request, Admiral A C Burke, deputy chief of staff to Admiral Joy, sent a signal to the divisional commander, Major-General O P Smith:

> British 41st Royal Marine Commandos available and anxious to join your division earliest. Suggest this excellent unit be employed.[22]

There was no reply for ten days. General Smith was anxious to have 41 Commando but X Corps headquarters was miffed at being bypassed. Trivial objections to the attachment had been raised.

'This need not deter us,' Admiral Burke remarked to the British naval *attaché*, Commander J M D Gray, RN. 'They [41 Commando] are being sent to the 1st Marine Division as replacements—this will get over the difficulty.'[23]

It did. The Commando embarked on the USS transport *Jackson* for Hungnam on Thursday, 16th November.

.   .   .   .   .

It had been General MacArthur's wish to revive his offensive on 17th November but the Eighth Army was unable to respond on this date. Despite further extraordinary efforts by the Army Engineers to extend the railways and improve the roads, supply lines were again overstretched. General Walker had hoped to bring Chinnamp'o, the port of P'yongyang, rapidly into his service, but the combination of United Nations bomb damage, North Korean demolitions, and mines delayed its use. In mid-November, 27 Brigade noted that it was short of fuel and rations on this account. Shortages were mitigated by use of the FEAF Combat Cargo Command: petrol and diesel were flown into Sinanju airfield for I Corps. This was not a system capable of sustaining an offensive, however, when the demand for motor fuel and artillery ammunition was expected to quadruple.* It was 22nd November before General Walker felt able to signal Tokyo that he was ready. The 23rd was Thanksgiving.† Special rations had been issued which commanders at all levels hoped their soldiers would be able to enjoy generally free of the alarms and excursions of the battlefield. D-day was thus to be on 24th November.[25]

---

*The Army required 4,000 tons a day for maintenance of offensive action.[24]
†The United States harvest festival, instituted by the Pilgrim Fathers in 1621, is celebrated on the fourth Thursday in November.

The strategic plan was broadly the same: the UN forces were to advance to the Yalu, after which there would be a withdrawal of the non-Korean elements, though the precise line to which they would retire had not been selected. It was a reasonable assumption that, if the main fighting elements could be drawn back safely, the high command would not be under pressure in making choices. Yet, for all his expressions of confidence, General MacArthur was aware that Chinese forces remained in Korea* and that the gap between Eighth Army and X Corps invited exploitation. Closer to the front, the experiences of the first week in November persuaded General Walker to abandon the methods of October. To avoid ambushes, he ordered 'a deliberate and thorough advance'. Immediately, objectives were limited to a range of twenty miles.[26]

The Army had three corps on the line: I in the western sector, with the 24th Division on the left, 1st ROK on the right, and 27 Brigade in reserve; IX with the 25th Division left, 2nd right, and the Turkish Brigade in reserve; and II ROK Corps on the eastern flank, comprising 7th and 8th ROK Divisions forward, the 6th in reserve. 1st Cavalry was the Army reserve.

On the east coast, the landing of General Almond's X Corps had been delayed for a week by the extensive mining of the approach channels. The amphibious force, which included British, French and New Zealand frigates, steamed up and down during costly clearance operations until 25th October. Landing then began on beaches held by I ROK Corps, marching up the east coast. Wonsan, Hungnam and Hamhung were secured within a wider bridgehead by the 1st United States Marine Division, overcoming North Korean and, later, Chinese forces. Relieved then by the 3rd Division, the Marines prepared to advance north west. Meantime, the 7th Division landed up the coast at Iwon. Its 17th Infantry Regiment reached the Yalu at Hyesanjin on 21st November. The corps commander, General Almond, had a photograph taken with General Barr, commanding the division, on its frosty southern bank. The ROK I Corps had captured Ch'ongjin. Its advanced guards were within twenty miles of the Soviet frontier.

General Almond's drive to the Yalu was matched by his determination to avoid subordination to General Walker. Liaison with his larger neighbour was minimal. However, at the bidding of General MacArthur, he was obliged to consider more precisely participation in a common strategy. In mid-November, he was able to show that movement west of his divisions was impracticable; the roads were poor, mined and cratered, with many of the bridges damaged.

---

*General MacArthur's intelligence chief, Major-General Charles Willoughby, estimated that there were up to 70,000 Chinese troops in Korea in the third week of November and, astonishingly, 82,799 NKPA[27].

He represented that X Corps could best help Eighth Army by being ready to strike westward when the main body of his corps was north of the Changjin and Pujon reservoirs. By the 24th, General MacArthur had accepted this, though he pushed X Corps boundary further west and south to draw its forces closer to General Walker's right flank. The 7th Division was to capture Changin, the Marines Mup'yong-ni and, beyond it, Manp'ojin.[28]

In frontage, this latter was less than the task originally intimated to General Smith of the Marines but still daunting. Assuming that he overcame the four Chinese divisions said to be in the area of Changjin reservoir, the advance to Manp'ojin would extend his line of communication to two hundred miles through a series of formidable passes. Throughout his operations his left flank would be wide open, inviting encirclement. He determined to advance deliberately, picketing important high ground as he advanced, and on arrival at the reservoir to make a main base at Hagaru-ri before pushing on to Mup'yong-ni.[29] The basic work was completed on 15th November.

The winter came on abruptly. In mid-November, the daytime temperature had dropped to minus 20° Celsius. Windproof clothing was still arriving from the United States but issues were completed by the 17th, and none needed it more than the ROK divisions. With troops in position and supply lines full, X Corps began to advance on 27th November at 0800 hours.

Meantime, the opposition had not been idle. It is an open question whether Mao and the Military Commission in Peking intended the 'First Phase Offensive' to be an offensive as such; more likely, a sortie in strength to give the UN forces a bloody nose, warning them to stay out of the Korean Yalu provinces. If so, they underestimated General MacArthur. But he also underestimated the Chinese high command. Later, he was to accuse it of introducing troops 'surreptitiously' into Korea, as if to imply that the use of military surprise was sharp practice. He also commented that his own offensive had coincided with an offensive by the Chinese People's Volunteers. All the evidence suggests that the resumption of his advance triggered a Chinese counter-attack which, routing the United Nations's forces, developed into an offensive.

It is far from clear whether this second offensive was launched with the expectation of the results achieved. It is likely that the joint headquarters in Shenyang were aware that the UN march to the frontier would be resumed in the second half of November, and certain from the range of prisoner-of-war information that dispositions had been made to wait for the UN forces to enter the ground chosen by P'eng Te-huai's army group commanders.

Subsequent events, however, give no indication of a grand manoeuvre unfolding. Contrary to a widespread impression, no attempt was made to exploit the gap between Eighth Army and X Corps.

By 10th November, 9 Army Group had entered Korea to direct operations in the eastern sector. The 42nd Army was transferred to the west, to which 13 Army Group responsibility was henceforward confined.

A thin screen of troops, North Korean and Chinese, had been left to cover the withdrawal of the Chinese Peoples' Volunteers from contact on 6th November. In disposing his eighteen divisions in the west, General Li T'ien-yu appears to have expected the strongest advance to be made in the western sector. Three armies of 13 Army Group were distributed in the mountains on either side of the main approach routes. The Fortieth Army lay north of Unsan. Further east, above Huich'on, he had placed the Thirty Eighth and Forty Second Armies. The army group had been reinforced to number one hundred and eighty thousand soldiers. General Sung Shin-lun's 9 Army Group deployed one hundred and twenty thousand against General Almond's X Corps. North Koreans were attached to both groups.

Air observers saw no sign of these forces on Eighth Army's front on 24th November. The land was as empty as the day before, when General MacArthur had made his own air reconnaissance to the Yalu. There was no opposition on the ground to the advancing UN columns apart from a few brief exchanges of fire with scattered and yielding enemy outposts. Occasional delays arose from mine-fields and demolitions. 'Deliberately and thoroughly', the army front, eighty kilometres in width, moved north between seven and ten miles on the first day of the advance. The 24th Division approached Chongju unchallenged.

On the 25th, however, the leading regiment of 1st ROK Division had several fire fights as it progressed north of T'aech'on in the afternoon. Villagers spoke of 'many Chinese' in the area. The divisional commander, General Paik Sun-yup, noted that groups of civilians were making their way south, carrying their belongings with them.[31] Elsewhere, there were increased contacts, warnings and sightings of enemy bodies; an aircraft reported 'hundreds of men' working on the road close to Tokch'on. Chinese outposts were stronger and fought more stubbornly before withdrawing. Late in the afternoon, a regiment of II ROK Corps, following the headwaters of the Taedong below steep mountain tops, found itself ambushed by 'one point, two sides'—the Chinese soldiers' name for a simple trap in which the advance is blocked, and as the force seeks to deploy against it, the enemy opens fire along each side.

A running battle followed. Some of the ROKs were able to escape in the darkness to join the remainder of their division.

That night, battalions of the ROK 7th and 8th Divisions heard drums, clanging gongs and clashing cymbals. The South Korean soldiers knew that presaged an attack. The warning sacrificed surprise but aroused dread. Soon after, fire fights began to blaze in and around them. Chinese artillery and mortar fire burst among the ROK defences from the foremost of which companies began to stream back to join those behind. More seriously, the right flank of the corps was driven in. The roads between the forward divisions and Corps headquarters were cut.

The 26th was an uneasy day. Apart from the 24th Division, which secured Chongju without opposition, there was fighting across the whole front. Though helped by the 5th Air Force, II ROK Corps was crumbling. The KMAG radio reported that several thousand Chinese were moving southwards through the mountains from Tokch'on. General Coulter, IX Corps Commander, was immediately anxious that these forces would cut in behind him, notably behind his right flank formation, 2nd Division. With General Walker's agreement, he committed the Turkish Brigade to take the narrow road to Tokch'on and block its western exit. 27 Brigade was moved from I Corps to IX as a consequence.

IX Corps headquarters was just west of Kunu-ri,* about twenty five miles from the brigade location at Pakch'on. When Brigadier Coad reported there at 10 o'clock on the morning of the 27th November, the operations staff were trying to discover the whereabouts of the ROK II Corps. Several hundred had come into the Turkish Brigade's night defences on the Tokch'on road—where they were at first mistaken for Chinese—and still more had begun to emerge on to the Kunu-ri–Sunch'on road. At least one Chinese army was known to be marching south west towards the corps rear area. Throughout the day, as reports came in, were confirmed or negated, the brigade was given a series of contingency orders. By evening, it became known that 1st ROK Division was being driven south from Taech'on, and that the Turks were in danger of being overwhelmed. The 25th and 2nd Divisions were engaged but holding, though enemy had broken past the latter's left flank. With pressure mounting across the whole front, particularly at night, there was no possibility of pulling out a division to restore the former II ROK Corps positions.

27 Brigade was put at immediate notice to move to any task, probably across the Ch'ongch'on, from 1930. Brigadier Coad protested that a reaction of that sort in darkness would be counterproductive. The corps' chief of staff agreed that they would not be

---

*This is also shown on maps as Kunmo'ri

committed until dawn. By then, as it happened, there was no requirement to move forward; the whole Army was withdrawing.[31]

Brigadier Coad was called to see the corps commander at 1100 on the 28th November. General Coulter put several counter-attack options to him but admitted that he had neither tanks nor artillery to spare except on a very temporary basis:

> . . . after a certain amount of suggestion on my part, it was decided to move the Brigade back to the area Chasan, some 35 miles south, to hold a defensive flank and to keep the road Chasan–Kunu-ri open, which was already reported cut. Transport would be provided after it had moved Corps HQ.
> At 1415 hours battalions started to march, with orders to fight their way through if the road was cut. By 0315, the Brigade was complete in the new area.[32]

This brief paragraph is an understatement. It was a difficult march. Every kind of vehicle was moving down the rutted, single track road, jeeps, light and heavy radio trucks, load carriers, tankers, engineer plant. There was no traffic control. *En route,* the columns passed a medium artillery battalion deployed on either side, switching frequently to fire in almost every direction, including south. As dusk approached, the traffic dwindled, then ceased. The British Commonwealth soldiers began to look anxiously at the hills on either side.

Generously, the Argylls had loaned a pair of pipers to the RAR and Middlesex, and their playing cheered the otherwise silent hours. From time to time, small groups of trucks appeared to ferry the marchers to Chasan, but part of the Middlesex were still on foot when the concentration area was reached at 0315. They were thankful to find tea and rum waiting.[33]

Chasan lies in open ground on the P'yongyang–Manp'ojin railway, close to a convergence of roads and ferry site. 3 RAR were ordered to deny this site to the enemy. The Middlesex was to patrol the road to Kunu-ri. The Argylls were in reserve.

Picture the joy of the Middlesex soldier, resting on the frozen paddy field, as he was wakened at 0830 on the 29th November to be told to make ready to patrol back up the road down which he had marched only a few hours previously. Fortunately, the cooks were at their work. A mess tin of hot water was provided for washing and shaving, and a hot breakfast was put into the same mess tin, rinsed out. American transport arrived at 10 o'clock.

The Middlesex now saw the southern half of the road in daylight. It ran through low hills north of Sunch'on to Chop-tong, a railway halt. Thereafter the hills closed in and rose higher. Colonel Man dropped off a radio relay station at Chop-tong and this soon passed a warning that aircraft had seen enemy at the exit from the pass on a ridge six miles to the north. The leading company passed the village of Yongwon-ni, approached the summit of the ridge and stopped:

> On the side of the road tilting into the ditch was a bullet ridden jeep. From inside sprawled the bodies of an American colonel and his driver . . . Then from nowhere appeared twenty or thirty men in dirty white clothes, strolling rather furtively towards us.[34]

These men were secured and found to be unarmed. They were soon followed by a column of refugees who were escorted down to Chop-tong. Colonel Man began to move his battalion forward a company at a time. Ahead, aircraft were striking at targets apparently at the other end of the pass. An attempt to cross the ridge was stopped by fire from higher ground to the right. A Company under Major R K Dowse was ordered to prepare a deliberate attack upon it, supported by mortars and machine-guns. The leading platoon commander, Second Lieutenant J M Lock, twice wounded on the ascent, was killed just below the crest, another officer and twenty four were wounded.[*][35]

During the afternoon, groups of Chinese had been seen on many of the hills east and west of the road. Colonel Man believed that he should not concentrate his battalion to attack because he would lose the high ground essential to a safe withdrawal. He had no artillery or armour in support and was almost twenty miles from the remainder of the brigade. With the approach of darkness, he began to pull back slowly, The movement was unimpeded until Major Willougby's D Company, the rearguard, was rushed by a group of about forty Chinese as they left their positions. The Middlesex turned and killed nine of the enemy at short range and wounded others at a distance for the loss of one casualty to themselves.[36]

The news from IX Corps headquarters that night, 29th November, was gloomy. The Turkish Brigade had extricated itself with difficulty from the Tokch'on area and was now to withdraw with the greater part of the 2nd Division down the road to Sunch'on and Chasan. The remainder of IX Corps and the whole of I was withdrawing down the western MSR.[†] The Middlesex, now strengthened by a platoon of tanks and a battery of 105-mm guns,

---

*He was the second RAOC officer serving with the Middlesex to be killed.
†Main supply route.

were ordered to return next morning, the 30th, to the end of the pass to assist the 2nd Division.

Somewhat to their surprise, they found the area empty on arrival at 1030, and were soon on the principal high points. From these they repulsed several attacks during the morning and harassed Chinese moving across the front.

The Middlesex observation posts were looking for the approach of a tactical sweep by the 2nd Division on either side of the road. What appeared from noon was a column of tanks, trucks, guns and gun towers all seeking to drive through with men clinging to whatsoever would carry them. Many at the head of the column succeeded in escaping but gradually through the afternoon the volume of Chinese fire in and beyond the sight of the British battalion reduced the numbers of Americans, Turks and ROKs emerging mounted or on foot. There were many dead and wounded on the vehicles. Some survivors were 'in an hysterical condition . . . who opened fire on our troops in error and Privates Freakley and Smillie were wounded, the former fatally.'[37]

The Middlesex did what they could to help with their own fire, in assisting the direction of air strikes, and in providing an elementary traffic control and report centre. Their medical sergeant at Chop-tong, the medical officer at Chasan, succoured several hundred casualties to the limit of their supplies. The battalion was drawn back before dark but the headquarters came under fire from the eastern hillside in the area of the gun battery. All weapons to hand were turned on the enemy, the American 105s over open sights, before the column moved away.

At Chasan, the brigade was preparing for rearguard duties with 1st Cavalry Division. Eighth Army was withdrawing without any clear idea of where it would stop to fight. General Walker and his corps commanders believed that their technical superiority had been overwhelmed by numbers, but this was not the prime cause of the defeat on the Ch'ongch'on and in the Taebaek mountains.* The Chinese had succeeded in destabilising the Army by exercising again the skills manifested in early November: mastery of conceal- ment and thus surprise; cross country marching over mountain and hill tracks remote from the roads which the United Nations' forces were reluctant to leave; persistent attack in flank and rear almost without regard for casualties. Most importantly, for the longer run of operations, they had established a moral ascendancy.

The idea also took root then that the cunning Chinese had deliberately used its numerical weight first against the green and

---

*The Chinese Communist Forces put more men into battle, less in support and adminis- tration than the United Nations, but only twelve of 13 Army Group's divisions actually fought in this offensive, say, 100,000 against 45,000 combat soldiers in Eighth Army.

perhaps politically unreliable ROK divisions. But the ROK soldiers had shown their political preference on the Pusan perimeter; even in the worst of times there, there had been no mass defections. Whilst they were certainly less seasoned, the 1st ROK Division on I Corps' front had been the first to clash with the Chinese forces because they had advanced due north. The 24th Division were advancing west initially. A huge ambush was waiting beyond Chongju but the division was recalled before reaching it. The ROK II Corps was in high mountains which offered the best concealment and cross country manoeuvre options to the Thirty Eighth and Forty Second Armies. IX Corps' problems were not alone due to the collapse of II ROK Corps; the right flank of the 2nd Division was broken shortly afterwards. Impulsive judgements in IX Corps wasted the potential of the Turkish Brigade and came close to doing the same with 27 Brigade. Underestimation of the Chinese numbers combined with a false confidence in the power of the Eighth Army and Fifth Air Force had precluded planning for a reverse. The speed and range of the Chinese riposte was such that, by the time he had sufficient information to make a judgement, General Walker had no option but to break away and reorganise. The faulty arrangements for the withdrawal of the 2nd Division and Turks enhanced the Chinese success. The division lost four thousand officers and men, and quantities of weapons, equipment and vehicles. It is probable that, but for the opening of the Yongwon-ni exit by the Middlesex, these would have been greater. The battalion kept open the road to Chop-tong against forces that were waning in power but were not wholly spent.[38]

They were waning in power there and elsewhere by the 30th November because of the inherent weakness of the Chinese Communist Forces (CCF) in Korea: their communications were poor so that comcomitantly their objectives had to be limited. As earlier, armies began to lose track of divisions, divisions of regiments as operations developed. It was not feasible to commit fresh troops to relieve those who had been weakened by ground and air fire because neither army group nor army headquarters knew their battle strength—often divisions did not immediately know it themselves. In the later stages, casualties among regiments and battalions increased as, spirits high, they prolonged the fighting and were caught in daylight by the Fifth Air Force. A halt was essential for reorganisation, the gathering of wounded, the burial of dead, and the collection of booty. In Shenyang, a halt was also necessary to consider the outcome of operations against General Almond's X Corps.

The news from the Eighth Army front on the night 25th/26th November was not encouraging to X Corps headquarters. It coincided with strong evidence of two Chinese armies in its own area. But the notion then developed that these forces were moving westward to reinforce the offensive against the Eighth Army. The X Corps plan was therefore to proceed unchanged.

In part, this optimistic view of enemy intentions was due to the run of the 7th Division's 17 RCT to Hyesanjin on the Yalu, and of a smaller body, Task Force Kingston, to Sing'alp'ajin eighteen miles to the west. But it was not P'eng Te-huai's intention that General Sung's 9 Army Group should be scattered into the bleak north east of Korea. The strategy was to draw the UN forces north west and then to cut the roads round and south of the Changjin reservoir, isolating those forward from their line of supply.

A task force of the American 7th Division was in position to advance along the eastern shore on 27th November. On the south west, the Marines had advanced beyond the Toktong Pass and secured Yudam-ni. Behind these advanced posts, the pass was picketed by a company, the base at Hagaru-ri was garrisoned. South of Hagaru-ri, General Smith kept the 1st Marine RCT at Koto-ri and Chinhung-ni, his long stops.

41 Commando arrived at Koto-ri on 28th November *en route* to Yudam-ni via Hagaru-ri. Yudam-ni was embattled; the road from Koto-ri to Hagaru-ri was cut. Colonel Lewis B Puller, commanding the 1st Marines, organised a task force under Lieutenant-Colonel Drysdale to open the road next day, and to escort a convoy of divisional headquarters trucks, specialists and stores into the Hagaru-ri perimeter. The Commando was to be joined by his G Company and a company of the 7th Division. Initially supported by the artillery at Koto-ri, and with a forward air controller, the task force set off at 0930 on 29th November in a bitter north east wind.

The Commando and G Company took the first two features in succession, the resistance stiffening on each. Enemy on twin heights close to the road stopped the column two and a half miles from Koto-ri. Air, and subsequently tanks, hastened the advance a further mile and a half. Unfortunately, the armour had not been placed under Colonel Drysdale and the company commander insisted that his force must all be at the front. He reported that a second tank company would catch up the rear, but the upshot was that there was no armour to complement the Commando detachment protecting the centre of the column.

They were now entering a long valley—'Hell Fire Valley'—which gave the Chinese an opportunity to close the engagement range. The tanks, Marine and Army infantry, made a way through by a series of attacks interspersed with skirmishing. Appreciating the depth of the enemy positions, Colonel Drysdale asked General

Smith whether he should push on with the likelihood of considerable casualties. The needs of Hagaru-ri weighed in favour of continuing. They pressed forward, Captain Sitter of G Company assuming command when Colonel Drysdale was wounded. At 1915, almost ten hours after leaving Koto-ri, the fighting element of the column entered the Hagaru-ri defences. They had advanced at about a mile an hour.

Behind them, the divisional troops they were escorting had been cut off. Their radios were destroyed by fire. The southern end of the convoy, aided by the second tank company, managed to return to Koto-ri while the central section fought on through the night until their ammunition was exhausted. Thanks to clever parleying by Major Jack McLaughlin, the senior United States Marine in their midst, a few groups including the Commando detachment managed to slip away, but he and the remainder, many of whom were wounded, were captured.[39]

In this small action, one hundred and sixty two were killed or missing, one hundred and fifty nine wounded and recovered. Among these, 41 Commando's casualties numbered sixty one, a quarter of its strength. Yet the American and British forces which reached Hagaru-ri were probably crucial to its survival, as General Smith had foreseen. Everywhere within his area, the full weight of the Chinese strength was apparent.

General Almond had been summoned to Tokyo on the night of the 28th where, with General Walker, General MacArthur and his staff, strategic options had been discussed. It was decided that X Corps should draw back to secure the Hamhung–Hungnam sector, while Eighth Army withdrew southwards 'successively'.[40] A staff proposal to send the 3rd Division across the Taebaek Range to reinforce General Walker was wisely discarded.

For General Almond, the withdrawal of his forces from the far north and north east would not be difficult. Those on the Yalu, and I ROK Corps on the east coast, were not under pressure. But the task force from the 7th Division—two battalions of infantry and one of artillery—sent earlier to relieve a Marine force on the eastern side of the Changjin reservoir, was isolated by a Chinese division and supported only by tactical air strikes and air resupply. Due to the leadership of the senior officer present, Lieutenant-Colonel Donald C Faith, and a remarkable recovery operation across the lake ice by the Marines in Hagaru-ri, almost half their number reached the garrison there between 2nd and 4th December, though Colonel Faith was mortally wounded on the march.[41] The 1st Marine Division, extended from Koto-ri to Yudam-ni, was surrounded at each point of occupation. Yudam-ni was seventy eight miles from Hungnam, fourteen from Hagaru-ri, twenty five from Koto-ri. Believed to be invested by four Chinese divisions—actually, seven—there were doubts at X Corps headquarters that the northernmost positions, Yudam-ni and Hagaru-ri, could be evacuated, even if they survived the attacks being mounted nightly against them.

General Smith had no intention of abandoning a single man. He planned to move back as he had advanced, from one consolidated area to another. As many wounded as possible were to be collected at Hagaru-ri and flown out from the air strip. Whatever weapons and equipment could not be carried or driven out would be destroyed. Nothing was to be left to the enemy.[42]

The first step was to reinforce the lone Toktong Pass picket, Fox Company of the 7th Marines. Succoured by parachuted supplies and air strikes, it had fought off repeated attacks. A composite battalion of the 7th left Yudam-ni at 2100 on 1st December on a black night with the temperature minus 24° Celsius. They were laden with ammunition for a march that was to take them twenty hours through the snow covered mountains, fighting a way through a series of Chinese positions. Fortunately, some of their foes, units of the 58th Division, were sheltering, chilled and exhausted, in rock shelters as they passed.

With the pass secured, the remainder of the Yudam-ni force, 5th and 7th Marines, had to break contact and fight south, clearing the road for their vehicles. While this was progressing, Hagaru-ri was again assailed by divisions of Liu Fei's Twentieth Army. What remained of 41 Commando formed a mobile reserve within the perimeter of 6 miles. A series of attacks in considerable strength were mounted between 2300 on the 30th to 0630 on 1st December At 0300 that morning, the line was broken in the south east corner and 41 was ordered to recapture the small but important feature captured by the Chinese. Lieutenant G F D Roberts was sent with B Troop.

Roused, the twenty seven Royal Marines made their way forward in the intense cold. Close by, artillery and mortars were firing. Small arms fire flashed at numerous points round the perimeter. At G Company headquarters, Roberts found Captain Sitter, wounded but still in command, anxious that the enemy would at any moment pour through the gap in his defences. There was no other reserve to hand; the last available reinforcement, a dozen members of battalion headquarters under the intelligence officer, had just joined him. A simple plan was made for supporting fire when B Troop clambered up through snow to a high point on the ridge above.

Just before 4 o'clock, with the perimeter silent and dark, the Commandos closed. With small arms and grenades they assaulted the Chinese position and recaptured it, losing three wounded. Mortar fire fell among those withdrawing. At 0630 the night battle ended. At 9 o'clock on 1st December, the Marine Air Wing resumed strikes upon the ring of Chinese positions.[43]

Within Hagaru-ri, the worst was over, though none there knew it. The Chinese 58th Division had lost 8,000 killed and wounded, its ammunition supplies were becoming exhausted.[44]

The tail end of the column from Yudam-ni and the Toktong Pass arrived in Hagaru-ri on 4th December. Fifteen hundred wounded came in with the two regiments. The Combat Air Command flew out four thousand, three hundred and forty two wounded and severely frostbitten casualties. A thousand walking wounded and those whose frostbite had not become disabling remained. Many of these were disposed as drivers for the next break out. The Chinese 76th Division, which had overwhelmed Colonel Faith's task force to the east of the reservoir, had meantime blocked the road to Koto-ri

In the struggle for Hagaru-ri, 41 Commando had taken a full part in the defence, twice being sent to feel out the Chinese positions on the road to Yudam-ni. They were ready, as part of the 7th Marines, to join the break out to Koto-ri on the morning of 6th December. Their American colleagues were surprised but not unimpressed to note that the Royal Marines assembled for inspection before moving, shaved, boots polished, weapons and equipment presented. Throughout the day, fighting intensified, requiring the return of 41 Commando to the Hagaru-ri perimeter, in which the artillery remained to support the advanced guard. Gradually, the whole body of ten thousand troops forced a way south. The reverse journey of eleven miles took thirty eight hours to complete. *En route*, the Commando recovered some of its dead from Hell Fire Valley and, more happily, Captain P J Ovens and eleven members of his troop who had slipped away from the centre of the column on 30th November, hiding for a week in the midst of the enemy. With others who had reached Koto-ri in small groups, 41 Commando's fighting strength rose to one hundred and fifty.[45]

The combination of forces from the three positions, Yudam-ni, Hugaru-ri, and Koto-ri was fourteen thousand officers and men. The break out from the latter began in darkness and heavy snow on 8th December with a thrust northward to capture the hairpin bend on the road over the Funchilin Pass.* Two Chinese divisions, the 60th and the 77th, were known to be in the vicinity, and had

---

*The 1st Battalion, 1st Marines, at Chinhung-ni, were ordered to make this sortie. They were relieved by a force from the 3rd Division. The transfer of the 3rd to the Eighth Army was cancelled on this account and to maintain a fresh force in the defensive perimeter.

they been in strength it is doubtful if the Marine Division, as a body would have survived. As it was, their numbers were much depleted by battle casualties and frostbite; the Marines lifted several hundred frostbitten prisoners from trenches during the next few days. Even so, those who were in position in bunkers dug into the hillsides fought stubbornly. The snowclouds prevented the intervention of marine and naval air but artillery from the 7th Division reinforced the Marine batteries at Chinhung-ni. As the hairpin bend defences and the summit of Hill 1081 were captured, units from Koto-ri fought slowly but persistently south. Bridging had been air dropped to span a demolished section of road at the head of the pass. Tracks and wheels passed over it to descend to the Sudong Valley and the Hamhung perimeter, held by I ROK Corps and the American 3rd and 7th Divisions. When all at last seemed completed, a final Chinese sortie cut the road briefly but expensively in Sudong. Chinese soldiers hiding among several thousand refugees seeking sanctuary in Hamhung, attempted to draw Marines into ambush. By the 11th, however, all were recovered. The 3rd Division artillery shelled the Koto-ri site to catch any enemy sheltering within.

41 Commando came out late on 10th December to be carried in lorries and open railway cattle trucks 'to a tented camp in Hungnam . . . in a sea of mud but after a 23 miles march over the mountains on an empty stomach and without sleep for 72 hours, we could not have cared less!' On the 12th, Colonel Drysdale noted, 'Whole unit embarked in USS *General Randall* with the remainder of 5th [Marine] Regimental Combat Team. 5,000 in a ship designed to carry 2,000 but it had sheets, baths, and plenty of food.'[46] They set sail for Pusan.

During these hard times in the east, the 29th Independent Infantry Brigade Group joined the Eighth Army front. In the first three weeks of November it completed disembarkation, concentrated its Centurion and Cromwell tanks in the north and advanced the administrative chain. As a first step to operations, units assisted 187 Airborne RCT in securing the main supply route of I and IX Corps. Brigadier Brodie detached the RUR to Uijongbu on 11th November and the Glosters to Kaesong in the following week. North Korean forces were certainly about. The RUR chased a band attacking Kapyong. Uniformed NKPA were reported to be preparing to block the Sibyon-ni crossroads on the central MSR. The Glosters, accompanied by the 25–pounders of 70 Field Battery and a detachment of 55 Field Engineer Squadron, were sent to relieve the area. On 25th November, one of its companies clashed with guerrillas to the east. A prisoner described his unit as a battalion, but they were evidently a roving body, for sweeps next day failed to find them.[47]

That was two days after the Eighth Army advance began. 29 Brigade began to feel that it would still be looking for guerrillas on the line of communication when the war ended. On the 28th November, however, portentous news came with an order from brigade headquarters. The force, less the Royal Northumberland Fusiliers and other units just arriving, was to move north of P'yongyang immediately by road and rail because 'large numbers of Chinese have entered the war'.[48] The end of the war seemed suddenly much further away.

Rail movement would be in box cars, a popular form of conveyance; sleeping bags could be spread across their floors, stoves could be improvised within them to boil water on the journey, and to keep the occupants warm with only a moderate danger of catching fire. The winter wind had persuaded everyone to put on the vests and long underpants mocked in Colchester. String vests, worn next to the skin, oiled sweaters and socks, frost protecting boots with removable insoles, windproof smocks and trousers, had been added as 'winter warfare items' to normal clothing scales.*

By 30th November, as the Middlesex pulled back from Yongwon-ni, as the Marines in Yudam-ni made ready to fight south to Hagaru-ri, 29 Brigade's two forward battalions took up positions between Sinanju and P'yongyang. Eighth Army advice was that the next move would be northward to the Ch'ongch'on. The continuous lines of marching and mounted troops moving south, however, suggested to the British soldiers near the road that if this took place they would be on their own. Long columns of 'battle stained Turks' passed the RUR at Yongyu. RUR and Glosters alike wondered what had happened to their advanced parties sent forward to a rendezvous in Anju.

On 1st December these venturers returned, full of brave stories, to be sent off south next day, the main body of the brigade following in a snowstorm. Now under command of General Milburn, Brigadier Brodie was ordered to cover the withdrawal of I Corps through P'yongyang. The RUR was to hold the north end of the main bridges, the Glosters the northern thresholds and southern exits, what is known in military language as the 'close bridge garrison'. Lieutenant-Colonel Carne, commanding officer of the Glosters, was the officer named as having the authority to order the bridge

---

*Some of these items had been manufactured to support the Archangel and Baltic expeditions immediately after the first world war. Apart from a few cases of cracked boot leather, they were in excellent condition.

demolition by United States engineers.* Tanks of the 8th Hussars and C Squadron, Royal Tank Regiment, supported the two battalions.

As night fell on 4th December, the refugees leaving the town with the United Nations' forces became almost uncontrollable; they guessed that the bridges would soon be demolished and the river ice was still thin. They were a pitiable spectacle, principally the elderly, younger women and children, carrying babies, household possessions, and often huge sacks or rice on wooden 'A frames'. There were, however, youths with some families and occasionally men of an age for military service. There were no Korean authorities to interrogate these men; none of the Americans or British in the area of the bridges spoke Korean. The RUR road posts searched men who might be soldiers in disguise and there were further checks by the Glosters. Inevitably, a number of agents and perhaps some troops slipped past the British check points.

Throughout 4th December, vehicles of I Corps and marching men of 1st ROK Division passed over the bridges. Among them was 27 Brigade. Major Shipster of the Middlesex remarked of this encounter,

> . . . we had assumed that the arrival of [29] Brigade would be the signal for our return to Hong Kong. It had therefore been rather natural, in our tired and more forlorn moments, to natter, 'Come on, 29 Brigade'. In fact, once or twice a few had gone so far as to infer that they were a bit slow in arriving. . . . Well, here they were at last . . . We were delighted to see them and they gave us a glorious welcome as we passed through them. Pretty well every basic sentiment and rugged epithet were joyfully hurled from one side to the other. The colourful texture of the soldier's vocabulary could not have been better displayed. Englishmen are not as a rule so communicative to each other when they meet in foreign places. Dr Livingstone would have been badly shaken. The 29th Brigade looked smart and business like.[49]

Englishmen apart, an officer of the Royal Ulster Rifles noted that,

> . . . the riflemen ran out to the roadside to shake hands and to make the usual ribald remarks, and to throw to the troops in

---

*To avoid premature or delayed demolition at bridges or in other defiles, it is common military practice to appoint by name in the operation order the officer or NCO who is to effect the demolition—invariably an engineer—and the officer who will give him the order in writing to carry it out.

their vehicles some of the 'PX'* stores and comforts which . . .
had that morning been rescued from the burning city . . . there
was a good deal of admiration, too, for the brilliant way in
which the Commonwealth Brigade had fought, in spite of all
the difficulties and shortage of equipment they had experienced
since their arrival in the theatre.[50]

P'yongyang was not actually on fire, but when night came, great
fires were burning in the railway yards where the Americans and
British had concentrated their stores, and on the airfield, where
flames rose forty feet into the air. All military stocks in the brigade
sector that could not be backloaded by road or rail was destroyed
by Captain B Baton-Evans of 55 Field Engineer Squadron. At 0110
on the morning of 5th December, the last American vehicles passed
over the bridges—or what was deemed to be the last; the American
liaison officer selected to confirm this to Colonel Carne failed to
appear. At 35 minutes past midnight, the RUR withdrew to the
south as demolitions began on the foot and highway bridges close
by, their last vehicle crossing at 0240. Then Colonel Carne gave
the demolition order to the United States 14th Engineers. Almost
simultaneously, they blew the single timber bridge and the Class
50 panel bridges running across the island in midstream. Just
beforehand, the refugee columns were stopped, and by extraordinary sign language and gestures brought to understand that they
would be blown up if they attempted to follow.[51]

At about 6 o'clock on 5th December, it was confirmed that 24th
Division had demolished the bridge upsteam. IX Corps was clear.
The Glosters withdrew south to join 29 Brigade, rearguard for I
Corps on the western MSR. In the centre, 27 Brigade was withdraw-
ing with IX Corps through Sibyon-ni.

X and Y Companies† of 1st Battalion, The Royal Northumberland Fusiliers, under the commanding officer, Lieutenant-Colonel
Kingsley Foster, occupied Sibyon-ni from 29th November. In
handing the position over, Colonel Carne gave one piece of advice.
Intelligence reports tended to describe the local enemy as 'bandits'
or 'guerrillas'. In his view, they should be regarded as trained
soldiers and arrangements made to deal with them accordingly.

The position lay a mile due east of Sibyon-ni village. A stream
and road ran along the south side. On the north was a small steep
hill, Point 138. Known as Gibraltar Hill in the Northumberland
plan, it dominated the defences. In the southwestern corner, one
thousand yards from Point 138, was a low mound, named 'The

*PX, the American post exchange, which provided canteen supplies.
†By regimental custom, the Northumberland rifle companies were designated W, X, Y,
and Z. The Regiment is also known informally as the 'Fifth Fusiliers'.

Hump' by the Glosters. At about 0300 on the 30th, an attack was launched on the Northumberland Fusiliers from east and west, simultaneously with an attempt to take Gibraltar Hill from the north. There was a half moon in a clear sky. It was bitterly cold though the wind was light.

The cold was largely forgotten as the Northumberland defences fought to keep out a force about 1,200 strong supported by mortar fire. The Hump was broken into after an hour and not fully recovered until dawn. The key to the position, however, was Gibraltar Hill, of which the summit was held by 4 Platoon under Lieutenant Malcolm Cubiss. The initial attack from the north into his platoon failed, though it was to be renewed several times, and joined by those approaching from the east.

The determination of the rifle companies and assault pioneer platoon threw back the initial surprise attack. Vickers machine guns and 3-inch mortars quickly added to the defensive fire. On the southern side of the perimeter was B Troop of 116 Battery, the Northumberland affiliated artillery from 45 Field Regiment. The four guns were commanded by a remarkable warrior, the one-eyed Captain D W V P O'Flaherty, who had won a DSO as he had lost his eye, fighting with a commando in the war. Over open sights, he supported the infantry, the troop pausing only when it became necessary to fight for the gun position with small arms and grenades.

Towards the end of the night, an attack from two directions bore into the small force on Point 138. The platoon showered those approaching with grenades. This thinned but did not halt their assault. Lieutenant Cubiss sprang up to throw a white phosphorous grenade at the foremost North Korean at about five yards range. The mass of exploding matter enveloped him. His blazing body illuminated a hand to hand battle which ejected the intruders.

By 7 a.m. 30th December, the fighting stopped. In the growing light, the Northumberland Fusiliers were able to see the North Koreans marching south east and Captain O'Flaherty's four 25-pounders followed them with salvoes.[52]

The attack had been made by a weak regiment of the NKPA, slightly more than Colonel Foster cared to accept with two companies. He had lost five killed, three wounded and three men missing.* Cutting his force on the MSR at Kaesong to a minimum, he summoned W Company and the remainder of 116 Battery to Sibyon-ni. The North Koreans returned at 1930, prowling about, seeking an opening from time to time. But the Northumberland

---

*The three Northumberland soldiers captured were returned, unharmed, with two other sets of prisoners on 17th December, three American and three ROK. They had all been reasonably treated, though subjected to political indoctrination.[53]

companies held their fire, giving no idea of their extended positions. From their midst the artillery forward observation officers and mortar fire controllers reported enemy movements. The 25-pounders and 3-inch mortars fired periodically at prime targets. Having lost a number of casualties and almost certainly being aware that the position had been reinforced, the regiment withdrew at 0230, 1st December.[54]

A ROK battalion took over the position on 2nd December and was still in occupation when 27 Brigade arrived at Sibyon-ni on the 8th. On that date, 29 Brigade were approaching Kaesong, where they arranged to pick up the Royal Northumberland Fusiliers and other brigade units which had completed forming up. Of the Chinese there was no sign. Eighth Army had not only broken contact, essential to an orderly withdrawal, but no attempt was then made to lie in ambush for the pursuing enemy. The only clashes were with North Korean groups such as the regiment at Sibyon-ni and what appeared to be an NKPA reconnaissance screen advancing down the central mountain spine. 27 Brigade had two minor brushes with guerrillas before it settled on 12th December into a reserve position at Uijongbu, ten miles due north of Seoul. 29 Brigade, complete as a group, drew south across the Imjin river on the western MSR and came to rest, as I Corps reserve, eight miles from Seoul.

Mail and newspapers from home were awaiting both formations. When these were opened, it became apparent to Australians and British alike that the reverse of arms in the north had led to a political storm at home.

SOURCE NOTES: CHAPTER 14

1. Written during the Long March, 1934–35. See *Heng-tao-li-ma P'eng Ching-chun* (Gallant General P'eng), Jen Min Ch'u-pa She, (Peking, 1979).

2. Brigadier T Brodie.

3. DEFE series, MO1 Collection, ACANTHUS Conference No 1, para 60.

4. Lieutenant Colonel D B A Grist, conversation with author. See also *Remembered with Advantage*, Grist, private publication, copy in RHQ, The Gloucestershire Regiment.

5. Major General A E Younger, conversation with author.

6. *The Royal Ulster Rifles in Korea,* (Belfast, 1953) pp 11–12.

7. CINC British Commonwealth Occupation Force (BCOF) to Australian COS, 4th August 1950, Australian Archives (Aust A) CRSA 5954, Box 1688, file marked 'Assistance to UN in Korea.

8. DEFE series, Korea CAB/TOK, see for example MOD (COS) to Tokyo (Bouchier) of 22nd August 1950.

9. Field-Marshal Lord Harding, conversation with author.

10. CINC BCOF to Australian CGS of 27th August 1950, Aust A CRSA 5954, Box 1661, file 2.

11. DEFE 11/198, UKSLSA Melbourne unnumbered to COS 091635 August 1950.

12. CGS Melbourne to CIGS, London of 31st August 1950, Aust A CRSA 5954. Box 1661, file 2.

13. CIGS, London to CGS, Melbourne of 2nd and 3rd September 1950, Aust A CRSA 5954, Box 1661, file 2.

14. DEFE series, MO1 Collection, for example, see MO2/330/50 and footnote of 6th September 1950, and attached VAG Minute.

15. DEFE 11/203, Agendum No 161/50, Supplement 1, British Commonwealth Force Korea (BCFK) Administrative Plan of 8th November 1950.

16. For an exposition of this problem and its resolution, see Dr Jeffrey Grey, *The Commonwealth in the Korea War*, (Manchester, 1988), Chap 4.

17. DEFE 11/203, SofS, CRO, to PM 72/50 of 17th November 1950.

18. DEFE series G/Kor/3 (Special Operations), 1stSL 1888 to MOD of 15th August 1950.

19. DEFE series G/Kor/3 (Special Operations).

20. Field, op cit, pp 226, 246. Letters Colonel D B Drysdale and Lieutenant Colonel G F D Roberts to author. 41 Commando WD, October 1950.

21. Case 11554, Vol 18 RoPs, UK Naval Adviser, Tokyo, Chapters III and IV. Letters, Drysdale and Roberts. See also Oral History of Admiral Arleigh Burke, USN in Library of Naval Academy, Annapolis, Maryland, (original in US Naval Archives).

22. Case 11554 Vol 18, RoPs, UK Naval Adviser cit Chapter V.

23. Ibid

24. EUSAK War Diary (WD) (G-4 Journal) November 1950, (USNARS, Suitland).

25. EUSAK G-3 Op Instruction of 211645 November 1950, (USNARS, Suitland).

26. EUSAK Op Plan 15 of 14th November 1950. See also Schnabel, op cit, p 272.

27. Schnabel, op cit, p 273.

28. X Corps Op Order No 6 of 11th November and No 7 of 25th November 1950, (USNARS, Suitland).

29. Lynn Montross and Captain Nicholas A. Canzona, USMC, *United States Marine Operations in Korea, 1950–53, Volume III, The Chosin Reservoir Campaign,* (Washington, 1957) pp 135–6.
30. General Paik Sun-yup, conversation with author.
31. Coad, conversation with author.
32. Ibid, and Coad Report, cit, Part IV, p 4.
33. Coad, conversation with author. O'Neill, op cit, pp 69–72. WDs, November 1950: HQ 27 Bde, 1 MX, 1 A&SH, 3 RAR. Coad Report, cit, Part IV.
34. Shipster, op cit, p 34.
35. Colonel A M Man, letter to author. 1 MX WD November 1950.
36. Ibid. Willoughby and Major G G Norton, conversations with author.
37. 1 MX WD, November 1950.
38. Estimates of losses may be culled from EUSAK prisoner-of-war interrogation reports, which are strikingly confirmed in interrogation by Huang Chen-hsia of former prisoners who opted to return to Taiwan, mentioned *passim* in William Whitson with Huang Chen-hsia, *The Chinese High Command,* (New York, 1973).
39. Montross and Canzona, op cit, Chap IX. 41 Commando WD, November and December 1950. Drysdale, letter and Report by Drysdale on operational Experience—41 Independent Commando, RM, (hereafter referred to as Drysdale Report), RM Archives. Major (now Lieutenant-General) J N McLaughlin, USMC, conversation with author.
40. CINC UNC C50095 and C50105 of 30th November 1950 to Department of Army for JCS, (USNARS, Suitland).
41. Captain Russell A Guegler, *Combat Actions in Korea,* (Washington, 1954) Chap 7. Montross and Canzona, op cit, pp 243–5.
42. Montross and Canzona, op cit, pp 251–5.
43. Ibid, p 242. Drysdale and Roberts, notes and Drysdale Report cit.
44. For a summary of Chinese losses during this period see Montross and Canzona, op cit, pp 351–5.
45. Ibid, Chapter XIII. Drysdale and Roberts, letters and Drysdale Report cit.
46. Drysdale Report, cit.
47. 1 Glosters WD, November 1950.
48. HQ 29 Bde WD, November 1950.
49. Shipster, op cit, p 40.
50. *RUR in Korea,* cit, p 19.
51. 1 Glosters WD, December 1950.
52. 1 RNF WD, November 1950 and report with WD December 1950. Brigadier D W V P O'Flaherty, conversation with author.
53. 1 RNF WD, December 1950, Appendix Q 3.
54. 1 RNF WD, November and December 1950.

CHAPTER 15

Tumult and Affright

The defeat of the United Nations's forces did not become apparent until 28th November. There was enough evidence for General Walker to judge at noon on the 27th that his line was under pressure, as his staff informed GHQ, but he could not then be sure whether the Chinese were offering a stiff defence or opening a counter-offensive.[1] Next day, he was in no doubt that it was the latter. The situation in II ROK and IX Corps areas, taken with the identification from prisoners of seven (of the nine) Chinese armies, made it equally plain to General MacArthur that his advance to the Yalu was overthrown. He sent a long situation report to the Joint Chiefs of Staff in the late afternoon of the 28th explaining that he was opposed by almost 200,000 Chinese with approximately 50,000 North Koreans.

For explanation there had to be in the light of his confident assertions that his ground and air strategy would bring a swift and victorious end to operations. The Joint Chiefs did not quarrel with his assessment of the enemy aim: 'the complete destruction of all United Nations forces in Korea'. The strategy to accomplish this had, in the C-in-C's view, been set in hand immediately after the Inch'on landing; troops had been concentrated in North East China for intervention. Some had been infiltrated by night across the border to check the UN advance in the autumn, screening the build up of 'overwhelming strength, presumably for a spring offensive'. By implication, the UN offensive had forced a precipitate reaction, which enemy reinforcement and supply would carry forward by night across the Yalu ice, 'which it is impossible for our air potential to interdict'.

It is quite evident that our present strength of force is not sufficient to meet this undeclared war by the Chinese with the inherent advantages which accrue thereby to them. The resulting situation presents an entire new picture which broadens the potentialities to world embracing considerations beyond the sphere of decision by the Theatre Commander. This command has done everything humanly possible within its capabilities but is now faced with conditions beyond its control and strength.

349

> As directed . . . [by JCS contingency instructions[2]] my strategic plan for the immediate future is to pass from the offensive to the defensive with such local adjustments as may be required by a constantly fluid situation.[3]

This was both a holding signal and a marker. General MacArthur had ordered Generals Walker and Almond to report to Tokyo that evening to discuss options. The GHQ staff had prepared a range running from the best—a X Corps strike westward to relieve Eighth Army's right flank—to the worst, a general disengagement. Very properly, the essential aim was damage limitation. Characteristically, General MacArthur hoped for a chance to snatch victory from the jaws of defeat.

If the holding nature of the report was not apparent to the Joint Chiefs of Staff, the marker was clear. It was clear to all the United States authorities concerned and to their international partners in the war. Setting aside the tautology, inconsistencies such as the unexplained drop in North Korean forces by 40,000, and disregarding the overblown confidence of the theatre commander, three unpleasant facts were manifest. The Chinese were not going to be defeated in the northern provinces of Korea. They had been preparing for offensive action. The United Nations' two bargaining counters, possession of territory and power of forces, were declining in value.

In London, the Chiefs of Staff were not impressed by Air Marshal Bouchier's conclusions on 28th November that the overall military position 'is not as bad as it will be represented in the press'.[4] They expected that the Chinese would reverse the Eighth Army as it had done in early November. Field-Marshal Slim had prepared a minute for his colleagues on the 27th, setting out questions to be resolved between Britain and the United States if it came to open war with China.[5] While the Service staffs considered these, first indications of withdrawal by the United Nations' forces reached London. The Chiefs signalled a catalogue of anxiety to Lord Tedder on the afternoon of the 28th of which the prime point was that any request by General MacArthur to bomb north east China should be resisted.[6] Next day, in Cabinet, the Foreign Secretary made the same point. They were all anxious to localise the conflict. Some of those present warned that 'there was a good deal of uneasiness among Government supporters which might be reflected in the foreign affairs debate in the House of Commons which was to open that afternoon'. Anticipating such a reaction, Mr Bevin had asked Mr Acheson for assurances that policy would continue to be developed by consultation, and for the latest politico-military information and policy proposals from Washington. He had had a sympathetic but limited response—Mr Acheson was looking himself for new ideas—which reiterated agreement on the need to localise hostilities, and included the 'unanimous and considered judgement . . . that the present Chinese offensive has been planned and staged over a considerable period of time'.[7] This latter point does not seem to have impressed Cabinet, Foreign Office or the Defence departments. The Prime Minister's view, expressed at the morning meeting, that 'General MacArthur had been over-optimistic about the course of the campaign; and the check which he had suffered might lead him to exaggerate the strength of this Chinese attack',[8] may have been general in White-hall. It may also have occasioned the curious consensus that 'there was perhaps some prospect that fighting would gradually come to an end if, as seemed likely, China's intervention was based mainly on considerations of self-defence and did not form part of Russia's world strategy'.[9]

The Prime Minister and Foreign Secretary led the defence of their ally against 'two or three persistent critics'.[10] They reminded colleagues,

> . . . in the last resort it would be difficult to decline to support a United States resolution condemning Chinese aggression. If we were to withdraw our support for United States strategy in the Far East, the United States Government would be less willing to continue their policy of supporting the defence of Western Europe; and without their full assistance in Europe, we had little chance of withstanding a major Russian aggression there. . . .
> (e) One of the main objectives of Russian policy was to provoke divergences of policy between the United Kingdom and the United States. We should be playing into Russian hands if we allowed this adverse turn of events in Korea to be a cause of ill-feeling between ourselves and the Americans. . . .[11]

Meantime, the Foreign Office and State Department were seeking individually and collectively to muster ideas as to what should be done to recover from the military reverse. Some members of the latter were indeed proposing that China should be declared an 'aggressor'. Britain, supported by France, Australia and Canada, opposed this successfully over the next few days. The Defense and State Departments resurrected the option of economic warfare, but the Foreign Office pointed out that a trade embargo would be difficult, if not impossible, to enforce. It might, besides, oblige China to become wholly dependent on Russian dominated markets. Yet in return the only British suggestion was withdrawal to a convenient defensive line, 'presumably across the narrowest part of Korea'—an identical presumption in the State Department—while hoping that the Chinese might respond favourably to the six power appeal to withdraw, perhaps even agree to discuss the establishment of a demilitarised zone.[12]

While discussing British objections to naming China as an 'aggressor', Mr Rusk remarked to Sir Oliver Franks that there were other problems to be discussed between the United States and United Kingdom. Assuming temporary stabilisation of a line in Korea,

1. How do we mobilise political and economic pressures on China?
2. . . . [how are we] to deal immediately with this disclosure of a larger threat and are the British and Americans estimates in this regard near alike? Also, how do we relate the UN General Assembly to the political and economic pressures needed to meet this threat?[13]

On the same day, 29th November, Lord Tedder replied to the Chiefs,

1. . . . I have seen Bradley . . . and thought it advisable to show him your message. He reiterated US determination to avoid extension of conflict. This had been discussed at length and emphasised in JCS meeting and [US delegation to] Security Council today. MacArthur's directives leave no ambiguity on the subject of not taking action across the Yalu.
2. They are worried at potential air threat. Recent Intelligence shows some two hundred medium or light bombers plus some seventy MiGs [in North East China and adjacent Russian territory]. Last night [enemy] air attack on P'yongyang did considerable damage. Bradley said that only consideration which would make air attack on air bases in Manchuria thinkable, would be if Communist air attack seriously endangered security of UN Forces and in such case it would only be done to cover withdrawal.
3. I pointed out that such action by bringing in Russian Air would probably make situation both in air and on ground worse than ever. The point was taken. I also pointed out and Bradley agreed that this would possibly if not probably lead to world war. I emphasised that a decision with such possible implications was one which must call for full consideration with other Governments and presumably with UNO. Bradley registered and agreed. He asked me to assure you that he and Joint Chiefs were in strong agreement with you on this issue.

4. My impression at this end is that political or party considerations are not playing a large part in US views regarding military
action in Korea. It is purely military considerations that have
weighed in the past and still are the decisive ones.[14]

In the sense that President and Cabinet were traditionally loathe
to interfere with their Commander-in-Chief in the field, Lord
Tedder's judgement was correct. But public opinion, moved by
disappointment, and by no means confined to Republican supporters, was rising against Mr Truman on the Korean issue. Many
editors and correspondents believed that he should dismiss Mr
Acheson because he was inclined to defer to the 'pro-Red British'.
Sir Gladwyn Jebb advised Mr Bevin that 'The present mood in
the United States is extremely bellicose'. Mr Acheson had assured
Sir Oliver Franks that 'any rumours of contemplated withdrawal
were baseless'.[15]

In these circumstances, President Truman made a statement to
a news conference on the morning of 30th November confirming
that the United States would continue to resist aggression in Korea
and elsewhere but had no aggressive intentions against the People's
Republic of China. During questions afterwards, this exchange
followed with a correspondent:

The President: We will take whatever steps are necessary to
meet the military situation, just as we always have.
Question: Will that include the atomic bomb?
The President: That includes every weapon that we have.
Question: Mr President, you said 'every weapon that we have'.
Does that mean that there is active consideration of the use of
the atomic bomb?
The President: There has always been active consideration of
its use. I don't want to see it used. It is a terrible weapon, and
it should not be used on innocent men, women and children
who have nothing whatever to do with this military aggression.
That happens when it is used.[16]

The President had told the simple truth. Press and radio made
much of it, adding to the consternation and anxiety of the United
States administration and the governments of its allies. Few of the
latter were aware that limited deployment of nuclear weapons had
already taken place.

As soon as the United States was engaged in the Korean war,
the Joint Chiefs of Staff outside and within the National Security
Council discussed the range of military options. At the first meeting
on 25th June, the use of nuclear weapons in Korea was rejected

but, in case Russia should intervene from its air bases in the Far East, the President said that plans should be prepared to destroy these bases with atomic bombs. He did not say they would be used, only that they should have a plan to use them if necessary; as noted earlier, the entry of Russia into the war was then half expected.

In Cabinet on 7th July, with the ROK Army and Task Force Smith scattered and the other advanced elements of 24th Division falling back, the President was anxious to 'let the world know that we mean business'. He declined advice to seek agreement in the United Nations for use of nuclear weapons, but agreed on the 8th to send to Britain two medium bomber groups with aircraft configured for nuclear bomb delivery together with fighter escorts. They would carry atom bombs without the the essential cores. This was partly to position a means of atomic retaliation if Russia suddenly attacked in Europe, but was equally meant to send a signal of deterrence to the Soviet Union, a ploy used previously.* Somewhat naively, General Vandenberg assumed that the Royal Air Force would accept these aircraft on British bases as a matter of course. Sir John Slessor replied that he could not receive them without political clearance and at once notified the Prime Minister. The latter was therefore ready for an approach by the American Embassy.

On the morning of 10th July, Mr Attlee put the proposal to the Cabinet, omitting some of the details. In keeping with the secrecy militating in such matters,† no mention was made of atomic weapons accompanying the aircraft. The explanation for the intended deployment was that,

> . . . in view of the strain which might be thrown on their transport facilities by the need to reinforce their troops in Korea, the United States authorities were anxious to accelerate the approved programme for stationing United States air forces in this country as part of the defence arrangements under the North Atlantic Pact. . . . it was agreed that it was important that these movements should not be related in any way to the situation in Korea but should be presented as routine movements giving effect to an agreed policy. From this point of view it was desirable that the announcement, and any necessary explanations of it,

---

*An American nuclear strike force was sent to Europe in 1948 as a deterrent to war during the Russian blockade of Berlin. No evidence has emerged to show that it affected the outcome.

†Mr Attlee committed Britain formally to an atomic development programme in January, 1947, but he did not inform more than a few members of his Government then or later.[17]

should be kept within the control of the United Kingdom authorities.

A press release was subsequently arranged which announced 'normal rotation' of aircraft. The Glosters and Royal Ulster Rifles were sent from Colchester to guard the aircraft and their weapons on East Anglian bases until more permanent arrangements could be made.[18]

As setbacks multiplied to critical proportions in Korea, a few hawks in the Pentagon, fewer in the State Department, proposed the use of nuclear weapons against the NKPA, but their advice went unheeded. During the visit of Generals Collins and Vandenberg to Tokyo at the end of July to discuss reinforcements, however, the latter prompted General MacArthur to remark a 'unique use for the atomic bomb' if the Chinese should enter the battlefield, though of this there was then no sign. Throughout this visit, General Vandenberg was frustrated by the apparent inability of the air force to halt the enemy in Korea; he failed to recognise that the US and ROK soldiers often owed their preservation to the 5th Air Force. Sending conventional B-29s from the Strategic Air Command to reinforce the Far East Air Force on his return to Washington, he persuaded his colleagues that they should include ten modified for nuclear weapons to the same bases in Guam. These carried atom bombs without cores.[19]

American and British arrangements had concealed these deployments by a secrecy which was to be criticised in later years. It is ironic that President Truman's ready admission that he had actively considered using nuclear weapons occasioned so much surprise and excitement. The United States had atom bombs; it was public knowledge. The Atlantic allies were comforted by it. They had good reason to believe that such weapons deterred Stalin from continuing his expansionism into western Europe, even though he had atom bombs of his own from 1949. Inevitably, their use was considered when the American forces were committed to operations, albeit of a limited nature; but their use in Korea had been rejected except for the abiding contingency of war with Russia.

After a hurried meeting in the White House, Charles—'Charlie'—G Ross, the President's Press Secretary, sought later on 30th November to cool the excitement by a statement which concluded,

> . . . by law, only the President can authorize the use of the atom bomb, and no such authorization has been given . . . In brief, the reply to the questions at today's press conference do not represent any change in the situation.[20]

This statement had little effect. The Presidential admission was a prize which the news industry was unwilling to discard. Surprising and sensational, it had also a potential for prolonged analysis and discussion. For those in government office concerned with the war, their officials and officers, it intensified the tumultuous and fearful atmosphere in which they were conducting their business, and nowhere with greater effect than at the United Nations. Some diplomatists were so convinced that a world war was about to start that they had tears in their eyes during discussions in offices and corridors.

Mr Truman's morning press conference overshadowed the 503rd Meeting of the Security Council in the afternoon and evening of 30th November. Three draft resolutions were voted upon. The Russian condemnation of the United States aggression against Taiwan was defeated by nine votes to one (Soviet Union), India not participating.* The condemnation of the United States by the People's Republic of China, submitted by their delegate, General Wu Hsiu-chuan, for 'criminal acts of armed aggression against the Chinese territory of Taiwan, and armed intervention in Korea', was defeated by an identical vote. Finally, as expected, the Soviet delegate vetoed the six-power resolution,† which would otherwise have been carried by nine votes.[21]

Shortly before the Security Council met, Mr Attlee called his Cabinet together in his room in the House of Commons to discuss President Truman's statement to the press. They began at 6.45 pm, a quarter to two in the afternoon in Washington and New York. Details of the press conference had been received by members of Parliament on news tapes. Labour, Conservative and Liberal back-benchers were not reassured by the clarification, some felt the nation was being drawn into a nuclear war. Mr Churchill, Leader of the Opposition, believed that European defence was endangered by a 'diversion' in Asia. Moderate and immoderate reactions were expressed at informal meetings but a common wish was that the Prime Minister should go to Washington to thrash out the nuclear weapons issue with the President. One hundred Labour members signed a letter to the Prime Minister with this advice.

Mr Attlee told the Cabinet that he did not believe that the United States was preparing to use the atom bomb but they could not ignore the alarm caused by the President's statement:

---

*The UK High Commissioner in New Delhi had been warned that unless the six-power resolution was amended to call for a cease fire and demilitarised zone, which the Indian delegate would then attempt to negotiate through General Wu, India would not participate in the vote. [22]

†See p 295.

. . . urgent action was necessary in order to allay public anxiety. Moreover, the military situation in the Far East had deteriorated seriously and the consequences of a possible war with China had to be faced. He therefore thought it desirable . . . that there should be direct consultation between the President and himself; and he proposed to suggest to the President that he should go immediately to Washington for personal consultations with him. . . .

(b) The impression should not be given that the only purpose of the visit was to discuss the use of the atom bomb. That question would, however, be discussed and the responsibility for deciding on the use of the atom bomb would have to be defined. A decision of this importance could not be left to the commander in the field or even to the United States Government alone. All nations which had contributed to the United Nations force in Korea should be consulted and there should be unanimity among them before a decision was taken to use the bomb.

(c) The Prime Minister would wish to discuss with the President the general situation in the Far East and its effect on defensive preparations in other parts of the world. The Americans should be pressed to establish the [NATO] supreme command in Europe without further delay, whatever the attitude of the French Government proved to be on the question of Germany's partici-pation in the defence of Western Europe. There was also urgent need for an exchange of views on raw materials. American action in this matter was seriously handicapping the efforts of other countries, including the United Kingdom. . . .[23]

Action was already in hand through Sir Oliver Franks and, shortly, also through Mr Holmes, American *Chargé d'Affaires* in London,* to obtain the President's agreement to a meeting, which came almost immediately.[24] A programme was developed for 3rd to 12th December, comprehending five days in Washington, a day in New York at the United Nations headquarters, a day in Ottawa with the Canadian Government, and return home via New York. Mr Bevin's heart condition prevented him from accompanying the Prime Minister. The Foreign Office was to be represented by a Deputy Under-Secretary, Sir Roger Makins, the Chiefs of Staff by Field Marshal Sir William Slim, and the Economic Planning Staff by its chief, Sir Edwin Plowden. Sir Oliver Franks, an indispensable

---

*Julius C Holmes, Minister in the United States Embassy in London, was acting in the absence of the Ambassador, Mr Douglas.

adviser, would be joining the Prime Minister's party* in Washington.

Friday and Saturday, 1st and 2nd December, were filled with preparations,[25] and consultations with Australia, Canada, India— Mr Nehru floated the idea that he might join the meeting in Washington—and France. To Mr Bevin's surprise, M. Pleven, the French Premier† and Foreign Minister, M. Schuman, came to London at their own suggestion. French public opinion favoured direct negotiations with the Chinese; there was anxiety that Chinese support for Ho Chi Minh in Indo-China was growing. The French Foreign Office inclined to the view that the hawks in the Defense and State Departments wished to identify China as an aggressor as a means of obtaining authority to bomb North East China— General MacArthur had just informed a journalist that constraint in this area put his forces under 'an enormous handicap, without precedent in military history'.[26] Mr Attlee saw no difficulty in representing these French views, inter-related in part with British sensitivity concerning Malaya and Hong Kong. He had hoped that the French had also come to say that they were ready to agree on West German rearmament and the appointment of a NATO supreme commander—that would have been welcome news in Washington—but he was disappointed.[27]

On the Saturday, Sir John Slessor, roused by General MacArthur's press statement, drafted a reiteration of the Chiefs' views on bombing policy for representation by Lord Tedder to General Bradley. But the First Sea Lord would not agree to its despatch:

I strongly oppose sending now any telegram of this sort. MacArthur, whatever his faults, has a very difficult situation at the moment and there is nothing we can do which can alter this. The Prime Minister and CIGS will arrive on Monday. . . .[28]

Meantime, the Defense and State Departments had been much occupied in seeking a means of countering the crisis in Korea, spurred in part by the need to coordinate ideas for the meetings with the British visitors.

By 3rd December, it was becoming apparent, both from the situation reports and General MacArthur's personal comments to

*The other members were Mr R H Scott, Foreign Office, Mr Robert Hall, Cabinet Office Economic Section, Mr D H F Rickett, Principal Private Secretary to the Prime Minister, and Mr Philip Jordan, the Prime Minister's Public Relations Adviser.
†Pleven, Rene Jean (1901–), Premier of France, July, 1950–March, 1951; August, 1951–January, 1952.

Washington and the press, that there was no prospect of holding the narrow neck of the North Korea peninsula or indeed any other line on the Eighth Army front. The Commander-in-Chief fairly pointed out that the Chinese would find a way through the wild, high country inland as a means of passing forces behind his own. In Washington and London, the Chiefs of Staff drew the inference that, if that was valid for the shortest line, it was more so for all others; a spine of high, jagged mountains extended south almost to Pusan. The only stable area appeared to be the X Corps enclave which General MacArthur insisted in maintaining as a threat to the enemy line of communication. It was the only area which offered an option for enterprise. Elsewhere, as he reminded the Chiefs, he was fighting a massive force with endless reinforcements and Russian supplies, in mountainous country which restricted air support, remote from the coasts and naval guns. His soldiers were tired after five months of fighting, his units under strength,

> This small command, actually under present conditions, is facing the entire Chinese nation in an undeclared war, and, unless some positive and immediate action is taken, hope for success cannot be justified and steady attrition leading to final destruction can reasonably be contemplated.[29]

Over the Saturday and Sunday and into the morning of Monday, the 3rd, the debate narrowed as senior members of the State Department—principally Mr Acheson and Mr Rusk—and the Defense Department, guided by General Marshall, recognised that handwringing and indecision were distorting their perspectives.

Mr Acheson determined that they should press the six-power resolution, vetoed in the Security Council, in the General Assembly. If nothing else, this would provide an opportunity to rally their allies. A cease fire without conditions might be acceptable but not on terms framed by China. The price would be exorbitant: abandonment of the South Koreans and the Nationalists on Taiwan, a majority share, with Russia, in the Japanese Peace Settlement. United States influence in Asia, particularly its ability to encourage resistance to Communism, would be fatally reduced. He thought of advising the President to appoint General Collins as the UN Commander-in-Chief, leaving General MacArthur as the *shogun* in Japan. At all events, he and Mr Rusk agreed that they must encourage the military to fight to establish a line, failing that one or more enclaves, and failing that to the point of evacuation.

Among the Services staffs, the dynamic force of the Chinese infantry and the threat of massive attacks from the airfields of North East China inhibited the development of plans. They doubted their ability to hold any territory; but all agreed equally that, currently, air attacks into China would be counter-productive. None supported General MacArthur's option of a general evacuation followed by a blockade of the China coast. In default of establishing a line, the consensus was that they should seek to hold one or more enclaves at, say, Hamhung, Seoul-Inch'on, and Pusan. Both Departments had come to accept the possibility of military defeat but were determined to continue fighting.

Writing in later years, Mr Acheson seemed to think that the American side had completed its policy reviews and decided on its course, ready if necessary to take that course alone before meeting the British visitors. But the records of the Defense and State Departments show that options were far from closed when the talks began on the afternoon of 4th December, and there are strong indications that, as in all the troubled matters of Korean security, the United States Government was as ready to consider British advice as to offer its own.[30] The two parties were like tennis playing friends, sometimes partners, sometimes opponents. In either relationship, each respected the other's skills and learnt from the other's game.

In this December match, Mr Acheson did not much like the idea of playing opposite Mr Attlee with the President as his partner. He had to defer to the latter and show some respect to the former; he much preferred playing the game with Mr Bevin, better still with Sir Oliver. They began at 4 p.m. in the Cabinet room at the White House.[31]

Their longstanding disagreement on the nature of the People's Government of China continued to divide them. The Americans believed that Mao's regime was the tool of the Soviet Union. The British believed that it was as fervently nationalist as Communist. The greater part of the meeting, which ran for an hour and a half, was occupied by the details of their difference. The President then read out a memorandum of Mr Acheson's policy proposals* embracing cease-fire options, fighting to the end if a cease fire could not be arranged, mobilisation of political and economic measures against China if the United Nations were defeated, action in Asia to counter Communism including acceleration of Japanese independence.[32]

There was a pause. All seemed to feel that, though the two sides had not drawn together, there was nothing more to be said. Sir Oliver Franks then asked if he might suggest the points which had emerged. He offered four:

---

*These were in the form of answers to questions drafted by Mr Acheson as 'Suggested procedure for First Meeting with Mr Attlee'. For details see *Foreign Relations of the United States, Vol VII, Korea*, p 1375.

a. The military situation was such that we ought not to assume that the bridgeheads could be held; and our position would be one not so much of diminishing strength as definite weakness.

b. The Prime Minister had tried to guess what would be in the mind of the Chinese if they came to negotiations They would go beyond Korea and bring in the question of Formosa and that might lead us on to a slippery slope.

c. Mr Acheson had outlined another possibility under which we would hold on to Korea as long as we could and leave, not as a result of negotiation, but because we were forced out. We should then have to consider what to do to the Power that had forced us out.

d. A proposal for a cease-fire, if possible at all, would have to be carried out very quickly. It to some extent cut across the two alternative courses already mentioned, but it seemed to be something which ought to be aimed at on its own merits.

The President and Mr Acheson agreed on the clarity and accuracy of this summary. The latter added that if the condition of a cease fire was withdrawal behind the 38th Parallel, that would be no concession at all.[33] Sir Oliver had made a common bridgehead for them all on a forbidding shore.

Immediately the principals had agreed a press statement and departed, their senior advisers moved to a meeting in Mr Acheson's office to chew the fat. The narrow bridgehead was extended a little. Mr Acheson asked whether, following talks with the Prime Minister that evening, his British associates could come over next morning to prepare recommendations for their respective chiefs so as to avoid a reiteration of their differences at the meeting in the afternoon. Sir Oliver said they would be in touch before the luncheon on board the President's yacht.[34]

On the evening of the 4th, some indication of Chinese ideas came from New York. Mr Lie, Secretary-General of the United Nations, and Sir Benegal Rau, had had informal talks with General Wu. The General had advanced three demands from his government: withdrawal of United Nations forces from Korea; withdrawal of the United States' Seventh Fleet from the Taiwan area; and the replacement of the Kuomintang representation in the United Nations by one from Peking. Mr Lie had asked him to propose a cease fire in Korea involving withdrawal of the Chinese to the Yalu and the United Nations below the 38th Parallel. General Wu had said it would take three days to get an answer.[35] This report confirmed the apprehensions of the State Department and Foreign Office.

On the morning of the 5th, the meeting was resumed in Mr Acheson's office, joined also by Mr Younger, who had come down from New York, John Hickerson and Averell Harriman. As a result of their discussions,[36] it was possible to begin the second afternoon conference, aboard the USS *Williamsburg*, with an agreement,

> (a) That the 6-Power [sic] Resolution vetoed in the Security Council should be filed and circulated as soon as the six Powers can agree on the minor editorial changes to put it into shape for General Assembly action.
>
> (b) If a cease fire resolution were introduced in the General Assembly, the United States and the United Kingdom should, in principle, be prepared to support it.

When the President remarked that he could not agree on voluntary withdrawal from Korea, Mr Attlee responded, 'We're in this with you, and we stand together'. His dry manner and exposition—'as a long withdrawing, melancholy sigh'—did not recommend him to Mr Acheson, but this statement manifested a warmth which impressed the Americans. It was thus unfortunate that the Prime Minister soon fell back on the old, divisive subject of the nature of the Chinese regime. Seeking new ground, Mr Acheson began to review what must be preserved in their strategy. The 'island chain' in the Pacific, for example—Japan, the Ryukus, Taiwan, and the Philippines—must not be lost to Communism.

Their discussions were briefly interrupted by a message from Lake Success that many Arab and Asian delegations were calling upon the Chinese and North Koreans not to cross the 38th Parallel. It was welcome news, promising support for their hopes of a cease fire. But it emphasised the need to seek agreement on what they would do if there was no cease fire and they were forced out.

Returning to the main discussion, Mr Acheson maintained that they must be consistent or they would lose public support for their overall security policy:

> At that point we would have to consider the possibility whether we would engage in warfare against China or would take some other action . . . Before coming to the long-range consideration regarding China, there was one thing which ought to be mentioned and that was the attitude of the American people. . . . As the President said yesterday no Administration in the United States could possibly urge the American people to take vigorous action in its foreign policy on one ocean front while on the other ocean front they seemed to be rolled back and to accept a

position of isolation. The public mind was not delicate enough to understand such opposing attitudes and even if it were that difference would be wrong.

We were up against a fundamental proposition: if we accepted the proposition that because an aggression is a very large one we can submit to it we have changed our attitude very deeply. This would affect our attitude to other things. This was not a question of logic but of the very integrity of the people. In common with other members of the UN we went out after a smaller aggressor. We are now faced by a bigger aggressor and we have been licked in this campaign. If we face that by saying we adjust ourselves to it it affects the whole stand of the people. In that case we must adjust ourselves to power and aggression everywhere. . . .

President, Prime Minister and Secretary of State then spoke on the discrete viewpoints and expectations of public opinion in the United States, United Kingdom and Asia. Sir Oliver Franks intervened:

. . . he thought a good deal had been agreed upon in connection with plans in the UN. If a cease-fire is suggested without strings, we like it. If there is no cease-fire, we don't wish to contemplate a voluntary withdrawal from Korea and allowing for our very different roles in Korea, the UK wanted to go along with the United States and therefore their units to help carry out the task. If resistance can be continued in Korea we may get to the negotiating stage later. If the cease-fire were not accepted there would be no chance for negotiations. The Chinese troops, by sheer force of numbers, may compel an honourable withdrawal. We would not then be giving way. Then the UN and United States which had suffered most would have done all they could for Korea even though that was not enough. . . . It had been said yesterday and elaborated by Secretary Acheson that we should follow up our attitude against aggression with determination to defend Korea as long as we could. We should maintain our attitude against aggression in the face of the greater aggression. In that connection, it had been suggested we should think of economic sanctions and aiding movements in China which might break down the Chinese Communist Government. For his part he was undecided and not convinced now that that attitude and that course of action was in the best interest of all of us. He did not see how even if we were both agreed on this course we could get much UN support. If there is little support in the UN, it is a ground for questioning this policy. It would be hard to go ahead without UN sanction. It would not be easy to bring damage to China quickly. On the other hand, considerable and rapid damage could be done to the UK in Hong Kong and Malaya. Would not the proposed course tend to provoke the Chinese to see what they could do against us in those places? It would increase the tempo of their action and he wondered whether we wished to do this. . . . He thought that should be clarified in these discussions. He wished to return to the question of negotiations if there were a cease-fire or if continuing resistance proves to be possible in Korea without a cease-fire. . . . On the question of whether or not Formosa should be involved in any negotiation, if he thought that this involved a stride on the slippery slope, he did not want to do that. Another question was Chinese Communist membership in the UN. This would probably come up in any negotiation on the Korean question and many Asiatics would support them. The United Kingdom had followed that position and was not changing it. . . .

They had returned to the point of disagreement between Mr Acheson and Mr Bevin at the beginning of the war. The British representatives believed their ideas were rooted in realism, the Americans thought they smacked of appeasement. The problem was that there seemed to be no accommodating middle ground. Mr Acheson remarked that,

He thought Sir Oliver Franks had very forcibly raised the question of what we did against the Chinese. He didn't think it was possible to know at this point. One aspect of the present situation was that any one who put up an idea subjected himself to powerful attack. It was hard to suggest any position which could not be successfully attacked. He agreed there might be great trouble in bombing China. This might lead to a chain of circumstances which had to be carefully considered. The question was not so much the ends of a policy but whether you start by accepting the results of aggression and say to the aggressors that they had licked us and then collect their price. Would we go on and say we are friendly to the aggressors, that we want to trade with them and seat them in the UN? The proposal had that flavour. If there is a cease-fire and negotiation, the approach should be that we would negotiate on the future of Korea. . . .

Nothing that followed that afternoon took matters beyond this point.[37] 'The British still seem to think that all should be given up in the Far East to save Europe,' Mr Truman wrote in his diary that evening. 'I said No! We talk some more tomorrow. The position of the British in Asia is, to say the least, fantastic. We cannot agree to their suggestions. Yet they say they will support us whatever we do!'[38]

On the 6th, the meetings were concerned with European defence, including economic questions. The British were planning to raise twenty regular and reserve divisions and they needed assistance. Domestically, the most pressing problem was the supply and transportation of raw materials, but they also wanted to see more American divisions in Europe, even if they came from the National Guard.* Their difficulties with the French over West German rearmament were discussed. These problems would have been outstanding even if there had been no war in Korea, but some were exacerbated by its course, notably manpower.

The fifth meeting was held at the White House once more from 3.45 to 5.10 p.m. Though two items on the agenda related to Atlantic Defence, the other two were interrelated: the Far East and the Atomic Bomb. By this time, Sir Gladwyn Jebb had had a luncheon meeting with Ambassador Wu,† at which all the Chinese requirements were repeated, though abandonment of Taiwan seemed to be paramount.[39] After dinner at the British Embassy that night, the principals discussed privately national political difficulties: the President mentioned that twenty-four Republican senators were demanding information about 'secret commitments' to the British; Mr Attlee responded by citing his own problems in foreign policy with some of his senior Party members, especially Aneurin Bevan. Then they were asked to join their senior advisers to talk about breaking the remaining barriers to a full NATO command in Europe. Mr Acheson, Field Marshal Slim and Lord Tedder hoped that, during this, the Prime Minister might finally demonstrate that Britain was contributing to the limits of its resources in manpower and materials. But Mr Attlee switched suddenly to a subject vexing him: General MacArthur's conduct of the campaign in Korea. The British wanted to use the Combined US and UK Chiefs of Staff to control the overall conduct of operations, an idea which stung the American partners. They were able to point out that they had frequently accepted British protests— in such matters as bombing policy, for example—quite apart from the folly of seeking to run a war by committee. Was this, the

---

*Because so much of the United States Army had been sent to Korea, the President had mobilised part of the Reserves and National Guard. He declared a national emergency in December.

†At the luncheon, given by Trygve Lie, the General let it be known that he preferred to be called 'Ambassador'

Americans asked, how they intended to direct a supreme commander in NATO when he was appointed? In any case, how would
the other states with forces in Korea—the French, for example—
take to Anglo-American military direction? This was an unwise
venture by the British delegation, prompted by frustration, lacking
the weight of deliberate consideration. It was uncharacteristic of
the Prime Minister, the Field Marshal, and Marshal of the Royal
Air Force Lord Tedder. It cooled a friendly atmosphere. The
American reaction may have been all the stronger because most
of them believed that General MacArthur would never submit to
direction. Somewhat at odds, they dispersed soon after midnight.
A preliminary meeting in the State Department next morning was
'gloomy and unproductive' in Sir Oliver Franks' view.[40]

These contacts did not promise any further advance at the fifth
meeting, that afternoon, 7th December. The omens were true. But
in one important matter, there appeared to be concord. In the
matter of nuclear weapons, the President promised Mr Attlee at a
private meeting that he would not use the bomb without consulting
him. Though he declined to commit this to writing—'if a man's
word isn't any good it isn't made any better by writing it down,'
said the President—the Prime Minister was satisfied.[41] This was
not well received later by Mr Truman's advisers.

So they came to the final meeting on Friday, 8th December,
attended by many members of Mr Truman's Administration, and
by General Collins, who had just returned from Korea. The latter
was able to give them a fuller and, as most thought, a more hopeful
picture of the situation there. General MacArthur considered that
he would be able to withdraw X Corps safely and reunite it with
Eighth Army to hold a line south of the Han, at any rate on the
Naktong. General Walker was equally confident. The briefing did
not mention that General MacArthur's view was based on being
reinforced, if necessary by divisions from Taiwan, and the removal
of all restrictions on bombing and blockading of China.

The only difficulty that morning was the phrasing of parts of the
communique. The objectives of the two nations in foreign policy,
it declared, were the same. 'They were in complete agreement that
there could be no thought of appeasement or of rewarding
aggression whether in the Far East or elsewhere'. They owned to
differences over China's seat in the United Nations, and found a
common formula for Taiwan—a measure of American success in
their debates. They affirmed support for and action to develop
NATO. Wording concerning the atom bomb resulted from a
last minute adjustment. The gentleman's agreement between the
President and the Prime Minister could not, in Mr Acheson's

view, be sustained. It contravened the MacMahon Act.* Mr
Acheson described events later thus,

> A whispered conversation with the President and a note passed
> across the cable to Oliver Franks brought the three of us
> [including Robert Lovett] and the Prime Minister together in
> the President's office, while others continued revision of the
> draft.
>
> I pointed out that . . . Congress would not permit it. . . .
> The suggestion he had made in the Cabinet Room would open
> a most vicious offensive against him and the British, whereas a
> program of keeping in close touch with the Prime Minister in
> all world situations that might threaten to move towards violence
> and hostilities of any kind would be widely approved.
>
> All agreed with this, albeit Mr Attlee a little sadly, and we
> began drafting a suitable paragraph, Oliver Franks acting as
> scribe. The President pulled out the slide to the left of his desk.
> Oliver left his chair and knelt between mine and Attlee's to
> write on it. 'I think this is the first time,' said the President, 'that
> a British Ambassador has knelt before an American President'.[42]

The *communique*[43] agreed, the summit ended—'my first,' Mr
Acheson wrote in a memoir, 'accompanied by an ungranted prayer
that I might be spared another . . .'.[44] Mr Attlee left for lunch with
Hume Wrong, the Canadian Ambassador, and Lester Pearson,†
Canadian Minister for External Affairs, and then briefed the
British Commonwealth representatives in Washington at the British
Embassy. The whole British party then flew to New York for a
day at the United Nations headquarters, and finally to Ottawa,
for consultation with the Canadian Cabinet. The latter were
particularly interested to know whether the informal understanding
between Mr Truman and Mr Attlee concerning use of nuclear
weapons included Canada and were told that nothing had been
said to the contrary.[45]
On the Tuesday morning, 12th December, Mr Attlee returned
home to report to the Cabinet and the House of Commons—and
in a sense—to the French; he had represented their views as well
as those of the Commonwealth. Sir Roger Makins was sent to

---

*The McMahon Act, signed by the President on 1st August 1946, was originally intended
to ensure that Russia did not have access to atomic secrets. Its effect was to counter the
agreement between Canada, the United Kingdom and United States to cooperate in this
field, and obliged the British Government to initiate its own atomic energy programme.
See Professor Margaret M Gowing, *Independence and Deterrence, Britain and Atomic Energy,
1945-52*, vol 1 (London, 1974).
†Pearson, Rt Hon Lester Bowles (1897-1972), Canadian Secretary of State for External
Affairs, 1948-57, Prime Minister, 1963-68.

Paris to round out the reports which had been passed in Washington to the French Ambassador.

What did the visit achieve? Within the eye of those who view most political ventures and all politicians' statements with cynicism, the air fares were wasted. It is an astigmatic judgement. All else apart, the event of meeting relieved a rising crisis of European and Commonwealth confidence in the conduct of the war by the United States.[46] It exposed to the Administration the weakness of pursuing economic operations against China if the UN forces were driven out of Korea. At the same time, it convinced the British that the United States was not going to become involved in war with the People's Republic. There was, in addition, some satisfaction of British requests for assistance in the supply and movement of scarce raw materials.

Despite the limitation of Mr Truman's agreement to consult the United Kingdom and, by association, Canada in their use of nuclear weapons in Korea, the President's spoken promise was not thereby annulled. He was an honourable man and, with Mr Acheson, already uneasy about the breach of agreement with these partners occasioned by the MacMahon Act. It is very unlikely indeed that atom bombs would have been used in Korea without prior consultation. Failure to do so would have broken the ties not only between Washington and London—and the British Commonwealth—but equally between western Europe and Washington. Honour and American political interest would have combined to militate against such a course. The British record of the understanding, sometimes derided as illusory, is thus a fair one.

Then, although some sort of combination as to future policy in Korea would have been possible by exchanges of telegrams and discussions between Sir Oliver Franks and Mr Acheson, it is doubtful whether there would have been such a clear understanding of each other's views without the personal contact of the principals and no less, their immediate subordinates. Mr Attlee's opinion that Communist China would be easier to deal with in the United Nations rather than outside struck home in the State Department even though the Secretary and his assistants could not bring themselves to agree in the circumstances of the time to turn the Kuomintang out. The British were obliged to recognise that removal of the Seventh Fleet from the Taiwan Strait as a bargaining counter would be to embark on 'the slippery slope' of appeasement. The United States was reassured that the British would stick with them politically and militarily in the fight for Korean territory. They valued that. As a consequence, British opinions continued to be sought and carried weight.

Personal opinions were, inevitably, formed or developed among the participants about one another during the meetings. A problem for Mr Acheson, as he later explained, was that Mr Truman and Mr Attlee liked one another. Whilst the Secretary of State thought of the Prime Minister as a 'Job's comforter', there were some advantages to the presidential friendship. 'Attlee certainly stiffened our resolve to stand no insubordination from MacArthur'.[47] Field Marshal Slim preferred General Marshall's 'quiet influence to Mr Acheson's sudden bursts of firecrackers'.[48] He also reported to the other Chiefs of Staff on 14th December that 'United States official opinion was in a confused state. They were surprised and indignant that they had suffered a serious reverse in Korea . . .'.[49]

No stranger himself to the problems of a retreat from an enemy which had secured a moral ascendancy, the CIGS recognised General Walker's difficulty. But he felt reasonably confident that a winter line would be established at some point because he believed that the Chinese could not supply an indefinite advance on the backs of porters.

As the field marshal returned, General P'eng's armies were seeking to do just that.

SOURCE NOTES: CHAPTER 15

1. Record of telephone conversation, GHQ (Maj-Gen Hickey) to Eighth Army (Col Landrum), 271250 November 1950—GHQ UNC Chief of Staff Daily Folders, (USNARS, Suitland).

2. Signal JCS 92801 to CINCFE 272240 September 1950), Signal JCS 93709 to CINCFE 092205 October 1950) Army Radio Files, (USNARS, Suitland).

3. Signal CINCFE C 699553 to JCS 281645 November 1950, (USNARS, Suitland).

4. DEFE series, CAB/TOK, Toyko (Bouchier) CAB 124 to MOD (COS) 280838 November 1950.

5. DEFE 11/204, Minute from CIGS to 1stSL and CAS, CIGS/BM/374065/2 of 27th November 1950.

6. Ibid, Ministry of Defence, COS(W)907 to BJSM, Washington (Tedder) 281530 November 1950.

7. London 3117 to State Dept, 28th November 1950, FRUS Vol VII op cit, p 1241, Secretary of State (SofS) 2810 to London 28th November 1950, FRUS Vol VII op cit, p 1249.

8. CAB 128/18, Cabinet 78 (50), Minutes of 29th November 1950.

9. Ibid. See also DEFE 11/204, FO proposed telegram to Washington of 30th November 1950 (f 1495).

10. Shinwell, conversation with author.

11. CAB 128/18, Cabinet 78 (50), Minutes of 29th November 1950.

12. DEFE 11/204, Paris 347 to FO 29th November 1950, FO 5327 and 5328 to Washington 30 November 1950, Washington 3225 to FO of 30th November 1950.
    (Australian Delegation to UN) New York 1084 to Canberra of 28th November 1950 and New York 1088 to Canberra of 29th November 1950, Department of Foreign Affairs (DFA) Masterset Inwards Cablegrams, series 1950, Canberra.

13. Memo of conversation Rusk/Franks, 29th November 1950, FRUS Vol VII op cit, p 1252. DEFE 11/204, Washington 3208 to FO 29th November 1950.

14. DEFE 11/204, BJSM Washington AWT(Tedder) 76 to MOD (COS) 290100 November 1950.

15. Ibid, New York 1894 to FO 29th November 1950, Washington 3219 and 3232 of 30th November 1950.

16. FRUS Vol VII, op cit, pp 1261-2.

17. See Professor Margaret M Gowing, *Independence and Deterrence, Britain and Atomic Energy, 1945-52,* Vol 1 (London, 1974), Chapter 6.

18. See Roger Dingman, *Atomic Diplomacy During the Korean War*, essay in *International Security,* Winter 1988/9, Vol 13, No 3 (Harvard/MIT, 1988). Although some of the British records are not wholly in accord with Mr Dingman's American sources, they do not detract from the main thrust of this essay. Shinwell, conversation with author. CAB 128/18, Cabinet 44 (50), Minutes of 10th July 1950. Author took part in this guarding event.

19. See Dingman, op cit, re Guam.

20. FRUS Vol VII, op cit, p 1262, Acheson, op cit, p 85.

21. UN Documents S/PV530 & S/1757, S/1921, S/1894.

22. DEFE 11/204, New Delhi 3372 to CRO 30th November 1950.

23. CAB 128/18, Cabinet 80 (50), Minutes of 30th November 1950. NB, these are dated 1st December and thus refer to 30th November as 'yesterday'. Shinwell,

conversation with author. For Prime Minister's announcement, see Hansard, 30th November 1950, cols 1442–48.

24. FRUS Vol VII op cit, the *Chargé* in the UK to SofS 3195 of 30th November 1950.

25. See also CAB 21/1783. DEFE 5/21, COS(50) 191st Meeting of 1st December 1950.

26. See *US News & World Report,* 1st December 1950.

27. For the record of the meetings, see FO800/465 (FR/250/23 and 24).

28. DEFE 11/205, 1stSL manuscript minute of 2nd December 1950.

29. Signal CINCFE C 50105 to Dept of Army for JCS 30th November 1950, Signal JCS C 97772 to CINCFE 1st December 1950 and Signal CINCUNC 50332 to Dept Army for JCS 3rd December 1950, (USNARS, Suitland).

30. FRUS Vol VII op cit, Memo of Pentagon Meeting, 3rd December 1950 and Report of conversation of Secretary of State with staff, 3rd December 1950. Minute, General Bradley to Defense Secretary of 4th December 1950. Acheson, op cit, Chapter IV.

31. CAB 21/1783, The PM's visit to Washington cit, New York and Ottawa and US documents on same subject 795.00/12-450, USNARS, Washington.

32. Ibid.

33. Ibid. See also Truman, op cit, p 425, DEFE 11/205, BJSM Washington FMS1 to MOD 050159 December 1950.

34. FRUS Vol VII op cit, Memo of conversation, Secretary of State/Franks *et al*, 4th December 1950. DEFE 11/205, Washington 3282 to FO 4th December 1950.

35. FRUS Vol VII op cit, New York 369 to Secretary of State 4th December 1950. DEFE 11/205, New York 1933 to FO of 4th December 1950.

36. FRUS Vol VII op cit, Memo of conversation, Secretary of State/Franks, Rt Hon K Younger etc, of 5th December 1950.

37. CAB 21/1783. 795.00/12-550, USNARS, Washington. PM's visit to Washington cit DEFE 11/205, Washington 3296 to FO 6th December 1950. Truman, op cit, pp 426.

38. Truman diaries, entry of 5th December 1950, USNARS, Washington.

39. DEFE 11/205 New York 1947 to FO 5th December 1950.

40. CAB 21/1783, PM's visit to Washington cit (date in these minutes is erroneous). FRUS Vol VII, Memo on meeting in British Embassy, evening 6th December 1950. Truman, op cit, p 434. Acheson, op cit, Chapter IV.

41. FRUS Vol VII op cit, Memo—excerpt from meeting between President and Prime Minister in the Cabinet Room, 7th December 1950.

42. Acheson, op cit, pp 90–91. (There appears to be a misdating of the event recorded at 41, above). CAB 21/1783, PM's visit to Washington cit FRUS Vol VII op cit, Annex (Memo for Record, by Mr R Gordon Arneson, Special Assistant to the SofS of 16th January 1951).

43. CAB 21/1783. 795.00/12-850, USNARS, Washington. PM's visit to Washington cit.

44. Acheson, op cit, p 91.

45. CAB 21/1783, White Paper, Cmd 8110. PM's visit to Washington cit.

46. See, for example, London 3200 to State Department 1st December 1950, FRUS Vol VII op cit, pp 1296–7.

47. See, for example, Harris, op cit, p 464.

48. Field-Marshal Slim, conversation with author.
49. DEFE 5/21, COS(50) 206th Meeting.

45. 2 Lt M N S McCord, RUR, checking suspicious refugees at a Battle Patrol road-block during the withdrawal, December 1950. (Brigadier M N S McCord)

46. HQ 27 Brigade, Uijongbu, December 1950. (Lt Col H R Jeffes)

47. RFA *Wave Laird* oiling HMS *Theseus*, January 1951. Due to high seas, the pipe line broke just after this picture was taken. (Douglas House Esq)

48. HMS *Theseus* in the typhoon, November 1950. (Douglas House Esq)

49.   Chinnamp'o under attack after enemy reoccupation. (Douglas House Esq)

50.   The same. (Douglas House Esq)

51.   On the flight deck of HMS *Theseus*, Christmas Day, 1950.
      (Douglas House Esq)

52.   The same, January 1951. (Douglas House Esq)

53. Sea Fury landing on HMS *Theseus*. The one that got home and (53a) the Firefly that didn't, October/November 1950. (Douglas House Esq)

54.   1 RUR Battalion Headquarters in battle positions,
      3rd January 1951. (Brigadier M N S McCord)

55.   Men of 1 NF moving up to battle positions, 3rd January 1951.
      (Imperial War Museum)

56. The Han river bridge demolished by 55 Field Squadron, RE, January 1951. (Maj Gen A E Younger)

57. Refugees crossing the Han river ice, January 1950, in 27 Brigade area. (Lt Col H R Jeffes)

58.   Refugees on the road south of Seoul, January 1950. (Lt Col H R Jeffes)

59.   Centurion tank of the 8th Hussars covers the withdrawal towards Suwon,
      January 1951. Its gun is pointing rearwards towards the enemy.
      (Lt Col H R Jeffes)

CHAPTER 16

Square One and a Half

During that period of high spirits when operations in Korea seemed to be in a final, victorious phase, when General Walker was asking that ammunition deliveries to his Army should be cut back, and General MacArthur was selecting forces for disposal to other theatres, the United States and Commonwealth navies thinned out their forces. The US carriers *Valley Forge* and *Boxer,* for example, departed for the United States,[1] *Theseus* (Captain A S Bolt, DSO DSC RN)—which had replaced *Triumph* in October—for Hong Kong. The contingent from the Royal Canadian Navy was under warning to return to home waters. Among the last to draw back, Admiral Andrewes sailed with a part of his force to Hong Kong on 26th November, expecting to be absent for rest and training for several weeks. Some of the original squadron had been engaged in operations continuously since late June and looked forward to leave as they arrived in the colony on 28th November. Yet, the news from Korea was disquieting as they came ashore. The admiral ordered certain measures in case they were called back at short notice. *Theseus,* engaged in local training, re-embarked her aircraft from Kai Tak airfield. All ranks, together with those in *Kenya* and *Constance* (Commander A G L Seale DSC RN), were ordered to remain in Hong Kong and to declare an address for contact.

At a luncheon party given by the French ambassador in Tokyo on 29th November for the officers of *La Grandière,** Admiral Joy took aside the British naval *attaché* to say that he was thinking of asking Admiral Andrewes and the carrier group to return immediately. Commander Gray was thus able to send a warning to Hong Kong and Singapore before a formal request was signalled by COMNAVFE on the 30th.[2] Captain Lloyd-Davies, deputising for Admiral Andrewes in Japan, was instructed to return all his ships in port to sea.

Admiral Brind was in Hong Kong. He reported to the Admiralty that despite the inevitable disappointment at recall from leave after thirty six hours ashore and an abrupt separation for many with

---

La Grandière was being withdrawn to Indo-China, where Viet Minh forces were advancing across the Chinese frontier on Hanoi.

families in the station, all those concerned loaded and embarked on 1st December 'with good cheer and vigour which greatly pleased me; there was no sign of depression'.[3] The warships put out into the chill force of a north easterly gale.

It was difficult for some of the wives left behind to understand why the Royal Navy was needed so urgently because of the sharp reverse on land in Korea. There had been no sudden appearance of Chinese coastal warships or merchant carriers in support of General P'eng Te-huai's army groups. Vice-Admiral Andrewes* could not, at the moment of sailing, have given precise reasons. These became apparent, however, when he arrived in *Theseus* at Sasebo on 4th December, delayed by the stormy passage.

Rear-Admiral A E Smith, commander of Task Force 95, told him that there were two immediate naval requirements. On the east coast, preparations had to be made to evacuate the 1st Marine Division, and probably the entire X Corps.[4] More pressing, General MacArthur's staff in Tokyo expected that a considerable number of United Nations troops were likely to be cut off to the west of the River Taedong as the Chinese took P'yongyang. Their only escape route lay through Chinnamp'o. In any case, considerable stocks of fuel, other supplies and stores, together with the port operating force, had to be evacuated from the city. On the west coast also, preparations had to be made for evacuation of Inch'on, the intermediate supply base of the Eighth Army. These operations were to be commanded by Admiral Doyle, whose amphibious craft would necessarily be the prime movers.† Admiral Andrewes' Commonwealth force was to continue its responsibilities but was also to assist the evacuation operations as required. *Theseus* would provide air cover overall. The Royal Air Force Sunderlands would increase the level of their patrolling.

Ships were already hastening to these tasks in an atmosphere of crisis. The apprehensions in Tokyo and Washington of attack by Russian and Chinese aircraft have already been noted, and these had been transmitted to subordinate commanders—the Joint Chiefs sent out a general warning to all United States forces on 6th December that the Soviet Union might initiate war at short notice.[5] Naval commanders raised the level of anti-submarine precautions. The port of Chinnamp'o lies twenty four miles upstream from the sprawling shoals of the Taedong estuary. The navigation channels, obstructed under the supervision of Russian officers in September with moored inertial and magnetic mines, had been swept by a UN force under American command augmented by Japanese

*He was promoted to vice-admiral on 1st December 1950.
†The amphibious force for the west coast was put under Rear-Admiral Lyman A Thackerey, USN, commander of Amphibious Group 3.

minesweepers.* Invaluable help in identification of mine locations was given by North Koreans who had taken part in the laying operation. Even so, it was difficult work, made the more hazardous by the shifting sand and mudbanks, and a current which often exceeded five knots. A channel was opened to Tank Landing Ships (LSTs) on 9th November. By the 20th, clearance of a deep channel enabled Lieutenant-Commander G V Gladstone DSC RAN† to pilot the US Hospital Ship *Repose* upstream, though the latter had less than a foot of water under her keel on several occasions during the journey. The intrepid pilot was not sorry to be instructed to stay with his charge overnight; the consequence was a rest aboard *Repose* in the company of fifty American nurses. By this date, port operations were fast expanding to support the final drive of Eighth Army to the north.

One week later, as the Eighth Army began to stream southward, this valuable advanced base was becoming a liability. By early December it was in jeopardy. The nearest naval force was Captain J V Brock's Task Element 95.12 on coastal blockade. It comprised his three Canadian destroyers and the Australian *Bataan* and *Warramunga*. On 3rd December *Cayuga* and *Bataan* were covering the mouth of the Yalu, *Athabaskan* and *Warramunga* were to the south. *Sioux* was escorting the Royal Fleet Auxiliary tanker, *Wave Laird,* to refuel the force at a rendezvous south of Ch'o-do island. Early on the morning of the 4th, a signal reached Captain Brock to assist United States amphibious forces *en route* to Chinnamp'o to withdraw forces and stocks. His prime task was to defend these transports. 'Be prepared to act in fire support of Eighth Army, entering Chinnamp'o River [sic] swept channel as necessary' [8].

Captain Brock at once hastened the arrangements to refuel his ships. The attachment of the US destroyer *Forrest B Royal* to his Task Element made it possible to maintain two destroyers on patrol while covering with the other four the transports as they passed from the south into the Taedong estuary. The transport group, under Captain S G Kelly, USN, comprised three attack transports (APAs), two attack cargo ships (AKAs) and a number of LSTs.‡ A further message, directly from Admiral Smith, advised Captain

---

*Before withdrawing to Hong Kong in late November *Theseus* provided air cover for the minesweeping and, initially, a base for United States helicopters. Twelve Japanese minesweepers, drawn from the body engaged in sweeping mines laid round Japan during the second world war, augmented the force.[6]

†Executive officer of *Warramunga,* one of several RAN and RN parties assisting the minesweeping operation, he was in charge of the officers concerned with pilotage—known locally as 'the Chinnamp'o Pilots' Association.[7]

‡These armed vessels were classified as warships and, as such, manned by members of the United States Navy. Captain Kelly, aboard the APA USS *Bayfield,* was also to command the port evacuation.

Brock that, as the Chinnamp'o area was endangered by enemy land forces, he should move up river with all his task group to assist in the defence of the port. *Ceylon* would be joining the destroyers on the 5th to add weight to the force.[9]

Captain Brock's inclination was to arrive in the estuary on the morning of the 5th so as to make the passage upstream in daylight. In this, he was strongly supported by the other ships' captains at a conference aboard *Cayuga* that afternoon; the swept channel was marked by unlit buoys, some of which had certainly been dragged from their original anchorage by tide and current. There were recurrent snowstorms—the gale had not yet blown itself out—and ice floes discharged from the Yalu river were drifting southwards. He decided to signal Captain Kelly for information as to the local situation, but while awaiting an answer received a message from the USS *Foss,* supplying power to Chinnamp'o: 'We are uncovered. Take necessary action immediately'.[10] Although the wording amused Task Element 95.12, it prepared its members for the answer from Captain Kelly which arrived at 2200: support was required at once; 'the local situation may reach emergency basis Tuesday [5th December] forenoon'.[11] Captain Brock gave orders for a night passage up the river.

As they entered the estuary, the tide was almost out. The advantage of a reduced current was outweighed by the low water level in the channel. Feeling a way through the darkness, each ship was on course for the first turning point, comforted by the presence there, as at each succeeding turn, of a minesweeper or ROK patrol vessel.

Warramunga, nearest to the estuary at the outset, was first to turn in, taking the Short Cut approach. At 2315, she ran aground in the centre of the channel where the chart indicated ten feet of water below the keel. The engines were run at full speed astern but the hull did not move. Commander Becher decided to wait until the rising tide refloated his ship.

Meantime, the remaining five destroyers were following in order *Cayuga, Athabaskan, Bataan, Forrest B. Royal, Sioux,* at intervals of half a mile,

In *Cayuga* the navigator, Lieutenant A L Collier, RCN , dashed back and forth between the radar screen and the chart table, rapidly and accurately plotting his 'fixes', and relaying his information to Captain Brock on the bridge and to the destroyers astern. During the four hour passage Lieutenant Collier made one hundred and thirty-two fixes, most of them by radar, showing the position of the ship in relation to the channel marker buoys and nearby landmarks. . . .[12]

Those astern were also making their own calculations. Though greatly helped by *Cayuga's* guidance, they could not follow precisely in her wake. Shortly after midnight, *Sioux* went aground in mid-channel, managed to draw off, but fouled her starboard propellor on the mooring wire of a drifting buoy. Commander Taylor turned back in order to free the propellor shaft in deep water. At 0330 on 5th December, the remaining four warships reached Chinnamp'o.

They half expected to find the port under fire, but it was peaceful. Seamen and soldiers were working under lights and a large crowd of civilians seemed to be gathering quietly along the edge of a wharf. Vexed that he had hazarded his destroyers on what appeared to be a false premise, Captain Brock was given a message from *Bayfield*: Captain Kelly asked him to a conference on board over breakfast at 0800.

When they met, the news was both good and bad. Army reports of Chinese advancing down the Taedong river—which had occasioned the *Foss*'s alarm and Captain Kelly's anxiety the previous day—were now known to be false, a product of battlefield qualms. However, the Army base commander had been warned that the field forces were withdrawing from P'yongyang that day and the line would retire to the south of Chinnamp'o by the evening of the 6th. One road remained open for twelve hours; selected road transport was moving back that afternoon. But the railway line, which ran north east to P'yongyang, was already cut; the rolling stock in the sidings, oil storage tanks and other facilities which there was no time to dismantle, would have to be destroyed where they stood. As much of the food, fuel, ammunition, clothing, equipment, tools, plant, vehicles and spare parts as they could outload were being put into the AKAs and LSTs. The Army and Navy shore parties, ROK forces including wounded, police and prisoners, totalling almost eight thousand, would be taken out in the transports. A large number of North Korean civilians, perhaps 50,000, mostly in families, were also anxious to be taken off.

Though responsible for all activities in the port evacuation, Captain Kelly proposed that he should attend to the embarkation and movement of the base while Captain Brock took entire charge of the defence. This plan was signalled to *Ceylon*.

Captain Lloyd-Davies had arrived off the Taedong estuary at 0900 on the 5th in *Ceylon* to take command of the Commonwealth ships in the evacuation operation. He planned to sail directly up to Chinnamp'o but fell in with *Warramunga*. Commander Becher told him of the difficulties of the channel and said that he had himself stood off after meeting *Sioux*, crawling downstream with eighteen inches of water under her keel on a falling tide. On this account and the news from *Cayuga* that there was no immediate threat to the port, Captain Lloyd-Davies sensibly decided to remain in deep water where, with the two destroyers, he would be able to cover Captain Kelly's ships as they emerged into the Yellow Sea.*

During the morning at Chinnamp'o, it had been agreed that the APAs, AKAs, and LSTs should sail in sufficient time to pass through the swept channel in daylight. One of the consequences was that the Army engineers would have insufficient time to demolish the standing installations and rolling stock. Captain Brock undertook to destroy them by bombardment.

Piecemeal, ships departed. Captain Kelly sailed in *Bayfield* at 1430. It soon became clear that time and tides were running against the destroyers; the last APA did not complete loading until 1700. Captain Brock decided that he would bombard the port as arranged and then withdraw for the night to an anchorage five miles downstream; he did not fancy another night passage through the estuary. *Athabaskan*, sent to secure the anchorage, became also the force watchman. Commander Welland put out his motor cutters to screen the crews and passengers in the multitude of junks and other local craft carrying North Koreans who wished to leave with the United Nations forces.

The bombardment began at 1735 on 5th December. Targets had been identified during the day with the Army base commander, great care being taken to avoid firing on housing areas. The 5-inch guns of *Forrest Royal* demolished the rolling stock and seriously damaged the railway marshalling yards and station. *Bataan* and *Cayuga* shot with their 4.7- and 4-inch guns respectively at the oil storage tanks, supply dumps, and dock installations, adding their fire to the railway yards. The targets areas were soon in flames which were to burn for many hours. The remaining small craft on the beaches were also to have been shelled but Captain Brock decided to leave them intact. Numerous refugees had pulled back into shelter when the firing started but were clearly hoping to escape by boat as soon as it seemed safe to re-emerge. After seventy minutes, the bombardment ended, though explosions continued for some time ashore, principally from the oil storage site. Against a background of flames, the three destroyers with the ROK minesweepers, YMS *301, 302*, and *306*, withdrew to join *Athabaskan*.

Next morning, the APA *Bexar* and several LSTs were discovered to be aground down the river, though all refloated on the rising tide. *Athabaskan* led the procession towards the estuary and open sea. *Cayuga* covered the rear.

'Mission successfully completed,' Captain Brock reported modestly through a snowstorm.[13]

Ceylon's divers were able to cut away the mooring wire on *Sioux's* propellor shaft during the day.

The whole force of Commonwealth and American ships moved south towards Inch'on during the remainder of the day. There they found that the port and base was being run down; Army engineers were preparing essential facilities for demolition. Captain P W Brock, RN, on *Kenya* was preparing a naval gunfire plan with Rear-Admiral Thackrey for the seaward evacuation. Admiral Andrewes called a conference of his captains at which he gave instructions for the foreseeable future:

There were four requirements.

1. *Coastal Blockade.* To be maintained by Task Element 95.12 under Captain Lloyd-Davies with *Ceylon, Bataan, Cayuga,* and *Sioux.*

2. *Anti-aircraft defence and naval gunfire support of Inch'on.* To be provided by Task Element 95.14 under Captain Brock RN with *Kenya, Athabaskan, Warramunga,* and H Neth MS *Evertsen.*

3. *Escort and anti-submarine cover.* To be provided by the frigates of Task Element 95.13 under Captain W L M Brown, OBE DSC RN on *Cardigan Bay,* with *Morecambe Bay* (Commander C C B Mackenzie RN), and HMNZSs *Rotoiti* (Commander B E Turner, DSC RNZN), and *Tutira.*

4. *Air cover for the Task Group and armed reconnaissance north of the bomb line.** To be provided by Task Element 95.11 under Captain Bolt with *Theseus,* carrying Admiral Andrewes' flag as Commander, Task Group 95.1 , and the destroyers *Concord, Constance,* and *Cossack* as escorts.[14]

The problems of *Triumph* during her tour of operations have been recorded. *Theseus,* a light fleet carrier of the same class, had been modified structurally and was better equipped for operations with her twenty one Sea Furies XI in place of the *Triumph's* Seafires, and twelve of the more modern Fireflies V.† Even so, she was overcrowded, her aircraft ammunition stowage was limited, and the aircraft lacked multi-channel Very High Frequency (VHF) radios in common use among the United States Navy, Marine and Air Force aircraft and controllers. Like *Triumph, Theseus* had only one catapult instead of the desired two, and this was limited to one thousand shots. Individual ingenuity and improvisation overcame these and other difficulties.

Theseus was launching an average of forty sorties a day—without an accident—between 7th and 15th December and only a little less

---

*The 'bomb line' was drawn daily on maps and charts to distinguish enemy from friendly territory. Coordinates tended to be well beyond the line of friendly land forces.
†17 Carrier Air Group (Lieutenant-Commander F Stovin-Bradford, DSC RN) comprised 807 Squadron—Sea Furies—(Lieutenant-Commander M P G Smith, DSC RN) and 810 Squadron—Fireflies—(Lieutenant-Commander K S Pattison, DSC RN).

in a second period on station during the month despite intermittent gales. Reconnaissance and combat air patrols were flown over the battlefield. Offensive sorties were made against enemy positions and troops, rail and road transport, bridges and tunnels for seventeen days through Christmas and Boxing Day. Not all these were without incident. There were alarms from the Fifth Air Force that an amphibious fleet was approaching from China but this turned out to be fishing boats. On 14th December, MiG-15s attacked a naval helicopter on the Ongjin peninsula which, in error, the Fury patrol had briefly uncovered. On the 24th, the engine of Lieutenant D W P Kelly's Sea Fury failed just after take off on 24th December—he was rescued by the *Sioux* four miles ahead of the carrier, numbed but otherwise unhurt after thirteen minutes in the icy water.[15]

All ships' companies operating in these conditions became tired and, between occasional incidents, bored; even the aircrew became weary if they were not flying. Admiral Andrewes made the following signal to his command on 12th December:

1. As China has intervened in the Korean War, it seems unlikely that she will limit her efforts to land operations, but will probably strike at naval forces by aircraft and submarine.

2. This has become more likely now that the front has moved south.

3. Any extension of the war could be helped by Russia with or without open intervention.

4. Commanding officers are to impress on all on board the individual responsibility that each man has to fight against boredom and over-confidence and keep ships in a high state of alertness.

5. This will be a hard task for everyone, but our strength and security depend upon it.[16]*

The brief appearance of two MiG-15s almost on the 38th Parallel was not the opening of the major enemy air offensive so widely expected in the UN high command. Daily aerial battles were indeed taking place, but they were almost exclusively confined to the northernmost limits of western and central Korea against aircraft launched from airfields in North East China. The arrival of a squadron of F86A Sabres and another of F-84E Thunderjets from the United States in November provided the Fifth Air Force with the means of meeting the MiG-15s on more or less even terms in technology, with an advantage to the American pilots in

---

*This order was commended by Admiral Joy a few days later as a guideline for American warships.

experience and skill. But Admiral Andrewes could not ignore the fact that his ships had thrice been hazarded by enemy aircraft, though briefly, in hit and run raids. He ordered *Ceylon,* and her successors in the blockade force, to keep as close as possible to *Theseus.*

After a month of intensive operations, the carrier was in need of a break for maintenance. No relief was available, however, during the evacuation of the east coast enclave through Wonsan and Hungnam, a huge task—105,000 US and ROK servicemen, 91,000 refugees, 17,500 vehicles, and 350,000 tons of stores and equipment—which was not completed until Christmas Eve.* Seven United States aircraft carriers supported the operation and as soon as it was over two, the USS *Badoeng Strait* and *Sicily,* escorted by six destroyers, moved to relieve *Theseus.* On 31st December, the ship's company was able to enjoy a delayed Christmas holiday.

·   ·   ·   ·   ·

In the second half of December, the Eighth Army settled into a line roughly following the 38th Parallel from the south bank of the Imjin river in the west, then eastward through Yongp'yong, Hwach'on, and Inje to Yangyang on the east coast. There was no tactical merit in this stretch of territory but strategically, certainly politically, the parallel had significance. Every yard conceded thereafter involved abandonment of South Korean territory, an outcome foreseen by President Truman and Mr Attlee at their meetings in Washington. The question remained open whether, as they were forced back through a series of lines, they could finally hold a perimeter covering Pusan. Reinforced by X Corps, General Walker believed that he would be able to do so. If not, he had Pusan as an escape hatch.[17]

In mid-December, however, there was no reason to withdraw from the parallel. There were daily reports of clashes from divisions, some alarming, but they lacked substance. The enemy in every case was North Korean. The guerrilla bands, once more in direct contact with their high command, had been instructed to operate as widely and intensively as means and opportunity permitted pending the arrival of the main forces. And the main forces were advancing slowly because General P'eng was content to let the United Nations command concede ground without a struggle, and determined, when the Eighth Army made a stand, to attack only with a sufficiency of supply and support. As previously, there were

---

*X Corps was not forced out from this enclave but withdrawn as a matter of strategic policy.

limits to the pace of his movement, principally vulnerability to air attack in daylight. American and Australian aircrew, and pilots from *Theseus*, were quick to strike any units foolhardy enough to march in the open between dawn and dusk. Men, trucks, and railway trains were hunted in these hours except when the weather closed flying visibility.

On medical advice, Brigadier Coad passed command of his brigade to Lieutenant-Colonel Man from 10th to 18th December. He had become exhausted, partly due to lack of rest, as much to exasperation. He was deeply worried by the practice in IX Corps headquarters of issuing a series of orders and counter orders without regard to the consequences to their subordinates; of being given tasks which were found by his battalions to be pointless or already in hand by others. He was worried by the defeatism among the corps staff. 'Morale at the Headquarters,' he wrote later, 'was . . . appalling. The axis was universally called the escape route and complete evacuation by sea openly talked about'.[18]

In both 27 and 29 Brigade, the lack of enemy pressure was widely discussed, the reasons for the long withdrawal from P'yongyang debated. Brigadier Brodie was on better terms with his commander and headquarters, General Milburn of I Corps, and had the advantage of comprehensive operational and administrative support. Brigadier Coad's needs were partially remedied when the 1st United States Artillery Observation Battalion was allotted permanently to him on 15th December. The unit had converted to 105-mm guns. And the 60th Indian Parachute Field Ambulance also joined the brigade in mid-December. The latter unit, under Lieutenant-Colonel A G Rangaraja, had already made a name for itself in the north. Arriving in P'yongyang as it was about to fall, scouts discovered that all their medical supplies were about to be destroyed. A railway engine was found, filled with water, fired by timber in the absence of coal, and coupled to the rolling stock. The train was then driven south by members of the unit just before the bridge was blown.

Each brigade continued to be the reserve of its parent corps and reconnoitred counter-attack contingencies. Inevitably, they also picked up a series of odd jobs. A standing duty of 27 Brigade was defence of corps headquarters, known as 'The Palace Guard'. Both formations sent detachments to guard sites in the Kimpo peninsula. Minor counter-guerrilla operations were frequent—6 Platoon of 3 RAR distinguished itself in a lone battle on the high peak of Unak-san, thirty miles north east of Uijongbu. During the remainder of December, planning continued for withdrawal through Seoul across the River Han and a number of positions were partially dug to cover bridges or to provide sites for others to occupy in case they were 'pushed back'. Major Younger's 55 Field Squadron, 29 Brigade's field engineers, was progressively drawn in from route maintenance to the preparation for demolition of the Han bridges between Seoul and Yongdongp'o. The aim within the Army was that, with the issue of a codeword, division by division, unit by unit, they would pass back in an ordered manner. Special arrangements were made with the ROK civil police to prevent a last minute rush on to the bridges by refugees. But the planners at Army and Corps levels would not leave the plan as it stood: a series of amendments and addenda were issued which soon eclipsed the original. These activities contributed to the notion that, whatever else the Army would do when the enemy finally caught up, it was not going to make any sort of stand.

Yet such reflections should not convey an impression of British Commonwealth forces dispirited by the burdens of active service. Tasks given at short notice were regarded as part of the soldier's trade. Coping with the intense cold, enjoying simple pleasures—a NAAFI supply line at last reached to 27 Brigade and was never more welcome—giving and taking in the abiding interaction of comradeship, these were the matters which were important to the men in the brigades. To the relief of everyone, Christmas Day was enjoyed without any new operational demands. Church services were held and heavily attended among all units. There were quantities of turkey and plum pudding for dinner at midday with beer that had been carefully sheltered to prevent it from freezing.

By Christmas, the command of the Eighth Army had changed. General Walker set out on the morning of 23rd December to pass to 27 Brigade a Presidential Citation from Syngman Rhee. The brigade was paraded but the general did not arrive. His jeep was run into by a truck attempting to overtake from the opposite direction. Mortally injured, the army commander died in hospital. His successor, from the Army staff in Washington, was Lieutenant-General Matthew B Ridgway.*

He arrived in Tokyo at midnight on Christmas Day and saw General MacArthur on the morning of the 26th. The Commander-in-Chief was at his best, welcoming, reasonable, practical. He made it clear that they should seek to salvage what they could in Korea. As to the means of doing it, 'Form your own opinions. Use your own judgement. I will support you. You have my complete confidence'.[19]

By the 27th, General Ridgway was in post. Over the next few days he spent much time touring the forward area, seeing as many

---

*Ridgway, (later General) Matthew Bunker (1895-1988), was then Deputy Chief of the Army Staff for administration.

members of his command as possible, returning to his headquarters each evening to issue instructions. He had hoped to turn the Eighth Army on to the offensive but rapidly came to see that many of its members lacked the motivation, the spirit, and the leadership that were necessary. To remedy that would take time. At any moment, it appeared that P'eng Te-huai would renew his offensive. His first task, therefore, was to demonstrate to his command competence as a commander in the field.

Immediately, he could only impress upon his formation commanders that he intended to make no withdrawal without a fight; and that he intended to hold Seoul. This latter decision was the product of his inexperience. Yet the two together impressed sufficient of his subordinates that they needed to close up for a battle rather than shake out for another retreat.

That battle was now upon him. General P'eng Te-huai had brought forward twenty four Chinese and four North Korean divisions to open his 'Third Phase Offensive': 237,000 soldiers were to break open the United Nations line at selected points between Munsan-ni in the west to Inje in the east. Behind this force were a further fifteen Chinese and three North Korean divisions, a further 152,000, whose task would be to pass through the broken enemy and complete destruction of the Eighth and ROK Armies. The attack began on 27th December in the ROK Army sector. The 9th ROK Division was broken at Hyon-ni, then the 8th and 3rd in succession. By the 29th, a huge gap had been opened in the eastern sector. To cover the flank of the Eighth Army, General Ridgway ordered the 2nd Division, retraining and re-equipping after its experiences at Kunu-ri, to occupy the area of Wonju.

Elsewhere, Chinese forces engaged in probing attacks over the next few days which grew stronger on the front of the 1st ROK Division in I Corps and its right hand neighbour 6th ROK in IX Corps early in the morning of 31st December.

General Milburn's I Corps had two divisions forward: the 25th on the left, with the Turkish Brigade under command, held the southern bank of the Imjin river from its confluence with the Han at the northern end of the Kimpo peninsula through Munsan-ni to the upper tidal limit; 1st ROK Division continued the defence upstream on a frontage of twenty thousand yards. Two of the ROK regiments were forward, covering prominent loops of the river bank in which lay fords. The third regiment was sited in rear, behind the towering mass of Kamak-san, astride a network of minor roads leading to the MSR in the west, and the Seoul–Uijongbu–Ch'orwon highway in the east.

This latter highway was in General Coulter's IX Corps. 6th ROK Division, on the right of the 1st, blocked it in the area of

Tongduch'on, approximately halfway between Seoul and Ch'or-won. The 24th Division was next in line to the right, covering P'och'on on the main road from Kumwha to Seoul. The western MSR and the two main roads running south to the capital through Uijongbu were regarded as the principal avenues of the coming Chinese attack on the Eighth Army, a fair judgement but one more natural to a western eye, accustomed to appraising the thrust lines of mobile armoured forces, than a general of the People's Liberation Army. The intermediate routes were better suited to the Chinese—and no less to the North Koreans, attacking in the mountainous east, whose armoured striking force had been largely destroyed in the summer and autumn.

After Christmas, the battalions of 29 Brigade had been sent forward to dig reserve positions for 1st ROK Division in case the line should be forced back in the offensive widely expected. General Milburn hoped to be able to withdraw the ROKs before they were broken up and relocate them in this site fifteen miles behind their Imjin positions. This would enable him to maintain a line roughly level with Uijongbu, for which IX Corps would surely make a stand. But 1st ROK Division had not yet recovered from its losses in the north, particularly of its middle ranking officers and senior non-commissioned officers. It had many new recruits, numerous unfledged leaders. When the Chinese attacked across the Imjin, the two forward regiments scattered to the south after a brief exchange of fire. At first light, a very large number of Chinese were seen from the air to be closing on the reserve regiment and divisional gun line.

These events took place during the night of 31st December into the first hour of daylight on 1st January 1951. General Milburn at first believed that he had lost only the forward edge of the ROK area and decided to counter-attack with his reserve, 29 Brigade. The Brigade was alerted at 0545 on New Year's Day[20] and ordered to move up the MSR and then by a branch track to Tongo-ri, the headquarters of 1st ROK Division. Brigadier Brodie went at once to see General Milburn and then drove to Tongo-ri to confer with his commanding officers. Colonel Burke, the deputy brigade commander, followed closely with unit reconnaissance parties. The aim was to identify enemy movements and counter-attack to restore the line as quickly as possible.

Events had moved too swiftly, however: the ROK divisional headquarters was pulling back in haste. Air reports indicated that the enemy were already south of Tongo-ri. A rapid change of plan was needed.

The brigade vehicle column was stopped on the MSR between 11 and half past. The trucks pulled off on to the ice bound paddy.

Some units wisely decided to eat their midday meal while waiting, and were glad of hot food in the biting wind. Commanding officers returned early in the afternoon with orders to move to the area the brigade had been preparing for 1st ROK Division. It was fortunate that the access tracks, north east through Koyang and Sindun-ni respectively, had been worked on by the engineers of 55 Squadron for several days. Both were still very narrow but just adequate for light wheels and tracks. The three battalions each settled into defences designed for thrice their number. The Fifth Fusiliers lacking W Company, which had been kept in rear to guard the Han crossings, was the right forward and most northerly unit in defence. The RUR with Cooper Force* were located to the west. The Glosters were in rear of each. 45 Field Regiment, recalled from guarding bridges, deployed its three gun batteries six thousand yards to the south, within the protection of the Thai Infantry Battalion.† The 4.2 mortar troops of 170 Battery dispersed to cover the battalions to which they were affiliated. Infantry 3-inch mortar and machine-gun platoons were laid out to cover approaches to the rifle companies. In the remaining hours of daylight, there was no sign of the enemy—air attacks had halted and dispersed them—but elements of 1st ROK Division drifted into the brigade area. Problems of language, exhaustion and anxiety made them unresponsive to requests, followed by orders, to adjust to defence requirements.

Returning to his headquarters at midday, Brigadier Brodie was prompted by the experiences of December and a talk with General Ridgway to write the following, which reached his command late in the afternoon:

ORDER OF THE DAY

At last after weeks of frustration we have nothing between us and the Chinese. I have no intention that this Brigade Group will retire before the enemy unless ordered by higher authority in order to conform with general movement. If you meet him you are to knock hell out of him with everything you have got. You are only to give ground on my orders.

T Brodie
Brigadier[21]

---

*Cooper Force, an *ad hoc* unit under Captain D Astley-Cooper of the 8th Hussars, was formed from the regimental reconnaissance troop and the six Cromwell tanks provided for artillery observation posts. The Centurions of the 8th Hussars were believed to be too heavy for the narrow tracks and local bridges.

†The Thai contingent, a reinforced infantry battalion, was under command of 29 Brigade on 1st January 1951.

The night of 1st January was quiet. The battalions passed the daylight hours of the 2nd improving their defences and patrolling. Contact was made by the RUR with E Coy of the American 35th Regiment, located in Koyang. This was part of the 25th Division, which had been moved back from the Imjin. Koyang was a mile and a half on the map from the nearest companies of the Rifles, B and D, but although these two were on a ridge, an intermediate feature screened the village. A patrol from the Fusiliers made contact with an American company of the 24th Division to the east. 'OC Z Company reported that the morale of this company was very low and that he was under the impression that they would not stay if attacked.'[22]

Concerned by the width of his front, in particular the distance between the Fifth Fusiliers and the 24th Division, Brigadier Brodie asked I Corps for units of 1st ROK Division as they reformed in rear. Two battalions came forward at 2115 and were put into unoccupied villages, in which they were advised to remain during the night so as to avoid being shot at in error. It seemed very unlikely that another night would pass without a battle.

Throughout the night of the 1st January and during part of the 2nd, elements of the Chinese break-in-force had infiltrated south and east, following the tracks towards Uijongbu. Two divisions from the reserve of the assault armies were then passed across the Imjin, the 116 Division to attack along the western MSR, the 149 to cut it near the edge of Seoul. The inner flanks of these divisions converged close to Koyang.

At 0315 on 3rd January, B and C Companies of the Rifles heard firing in the direction of Koyang. A little later, it was learned that the American company there had been driven out. Other positions of its parent, 35th Regiment, were under attack. Major Blake, commanding the battalion in the absence of Colonel Carson, decided to stand to arms. Almost at once, Major Joe Ryan's company, A, north east in the defences, saw shadowy figures close to its wire. Flares were fired and the Vickers section dispersed what appeared to be a group in civilian clothes. On the western side of the valley, B Company fired on a similar target.

Towards dawn, a patrol under Second Lieutenant Robin Bruford-Davies set off to see whether the enemy had occupied the ridge overlooking Koyang. Bursts of fire, explosions and shouting along the patrol's route suggested that it was fighting, but no one returned to the company position and radio contact with this small party was lost. Ideas of an investigation had to be set aside because, shortly after these ominous noises, B and D Companies were approached by men with white flags crying 'South Koreans—we surrender!', a ruse rapidly negated by bugle accompaniments and

387

bursts of fire. Numerous Chinese then rose from the scrub and broke into part of each company's position. B Company was pushed off the high point of the western ridge, Point 195, but held a spur to the north east. A Chinese bugle sounded a victory blast from the height.

The 25-pounders of 45 Field, the 4.2 mortars of 170 Battery and the battalion's 3-inch mortars now fired on to the ridge, augmented by the tank guns of Cooper Force. The two companies gave no more ground. Four F-80s arrived to add napalm, rockets and cannon fire to the battle, striking enemy coming forward to join the battle from the west and north.

Major Blake decided to sweep the ridge. He stretched C Company to take over the north eastern locality and withdrew A for the counter-attack. The Battle Patrol, ninety strong, was sent off to secure a start line. At 1145, its commander, Captain G W H Cocksedge, reported that the supporting fire had destroyed or dispersed most of the enemy. B Company was able to recover Point 195 and, combing the hillside with D, discovered almost fifty Chinese bodies. Major Blake sent a reassuring signal to Brigade Headquarters, 'Positions restored'.[23]

Behind the Royal Ulster Rifles, the Glosters' area remained quiet. A steep ridge of mountains separated the two battalions which witheld the noise of the Rifles' battle. But at 0610, an hour before dawn, small arms and mortar fire were heard to the north, and the rear link radio operator reported that the Fifth Fusiliers were informing brigade headquarters of an attack.

One hour before this, a company of Chinese had entered the village lying in the valley between the hills occupied by Y and X Companies, killing the signallers manning the telephone exchange in the schoolhouse, capturing others. This surprise action, accomplished with very little firing, was not heard by the remainder of the battalion. At 0610, another, larger, party attacked Major R Pratt's X Company, and the battalion stood to arms.

X Company, and the Support Company base close by, stood firm. The enemy drew off. The signals officer came up the track towards the village to see why the telephone exchange was not answering and found several of his men with the Support Company base just below X Company. They reported that the roadblock and exchange had been overrun. Inexplicably, there was a brief burst of firing suddenly from within the village at that moment. Just before dawn, Z, the right hand company under Major John Wynn was attacked and, half an hour later, Major R Leith-McGregor commanding Y, on the left, said that there was firing in the valley immediately behind him—a Chinese detachment had captured Y Company's little administrative base in the village immediately below.

From the Glosters, the track ran north through the Fifth Fusiliers headquarters and came to a T junction below X Company. The top of the T ran west behind Y, east in front of X and Z Companies. While it was still dark, the Chinese placed two machine-guns in the village below Y Company. Facing east, they could cover the T junction, village, and road block they had captured earlier but could not be seen by any of the Fusiliers' positions. These weapons prevented any attempt to get to the telephone exchange and roadblock.

As further attacks were made, the Chinese also attempted to capture Y Company. Supported by 45 Field Regiment's 25-pounders and the two sets of mortars, all companies threw back their assailants. An air strike by F-80s destroyed a mortar position identified by Y Company. Between attacks, their positions were sniped from the scrub. Counter-sniping reduced the effect of this.

Colonel Foster's dilemma was that he could hold firm during daylight but had no means of clearing the enemy away. He asked Brigadier Brodie to send him some tanks. At brigade headquarters, Major Trevor, the brigade major, had been seeking the relief of W Company, guarding three of the Han bridges. This was agreed as Colonel Foster requested tanks. The brigadier said that a troop of C Squadron, 7th Tanks, and W Company, should be moved forward as swiftly as possible.

The four Churchill tanks reached the Fusilier's headquarters at 1125. W Company arrived at 1430. Everything was ready: a fire plan had been prepared using the whole of 45 Field's guns—the RUR battle was over—the 4.2- and 3-inch mortars. With the infantry on the left of the track, the tanks on the right, the clearing operation began just before 1445. Major Charles Mitchell, commanding W Company, wearing a woollen hat sent by his mother and smoking a large cigar, followed closely behind his two leading platoons.

There was a brief check as the two platoons closed on the track junction. Chinese machine-gun and mortar fire came from the western arm. Fragments of shrapnel from a distant burst hit Lieutenant S W Cooper lightly in the face, and he reflected momentarily that this might be his first and last action. The tanks, obliged at this point to follow the track, moved ahead and began to fire their guns into the enemy positions to the west and on the slopes below Y Company. Almost at once, the enemy resistance began to crumble. Some drew off westward, others to the north, pursued by fire. The tanks drove on past X to stop below Z Company. By 1630, the battalion area had been cleared for the loss of one member of W Company wounded. Two hundred Chinese dead were found in the villages and on the hill slopes. The Fifth Fusiliers were able to bring out their dead and wounded from the morning actions.

By this time, the Army battle position had become serious. 27 Brigade had been ordered to abandon Uijongbu. The 24th and 1st Cavalry Divisions were covering the outskirts of Seoul. Kapyong-ni had been lost across the arc to the east. Having reluctantly agreed to fall back into a close defence of Seoul after the first day of fighting, General Ridgway recognised on 3rd January that he would have to withdraw completely behind the Han.

29 Brigade was ordered to withdraw in company with 25th Infantry Division but attempts to coordinate timings closely were impracticable. The division was moving to its own timetable and had lost touch with many of its units. As a consequence, the MSR above the British access points was open to the enemy. Brigadier Brodie decided to withdraw the Fifth Fusiliers at once. The Glosters and Rifles were to follow.

The Fusiliers' war diary indicates the demand and response for a quick retirement:

1710. Brigade commander informed [battalion] second-in-command that withdrawal would start almost immediately.
1730. Brigade major to adjutant. Aim to have battalion clear of positions by 1800 hours. Companies to march to embussing point on MSR (approx. 11 miles). RASC transport would lift battalion to Suwon. I RUR withdrawing at 1830 hours. . . .

By 2355, the whole battalion had reached the RASC trucks and departed for Seoul and the Han crossings. The enemy had been seen occupying their positions as they moved down the track, though there had been no engagement in the gloom. The track below Z Company had been cut as they prepared to move and Major Wynn had moved across country to avoid a late encounter.

The Glosters began their march at 1915, as soon as the Fifth Fusiliers had cleared their position. They destroyed three carriers which had broken down in the last hour but were otherwise complete. The adjutant followed the column and saw it through the brigade check point in the northern outskirts of Seoul. There, by a blazing fire, at 0230 on the 4th, he encountered Captain Hugh Hamill, adjutant of the Royal Ulster Rifles. The latter had been expecting his battalion for some time and was concerned that they had been delayed.[24]

The Rifles did not actually receive the order to move until 1830. All its arrangements had therefore to be made in darkness. By 2100 hours, a strong standing patrol under Second Lieutenant Mervyn McCord was established one thousand yards north of the battalion headquarters village of Chaegunghyon. He was to remain in position until 2230, then to rejoin the departing battalion. The first company to move was B Company and this reached the start point at 2130, as ordered. It was followed by the headquarters and A echelon vehicles, then C, D and A. The 3-inch mortars fired their remaining ammunition into likely enemy areas and were loaded into their tracked carriers. The 4.2 troop joined the column. It was another cold, clear night with a keen wind. Snow on the paddy aided vision.

About a mile south of Chaegunghyon, the track wound round Hill 127, passing through the village of Pulmiji. B Company was among the houses when bright flares appeared suddenly overhead— dropped by aircraft to discover enemy on the snowy ground. But now these flares disclosed the RUR movement to the Chinese. By the time the centre of the column was in Pulmiji, machine-guns and mortars had been brought on to Hill 127. These were fired into the Rifles. Hundreds of Chinese soldiers came running down from the hills to establish close firing positions, some in the river bed over which the track passed towards the MSR, others in the village.

Major Blake's aim was to keep the column moving. Though he briefly discussed with Major Ryan a counter-attack by A Company, the two men parted when this was seen to be impracticable. Small battles raged along and around the river bed. Broken and burning vehicles blocked the track through Pulmiji. Approaching the village, Captain James Majury's carrier sped him away several times from pockets of Chinese until an abandoned truck blocked him altogether and he was captured with his crew. Cooper Force closed up, trying to drive the enemy back with the tank 75s and Besa machine-guns. The Chinese closed in on the tanks with pole charges, setting several on fire. Captain Astley-Cooper ordered one troop to break out with a platoon of infantry but they were quickly stopped. Major John Shaw, Support Company commander, gathered a number of soldiers and forced a way through the enemy ring. Second Lieutenant McCord, Sergeant Campbell, and Corporal Blackstock entered the *melée* with the rearguard patrol to destroy an enemy post blocking the route to the west. McCord then found a Cromwell tank to accompany another part of the column westward before he disengaged his patrol to lead them away over the hills.[25]

At 0400 on 4th January, when the battalion roll was checked, two hundred and eight of the Rifles were missing.* A conference

*These losses were reduced to one hundred and fifty seven by individuals who had reached other units or were otherwise rescued, and those returning from hospital after wounds.

gathered at the headquarters of the United States 27th Infantry later that morning to discuss the option of a sortie to rescue any groups still holding out. But though General Ridgway was willing to delay final withdrawal to this end, Brigadier Brodie realised that such an operation, involving at least the whole of 27th Infantry, would endanger a far greater number than might be recovered. He decided that those remaining, if they were still free, must fight their own way out.

A helicopter, sent by General Milburn to the area of Pulmiji at midday, found two small groups of soldiers, seven in all. These were recovered by the gallant pilot, landing close to burned out tanks of Cooper Force. Captain Astley-Cooper and his small command had been destroyed in a devoted action, though a few among the crews managed to escape on foot. Captain John Lane, commanding the 4.2 Mortar Troop of 170 Battery was dead. Major Blake had been killed in the exercise of his command.* The battle was a blow to the Brigade, but it had been fought with valour.

To the east, 27 Brigade had again demonstrated its reliability in operations. At 0615 on 1st January, IX Corps ordered Brigadier Coad to put into force one of his contingency tasks: blocking the road at Tokchong. This was to be held until 6th ROK Division, which was believed to be withdrawing prematurely, and the 24th on the road to the east had passed through Uijongbu. The 6th Medium Tank Battalion, equipped with M46 Pattons, was placed under the brigadier's command for the operation, and a promise was made to return the artillery battalion, which had been sent to reinforce the 6th ROK Division. Immediately, the only artillery support was B Company of the 2nd Chemical Mortar Battalion, equipped with 4.2 mortars, which had been attached since November. Coad asked the corps chief of staff to return at least one of the two companies of Argylls guarding rear corps head-quarters, fifty miles to the south.

He remarked later,

> I always seemed to be asking for things, which I hated doing, but IX Corps staff continually overlooked our lack of resources until I pointed them out. They promised me some armoured personnel carriers but none were sent. I did not mind this too much because we were allowed to hold on to our American trucks. Without these, we should have been left behind.[26]

Tokchong was understood to be held by 6th ROK Division. Driving towards it from Uijongbu, the Australian column were

---

*The Royal Ulster Rifles have placed a fine memorial overlooking the battle site, to the south of Chaegunghyon.

fired upon by what were at first thought to be ROK stragglers but, as the range closed, were seen to be Chinese. The tanks, ably supported by small arms fire from the American mortarmen, dispersed this group, though snipers returned later. Leaving a liaison officer with the ROKs in the town, Lieutenant-Colonel Ferguson deployed his companies to cover the highway and the branch road to Solma-ri and Choksong. Elements of both 1st and 6th ROK Divisions were using the latter. South of Tokchong, the Middlesex and Argylls held the head of the pass to Uijongbu.

The abrupt retreat of 1st ROK Division accelerated the movement of the 6th. Marching men, interspersed with groups of fast moving vehicles, passed the Australians, Argylls and Middlesex. The apparently endless refugee column passed among them. About 1500 on the 1st, IX Corps ordered a general withdrawal. 3 RAR fell back through the other two battalions to cover Uijongbu, through which the 24th Division would also be retiring.

Following the usual deployment practice, Colonel Ferguson set off to reconnoitre and arranged to meet the members of his 'Orders Group' at a rendezvous. The group soon followed him, leaving Lieutenant A G W Keys to bring the remainder of the battalion in American transport to the new location. South of Tokchong, the colonel's 'R Group', then the 'O Group', ran a gauntlet of enemy fire, losing one vehicle as they raced through. When the main column approached this enemy position, Lieutenant Keys dismounted the battalion, attacked the roadblock with two companies, killed seven of the enemy for the loss of four wounded, and continued the journey.

By 2100 that evening, the groups of stragglers from the two ROK divisions from the north and north west, and 24 Division from the north east, had cleared Uijongbu. The decision for abandonment lay with the brigadier. He decided to withdraw the Middlesex and Argylls through the night, followed by the Australians. 3 RAR began to pull back at 0300 on the 2nd, joining a brigade concentration area behind the 1st Cavalry and 24th Divisions, who held the IX Corps share of the perimeter round Seoul. This was attacked by the Chinese after darkness on the night of the 2nd/3rd.

27 Brigade was placed under command of 24th Division as rumours spread that heavy fighting was taking place on the perimeter. A company of 3 RAR with twenty tanks and a Mosquito light aircraft was sent out to reconnoitre beyond the forward localities but found only 'two American battalions . . . in a good deal of confusion'.[27] This confusion was made worse when the area was struck by F-80s. There was no sign of Chinese, fighting or otherwise, as the group was recalled urgently.

At 1415, Brigadier Coad was ordered to report to divisional headquarters. 'Coad,' said General Church, 'we are going to pull'.[28]

Headquarters, 27 Brigade, dusted off the Army and Corps plan for crossing the Han river. But for reasons never made apparent this was quickly abandoned in IX Corps. The brigade was to form the rearguard, covering the north and north east approaches to the standing and temporary bridges, with 27 RCT of the 25th Division guarding the I Corps bridges downstream. The Middlesex position was on a bare peak and the night was 'agonisingly cold'. Sentries had to be changed frequently, though the acute discomfort denied rest to those off duty. Throughout the evening, units of 1st Cavalry and 24th Division came back across the bridges in good order. Refugees were held back from the bridgeheads by civil police working with the United States Provost.

Early on 4th January, divisional headquarters warned 27 Brigade that it would be kept in position for most of the day if the enemy did not close up; the aim was to recover as much of the temporary bridging as possible. In any case, all units would now use the railway bridge to cross the Han, which would be destroyed as soon as the last man was over. By 0430, there were signs that the enemy was indeed approaching: Chinese patrols had been moving and probing round 3 RAR since 0230 and a fire fight had developed by 0430. An hour later D Company drew in its outposts because enemy numbers close by were growing. In these circumstances, Brigadier Coad reminded General Church that he had deployed his battalion in temporary night positions. If they were to remain during the day, he needed to make changes. There was no response to this point, made by radio with considerable electronic interference. But by 0730, IX Corps had completely withdrawn. Headquarters 25th Division, in command of the final elements north of the river, agreed that 27 Brigade might follow.

Almost all the brigade's vehicles had already been sent to a rendezvous south of the Han. 3 RAR and the Middlesex pulled back, the latter under mortar fire, and crossed the river with brigade headquarters. The Argylls held the last positions. D Company, the rearguard, crossed at 1000 and the American engineers blew apart the spans of the railway bridge and part of the piers.

To the west, 55 Field Squadron was in process of blowing the standing and temporary bridges in the I Corps sector. From 0355 to 0930 they destroyed floating rafts, a footbridge, a naval cube bridge, and the lower railway bridge on which a pier and two spans were demolished. Finally, at 1300, they blew the charges on the 'Shoefly' timber and trestle bridge. This was the only part of the grand evacuation plan which remained unchanged. The Royal

Engineers had laboured for many days placing and connecting over eight thousand pounds of explosive. None of their circuits failed. The squadron followed 29 Brigade to Suwon.[29]

27 Brigade moved slowly to Suwon also. The road was packed with the vehicles of both I and IX Corps, but at Suwon the latter turned off for Ich'on. Brigadier Coad was only half pleased to be told by General Church that he liked the British troops to undertake rearguards as they were a steadying influence on American soldiers.[30] He decided it would be tactful to keep this remark to himself for the time being.

So contact was broken across the front. Admiral Andrewes, preparing to send a note of congratulations to the Argylls on the posthumous award of the Victoria Cross to Major Muir, announced at this time, asked a member of his staff as a matter of interest precisely where the defensive line had settled. When he looked at the map he remarked,

'Why, we are back to square one.

'Oh, it's not as bad as that, sir.'

'Well, call it square one and a half.'

This was the sum for the United Nations Command of the bitter struggles and vain hopes of six months.

SOURCE NOTES: CHAPTER 16

1. Field, op cit, pp 252–3.

2. COMNAVFE signal to FO2i/c FES, repeated CTF 90 and COM 7th Fleet of 300515Z Nov 50, US Naval Archives, NAVFE Command & Historical Report, Sep-Nov 50. Also Report of Proceedings, UK *Naval Attaché*, Tokyo, Chap 5, p 6, Case 11554 Vol 18

3. Qu. *British Naval Staff History* op cit, p 98 and fn.

4. Foreseeing the possibility of withdrawal of the forces in the east coast enclave, Admiral Joy warned Admiral Doyle on 28th November. See US Naval Archives, COMPHIBGRUONE *Action Report for Hungnam Redeployment, December, 1950.* Also Field op cit, pp 268–9, and Cagle and Manson, op cit, p 180.

5. Rad JCS 98172, all Commands, 6th December 1950, (USNARS, Suitland).

6. Cagle and Manson, op cit, Chap 5. Also O'Neill, op cit, vol ii, p 430.

7. Ibid.

8. Signal CTG 95.1 of 032015Z December 1950 (for connected signals see Canadian National Archives (CNA) NS 1926–DDE-218, Vol 2).

9. Signal CTF 95 of 032015Z December 1950, CNA as above. Also Field op cit, p 272.

10. Captain J V Brock *Patrol Report of 20th November to 6th December 1950 to FO2i/c FE Station* (CTG 95.1) CNA NS 1926–DDE-218, vol 2.

11. Thor Thorgrimsson and E C Russell, *Canadian Naval Operations in Korean Waters, 1950–55,* (Ottawa, 1965), pp 31–32.

12. Ibid, p 32. See also Captain J V Brock's *Patrol Report* cit, retained with FO2i/c FES Report of proceedings for this period.

13. Captain J V Brock's *Patrol report* cit. Also HMS *Ceylon,* RoPs of 23rd December 1950, Admiralty Case 11554, vol 4, Thorgrimsson and Russell op cit, pp 34–36, and Lieutenant A J Ploscz, RCN, writing as 'A J P' in the Canadian Naval Journal, *Crowsnest,* February, 1951, pp 4–6, *The Chinnamp'o Affair.*

14. Case 11554, Vol 19, FO2i/c FES RoPs No 26.

15. HMS *Theseus,* RoPs December 1950, Case 11554 Vol 15. Also, Field op cit, p 308, and FO2i/c FE Station, Special RoPs in Korean Operations, July 1950–December 1951, Admiralty Case 11554, Vol 21, Section 1, Part III.

16. Qu. *British Naval Staff History* op cit, p 101.

17. For the complementary view in Washington, see USNARS Suitland, Department of the Army, G-3 file 091 Korea, Case 134.

18. Coad Report, cit, Part IV, p 7. Also 27 Bde War Diary (WD) of December 1950, Appendix H.

19. Ridgway, op cit, p 83.

20. 29 Bde WD of January 1951 states 0700 but units (eg 1 GLOSTERS), show 0545. 1 RUR mentions 0300.

21. 29 Bde WD of 1st January 1951, Appendix A.

22. 1 NF WD of 2nd January 1951.

23. 1 RUR WD of 3rd January 1951 and *RUR in Korea,* Chap 3. 45 Fd Regt RA and 170 Mor Bty RA WDs of 3rd January 1951.

24. WDs of 3rd January 1951: 1 NF, 1 GLOSTERS, 45 Fd Regt RA, 170 Mor Bty RA. Author's conversations with Captain (now Major) J E Dunning, Lieutenant (now Major) S W Cooper, and Major P W Weller.

25. 1 RUR WD, 3rd/4th January 1951 and *RUR in Korea,* Chap. 3. Author's conversations with Captain (now Major-General) J H S Majury, Lieutenant (now Brigadier) M N S McCord, and Major (now the Revd.) E M Ryan.

26. WDs of 1st January 1951: 27 Bde, 1 Mx, 1 A&SH, 3 RAR. Coad Report, cit, Pt IV, p 7, Coad, conversation with author. Captain John G Westover, *Combat Support in Korea,* (Washington DC, 1987), pp 77-8.

27. Coad Report, cit, Pt IV, p 8. 3 RAR WD of 1st January 1951.

28. Coad Report, cit, Pt IV, p 8.

29. WDs, 4th January 1951: 27 Bde, 55 Fd Sqn RE. Author's conversations with Alan Moody, Wilson and Younger.

30. Coad Report, cit, Part IV, pp 8-9, Author's conversation with Coad and Jeffes.

APPENDIX A

United Nations Security Council Resolution of 25th June, 1950 at the 473rd Meeting

THE SECURITY COUNCIL

Recalling the finding of the General Assembly in its resolution of October 1949 that the Government of the Republic of Korea is a lawfully established government having effective control and jurisdiction over that part of Korea where the United Nations Temporary Commission on Korea was able to observe and consult and in which the great majority of the people of Korea reside; and that this Government is based on elections which were a valid expression of the free will of the electorate of that part of Korea and which were observed by the Temporary Commission; and that this is the only such Government in Korea;

Mindful of the concern expressed by the General Assembly in its resolutions of 12 December 1948 and 21 October 1949 of the consequences which might follow unless Member States refrained from acts derogatory to the results sought to be achieved by the United Nations in bringing about the complete independence and unity of Korea; and the concern expressed that the situation described by the United Nations Commission on Korea in its report menaces the safety and well being of the Republic of Korea and of the people of Korea and might well lead to open military conflict there;

Noting with grave concern the armed attack upon the Republic of Korea by forces from North Korea,

Determines that this action constitutes a breach of the peace,

I.   *Calls* for the immediate cessation of hostilities; and *Calls upon* the authorities of North Korea to withdraw forthwith their armed forces to the thirty-eighth parallel;

II.   *Requests* the United Nations Commission on Korea
(a) To communicate its fully considered recommendations on the situation with the least possible delay;
(b) To observe the withdrawal of the North Korean forces to the thirty-eighth parallel; and
(c) To keep the Security Council informed on the execution of this Resolution;

III. *Calls upon* all Members to render every assistance to the United Nations in the execution of this Resolution and to refrain from giving assistance to the North Korean authorities.

Notes:

1. This resolution was adopted by 9 votes (Nationalist) China, Cuba, Ecuador, Egypt, France, India, Norway, the United Kingdom and United States] to 0 with 1 abstention (Jugoslavia) One member was absent (USSR).

2. Immediately following the adoption of the resolution, Jugoslavia proposed a second resolution, namely:

THE SECURITY COUNCIL

Noting with grave concern the outbreak of hostilities in Korea, and anxious to obtain all the necessary information enabling it to pass judgement on the merits of the case,

Calls for an immediate cessation of hostilities and withdrawal of forces,

Invites the Government of North Korea to state its case before the Security Council.

1 vote in favour [Jugoslavia] with 3 abstentions [Egypt, India, Norway]. One member was absent [USSR].

UN Doc. S/1500 and 1501

United Nations Security Council Resolution of 27th June, 1950 at the 474th Meeting

THE SECURITY COUNCIL

Having determined that the armed attack upon the Republic of Korea by forces from North Korea constitutes a breach of the peace;

Having called for an immediate cessation of hostilities; and

Having called upon the authorities of North Korea to withdraw forthwith their armed forces to the 38th parallel; and

Having noted from the report of the United Nations Commission for Korea that the authorities in North Korea have neither ceased hostilities nor withdrawn their armed forces to the 38th parallel, and that urgent military measures are required to restore international peace and security; and

Having noted the appeal from the Republic of Korea to the United Nations for immediate and effective steps to secure peace and security,

Recommends that the Members of the United Nations furnish such assistance to the Republic of Korea as may be necessary to repel

the armed attack and to restore international peace and security
in the area.

Notes:

1. The resolution was carried by 7 votes to 1 (Jugoslavia), with 2
abstaining (Egypt and India).

2. Immediately afterwards, the Jugoslav delegate put a contrary
resolution, reiterating the call for a cease fire, initiating mediation
and inviting the attendance of a representative from North Korea
to take part in it. This was rejected by the reverse order of votes
in paragraph 1, above. Egypt and India continued to abstain. The
USSR remained absent.

UN Doc. S/1511 and 1509.

APPENDIX B

United Nations General Assembly Resolution 112(II) of 14th November, 1947

Inasmuch as the Korean question which is before the General Assembly is primarily a matter for the Korean people itself and concerns its freedom and independence, and

Recognizing that this question cannot be correctly and fairly resolved without the participation of representatives of the indigenous population,

THE GENERAL ASSEMBLY

1. *Resolves* that elected representatives of the Korean people be invited to take part in the consideration of the question;

2. *Further resolves* that in order to facilitate and expedite such participation and to observe that the Korean representatives are in fact duly elected by the Korean people and not mere appointees by military authorities in Korea, there be forthwith established a United Nations Temporary Commission on Korea, to be present in Korea, with right to travel, observe and consult throughout Korea.

II

THE GENERAL ASSEMBLY

Recognizing the urgent and rightful claims to independence of the people of Korea;

Believing that the national independence of Korea should be re-established and all occupying forces then withdrawn at the earliest practicable date;

Recalling its previous conclusion that the freedom and independence of the Korean people cannot be correctly or fairly resolved without the participation of representatives of the Korean people, and its decision to establish a United Nations Temporary Commission on Korea (hereinafter called the 'Commission') for the purpose of facilitating and expediting such participation by elected representatives of the Korean people:

1. *Decides* that the Commission shall consist of representatives of Australia, Canada, China, El Salvador, France, India, Philippines, Syria, Ukrainian Soviet Socialist Republic;

2. *Recommends* that the elections be held not later than 31st March, 1948, on the basis of the adult suffrage and by secret ballot to choose representatives with whom the Commission may consult regarding the prompt attainment of the freedom and independence of the Korean people and which representatives, constituting a National Assembly, may establish a National Government of Korea. The number of representatives from each voting area or zone should be proportionate to the population, and the elections should be under the observation of the Commission;

3. *Further recommends* that, as soon as possible after the elections, the National Assembly should convene and form a National Government and notify the Commission of its formation;

4. *Further recommends* that immediately upon the establishment of a National Government, that Government should, in consultation with the Commission:

(a) constitute its own national security forces and dissolve all military or semi-military formations not included therein;

(b) take over the functions of government from the military commands and civilian authorities of North and South Korea, and

(c) arrange with the occupying Powers for the complete withdrawal from Korea of their armed forces as early as practicable and if possible within ninety days;

5. *Resolves* that the Commission shall facilitate and expedite the fulfilment of the foregoing programme for the attainment of the national independence of Korea and withdrawal of occupying forces, taking into account its observations and consultations in Korea. The Commission shall report with its conclusions to the General Assembly and may consult with the Interim Committee (if one be established) with respect to the application of this resolution in the light of developments;

6. *Calls upon* the Member States concerned to afford every assistance and facility to the Commission in the fulfilment of its responsibilities;

7. *Calls upon* all Members of the United Nations to refrain from interfering in the affairs of the Korean people during the interim period preparatory to the establishment of Korean independence, except in pursuance of the decisions of the General Assembly; and thereafter, to refrain completely from any and all acts derogatory to the independence and sovereignty of Korea.

APPENDIX C

United Nations General Assembly Resolution 195 (III) of 12th December, 1948

THE GENERAL ASSEMBLY

Having regard to its resolution 112 of 14th November, 1947, concerning the problem of the independence of Korea,

Having considered the report of the United Nations Temporary Commission on Korea (hereinafter referred to as the 'Temporary Commission'), and the report of the Interim Committee of the General Assembly regarding its consultation with the Temporary Commission,

Mindful of the fact that, due to difficulties referred to in the report of the Temporary Commission, the objectives set forth in the Resolution of 14th November, 1947, have not been fully accomplished, and in particular that unification of Korea has not yet been achieved,

1. *Approves* the conclusions of the reports of the Temporary Commission;

2. *Declares* that there has been established a lawful government (the Government of the Republic of Korea) having effective control and jurisdiction over that part of Korea where the Temporary Commission was able to observe and consult and in which the great majority of the people of all Korea reside; that this Government is based on elections which were a valid expression of the free will of the electorate of that part of Korea and which were observed by the Temporary Commission; and that this is the only such Government in Korea;

3. *Recommends* that the occupying Powers withdraw their occupation forces as early as practicable;

4. *Resolves* that, as a means to a full accomplishment of the objectives set forth in the resolution of 14th November, 1947, a Commission on Korea, consisting of the same Member States which composed the United Nations Temporary Commission on Korea, be established to continue the work of the Temporary Commission and carry out the provisions of the present resolution, having in mind the status of the Government of the Republic of Korea as herein defined, and in particular to:

(*a*) Lend its good offices to bring about the unification of Korea and the integration of all Korean security forces in accordance with the principles laid down by the General Assembly in the resolution of 14th November, 1947;

(*b*) Seek to facilitate the removal of barriers to economic, social and other friendly intercourse caused by the division of Korea;

(*c*) Be available for observation and consultation in the further development of representative government based on the freely expressed will of the people;

(*d*) Observe the actual withdrawal of the occupying forces and verify the fact of withdrawal when such has occurred; and for this purpose, if it so desires, request the assistance of military experts of the two occupying Powers;

5. *Decides* that the Commission:

(*a*) Shall within thirty days of the adoption of this resolution, proceed to Korea, where it shall maintain its seat;

(*b*) Shall be regarded as having superseded the Temporary Commission established by the resolution of 14th November, 1947.

APPENDIX D

ORDERS OF BATTLE

The North Korean People's Army and The Armed Forces of the Republic of Korea

The North Korean People's Army—In Min Gun

1. Field Army Headquarters (including signal and administrative units) — 2,700

2. Headquarters, I Corps ⎫ including — 1,790
   II Corps ⎬ signal units — 1,680

3. *Formations, assembly dates, and strengths*

1st Division (Feb 48) (one regiment from Chinese Communist Forces (CCF) veterans)	11,000
2nd Division (Feb 48)	10,838
3rd Division (Oct 48)	11,000
4th Division (Oct 48) (one regt from CCF vets)	11,000
5th Division (Aug 49) from 164 CCF Division	11,000
6th Division (Jul 49) from 166 CCF Division	11,000
7th Division (formerly titled 11th) (Apr 50) from 7th Border Constabulary Brigade	12,000
10th Mechanised Infantry Division (Mar 50)	6,000
12th Division (formerly titled 7th and 15th) (Apr 50) from 139, 140, 141, 156 CCF Divisions	12,000
13th Division (Jun 50)	6,000
15th Division (Jun 50)	11,000
105th Armoured Brigade (Aug 49)	6,000
956 Independent Marine Regiment (Jul 49)	3,260
766 Independent Infantry Regiment (Raiding Force)	1,500
12 MTsP ('Motorjik') Regiment	2,000

Border Constabulary

4. 1st Brigade — 5,000
   2nd Brigade — 2,600
   3rd Brigade — 4,000
   5th Brigade — 3,000

   Total, field force: — 146,368

5. *Naval Force* (see Note G, below)   2,280

6. *Air Force* (see Note H, below)   3,877

    Total, fighting forces: 152,525

Notes:

A. The Field Army Headquarters was distinct from the national General Headquarters within the Ministry of Defence in P'yongyang.

B. The establishment of a North Korean Division was 10,381. Over and under posting arose as a result of regimental strengths at the time of formation. For example, the 13th Division was formed in the first week in June from regiments trained and formed in the 1st, 2nd and 3rd Democratic Youth Training Centres at Sinuiju and Yongamp'o. Similarly, the 15th was formed from the 3rd People's Training Centre at Hoeryong and the Democratic Youth Training Centre at Najin. As a part of the security arrangements, none of the regimental officers and other ranks knew that they were part of a divisional organisation until 24th June, 1950.

C. The Border Constabulary (*Bo An Dae* as distinct from the NKPA, *In Min Gun*) was a special security force trained directly by Russian instructors. Its officers were trained in a special school. Candidates were accepted only on the basis of noted political reliability.

D. 1st and 3rd Border Constabulary Brigades were subsumed by the Field Army (forming the basis of 8th and 9th Divisions) in July, 1950.

E. 7th Border Constabulary Brigade is not shown separately as it had already been converted as cadres for the 7th Division prior to the outbreak of war.

F. Prisoners-of-war reports refer to the '17th Motor Cycle Regiment' as well as the 12th. This is due to the fact that the original motor cycle reconnaissance unit was the 17th Motor Cycle Battalion. Only one such regiment, the 12th has been positively identified. 'Motorjiks' were equipped with motorcycle and side car vehicles.

G. The North Korean Navy was an element of the NKPA (on the same basis that all armed forces in Russia are part of the 'Red Army'). On the outbreak of war it comprised:

    one (former Japanese) escort
    five (former Finnish) motor torpedo boats
    five Russian minesweepers
    seven (former German) R-boats
    one (former German F-type) landing craft
    fifteen miscellaneous Russian and former Japanese motor launches and patrol craft

H. The North Korean Air Force was similarly a section of the NKPA. A re-equipment programme accelerated from April, 1950 as aircrew became available from advanced training. An air division was formed, expanding from 1,675 all ranks to the figure given above in June, 1950. All these were volunteers with the exception of the anti-aircraft units on air bases. Training aircraft apart, the operational aircraft numbered:

78 YAK-7B fighter
70 Il-10 bombers

J. GHQ troops, coastal defence artillery, later 24, 25 and 26 Mechanised Artillery Brigades and other coastal defence forces, and anti-aircraft artillery in North Korea are not shown in the figures above.

The Armed Forces of the Republic of Korea

1.	*Headquarters*	27,558
2.	*Divisions*	
	1st Infantry Division	9,715
	2nd Infantry Division	7,910
	3rd Infantry Division	7,059
	5th Infantry Division	7,276
	6th Infantry Division	9,112
	7th Infantry Division	9,698
	8th Infantry Division	6,866
	Capitol Infantry Division	9,561
	Total, land forces:	94,755
3.	*Coast Guard*	7,715
4.	*Air Force*	1,865
	Total, ROK armed forces:	104,335

Notes

A. There was no Army headquarters in the field for the Republic of Korea and, equally, there were no corps headquarters in being. The land force was conceived, organised and equipped by the United States as a constabulary force to secure the frontier on the 38th parallel. Overall command was vested in the Chief of the General Staff in Seoul, within the Ministry of Defense. The two corps headquarters were not organised until the first and second weeks of July respectively. They were manned, at a total of 6,000 all ranks, at the expense of the already depleted divisions. There was a relatively large element of base and line of communication forces following United States practice. These, together with the military forces in the Ministry and its associated signals units are included in the number in 1., above.

B. The strength of the 17th Regiment, detached to cover the ROK fragment of the Ongjin Peninsula, was 2,500. These are included in the figures for the Capitol Division, its parent.

C. The 3rd and 5th Divisions—there was no 4th Division—had neither artillery nor engineer units.

D. The Coast Guard, conceived as a maritime constabulary, and organised on the basis of the United States service, became the ROK Navy. Its numbers included 1,241 marines at the outbreak of war. It comprised:

> four United States PC (patrol craft)
> six United States YMS (motor minesweepers)
> fifteen (former Japanese) minesweepers
> ten (former Japanese) minelayers
> one United States LST
> eleven picket boats

It is notable that, due to lack of official funds, one of the patrol craft was bought by subscription organised by the officers and ratings.

E. The Air Force consisted of:

> twelve light liaison aircraft
> ten advanced training aircraft (T-6).

The KMAG air adviser had approximately ten F-51 Mustangs to dispose to the ROK Air Force but the latter were awaiting crews for them. These were handed over formally on 26th June but some months elapsed before crew training was completed.

Comparative table of weapons

Weapon/weapon system		NKPA	ROK Army
Tanks		242 T-34	none
Armoured cars		54	27
Self-propelled artillery		176 SU76	none
Howitzers, towed,	122-mm	172	none
	105-mm	none	91
	76-mm	380	none
Anti-tank guns	57-mm	none	140
	45-mm	550	none
Anti-aircraft guns,	85-mm	12 (excludes those on airfields)	none
	37-mm	24	none

Mortars,	120-mm	225	none
	82- or 81-mm	1,142	384

Sources

United States Far East Command (FECOM) Intelligence Publications (1952):
  History of the North Korean Army
  North Korean Air Force

Roy E Appleman, *South to the Naktong, North to the Yalu*, (Washington, 1961).

James A Field jr, *History of United States Naval Operations, Korea*, (Washington, 1962).

Robert F Futrell, *United States Air Force Operations in the Korean Conflict, 25 June–1 November, 1950*, USAF Historical Study No 71 (formerly secret, now unclassified), (Washington, 1952).

United States Allied Translator and Interpreter Section (ATIS) Interrogation Reports series from inclusive 1951 to 1954 (US National Archives, Suitland).

The Ground Battle History Institution of Japan, *Korean War*, vol i, (Tokyo, 1969).

National Affairs Institute, Seoul. Details supplied to author October 1987.

APPENDIX F

Extracts from the Charter of the United Nations

A. *From Chapter V—The Security Council*

Procedure

ARTICLE 28

1. The Security Council shall be so organised as to be able to function continuously. Each member of the Security Council shall for this purpose be represented at all times at the seat of the Organisation.
2. The Security Council shall hold periodic meetings at which each of its members may if it so desires, be represented by a member of the government or by some other specially designated representative.
3. The Security Council may hold meetings at such places other than the seat of the Organisation as in its judgment will best facilitate its work.

B. *From Chapter VII—Action with Respect to Threats to the Peace, Breaches of the Peace, and Acts of Aggression*

ARTICLE 39

The Security Council shall determine the existence of any threat to the peace, breach of the peace, or act of aggression and shall make recommendations, or decide what measures shall be taken in accordance with Articles 41 and 42, to maintain or restore international peace and security.

ARTICLE 42

Should the Security Council consider the measures provided for in Article 41 would be inadequate or have proved to be inadequate, it may take such action by air, sea, or land forces as may be necessary to maintain or restore international peace and security. Such action may include demonstrations, blockade, and other operations by air, sea, or land forces of Members of the United Nations.

ARTICLE 43

1. All Members of the United Nations, in order to contribute to the maintenance of international peace and security, undertake to make available to the Security Council, on its call and in accordance with a special agreement or agreements, armed forces, assistance, and facilities, including rights of passage, necessary for the purpose of maintaining international peace and security.

2. Such agreement or agreements shall govern the numbers and types of forces, their degree of readiness and general location, and the nature of the facilities and assistance to be provided.

3. The agreement or agreements shall be negotiated as soon as possible on the initiative of the Security Council. They shall be concluded between the Security Council and Members or between the Security Council and groups of Members and shall be subject to ratification by the signatory states in accordance with their respective constitutional processes.

ARTICLE 46

Plans for the application of armed force shall be made by the Security Council with the assistance of the Military Staff Committee.

ARTICLE 47

1. There shall be established a Military Staff Committee to advise and assist the Security Council on all questions relating to the Security Council's military requirements for the maintenance of international peace and security, the employment and command of forces placed at its disposal, the regulation of armaments, and possible disarmament.

2. The Military Staff Committee shall consist of the Chiefs of Staff of the permanent members of the Security Council or their representatives. Any Member of the United Nations not permanently represented on the Committee shall be invited by the Committee to be associated with it when the efficient discharge of the Committee's responsibilities requires the participation of that Member in its work.

3. The Military Staff Committee shall be responsible under the Security Council for the strategic direction of any armed forces placed at the disposal of the Security Council. Questions relating to the command of such forces shall be worked out subsequently.

4. The Military Staff Committee, with the authorisation of the Security Council and after consultation with appropriate regional agencies, may establish regional sub-committees.

C. *From Chapter XVII—Transitional Security Arrangements*

ARTICLE 106

Pending the coming into force of such special agreements referred to in Article 43 as in the opinion of the Security Council enable it to begin the exercise of its responsibilities under Article 42, the parties to the Four-Nation Declaration, signed at Moscow, October 30, 1943, and France, shall, in accordance with the provisions of paragraph 5 of the Declaration, consult with one another and as occasion requires with other Members of the United Nations with a view to such joint action on behalf of the Organisation as may be necessary for the purpose of maintaining international peace and security.

APPENDIX G

ACANTHUS—MEETING No 1

Minutes of the first meeting held in the
War Office, Room 415, Main Building,
at 1030 hrs, Tuesday, 8 August 1950

Those present:

Lt-Col H A Prince,	SD 2 (Chairman).
Brigadier T Brodie,	HQ, 29 Inf Bde.
Colonel C F Hutt,	MT 1. [Training]
Colonel W B Radford,	RAC 1. [Royal Armoured Corps]
Colonel D S Gordon,	Inf (a). [Infantry]
Colonel F R Armitage,	AG 1(a). ⎤ [Adjutant-
Colonel G P L Weston,	AG 5(Mob). ⎬ General's
Colonel H V McNally,	AG (PM). ⎦ Branches]
Colonel C E Eccles,	AMD 2. [Medical]
Colonel I L W D Laurie,	Q(Ops) 3. [Quartermaster-General's Operations]
Colonel B J O Burrows,	Col (P) Mov. [Movements]
Colonel L H Gordon,	ME 4. [Electrical & Mechanical Engineers]
Colonel J N Drew,	DDAPS. [Postal]
Lt-Col C T W Hill,	G(SD), Eastern Comd.
Lt-Col B M Wood,	G(Trg), Eastern Comd.
Lt-Col J D Palmer,	AAG, Eastern Comd.
Lt-Col S G Slingsby,	ADOS, Eastern Comd.
Lt-Col G Lerwill,	G(SD), East Anglian Dist.
Lt-Col N W Finlinson,	AQMG, East Anglian Dist.
Lt-Col N M H Wall,	G(SD), Southern Comd.
Lt-Col J E Hill,	G(SD), AA Comd. ⎤ [Anti-
Lt-Col G M T Morphew,	G(SD), 1 AA Group, ⎦ Aircraft]
Lt-Col R N Lyons,	49 A Tk Regt.
Lt-Col A M Field,	MO 2. [General Staff Military Operations]

Lt-Col P H W Brind,	SD 2. [General Staff, Staff Duties]
Lt-Col L T S Shawcross,	Sigs 5. [Signals]
Lt-Col R W O Daltry,	Q 4. [Quartering]
Lt-Col C J Tobin,	Ord 1. ⎱ [Ordnance Services]
Lt-Col G J Mitchell,	Ord 2. ⎰
Lt-Col G C Richardson,	Ord 7.
Lt-Col E Matthewman,	Ord 9.
Lt-Col F W G Benemy,	Ord 13.
Lt-Col J C Murphy,	Ord 21.
Lt-Col W H Summers,	ST 1. [Supply & Transport]
Major W Roberts,	G(SD), Eastern Comd.
Major T C T Mossman,	G(Trg & Int), Eastern Comd.
Major F F Laugher,	DAQMG, Eastern Comd.
Major Chester Williams,	Q(Ops) Southern Comd.
Major B C Withers,	'A', Southern Comd.
Major H F L Fox,	G(SD), AA Comd.
Major B J Eastwood,	DAA&QMG, 29 Inf Bde.
Major T V Fischer-Hoch,	170 Fd Baty RA.
Major E V M Strickland,	MI 1. [Military Intelligence]
Major C B Franklin,	GS(W) 1. [Weapons technology]
Major P H Moir,	SD 1.
Major F D Pile,	SD 4.
Major I R Graeme,	RA 1. [Artillery]
Major G H Chambers,	E 1. [Engineers]
Major D P K Rennick,	Sigs 3.
Major G R Price,	Sigs 3.
Major P J E Rowell,	Q(AE). [Army Equipment control]
Major M E MacWilliam,	Q(Ops) 1.
Major L R Rees,	Q(M) 1.
Major S J Cornfoot,	Q(M) 1.
Major A F Hicks,	Q(M) 3.
Major W T Laybourn,	Q(M) 5.
Major C Harston,	ST 5.
Major C W L Minister,	ME 2.
Major D E Grant,	F 9. [Finance]
Capt M J Smith,	RA 1.
Capt T Pearce,	F 9.
Capt F H Smith,	ME 2.
N E Crawshaw Esq,	QMGF. [Finance]
P A S Sale Esq,	Sc 1. [Scientific Advisory Branch]
Major M G McComas,	SD 2 (Secretary)

AUTHORITY FOR EXECUTIVE ACTION

1. *Minutes of Meetings*
   (a) The minutes of this and all subsequent meetings on the same subject will be taken as authority for executive action.
   (b) The minutes of meetings will form the basis of the Agenda for subsequent meetings.
   (c) Command representatives are warned that it may be necessary to take urgent action, on their return to their own HQ, to put their staff and service representatives in the picture, since War Office branches represented at the meeting are liable to initiate action on their own nets as soon as possible.

ORDER OF BATTLE

2. *Staff Table*
   Attached at Appendix 'A' is the provisional Staff Table for the force. The next edition of the Staff Table will include locations of all units.

   Action by SD 2

PLANNING DATA

3.

Planning Dates		*Action by*
'D' Day.	1 November	
1st Estimate Tonnage required and vehicle details.	21 August	Comds. concerned
Firm estimate tonnage and vehicles	26 August	—do—
Firm Staff Tables	5 September	SD 2.
Allocation to Ships.	15 September	Comd, 29 Bde.
Final adjustment by	22 September	SD 2.

Loading of Vehicles:
† 'A' [armoured] vehicles any time after   1 October
'B' [unarmoured] vehicles any time after   7 October
(NOTE: † Q(Movements) 3 will ensure that vehicles are NOT called forward until as late as possible).

Action by Q(M) 3

4. Planning is based on:
   (a) Destination teeth arms is KOREA not JAPAN. Although there is no question of 'tactical loading' Q(M) 2 and 3 will

ensure that ships are loaded so that the force can be assembled as rapidly as possible, for operations on arrival.

Action by Q(M) 2
Q(M) 3

(b) Stores must arrive simultaneously or immediately after personnel.

(c) Two base areas: one in KOREA one in JAPAN.

(d) Normal maintenance of FARELF must not be interrupted.

PREPARATION OF UNITS

5. *RAC*

(a) 8H will remain in Southern Command sending one squadron at a time, beginning 7 September, for training to STAMFORD.

(b) Crocodiles [flamethrowing tanks]—will be sent to STAMFORD for training by 7 September.

(c) Bridge Layers—must be Churchill and not Valentines [tank types].

6. *RA*

(a) *45 FD Regt.*—A Radar Troop and five additional OP [observation post] parties, to work with armour, have been added to the unit. The Radar Troop will be available by about 1 September.

(b) *170 Mortar Battery*—Must be concentrated in Eastern Command for training by 6 September. It will move back to Western Command after training. Operational vehicles must be issued to this unit as a matter of urgency. No training vehicles can be provided.

Action by Ord 13

(c) *11 LAA Battery.*

(i) To move to STAMFORD by 15 September for training. Unit will return to its present location after training.

(ii) Unit has NO SP [self propelled] guns at present. These to be issued soonest.

Action by Ord 13

(iii) NO OP parties will be provided for the LAA Battery.

(d) There will be NO Air OP element in the force.

(e) *Practice Camps.* Eastern Command confirmed that all arrangements for practice camps are well in hand.

(f) *RA Order of Battle.*

(i) It has been ruled that there will not be a HQ RA.

    (ii) The question of a Composite Anti-tank Battery being added to the Order of Battle is being referred to the ECAC. [Executive Committee of the Army Council]

Action by SD 2

7. *RE*

55 *Fd Sqn* to be at STAMFORD for brigade training by 3 September. One troop to be sent up as soon as possible after 20 August. The unit to move back to its present location afterwards.

8. *INF*

  (a) *17 prs.*

    (i) All operational and reserve guns will be at CASTLE MARTIN by 28 August.

Action by Ord 9

    (ii) The Practice Camp period, for Infantry platoons, will be 28 August to 10 September. During this time reserve guns will also be 'zeroed'.

    (iii) No HE ammunition for 17 prs will be taken abroad.

    (iv) 29 Brigade confirmed that no RA reservists will be required for Infantry Anti-tank Platoons. If any experienced RA serjeants were available they should be loaned to Infantry Platoons to assist in training and firing.

Action by Eastern Command

  (b) *Training of Infantry Signallers.*

Eastern Command to liaise with MT, War Office [Directorate-General of Military Training] regarding the training of reservist signallers.

Action by Eastern Command

  (c) *Anti-tank mines.*

Anti-tank mines Mk V will be taken in addition to the 'Hawkins' grenades.

  (d) *Rocket Launchers.*

Inf (a) to arrange for necessary training to be carried out at STAMFORD. It is understood that 40 launchers and 100 live rounds should arrive shortly. These would be despatched to STAMFORD.

Action by Inf (a) and GS(W)1

9. *Field Ambulance.* (incl FTT, FST, Mob Dental Teams and Fd Hyg Sec).

To move to STAMFORD for brigade training by 1 September. After training is completed units will remain in Eastern Command. Detailed locations will be decided by Eastern Command.

Action by Eastern Command

10. *Workshops*

It was confirmed that 10 Infantry Workshops will not be under command of 29 Brigade for all purposes forthwith.

11. *New Units*

Command concerned will keep War Office, SD 2, informed on the progress made in the formation of new units. As soon as these are up to strength in men and equipment Brigade Commander will be consulted on their future.

Action by Commands concerned

12. Movement of all units coming to STAMFORD for training will be co-ordinated between Eastern Command and the Command concerned.

13. *Mules*

The question of whether a Mule unit will be required is to be referred to Washington.

Action by MO2
[corrected to SD 2]

14. *Operational Research Unit*

It is hoped to despatch two officers to liaise with the Americans to whom they will be attached.

Action by Sc 1

15. *Reinforcement Holding Units*

Two such units would be mobilised by 31 August. These would be:

(a) *'K' Holding Unit (to be raised by Eastern Command.)*

This unit will eventually function in KOREA. It will include a Forward Delivery Squadron (Special) and will initially hold all the first reinforcements. These first reinforcements will train with their own units but travel with the RHU. The Forward Delivery Squadron (Special) will be mobilised by Southern Command. The tanks required by 'K' Holding Unit for training in Korea will be provided from those held in reserve in JAPAN.

(b) *'J' Holding Unit (to be raised by Northern Command.)*

This unit will eventually function in Japan and will initially hold the first month's wastage rates. It will incl the 02E organisation. 'First month's wastage' will train under arrangements NORCO and travel with the unit.

Action by MT 1 and
Commands concerned

16. *Battle School*

This will be organised as a training team consisting of approximately five officers and 7 other ranks under command of a Lt-Colonel. Its tasks will be:

(a) To assist Commander 29 Brigade.

(b) To co-ordinate the training of 'J' and 'K' Holding Units.

(c) Training liaison with the Americans.

(d) To correspond with the War Office, on behalf of Commander, 29 Brigade, on any shortcomings revealed in British training methods and on any new ideas.

Action by MT 1

VEHICLES AND EQUIPMENT

17. *Paint*

(a) *IT IS NOW CONFIRMED* that all vehicles will be painted with COLOUR NO 15 OLIVE DRAB. As far as possible vehicles will be painted before issue, but issues will NOT be held up on this account. Where this has not been possible Commands concerned will assist units to get their vehicles spray painted. Spray paint guns will be issued to Commands as under:

12 to Eastern Comd

3 to Southern Comd

*Actions by Q(AE) and
Commands concerned*

(b) All vehicles will have a five pointed white star on tops and sides, the star being as large as available space will allow.

Action by Commands concerned

18. All existing units will be made up to strength with operational vehicles by 28 August. It should be noted that some vehicles will be issued ready for loading on ships and units should, as far as possible, leave these alone.

Action by Ord 13

19. It was confirmed that B Echelon, 8H, would not be increased.

20. The possibility of improving the conversion of certain unit vehicles so that stretchers can be carried will be investigated by ME 2 who will report at the next meeting.

Action by ME 2

21. The question of charging vehicle and wireless batteries on arrival would be investigated by Ord 1. Sigs 5 to let Ord 1 know the size of the wireless battery commitment direct.

Action by Ord 1 and Sigs 5

22. It was confirmed that Carriers would be loaded with 'B' vehicles.

23. It was confirmed that G 1098 equipment would NOT be loaded in vehicles for the voyage.

24. All War Office branches producing new AF G 1098 details must forward them to Ord 2 as soon as possible so that equipment could be issued to units in time for tonnage details to be submitted by 21 August as requested.

25. It is confirmed that all FAMTOs [items for first aid to mechanical transport] will be taken in bulk NOT on MT ships.

26. *Maps*
Commander, 29 Brigade to inform the War Office, SD 2, what scale of issue he requires.

27. *Wireless Sets*
Sigs 5 to produce a specimen layout showing recommended nets and wireless sets, within the force, between JAPAN and SINGAPORE, and between JAPAN and UK.

Action by Sigs 5

28. *Flame Thrower Fuel*
GS(W) 1 to draft a signal for transmission to Washington on the question of the provision of flame thrower fuel and industrial and inert gases.

Action by GS(W) 1

29. *Anti-Freeze*
Ord 13 to say how much anti-freeze will be required to fill all radiators on arrival. Washington will be asked to ensure sufficient is available.

Action by Ord 13 and SD 2

30. *POL [Petrol, oil and lubricants] etc*
It was agreed that the Americans should provide all POL less:
Buffer oil.
Hydraulic fluid for AFVs. [armoured fighting vehicles]
C 600 for 'A' vehicle gear boxes.
Washington to be asked to confirm this.

Action by SD 2

31. *Sulphuric Acid*
Sigs 5 to inform SD 2 on amounts required on arrival and for maintenance. Washington is to be warned to have necessary amount available.

Action by Sigs 5 and SD 2

32. *Accommodation Stores*
Q(Ops) 1 to co-ordinate services queries and draft a signal for transmission to Washington.

Action by Q(Ops) 1

CLOTHING

33. All reservists to be issued with Home Scales on arrival in units.

32. The scale of clothing to be taken will be announced later.

35. Steel helmets taken will be BRITISH Mk IV.

36. All units will wear 29 Independent Infantry Brigade sign. [a rectangular patch on each arm bearing a white circle on a black background]

MISCELLANEOUS POINTS

37. *Delegation of Command*
    It is confirmed that:
    (a) GOC-in-C, Eastern Command is responsible for the training of 29 Independent Infantry Brigade Group.
    (b) Commander, 29 Independent Infantry Brigade Group can correspond direct with and visit all units under his command.
    (c) Responsibility for local administration and mobilisation remains with the Command in which the unit is located subject to any wishes expressed by Commander, 29 Independent Infantry Brigade Group.

38. *Services Royal Review*
    It was confirmed that 29 Independent Infantry Brigade Group would not be required.

39. *Anti-Gas Equipment*
    Anti-Gas equipment would be taken by units in bulk.

40. *Transport Ships*
    Q(M) 3 will take up the question of provision of guards in MT ships. Guards up to 1 [senior NCO] plus 10 [junior ranks] will be required.

    Action by Q(M) 3

41. *Married Families*
    (a) Q 4 to inform Commands concerned as soon as possible on the policy regarding [retention of married quarters by] families of units of 29 Independent Infantry Brigade Group.

    Action by Q(M) 3

    (b) It was noted that the movement of families to all parts of the world would be held up as the result of the move of 29 Independent Infantry Brigade Group.

42. *Evasion and Escape*
    MI 1 to organise training in evasion and escape. Details to be notified to Commands direct.

    Action by MI 1

43. *Armoured OPs*
    Armoured OPs for 45 Fd Regt will be CROMWELLS.

44. *Field Documentation*
    (a) A Field Documentation Unit will be raised forthwith at READING by Royal Berks Depot. The unit will move to COLCHESTER on 14 September and the whole FORCE will go on to field documentation wef [with effect from] midnight 17/18 September.

(b) The date on which field accounting will be instituted has still to be decided. Q(AE) to let SD 2 know the date as soon as possible.

Action by Q(AE) and SD 2

45. *Administrative Increments for FARELF*
Certain administrative assistance will have to be provided at HONG KONG and SINGAPORE. Q(Ops) 1 to draft a signal, for despatch by SD 2, defining what assistance will be required.

Action by Q(Ops) 1 and SD 2

46. *PsIAT [projectors, Infantry, anti-tank]*
Will be taken unless instructions to the contrary are given. [They were not taken: the American 3.5-inch rocket launcher superseded them]

Action by Inf (a)

47. *Despatch of subsequent drafts*
It is planned that a further 'maintenance' draft of about 300 will sail about 7 December. This draft will be assembled about 14 September.

48. *Formation of HQ, 19 Brigade*
This HQ is likely to form about 1 September [in replacement of 29 Brigade] SD 1 to confirm this date later.

Action by SD 1

49. *Courses*
(a) It was confirmed that officers down to attend the next Staff College and Joint Services Staff College courses would NOT move abroad. Personnel due to attend other courses (including the Senior Officers School) will accompany their units abroad.
(b) Eastern Command will co-ordinate any extra courses which Commander, 29 Independent Infantry Brigade Group required. This will include photo interpretation courses which will be arranged by MI 1.

Action by Eastern Command and MI 1

50. *Brochures*
It was understood that the Chief of Staff, Eastern Command was arranging with DMI [Director of Military Intelligence] for the production of the necessary Intelligence Pamphlets.

51. *Training*
(a) The question of training films en voyage will be dealt with later.

Action by MT 1

(b) Q(M) 2 will take up the question of live firing (.303) [ie, small arms only] from troopships.

Action by Q(M) 2

(c) MT 1 will produce details of special training manuals recommended, including training in mountain warfare.

Action by MT 1

(d) *Training Ammunition*

It was agreed that Commander, 29 Independent Infantry Brigade Group should be issued with such training ammunition as he required other than 20 pr AP [armour piercing] shot. 20 pr AP shot was in short supply and GS(W) 1 would work out a suitable training scale notifying Eastern Command direct.

Action by GS(W) 1

52. *Baggage*

(a) It was agreed that units might increase personal scales by 50%.

(b) Q(M) 1 will issue unit serial loading numbers direct to Commands concerned as soon as possible.

Action by Q(M) 1

(c) It was laid down that the code word ACANTHUS would NOT appear on unit baggage. Specific instructions for the marking of baggage would be issued to Commands concerned by Q(M) 1 after clearance with MI 1

Action by Q(M) 1 and MI 1

(d) Q(M) 1 will liaise with AG 5 (Mob) and issue distinguishing colours for units' baggage as soon as possible.

Action by Q(M) 1

(e) Q(M) 2 were asked to ensure that copies of all relevant movement instructions were sent to Anti-Aircraft Command.

Action by Q(M) 2

53. *Advanced Parties*

Details would be provided later.

Action by SD 2

54. *Liaison Party*

MO 2 to arrange with Washington for the Deputy Commander, 29 Independent Infantry Brigade Group and one RAC and one RA officer to fly to KOREA in order to gain first hand experience of operational conditions. This party to return to UK not later than mid-September. [In the event, this party was enlarged and overlapped the Battle Indoctrination Teams at paragraph 60, below]

Action by MO 2 and SD 2

55. *Establishment 29 Infantry Brigade Group*

It will probably be necessary to increase the size of 29 Infantry Brigade HQ when the final command organisation has been agreed. Commander, 29 Independent Infantry Brigade Group to raise the matter again.

Action by 29 Inf Bde

56. *Stopping of National Service volunteers*
AG 1(a) to investigate the reason why there is a 'standfast' on obtaining national service volunteers and to take what action is necessary.

Action by AG 1(a)

57. *Warning Orders*
AG 1(a) will ensure that Personnel branches keep Staff branches in Command HQs warned of the raising of any new unit.

Action by AG 1(a)

58. *Postal Address*
The Postal Address of all units will be:
Number—Rank—Name,
   Unit,
Army Post Office No 3

59. *Priority Tables*
Commander, 29 Independent Infantry Brigade Group will produce a priority table of units showing the order in which 'A' and 'B' vehicles may be taken for loading.

Action by 29 Inf Bde

60. *Battle Indoctrination*
Commander, 29 Independent Infantry Brigade Group to forward to War Office, SD 2, details of parties he would like despatched to KOREA to experience operational conditions. These parties to rejoin the main force at SINGAPORE to pass on their experiences. Washington to be consulted on whether it will be possible for these parties to be received.

Action by Brigade Commander, SD 2

61. *Next Meeting*
The next meeting will be held at 1030 hrs on Wednesday 16 August 1950 in Room 350, Main Building.

M G McComas
Major, GS,
Secretary.

Copies to:
   Those present.
   Additional copies to:
   Headquarters, Eastern Command (30).
   Headquarters, East Anglian District (10).
   Headquarters, Western Command (3).
   Headquarters, Southern Command (10).

Headquarters, Northern Command (3).
Headquarters, Anti-Aircraft Command (3).
Headquarters, 29 Infantry Brigade (10).
MS 1. [Military Secretary]
Q 1.
AMD 6.
QMGF.
MGOF. [Master-General of the Ordnance Finance Branch]
F 1, 6.

Notes:

A. This document is appended *in extenso* principally because it reveals considerable information about the preparation for and expectations of operations and administration in the developing Korean war. However, it also illustrates aspects of the mobilisation process of the War Office and the British Army at home in that period.

B. For example, although there were many officers senior to the chairman, a lieutenant-colonel, he took charge because he represented the Director of Staff Duties, head of the General Staff division responsible for organisation policy and coordination throughout the War Office and Army.

C. Errors of syntax and consistency notwithstanding, the minutes reflect well the range of the meeting. It ran to a prepared agenda relative to paragraphs 1 to 36 but, thereafter, the items were those raised by individuals round the table, hence the random nature and order of subjects.

D. A second meeting was notified at the end of the first but was not held: sufficient direction had been given and information passed to enable all concerned to move ahead, guided by supplementary orders—for example, movement instructions—and informed by day to day communications. Minor corrections necessary in the Staff Table were completed within ten days.

E. References to 'Washington', occurring in the Minutes indicate consultation with the British Army Staff within the British Joint Services Mission there. This was the agency for contact with the United States Army.

F. The original was classified as Secret, and marked as such at the top and bottom of each page.

No.	Unit		WE	Offr	OR	Ref	Remarks
39.	5 Med Wksp Stores Sec RAOC	1st Rfts	II/956/1	1	18	536o/1	
					1		
40.	29 Inf Bde Sp Tps LAD	1st Rfts	II/1007/1	1	26	5018/2	For Mortar Bty, LAA and Sqn Crocodiles.
					1		
41.	MC Increment. [Movement Control]	1st Rfts		3	14		
					1		
42.	102 Postal Unit Type 'B'	1st Rfts	IV/113/1	2	25	3367/1	One offr and one cpl to be att to Bde HQ.
					1		
43.	73 Fwd Base Pay office		IV/113/1	2	5	3919/1	
44.	208 Fd Cash Office	1st Rfts	III/57/4	1	2	3431/1	
45.	Comd Pay office.			13	111		
46.	Battle School: (a) 'J' RHU. (b) 'K' RHU.		II/806/1 II/806/1	Less Battle School			
47.	Det Fwd Del Sqn [Forward delivery squadron for armoured vehs]	1st Rfts		1	24		To be confirmed, further details later.
48.	HQ Fd Records.	1st Rfts		3	43		
49.	No 1 HQ NAAFI RASC/EFI			4	90		
50.	NAAFI			4	98		To follow up when force is established.

APPENDIX J

Directive to Air Vice-Marshal
C H Bouchier, CB, CBE, DFC, RAF

You are appointed to General MacArthur's Headquarters as Senior British Military Liaison Officer between him in his capacity as Commander-in-Chief of the United Nations forces operating in support of South Korea, and the British Chiefs of Staff.

2. Sir A Gascoigne, the Head of the United Kingdom Liaison Mission in Japan, is the Senior British representative in Japan. You will therefore act in close co-operation with him and his staff and keep him generally informed of your work.

3. You will be responsible for:-

    (a) The despatch of periodical reports on the battle situation as seen by you.

    (b) The despatch of periodical appreciations of the general situation as seen by the Commander-in-Chief himself.

    (c) Keeping the Chiefs of Staff informed of future American plans including expected reinforcements, both American and Allied, and the forecast dates of this deployment in the theatre.

    (d) The despatch of information concerning the tactics and technical equipment employed by the enemy. You should also report on Allied tactics and weapon effectiveness. You should in due course inform the British Chiefs of Staff whether you want any specialist staff for this purpose.

    (e) Providing General MacArthur with any detailed information he may require concerning British forces placed at his disposal; this may include making preliminary arrangements for the arrival of the advanced parties of any ground forces which may be allocated to the theatre.

    (f) In certain circumstances representing the views of the British Chiefs of Staff to General MacArthur, but the normal channel of communication from the British Chiefs of Staff will continue to be through the US Chiefs of Staff.

4. Sir A. Gascoigne has been asked to arrange for you and your staff to be housed and administered as part of General MacArthur's Headquarters. You will be paid under Air Ministry arrangements.

Notes

a. The Directive was issued under authority of the Chiefs of Staff COS (50) 284 of 1st August, 1950.

b. On the appointment of Lieutenant-General Sir Horace Robertson as non-operational Commander-in-Chief, British Commonwealth Forces in Japan and Korea, the following amendment was issued under COS (50) 494 of 27th November, 1950:

'(a) Delete paragraph 3 (e). Renumber existing paragraph 3 (f) as 3 (e).

(b) Insert new paragraph 4:-

4. You will maintain a close liaison with C-in-C, BCOF in his capacity as non-operational Commander of those Commonwealth Forces in JAPAN and KOREA for which he is responsible on all administrative matters.

(c) Re-number existing paragraph 4 as paragraph 5.'

APPENDIX M

United Nations General Assembly Resolution 376(V) of 7th October, 1950

The General Assembly

Having regard to its resolution of 14 November 1947 (112(II)), of 12 December 1948 (195(III)), and of 21 October 1949 (293(IV));

Having received and considered the Report of the United Nations Commission on Korea;

Mindful of the fact that the objectives set forth in the resolutions referred to have not been fully accomplished and in particular that the unification of Korea has not yet been achieved, and that an attempt has been made by an armed attack from North Korea to extinguish by force the Government of the Republic of Korea;

Recalling the General Assembly declaration of 12 December 1948 that there has been established a lawful government (the Government of the Republic of Korea) having effective control and jurisdiction over that part of Korea where the United Nations Temporary Commission on Korea was able to observe and consult and in which the great majority of the people of Korea reside; that this government is based on elections which were a valid expression of free will of the electorate of that part of Korea and which were observed by the Temporary Commission; and that this is the only such government in Korea;

Having in mind that United Nations armed forces are at present operating in Korea in accordance with the recommendations of the Security Council of 27 June 1950, subsequent to its resolution of 25 June 1950, that Members of the United Nations furnish such assistance to the Republic of Korea as may be necessary to repel the armed attack and to restore international peace and security in the area;

Recalling that the essential objective of the resolutions or the General Assembly referred to was the establishment of a unified, independent and democratic Government of Korea;

1. *Recommends* that

(a) All appropriate steps be taken to ensure conditions of stability throughout Korea,

(b) All constituent acts be taken, including the holding of elections, under the auspices of the United Nations for the establishment of a unified, independent and democratic Government in the sovereign State of Korea,

(c) All sections and representative bodies of the population of Korea, South and North, be invited to cooperate with the organs of the United Nations in the restoration of peace, in the holding of elections and in the establishment of a unified Government,

(d) United Nations forces should not remain in any part of Korea otherwise than so far as necessary for achieving the objectives specified at (a) and (b) above,

(e) All necessary measures be taken to accomplish the economic rehabilitation of Korea;

2. *Resolves* that

(a) A Commission consisting of Australia, Chile, Netherlands, Pakistan, Philippines, Thailand and Turkey, to be known as the United Nations Commission for the Unification and Rehabilitation of Korea be established to (i) assume the functions hitherto exercised by the present United Nations Commission in Korea, (ii) represent the United Nations in bringing about the establishment of a unified, independent and democratic Government of all Korea, (iii) exercise such responsibilities in connexion with relief and rehabilitation in Korea as may be determined by the General Assembly after receiving the recommendations of the Economic and Social Council. The United Nations Commission for the Unification and Rehabilitation of Korea should proceed to Korea and begin to carry out its functions as soon as possible;

(b) Pending the arrival in Korea of the United Nations Commission for the Unification and Rehabilitation of Korea, the Governments represented on the Commission should form an interim committee composed of representatives meeting at the Seat of the United Nations to consult with and advise the United Nations Unified Command in the light of the above recommendations; the interim committee should begin to function immediately upon the approval of this resolution by the General Assembly;

(c) The Commission shall render a report to the next regular session of the General Assembly and to any prior special session which might be called to consider the subject matter of the present resolution, and shall render such interim reports as it may deem appropriate to the Secretary-General for transmission to its Members;

The General Assembly furthermore,

Mindful of the fact that at the end of the present hostilities the task of rehabilitating the Korean economy will be of great magnitude;

3. *Requests* the Economic and Social Council, in consultation with the specialised agencies, to develop plans for relief and rehabilitation on the termination of hostilities and to report to the General Assembly within three weeks of the adoption of this resolution by the General Assembly;

4. *Also recommends* the Economic and Social Council to expedite the study of the long-term measures to promote the economic development and social progress of Korea and meanwhile to draw the attention of the authorities which decide requests for technical assistance to the urgent and special necessity of affording such assistance to Korea;

5. *Expresses* its appreciation of the services rendered by the members of the United Nations Commission on Korea in the performance of their important and difficult task;

6. *Requests* the Secretary-General to provide the United Nations Commission for the Unification and Rehabilitation of Korea with adequate staff and facilities including technical advisers as required; and authorises the Secretary-General to pay the expenses and per diem of a representative and alternate from each of the States members of the Commission.

Notes:

1. This was the final form of the draft of the 'eight nations' (sometimes also called the '8–Powers')—Australia, Brazil, Cuba, the Netherlands, Norway, Pakistan, the Philippines and the United Kingdom, carried previously in the First Committee by 47 votes to 5, Russia, Byelorussia, Ukraine, Czechoslovakia and Poland, with seven abstentions, Egypt, India, Lebanon, Saudi Arabia, Syria, Yemen, Yugoslavia. This voting was repeated in the General Assembly vote on 7th October 1950. (See p 222 in main text).

2. Immediately afterwards, the Assembly voted on the five nation or 5–Power draft, defeated in the First Committee 46:5. It was defeated in the General Assembly 52:5 with 3 abstentions. Similarly, a Russian draft resolution calling for the disbandment of UNCOK was defeated 55:5.

3. See UN Documents:
   A/PV294
   A/1426–8

APPENDIX P

Sea Movement of 29th Independent Infantry Brigade Group to Korea, 1950

Serial	Ship	Carrying:	Destination	Planned Date of:– departure (actual)	arrival dates)	Remarks
I.	*Peleus**	Vehicles 13 (reserves)	Hong Kong	13 Sep (as scheduled)	16 Oct	For transhipment to KURE
2.	*Singalese Prince*	Stores 606 dwt Ammunition 490 dwt Vehicles: 281 24 × 25-pr field guns	Pusan	21 Sep (21 Sep)	3 Nov 3 Nov)	16 armoured For 45 Field Regt RA
3.	*Pine Hill*	Stores 166 dwt Ammunition 422 dwt Vehicles: 158	Pusan	21 Sep (22 Sep)	9 Nov 3 Nov)	incl 7 Centurion, and 4 Cromwell tks
4.	*Maple Hill*	Stores 373 dwt Vehicles 173	Pusan	21 Sep (24 Sep)	10 Nov 10 Nov)	18 armoured incl 8 Crocodile tks
5.	*John Star*	Stores 459 dwt Ammunition 952 dwt Vehicles 185 6 × 17pr anti-tanks guns	Pusan	21 Sep	10 Nov	11 armoured For 1 GLOSTERS
6.	*Stratidore*	Stores 520 dwt Ammunition 971 dwt Vehicles 178 6 × 17-pr anti-tank guns	Pusan	21 Sep (as scheduled)	10 Nov	24 armoured For 1 RUR
7.	*Lord Lloyd George*	Stores 471 dwt Ammunition 1,000 dwt Vehicles 174	Pusan	21 Sep (as scheduled)	10 Nov	29 armoured
8.	*Bangor Bay*	Stores 902 dwt Ammunition 637 dwt Vehicles 172	Pusan	23 Sep (as scheduled)	9 Nov	35 armoured
9.	*Thistlemuir*	Stores 80 dwt Vehicles 126	Pusan	26 Sep (as scheduled)	13 Nov	46 armoured, incl 6 Centurion, 4 Cromwell and 2 Churchill tks.
10.	*Benarty**	Vehicles 110 (reserves)	Kure	27 Sep (as scheduled)	10 Nov	
11.	*Fry Hill*	Stores 541 dwt Vehicles 77	Pusan	1 Oct (as scheduled)	24 Nov	9 armoured: 8 Crocodile, and 1 Centurion tanks.

Serial	Ship	Carrying:	Destination	Planned Date of:– departure (actual)	arrival dates)	Remarks
12.	*Empire Pride*	*Troops:* 1 RUR 51 Army Postal Unit, RE 26 Fd Amb, RAMC 4 Ord Depot, RAOC (part) 10 Inf Wksps, REME & Stores Sec, RAOC 208 Fd Cash Office, RAPC Command Pay Office	Pusan	1 Oct (as scheduled)	5 Nov	
13.	*Empress of Australia*	*Troops:* HQ 29 Indep Inf Bde Gp Def & Emp Pl LAD Type 'B', REME 904 Field Security Sec, Int Corps 29 Indep Inf Bde Sig Sqn, R Sigs 45 Fd Regt, RA Sig Tp, R Sigs LAD, Type B 57 Coy, RASC X Supply Sec, RASC 22 Field Surgical Team, RAMC 9 Field Transfusion Team, RAMC 10 Fd Hygiene Sec, RAMC 223 Mob Dental Teams, RADC 29 Inf Bde Ord Field Park, RAOC 29 Inf Bde Sp Tps LAD 23 Heavy Recovery Section, REME 249 GHQ Provost Coy, RMP Det, Sepcial Investigation Branch, RMP Movement Control Increment, RE 102 Postal Unit, Type B, RE No 1 Battle Training Team, HQ Field Records, No 2 Public Relations Service	Pusan	2 Oct (as scheduled)	3 Nov	

SEA MOVEMENT OF 29th INDEPENDENT INFANTRY BRIGADE GROUP TO KOREA, 1950

Serial	Ship	Carrying:	Destination	departure (actual)	arrival dates)	Remarks
14.	*Empire Windrush*	*Troops:* 1 GLOSTERS 55 Fd Sqn, RE Fwd Delivery Sqn, RAC	Pusan	2 Oct (as scheduled)	7 Nov	
15.	*Benwyvis**	Vehicles 59 (reserves)	Kure	2 Oct (as scheduled)	17 Nov	5 armoured. See also serial 31.
16.	*London Dealer*	Stores 515 dwt Ammunition 500 dwt Vehicles 180	Pusan	3 Oct (as scheduled)	20 Nov	29 armoured
17.	*George K*	Stores 469 dwt Ammunition 912 dwt Vehicles 149 6 × 17-pr anti-tank guns	Pusan	4 Oct (as scheduled)	22 Nov	17 armoured For 1 NF
18.	*Aeneas**	Vehicles 27 (reserves)	Kure	4 Oct (as scheduled)	10 Nov	18 armoured
19.	*Glenartney**	Vehicles 64 (reserves)	Kure	4 Oct (as scheduled)	16 Nov	42 armoured
20.	*Inagua*	Stores 177 dwt Vehicles 101	Pusan	6 Oct (as scheduled)	25 Nov	12 armoued: 8 centurions, 2 Cromwells and 2 Crocodiles
21.	*London Statesman*	Ammunition 481 dwt Vehicles 110	Pusan	6 Oct (as scheduled)	21 Nov	Incl 8 Centurions
22.	*City of Coventry**	Vehicles 98 (reserves)	Kure	7 Oct (as scheduled)	28 Dec	
23.	*Surat**	Vehicles 70 (reserves)	Kure	7 Oct (as scheduled)	22 Nov	2 armoured
24.	*Benalbanach*	Stores 930 dwt Vehicles 34	Pusan	9 Oct (as scheduled)	13 Nov	24 Centurions, 6 Churchills, 4 Crocodiles.
25.	*Nimaris*	Stores 140 dwt Ammunition 1,003 dwt Vehicles 112	Pusan	10 Oct (as scheduled)	29 Nov	
26.	*Empire Halladale*	*Troops:* 1 NF 170 Mortar Battery, RA 4 Ord Depot, RAOC (part) 5 Med Wksps Stores Sec, RAOC HQ, British Element, Korean Base	Pusan	11 Oct (as scheduled)	18 Nov	

449

Serial	Ship	Carrying:	Destination	Planned Date of:– departure (actual)	arrival dates)	Remarks
27.	*Empire Fowey*	*Troops:* 8th Hussars Sis Tp, R Sigs LAD, Type 'C' C Sqn, 7 R Tks 11 LAA Bty, RA Sig Tp, RSigs 78 Motor Ambulance Convoy, RASC 5 Medium Wksp, REME 224 Mobile Dental Team, RADC	Pusan	2 Oct (as scheduled)	11 Nov	
28.	*Lancashire*	*Troops:* K Reinforcement Unit 104 Air Photo Interpret-ation Sec No 1 NAAFI, RASC/ EFI	Pusan	12 Oct (as scheduled)	18 Nov	1st reinforcements
29.	*Empire Medway*	*Troops:.* 29 General Hospital, RAMC J Reinforcement Unit	Kure	14 Oct (as scheduled)	23 Nov	
30.	*Empire Viceroy*	Stores 728 dwt Vehicles 34 (reserves)	Pusan	26 Oct (as scheduled)	2 Dec	11 Centurions, 2 Churchills. 13 Centurions 8 Churchills
31.	*Benalder* *	Vehicles 37 (reserves)	Singapore	—	31 Oct	31 armoured, all trans-hipped to *Benwyvis* 9 Nov 50.

Notes:

a. This appendix manifests the shipping and passage time required to move an independent infantry brigade group at war strength with line of communication and base support to the Korean/Japanese theatre in 1950. Men apart, figures shown are for the force with a theatre reserve for 30 days. Shipping followed carrying 90 days maintenance and a repair pool.

b. Total tonnages excluding troops were:

  Stores: (i) including unit heavy weapons other than guns, and equipment
                         4,539 dead weight tons (dwt)

      (ii) tinned and dry rations   2,538 dwt

  Ammunition   7,368 dwt

c. *Vehicles A/C* (tanks and other heavy tracked vehicles, scout and armoured cars, light tracked vehicles, plant and specialist trailers)   431

d. *Vehicles B* (heavy, medium and light wheeled vehicles, general service and specialist trailers)   2,291

e. *Trailers* formed about 20% of total vehicles.
  In addition, 277 motor cycles were carried in vehicle ships.

f. Ships marked * were taken up temporarily from trade, wholly or partly.
  The remainder belonged to or were on long-term contract to HM Government.

APPENDIX Q

Directive to Lieutenant-General Sir Horace Robertson, KBE, DSO, Commander-in-Chief, British Commonwealth Occupation Force

INTRODUCTION

His Majesty's Governments in the United Kingdom, Australia, Canada, and New Zealand have agreed that [in accordance with the principles and procedure established in connection with the British Commonwealth Occupation Force in Japan] responsibility for non-operational control and the general administration of the United Kingdom, Australian and New Zealand Army and Air Forces, and the Canadian Army Force, which have been or may be made available to the United Nations for operation in Korea, should rest with the Australian defence machinery together with the accredited representatives in Australia of the United Kingdom, Canadian, and New Zealand Chiefs of Staff.

2. This directive, which defines your responsibilities as Commander-in-Chief British Commonwealth Occupation Force in relation to such forces, is issued to you by the Australian Government in accordance with the assignment of responsibility referred to in paragraph 1 above.

3. This directive is additional to and, where it conflicts with it, supersedes your existing directive as Commander-in-Chief, British Commonwealth Occupation Force, dated 21st April 1949.

APPOINTMENT

4. You are appointed the representative of the Australian Chiefs of Staff to the Commander-in-Chief of United Nations Forces operating in Korea in respect of non-operational control and general administration of the forces set out in paragraph 1 above.

COMMAND AND CONTROL

5. (a) The operational control of the forces referred to in paragraph 1, above, will be exercised by the United Nations unified command.

(b) Non-operational control and administration of the forces referred to in paragraph 1, above, will be your responsibility as Commander-in-Chief, British Commonwealth Occupation Force.

6. In relation to non-operational control and administration of the Commonwealth Forces concerned, policy directions to you will be issued from the Australian Chiefs of Staff Committee.

7. You will be the representative of and responsible to each Commonwealth Service Headquarters concerned for administrative matters which concern them alone, and you will communicate with them in relation thereto. This does not prejudice the right of Commanders of national components to communicate direct with their own Governments in accordance with the directives they have received from them.

BASE ORGANISATION

8. To maintain the British Commonwealth Forces in Korea a British Commonwealth advanced base is to be established in Korea with an element in Japan. This base is to be stocked from the main base in Singapore, the existing British Commonwealth Occupation Force base in Japan, and other British Commonwealth sources as may be decided from time to time.

9. The existing British Commonwealth Occupation Force base in Japan will be responsible for maintaining such elements of the advanced base as may be located in Japan in all respects except for ordnance equipment and stores.

SAFEGUARDING INTERESTS OF BRITISH COMMONWEALTH FORCES

10. As the representative in Japan of the Australian and New Zealand Chiefs of Staff, and the United Kingdom and Canadian Service Departments concerned, you are to interest yourself in the operational tasks allotted to the United Kingdom, Australian and New Zealand Forces, and the Canadian Army Force, and for this purpose you are to maintain close contact with the Commander of the British Commonwealth Force in the field.

If the Commander of the British Commonwealth Force in the field in Korea makes representation to you in regard to the operational employment of his force, you are to represent the case to the Commander-in-Chief of the United Nations Forces in Korea, and report to the Australian Chiefs of Staff Committee.

FINANCIAL RESPONSIBILITIES

11. Your financial responsibilities in relation to the employment of the British Commonwealth Force in Korea will be communicated to you at a later date.

REPORTS

12. You will be responsible to the Canadian, Australian and New Zealand Chiefs of Staff Committee for:
   (a) the despatch of authoritative periodical reports on the battle situation with such comments as you deem necessary.
   (b) the despatch of periodical appreciations of the general situation as seen by the Commander-in-Chief, United Nations Forces in Korea.
   (c) keeping them informed of future plans, including expected reinforcements and the forecast dates of their deployment in the theatre.
   (d) the despatch of information concerning the tactics and technical equipment employed by the enemy. You should also report on Allied tactics and weapon effectiveness.

13. You will be responsible for providing the Commander-in-Chief, United Nations Forces in Korea, with any detailed information he may require concerning British Commonwealth Forces placed at his disposal.

Notes:

a. This directive was issued by the Australian Government over the signature of Lieutenant-General Sir Sydney Rowell, Chairman of the Chiefs of Staff. It carried the authority of the four governments concerned. It was cleared by the New Zealand Government on 22nd November 1950 with a preference for the exclusion of the words in brackets in paragraph 1. British and Canadian clearance was completed by the end of the month, when the Australian Chiefs of Staff despatched it to General Robertson. It became immediately effective.

b. Reference to a single British Commonwealth Force Commander in Korea was based on the expectation that 27 Brigade would shortly leave the theatre, when 29 Brigade would function alone as the operational force.

c. For financial arrangements, see Appendix R, following.

d. The United Kingdom was excepted from the provisions of paragraphs 12 and 13 because Air Vice-Marshal Bouchier had been retained as representative of the British Chiefs of Staff.

APPENDIX R

British Commonwealth Forces in Korea
Provisional Administrative Plan

GENERAL

This paper sets out the provisional administrative plan for the maintenance of the British Commonwealth Ground Forces operating as portion of the United Nations Forces in Korea hereinafter referred to as the FORCE. It incorporates the War Office plan for the maintenance of the British 29th Independent Infantry Brigade Group and the British Element Korean Base.

It is proposed that the existing administrative and maintenance arrangements for the British Commonwealth Air Force contingents supporting the United Nations in Korea should not be disturbed.

FORCE TO BE MAINTAINED

2. Initially THE FORCE will comprise:—
   (a) United Kingdom—29 Indep Bde Gp.
                       British Element Korean Base.
   (b) Australian   —3 Bn RAR.
                       Australian Element Korean Base.
   (c) New Zealand   —16 Fd Regt RNZA and attached sub-
                       units.
3. It is possible that some maintenance of the British 27 Inf Bde will require to be undertaken during its relief in Korea by 29 Bde Gp. Provision may need to be made for small elements of Allied Forces with British equipment.
4. The detailed Order of Battle of THE FORCE referred to in para 2 above are shown in Appendix A attached.
5. Planning strengths:—
   (a) Personnel—
       British: 10,500 (incl 1st reinforcements).
       Australian (less BCOF): 1,800 (incl reinforcements).
       New Zealand: 1,100 (incl reinforcements).

(b) Vehicles (H. E.) (excl M/c).

		British	Australian	NZ	Total
(i)	Heavy A	118	–	–	118
(ii)	Light A	203	41	3	247
(iii)	'B'	1,803	111	291	2,205
(iv)	'C'	4	–	2	6

COMMAND AND CONTROL

6. (a) Operational Command of THE FORCE is vested in the Commander-in-Chief, United Nations Unified Command, KOREA.
   (b) Non-operational control and general administration of THE FORCE is the responsibility of the Commander-in-Chief, British Commonwealth Occupation Force, Japan.
7. Except where otherwise indicated in this plan, maintenance support for the components of THE FORCE will be provided as follows:—
   (a) United Kingdom Formations and Units—GHQ FARELF SINGAPORE
   (b) Australian Units—
       (i) British Common User Items—GHQ FARELF SINGAPORE
       (ii) Non-Common User Items—AHQ AUSTRALIA
   (c) New Zealand Units—
       (i) British Common User Items—GHQ FARELF SINGAPORE
       (ii) Non-Common User Items—AHQ NEW ZEALAND
8. Details of the procedures to be adopted for the provision and meeting demands are set out in the appropriate Service paragraphs below.
9. A plan showing the proposed chain of supply and administrative control is attached as Appendix C.

MAINTENANCE AREA

10. THE FORCE is to be maintained from British Commonwealth sources (see para 7 above) through an advanced base which is to be established in KOREA with a transit area at Kure (JAPAN).

THEATRE RESERVES

11. (a) Ammunition:—
        all natures less tank   —30 days contact
        tank ammunition   —90 days contact
    (b) Heavy 'A' vehicles   —see para 13 below

(c) Light 'A' and 'B' vehicles   —30 days contact
(d) 'C' vehicles   —100% Unit equipment
(e) Ordnance stores less ammunition—30 days contact
    and vehicles
(f) Supplies including miscellaneous—30 days
    ST items

12. Special reserve of tanks and other heavy 'A' vehicles:
    (a) Tanks and Crocodiles   —50% Unit equipment
    (b) Other heavy 'A' Vehicles   —100% Unit equipment

MAINTENANCE STOCKS

13. (a) Ammunition:
        (i) 25 pr
           3-in mortar
           4.2-in mortar
           Explosives   —210 days contact
        (ii) Other natures   —90 days contact
    (b) Light 'A' and 'B' /vehicles/   —90 days contact
    (c) Ordnance stores   —90 days contact
    (d) Medical stores   —90 days contact
    (e) Supplies and miscellaneous
        ST items   —45 days

REPAIR POOLS

14. (a) Light 'A' and 'C' vehicles   —25% Unit equipment
    (b) 'B' vehicles   —15% Unit equipment

DISTRIBUTION OF THEATRE RESERVES AND MAINTENANCE STOCKS

15. In principle, all stocks except medical stores (see paragraph 30) will be held in KOREA. The transit area in JAPAN will only be used for transhipment of stores arriving in commercial shipping. Requirements for all units in the transit area that are not met by British Commonwealth Occupation Force, (see paragraph 17a) will be demanded on KOREA.

UNITED KINGDOM ASSISTANCE

16. GREAT BRITAIN either by direct shipment or from SINGAPORE is to provide—
    (a) Stocks required for theatre reserves, maintenance and repair pools on the scales set out in paras 11 to 14 above for THE FORCE except as stated in paras 17 and 18 below.

457

(b) Complete maintenance of all components of THE FORCE except as stated in para 17(a) below in other than the following:—
  (i) Non-common user items of ordnance stores and equipment except as in para 19 below.
  (ii) Vehicles and vehicle spare parts (for the Australian component of THE FORCE).
  (iii) Fresh rations for 3 BATTALION ROYAL AUSTRALIAN REGIMENT.
  (iv) Tea milk and sugar for THE FORCE when on Fresh Rations.
(c) Stocks of Ordnance equipment necessary for re-equipment of 3 BATTALION ROYAL AUSTRALIAN REGIMENT to reduce the non-common user items of equipment with which it is at present equipped to an agreed minimum.

AUSTRALIAN ASSISTANCE

17. AUSTRALIA is to provide:—
  (a) Complete maintenance in other than ordnance stores and equipment and medical and dental stores for such portion of THE FORCE as may be located in JAPAN.
  (b) Fresh rations for the Australian component of THE FORCE.
  (c) Tea milk and sugar for THE FORCE when it is on fresh rations.
  (d) Theatre Reserves, Maintenance Stocks and Repair pools in accordance with paras 11–14 above for those items of equipment with which the Australian component is ultimately equipped and which are available from Australian sources.
  (e) The maintenance at prescribed levels of stocks of non-common user items of Ordnance Stores, clothing and equipment, plus vehicles and their necessary scaling of spare parts, for the Australian component.

NEW ZEALAND ASSISTANCE

18. NEW ZEALAND is to provide—
Reserves and maintenance stocks, for the New Zealand Component of THE FORCE as follows:
  (a) Vehicle spare parts—90 days
  (b) One first line of all types of ammunition.
  (c) Clothing (other than cold weather clothing, source of supply not yet clear) and personal equipment—Estimated 6 months requirements.

19. NEW ZEALAND has stated its inability to maintain the required stock levels except in clothing.

UNITED STATES ASSISTANCE

20. UNITED STATES ARMY has agreed to provide in KOREA:
    (a) Engineer stores, including timber, less rafts and hutting.
    (b) Petrol oil and lubricants including 70 octane, MT Gasoline, less C 600.
    (c) All transportation behind 29 Infantry Brigade Group including tank trasporters, and including facilities for the necessary transit work in JAPAN.
    (d) Casualty evacuation between 29 Infantry Brigade Group and 29 General Hospital.
    (e) All work in connection with port operating.
    (f) Labour.
    (g) Works services.
    (h) Industrial and inert gases.
    (j) Wet-cold weather clothing for the Australian Component.

MOVEMENT

21. *Freight (Sea Movement)*
    (a) *SINGAPORE/KOREA*
        FARELF is providing:
        (i) WD LST [Tank Landing Ship] to operate one sailing per month. It will be available for limited shuttle service JAPAN/KOREA if so required.
        (ii) One chartered Coaster—estimated turn round SINGAPORE-KOREA two services per month.
        (iii) Commercial shipping as available and required.
    (b) *UNITED KINGDOM—SINGAPORE—JAPAN*
        (i) Commercial opportunities estimated at two services per week.
        (ii) Voyage times—UNITED KINGDOM to
                        SINGAPORE—6/7 weeks
                        SINGAPORE to JAPAN—2 weeks.
    (c) *NEW ZEALAND—AUSTRALIA—JAPAN*
        Commercial opportunities.
        NEW ZEALAND—AUSTRALIA: approximately 2 per month
        AUSTRALIA—JAPAN: approximately 1 per month.
    (d) *JAPAN—KOREA*
        As arranged by Commander-in-Chief, British Commonwealth Occupation Force

22. *PERSONNEL (SEA MOVEMENT)*
    (a) *UNITED KINGDOM*
        All reinforcements ex UK will normally be disembarked at SINGAPORE for onward passage in SS HONG SIANG (under FARELF Charter). Any troopship just missing scheduled sailing of this vessel will, if necessary, be routed on to JAPAN. Casual traffic will be commercial and Naval opportunities.
    (b) *AUSTRALIA and NEW ZEALAND*
        Movement of personnel will be by commercial opportunities:

NEW ZEALAND—AUSTRALIA: approximately 2 per month
    AUSTRALIA—JAPAN: approximately 1 per month
    (c) *JAPAN—KOREA*
        Movement of personnel, JAPAN—KOREA, will be as arranged by Commander-in-Chief, British Commonwealth Occupation Force.
23. *Freight and Personnel (Air Movement)*
    (a) *UNITED KINGDOM—SINGAPORE—JAPAN*
        (i) BOAC—two passenger and two freight flights per month.
        (ii) RAF—emergency light freight and casualty evacuation (see also para 29).
    (b) *NEW ZEALAND—AUSTRALIA—JAPAN*
        Chartered aircraft as necessary and commercial opportunities (see also para 29).

ACCOMMODATION

24. (a) Such arrangements as may be necessary are to be made by Commander-in-Chief, British Commonwealth Occupation Force for the accommodation of THE FORCE in KOREA.
    (b) British Commonwealth Occupation Force is to provide accommodation for such elements of THE FORCE as may be stationed in JAPAN.
    (c) FARELF is to provide hutted accommodation for 3,000 men for the Korean Base.
    (d) US Army are providing transit facilities in KOREA.
    (e) Tentage and accommodation stores for 10,000 men are being shipped with the UNITED KINGDOM Component.

SUPPLIES

25. *Rations*
    (a) Holdings—see paras 11 and 13. (Note: NEW ZEALAND is not providing reserves of rations.)

(b) Whilst the US Forces remain on tinned rations, THE FORCE in Korea will be provided with British Compo-[site] rations.

(c) United States is providing fresh bread for THE FORCE in Korea.

(d) FARELF is providing requirements of THE FORCE in Korea in respect of:
Cigarettes/Tobacco
Rum
Cocoa

(e) The portions of THE FORCE stationed in JAPAN are to be rationed by British Commonwealth Occupation Force in accordance with Australian Rations Scale (Fresh).

(f) If United States Army changes to fresh rations—
  (i) early advice is to be given by Commander-in-Chief, British Commonwealth Occupation Force to FARELF who are to provide British fresh rations (less bread) for the Force in Korea less the Australian Component.
  (ii) War Office [United Kingdom] is to provide such extra supply personnel as necessary.

(g) Subsequent maintenance:
  (i) Food requirements other than Australian fresh rations and bread will be by demand on FARELF, repeated War Office.
  (ii) Australian fresh rations will be by demand through British Commonwealth Occupation Force on Army Headquarters, AUSTRALIA.

26. *Miscellaneous ST supplies*
  (a) UNITED KINGDOM is to provide initially 60 days stocks for 10,500 personnel of:
    (i) Disinfectants
    (ii) Filter and sterilising powder
    (iii) Miscellaneous items
    (iv) Hospital rations
  (b) AUSTRALIA is to provide initial stocks (60 days) for the Australian component.
  (c) NEW ZEALAND is to provide no stocks of miscellaneous S & T supplies.
  (d) Subsequent maintenance is to be by demand on FARELF repeated War Office.

PETROL OIL AND LUBRICANTS

27. All POL including antifreeze, less C 600 in Korea, is being provided by United States Army in KOREA or by British Commonwealth Occupation Force in JAPAN. War Office is arranging

to supply stocks of C 600 pending investigations of suitability of US SPIRAX 90.

28. *Flame-thrower fuel*

United States Army is to supply.

MEDICAL AND HYGIENE

29. *Casualty evacuation*
   (a) KOREA—JAPAN
       Between units of THE FORCE in KOREA and 29 General Hospital in JAPAN, casualty evacuation will be through United States Army medical channels.
   (b) JAPAN—UNITED KINGDOM
       (i) Royal Air Force likely to provide 60 passengers per month by air to United Kingdom.
       (ii) Evacuation of overflow from (i) above will be through FARELF, SS HONG SIANG being used to SINGAPORE.
   (c) JAPAN—AUSTRALIA—NEW ZEALAND
       By commercial shipping and/or chartered aircraft as necessary.
30. *Medical and Dental Stores*
   (a) 90 days holdings for all medical and dental units are to accompany British 29 General Hospital for use by THE FORCE.
   (b) Subsequent maintenance is to be demanded on FARELF.

ORDNANCE

31. *Holdings*—see paras 11 to 19 above.
32. *Initial Supply and re-supply*
   (a) UNITED KINGDOM Component: Four months require-ments will accompany Component from UNITED KINGDOM and further requirements, less major items, for a further period of four months will be shipped two months later to KOREA by chartered shipping or to KURE by commercial opportunities.
   (b) Australian Component: Eight months requirements of items with which the Australian Component is ultimately equipped (see para 16 (c)) and which are available from Australian sources will be phased into 4 Ord[nance] Depot as arranged with British Commonwealth Occupation Force.
   (c) NEW ZEALAND Component: Stores as stated in para 18 are accompanying the NEW ZEALAND Component to the theatre.

462

34. *Layout*
    (a) 4 Ord Depot will be located in KOREA and will consist of:
        Ordnance store depot
        Ammunition depot
        Vehicle and Gun Park
        Laundry and Bath Platoon
        with a small element at KURE to deal with transhipment of stores that cannot go directly to KOREA.
    (b) 29 Infantry Brigade Ordnance Field Park will move with 29 Brigade Group and is to be increased by one ordnance brigade platoon.
    (c) Stores sections will accompany 10 Infantry Brigade Workshops, 5 Medium Workshops and 444 Forward Delivery Squadron, Royal Armoured Corps.
    (d) Port ordnance detachments will be provided by 4 Ordnance Depot as required.
35. *Clothing replacements*
These will be in accordance with orders issued by National Component Commanders.

ELECTRICAL MECHANICAL ENGINEERS

36. *Layout*
    Korea
    10 Infantry Workshops will be in immediate support of 29 Infantry Brigade Group and 5 Medium Workshops will operate under the control of HQ Korean Base.
37. *Repair policy*
    (a) First and second echelon repairs, less Army Service Corps. will be carried out by 10 Infantry Workshops and 5 Medium Workshops in KOREA. Limited repair beyond this range will be carried out in KOREA provided that spares are held in accordance with agreed Ordnance/Electrical Mechanical Engineer range. First and second echelon repairs to vehicles in JAPAN will be carried out by British Commonwealth Occupation Force.
    (b) Vehicles and equipment of other than Australian, Canadian or United States origin requiring third and fourth echelon repairs will be backloaded to SINGAPORE, less Centurion tanks and other heavy 'A' vehicles except Comet tanks, and less repairs catered for at para 37(a) above.
    (c) Vehicles of Australian, Canadian or United States origin for third or fourth echelon repairs will be backloaded to JAPAN.

(d) Centurion tanks and other heavy 'A' vehicles, except Comet tanks, requiring repairs beyond the scope of 5 Medium Workshops, will be backloaded to United Kingdom.

(e) FARELF is to undertake repairs to Comet tanks.

(f) Main engine assemblies of Centurion tanks will, except in emergency, be backloaded by sea to United Kingdom. If operational wastage rates prove high, arrangements will be made with the War Office for their air freightage.

ENGINEER STORES

38. *Bridging equipment*

The following equipment is accompanying the UNITED KINGDOM Component to the theatre:

 20 modified Class 50/60 rafts

 20 trailers

This equipment will be handed over to United States Army on arrival. United States Army are providing prime movers for the trailers.

39. *Explosives*

240 days contact rates (theatre and maintenance stocks) are being despatched with the UNITED KINGDOM Component.

Commander-in-Chief, British Commonwealth Force will confirm to FARELF, repeated War Office, whether United States Army will replenish or whether maintenance is required from SINGAPORE.

40. *Mine Detectors*

Replacements of mine detectors will be with American types to be supplied by United States Army.

41. *Engineer Stores*

All other engineer stores requirements, including bridging and timber but less huttings, is to be provided by United States Army.

POSTAL

42. (a) 102 Army Postal Unit located in KOREA will perform the functions of a Base Postal Depot with Forward Army Post Offices set up to serve the Force. Detachments will also be provided as required.

(b) 51 Army Postal Unit will operate in the Korean Base.

(c) Air mail will be forwarded between United Kingdom and Japan by scheduled BOAC (twice weekly) services and between NEW ZEALAND—AUSTRALIA and JAPAN by scheduled services. Connecting Air services between JAPAN and KOREA will be used.

(d) Surface mail will be handled through fastest normal routes.

LABOUR

43. (a) Skilled and unskilled local civilian labour will be provided by the South Korean Government through the existing US Army organisation
    (b) Methods of indenting for, conditions of service, hours of work, and rates of pay of civilian labour will be as decided by Unified Command, KOREA for all local labour employed by United Nations forces, and will be promulgated by the Commander-in-Chief, British Commonwealth Occupation Force.
    (c) Authority for employment of civilians in KOREA will be exercised as follows:
        (i) Professional, administrative, supervisory and clerical staff, Motor Transport drivers and mess staff and servants (such as waiters, cooks and orderlies) may be employed within War Establishment in replacement of military personnel on the authority of Officer Commanding Unit or installation. In exceptional circumstances civilians of these grades may be employed in excess of War Establishment on the authority of the Commander-in-Chief, British Commonwealth Occupation Force.
        (ii) Interpreters, hotel staff, marine grades, artisans and unskilled labour necessary for the functioning of the respective Services may be engaged and discharged at the discretion of the authority of the heads of the Services or their authorised delegates. In an emergency civilians may be engaged by units, but application for covering authority will be made immediately.
        (iii) The cost of the following categories will be borne by the agency employing such labour:
        barbers and gardeners; employees of NAAFI/EFI; or employees in hotels or clubs controlled by NAAFI/EFI; mess cooks, waiters and orderlies employed in excess of WE, unless authority has been granted, employees of voluntary organisations, eg, Red Cross.

NAVY ARMY AIR-FORCE INSTITUTE/EXPEDITIONARY FORCE INSTITUTE

45. *Layout*
No 1. Headquarters Royal Army Service Corps/Expeditionary

Force Institute will accompany THE UNITED KINGDOM Component and will operate:

KOREA: One canteen base depot

Three bulk issue stores

Six mobile canteens

JAPAN: One transit detachment.

46. *Additional facilities*

Navy, Army, Air-Force Institutes are prepared to send additional detachments to provide wider facilities, eg, static canteens, to follow from United Kingdom when required. Headquarters Korean Base will advise Commander-in-Chief, British Commonwealth Occupation Force of further requirements after arrival in KOREA.

47. *Supplies*

Navy, Army, Air-Force Institutes supplies will include the requirements of the Force in KOREA in respect of regimental necessities, including razors, brushes etc. Arrangements are also being made for the provision of a limited range of sports goods for sale by the Navy, Army, Air-Force Institute.

AACS

47. The Australian Army Canteen Service will cater for such portions of the Force as may be located in JAPAN. It will extend its present activities as may be decided from time to time by C-in-C BCOF.

FINANCIAL SECTION

48. Issued separately.

Notes on the Plan and its appendices

a. This plan is shown *in extenso* because it manifests the principles on which the Commonwealth land forces were supplied and administered during the Korean war, and the detail from November, 1950, to February, 1951. *It should be read in conjunction with Appendix N.* It also demonstrates the advantages of common weapons, equipment and procedures in an international force. Although these were apparent in later military operations and other cooperative ventures in Borneo and Malaya in the 1950s and 1960s, and in the Rhodesian Monitoring Force in 1980, all were on a smaller and narrower basis.

b. The plan was presented to the Australian Defence Committee on 8th November by the Joint Administrative Planning Committee under reference Report No. 8/1950, and the Defence Committee's Agendum No 161/1950, Supplement No. 1, under Secret cover. (See also UK PRO Reference DEFE 11/253). It was the work of military and civil staff officers in Australia, New Zealand and the United Kingdom which accounts for its irregular style and phraseology. United Kingdom agreement to its adoption is contained in DEFE 11/204 (Commonwealth Relations Office 217 of 18th November 1950), and although it was still referred to as 'provisional', the plan above was implemented almost wholly as drafted. British agreement was interconnected with the terms of Lieutenant-General Sir Horace Robertson's appointment as Commander-in-Chief of the Commonwealth Base, which became subordinate to the British Commonwealth Occupation Force in Japan. (See Appendix Q).

c. Although the New Zealand field artillery regiment RNZA and transport platoon of the RNZASC did not enter operations until 1951, the decision to form and despatch them had been taken in sufficient time to ensure full coverage of arrangements for their component in the plan. Canadian participation had also been agreed in 1950 but the Canadian Government did not wish to enter joint administrative (or financial) arrangements, as they saw it, precipitately, for several reasons. Political reservations apart, Canada had long since divorced herself from ties to sterling, and some of the Canadian Army's equipment was of United States origin.

d. The foregoing notes apply generally to the agreement on financial arrangements between the Commonwealth nations concerned, but these will be discussed more fully in vol ii.

e. The appendices to the Administrative Plan were threefold:

A—the British Commonwealth Order of Battle in Korea.
    This is not reproduced as the final deployment of units to Korea is shown fully in Appendix N to this volume.
B—Units located in the Transit Area, Kure, Japan.
    Attached—shown as recorded.
C—Chain of Operational, Supply and Administrative Control.
    Attached—shown as recorded.

APPENDIX B to Provisional Administrative Plan

DETAILS OF UNITS TO BE LOCATED IN TRANSIT AREA: KURE

HQ	Transit Area HQ (detached from HQ Korean Base)
ST	78 Motor Ambulance Convoy, less one platoon
Med	29 General Hospital
	10 FIT
Ord	Detachment, 4 Ordnance Depot
Provost	One section, 249 GHQ Provost Company
Pay	31 Command Pay Office
Postal	Detachments, 102 Army Postal Unit

Records   1st Independent Field Records
Misc   1 Battle Training Team
           'J' Reinforcement Unit
           One Reinforcement Training Unit (New Zealand)
           One Reinforcement Training Unit (Australian)
           Detachment, 1 HQ RASC/Expeditionary Force
           Institute

Note

Although the original intention was to locate 1st Independent Field Records in Korea, it was established in Kure from November 1950. A detachment was sent to the British Commonwealth Korean Base in Korea.

APPENDIX C to Provisional Administrative Plan

BRITISH COMMONWEALTH KOREAN FORCE

CHAIN OF OPERATIONAL, SUPPLY AND ADMINISTRATIVE CONTROL

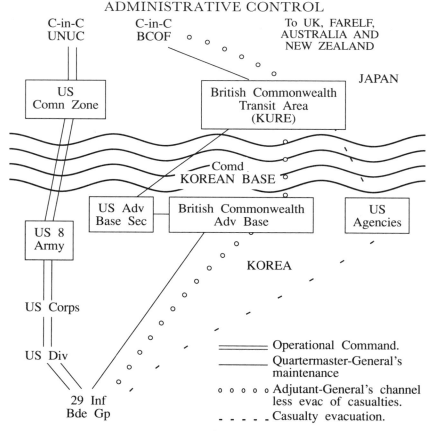

SOURCE DOCUMENTS AND BIBLIOGRAPHY

Source documents

United Kingdom
In the United Kingdom, the author has had unrestricted access to the files of all Departments of State and ministries involved in the events of the Korean War. In so far as this volume is concerned, they were:

Cabinet Office
Foreign Office
Commonwealth Relations Office, and Dominions Office
Treasury
Defence
Admiralty
War Office
Air Ministry
Supply
Board of Trade
Transport

The process of selecting records to be permanently preserved, or not, which is carried out in all Government Departments has, in respect of the records of the United Kingdom's part in the Korean War, inevitably left some gaps. Rationalisation of working papers has, for example, resulted in the reduction of those of the Staff Duties and Military Operations Directorates in the War Office to a single volume, the MO1 Collection.

However the Chiefs of Staff collection has, with few omissions been preserved. The series, originally under reference G/Kor/1, 2 or 3, contains the working papers of the Chiefs' secretariat. These include the minutes of the Chiefs of Staff meetings in connection with the war, and the relevant 'diptels', the Foreign Office and Commonwealth Relations Office telegrams. The full range of minutes of the Chiefs of Staff meetings are held separately in bound volumes and, similarly, the run of diplomatic telegrams. However, in order to obviate the need for the researcher in the Public Record Office to call for numbers of departmental documents, many of the source notes in this volume locate the Chief's meetings and diplomatic telegrams in the Chiefs of Staff's file relevant to the period. Where there is a requirement to see departmental minutes to telegrams, and the range of policy papers and memoranda of the Foreign and Commonwealth Relations Offices, it will be necessary to draw upon the series shown below.

Some of the documents relating to defence and overseas policy are still withheld from public view. I have had access to and taken account of all of them.

Minutes of Cabinet and Cabinet Committee meetings, including preparatory papers for agenda items, have all been preserved and their descriptions for reference are shown below. The same applies to records of standing inter-departmental committees or those formed to deal with business arising from the war.

Service unit and command diaries have been preserved intact, though a few attached papers or maps have been lost in handling. This is a common mishap with papers which are compiled on active service, frequently on the move, in all weather, sometimes in poor accommodation and light. It may be helpful to point out that these documents are not hour to hour records. That is the function of the operations log. But the latter is completed in manuscript and often, by the very fact of its immediacy, is subject to errors of understanding or reporting which become apparent later. A Report of Proceedings or war diary is sometimes made up daily, more often once a week or month, depending on when the officer responsible for its compilation is able to find a quiet moment. The diary is based on the unit operations log, complemented by his own enquiries, and connected papers, charts or maps, together with administrative details required by higher headquarters—for example, the names of officers and the numbers by rank and duty of all members of a unit are expected to be shown in an annexure to all Army war diaries. Operational logs are not preserved.

Copies of Reports of Proceedings for all Commonwealth warships, and the war diaries of all Commonwealth land force units, are held in the United Kingdom Public Record Office, though these do not include all attached papers for Australian, Canadian, and New Zealand units. On this account, some of the references to these records relate to the originals in the national archives of the Commonwealth country concerned.

Series References
Prime Minister's Office—

PREM 8
notably 1405 Part 1

Cabinet Office—

CAB 21
CAB 65
CAB 66
CAB 69
CAB 79
CAB 80
CAB 84
CAB 99
CAB 120
CAB 124
CAB 126
CAB 128
CAB 129
CAB 130
CAB 131
CAB 133
CAB 134
CAB 139

Foreign & Commonwealth Office—

FO 371
(Far Eastern Department (F) 83008–84700
inc (1950) 92058–93122
inc (1951))
FO 800
DO 35

Defence departments—

DEFE 4
DEFE 5
DEFE 7
DEFE 11

Admiralty Case 11554
ADM 1
ADM 116
ADM 167

WO 32
WO 36
WO 163
WO 193
WO 203
WO 208
WO 216

	WO 242
	WO 259
	WO 281
	AIR 8
	AIR 19
	AIR 20
	AIR 27
	AIR 28
Treasury—	T171/397–402
Board of Trade—	BT 11

Commonwealth

Thanks to the generosity of the Australian and Canadian Governments, I have had access to their archives containing ministerial, external affairs, and defence documents. I exclude New Zealand only because I have not required to research there in connection with this volume, but I have had full responses to written requests for help. Principal series references in Australia and Canada are shown below.

Australia

Mitchell, ACT (Political, External	CA 12
Affairs, Defence, and Treasury)	CA 18
	CA 46
	CA 68
Australian War Memorial, Canberra,	AWM 85
ACT (War diaries, BCOF, Defence	AWM 89
Committee, Naval History, Professor	AWM 114
O'Neill's papers)	AWM 123
	AWM 124
Defence Archives & Hist., Russell,	JAPC agenda and
ACT (Joint Administrative Plans)	reports, 1950

Canada
Ottawa

Political and External Affairs	RG 2
Naval History series	1480
	1650
	1926

Naval Reports of Proceedings
NB. During the writing of this volume, many state papers relating to the Korean War were still held in the Departments of National Defence and External Affairs, eg DoEA 8254, 1941–51.

United States

The accessibility of national records in the United States is well known. I received every assistance in searching State Department records in the National Archive building in Washington, DC, and the military records centre at Suitland, Maryland. I was fortunate to find the full range of naval signals and orders in the Naval Records in Washington, DC, but there are no Records of Proceedings or the equivalent for United States warships; it was not then the custom to make such records. I was given full details of records available by the (then) Chief of United States Air Force History, Major-General J Huston together with a copy of the history of the Far East Air Force in the Korean War and FEAF Intelligence Roundup during my visit to his headquarters in Washington, DC.

Full details of the State Department series is contained in the publication 'Foreign Relations of the United States, volume VII, Korea.' Papers omitted from this collection lie within these references in the Archives building on Pennsylvania Avenue, Washington, DC.

The National Security Council Papers are in the same location in the series RG 407.

The Joint Chiefs of Staff files at Suitland are contained in a series of case files under the prefix 'CCS' (Combined Chiefs of Staff), with which are associated notes and memoranda by the Chairman and members, and copies of documents relating to action on matters such as Presidential or National Security Council decisions.

The Army records are at Suitland also. There is a good deal of overlapping between the extensive sets of series. They are not therefore listed. The researcher would be advised to decide whether to seek first a *resumé* of a particular item or period of interest in the form of the Army or a corps monthly summary of events, or to ask directly for the formation or unit war diary concerned, with which will be connected operation orders and message files. These are not always continuous at lower levels for the same reasons that applied to British war diaries. Intelligence information ranges from immediate reports to the specialist productions of the Allied Translator & Interpreter Section following interrogations of prisoners-of-war. At the high levels—GHQ in Tokyo and in Headquarters, Eighth Army and X Corps, journals, chiefs of staff memoranda etc, supplement the picture of policy making, reaction to events, and the day to day working of the commander and his staff.

Further information is available in personal papers (and some official papers retained by senior commanders) at the following sites:

US Army Military History Institute, Carlisle, Pa
Lieutenant-General Edward Almond—papers and oral history
(OH)
General Matthew B Ridgway—papers
S L A Marshall—papers

Douglas MacArthur Memorial Library, Norfolk, Va
This contains the MacArthur Memorial Bureau Archives,
including both the General's extensive official, demi-official,
and personal papers, and those of his personal staff. Of note
are:

RG 5—SCAP records 1945-51
RG 6—GHQ FECOM, records, 1947-51
RG 9—Signals collection, 1945-51
RG 10—General MacArthur's personal letters, 1932-64

Official Publications

United Kingdom

Naval Staff History, *British Commonwealth Naval Operations, Korea,
   1950-53*(Ministry of Defence, 1967)
Linklater, Eric *Our Men in Korea* (HMSO, 1952)

Australia
O'Neill, Professor Robert, *Australia in the Korean War*, Australian
   War Memorial, Canberra
      Volume 1: *Strategy and Diplomacy* (1981)
      Volume 2: *Combat Operations* (1985)

Canada
Thorgrimsson, Thor and Russell, E C, *Canadian Naval Operations
   in Korean Waters, 1950-55* (Department of National Defence,
   Ottawa, 1965)
Wood, Lieutenant-Colonel Herbert Fairley, *Strange Battleground,
   Operations in Korea and their effects on the Defence Policy of Canada*
   (Ottawa, 1966)

Democratic People's Republic of Korea
Documents and Materials Exposing the Instigators of the Civil War in Korea
   (Ministry of Foreign Affairs, P'yongyang, 1950)

Republic of Korea
The History of the United Nations Forces in the Korean War, six volumes
   (Ministry of National Defence, Seoul, 1973)

United States of America
United States Joint Chiefs of Staff. The history of the Joint Chiefs of Staff series (Wilmington)
Schnabel, James F, and Watson, Robert, Volume 3 *The Joint Chiefs of Staff and National Policy* (1979)

United States Naval History Division
Field, James A, *History of United States Naval Operations, Korea* (Washington, DC, 1962)

Headquarters, United States Marine Corps
Montross, Lynn and Canzona, Captain Nicholas A, USMC, *US Marine Operations in Korea,* volumes I to III (Washington, DC, 1954–57)

Office of the Chief of Military History, Washington, DC,
The United States Army in the Korean War series:
1. Schnabel, James F, *Policy and Direction, The First Year* (1972)
2. Appleman, Roy E, *South to the Naktong, North to the Yalu* (1961)
3. Mossman, William, *Ebb and Flow* (1990)
4. Hermes, Walter G, *Truce Tent and Fighting Front* (1966)
Cowdrey, Albert E, *The Medics' War* (1987)
Gough, Terence J, *US Army Mobilisation in the Korean War* (1987)
Gugeler, Captain Russell A, *Combat Actions in Korea* (1954)
Sawyer, Major Robert K, *Military Advisors in Korea: KMAG in Peace and War* (Washington, DC, 1962)
Westover, John G, *Combat Support in Korea* (1987)

United States Air Force History Branch
Futrell, Robert E, *The United States Air Forces in Korea, 1950–1953* (New York, 1961)

United States Department of State
Foreign Relations of the United States, 1950 Volume VII, Korea (Government Printing Office).

Books

Acheson, Dean, *Present at the Creation* (London, 1969).
Anderson, Brigadier R C B, *History of the Argyll and Sutherland Highlanders, 1st Battalion 1939–54* (Edinburgh, 1956)
Barclay, Roderick, *Ernest Bevin and the Foreign Office 1932–69* (London, 1975)
Baldwin, Frank (ed), *Without Parallel* (New York, 1973)
Barker, Elizabeth, *The British between the Superpowers* (London, 1983)
Bartlett, Norman (ed), *With the Australians in Korea* (Australian War Memorial, Canberra, 1954)
Baylis, John, *Anglo-American Defence Relations 1939–84* (London, 1984)

Berger, Carl, *The Korean Knot* (Philadelphia, 1957)

Beloff, Max, *Soviet Policy in the Far East 1944–51* (London, 1953)

Bullock, Alan, *Ernest Bevin, Foreign Secretary* (London 1983)

Cagle, Malcolm W and Manson, Frank A, *The Sea War in Korea* (USNI, Annapolis, 1957)

Cotton, James and Neary, Ian (eds), *The Korean War in History* (Manchester, 1989)

Cummings, Bruce (ed), *Child of Conflict, The Korean-American Relationship 1943–53* (Seattle, 1983)

Cutforth, Rene, *Korean Reporter* (London, 1952)

Dean, Major-General William F, *General Dean's Story* (London, 1954)

Deane, Philip, *Captive in Korea* (London, 1953)

Domes, Jurgen, *P'eng Te-huai, The Man and the Image* (London, 1985)

Foster, D F, see Pickersgill, J W

George, Alexander L, *The Chinese Communist Army in Action* (London, 1967)

Goodrich Leland M, *Korea, A Study of US Policy in the United Nations* (New York, 1956)

Goodwin, Geoffrey L, *Britain and the United Nations* (London, 1957)

Gowing, Margaret, *Independence & Deterrence, Britain and Atomic Energy 1945–52* (London, 1974)

Grey, Dr Jeffrey, *The Commonwealth in the Korean War* (Manchester, 1988)

Griffith, Brigadier-General Samuel B. II, *The Chinese People's Liberation Army* (London, 1967)

Gunther, John *The Riddle of MacArthur* (New York, 1951)

Harris, Kenneth, *Attlee* (London, 1982)

Hastings, Max, *The Korean War* (London, 1987)

Hayes, Richard F, *The Awesome Power, Harry S. Truman as Commander-in-Chief* (Baton Rouge, 1973)

Heinl, Colonel Robert Debs jr, *Victory at High Tide* (Washington, DC, 1979)

Henderson, Gregory, *The Politics of the Vortex* (Cambridge, Mass, 1968)

Higgins, Marguerite, *War in Korea* (New York, 1951)

Hiscocks, Richard, *The Security Council. A Study in Adolescence* (London, 1973)

Huang Chen-hsia, *Chung-kung chun-jen chi* (Hong Kong, 1968) see also Whitson, William

Inglis, A I, see under Munro, J

Jackson, Robert, *Air War Over Korea* (London, 1973)

Karig, Captain Walter, *Battle Report* (New York, 1952)

Kemp, Lieutenant-Commander Peter, *The Middlesex Regiment 1919–52* (Aldershot, 1956)

Kennan, George F, *Memoirs 1925–63* 2 volumes (Boston, 1967 and 1972)

Khruschev, Nikita, *Khruschev Remembers* (London, 1971)

Kim Ch'ang-sun, *Puk Han siponyon-sa* (Seoul, 1961)

Kim Chun-kon, *The Korean War* (Seoul, 1973)

Kim Hak-joon, *Unification Policies of South and North Korea* (Seoul, 1978)

Kolko, Joyce and Gabriel, *The Limits of Power. The World and US Foreign Policy 1945–54* (New York, 1972)

Korean War, The Ground Battle History Institution of Japan, (Tokyo, 1969)

Ladd, James D, *The Royal Marines* (London, 1980)

Leckie, Robert, *The Korean War* (London, 1962)

Lee, Chong-sik, *The Politics of Korean Nationalism* (Berkeley & Los Angeles, 1965) see also under Scalapino

Lie, Trygve, *In the Cause of Peace* (New York, 1954)

Long, Gavin, *MacArthur as Military Commander* (London, 1969)

Lowe, Peter, *The Origins of the Korean War* (London, 1986)

Luard, Evan, *Britain and China* (London, 1962)

MacFarquhar, Roderick, *The Origins of the Cultural Revolution*, two volumes (London, 1974 and 1983)

MacDonald, Callum A, *Korea: The War Before Vietnam* (London, 1986)

McClellan, David S, *Dean Acheson, The State Department Years* (New York, 1976)

McCormack, Gavan, *Cold War, Hot War* (Sydney, 1983)

McCune, George, *Korea Today* (New York, Cambridge, Mass, 1950)

Manchester, William, *American Caesar, Douglas MacArthur* (London, 1979)

Manson, Frank A, see Cagle, Malcolm W

Marshall, Brigadier-General S L A, *The River and the Gauntlet* (New York, 1953)

Meade, E. Grant, *American Military Government in Korea* (New York, 1951)

Monat, Pawel, *Spy in the United States* (London, 1962)

Mosley, Leonard, *Dulles* (New York, 1978)

Munro, J A and Inglis, A I (eds), *Lester Pearson Memoirs, 1948–57* (London, 1974)

Neary, Ian, see Cotton, James

Nicholas, H G, *The United Nations as a Political Institution* (second edition, London, 1962)

O Yon-jin, *Hana ni chung-on* (Pusan, 1952)

Oakley, Derek, see Smith, Peter.

Odgers, George, *Across the Parallel* (London, 1953)

Oh, John Kie-chang, *Korea: Democracy on Trial* (New York, 1968)

Oliver, Robert T, *Syngman Rhee. The Man behind the Myth* (New York, 1954)

Paige, Glenn D, *The Korean Decision* (New York, 1968)

Panikkar, K M, *In Two Chinas* (London, 1955)

Pickersgill, J W, and Foster, D F, *The Mackenzie King Record, IV, 1947–1948* (Toronto, 1970)

Rees, David, *Korea: The Limited War* (London, 1964)

Ridgway, General Matthew B, *The Korean War* (New York, 1956)

The Royal Ulster Rifles in Korea (Belfast, 1953)

Scalapino, Robert A, and Chong Sik-lee,*Communism in Korea* vol 1 (Los Angeles, 1972)

Shipster, Colonel J N, *The Diehards in Korea* (Middlesex Regiment, 1979)

Simmons, Robert R, *The Strained Alliance, Peking, Pyongyang, Moscow and the Politics of the Korean War* (New York, 1975)

Smith, Gaddis, *Dean Acheson* vol XVI in Robert E. Ferrell (ed), *The American Secretaries of State and their Diplomacy* (New York, 1972)

Smith, Peter C, and Derek Oakley, *Royal Marines, a Pictorial History* (Tunbridge Wells, 1988)

Stairs, Denis, *The Diplomacy of Constraint, Canada, the Korean War and the US* (Toronto, 1975)

Stone, I F, *The Hidden History of the Korean War* (London, 1952)

Suh, Dae-sook, *The Korean Communist Movement* 2 vols (Princeton NJ, 1967 and 1970)

Thompson, Reginald, *Cry Korea* (London, 1951)

Truman, Harry S, *Memoirs* 2 vols (New York, 1955 and 1956)

Whiting, Allen S, *China Crosses the Yalu* (New York, 1960)

Williams, Francis (with Lord Attlee), *A Prime Minister Remembers* (London, 1961)

Williams, Philip M, (ed), *Hugh Gaitskell* (Diary) (London, 1983)

Whitson, William W, and Huang Chen-hsia, *The Chinese High Command, A History of Communist Military Politics, 1927–71* (London, 1973)

Newspapers and news agencies, magazines and journals

Age (Australia)

American Mercury (US)

Army (US)

Asian Survey (US)

Associated Press (UK)

Australian Defence Force Journal

Bulletin (USSD—US)

China Quarterly (UK)
Colliers (US)
Crowsnest (Royal Canadian Navy Journal—Canada)
Daily Express (UK)
Daily Mail (UK)
Daily Telegraph (UK)
Daily Worker (UK)
International Security (US)
Economist (UK)
Foreign Affairs (US)
Jen Min Pao (People's Daily) (China)
Life (US)
Manchester Guardian (UK)
Newsweek (US)
New York Herald Tribune (US)
New York Times (US)
Ottawa Citizen (Canada)
Pacific Historical Review (US)
Political Quarterly (US)
Reuters
RIIA publications (UK)
RUSI Journal (UK)
Saturday Evening Post (US)
Sydney Morning Herald (Australia)
Time Magazine (US)
Times (UK)
Toronto Daily Star (Canada)
Twentieth Century (UK)
US News & World Report (US)
Washington Post (US)

Cinema and Television—news and international affairs

Gaumont British News (UK)
Pathe Gazette (UK)

The Korean War, Produced by Phillip Whitehead for Thames
(6 Parts)   TV/Channel 4/WGBH Boston/ABC

Index

fn—footnote   sn—source note

Q

Queen's Own Royal Regiment, The *see* ARMIES

R

Radford, Admiral Arthur William, USN, Commander-in-Chief of the United States Pacific Fleet 266

Rangaraja, Lieutenant-Colonel (later Colonel) A G, IAMS, commanding officer, 60th Indian Parachute Field Ambulance 382

Rankin, Squadron-Leader (later Wing-Commander) Ronald John, Royal Australian Air Force 40 and fn

Rau, Sir Benegal Rama, Indian Permanent Representative at the United Nations 45, 46, 222, 361

Reardon Smith Line 71fn

Redman, Major-General (later Lieutenant-General Sir) Harold, Director of Military Operations (DMO) 99 fn, 101

Reith, Major Douglas, Argyll & Sutherland Highlanders, Brigade Major, 27th British Commonwealth Brigade 173, 257 fn

Rendell, Major (later Brigadier) D B, Middlesex Regiment 262 sn6 and 27

Repose, USS Hospital Ship 375

Republic of Korea: formation 1, 18–20; second elections in 30–31; status 21–9, 46; recognised by US and UK 29; supported by UK 33; ministers excluded from settlement by Kim Il-sung 39; US suspects motives of 30 and fn, (persists in support of) 267; ROK Government quits Seoul for Taejon 37; *passim* 31, 32, 46, 83, 93, 100, 186, 203, 204, 219

National Assembly 16, 19, 26, 30 fn, 31, 39, 136, 196, 222, 267

Republican Party (United States) 299

Reuter's News Agency 50, 270, 302, 303

Rhee, Syngman (also Li Seung-man), President of the Republic of Korea 19, 22, 23, 24, 29, 30, 38, 39, 192, 196, 216, 229, 266 fn, 267

Rickett, D H F, Principal Private Secretary to the Prime Minister 358 fn

Ridgway, Lieutenant-General (later General), Matthew B, US Army, Deputy Chief of Army Staff, later Commander, 8th US Army in Korea 383, 384, 386, 390, 392

Rimuon-ma Cape (also Imwon-jin) 67

Roberts, Lieutenant (later Colonel) G F D, Royal Marines, 41 Commando 339

Robertson, Lieutenant-General Sir Horace, Australian Army, Commander-in-Chief, British Commonwealth Occupation Force, and non-operational Commander British Commonwealth Forces in Korea 285 fn, 319, 322, 323, 324, 325, 326

Robertson, Sergeant J, 1 A&SH 164

Rochester, USS (cruiser) 63, 150, 154

Romanenko, Major-General A A, Political Staff, Russian Far Eastern Front 6

Roosevelt, Franklin Delano, President of the United States 2 and fn, 3, 5, 7, 88

Ross, Charles (Charlie) G, Press Secretary to President Truman 267 fn, 355

Rotoiti, HMNZS (frigate) 379

Rowell, Lieutenant-General Sir Sydney Fairbairn, Chief of the Australian General Staff 324, 325, 326

Rowlandson, Colonel (later Brigadier) A M, British Army, commander of the British Commonwealth Korean Base 322 and Appendix N

Royal Air Force, *see* AIR FORCES

Royal Army Dental Corps, units *see* ARMIES

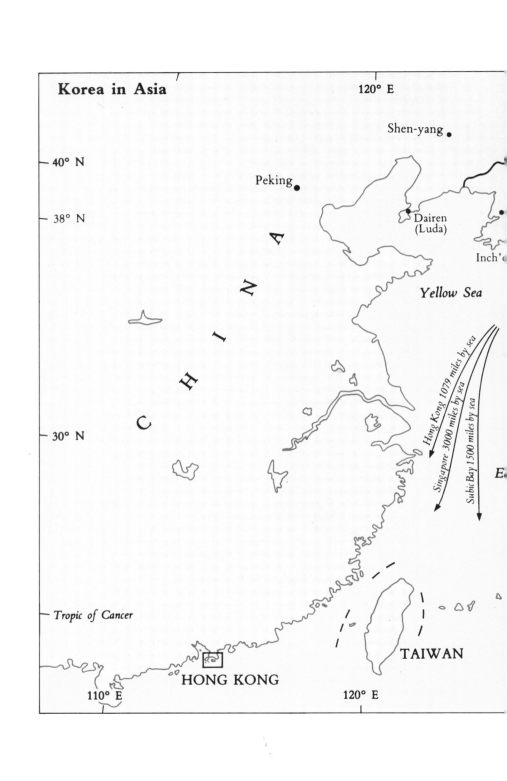

Korea in Asia

120° E

Shen-yang •

40° N

Peking •

38° N

Dairen
(Luda) •

Inch'

CHINA

Yellow Sea

Hong Kong 1079 miles by sea

Singapore 3000 miles by sea

Subic Bay 1500 miles by sea

30° N

E

Tropic of Cancer

TAIWAN

HONG KONG

110° E

120° E